CAPITAL CANOEING AND KAYAKING

A Complete Guide to Whitewater Streams within Two Hours of Washington DC

Stephen Ettinger

Copyright © 2013 Stephen J Ettinger
All Rights Reserved

ISBN: 1478317752
ISBN-13: 9781478317753

Table of Contents

PART I. BACKGROUND 1

Chapter 1. The Whys and Wheres (of this Book) 3

Chapter 2. The Who's and What's (in a Name) 9

Chapter 3. The How and When (to Paddle Small Streams) 13

PART II: METROPOLITAN BALTIMORE 21

Chapter 4. Southern Harford County 23
   Swan Creek, James Run, Bynum Run, Winters Run, *West Branch Winters Run*, East Branch Winters Run

Chapter 5. Gunpowder Falls Basin 31
   Gunpowder Falls, *Grave Run*, Georges Run, Little Falls, Beetree Run, Third Mine Branch, Piney Creek, Western Run, Blackrock Run, Long Green Creek, Little Gunpowder Falls

Chapter 6. Back River Basin 45
   Herring Run, West Branch Herring Run, *Chinquapin Run*, Moores Run, Redhouse Creek, Stemmers Run

Chapter 7. Jones & Gwynns Falls Basins 51
   Jones Falls, *North Branch Jones Falls*, Roland Run, Western Run, Stony Run, Gwynns Falls, Red Run, Scotts Level Branch, Powder Mill Run, Dead Run, *Maidens Choice Run*, Gwynns Run

Chapter 8. Patapsco River Basin 65
   Patapsco River, North Branch Patapsco, West Branch Patapsco, East Branch Patapsco, *Deep Run [north]*, Beaver Run, Morgan Run, South Branch Patapsco, Gillis Falls, Piney Run, Brice Run, Bens Run, Deep Run [south], West Branch Herbert Run

Chapter 9. Patuxent River Basin 79
   Patuxent River, Cabin Branch, Cattail Creek, Hawlings River, Little Patuxent, Middle Patuxent, *'Clarksville Branch'*, Hammond Branch, Western Branch

PART III: WILLS CREEK TO CATOCTIN CREEK 91

Chapter 10. Wills Creek Basin 93
Wills Creek, Brush Creek, *Hillegas Run, Shaffers Run,* Little Wills Creek, Wolfcamp Run, Gladdens Run, Jennings Run, North Branch Jennings Run, Braddock Run

Chapter 11. Evitts Creek to Licking Creek 103
Evitts Creek, Town Creek, *Wilson Run,* Flintstone Creek, Fifteenmile Creek, Sideling Hill Creek, *West Branch Sideling Hill Creek,* East Branch Sideling Hill Creek, Piney Creek, *Little Tonoloway Creek [south],* Tonoloway Creek, Little Tonoloway Creek [north], Licking Creek, *Patterson Run,* Big Cove Creek, Esther Run, *Little Cove Creek.*

Chapter 12. Conococheague & Antietam Creek Basins 117
Conococheague Creek, *Rocky Mountain Run, Carbaugh Run, Marsh Run [south],* Antietam Creek, West Branch Antietam Creek, East Branch Antietam Creek, Red Run, Little Antietam Creek [north], Marsh Run [north], Beaver Creek, Little Antietam Creek [south]

Chapter 13. Catoctin Creek Area 131
Israel Creek, Little Catoctin Creek [south], Catoctin Creek, *Little Catoctin Creek [north],* Middle Creek, *Grindstone Run,* Little Catoctin Creek [central], Cone Branch, Broad Run, Tuscarora Creek

PART IV: MONOCACY BASIN 141

Chapter 14. Monocacy North 143
Marsh Creek, Little Marsh Creek, Rock Creek, White Run, Littles Run

Chapter 15. Monocacy West 149
Toms Creek, Miney Branch, Friends Creek, Middle Creek, Owens Creek, Hunting Creek, Little Hunting Creek, Fishing Creek, Tuscarora Creek

Chapter 16. Monocacy East 165
Alloway Creek, Piney Creek, Double Pipe Creek, Big Pipe Creek, Silver Run, *Bear Branch, Meadow Branch,* Little Pipe Creek, Sams Creek, *Israel Creek,* Linganore Creek, North Fork Linganore Creek, *Bens Branch,* Bush Creek, Bennett Creek, Little Bennett Creek

PART V: WASHINGTON D.C. & MARYLAND SUBURBS 175

Chapter 17. Potomac River 177
Chapter 18. Western Montgomery County 185
Little Monocacy River, Seneca Creek, Great Seneca Creek, Wildcat Branch, Goshen Branch, Little Seneca Creek, Bucklodge Branch, Dry Seneca Creek, Muddy Branch

Chapter 19. Southern Montgomery County 193
    Watts Branch, Piney Branch, Rock Run, Cabin John Creek, Old Farm Creek, Snakeden Branch, Buck Branch, 'Kentdale Branch', Booze Creek, *Minnehaha Branch*, Little Falls Branch

Chapter 20. Rock Creek Basin 207
    Rock Creek, North Branch, *Croyden Park Branch*, Turkey Branch, Josephs Run, 'Cedar Lane Branch', Kensington Hills Branch, 'Forest Glen Branch', Coquelin Run, Fenwick Branch, Portal Branch, Luzon Branch, Broad Branch, *Soapstone Valley Branch*, Piney Branch

Chapter 21. Anacostia River Basin 225
    Northwest Branch, Batchellors Run, Bel Pre Creek, Sligo Creek, Long Branch Sligo Creek, 'Michigan Park Hills Branch', Northeast Branch, Paint Branch, Little Paint Branch, Still Run, Brier Ditch, *Watts Branch*

Chapter 22. Southern Maryland 241
    Henson Creek, Piscataway Creek, Tinkers Creek, Port Tobacco Creek, *Clark Run/Zekiah Swamp Run, Gilbert Swamp Run*

PART VI: CACAPON & WEST VIRGINIA PANHANDLE BASINS 251

Chapter 23. Cacapon River Basins 253
    North Fork Little Cacapon River, Cacapon River, Lost River, *Kimsey Run*, Baker Run, Trout Run, Waites Run, North River, *Grassy Lick Run*, Tearcoat Creek

Chapter 24. Sleepy Creek Area 263
    Sir Johns Run, Sleepy Creek, *Middle Fork, South Fork*, Mountain Run, Meadow Branch

Chapter 25. Back Creek Basin 269
    Back Creek, Isaacs Creek, Little Isaacs Creek, Hogue Creek, Brush Creek, *Little Brush Creek*, Babbs Run, Tilhance Creek

Chapter 26. Opequon Creek Area 277
    Opequon Creek, *Abrams Creek*, Mill Creek, *Middle Creek, Tuscarora Creek, Rockymarsh Run, Elk Branch/Elks Run*

PART VII: SHENANDOAH BASIN 283

Chapter 27. North Fork Shenandoah Basin 287
    North Fork Shenandoah River, Mill Creek, Stony Creek, *Laurel Run, Riles Run, Little Stony Creek,* Narrow Passage Creek, Pughs Run, Toms Brook, *Tumbling Run,* Cedar Creek, Paddy Run, Fall Run, Furnace Run, *Froman Run,* Passage Creek

v

Chapter 28. South Fork Shenandoah Basin.. 307
    South Fork Shenandoah River, Naked Creek, East Branch Naked Creek, Big Creek,
    West Branch Naked Creek, South Branch Naked Creek, *Cub Run, Stony Run, Big Run,*
    Hawksbill Creek, East Hawksbill Creek, Dry Run, Pass Run, Flint Run, Gooney Run

Chapter 29. Main Stem Shenandoah Basin... 323
    Shenandoah River, Happy Creek, Crooked Run, Manassas Run, *Borden Marsh Run,*
    Venus Branch, Spout Run, Evitts Run

PART VIII: NORTHERN VIRGINIA 335

Chapter 30. Northwest Loudoun County 337
    Piney Run, *Dutchman Creek,* Catoctin Creek, North Fork Catoctin Creek,
    South Fork Catoctin Creek, 'Morrisonville Creek', Milltown Creek, 'North
    Limestone Branch'

Chapter 31. Goose Creek Basin 345
    Goose Creek, Crooked Run [south], Gap Run, Panther Skin Creek, Jeffries Branch,
    Cromwells Run, North Fork Goose Creek, Crooked Run [north], Beaverdam Creek, North
    Fork Beaverdam Creek, Little River, Sycolin Creek, Tuscarora Creek

Chapter 32. Above Great Falls 357
    Broad Run, *Beaverdam Run,* Sugarland Run, Nichols Run, Clarks Branch,
    Mine Run Branch

Chapter 33. Difficult Run Basin... 363
    Difficult Run, *Little Difficult Run,* Wolftrap Creek, *Colvin Run,* Captain
    Hickory Run, Rocky Run

Chapter 34. Virginia Palisades 371
    Bullneck Run, 'West Branch Bullneck Run', Scott Run, Dead Run, *Turkey Run,*
    Pimmit Run, Little Pimmit Run, *Gulf Branch, Donaldson Run, Windy Run, Spout Run*

Chapter 35. Virginia Suburbs South... 383
    Fourmile Run, *Long Branch,* Holmes Run, Tripps Run, Backlick Run, Indian Run,
    Turkeycock Run, Pike Branch, Accotink Creek, Pohick Creek, South Run, Giles Run

Chapter 36. Occoquan River Basin.. 399
    Occoquan River, Broad Run, Kettle Run, Cedar Run, *Mill Run,* Turkey Run,
    Licking Run, Bull Run, Chestnut Lick, Little Bull Run, Cub Run, Elklick Run, Big Rocky
    Run, Popes Head Creek

Chapter 37. South of the Occoquan 415
    Neabsco Creek, Powells Creek, South Fork/Quantico Creek, Chopawamsic
    Creek, Aquia Creek, *Accokeek Creek,* Potomac Creek, *Long Branch,* Potomac Run

PART IX: RAPPAHANNOCK BASIN 427

Chapter 38. Upper Rappahannock Basin 429
Rappahannock River (upper), Fiery Run, Jordan River, Hittles Mill Stream, Thumb Run, Great Run

Chapter 39. Hazel River Basin 435
Hazel River, Hughes River, Thornton River, North Fork Thornton River, Piney River, Rush River, Covington River, *Battle Run*

Chapter 40. Rapidan Headwaters 449
Rapidan River (upper), Garth Run, Conway River, South River, Robinson River, Rose River

Chapter 41. Rappahannock Tailwaters 465
Rappahannock River (lower), Marsh Run, Mountain Run, Deep Run, Rapidan River (lower), Cedar Run, Mountain Run, Mine Run, Rocky Pen Run, Hazel Run, Massaponax Creek

Index of Streams 479

Total of 372 creeks, 521 sections, 48 maps

Dedication

This book is dedicated to the memory of RC Forney, a fellow creek explorer who died tragically under a strainer at Pete Morgan's Rapid on the Cheat Canyon on a Thursday Paddle on November 3, 2005, leaving behind a wife and two small children. RC's enthusiasm and *joie de vivre* made it a special pleasure to paddle with him, and he is still sorely missed by many of us in the Thursday Paddlers and beyond.

Acknowledgements

Many paddlers have helped my work on this book, but I want to especially acknowledge those who have done the most. Alf Cooley and Ed Evangelidi have kindly reviewed and edited it for me – Alf by catching my mistakes and asking questions, Ed by providing lots of additional information on the creeks and their vicinities. Ed Grove generously shared with me his experience in writing paddling guidebooks, and Ed Gertler gave me useful information on a number of Maryland creeks. Those who were with me on at least 3 exploratory trips were, in order of frequency, Ed Evangelidi, Jamie Deehan, Larry Lempert, Alf Cooley, Jon Hauris, RC Forney, Ernie Katz, Al Cassell, Gisela Zarkovsky, Dick Pierce, Tim Tilson, Chris Oberlin, Barbara Brown, Jane Collins, Frank Fico, Dave Singer, Bob Youker, Rusty Dowling, Phil DeModica and Ron Knipling.

More broadly, I want to thank all the members of the Thursday Paddlers, whose recurring hopes of running a reasonable stream with enough water were often derailed by my dragging them off to explore some bony, strainer-laden storm drain. Special thanks goes to Barbara Brown for the skill, time and effort she took to produce the photos on the covers.

My two sons, Jonathan and Kenneth, gave me sage advice regarding maps. And my wife Ronie tolerated my many misadventures, kept pushing me to finish the book, and provided invaluable moral support throughout.

The existing paddling guidebooks to the area have been important sources of inspiration, information and ideas: Ed Gertler's *Maryland and Delaware Canoe Trails*, Roger Corbett's *Virginia Whitewater*, Ed Grove's *Classic Virginia Rivers*, Paul Davidson's et al *A Canoeing and Kayaking Guide to West Virginia* and Ron Canter's out of print *Nearby Canoeing Streams*. Mainly for some of the larger and flatter rivers and creeks that I have not personally paddled, I have summarized (and referenced) information obtained from those books.

I have quoted parts of trip reports by others as follows: Mike Soukup on Long Green Creek; Steve Revier on Middle Creek, Catoctin Basin (section 2); Bobby Miller on Hunting Creek; Ron Knipling on

Little Pimmit Run; John Alden on Scott Run (section 3); and Larry Gladieux on Neabsco and Powells creeks. I have also utilized other trip reports, such as by Erik Amason on Donaldson, Windy and Dead runs, Frank Fico on Sugarland Run and Ron Canter on Thumb Run. I want to thank them all.

Finally, I want to thank the staff of numerous county historical societies in the area for helping me locate historical and geographical information on the creeks.

Disclaimer

The information contained herein is as accurate as I could make it at the time that I paddled or scouted the stream. However, rivers and especially small creeks change over time, and in particular, new hazards such as fences, low-water bridges and other strainers may appear. Whitewater canoeing and kayaking are inherently dangerous sports, and the participants need to assess carefully their capabilities and take all appropriate precautions, including scouting and portaging when they have doubts. Unlike Mitt Romney's infamous 47%, they must take responsibility for their own lives.

About the Author

Steve Ettinger has been paddling canoes since he went to summer camp as a child to escape from the Bronx, and it seems like he's been writing this book for almost as long. He shifted from lakes to whitewater soon after arriving in Washington DC in 1972 to work as an economist for the World Bank. It was a sport he and his wife could do tandem – fortunately, his marriage has survived better than his tandem.

After taking early retirement from the World Bank, Steve joined and soon began organizing the Thursday Paddlers – currently about 130 canoeists and kayakers who are retired, unemployed, underemployed, free during the summer or simply willing to sacrifice an occasional workday to go whitewater paddling. A few even tell their employers not to expect them on Thursdays.

In keeping with broader trends, the large majority of the group are now kayakers. When asked why he too has not switched to that easier and more maneuverable craft, Steve's favorite reply is that "any fool can make it down a whitewater creek in a kayak, but it takes a special kind of fool to canoe it."

He always liked exploring new creeks, and discovered that he was onto something of wider interest when the *Wall Street Journal* published a page one article (by Thomas Ricks) on July 2, 1991, about his "brown water" adventures on Rock Creek tributaries. A few years later, Angus Phillips, the "Outdoors" reporter for the *Washington Post* sports section, discovered the Thursday Paddlers, and began joining and writing up some of his trips. Alas, after Angus' retirement, Steve slipped back into journalistic obscurity – hence the need to publish this potential best seller.

CAPITAL CANOEING and KAYAKING

A Complete Guide to Whitewater Streams within Two Hours of Washington DC

PART I: BACKGROUND

The original intended title of this book was "Washington's Other Whitewater" (WOW – sort of catchy!). But as Angus Phillips, outdoor columnist of the *Washington Post* wrote presciently back in 1996: "President Clinton's real estate woes will probably be long forgotten before he finishes" this book. So unlike George Stephanopoulos, Dick Morris, and "that woman," I decided not to cash in on the peccadilloes of the Clinton administration. Besides, there's been so much good stuff in the W and Obama years.

The biggest change in my approach over the intervening years has been in regard to **maps**. Before, I was planning to include detailed shuttle maps for every creek – over 250 pages of maps. But with the advent on on-line mapping, especially Google Maps, I shifted to giving the GPS coordinates and letting users of this book print their own maps including directions to their targeted creeks before setting out. This not only saved me a lot of work (although I had already drawn over 190 creek-level maps) but made the book much less bulky. Now I include maps only at the chapter level and above, so as to give a general idea of the streams' locations.

Rain, Rain, Come Again.

It's a steamy late summer afternoon in Washington, the clouds are building up, the air is more electric than a Tim Geithner speech, and a thunderstorm is imminent. (Almost) everyone looks and sounds worried; however, I'm excited. This could be a chance for a first descent of a local storm drain. But there is no time to waste. I must get home, load my canoe and fight through rain-induced gridlock worse than Congress to reach the put in no later than a few minutes after the downpour ends, in that brief window when there might be sufficient water to float a boat.

It's a cool, soggy spring morning, after heavy rains have soaked the region. The Weather Channel reports flooding in the Blue Ridge, and the National Weather Service warns that all rivers and creeks are above safe levels. Again, time is short, although not quite as short. During the next hour or two, I must put together a trip to catch those tiny, swollen mountain creeks, before their water levels fall faster than Rick Perry's campaign when he couldn't remember the third government department he wanted to abolish.

> **Rain, Rain, Go Away.** The English language suggests that rain is evil. We have expressions like "save for a rainy day," "don't rain on my parade," and "into each life a little rain must fall." It's rather like black hat, blackguard, and black mark. Weather news on TV and radio is also as objective as Fox on politics, with reports such as "the bad news is that rain is predicted for tomorrow, but the good news is that it will clear up later in the week." I much prefer the approach of the people in arid Botswana, who greet each other with "*pula!*"– "may it rain!"

Chapter 1:

The WHYS and WHERES (of this Book)

A River Runs Through It

Rivers have always been important for Washington and Baltimore. The former's location was set by the fall line of the Potomac River, its southern boundary is that river, and its strongest Civil War force was the Army of the Potomac. Baltimore was built where Jones Falls and Gwynns Falls reach an estuary of the Chesapeake Bay. Rivers form the boundary between Maryland and Virginia/West Virginia, and part (but, of course, never all) of the boundary of every county in Maryland and northern Virginia. Where the rivers themselves do not form the boundaries (e.g. between Virginia and West Virginia), it is often their watersheds instead.

Native Americans settled along rivers and creeks, and for long-distance travel used canoes dug out of tulip poplar, cypress or yellow pine. Some reached 50 feet and could carry up to 40 people. This rather limited their maneuverability in rapids.

In the early years of **European settlement**, waterways provided a main means of transportation. In 1608, John Smith sailed up the Potomac, Patuxent and Patapsco rivers. One of the first books on the area, "A Relation of Maryland" (1635), reported that: "It's full of Rivers and Creekes and hath store of Springs and small Brookes." The original settlements were along the flat creeks of the coastal plain. The rapids of the fall line (where the Piedmont drops down to the coastal plain) later became the site for the major cities, as it was the limit of access of ocean-going ships.

Once substantial settlement moved above the fall line, interest in building **canals** began. In 1785, Maryland and Virginia chartered the Potomac Company, with George Washington as its president (he owned interests in western lands), to develop a trade route along the river, with a canal and locks to bypass the rapids. Pennsylvania also expressed interest, because of its link to the Potomac via the Monocacy River. This helped lead to the **Annapolis trade convention**, called to address the regulations which hampered interstate commerce, and that was followed by the Constitutional Convention to correct all of the shortcomings of the Articles of Confederation. The great age of canal building in the early 19th Century included passages along many local rivers, but railroads soon reduced these to mainly historical interest.

In the **War of 1812**, the Patuxent and Patapsco rivers were the British avenues of naval attack on Washington and Baltimore, respectively. During the **Civil War,** rivers and creeks in the area figured prominently in the clashes between the armies of the Potomac and of Northern Virginia (e.g., Bull Run and Antietam Creek), as well as in the Shenandoah Valley campaigns (e.g. Cedar Creek).

Until the 1870s, creeks provided the chief source of **power for industry**. Hundreds of gristmills, sawmills, paper mills, woolen mills etc. were built along them – fourteen on Rock Creek (in and near DC) alone, for example. Mills were often multi-purpose (especially gristmills, because grain availability was seasonal), and became production centers of villages and towns. Baltimore's initial industrial development was based on the water-driven mills in the basins of the Gunpowder Falls, Back River, Jones Falls, Gwynns Falls and the Patapsco River. Governments encouraged this development; for example, in 1669, Maryland granted free land to anyone erecting a flour mill. These mills required a sufficient vertical drop for power, and so small dams/weirs and diversion channels were built. These changed the hydrology of the creeks, by trapping lots of silt. This is still evidenced in high, sheer stream banks with horizontal layers of sediment.

Water-powered mills were eventually undone by new technologies, economies of scale, and less dependable water flow (as land development reduced the forest cover). In particular, the development of metal rollers in the 1880s enabled the hard red wheat grown in the plains states to be milled economically, and flour from there quickly undercut the wheat industry in the east. Maryland had some 550 flour mills in 1880, but 60% of them were gone eight years later and only one survives now (except for those refurbished as historical sites).

Streams also provided the power for the bellows in the blast furnaces that produced pig iron, and they floated the wood that provided the heat. Less romantically, they were wonderful sites for tanneries, slaughterhouses etc. that wanted easy and free disposal of noxious wastes.

In the second half of the 19th Century, the building of **dams** commenced on the larger creeks and rivers, for generating power, ensuring year-round water to the burgeoning cities, and protecting against floods. Now that there are cheaper sources of power and more interest in the environment, these dams are starting to come down.

Rivers and creeks are now important for their **recreational potential**. This is one of the country's best areas in terms of the variety and accessibility of whitewater. The large number of local paddlers and the presence of the US Olympic Canoe and Kayak Slalom Team are evidence of this. The main reasons are the rapids of the fall line and the eastern ranges of the Appalachians, the relatively high precipitation and the mild climate. Whereas paddlers in many other parts of the country routinely drive 5-10 hours to get to good whitewater, here there are dozens of choices, of all difficulty levels, virtually at our doorstep. But, as is repeated obsessively in the remainder of this book, one has to be very opportunistic to take full advantage of this paddling cornucopia.

Genesis

The idea for this book arose gradually. I used to drive and bike along tributaries of Rock Creek near my home in Washington DC, and began to wonder whether such tiny streams could ever be paddled. Then, during a heavy storm in July 1985, I found one of them (Broad Branch) deep enough, launched and got hooked. Soon I was investigating all of the Rock Creek tributaries and, as time and rainfall permitted, running them. Word of this strange behavior leaked out, and on July 2, 1991, the *Wall Street Journal* highlighted my unusual avocation in a page 1 article by the not-yet-famous Tom Ricks on "brown-water" paddling" (see chapter 20). Suddenly I realized that this peculiar activity might be of interest to a wider audience, and I thought of writing an article on the Rock Creek basin. But, following the example of Independent Counsel Kenneth Starr (younger readers might want to Google him), I instead expanded my whitewater investigations to more and more neighboring areas, and kept at them doggedly for many years.

How Small Is Small?

This book differs from existing paddling guidebooks mainly in its comprehensive **inclusion of tiny creeks**. I have written up 521 sections on 372 rivers and creeks, for a total of 2,050 miles. Of these, 365 sections (70%) covering 960 miles (47%) were too small for he existing guidebooks. On the other hand, because my focus is whitewater, I have left out tidal water, as well as the flat sections of the larger rivers (Potomac, Shenandoah, Rappahannock, Rapidan, Patuxent, Monocacy, Cacapon etc.), all of which are well described in those guidebooks.

I did not set specific minimum size limits in advance, but instead investigated all creeks that appeared even occasionally runnable. Once I had settled on drainage area as the best measure of size, and found a program for measuring it on my computer, I looked to see what minimums I had used. It turned out that for **rural areas**, I had included most streams with at least seven square miles (provided they were accessible, had decent gradients, were not obviously overrun by strainers, and could be run for at least a mile or so), and a smattering of even smaller ones which had piqued my interest because their gradients suggested good whitewater, or which I had happened to find up after a heavy rain.

In **urban areas**, there was essentially no lower limit (about a dozen creeks were below 1 square mile, with the smallest being just 0.3 square miles), for three reasons. First, these streams are so flashy that even the tiniest occasionally come up. Second, many urban streams pass through neither dense woods nor private property, and therefore have few of the tree or fence strainers that bedevil their rural counterparts. And third, proximity to most paddlers' homes means that these creeks can be reached quickly enough to catch them immediately after a heavy rainfall.

Geographic Coverage

To make this guidebook as useful as possible to the largest number of paddlers (inspired by John Stuart Mill, before he went out of fashion), I have based the geographic coverage not on state boundaries but on accessibility from the Washington area – with roughly two hours' drive as the limit. Within that, I have used watershed boundaries to set the exact range. The books thus cover most of Maryland (except Garrett County in the far west and the flat Eastern Shore) and northern Virginia, and the nearer parts of Pennsylvania and West Virginia. The total area is about 13,000 square miles.

To the northeast, I include the small basins past Baltimore but nothing in the vast Susquehanna watershed. To the southwest, I cover the Rappahannock basin, but not beyond; the York River watershed, which is the next to the south, has whitewater only on the fall line (and this is covered adequately in existing guidebooks), because it rises in the Piedmont rather than the Blue Ridge. In the northwest, I have included the Wills Creek basin, up to three hours away, because of its excellent whitewater. To the west, I go as far as the Cacapon basins, stopping just short of Romney (aha!) WV and the South Branch of the Potomac. Within the Shenandoah Valley, the two-hour rule brought me as far upstream as Mill Creek on the North Fork and Naked Creek (oho!) on the South Fork.

CAPITAL CANOEING AND KAYAKING

GEOGRAPHIC COVERAGE

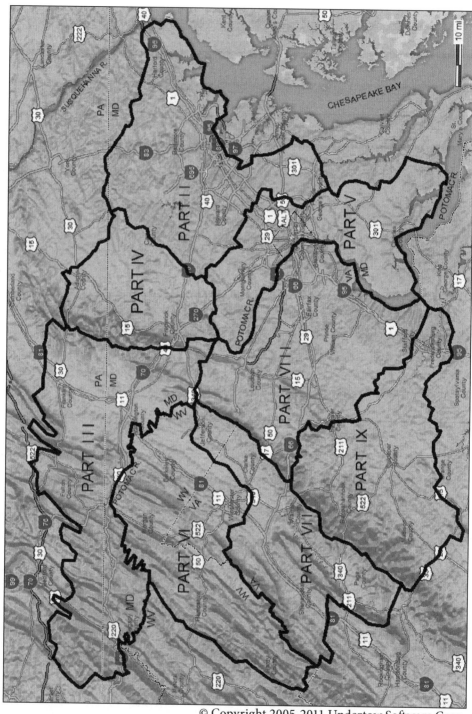

© Copyright 2005-2011 Undertow Software Corp.

Town and Country

This geographic scope includes streams all along the downtown-wilderness continuum. At one end is a cluster of storm drains (sometimes mislabeled "sewers") in Washington and Baltimore that carry street run-off. At the other extreme are the relatively pristine brooks that flow out of Shenandoah National Park or Catoctin Mountain Park. In between are creeks in the north-south valleys of the Appalachians, agricultural areas of the Piedmont ("foot of the mountains"), woodlands of the coastal plain and suburban parks.

Urban storm drains, such as in the Rock Creek and Anacostia basins, rise and fall extremely fast, because water gushes down paved surfaces. A day of light rain may produce only a trickle, but a ten-minute thunderstorm can bring them to bank-full – for the next ten minutes. They are heavily polluted and can be pretty ugly, but on the positive side, they are close to most paddlers' homes and tend to have easy access and no fences.

Mountain streams are the reverse in most ways. It takes hours of rain to bring them up, and they fall more slowly, despite their steep gradients. They are most often runnable in the winter or early spring, as snow melts and before vegetation begins to absorb the water. Water quality and scenery are generally fine. Fences may be a problem and tree strainers even more often so. These creeks congregate in the Monocacy basin west, the North and South branches of the Shenandoah, the Rappahannock headwaters, and the Wills Creek and Cacapon basins.

North-south valley and **Piedmont streams** have moderate gradients, stay up longer and are blocked less by trees but more by farm fences. The water may be polluted by cattle and agricultural runoff, and the scenery tends to be unexciting. Most have relatively steady gradients without major rapids, but some have steep gorges as they make their final descents into the larger rivers. There are many of these creeks in the Gunpowder, Patapsco, Monocacy east and WV Panhandle basins, as well as those from Evitts Creek through the Catoctin area.

Coastal plain woodland creeks have low gradients and few fences, but many tree strainers. Southern Maryland is the one chapter that covers only the coastal plain, although several streams in other chapters are found there as well.

Suburban parkland brooks are in between Piedmont creeks and urban storm drains; look at Southern Harford and Western Montgomery counties.

Gone Are the Days

I have carried out considerable research into the history of these streams, covering such matters as their names, early settlement, role in the Civil War and other conflicts, economic significance and interesting places nearby. I was inspired in this by Roger Corbett's treatment of Civil War and other historical aspects of Virginia's rivers. This information is enclosed in boxes (except when very brief), so as to distinguish it from the more paddling-related text. In addition to the wealth of information that is now on line, I found visiting county historical societies useful. To avoid the need to submit this book for clearance, I have omitted matters related to national security, such as how to paddle to Camp David or the CIA, or good spots along creeks to hide secret documents.

According to a Usually Reliable Source

Originally I had hoped to paddle or at least find trip reports on each creek. But given how seldom the smaller streams are up, and how few people have paddled them, that proved too ambitious. So making a virtue of necessity, I include *"explorers' specials,"* scouted from topographic maps and no-water visits. This seemed a better solution than leaving out many streams or postponing completion of the book until the Chelsea Clinton administration. In total, of the 521 river sections in this book, 91 (17.5%) are *"explorers' specials."* So there is lots of scope for any of you who are explorer types to check out these streams. They are more common in the areas farther from DC, especially in those chapters more recently added to my coverage.

The Joy of Creeking

What is the appeal of micro-streams? First is the adventure of paddling where few have paddled before, and making what may be **first descents** (although one can never know for sure). Besides, where else in the Great Northeastern Megalopolis can one go **"exploring"**? Some trips even result in "discoveries" such as unknown rapids. In addition, I have always liked the **variety** of paddling different streams. This also gives the opportunity to visit out of the way places, and to see them from a different (and usually more attractive) perspective than most people. A final special attraction is the **proximity** of many of these creeks to the Washington area, which minimizes driving.

Of course, this list is only what is special about micro-streams. The other pleasures of paddling – rapids, scenery, exercise, wildlife, peace and quiet, and the company of like-minded people – also apply.

Up the Creek

So why have so few people taken advantage of this recreational resource? First is the **difficulty of catching the creeks up,** as tiny streams rise and fall so fast. The recorded river gauges used to be of little value; however, this has changed dramatically (see chapter 3), so catching these streams is much more feasible now. But even when you know where to go, catching these creeks right after a heavy rain (the only time to run the smallest of them) presents its own problems. For example, thunderstorms usually occur just around, and exacerbate, the evening rush hour. It's a helpless feeling to sit in a traffic jam as the water drains out of your intended destination.

The second problem area is the **quality of paddling** on many of these streams. The density of strainers is inversely related to the size of the stream. And cutting out tree strainers is like a crash diet: almost certain to succeed in the short run but fail eventually. The other serious negative, especially for urban (and ranch area) creeks, is water quality. Not only does one get the run-off from city streets (or pastures), but after very intense rains, some urban sewer systems get overloaded, which results in the creeks smelling rather like the electoral campaign financing system.

So in the end, the micro-stream focus of this book is mainly for those who will put up with the negatives because of their love for whitewater and/or adventure. So be it. I just lay out the options and you can be The Decider.

Chapter 2:
The WHO'S and WHAT'S (in a Name)

Since 1890, the United States Board on Geographic Names has had the final say over the names of all rivers and creeks. It is composed of representatives of various federal agencies and coordinated by the US Geological Survey, in the Department of the Interior. Their decisions comprise the Geographic Names Information System (GNIS). To the best of my knowledge, it has not yet been politicized (although there is many a Bush Creek and no Obama River).

First Names

With few exceptions, the rivers' and creeks' "first names" come from one of three sources: Indian words, early settlers' names, and aspects of the creek or its vicinity. **Native American** names are used primarily for the larger rivers and for streams along the coast, as the English came upon those very early in their exploration, before they had much basis for attaching other names. In this region, it is mainly in the rivers (rather than the towns, counties or even mountains) that Native American names are preserved. For example, in Maryland, there are 45 Indian stream names – twice as many as for any other category of place. Still, they constitute only 6% of the 770 named streams in the state. The Native American names are of two sorts:

a) Those given to the creeks by the Indians themselves, such as Accotink, Alloway, Antietam, Aquia, Cacapon, Catoctin, Chinquapin, Chopawamsic, Conococheague, Linganore, Monocacy, Neabsco, Occoquan, Opequon, Pohick, Quantico, Rappahannock, Shenandoah and Zekiah; the original meanings of some of these names are known, and there are one or more hypotheses about all of the others, often based on arcane interpretations of the original pronunciation and meaning of each syllable. (Virginia Algonquian, the main local language, was last spoken in 1785.) The known or hypothesized names usually relate to some aspect of the river or creek; and

b) Names of local tribes or villages, such as Anacostia, Massaponax, Patapsco, Patuxent, Piscataway, Potomac, Seneca, Tonoloway and Tuscarora. There are four Tuscarora creeks in this book, because the name is mellifluous. The Seneca ("mountain people") and Tuscarora ("shirt-wearing people"), members of the Iroquois Federation, passed through the area but did not settle in it.

Early settlers (mostly English) in the area are widely represented in river names – about 100 in this book. Examples include the Robinson, Hughes (Hugh's), Hazel, Thornton, Conway, Rose (Rowe's), Covington and Rush rivers in the Rappahannock basin, and Jones, Gwynns and Gillis falls near Baltimore. In a few cases, first names were used, such as Roland Run, Giles Run, Toms Brook, Sams Creek and Bens Run, and in even fewer cases the names of groups rather than individuals, such as Friends and Dutchman creeks. Only a few creeks were also named after important people, such as Braddock (the British commander in the French and Indians War) and Hillegas (the first Treasurer of the United States) runs.

But the most common source is some **aspect of the creek** itself or its vicinity. This large group of names can be subdivided as follows:

a) **Flora, fauna, minerals or man-made structures** seen in or near the creek. The flora include Brier Ditch, Brush Creek, Bush Creek, Cedar Creek, Chestnut Lick, Piney Branch, Laurel Run, Beetree Run and Cattail Creek. The simple fauna category has Bear Branch, Bull Run, Buck Branch, Elks Run, Cub Run, Beaver Creek, Pike Branch, Swan Creek, Goose Creek, Trout Run, Turkey Run, Turkeycock Run, and Wildcat Branch. Names involving something about animals are Snakeden Branch, Panther Skin Creek, Bucklodge Branch, Wolftrap Creek, Elklick Run, Beaverdam Creek and Bullneck Run. The minerals group includes Flint Run, Limestone Branch, Soapstone Valley Branch, Blackrock Run, Grindstone Run and Paint Branch (dyes were made from the soil). And the man-made structures are in Redhouse Creek, Powder Mill Run, Grave Run, Cabin Branch, Furnace Run, Mine Run, Hittles Mill Stream and the plain old ubiquitous Mill Creek.

b) **Location**, such as Big Cove Creek, Middle Creek, Back Creek, North Branch, Gulf Branch, Western Run, Hawksbill Creek (next to Hawksbill Mountain), Mountain Run, Meadow Branch, Old Farm Creek, Rocky Pen Run, Sugarland Run, Pass Run, Portal Branch, Gap Run and Narrow Passage Creek, or the name of a nearby town, such as Long Green Creek, Maidens Choice Run, Kensington Hills Branch, Milltown Creek, Sligo Creek and Port Tobacco Creek; and

c) **Natural aspects of the creek itself**, such as Muddy Branch, Tumbling Run, Long Branch, Lost River, Rock Creek, Dry Run, Difficult Run (hard to cross, although it would also work as a paddling reference), Falls Run, Windy Run, Red Run, Crooked Run, Broad Run, Still Run, Sleepy Creek, Big Run, Deep Run, Little Falls, Stony Creek, Dead Run or Naked Creek (bare of trees).

Of course, there are a few **exceptions** to these three categories: Goshen Branch, Manassas Run, Israel Creek and Jeremys (originally Jeremiahs) Run have Biblical names; Gooney Run is named after Lord Cromwell's dog, the Rapidan River after Queen Anne (the Rapid Anne), Minnehaha Branch after Longfellow's poem, Luzon Branch after the Philippine island and Venus Branch after the tennis player. And I could not find out, or there is some dispute about, the original reference in Happy Creek, Gunpowder Falls, Kettle Run, Big/Little/Double Pipe Creek and Cone Branch.

Last Names

River, **creek**, and **run** are all used to refer to flowing water. In general, a river is larger than a creek, which in turn is larger than a run. For example, South Run flows into Pohick Creek, a tributary of the Potomac River. (But there are exceptions, as where Wolftrap Creek flows into Difficult Run, or Falls Creek into Red Run, and the unique case of the Little River being a tributary of Goose Creek.) Around Baltimore, **falls** is used for six waterways, of varying sizes, which contain rapids but no real waterfalls.

Then there are **branches** and **forks**. One common use of these terms is to refer to the main headwaters. For example, the Potomac River begins at the confluence of its North and South branches, the Shenandoah at the meeting of its North and South forks. But these terms are also used just to mean tributary. Almost all of the Rock Creek tributaries are "branches," and the Potomac itself has many other "branches," such as Muddy, Watts, Minnehaha and Little Falls in southern Montgomery County.

And, finally, there are the seldom-used oddities – **brook**, **stream**, **lick**, **ditch** (each of which is represented once in this book), **prong, waters, gut** and **rill**. The one thing they all have in common is being small.

> The **geographic differences** are striking. Of the 22 "rivers" written up in this book, 13 are in the Rappahannock basin – in the old English usage, only "rivers" and "runs" flow, so anything too big to be a "run" becomes a "river." Maryland's Potomac tributaries include many more "creeks" and "branches" than "runs," but in the Shenandoah Basin, Northern Virginia and from the Patapsco northward, the situation is reversed.

Prefixes

Many creek names start with "**Little**." It is generally used to denote a side stream, such as Little Isaacs Creek, Little Pimmet Run, Little Hunting Creek, Little Difficult Run, Little Bull Run, Little Patuxent River, Little Wills Creek or the two Little Antietam creeks. Rarely, it designates a parallel stream, such as Little Monocacy, Little Cacapon or one of the two Little Tonoloway creeks. In a few cases, it refers to the smaller headwater, such as Little Seneca Creek (which joins Great Seneca Creek to form Seneca Creek) or Little Pipe Creek (which joins Big Pipe Creek to form Double Pipe Creek). There are three Little Catoctin creeks, one in each category. Little Gunpowder Falls is somewhere between the first two categories, as it joins the Gunpowder Falls only after both have become tidal. "Little's" antonyms, "**Big**" and "**Great**," are seldom used – Great Seneca Creek and Big Pipe Creek are the only ones in this book (in Big Cove Creek, the "Big" modifies Cove), although there are inaccurate road signs to "Big [sic] Gunpowder Falls."

> This being the National Capital area, you can expect lots of creeks with names linked to **political figures**. This book includes, for example, (George W.) Bush Creek, Bens (Bernanke) Branch, (Ollie) North Branch, James (Carville) Run, Deep (Throat) Run, (Colin) Powells Creek, Toms (Daschle) Brook, Sams (Rayburn) Creek, and the West Branch of Herbert (Hoover) Run. And, of course, there are the **Whitewater scandal** streams: (Paula) Jones Falls, (Linda) Tripps Run, the Rose (Law Firm) River and the Monicacy [sic] River.
>
> Then there are creeks named after those matters which really **make politics in Washington tick**, such as Friends (of Barack) Creek, Old Farm (Lobby) Creek, Happy (Days are Here Again) Creek, Fiery (Speech) Run, (Income) Gap Run, (Don't) Rock (the Boat) Creek, Rush (to Recess) River, (Confirmation) Battle Run, (Scratch My) Back Creek, Indian (Casino) Run, (Pass the) Buck Branch, Maidens (Freedom of) Choice Run, Dead (on Arrival) Run, Middle (of the Road) Creek and Hunting (Accident) Creek. And finally we get down to the **bedrock** Washington political names – Booze Run, Silver Run, Bull Run, Naked Creek and Crooked Run. I wonder why there are several Crooked runs, but no Straight Run.

A Winter's Worries, with no Snow Flurries

It's just February, a time to be merry, the canoeing season's ahead,
But there's no snow cover, so this water lover is looking ahead with some dread.
For surely you know how important is snow, for March, April, May, even June,
So here's what I fear for the rest of the year if we don't get some precip right soon.

The **Tye** will be dry and the **Dry** won't be high and the rivers won't be racin',
Sideling Hill will not fill and the **Wills** won't give thrills in the drained **Potomac** basin.
Pohick won't float a stick and **Cub Run** won't be fun, all the rivers will be scrapin',
I fear that the **Hazel** won't pass your appraisal, nor will **Catoctin** or **Cacapon**.

There won't be a lotta water on the **Otter** and you'll see every rock,
Passage Creek will be meek and the **Cheat** won't be neat, we won't even have the **Yough**.
When there's naught but slack water along the **Blackwate**r it won't be fun and games,
Only the obtuse would put in on the **Goose** or even the mighty **James**.

Seek no glory on the **Maury** with **Hell's Kitchen** barely twitchin', the rivers will be ever lower,
So you'll hardly see a, trickle on **Pequea**, or even the **Shenandoah**.
As the wailing gets louder along the **Gunpowder**, paddlers will climb the walls,
When they only can walk **Laurel Hill**, **Laurel Fork**, and even our own **Little Falls**.

With **Big Sandy** not dandy, the "**Golly**" not jolly, how will we find a thriller?
No one will be tossed by the waves on the **Lost** or even **North Branch at Kitzmiller**.
No paddler will smile along **Fifteenmile** unless rain falls like manna,
It will take Flash Gordon to get down the **Jordan** or even the **Susquehanna**.

Don't dream of the **Lehigh**, it won't quite be knee-high, I fear a great disaster,
In which even rapid becomes rather vapid, from **Bull Falls** to the **Bullpasture**.
On the **New** you'll feel blue, the **Hughes** won't float canoes, do we face a year-long drought?
With no flows on the **Rose** and the **Deer** looking sere, don't even think about **Trout**.

Then even the **Muddy** will be rather cruddy, its rapids they will bore us,
The lovely **Tohickon** will hardly be kickin', nor will the **Conway** or **Codorus**.
When waters don't gush down the **Brush** or the **Rush**, paddlers will become manic,
Shrinks will have to treat 'em along the **Antietam**, and down on the **Rappahannock**.

Nerves will get frayed on the **Clear and Dark Shade**, as kayakers go bananas,
Paddlers will get whiney just thinking of **Piney**, or even the **North and South Annas**,
Drought will ravage the **Savage**, the **North** won't gush forth, the rivers will be at their worst,
So when **Rocky Island** is nothing but dry land, remember I warned you first.

Chapter 3:

The HOW and WHEN (to Paddle Small Streams)

Small creeks can be difficult to catch. Not only are they up only briefly and seldom, but by the time recorded gauges show high enough levels, it may be too late. That said, it is possible to catch even the tiniest tributaries. During the first half of 1998, for example, during a very wet period, I ran 35 creeks that were too small for the existing guidebooks. (But during the next six months' drought, my score was zero!)

The keys to catching micro-streams are being: (a) **flexible** in targeting creeks, based on rainfall; (b) **prepared** to go out on short notice, with your put ins and take outs pre-selected; and (c) **current** on water-level and rainfall information. This chapter discusses the state of hydrological information (as of 2012) and how to use it, and then lays out the structure of this book and the data presented in the summary tables.

Data Sources

For predicting creek levels, both river-gauge and rainfall information are important. The smaller the stream, the more central the latter, because the water rises and falls so rapidly. Unfortunately, rainfall data are very difficult to use quantitatively. But fortunately, you have this book by a wannabe Nate Silver of creek-level forecasting.

Phone and TV. Until the late 1990s, paddlers had to rely on the telephone river gauge data that were updated twice daily. The morning gauges were not reported until 10-11 AM, so one had to head out based on the previous day's levels. For rainfall, the radar pictures on TV were useful for tiny urban creeks, which require intense downpours; however, it was virtually impossible to convert those images into rainfall totals.

River-levels.com. As in so many aspects of life, Al Gore's invention of the Internet revolutionized small-creek paddling by making more detailed and up-to-date data available. For river levels, the USGS sites (by state) are updated every one to four hours, and show graphically the changes over the past days. There are many more gauges than before, including on small creeks. As of mid-2012, in the area covered by this book, there were 110 gauges (75 in Maryland, 26 in Virginia, 6 in West Virginia, 2 in DC, 1 in Pennsylvania) with drainage areas of less than 100 square miles, whereas the smallest telephone gauge, Seneca Creek, has 101 square mile drainage, and the next smallest 210 square miles. And they give data in cfs, which are more comparable. You can access the sites via www.AmericanWhitewater.org or www.MonocacyCanoe.org, and then click on river levels. However, the coverage varies a great deal. The densest networks are in the small basins that comprise Metropolitan Baltimore and Northern Virginia, while many other areas are poorly served.

It costs about $12,000/year to operate a gauge, mainly for someone to go out periodically to recalibrate the cfs figures from the gauge height readings. USGS requires that another agency (usually part of a local government) share the cost 50-50, so gauges get added or dropped each year depending largely on local interest. As a result, some of the ones referenced in this book may be unavailable or superseded in a few years.

Rainfall.com. For rainfall, the Advanced Flood Warning System (AFWS) site http://afws.erh.noaa.gov/afws/national.php gives cumulative rainfall data for many gauges for the previous 15 minutes up to 24 hours. The main limitations of this site are its limited coverage, clunkiness and frequent unavailability. In Maryland, it includes only Baltimore, Howard and Prince Georges counties. In Virginia, the coverage is mainly the Blue Ridge. For other areas and an overall visual picture, ***http://radar.weather.gov/radar_lite.php?rid=lwx&product=NTP&loop=no*** gives detailed maps showing cumulative rainfall during the current storm, based on radar. One limitation is that they only show sums for the entire storm and for the past hour, so you may need to monitor this site several times during an extended storm, to know how recent the rainfall is. A second is that they are not fully accurate, both around the fringes and in the center of the map; to see this, compare the maps centered on adjacent areas.

Snowmelt is much harder to deal with, as it depends on snow pack depth, sunshine and air temperature. Snow melts mainly when the sun is high, so creeks rise each afternoon and then fall overnight. You may as well sleep late.

From Rainfall to Stream Flow (CFS)

Using rainfall figures to estimate river flow is a challenge, because how much of that rain makes it into the streambeds depends upon (a) the season, as much more gets absorbed by vegetation from late spring through mid fall, (b) soil moisture beforehand, and (c) how developed the area is, because runoff is more complete from paved surfaces. Furthermore, runoff speed depends upon gradient and land use. The National Weather Service has complicated computer models for predicting river levels, but anyone who has compared their predictions with what later eventuated knows how inexact that science is, even for the larger rivers. And for the smaller creeks, timing is more critical than total amounts of rainfall. In this book, while I list the most relevant rainfall gauges for each creek, I therefore generally refrain from giving any specific numbers to look for.

> Here is a brief **sample calculation**. One inch of rainfall on one square mile provides 2.32 million cubic feet of water (ah, the wonders of our English measures). On average, in this area, one-third flows into the streams, while the rest returns to the atmosphere via evaporation or plant transpiration. If these 773,000 cubic feet pass some gauge over a twelve-hour period, the average resultant flow from that square mile would be 18 cfs. For 5 sq. mi. drainage, for example, that would give 90 cfs flow, low but normally enough (see table below). Faster runoff results in brief high flows. The run-off is over half of precipitation in February to April, but below a quarter in July to September, which explains why the creeks are up much more during the former period, despite somewhat less total precipitation then.

In the area covered, average rainfall ranges from 33 to 55 inches per year. The highest rainfall is in the Rappahannock headwaters and the Gunpowder basin. The driest basins are those farthest west: Wills Creek to Antietam Creek, the Cacapon, the WV Panhandle creeks and the North Fork of the Shenandoah. (However, west of that, outside the scope of this book, rainfall picks up again significantly.)

> **How the USGS Measures River Flow** (as observed by Tom Gray). For large streams, it takes a team of four people about 30 minutes to measure the flow at any given point, to correlate gauge levels with cfs flows. They string a cable across the river, marked off in two-foot intervals. Working largely from canoes, they lower a gadget shaped like a fish with a pinwheel at its tail to three depths within each interval, and use a headphone to hear the clicks of each rotation of the pinwheel. The number of clicks per minute gives the speed of the water, the three speeds for each interval are averaged, the depth is measured at each interval, and the rest is arithmetic. This measurement has to be repeated at a number of different water levels in order to estimate the complete correlation. For tiny creeks, a single person can usually handle the task.

From Stream Flow (CFS) to the Zero Level

The critical calculation in paddling is the **zero level** (the minimum flow required), using river gauge readings. (Of course, zero level is not quite the same for everyone, as it depends upon boats, skills and tolerance for scraping.) Traditionally, eastern paddlers were familiar with cfs data primarily for dam releases, but used gauge height (in feet) elsewhere. Nowadays cfs data are widely available, and they have the advantage of being more comparable over time and between different creeks.

The **AW web site (*www.americanwhitewater.org*)** provides a quick way of scanning to see what creeks are above zero level. Its limitations are that it (a) does not include the smallest streams, (b) is based only on latest readings, not trends, and (c) uses just one reference gauge per creek.

For the larger rivers, the estimation of whether there is enough water is simple, because (a) there are gauges on most of them, (b) the levels change relatively slowly and (c) there is lots of empirical evidence of the zero level. For tiny streams, none of these are likely to apply. One must usually extrapolate from the nearest creeks with gauges, and look not just at current gauge levels but also at their trends and the recent rainfall. And to offset the lack of creek-specific data, one must apply some general rules.

The two main determinants of the flow needed are (a) the size of the drainage area above the put in, and (b) the gradient of the rapids. Point (a) is explained nicely on pages 14-15 of the 2000 edition of Corbett's *Virginia Whitewater*. In essence, the drainage area determines the average annual flow, which in turn affects the width of the streambed. Whitewater paddlers learn point (b) quickly; the steeper the rapids, the faster and therefore shallower the water (except where the stream is narrower at the rapids).

For the larger streams, I have based the zero-level figures on both my own experience and other sources. For the smaller ones, where I had no other reliable source, I have estimated as shown in the following table, using the difficulty of the rapids as a proxy for their steepness. Most small creeks for which there are reliable data are roughly consistent with this table. Remember, of course, that these are minimums to get down the creek without much scraping; optimal levels are in most cases considerably higher.

Where relevant, I also indicate the **time adjustment** to make. In the more common case, where the gauge is downstream or on a larger creek than the one being considered, this requires projecting what the gauge level will be a few hours after put in. Such projection is necessary because small creeks both rise and fall faster than large ones.

Zero-Level Flow Estimates

Drainage Area	Class I	Class II	Class III	Class IV
1 sq. mile	35 cfs	40 cfs	50 cfs	60 cfs
2 sq. miles	40 cfs	50 cfs	60 cfs	70 cfs
5 sq. miles	50 cfs	60 cfs	75 cfs	85 cfs
10 sq. miles	60 cfs	70 cfs	85 cfs	100 cfs
20 sq. miles	70 cfs	85 cfs	105 cfs	125 cfs
40 sq. miles	85 cfs	100 cfs	125 cfs	150 cfs
80 sq. miles	100 cfs	120 cfs	150 cfs	180 cfs

Once you have the zero level for the creek, you can estimate the required reading on the nearest gauge(s) based on the ratio of their drainage areas. I have not stipulated maximum safe levels, as these vary too much by paddler skill level. Personally, I am reluctant to paddle small whitewater creeks at more than three times the minimum – at least until I am familiar with them.

Winter, Spring, Summer or Fall

Small creeks might be paddled any time of the year. Late winter and spring normally have the highest levels, as there is snowmelt to supplement the rain, and little vegetation to soak it up. For urban creeks, summer thunderstorms provide very brief windows of opportunity. In the fall, tropical storms may bring heavy rain. Here is a summary of my personal paddling data. The numbers are of creeks/sections not in previous paddling guidebooks – as a proxy for smallness. As you can see, the best months were March-June, but this varied year by year – in fact, the most productive month is different in almost every column. (Some columns combine several years, as when I had less time for paddling or there was below-normal rainfall.)

Personal Trips on Micro-Streams, by Month

	1985-90	1991-95	1996	1997	1998	1999-00	2001-02	2003	2004	2005-11	Total
Jan.	0	1	1	3	**10**	1	0	1	0	1	18
Feb.	2	0	0	3	7	2	0	2	6	3	25
Mar.	0	5	1	6	4	5	2	2	1	**12**	37
April	3	5	**6**	2	3	3	4	-	**8**	4	38
May	**7**	1	5	1	9	1	6	4	1	2	37
June	2	3	4	6	3	3	**8**	5	2	4	40
July	1	**6**	1	1	0	0	0	1	2	5	17
Aug.	2	3	1	2	0	0	1	0	0	1	10
Sept.	0	0	4	1	0	**7**	1	**7**	6	3	29
Oct.	0	1	3	0	0	**3**	1	4	0	2	14
Nov.	0	1	1	**8**	0	0	0	1	1	2	14
Dec.	2	2	5	0	0	0	1	2	1	1	15
Total	19	28	32	33	36	26	25	28	28	39	*294*

THE HOW AND WHEN (TO PADDLE SMALL STREAMS)

Dam Releases

Four Maryland creeks covered here have dam releases. Jones Falls (chapter 7) has two to four brief releases annually, for the benefit of paddlers. The upper Gunpowder Falls (chapter 5) has releases to course water for Baltimore down from the Prettyboy Reservoir to the Loch Raven Reservoir, and may be runnable for weeks during a dry summer or fall. There are also much rarer and less predictable summer or fall drought releases on Little Seneca Creek (chapter 18) to help maintain the minimum flow requirement on the lower Potomac, and on the middle and lower sections of the Patuxent River (chapter 9), mainly for power generation.

Creek Access

Few landowners object if you just paddle through their property (especially as they would seldom see you!), but access to put ins and take outs can be an issue, particularly when you must cross private property or climb over fences. The best practice is to seek permission from the nearest house; if no one is home, leave a note. Some refuse because of concerns about liability; others won't formally give permission, but will not object if you launch anyway.

Canoe and Kayak Clubs in the Area

Paddling clubs organize formal and informal trips, as well as social events, that enable one to find like-minded river companions. Some of them run paddling skill and safety classes, and work to preserve river access and the environment. Their newsletters and Internet sites provide a wealth of paddling-related information.

The creeks in this book are within the home territories of six paddling clubs:

- Blue Ridge Voyageurs (DC area): www.blueridgevoyageurs.org
- Canoe Cruisers Association (DC area): www.canoecruisers.org
- Coastal Canoeists (Virginia): www.coastals.org
- Greater Baltimore Canoe Club: www.baltimorecanoeclub.org
- Mason-Dixon Canoe Club (Harpers Ferry area): www.masondixoncanoeclub.org
- Monocacy Canoe Club (Frederick Md. Based): www.monocacycanoe.org

Just the Facts, Please

At the start of each chapter, I summarize the area, the creeks covered and the relevant gauges, and provide a summary table of the following basic data on each creek:

(a) **Gradient**, in feet/mile, calculated from USGS topographic maps/programs. Whenever there is a stretch with much steeper gradient than the average, I put the higher gradient in parenthesis.

(b) **Difficulty**, following the international scale of river difficulty, as revised September 1997 (see box below) – rather than the current macho tendency to downgrade rapids. The table shows the highest level of difficulty at which there are several rapids; when there are one or two rapids more difficult than the others, I put this into parenthesis [e.g., II+ (III) means that there are several class II+ rapids and one or two class IIIs]. The difficulty ratings refer to low to moderate water levels; in high water, most are greater. I do not use ranges, such as "I-III," or "II-III" as do some other sources; every class III river also has class I and II rapids on it, and "class II-III" is ambiguous about whether the hardest rapids are class II-III or there are a mix of class II and class III rapids.

(c) **Length/distance** of the run, in miles, between the recommended put in and take out. Where there are alternative trip distances, this is explained in the text.

(d) **Area**, meaning catchment/drainage area above the put in. While imperfect, this is the best measure of how easy it is to catch the creek. As this statistic is not in any other local guidebooks, the absolute numbers may not yet mean much to most paddlers; however, the relative numbers should be useful immediately.

(e) **Gauge**, showing the reading that corresponds to zero-level paddling for the one or two specified gauges that are most relevant for the majority of the creeks in the chapter.

(f) **Rating**, from zero indicated by a dash (-) to four stars (****). This is obviously subjective, and is from the point of view of a high-intermediate paddler. The greatest weight is given to the challenge and frequency of the rapids, followed by the density of strainers, the scenery and the length of the run. The rating is given in exclamation points (!!!!) where the creek is class IV- or above in difficulty.

While the chapter tables lack room for more columns, under the individual creeks/sections I add the following data.

(g) **Scenery**, from A to D. This is also subjective, and may be distorted by the time of year (and even the weather) when I paddled the creek.

(h) **Strainers**, showing a range around the number per mile that I encountered. This includes trees and fences, but not low-water bridges (which are described in the text). Of course, strainers come and go, so these figures may be quite irrelevant when you run the stream. Nevertheless, certain creeks, because of their narrowness, topography, surrounding land use, beaver populations etc., tend to have higher densities of strainers.

On a separate line below the other data, I name the relevant USGS 1:24,000 **topographical map(s)** and give the **source of my information** on the creek, including the month and year of my last trip on it, so readers can know how up to date it is.

I have also added the **GPS locations** of the nearest road access to the put in and take out; **using Google Maps, you can then print out a map of the route from any location to the creek**. As a result, I have not had to include detailed shuttle maps in this book, and have been able to limit the **maps** to general ones covering each part and each chapter, that indicate the location of the streams.

I have not included two statistics often found in paddling guidebooks: time and stream width. The **time** spent depends on the water level, the size of the group and the amount of playing and/or scouting. For flat creeks or those with occasional strainers, two mph is a good average; on others, four mph or even more is feasible. Creek **width** has never seemed particularly important, and many creeks vary greatly in width. Furthermore, the catchment area is a reasonable proxy for flow, which correlates with average width.

Where there are (a) significant differences in difficulty between parts of a creek, or (b) long physical interruptions such as reservoirs, I have divided the creek into **sections**.

THE HOW AND WHEN (TO PADDLE SMALL STREAMS)

> **Revised International Standards of River Difficulty (Summarized)**
>
> **Class I: Easy.** Fast water with riffles and small waves. Few obstructions, all obvious and easily missed with little training. Risk to swimmers is slight; self-rescue is easy.
>
> **Class II: Novice.** Straightforward rapids with wide, clear channels which are evident without scouting. Maneuvering may be required, but rocks and medium-sized waves are easily missed by trained paddlers. Swimmers are seldom injured and group assistance is seldom needed.
>
> **Class III: Intermediate.** Rapids with moderate, irregular waves which may be difficult to avoid and which can swamp an open canoe. Complex maneuvers in fast current and good boat control in tight passages or around ledges are often required. Scouting is advisable for inexperienced parties. Injuries while swimming are rare, but group assistance may be required to avoid long swims.
>
> **Class IV: Advanced.** Intense, powerful but predictable rapids requiring precise boat handling in turbulent water. May have large, unavoidable waves and holes or constricted passages. A strong Eskimo roll for closed boats and a fast, reliable eddy turn needed. May require scouting and "must" moves above hazards. Moderate to high risk of injury to swimmers. Group assistance for rescue often essential, and requires practiced skills.
>
> **Class 5: Expert.** Extremely long, obstructed or violent rapids with added risk. May contain large, unavoidable waves and holes or steep, congested chutes with demanding routes. Any eddies may be small, turbulent or difficult to reach. Swims are dangerous, and rescue difficult, even for experts. Class 5 is an open-ended scale designated class 5.0, 5.1, 5.2 etc., with the increased difficulty from class 5.0 to 5.1, for example, the same as from class IV to 5.0.
>
> **Class VI: Unrunnable.**

From Top to Bottom

The remainder of the book has eight parts. Part II is the **Metropolitan Baltimore** basins (of which the Gunpowder, Patapsco and Patuxent basins are the largest). Part III covers **Wills Creek to Catoctin Creek** in central and western Maryland and adjacent parts of Pennsylvania. The Wills Creek basin is beyond the book's 2-hour range, but is included because of its excellent whitewater. Part IV describes the **Monocacy River Basin**. Part V on **Washington DC & the Maryland Suburbs** completes the north bank of the Potomac. Part VI is on the **Cacapon & West Virginia Panhandle Basins** (which mostly start in Virginia and flow into the "Eastern Panhandle" of West Virginia). The **Shenandoah Basin** (excluding the headwaters farthest from Washington DC) forms Part VII, while Part VIII covers watersheds in **Northern Virginia** which drain into the south bank of the Potomac. Finally, Part IX is on the **Rappahannock River Basin**. Parts II, V and VIII are heavily urban and suburban, whereas the others are mostly rural.

Within each part, the chapters generally cover a single large river basin or several smaller, adjacent basins. In general, sequences are from north to south, from upstream to downstream, and from main stem to tributaries.

The **Geographic Coverage map** (page 6) gives an overview of the the division into parts, the **8 part coverage maps** show the division into chapters, and the **39 chapter maps** show all of the individual creeks (plus others that are referred to, even if not included).

METROPOLITAN BALTIMORE

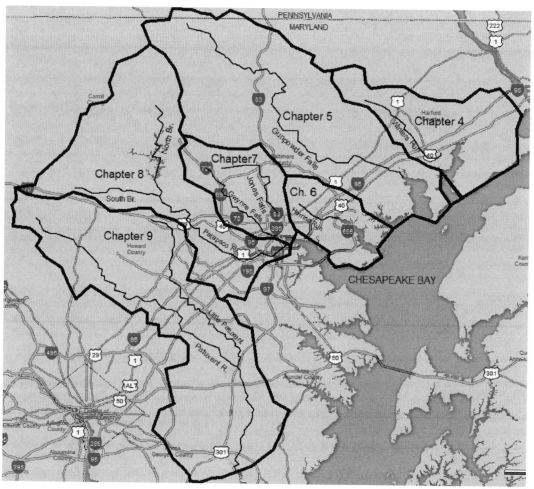

© Copyright 2005-2011 Undertow Software Corp.

PART II: METROPOLITAN BALTIMORE

Between the vast Susquehanna basin (28,000 sq. mi.), outside the scope of this book, and the Potomac basin (14,600 sq. mi.), which is the subject of Parts III to VIII, lie some much smaller watersheds, of which those of the Patuxent River (925 sq. mi.), Gunpowder Falls (415 sq. mi.) and the Patapsco River (370 sq. mi.) are the largest, that are roughly congruent with Metropolitan Baltimore (except that the lower Patuxent basin extends much too far south). This area has about 2.2 million people (38% of Maryland), from the outer suburbs to the inner city. And it has excellent paddling quality and variety when the creeks are up, for all skill levels.

While the Gunpowder basin extends slightly into Pennsylvania, those headwaters are too small to paddle, so all of the trips in Part II are in Maryland – in Baltimore City and County, Howard County, southern Harford County, eastern Carroll County and parts of Montgomery and Prince Georges counties. As for Baltimore City itself, its 80 sq. mi. of land are divided equally (22 sq. mi. apiece) between the Back River, Jones Falls and Gwynns Falls basins, with the remaining 14 sq. mi. draining directly into the Patapsco River estuary of the Chesapeake Bay.

Chapter 4, on **Southern Harford County** (the northern part of the county is in the Susquehanna basin), includes three excellent intermediate paddles, Swan Creek, James Run and Bynum Run, none of which are in previous guidebooks, as well as the larger and easier Winters Run and its tiny branches.

Chapter 5 is on the **Gunpowder Falls Basin**. The lower Gunpowder Falls is a delightful intermediate trip and Long Green Creek is a premier advanced paddle. Other fine intermediate runs include parts of Little Falls and Little Gunpowder Falls, and two upper sections of (big) Gunpowder Falls, one of which is often up (because of dam releases) during dry periods.

Chapter 6 is on the small **Back River Basin**. Herring Run is the largest creek (which shows how tiny everything else is) and a long and enjoyable albeit polluted paddle, while Chinquapin Run, Stemmers Run and the West Branch of Herring Run are interesting micro-streams. This, and chapter 7, are the most "brown water" (i.e. polluted) portions of Part II.

Chapter 7 covers the adjacent **Jones & Gwynns Falls Basins**, which drain the western and central parts of Baltimore City and have a surprising number of steep, runnable tributaries. Gwynns Falls has excellent whitewater, Jones Falls has regular releases and even races, and Dead Run and Western Run are the best of their tributaries.

Chapter 8, on the **Patapsco River Basin**, includes the North and South branches and their tributaries, as well as some tiny but interesting streams nearer Baltimore. Piney Run is the most challenging creek in this chapter, but there are fine intermediate paddles on parts of the main stem and the North and South branches, as well as Morgan, Beaver and Bens runs.

Finally, chapter 9 is on the **Patuxent River Basin**, which divides the Baltimore and Washington spheres of influence. The lower Little Patuxent is the only good whitewater trip in this watershed, and its Savage Falls is one of the most interesting and challenging rapids around.

These basins are remarkably well supplied with **river gauges** – 56 as of January 2013 – a huge help for catching their many fine creeks, and far more than for any other part of this book. This is largely because of concerns about both flooding and water quality in Metropolitan Baltimore. Most of the area also has on-line rain gauges. Unfortunately, for two of the largest and most popular waterways, the lower Gunpowder Falls and the Patapsco River, there are no on-line river gauges.

SOUTHERN HARFORD COUNTY

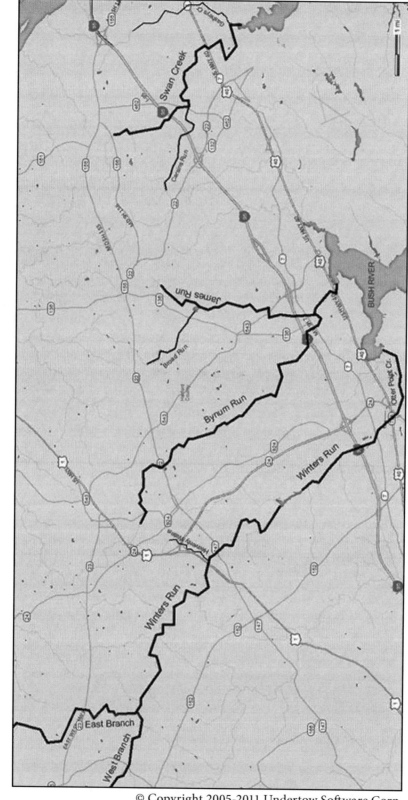

© Copyright 2005-2011 Undertow Software Corp.

Chapter 4:

SOUTHERN HARFORD COUNTY

Harford County, the northeastern end of the Baltimore Metropolitan Area, is a prosperous, generally rural area of 245,000 people that is increasingly being drawn into the Great Northeastern Megalopolis. In southern Harford County, just south of the once-mighty but now heavily-dammed Susquehanna River, are **Swan Creek** and the basin of the Bush River estuary. The latter was explored by Captain John Smith in 1608 and was the site of a 1663 peace treaty between English settlers and the Susquehannock, to counter their common enemy, the Seneca. The three main creeks that flow into it are **James, Bynum** and **Winters runs**. In turn, Winters Run, the largest of them, has runnable **East** and *West* **branches** (*italics* means this is an "explorers' special"). Little Gunpowder Falls, which forms the southwestern boundary of Harford County (with Baltimore County), is in chapter 5 on the Gunpowder Falls basin.

Swan Creek, Bynum Run and James Run all have excellent whitewater as they descend the fall line. Bynum Run offers the longest trip and two gorges, Swan Creek the hardest rapid and James Run the best scenery. Winters Run has two decent novice trips (separated by a reservoir), the first worth starting (when you have enough water) on its East Branch. I don't know much about the *West Branch* – it's an "explorers' special."

Bel Air, the county seat, located between upper Bynum and Winters runs, is the largest city, with 88,000 people (including adjacent unincorporated areas). Aberdeen (15,000), near the mouth of Swan Creek, is a distant second.

> **Henry Harford**, the last lord proprietary of Maryland, was the "love child" of Frederick Lord Baltimore, who died in 1771 without legitimate children and willed his possessions to his only son. Henry Harford was a British loyalist during the American Revolution; as a result his Maryland properties were all confiscated, although the county's name was not changed.

GAUGES: The seven river gauges in this area provide excellent coverage: Swan Creek (13.2 sq. mi.), James Run (9.2 sq. mi.), Bynum Run (8.5 sq. mi.), Winters Run (35 sq. mi.), Plumtree Run and Wheel Creek (tiny Winters Run tributaries, with 2.5 and 0.7 sq. mi., respectively, which serve almost like rain gauges) and Otter Point Creek (the continuation of Winters Run, 56 sq. mi.). There are no rain gauges reported. In the table below, **the zero-level gauge reference is to Bynum Run** (because of its central location).

name	gradient	difficulty	length	area	gauge	rating
Swan Creek	45 (100)	II+ (III)	2.7	11	75 cfs	***
James Run	50 (80)	II+ (III-)	4.0	7	110 cfs	***
Bynum Run - Section 1	42 (80)	III-	3.6	8	90 cfs	****
- Section 2	23	II	2.8	14	65 cfs	**
Winters Run - Section 1	20	I (II)	9.4	19	50 cfs	**
- Section 2	19 (30)	I	2.7	47	25 cfs	*
West Branch	35	?	2.5	5	100 cfs	?
East Branch	28	II-	2.5	7	75 cfs	**

SWAN CREEK: Carsins Run (Md. 462) to Post Road (Md. 132)

Gradient	Difficulty	Distance	Area	Scenery	Strainers	Rating
45 (100)	II+ (III)	2.7	11	B-	0-2/mi.	***

USGS Quad – Aberdeen; Source – Personal descent 9/11
N39 32.02, W76 10.09 to N39 31.22, W76 8.39

Swan Creek is the first stream to flow into the Chesapeake Bay below the Susquehanna River. The wide inlet called Swan Creek forms the northern border of the US Army's Aberdeen Proving Ground. The whitewater Swan Creek rises five miles north of Aberdeen (home of the Baltimore Orioles' Cal Ripken, the Ripken Museum and Ripken Stadium) and flows southeast. It is still tiny when it passes beneath I-95, but in the next mile it picks up its main tributary, Carsins Run, plus a pair of smaller branches.

You can put in on Carsins Run (100 yards above the confluence), which contributes about half the water, or on Swan Creek itself (350 yards above the confluence). This is an enjoyable and interesting trip, with only a few creek-wide strainers, mostly in the early part before the main rapids, although wood may also complicate some rapids. Especially in high water, be very cautious about blind turns.

There are only a few short class II- drops in the initial mile. Then, after a large island (most of the water goes to the right), the creek gets more interesting, with a mile of long class II and II+ rock gardens that approach class III in higher water. The gradient then eases up a bit, and you reach a culvert which can be run at very low water but requires catching a tiny eddy just above it on river left at higher levels.

At the next bridge, pull over on the right to scout a pair of class III ledges, 50 yards apart, which run together at higher levels. Both are 5-foot drops through boulders and concrete slabs. The first ledge is easiest on the right. Both ledges are easier with more water (up to a point), require sharp left turns and can be portaged. Nice rapids then continue to the end.

The scenery is pretty wooded hillsides for the first two miles, with Old Robin Hood Road alongside. We saw ducks and herons, but no swans. The final half mile, however, includes an upscale trailer park alongside the class III drops, US 40, two railroad tracks and a fair bit of trash.

Below the Post Road take out, the creek soon becomes flat, enters a swampy area, picks up its final tributary, Gasheys Creek, and widens out into a Chesapeake Bay inlet.

GAUGE: You can check the level from the road. Look for 115 cfs on the Swan Creek gauge at US 40, shortly above the take out. At 300 cfs, this is a very lively run.

Aberdeen Proving Ground is the Army's oldest weapons training and testing center. Every year, it teaches 20,000 recruits, right after their basic training, how to maintain and repair virtually all military equipment. It tests everything from submarines to boots. The rifle used to kill President Kennedy was brought here for ballistics testing after the assassination. The US Army Ordnance Museum contains the world's most extensive collection of military materiel.

The Swan Creek Restoration Partnership was initiated in 1994 by the Aberdeen city, Harford County and Maryland state governments, the US Army Corps of Engineers and the Aberdeen Proving Grounds. Community support was enlisted for activities such as tree planting, trash clean-up and water quality monitoring, and priority was given, within the limited funding available, to removing barriers to herring and alewife spawning runs. I have no idea how successful it was.

JAMES RUN: James Run Road to Philadelphia Road (Md. 7)

Gradient	Difficulty	Distance	Area	Scenery	Strainers	Rating
50 (80)	II+ (III-)	4.0	7	A-	0-2/mi.	***

USGS Quad – Bel Air/Edgewood; Source – Personal descent 10/06
N39 31.51, W76 15.43 to N39 28.59, W76 15.63

This is a beautiful intermediate run, mostly through a mini wilderness. Put in on James Run Road, 150 yards above the confluence with Broad Run (which is actually the larger of the two by far – 5 vs. 2 sq. mi. drainage). That first short stretch parallels James Run Road and is extremely narrow, until Broad Run pours in through two huge culverts, from a lake that provides water for a blacktop plant and gravel quarry.

The next 1.6 miles are virtually continuous class II and II+, at 65 ft/mile, getting harder towards the end. The streambed is wide enough to give a choice of routes, and there are no memorable drops – just constant maneuvering. In 2002, I encountered 8 creek-wide strainers here (all easy to spot and portage); in 2006, we never had to leave our boats, although several partial strainers required precise maneuvering. The next mile, alongside and then below Nova Scotia Road, is class II with a 40-ft/mile gradient and occasional views of barns, fields and houses. After Creswell Road (the USGS gauge is just below on river right), the gradient picks up again, and there are several nice rapids, including a class III- on a left turn. The creek does not flatten out until the final one-third mile, from I-95 to the take out at Philadelphia Road (Md. 7).

Below Md. 7, it is just a further flat one-third mile to the confluence with Bynum Run to form the Bush River, and another mile until that widens into the Bush River estuary of the Chesapeake Bay.

GAUGE: If you have enough water to run the first 150 yards to the confluence, you should be OK. You can also check the level from the rapids alongside Nova Scotia Road or Creswell Road. The James Run gauge should be over 125 cfs. Look for 35 cfs on Plumtree Run as a leading indicator, 2-3 hours before you start.

The first part of the run is along the edge of the **Stoney Forest Demonstration Area**. This forest of tulip poplar, beech, oak and hickory was purchased by the Maryland Department of Natural Resources in 1981, to educate private landowners in forestry management practices.

Half a mile above Creswell Road, on river right, are the remains of the **Harford Furnace**. Established in 1833, this iron works and industrial center once employed 6,000 people.

🛶 BYNUM RUN

Until I blew the whistle, Bynum Run had been a better-kept secret than who met with Dick Cheney's energy task force. It flows southeast for 14 miles, past Bel Air.

> **James Bynum** was killed by Indians along the creek in 1673. On Md. 7 between Bynum and James Runs is the hamlet of Bush, once the seat of Harford County; here, on March 22, 1775, was issued the **Bush Declaration**, the first call for independence by an elected body.
> Bel Air was the birthplace of the **Booth brothers** – Edwin, the greatest American tragedian of the mid-19th Century, and John Wilkes, who carried out its greatest tragedy. Their father, Junius Brutus Booth, was an actor who came from England and established a Shakespearian touring company. Their childhood home, Tudor Hall, became a bed and breakfast which was also used for performances and conferences, until its sale as a private residence in 1999.

Section 1: Churchville Road (Md. 22) to Wheel Road

Gradient	Difficulty	Distance	Area	Scenery	Strainers	Rating
42 (80)	III-	3.6	8	B+	0-2/mi.	****

USGS Quad – Bel Air; Source – Personal descent 7/06
N39 32.48, W76 19.84 to N39 30.20, W76 18.34

The put in is in Bynum Run Park; the on-line gauge is just below the bridge. You soon enter the first gorge, which is a half-mile long and up to class III-. After 1.5 miles you pass E. Macphail Road and then a closed low-water bridge. The next mile is class I, through woods and the Bel Air golf course. This is followed by a mile-long gorge of virtually continuous class II+ to III- rapids, with a total drop of 65 feet. It reminded me of the stretch of rapids on Rock Creek in DC; although this Bynum Run gorge is not quite as steep, it is twice as long. Wheel Road marks the end of the best rapids.

  GAUGE: The Bynum Run gauge should be over 90 cfs; 25 cfs on Plumtree Run would be a leading indicator, 2-3 hours before you start. The visual USGS gauge at the put in should be over 1.3.

Section 2: Wheel Road to Hookers Mill Road

Gradient	Difficulty	Distance	Area	Scenery	Strainers	Rating
23	II	2.8	14	B	0-2/mi.	**

USGS Quad – Bel Air/Edgewood; Source – Personal descent 7/06
N39 30.20, W76 18.34 to N39 28.73, W76 16.81

Below Wheel Road there are no more gorges, and the rapids, though frequent, are easier. One can find bald eagles, great blue herons and lots of geese and mallards.

  Take out at Hookers Mill Road, shortly above I-95. There is an enticing rapid just below, but the mile to Md. 7 is through ranchland with barbed wire fences. The creek is flat below Md. 7, and in 0.6 miles it meets James Run to form the Bush River.

  GAUGE: You need 4 inches less than for section 1, or about 65 cfs on the Bynum Run gauge. Check the rapids at the put in.

WINTERS RUN

Winters Run (named for the colonial family of Elisha Winter) is formed at the confluence of its East and West branches. Between sections 1 and 2 is the 1.5-mile Atkisson Reservoir, built in World War II to provide water to the nearby military base. Below section 2 is a smaller reservoir for water treatment, and then, at tidewater, the name changes to Otter Point Creek. In another 3 miles, that becomes a Chesapeake Bay estuary, which 2 miles later merges into the Bush River estuary.

Section 1: Pleasantville Road to Ring Factory Road

Gradient	Difficulty	Distance	Area	Scenery	Strainers	Rating
20	I (II)	9.4	19	B	1/mi.	**

USGS Quad – Jarrettsville/BelAir/Edgewood; Source – Personal descent (first 4.4 miles) 11/04; Gertler
N39 33.04, W76 26.17 via N39 32.00, W76 23.49 (mile 4.4) to N39 29.68, W76 21.46

This scenic novice trip has a rather steady gradient, lots of long riffles, one class II rapid and a dangerous weir. The first access is Pleasantville Road, 0.4 miles below the confluence. The next 3.8 miles, to Carrs Mill Road, are through woodland with fern-covered cliffs and frequent riffles, but also some downed trees. There is a class II rock garden through the ruins of an old milldam just above Carrs Mill Road, and good access 0.6 miles later at Watervale Road (mile 4.4).

Just above US 1, at mile 6.5, is a **4-foot sloping weir with a strong hydraulic**. At low levels, experienced paddlers can run this with speed, close to the right bank; others should portage on the left. Just below US 1, a tiny, strainer-filled tributary misnamed Heavenly Waters enters. Take out at Ring Factory Road, above the reservoir.

GAUGE: At Pleasantville Road, if the level looks adequate upstream, it will be so downstream as well. You need to project that the level on the Winters Run gauge (just below US 1) will be at least 200 cfs, some 2-3 hours after you put in.

Section 2: Singer Road to Philadelphia Road (Md. 7)

Gradient	Difficulty	Distance	Area	Scenery	Strainers	Rating
19 (30)	I	2.7	47	C+	<1/mi.	*

USGS Quad – Edgewood; Source – Personal descent (1st mile) 10/06; scouting
N39 28.47, W76 20.23 to N39 26.59, W76 18.93

For a long time, I ignored this section because Gertler reported that "the scenery degrades to a drab and trashy condition." But when I looked for myself, I was pleasantly surprised. The right bank has some rundown houses, but the left bank is wooded, with a few bamboo curtains. The gradient is 30 ft/mile for the first mile; its long riffles produce class II- waves when the water is high. There is a one-foot weir to be run. After that mile, the gradient drops to 12 ft/mile. Scout from and park along Winters Run Road.

GAUGE: Look for 100 cfs on Winters Run, 2-3 hours before you start, and 160 cfs on Otter Point Creek (half a mile below the take out) by the time you finish.

WEST BRANCH, WINTERS RUN: Charles St. to Confluence

Gradient	Difficulty	Distance	Area	Scenery	Strainers	Rating
35	?	2.5*	5	?	?	?

USGS Quad – Jarrettsville; Source – Partial scouting from road
N39 33.90, W76 26.36 to N39 33.04, W76 26.17

*(plus 0.4 miles on Winters Run)

This *"explorers' special"* is the somewhat smaller and steeper Winters Run headwater. You can put in at Md. 165, 1.5 miles above the confluence, or go up Charles Street to any of a number of put ins above that. One good option (used for the above data) is the low-water bridge of the Walnut Grove Tree Farm, 1 mile up Charles Street, which otherwise could be a hazard. Be alert for fences in this first mile, just below the confluence, and at Putnam Road shortly before the confluence, by the Addition to Conclusion estate (owned by logicians or political fund-raisers?), next door to which is, logically enough, the Subtraction from Addition to Conclusion property. Pleasantville Road, 0.4 miles below the confluence, is the first take out on Winters Run, but it is a steep climb, so you might as well keep going down to Watervale Road.

GAUGE: Check from Charles Street. You will want the Winters Run gauge to be projected to stay over 400 cfs, 3-4 hours after you put in, and the Bynum Run gauge to be projected to read at least 100 cfs an hour after you start. Some 35 cfs on Plumtree Run, an hour before you put in, would be the initial indicator.

EAST BRANCH, WINTERS RUN: Poteet Road to Confluence

Gradient	Difficulty	Distance	Area	Scenery	Strainers	Rating
28	II-	2.5*	7	C	1-2/mi.	**

USGS Quad – Jarrettsville; Source – Personal descent 11/04
N39 34.63, W76 26.36 to N39 33.04, W76 26.17

*(plus 0.4 miles on Winters Run)

The East Branch runs for 10 miles through a narrow valley. Put in at Poteet and Phillips Mill roads, a few yards above where Md. 23 passes high overhead. The creek has good current and lots of long riffles, with a few that reach class II-. After 1.5 miles, you pass Cosner Road, leave the woods and enter more open countryside. The biggest drop, a straightforward 3-foot ledge, is in this final mile. We encountered a wire and wood fence half a mile before the confluence, and its mate shortly below the confluence; fortunately, there were eddies above both. Pleasantville Road is 0.4 miles below the confluence, but most paddlers will want to continue down Winters Run at least to Watervale Road.

GAUGE: The riffles at the put in should be cleanly runnable. The Winters Run gauge should be projected to be at least 300 cfs, 3-4 hours after you put in, and the Bynum Run gauge over 75 cfs, about one hour after starting. Some 25 cfs on Plumtree Run, an hour beforehand, would be the first indicator of enough water being likely.

GUNPOWDER FALLS BASIN

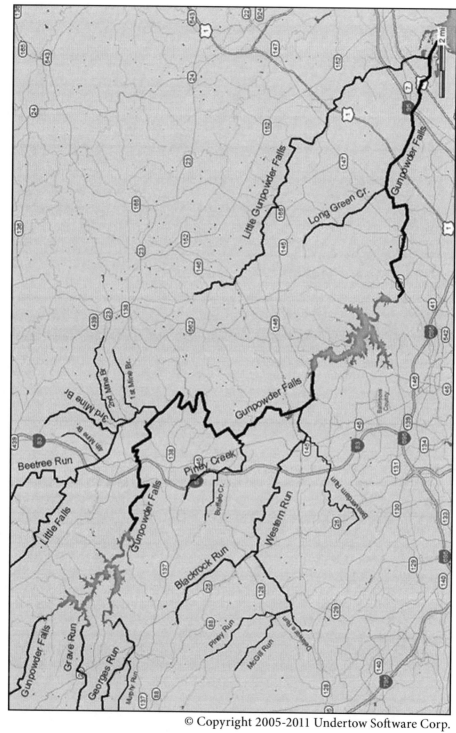

Chapter 5:
GUNPOWDER FALLS BASIN

Gunpowder Falls drains 415 square miles, in Baltimore County and bits of Harford and Carroll counties, Md., and York County, Pa. It is a basin of rolling hills, farms, stately homes, Republicans and good paddling variety, which covers most of the land from the Baltimore Beltway north to (and in places just beyond) the Pennsylvania state line. Hampstead (6,000) is the largest town in the northern part of the watershed, while Cockeysville (21,000) and Joppa (13,000) are much closer to Baltimore.

Gunpowder Falls itself can be run for a total of 31.5 miles, not counting its two reservoirs. The first runnable tributary, *Grave Run* (an "explorers' special"), rushes into Prettyboy Reservoir, followed a few miles later by the gentler **Georges Run**. Below Prettyboy Dam enters **Little Falls**, which can be paddled for over 10 miles, includes a delightful class III gorge, and has a class II- feeder named **Beetree Run** and a tiny and strainer-strewn class III tributary called **Third Mine Branch**. Then comes a thoroughly mediocre **Piney Creek**.

Into Loch Raven Reservoir flows the class I and relatively easy to catch **Western Run**, which has an interesting tributary, **Blackrock Run** (section 1 of which is a steep "explorers' special"). Below the reservoir is the most challenging water in the basin, **Long Green Creek**, the favorite local advanced trip of Baltimore kayakers. Its first class IV stretch can be scouted from the road, while the second is a longer and more beautiful wilderness adventure. Finally, where Gunpowder Falls is already tidal, **Little Gunpowder Falls** enters, after its 17 runnable miles, consisting of a long novice section 1 and an excellent section 2 with miles of continuous rapids, including a class III stretch.

> Over 17,000 acres along big and Little Gunpowder Falls are protected within **Gunpowder State Park**, largely to ensure the quality of Baltimore's drinking water. Swimming, hiking, picnicking and horseback riding are promoted. The **Northern Central Railroad Trail** is a scenic bicycle route that follows Beetree Run, Little Falls and Gunpowder Falls.
>
> **Gunpowder? Falls?** There are three theories concerning the river's name. One, now generally considered apocryphal, is that Native Americans, believing the gunpowder they had received from the colonists to be seeds, planted it along the creek. More likely is that the colonists named it after the deposits of saltpeter, a key ingredient of gunpowder, found near its mouth (a little south of there is Saltpeter Creek). The other contestant is that the popping sound from burning the local willow branches reminded early explorers of the discharge sound of gunpowder. "Falls" is a Baltimore regionalism, now used for only six streams – Gunpowder, Little Gunpowder, Little (chapter 5), Gwynns, Jones (chapter 7) and Gillis Falls (chapter 8).

GAUGES: Estimating water levels in this basin was once problematical but is now generally a breeze. There are (as of 2012) fifteen electronic gauges, with one or more on almost every creek covered in this chapter. The only real difficulty is for sections 5 and 6 of the Gunpowder Falls. The best source for that is usually the Greater Baltimore Canoe Club bulletin board, or, if Loch Raven Reservoir was full, you can calculate based on the water flowing into that reservoir. Rainfall is reported from a dozen sites in Baltimore County, although not from the rest of the basin. In the table below, **the gauge column refers to Beetree Run** (10 sq. mi.), except that the figures in ***bold italics are for the Little Falls gauge*** (53 sq. mi.).

name	gradient	difficulty	length	area	gauge	rating
Gunpowder Falls - Sec. 1	18	I	2.6	19	40cfs	*
- Sec. 2	31	II+	2.5	25	40cfs	***
- Sec. 3	35	III-	1.3	81	n.a.	***
- Sec. 4	8	I (II-)	15.3	83	n.a.	*
- Sec. 5	10	I	7.0	306	n.a.	*
- Sec. 6	23 (40)	III- (III)	3.4	340	n.a.	****
Grave Run	68 (100)	?	1.7	6	125cfs	?
Georges Run	25	I	1.6	13	40cfs	*
Little Falls - Section 1	52	II	2.3	11	65cfs	**
- Section 2	24	II-	3.1	24	40cfs	*
- Section 3	35 (60)	III- (III)	2.0	32	*175cfs*	****
- Section 4	10	I	2.9	41	*100cfs*	*
Beetree Run	30	II-	1.5	9	70cfs	*
Third Mine Branch	40 (80)	III	2.4	6	150cfs	*
Piney Creek	23	II- (II)	3.5	8	85cfs	*
Western Run	11	I	10.9	21	30cfs	*
Blackrock Run -Sec.1	33 (160)	?	2.4	5	150cfs	?
-Sec.2	30 (65)	II+	1.6	12	70cfs	**
Long Green Creek	85 (200)	IV	1.9	9	110cfs	!!!!
Little Gunpowder-Sec.1	15	II- (II)	11.5	20	45cfs	**
-Sec.2	33 (75)	III-(III+)	5.5	43	*160cfs*	****

GUNPOWDER FALLS

Gunpowder Falls is a special river to Baltimore-area paddlers; for example, the newsletter of the Greater Baltimore Canoe Club is *The Gunpowder Gazette*. Because of its two reservoirs and of variations in difficulty, I have divided Gunpowder Falls into 6 sections. Above Prettyboy Reservoir, the low-intermediate section 2 flows through a hemlock-shaded gorge, and is far better than the novice section 1. Section 3, just below Prettyboy Dam, is the lovely and exciting but short Gunpowder Gorge. It and the novice section 4 are often up during dry summers because of dam releases. Below Loch Raven Reservoir are a beginner stretch (section 5) and the popular, intermediate fall-line rapids (section 6). The Big G (as it is affectionately called) has been the main source of drinking and other water for Baltimore City and County since the Loch Raven (1912) and Prettyboy (1933) dams were built, after Lake Roland on Jones Falls had become too polluted. The North Branch of the Patapsco now supplements the supply.

> **Captain John Smith** sailed up Gunpowder Falls in 1608, until he was stopped by the rapids. He found iron ore and met with the Susquehannock and Massawomek tribes.
> Power from Gunpowder Falls made this an **industrial center** during the 19th Century. The Gunpowder Copper Works at Harford Road provided the original roofing for the US Capitol dome. Near Perry Hall, on US 1, were four iron furnaces and forges, the oldest dating to 1731. The Joppa Iron Works, further downstream near Philadelphia Road, were a leading supplier of nails and other iron goods from 1817 until 1865. Appropriately, there were also gunpowder mills, which blew up from time to time due to lightening and accidents.

Section 1: Old York Road to Grave Run Road

Gradient	Difficulty	Distance	Area	Scenery	Strainers	Rating
18	I	2.6	19	C	2-3/mi.	*

USGS Quad – Lineboro; Source – Personal descent 6/01
N39 42.87, W76 49.79 to N39 41.81, W76 48.34

Gunpowder Falls rises in York County, crosses the Mason-Dixon Line in 2 miles, and picks up its (much larger) South Branch. Put in 0.4 miles below the confluence, at Old York Road, alongside the railroad tracks. The first half of this run follows the tracks south, before the creek swings east. There are frequent riffles, occasional strainers, a private bridge and two heavy wooden fences (shortly above Grave Run Road). At low levels, the fences can be squeezed through, but with higher water they require portages.

GAUGE: On the staff gauge on river left just above Gunpowder Road, 2.0 is zero level. Look for 100 cfs on the Gunpowder Falls at Hoffmanville and 200 cfs on Little Falls. The rain gauge is Freeland in Baltimore County.

Section 2: Grave Run Road to Gunpowder Road

Gradient	Difficulty	Distance	Area	Scenery	Strainers	Rating
31	II+	1.5	25	A	0-2/mi.	***

USGS Quad – Lineboro; Source – Personal descent 6/01
N39 41.81, W76 48.34 to N39 41.41, W76 46.89

Put in, with permission, 50 yards downstream of the bridge. The run is through the beautiful Hemlock Canyon, where fern-covered rocks complement the extensive stands of 200-year old hemlocks. The class II and II+ rapids come in one gorge, and include rock gardens and small ledges. Expect a few trees blocking the creek (beavers are common).

If you continue past Gunpowder Road (site of the gauge), you go through a second gorge that is more dramatic, as the cliffs come down almost to the water. Alas, after almost a mile, you end up just inside Prettyboy Reservoir, for which boating permits are sold on an annual basis ($60 now), and only if you sign an agreement not to use your boat anywhere else. This is to prevent the introduction of zebra mussels, and even though these have not been known to attach themselves to plastic boats, **you will be fined if you are caught without a permit.** To avoid this risk, skip the second gorge and take out at Gunpowder Road.

GAUGE: The minimum levels are the same as for Section 1.

Hoffmanville, just upstream of the reservoir, is the site of the **first paper mill** in Maryland (1775-1893), and may have made the first paper for currency in the US. The water was pure enough because limestone filtered it and because the mill was upstream of most farms. Three mills were built, with 100 workers producing some 4 tons of paper per day, but fires and floods damaged them badly starting in the 1880s. The remains of the buildings, dam and diversion canal are on river right.

Section 3: Prettyboy Dam to Falls Road (Gunpowder Gorge)

Gradient	Difficulty	Distance	Area	Scenery	Strainers	Rating
35	III-	1.3	81	A	0-2/mi.	***

USGS Quad – Hereford; Source – Personal descent often
N39 37.17, W76 42.45 to N39 37.14, W76 41.43

This beautiful trip would earn four stars were it not for the carry to the put in. The dramatic way to enter is via the long staircase at the base of Prettyboy Dam; park just across the bridge. The alternative is to park in a gravel area on Falls Road, a half mile west of the take out, and carry/drag in a quarter mile, turning right at both intersections.

The first half of the trip from the dam is class I, with frequent riffles. Then come half a dozen interesting class II+ to III- rapids, before the creek calms down as it approaches Falls Road. All can be boat-scouted, but beware of strainers.

This trip is dependent upon water releases from Prettyboy Reservoir, which occur either: a) when there has been so much rain that Prettyboy Reservoir is full, or b) when there has been so little rain that Loch Raven Reservoir is low, and water must be coursed down there to supply Baltimore. Because the water usually comes from the bottom of the dam, it is pretty chilly, so you will enjoy this trip most on hot summer days.

For an easier take out (the climb up at Falls Road is a bit steep) or a somewhat longer trip, continue 0.7 miles down section 4 to Masemore Road.

GAUGE: Look for at least 100 cfs on the on-line gauge for Gunpowder Falls near Parkton. On the staff gauge on river left, 30 yards below Falls Road, 1.8 is zero level. This means at least one full tube is open at the dam. They do not announce release levels in advance, but generally the Friday afternoon levels are continued through the weekend.

My first attempt to run this, on what turned out to be the **first day of trout season**, was foiled by elbow-to-elbow anglers upstream of Falls Road. In 1986, however, the fishing regime changed to year round catch-and-release, made feasible by constant cold water releases from the dam of at least 11.5 cfs. Since the early 1990s, stocking has been discontinued, but natural breeding maintains a population of some 1,500 adult brown trout and 200 rainbow trout per mile.

Prettyboy Branch is a small Gunpowder Falls tributary near the site of the dam. It was named by the local landowner after his favorite riding horse, which drowned there.

Section 4: Falls Road to Phoenix Road

Gradient	Difficulty	Distance	Area	Scenery	Strainers	Rating
8	I (II-)	15.3	83	B-	<1/mi.	*

USGS Quad – Hereford/Phoenix; Source – Personal descent often
N39 37.14, W76 41.43 via N39 35.92, W76 37.57 to N39 31.37, W76 37.47

This mellow and pretty trip, like section 3, may be up during dry summers. The water is cool, a great bonus on hot summer days. There are frequent riffles and a long class II- rapid shortly below Big

Falls Road (mile 5.1). There are nine intermediate bridges; Blue Mount Road (mile 6) and Monkton (mile 8.5) are popular take outs, as the gradient drops a bit after that. In November 2007, paddlers sawed out some nuisance strainers without permission, leading to legal problems and bad publicity. Tubers are common. About a mile below Phoenix Road, the creek enters the Loch Raven Reservoir.

    GAUGE: Zero level is the same as for section 3.

Section 5: Cromwell Bridge Road to US 1

Gradient	Difficulty	Distance	Area	Scenery	Strainers	Rating
10	I	7.0	306	B	0	*

USGS Quad – White Marsh; Source – Gertler
N39 25.46, W76 31.85 via N39 25.33, W76 30.13 (Md. 147) to N39 25.64, W76 26.68

This pretty but rather dull trip begins shortly below the Lock Raven Reservoir, and the river is similar to but wider than in section 4 above. For a shorter trip, put in at Md. 147 for the last 4.5 miles of this section. The mouth of Long Green Creek is 1.3 miles above US 1; to see some advanced whitewater, take a side hike up that little terror.

    GAUGE: You need 4 inches less than for section 6, i.e. minus 4 inches at the RC gauge at US 1 (see below), but are still dependent upon rainfall while Lock Raven dam is full.

Section 6: US 1 to US 40 (Gunpowder Fall Line)

Gradient	Difficulty	Distance	Area	Scenery	Strainers	Rating
23 (40)	III- (III)	3.4	340	B+	0	****

USGS Quad – White Marsh; Source – Personal descent often
N39 25.64, W76 26.68 to N39 24.74, W76 23.31

This is a delightful intermediate run through Gunpowder Falls State Park. The longest rapid is the class III Gunpowder Falls, but two class III- rapids probably cause more spills. Even at zero level, these three rapids stay interesting, although other spots get bony. Potts Rock rapid, a mile into the trip, starts easy but gets tricky. You can eddy out right and then ferry past the hole (or pillow, in low water), before turning downstream.. In higher water, an easier routes opens up on the far left.

    On the main falls, which is a 150-yard rock garden shortly below Md. 7, the easiest route is left of center. The upper half has more rocks (holes at higher water), and ends with a pair of large eddies, left and right. The lower half has bigger waves but is more open. Below 6 inches this rapid is only class III-, but by 2 feet it is class IV.

    The other class III- rapid, S-Turn, is near the end. Just below the first drop, you can catch the large eddy on river left and then ferry across the main current above the hole. There is lots of play here, including eddy hopping back up the rapid.

    Because there is no parking nearby along US 40, take out by the river left trail network about 50 yards upstream of US 40, and then carry a quarter mile (along a trail upgraded by the Greater Baltimore Canoe Club) to the parking lot off Jones Road.

Shortly below US 40, the river becomes tidal, and 2 miles later it flows into the Gunpowder River estuary of the Chesapeake Bay. Paddlers who enjoy scenic flat water and bird life can continue 4 miles through Maryland's only river delta, to Mariners Point (reached by car via Joppa Farm Road and Kearney Drive), but should keep maps handy.

GAUGE: There is an RC gauge at the put-in bridge, downstream river left. Because of the reservoir, this section may stay up several days after a good rain. But if the reservoir was not full, it will only come up very briefly, from the 40 sq. mi. catchment below the dam (look for 90 cfs on Long Green Creek). When the Loch Raven reservoir is full, add the cfs for the Gunpowder (at Glencoe), Western Run and Beaverdam Creek, and subtract 125 cfs for Baltimore's consumption (150 cfs when lawns are being watered). Some 375-400 cfs correlates with zero level 1-2 days later, and you get about one inch from every 40 cfs above that. Given these variables, most paddlers rely instead on visual inspections reported on the Greater Baltimore Canoe Club bulletin board.

GRAVE RUN: Falls Road (Md. 25) to Prettyboy Reservoir

Gradient	Difficulty	Distance	Area	Scenery	Strainers	Rating
68 (100)	?	1.7	6	?	?	?

USGS Quad – Hampstead/Lineboro; Source – Scouting access points
N39 39.30, W76 48.47 to N39 39.28, W76 46.76

This tiny *"explorers' special"* has its own on-line gauge. Put in at the confluence with Indian Run, where Grave Run Road turns east. The trip starts out steep and through the woods. After 0.4 miles, you come to Resh Mill Road (the remains of the mill are on river left), where you can expect strainers near the bridge. The next 0.8 miles is mostly through fields, with fences possible as well as a small dam. The first part of this has a mild gradient, but then it steepens. The final half mile is through the woods again. Shortly above the reservoir (and visible from Gunpowder Road) is a very tight drop with pinning potential. As there are usually strainers in the final 200 yards from there to the bridge, scout this final bit beforehand and take out above it if necessary.

GAUGE: The Grave Run gauge (near the take out) should read at least 100 cfs. The nearest rain gauges are Freeland and Butler in Baltimore County.

GEORGES RUN: Gunpowder Rd (off Md. 25) to Georges Run Road

Gradient	Difficulty	Distance	Area	Scenery	Strainers	Rating
25	I	1.6	13	C	0-2/mi.	*

USGS Quad – Lineboro; Source – Personal descent 6/04
N39 36.98, W76 47.56 to N39 37.56, W76 46.36

Georges Run is tiny until it picks up Murphy and Peggys runs. Put in 20 yards above the confluence with the latter, 200 yards west of Falls Road (Md. 25), on Gunpowder Road. The stream parallels the road for a half mile and reaches Georges Run Road a mile after that, shortly above the backwater from Prettyboy Reservoir. It has a steady gradient with lots of riffles. Watch out for the overhanging thorn bushes, which forced one kayaker to do a literally face-saving roll. The first half is through farmland, with one cabin right alongside the creek, but then you enter the woods.

GAUGE: There are three USGS staff gauges on this tiny creek; the put in needs 2.25, the take out bridge 2.5 and the take out on river left 1.0. Look for 65 cfs on the Georges Run gauge near the take out. The nearest rain gauges are Freeland and Butler.

LITTLE FALLS

Little Falls can be paddled for over ten miles. Its best feature is a beautiful mile-long gorge in section 3. Section 1 would be a delight as well, were it not for the strainers, while sections 2 and 4 have little whitewater. The on-line river gauge at Blue Mount is towards the end of section 4.

Section 1: Gore Mill Road (2nd bridge) to Eagle Mill Road

Gradient	Difficulty	Distance	Area	Scenery	Strainers	Rating
52	II	2.3	11	B	3-5/mi.	**

USGS Quad – New Freedom; Source – Personal descent 3/00
N39 40.85, W76 42.04 to N39 40.11, W76 40.25

Gore Mill Road crosses Little Falls three times. Just above the middle bridge is an 8-foot dam (for the millrace to Gores Mill), with boulders below. Put in at its base, after asking permission at the nearby house; if no one is home, leave a note on your car. The creek starts out barely 10-feet wide, but broadens as it flows through an attractive, shallow gorge, over nearly continuous riffles and easy rapids, with few intrusions of civilization. Unfortunately, beavers have been at work felling trees across the creek. After one mile you cross Valley Mill Road, and 1.3 miles later, Eagle Mill Road (guess what the creek used to be used for!) marks the end of the gorge.

GAUGE: Judge from the lower bridge over Gore Mill Road (at the put in, the creek looks runnable even when it is not). You will need about 65 cfs on Beetree Run (when you put in) and 350 cfs on Little Falls at Blue Mount (projected to 4 hours afterwards). The rainfall gauge is Freeland (Baltimore Co.)

Section 2: Eagle Mill Road to Parkton (York Road)

Gradient	Difficulty	Distance	Area	Scenery	Strainers	Rating
24	II-	3.1	24*	C	0-2/mi.	*

USGS Quad – New Freedom; Source – Personal descent 3/00
N39 40.11, W76 40.25 to N39 38.39, W76 39.60

*(including Beetree Run, which enters 0.4 miles later)

The creek has lost half its gradient by Eagle Mill Road. Soon, Beetree Run enters, widening the creek and almost doubling the flow. You are out of the woods; this hurts the scenery but helps the strainer situation. This trip is class I except for three 2-foot ledges. Civilization intrudes more and more, including I-83 high overhead.

GAUGE: Look for 40 cfs on Beetree Run (an hour before you put in) and 200 cfs on Little Falls (3 hours after you start). Freeland (Baltimore Co.) is the rainfall gauge.

Section 3: Parkton (York Road) to Wiseburg Road

Gradient	Difficulty	Distance	Area	Scenery	Strainers	Rating
35 (60)	III- (III)	2.0	32	A	<1/mi.	****

USGS Quad – New Freedom; Source – Personal descent often
N39 38.39, W76 39.60 to N39 37.59, W76 38.09

The first mile (visible in part from the NCR trail) is wonderful, while the next, although still pretty, is an anti-climax. Immediately after the put in, you enter a beautiful wooded gorge, with class II to III chutes and rock gardens. Early on is a steep, twisting set of drops between boulders; just go with the flow. Right after that comes a second class III-: a chute on the far right, where you cut back hard left. The class III main falls gives you some choices. The most obvious route is straight ahead over the 4-foot drop, best run about 4 feet from the right bank. A more gradual route down the middle requires a sharp left turn into a very tight channel, while higher water opens up a third possibility at the top of the rapid on river left. I spell these options out here, because the sheer walls make scouting difficult, and the routes are not obvious until you are well into the rapid. Right below, a long class II+ rock garden marks the end of the best whitewater, but there are several more easy rapids as the scenery opens up and the gradient drops.

    GAUGE: For a clean run down the main falls you need 175 cfs at Blue Mount, two hours after you put in. However, at just 125 cfs, all of the other rapids are OK, and you can bump your way down the falls (on the right side). Freeland (Baltimore Co.) is the nearest rain gauge.

Section 4: Wiseburg Road to Gunpowder Falls (Blue Mount Road)

Gradient	Difficulty	Distance	Area	Scenery	Strainers	Rating
10	I	2.9	41	C+	<1/mi.	*

USGS Quad – New Freedom/Hereford/Phoenix; Source – Personal descent 3/85
N39 37.59, W76 38.09 to N39 36.02, W76 37.52

This beginner trip has **one hazard – a 5-foot dam after a half mile**, best portaged on river left. The creek twists between high banks, then returns to a pretty gorge, past the Blue Mount gauge and down to Gunpowder Falls. Blue Mount Road is a quarter mile past the bridge and just above the confluence.

    GAUGE: Judge from the riffles upstream of the put in. About 100 cfs on Little Falls at Blue Mount will suffice. Freeland (Baltimore Co.) is the nearest rainfall gauge.

BEETREE RUN: Beetree Road to Little Falls

Gradient	Difficulty	Distance	Area	Scenery	Strainers	Rating
30	II-	1.5*	9	C	1-4/mi.	*

USGS Quad – New Freedom; Source – Personal descent 10/02
N39 41.04, W76 40.00 to N39 39.53, W76 40.25

*(plus 1 mile on Little Falls section 2, to Walker Road)

Beetree Run rises just north of the Mason-Dixon Line, and flows south for 6.5 miles, with the Northern Central Railroad (NCR) Trail alongside. Put in on Beetree Road, just off Kauffman Road. The first quarter mile is narrow and twisty, the next narrow and straight, to where Bentley Road comes alongside. In the next half mile, to Bentley Springs, you pass under the NCR Trail four times and through a front lawn. This section is typical in terms of width (5-25 feet) and rapids (long riffles, with a few 1-2 foot weirs and chutes). The final half mile is again through a more natural setting. Fortunately, the narrowest parts are through grass and bushes, so the few strainers are mostly in wider spots where it is easier to see them. From the confluence, it is a mile to the take out at Walker Road (and another two miles to Parkton), passing under two more NCR Trail bridges and over a 2-foot ledge.

GAUGE: Beetree Run has its own gauge, at Bentley Springs; you need at least 70 cfs. The nearest rainfall gauge is Freeland (Baltimore County).

THIRD MINE BRANCH: Stablersville Road to Little Falls

Gradient	Difficulty	Distance	Area	Scenery	Strainers	Rating
40 (80)	III	2.4*	6	C	3-5/mi.	*

USGS Quad – New Freedom; Source – Personal descent 7/04
N39 39.12, W76 37.58 to N39 37.59, W76 38.09

*(plus 0.5 miles of class I on Little Falls to section 3 take out)

The first two-thirds of this trip is dismal, the last third excellent; alas, it is one package. The earlier part is class I to II and was replete with strainers, including 2 fences and 4 I-beam footbridges. Numerous branches and bushes hung over the current. In high water, the strainers would be dangerous.

And then you make a sharp right turn and the creek becomes a whitewater delight through a deepening gorge. This starts with a long class III rock garden, and then the stream becomes continuous class II and III, with few if any strainers, all the way to Little Falls, from where it is half a mile of class I water to the section 3 take out. Kayakers might want to run this part of Third Mine Branch by carrying up from Little Falls.

GAUGE: This creek is very hard to catch, because it has a tiny watershed and is quite wide in the rapids section. Look for at least 150 cfs on Beetree Run (projected an hour after you put in) and 800 cfs on Little Falls (4 hours after you start). The riffles below the put-in eddy should be clean. Try to catch this stream while it is still rising, as you want lots of water in the class III section, but not too much where there are strainers up above. The rainfall gauge is Freeland (Baltimore County).

In the late 18th Century, this area was called the "Mine Run Hundred" (the "Hundred" was the smallest administrative unit, theoretically with 100 families), due to the mining of **magnetite**, an iron ore with magnetic properties, for local furnaces. **Fourth Mine Branch** enters at the Little Falls section 3 put in at Parkton, followed 1.5 miles later by Third Mine Branch, and then Little Falls section 4 gets **Second Mine Branch** and **First Mine Branch**. With enough rain, you might explore the final 2.1 miles of First Mine Branch, from Hunters Mill Road, at 35-ft/mile and with 4 sq. mi. drainage area, or the last 2.8 miles on Second Mine Branch, from Stablersville Road, with similar statistics. Fourth Mine Branch is even smaller (2.5 sq. mi.).

PINEY CREEK: Ensor Mill Rd. to Gunpowder Falls (Sparks Rd)

Gradient	Difficulty	Distance	Area	Scenery	Strainers	Rating
23	II- (II)	3.5	8	C-	2-3/mi.	*

USGS Quad – Hereford; Source – Personal descent 11/06
N39 33.23, W76 39.90 to N39 32.39, W76 38.38

This stream flows south for 2 miles alongside I-83 to the put in, shortly below the confluence with its main tributary, Buffalo Creek. The first three-fourths mile is fine, with lots of class II- rapids, through pretty woods. But then, after Belfast Road and Belfast Avenue, comes an ugly half mile along I-83, with strainers around blind turns. The one class II rapid is a short, steep drop, where the creek leaves the highway.

The scenery improves a bit as you head east to York Road (Md. 45), but there are also more strainers and fewer rapids. Below York Road, the creek becomes twisty, the gradient drops, and you pass the Sparks High School playing fields. The final quarter mile is backwater from Gunpowder Falls. Take out just below the confluence, where Sparks Road crosses the Gunpowder, on downstream river left. The Gunpowder Falls State Park signpost summarizes the history of Sparks.

GAUGE: Look for 85 cfs on Beetree Run and 100 cfs on Piney Run. Freeland and Butler are the rain gauges. If the riffles by the put in can be run cleanly, everything can be.

WESTERN RUN: Confluence (Mantua Mill Road) to Md. 145

Gradient	Difficulty	Distance	Area	Scenery	Strainers	Rating
11	I	11.7	21	B-	<1/mi.	*

USGS Quad – Hampstead/Hereford; Source – Personal descent (middle 3.5 mi.) 2/98; Gertler N39 30.83, W76 46.02 to N39 29.60, W76 38.66

Western Run starts at the confluence of Piney and McGill runs (with two-thirds of the flow being from the former) and heads east. A mile later, Delaware Run adds about 50% to the flow, and at 4.5 miles, just after Falls Road, Blackrock Run joins.

This is the flattest significant tributary of Gunpowder Falls, but it is nevertheless a pleasant cruise, with few strainers. Just before Western Run Road are two series of lively riffles. Paper Mill Road (Md. 145) is the last access before the Loch Raven Reservoir.

GAUGE: You will want 30 cfs on Piney Run and 150 cfs on Western Run (near the take out, projected five hours ahead) to start at the confluence. Below Falls Road, just over half of this will suffice. The rain gauges are Butler, Baptist Home and Freeland.

Piney Run might be paddled for 3.4 miles, with a catchment of 9 sq. mi. and a 25-ft/mile gradient, but it has two fences visible from the road and probably quite a few more. **Delaware Run** has 10 sq. mi. drainage and a 20-ft/mile gradient for its final mile, but also goes through farmland. A 4.5-mile trip, starting on Falls Road, might be had on **Beaverdam Run**, which enters Western Run just before Loch Raven Reservoir. Its gradient averages an interesting 45 ft/mile, but its drainage area is only 5 sq. mi., and the landowner at Falls Road was hostile

BLACKROCK RUN

Section 1: Benson Mill Road to Stringtown Road

Gradient	Difficulty	Distance	Area	Scenery	Strainers	Rating
33 (160)	?	2.4	5	?	?	?

USGS Quad – Hereford; Source – Scouting put in and takeout
N39 34.14, W76 44.67 to N39 32.61, W76 43.97

This *"explorers' special"* is tiny at the put in, but it picks up about 40% more water after half a mile. It won't impress you in its first mile, but then it suddenly drops 40 feet within a quarter mile. That must be exciting, but I have no idea whether it is runnable. And then the creek returns to its leisurely pace of about 20 ft/mile.

GAUGE: You need at least 150 cfs on Beetree Run and 175 cfs on Piney Run, projected one hour forward. The rain gauges are Butler, Baptist Home and Freeland.

Section 2: Stringtown Road to Western Run

Gradient	Difficulty	Distance	Area	Scenery	Strainers	Rating
30 (65)	II+	1.6*	12**	C	2-4/mi.	**

USGS Quad – Hereford; Source –Personal descent 3/00
N39 32.61, W76 43.97 to N39 31.59, W76 42.93

*(plus 0.4 miles on Western Run); **(includes Indian Run, which enters in 200 yards)

Some 200 yards below the put in, the creek picks up its largest tributary, Indian Run, and then has a nice 65-ft/mile gradient for a third of a mile. You can see most of this from Falls Road. There is a twisty class II+ rapid early on, approaching the lodge and antique shop (formerly a flour mill), followed by a runnable 2-foot dam. A second class II+ comes as the creek approaches the road, with a sharp left turn. The rapids end after 1 mile, at Western Run Road. There is little in the remaining 0.6 miles except some riffles, a few strainers and a pair of fences (broken down when we ran the creek). The next take out is Cuba Road, 0.4 miles down Western Run.

GAUGE: If the rapid beneath Western Run Road is runnable, everything is. You will need some 70 cfs on Beetree Run, 80 cfs on Piney Run, and 400 cfs on Western Run (projected 3 hours forward). Baptist Home and Freeland are the rain gauges.

LONG GREEN CREEK: Glenarm Road East to Gunpowder Falls

Gradient	Difficulty	Distance	Area	Scenery	Strainers	Rating
85 (200)	IV	1.9*	9	B+	0-2/mi.	!!!!

USGS Quad – White Marsh; Source – Trip report (Mike Soukup); Partial scouting
N39 27.44, W76 28.85 to N39 25.64, W76 26.68

*(plus 1.3 miles on Gunpowder Falls to Belair Road – US 1)

This is THE local steep creek near Baltimore. By Long Green Station (named after an Irish town and on the National Register of Historic Places for its many 19th Century buildings), the main arms have joined. After a lazy mile and a half, it crosses Glenarm Road East (the put in), and soon plunges 12 feet over a class IV broken ledge (Pinball), usually run on the right. There is a small pool, 50 yards of class II, another small pool, and then an 8-foot, class IV- sloping ledge (Pillow) with most of the water on the right. Then the creek is class II+ for the rest of the three-quarter mile stretch to Harford Road (Md.147). This section can be scouted from Hartley Mill Road, but park on Glenarm Road East.

Soon the creek enters its second gorge, and the gradient grows and grows until Chowder Hole, just above Gunpowder Falls, from where it is 1.3 miles of class I down to Bel Air Road (US 1). To scout the lower part in advance, park at the take out, and follow the trail upstream, past the much smaller and even steeper Sweathouse Branch.

According to Mike Soukup, Long Green Creek is usually up about a dozen times a year, for an average of 4 hours. Here is an abridged version of his trip report:

"Below Harford Road, the stream enters a beautiful gorge. At high water, this is a quickly moving class III-IV creek, replete with cool drops, tight moves and numerous pinning possibilities – both on rocks and strainers. The first two drops can be scouted from the road. If you can handle them, the rest is not much more difficult.

'The first drop, a ten foot, 50 degree angular slide/rock pile, was bony but still lots of fun. The second drop is a 6-foot ledge, sloping on the left, sheer on the right. The left side was shallow, and I bounced down the slide to the bottom. Everyone else went to the right – where there was definitely more water and a better line. The next drop of any consequence is about half a mile below Harford Road. It is not normally difficult, but today, with a huge tree blocking most of river right (where all the water goes), you had to cut across the current and kind of boof into an eddy on river left.

'The next drop is my personal favorite. I went first, running it blindly down the far right hand side. When I got down, I noticed that the left side might be a very cool move. Soon everyone was running and re-running this rapid.

'There are two other cool rapids. One of them is very rocky, with pinning spots everywhere. You work from right to left, and bounce off a rock at the bottom right (watch your elbows!). The last rapid is a wonderful 15-foot long, 30 mph flume into a big hole. Several people also carried back up this one to run it again."

GAUGE: Check from Hartley Mill Road. On the Long Green Creek gauge, minimum is 100 cfs (2.5 feet). The USGS stick gauge at the second rapid approximates the on-line gauge. The closest (but still far) rain gauge is Ridge School in Baltimore Co.

LITTLE GUNPOWDER FALLS

This creek flows for 25 miles, mostly within Gunpowder Falls State Park, as the Harford - Baltimore County line. Joppa, near its mouth, was the Baltimore County seat from 1707-68 and a major port for tobacco exports, until siltation did it in. The creek merges with (big) Gunpowder Falls just above the Gunpowder River estuary of the Chesapeake Bay. Although Baltimore City has the right to dam up the Little Gunpowder for its water supply, it has (fortunately) not found this necessary.

Section 1: Md.146 (Jarrettsville Road) to US 1 (Bel Air Road)

Gradient	Difficulty	Distance	Area	Scenery	Strainers	Rating
15	II- (II)	11.5	20	B	1/mi.	**

USGS Quad – Phoenix/Jarettsville/White Marsh; Source – Personal descent 11/99
N39 32.63, W76 31.84 via N39 30.44, W76 27.57 (mile 6.1) to N39 28.59, W76 24.51

This scenic novice trip features high cliffs and rocky outcroppings. For shorter trips, you can use Greene Rd. (mile 3.0), Md. 165 (mile 4.6), Pleasantville Rd. (mile 6.1) and Bottom Rd. (mile 8.2; site of the on-line gauge). There is a runnable 2-foot weir a quarter mile below Md. 146, but otherwise the stream is class I for the first 8 miles, until three short rock gardens (class II- and II) around Bottom Road. Three miles later, in the last half mile, the riffles become continuous. Although the volume increases from small tributaries, the stream widens out and doesn't get much deeper. Higher levels are more fun, with faster current and bouncier waves.

    GAUGE: To start at Md. 146, look for 150 cfs on the Little Gunpowder Falls gauge; for the bottom part, two-thirds of that would suffice. The rain gauges are Butler and Freeland.

Section 2: US 1 (Bel Air Road) to US 40

Gradient	Difficulty	Distance	Area	Scenery	Strainers	Rating
33 (75)	III- (III+)	5.5	43	B-	<<1/mi.	****

USGS Quad – White Marsh; Source – Personal descent 10/06
N39 28.59, W76 24.51 via N39 26.84, W76 22.80 (FrnkInvl) to N39 25.29, W76 22.42

This trip starts out as a continuous class II- rock garden, and then gets harder. After Jericho Road (mile 2.2) is a series of class III- rapids. The first is a 4-foot ledge, easily scouted on the right and best run in the middle at low levels; the chute on the left has a sharp rock just below. The next splits around an island; the left side tends to catch trees. Then comes the class III+ Belko Factory Falls (the ruins are on river right), a ragged 6-foot drop that should be scouted from the left and used to be run on the right; **however, as of 2010, a shifted rock made this dangerous.** The remaining class III- rapids start with a twisty rock garden and a steep chute just above Franklinville Road (where parking is restricted, but there is one space 100 yards up the hill), followed by a rock garden below. Class II water then resumes, for the mile to I-95. The final 1.5 miles has only a pair of class II+ rapids, straddling Philadelphia Road.

    The surrounding woodlands are full of deer and quite pretty, except where buildings are close to the creek. Park at the shopping center by the take out. Below there, it is two flat miles to big Gunpowder Falls.

    GAUGE: Minimum would be 115 cfs on the Little Gunpowder Falls gauge (and on the Winters Run gauge). Use the Butler and Freeland rain gauges.

Near mile 2, the **Jerusalem Mill** (at Jerusalem Road) was built circa 1772 and features a rare vertical shaft. It has been rebuilt, and is now the headquarters of the Gunpowder State Park. The museum in the basement is open on weekends. At the next crossing, the **Jericho Road Covered Bridge** dates from 1865, except for the steel reinforcing girders beneath it.

CAPITAL CANOEING AND KAYAKING

BACK RIVER BASIN

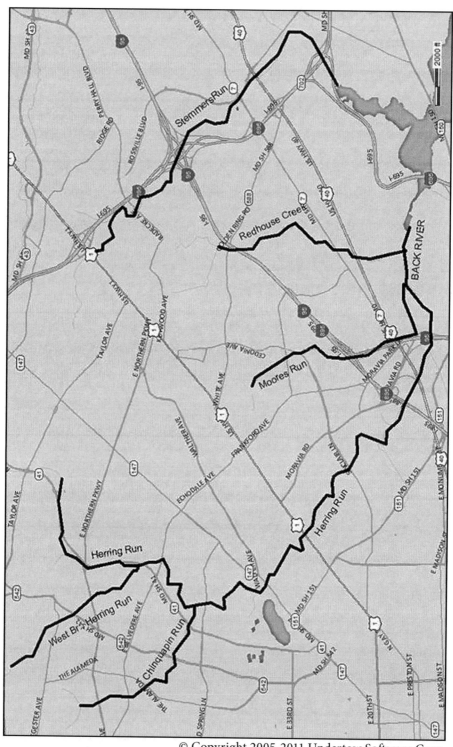

Chapter 6:

BACK RIVER BASIN

The Back River's tiny basin drains the northeastern quarter of Baltimore City, plus neighboring areas in Baltimore County, primarily Overlea (12,000), Rosedale (19,000) and Essex (39,000) – only some 55 square miles in all. The Back River itself is an inlet of Chesapeake Bay. Its western arm forms where Herring Run, its main tributary, meets Moores Run and Redhouse Creek, and becomes tidal, in a swampy area between railroad tracks, just east of the city limits. Its northeastern arm begins a few miles away where Northeast Creek becomes tidal. Northeast Creek is just a one-mile ooze, formed by Stemmers Run and the tiny and dull Brien Run.

Herring Run is by far the longest and easiest to catch trip in this basin, and it is a fine paddle, despite its poor water quality and the plastic that festoons the riverbanks. It has an enjoyable **West Branch**, which is an excellent place to start a Herring Run trip when there is enough water, as well as a short but steep "explorers' special" tributary named *Chinquapin Run*, which will challenge even advanced paddlers who manage to catch it up. **Moores Run** and **Stemmers Run** both also have nice whitewater for their first mile, before flattening out. **Redhouse Creek** is less appealing. Not surprisingly, the water in this basin is all rather polluted, especially from leaky old sewer pipes, so just keep your mouth shut and enjoy the paddling – on those rare occasions when intense rainfall brings these little streams up.

The land between the Patapsco and Back Rivers was the scene of the **Battle of North Point**, on September 12-13, 1814, which took place simultaneously with the attack on Fort McHenry, as part of the British attempt to capture Baltimore. Although the 5,000 British troops managed to drive the Americans back, they lost their commanding general and were unable to break through the defenses on Hampstead Hill. When the naval attack also failed, all the British forces withdrew.

GAUGES: There is an Internet gauge on **Moores Run**, at Radecke Avenue (one-third mile below the put in), with a 3.5 sq. mile catchment, which is the **zero-level gauge reference** in the table below, as well as one on the West Branch of Herring Run (2.1 sq. miles; half a mile above the put in). For Redhouse Creek and Stemmers Run, the gauge on Whitemarsh Run near Fullerton (2.7 sq. miles) is relevant. (There is also a gauge, of little usefulness, on an unnamed tributary of Moores Run, with just 0.21 sq. miles.)

name	gradient	difficulty	length	area	gauge	rating
Herring Run	35 (75)	II+ (III)	5.7	8.5	35cfs	***
West Branch	47	II+	0.8	2.5	80cfs	***
Chinquapin Run	85 (200)	III+ (IV)	1.1	2.1	200cfs	?
Moores Run	45 (70)	II	1.1	3.2	100cfs	**
Redhouse Creek	20	I	1.4	2.5	65cfs	-
Stemmers Run - Section 1	60	II (III-)	1.0	2.5	90cfs	***
- Section 2	20	I (II-)	1.4	3.3	55cfs	-

⋙ HERRING RUN: Echodale Avenue to US 40

Gradient	Difficulty	Distance	Area	Scenery	Strainers	Rating
35 (75)	II+ (III)	5.7	8.5	D	<1/mi.	***

USGS Quad – Baltimore East; Source – Personal descent 4/04
N39 21.24, W76 34.40 to N39 18.30, W76 32.31

This is a surprisingly pleasant, long run through east Baltimore. The creek (named for a family rather than a fish) begins as two branches: the West Branch coming south from Towson and the main stem from Parkville. The West Branch (see below) is a good place to start if it has enough water; the main stem is flatter (25 ft/mile) and ugly, as it is channeled alongside Perring Parkway. Unless starting on the West Branch, put in at Echodale Avenue, one-third mile below the confluence.

Herring Run is up to class II in its first mile, past Chinquapin Run and down to Cold Spring Lane. It enters the fall line alongside Morgan State University, and the rapids become longer, steeper and more frequent, culminating in a long, twisting class III rock garden. The action then gradually slows down, except for man-made ledges straddling Harford Road (Md. 147) at mile 2.1.

The following mile has just a few minor weirs and some long riffles, until a 70-yard, class II rapid just above Belair Road (US 1). The next 0.3 miles, to Mannasota Ave., contains a pair of long class II+ rock gardens, the latter one ending in a tricky drop just below the bridge. The 0.8 miles to Sinclair Lane (mile 4.2) are class I. Below there, the gradient drops to 20 ft/mile and the creek is flat, except for a few more man-made ledges of up to class II+. Take out just upstream of US 40, on a side road to the auto impoundment facility – park across from the office up above. (A major iron furnace opened here in 1744 – a progenitor of Baltimore's steel industry.)

On the negative side is the pungent odor of unprocessed sewerage pouring out of one pipe. The scenery changes from rocky gorge to open fields to more urban sights, and would be decent if not for the plastic ("witches' knickers") that festoons every rock, bush and eddy. (In Alan Fisher's *Country Walks near Baltimore*, there is a photo of old car tires along the creek, with the wry caption "Herring Run Park, a multiple-use facility.")

GAUGE: About 35 cfs on Moores Run and 20 cfs on the West Branch of Herring Run are needed. Lake Roland (Baltimore Co.) and Hazelwood (Baltimore City) are the rain gauges. The staff gauge at Echodale Avenue should be at least 1.2.

⋙ WEST BRANCH, HERRING RUN: Northern Pkwy to Herring Run

Gradient	Difficulty	Distance	Area	Scenery	Strainers	Rating
47	II+	0.8	2.5	C-	0-2/mi.	***

USGS Quad – Baltimore East; Source – Personal descent 4/04
N39 22.04, W76 34.80 to N39 21.24, W76 34.40

This little creek makes a nice start to a long trip down Herring Run. There is good access on the upstream side of Northern Parkway, and a lively class II+ drop at the culvert exit, but the entrance to the culvert tends to be blocked by fallen trees. On the downstream side, access is via a steep, trash-strewn trail, with parking around the corner. Farther upstream, the creek is a cement channel.

The trip starts out with class II and II+ rapids, in a wooded setting. Midway, you pass under Hillen Road and enter Mount Pleasant Park. Here the stream is constrained by riprap, but the gradient remains lively and the rapids varied. Be careful in high water, because eddies are few. The trickiest rapid, which would be class III with more water, is just below a high footbridge, where a 2-foot drop funnels you left toward a tree leaning over the creek. Scout this in advance from Edgepark Road. At the confluence, the two branches have about equal amounts of water. Continue a mild quarter mile to Woodbourne Avenue, or as far as you want to go on Herring Run.

GAUGE: Check from Hillen and Edgepark Roads. The West Branch gauge (half a mile above the put in) should be at least 50 cfs, and the staff gauge at Hillen Road at least 2 feet. Lake Roland (Baltimore Co.) is the nearest rain gauge.

CHINQUAPIN RUN: The Alameda to Herring Run

Gradient	Difficulty	Distance	Area	Scenery	Strainers	Rating
85 (200)	III+ (IV)	1.1	2.1	D	1-3/mi.	?

USGS Quad – Baltimore East; Source – Almost complete scouting on foot
N39 21.39, W76 35.76 to N39 20.72, W76 34.85

Chinquapin ("big nut") Run, an *"explorers' special,"* heads southeast from the Baltimore Co. line. Its banks are strewn with litter. It passes through a dark tunnel. But it has excellent whitewater. One might put in at Northern Parkway, but after 0.3 miles of fast class II water, the creek becomes concrete bound for 0.4 miles until The Alameda.

Shortly below The Alameda, with little warning, is a class IV chute, where the water gets channeled to river left. Catch the eddy above it to scout and/or carry. This is followed by 0.2 miles of class II, to Woodbourne Ave. Scout the 2-ft. ledge entry as well as the exit from the tunnel – a 4-foot drop from the right culvert, 3-foot from the left. Run far left or far right, to avoid a rooster tail. Then the creek drops 20 ft in about 175 yards, through a class III+ rock garden, which is followed by class III for 0.3 miles to Loch Raven Boulevard and class II for the next 0.4 miles to Perring Parkway.

The curved passage under Perring Parkway is 50 yards long, and you cannot see through it. Fortunately, it is wide enough to usually be clear. As you enter, stay away from the right wall, where two large pipes pour out less-than-pristine water. Shortly below the Parkway, a large sign announces "Polluted Water," as if one could have any doubts in the middle of Baltimore. The final 0.2 miles is through Morgan State University. Twenty-foot high riprap on river right protects the campus from the creek, which is class II+ here. You can take out at the confluence with Herring Run, continue an eighth of a mile to Cold Spring Lane, or keep paddling down the best part of Herring Run (if it is too high, just wait a short while for it to drop).

GAUGE: Moores Run should be over 200 cfs and the West Branch of Herring Run 120 cfs. The rain gauge is Lake Roland in Baltimore Co.

🛶 MOORES RUN: Above Radecke Avenue to end of Denview Way

Gradient	Difficulty	Distance	Area	Scenery	Strainers	Rating
45 (70)	II	1.1	3.2	C-	0-2/mi.	**

USGS Quad – Baltimore East; Source – Personal descent 6/03
N39 20.10, W76 32.28 to N39 19.30, 76 32.12

Moores Run emerges from underground in the Gardenville area of east Baltimore, flows south for 2.5 miles, just inside the city limits, and then east for its last half mile to the Back River. Put in off of Moores Run Drive, 0.4 miles above Radecke Ave., as close to where the creek emerges as you can get. Above Radecke Ave. are long class II rock gardens. From Radecke Ave. to Sinclair Lane, the class II rapids are shorter and the visibility is reduced. Below Sinclair Lane, the creek is class I. Take out on river right at the end of Denview Way, half a mile after Sinclair Lane, shortly after the only island.

If you go farther, at 1.4 miles you pass under JFK Memorial Highway, followed by I-95 and Pulaski Highway. Just after the last (at 2 miles), you can take out on river left, and climb the steep bank to 62nd Street. This stretch is all pretty flat.

The water quality is poor, and the various outflow pipes you see probably do not help. On the positive side, I encountered few strainers and surprisingly little trash.

GAUGE: You need about 100 cfs on the Moores Run gauge at Radecke Ave. This equals 1 foot on the large painted yellow gauge on the upstream side of the bridge on river right. Because this creek is street run-off, it rises and falls extremely fast. The rain gauges are Caroline (Baltimore City) and Lake Roland (Baltimore County).

🛶 REDHOUSE CREEK: Weyburn Road to Pulaski Highway (US40)

Gradient	Difficulty	Distance	Area	Scenery	Strainers	Rating
20	I	1.4	2.5	D+	1-2/mi.	-

USGS Quad – Baltimore East; Source – Personal descent 12/02
N39 20.11, W76 30.78 to N39 19.01, W76 30.96

This dull stream flows south through the Rosedale neighborhood of Hillcreek Camelot. There are frequent riffles, three small ledges and a few strainers, but the only tricky spot is after the first bridge, where the riffle tries to propel you into a low-leaning tree. The first mile is through a suburban park, with just a thin margin of trees to screen out the houses. Then the creek reaches the commercial strip, and both the visual and olfactory conditions deteriorate. Access is problematical at Philadelphia Road (Md. 7), so continue a quarter mile to Pulaski Highway, where the banks are not as steep and there is better parking. Below there, it is a flat half mile to the Back River. You could also add half a mile at the beginning of the trip by starting off of Hazelwood Road, but the put in would be more difficult and you would begin with a dark passage under I-95.

GAUGE: Look for 50 cfs on Whitemarsh Run near Fullerton, 65 cfs on Moores Run. The rain gauges are Caroline (Baltimore City) and Lake Roland (Baltimore Co.)

STEMMERS RUN

Stemmers Run (Captain Ulric Stemmer bought a plantation there in 1795) winds southeast for 5.5 miles, from the northeast corner of Baltimore City, through Double Rock Park in Overlea/Fullerton, and becomes runnable in Linover Park. It then roughly parallels I-695 until it joins tiny Brien Run to form Northeast Creek, which flows for less than a mile until it becomes an inlet of the Back River.

Section 1: Linover Park (Lillian Holt Drive) to Trump Mill Road

Gradient	Difficulty	Distance	Area	Scenery	Strainers	Rating
60	II (III-)	1.0	2.5	C+	0-2/mi.	***

USGS Quad – Baltimore East; Source – Personal descent 6/03
N39 21.64, W76 30.37 to N39 21.13, W76 30.00

This is an excellent short run after a heavy rainfall. The scenery is pleasant and the water does not smell, but the noise from I-695 reminds you of where you are. Put in just inside the entrance of Linover Park, near Essex Community College. The first quarter mile is class I, but as the creek turns back towards Lillian Holt Drive, its gradient picks up. After a short class II rapid comes the main action: a class III- boulder garden with alternative routes depending upon the water level. Below the bridge are a half dozen more class II rapids, a mixture of rock gardens, gravel bars and chutes, along the edge of the Garden of Faith Cemetery. There is good visibility for spotting any strainers. The fun comes to a sudden end after one mile, at Trump Mill Road. Take out on river right.

    GAUGE: About 90 cfs on Moores Run, 70 cfs on Whitemarsh Run near Fullerton and 50 cfs on the West Branch of Herring Run should suffice. The rain gauges are Caroline in Baltimore City and Lake Roland in Baltimore County. Because it drains parkland, Stemmers Run rises and falls more slowly than Moores Run.

Section 2: Trump Mill Road to Philadelphia Road (Md. 7)

Gradient	Difficulty	Distance	Area	Scenery	Strainers	Rating
20	I (II-)	1.4	3.3	D+	1-2/mi.	-

USGS Quad – Middle River; Source – Personal descent 6/03
N39 21.13, W76 30.00 to N39 20.35, W76 29.24

First you traverse the intersection of I-95 and I-695 through four long, wide, straight culverts. At the bottom of the last one is a two-foot drop and a short class II- rock garden. Then you enter parkland, with high banks, deer and dense vegetation. There is a decent current and one more two-foot weir. Take out just above Md. 7, as strainers tend to block the passage. One could continue another mile past the confluence with Brien Run down to Golden Ring Road, but the gradient keeps diminishing, and I saw two strainers in the first 200 yards.

    GAUGE: You need 55 cfs on Moores Run and 40 cfs on Whitemarsh Run near Fullerton. The rain gauges are Caroline and Lake Roland.

JONES & GWYNNS FALLS BASINS

© Copyright 2005-2011 Undertow Software Corp.

Chapter 7:
JONES & GWYNNS FALLS BASINS

Many East Coast cities sprung up at the limit of passage of ocean-going vessels. There, where imports and exports had to be transshipped, warehouses, shops, factories and homes were built. In the case of Baltimore, this was where Jones Falls and Gwynns Falls reached the Patapsco River estuary of the Chesapeake Bay. Development got a major boost from the gradient of these creeks, which provided the muscle for industry. In the first half of the 19th Century, Baltimore's water-driven mills made it the largest flour center in the country. The textile industry soon followed.

Gwynns Falls (which flows into the Middle Branch) and Jones Falls (which empties into the Inner Harbor) drain central and western Baltimore City plus part of Baltimore County. Their adjacent basins, each only about 60 square miles, contain a fantastic variety of ephemeral whitewater with challenging rapids, convenient gauges and even dam releases. Once the water quality is improved, this should become a paddling Mecca; in the meanwhile, it has been more like a paddling Baghdad.

Gwynns Falls has extensive and interesting rapids, and its section 2 would be an outstanding whitewater run were it not so polluted. Ron Canter called it "probably the longest continuous whitewater run in the entire Piedmont." **Jones Falls** has recently been given new life as a paddling stream by releases from Lake Roland. Six of these creeks' tiny tributaries – **Western, Stony,** *Maidens Choice* (an "explorers' special"), **Gwynns** and **Dead runs,** and **Scotts Level Branch** – have sections exceeding 100 ft/mile. Milder but still interesting are **Roland** and **Powder Mill runs,** and the *North Branch of Jones Falls* (the other "explorers' special"), while **Red Run** is the dog of the group. (In the Gwynns Falls basin, it's "better Dead than Red.") Washingtonians will have to move very fast, often in anticipation of rainfall, to catch these tributaries; Baltimoreans are, of course, much better located to take advantage of this paddling cornucopia.

As an old industrial city, Baltimore has not been kind to its streams. To utilize the power of the flowing water, mills were constructed along the creeks, and the valleys became industrial centers. Later, to control flooding, streambeds were moved and/or encased in cement and riprap. Worst of all, the streams were used as sewerage drains, and still today, due mainly to leaking sewer pipes, they are among the most polluted waterways in the region, especially where within or adjacent to Baltimore City. While stretches flow through parks, these parks have often not been well maintained, so there is little of the charm of, for example, Rock Creek Park in Washington D.C. or Cabin John Park in southern Montgomery County.

But, finally, the prospects are improving. Each of the two basins now has its own Watershed Association. Events like the Jones Falls Celebration and investments like the Gwynns Falls Trail hold out hope that the recreational value of these creeks will eventually be realized. And given the steep gradients and good rapids, that potential is certainly worth developing from a paddling perspective.

This is, of course, a heavily populated area. The Gwynns Falls basin has some 250,000 people and the Jones Falls watershed 200,000. As a result, about 75% of the land is developed, and some 40% consists of impervious surfaces, resulting in fast runoff and highly ephemeral streams.

GAUGES: Since 2003, a slew of gauges have been added, so that there are now 13 in the Gwynns Falls basin alone, of which 4 are on Gwynns Falls itself and 6 in its Dead Run sub-basin. The useful gauges are Gwynns Falls at Delight (4.3 sq. mi.) and Villa Nova (32.5 sq. mi.), Scotts Level Branch (3.2 sq. mi.), Powder Mill Run (3.6 sq. mi.), Dead Run at both Woodlawn (2.4 sq. mi.) and Franklintown (5.5 sq. mi.) and Jones Falls at Sorrento (25 sq. mi.). Just outside this chapter's coverage are helpful gauges on Moores Run (3.5 sq. mi.) to the southeast and Minebank Run (2.1 sq. mi) to the northeast. **The Dead Run gauge at Franklintown is the reference** in the table below, because of its central location and the fact that its drainage area is typical of most of the streams covered. Jones Falls sections 2 and 3 are usually run during dam releases. For the Jones Falls tributaries, primary reliance must often be placed on rainfall data; fortunately, the area is also well covered by AFWS rainfall gauges.

name	gradient	difficulty	length	area	gauge	rating
Jones Falls - Section 1	17	I (II-)	3.5	16	25cfs	*
- Section 2	19	II-	4.0	39	n.a.	*
- Section 3	33	II (III+)	1.9	50	n.a.	**
North Branch	53	?	2.0	6.0	55cfs	?
Roland Run	25	I	1.2	4.5	65cfs	*
Western Run	70 (130)	III+	3.0	1.6	225cfs	***
Stony Run	85 (190)	III+(5.0)	1.7	2.4	150cfs	*
Gwynns Falls - Section 1	22 (55)	II	2.5	32	25cfs	**
- Section 2	45 (150)	III (IV-)	5.6	39	25cfs	***
Red Run	25	I	3.0	4.6	60cfs	-
Scotts Level Branch	50 (150)	III	1.7	3.0	125cfs	**
Powder Mill Run	55	II (II+)	0.8	3.5	90cfs	**
Dead Run	55 (110)	III+	3.2	5.0	100cfs	***
Maidens Choice Run	60 (190)	?	2.0	1.0	300cfs	?
Gwynns Run	110	III- (III)	0.4	1.8	200cfs	**

JONES FALLS

Jones Falls rises in the mansion-strewn horse country of Baltimore County (where the Clintons might have moved if Paul Sarbanes had retired before Daniel Moynihan), northwest of the city. It flows east for 4 miles through the Green Spring Valley and then south for 8 miles, but its runnable path is interrupted twice: first by man-made Lake Roland, which forms the centerpiece of Robert E. Lee Park and was a source of drinking water until it became too polluted, and then by being submerged for its final 1.7 miles underneath downtown Baltimore, before entering the Inner Harbor subterraneously. Furthermore, once within Baltimore city limits, the Jones Falls Expressway (I-83) is alongside or even over the creek, which is channeled between 12-ft high, sloping cement and riprap walls. Gertler calls Jones Falls (sections 2 and 3) "the ultimate loser stream." But perhaps his judgment is too harsh, for devastated though it be, the creek can still provide paddling enjoyment. And now that there are regular annual races and 2-4 brief releases each year, this has actually become quite a popular stream.

The land on the west side of Jones Falls was surveyed in 1661 for a planter, **David Jones**. Rockland was settled in 1706. Baltimore was started along the west bank of Jones Falls in 1729, and Jones Town, on the east bank, three years later. They merged in 1745. In 1768, the Baltimore County courthouse and prison (now the site of the Battle Monument) were built overlooking Jones Falls, and this was the location of the last pillory and whipping post in Maryland, used until 1819. The river powered over a dozen mills. When the Bellona Powder Mill exploded in 1820, the shock waves were felt as far away as Washington DC; a decade later, E.I.DuPont called this mill his chief competition. Nearby gneiss quarries were a major source of building material (as well as of minerals for scientists and collectors).

Floods on Jones Falls wreaked havoc on Baltimore during the 18th and 19th centuries. In revenge, the lower part of the creek was moved eastward by a diversion canal (starting in 1786), its banks were encased in concrete and riprap, and finally, the last 1.7 miles were paved over. At the 1915 dedication ceremony of the Fallsway, the emcee joked: "We have come to bury the Jones Falls, not to praise it." But the stream had the last laugh, in June 1926, when its oily surface caught fire underground, blowing open manholes and damaging structures above.

To increase the awareness of the recreational benefits of the watershed, the first **Jones Falls Celebration** was held on Sept. 19-20, 1998, including a release from Lake Roland. Over 50 canoes and kayaks descended section 2, and about 10 of them continued down section 3. The festival and releases (200-300 cfs) have been repeated each year, including races coordinated by the Greater Baltimore Canoe Club. Baltimore has apparently rescinded its 1976 classification of Jones Falls as a sewer.

Section 1: Greenspring Avenue to above Lake Roland

Gradient	Difficulty	Distance	Area	Scenery	Strainers	Rating
17	I (II-)	3.5	16	D	1-3/mi.	*

USGS Quad – Cockeysville; Source – Personal descent 2/97
N39 24.87, W76 41.31 to N39 23.29, W76 39.56

The put in is one mile west of the intersection of I-83 (Jones Falls Expressway) and I-695, below the confluence with the North Branch. For 1.2 miles, you paddle east, to near the interstates' intersection. This part is very narrow; however, to our pleasant amazement, we were able to maneuver around or under the few fallen trees. A horseman who had lived there for 35 years said he had never before seen paddlers on the creek.

Soon afterwards, the woods end and the creek turns south into the world of highways and backyards. The middle third of the trip is marred by strainers and poor scenery. The final third has bridges instead of strainers – Falls Road, Ruxton Road, Falls Road, I-83, Falls Road – but is more polluted. The class II- rapid is within sight of the restored settlement of Rockland, just below one of those bridges. Take out alongside Falls Road, just as it bends away from the creek. (If you continue 0.2 miles farther to Lake Roland, you must then paddle a mile across the lake.)

GAUGE: Zero level is 1.6 feet on the gauge on a Falls Road crossing and 3.9 feet on the one alongside Falls Road shortly above the take out. The latter is on the Internet as Jones Falls at Sorrento, and needs to read over 110 cfs by the time you get there. The closest rain gauge is Baptist Home (Baltimore Co.).

Section 2: Lake Roland Dam to Ash Street (below Union Avenue)

Gradient	Difficulty	Distance	Area	Scenery	Strainers	Rating
19	II-	4.0	39	D	<1/mi.	*

USGS Quad – Cockeysville/Baltimore West; Source – Personal Descent 6/02
N39 22.66, W76 38.65 to N39 19.65, W76 38.40

As Baltimore no longer draws water from Lake Roland, the lake is often close to full and the outflow reflects the inflow, with a few hours' delay. But the best time to plan a trip here is during the September dam releases for the Jones Falls Festival or the summertime races. (Of course, it takes some time for the dam to re-fill following those.)

After a quarter mile, the creek leaves the woods, flows beneath Falls Road, enters Baltimore City and becomes degradedly urban, with cement and riprap along its banks, and the backsides of commerce and industry beyond. Natural rocks and trees are rare. Don't worry about the vinegary waterfall on the left as much as the unseen sewer drains.

Most of this trip is class I, but there are a few livelier places. In the first mile, beware of a steep, narrow chute with low branches overhanging from the left. Two miles later comes a short class II- rock garden, followed by more riffles, which continue into and through the final half mile beneath I-83, with the main flow first one side and then the other of the massive support pillars; because of its uniqueness, I enjoyed this.

You can take out (a) upon emerging into sunlight, on river right at Meadow Mills, just after Union Avenue, (b) up the riprap on river left towards the end of the second stretch beneath I-83, or (c) 200 yards further on, just across from the prominent gauge (18 inches is zero level) at the end of Ash Street. And if you don't want to waste time setting up a shuttle, just catch the Light Rail at Union Avenue (on river right).

GAUGE: Look for a dam release of at least 100 cfs. Currently, no on-line gauge is available. Baptist Home (Baltimore Co.) is the nearest rain gauge.

Section 3: Ash St. to Lafayette Ave. & Falls Road (just below North Ave.)

Gradient	Difficulty	Distance	Area	Scenery	Strainers	Rating
33	II (III+)	1.9	50	D+	<1/mi.	**

USGS Quad – Baltimore West/Baltimore East; Source – Personal descent 6/02
N39 19.65, W76 38.40 to N39 18.65, W76 37.18

This is the descent of the fall line. After a quiet start, there are four good class II rapids in a row, alongside Clipper Mill Road. Then, a lively riffle leads, at 0.6 miles, to the class III+ Factory Falls. Most kayaks head right, to a sheer 6-foot drop that is hard to scout; in this channel, stay far right (which takes some work), because the center leads to a deep hole that tends to fill open canoes and flip all kinds of boats. Open boaters tend to prefer the somewhat more gradual but twisting chute on river left, which needs a little more water and a right brace in the boiling hole at the bottom of the final 4-foot drop. The middle channel consists of several small, tight drops, but requires much more water, and is not runnable during releases; however, you can use it to portage. Factory Falls can be scouted from Falls Road, by parking at Mill Centre and walking upstream.

A quarter mile of class II thereafter is the 13-foot Round (or Horseshoe) Falls dam. (This drop is sometimes reduced by a pool formed by debris below.) There is calm water and not much of a hydraulic below. It is best run in the middle, with speed; boats that drop too vertically may hit the river bottom. There is a viewing platform on the left, next to which you can portage or take out. The races normally end at the bottom of this falls. It is then a 50-yard carry up to Falls Road.

Below the dam comes a final mile of class I. Take out alongside Falls Road soon after passing the Baltimore Streetcar Museum and the North Street (US 1) bridge; instead of going below Howard Street, pull over on the left. **Not long afterwards, the stream disappears underground; so don't miss this final takeout!** From there you can cross the creek and catch the light rail at the North Street station, back to Robert E. Lee Park.

GAUGE: You need a dam release (or natural flow) of at least 125 cfs, but there is no river gauge. Baptist Home (Baltimore Co.) is the nearest rain gauge.

The dam release began at 8:00 and the first racers at 9:30. But the **paddlers caught up with the release**, and at Factory Falls they had to wait for enough water. The challenge to the race results was rejected 5-4 by the U.S. Supreme Court, which added that this was not a precedent.

NORTH BRANCH, JONES FALLS: Shady Brook Ct. to Jones Falls

Gradient	Difficulty	Distance	Area	Scenery	Strainers	Rating
53	?	2.0*	6.0	?	?	?

USGS Quad – Cockeysville; Source – Scouting access points
N39 26.09, W76 43.45 to N39 24.86, W76 41.31

*(plus 1.2 miles on Jones Falls, to Greenspring Ave, at 25 ft/mile)

This *"explorers' special,"* on the largest Jones Falls tributary, begins in the Caves Park neighborhood. The first 1.2 miles is at 65 ft/mile, mainly through the woods. After the creek enters an estate, a pair of board fences in fast water just above Md. 130 needs to be portaged, probably along the driveway on river right (there is another fence on river left), which requires about 40 yards of trespassing, near a busy road. Below Md. 130, the gradient drops in half for the final, twisty 0.8 miles, and then you have a straight 1.2 miles on Jones Falls, passing two private roads, to the put in for section 1.

GAUGE: Look for 35 cfs on Moores Run, 55 cfs on Dead Run at Franklintown, 40 cfs at Gwynns Falls at Delight. Baptist Home and Ridge School are the rain gauges.

ROLAND RUN: Essex Farm Road to Circle Road

Gradient	Difficulty	Distance	Area	Scenery	Strainers	Rating
25	I	1.2	4.5	B-	0-2/mi.	*

USGS Quad – Cockeysville; Source – Personal descent 6/01
N39 24.89, W76 38.78 to N39 23.91, W76 38.96

Roland Run begins just west of Timonium and heads south for 2.5 miles to Lake Roland. At Essex Farm Road, south of I-695, its main tributary joins. It flows through parks and past elegant houses; however, it is polluted from leaking septic tanks. Despite its narrowness and the presence of beavers, it is relatively free of strainers, although not of overhanging branches. About halfway, just past Joppa Road, is a bouncy quarter-mile riffle. Then the creek slows down, and by Ruxton Road it is flat. The next bridge, Circle Road, just off Ruxton Road, is an easier take out.

GAUGE: Check the riffles at the put in. This creek falls rapidly. Moores Run should read over 40 cfs, Dead Run at Franklintown 65 cfs and Gwynns Falls at Delight 50 cfs. The rainfall gauge is Ridge School (Baltimore Co.).

Roland Thornberry obtained a land grant in the area in 1694. Lake Roland, created in 1858, was Baltimore's main source of water until 1915, when it was replaced by reservoirs on Gunpowder Falls. It is now the centerpiece of Robert E. Lee Memorial Park, and serves an important environmental function by settling out pollutants from Jones Falls.

WESTERN RUN: Labyrinth Road to Jones Falls

Gradient	Difficulty	Distance	Area	Scenery	Strainers	Rating
70 (130)	III+	3.0	1.6	D	1-2/mi.	***

USGS Quad – Baltimore West; Source – Personal descent 5/03
N39 21.91, W76 41.97 to N39 22.05, W76 39.13

Oh, ye lovers of "brown water," do not miss Western Run. The scenery is drab, the water quality is worse (especially after several sewers visibly discharge their noxious-smelling effluent), the strainers can be dangerous, and the creek is rarely up. But when it is, there are three miles of continuous white water, ranging from class II- to III+.

Put in where the creek emerges from its mile-long subterranean passage, in the northwest corner of Baltimore city. (An upper one-mile section in Pikesville, through the Druid Ridge Cemetery, should be allowed to r.i.p.) Western Run then flows due east through narrow Western Run Park, bordered for most of the way by Western Run Drive on the north and Cross Country Boulevard and later Kelly Avenue on the south. The first 1.5 miles and the last half mile can be scouted from these streets.

The first half of the run is mainly class II, except for a class III- ledge just below the third bridge (Strathmore Ave.). After you pass Greenspring Ave. midway, the creek and park widen out, woods replace gabions and walls as the predominant view, and there is a series of long, steep class III and

III+ rock gardens, with the gradient up to 130 ft/mile. Shortly below the large yellow gauge at Lochlea Road comes the last class III section, as the scenery becomes totally urban, entering upscale Mt. Washington Village.

One can take out on river right, between the Mt. Washington Inn on the right and the blue house. If you paddle the final 0.2 miles down the man-made drop to just above the confluence with Jones Falls, you would have to climb up an 8 ft, 35 degree cement embankment (feasible but tricky), or continue down section 2 of Jones Falls.

GAUGE: The visible gauge at Lochlea Road should read at least 3.0 ft. Powder Mill Run needs 150 cfs, Gwynns Falls near Delight 175 cfs, and Dead Run at Franklintown 225 cfs. The Pikesville rain gauge (Baltimore Co.) is in the headwaters.

It was surely no Western Run paddler who ever called **city folk** less friendly than their country cousins. A local teenager helped us clear a strainer, the family across from the put in came to watch us launch, and the kitchen staff at the Mt. Washington Inn asked if we could take them for a trip. It helped that we paddled through city parkland, not private property.

Mt. Washington was the site of the last cotton mill in Maryland. In 1996, it was converted into Fresh Fields, Starbucks and Smith & Hawken stores.

STONY RUN: Above Cold Spring Lane to Wyman Park Drive

Gradient	Difficulty	Distance	Area	Scenery	Strainers	Rating
85 (190)	III+ (5.0)	1.7	2.4	D	2-3/mi.	*

USGS Quad – BaltimoreWest/BaltimoreEast; Source – Personal descent 5/03
N39 20.71, W76 37.59 to N39 19.44, W76 37.55

Like Western Run, this steep urban stream has been mostly channelized. But it is more dangerous and less fun. It flows south for four miles, from the Baltimore County line to the geographic center of the city, through skinny Stoney [sic] Run Park and then wide Wyman Park. Put in 100 yards above Cold Spring Lane, at the confluence with its Homeland Branch, by a Loyola College parking lot. The creek starts off class II+ and very narrow, and then goes over several 2-3 foot man-made drops (evidence of early mills and later fishponds). In a quarter mile, it enters a 70-yard tunnel under Overhill Road; look through in advance for strainers. The next half mile, alongside Linwood Road, is narrow and alternately paved and hemmed in by riprap, so be cautious about strainers here too, as the stream is continuous class II (60 ft/mile) with few eddies.

Just beneath University Parkway is a steep class III+, twisting to the left, over rocks and concrete. After a short eddy comes another class III+ ending in a rocky drop, and 30 yards later is the big rapid. This complex 8-foot drop should be scouted from river right and portaged (by most paddlers), starting alongside the second class III+. (At the rapid itself, the left bank is very steep and the right bank is a 12-foot wall.) The creek then reverts to class II+, as it skirts Johns Hopkins through Wyman Park and flows beneath Remington Ave., followed 0.2 miles later by Wyman Park Drive. Take out on river right. Shortly below, **the creek goes underground** (you can see the entrance from the bridge), until it enters Jones Falls through a pipe a third of a mile later. Skip that.

GAUGE: Moores Run should be at least 100 cfs, Dead Run at Franklintown 150 cfs, Minebank Run 60 cfs, and Gwynns Falls near Delight 120 cfs. The rain gauges are Lake Roland in Baltimore Co. and Jones Falls in Baltimore City. Both branches at the put in need to be runnable; the section just below is not an adequate guide, as the creek widens out later.

> Stony Run is a most **educated creek**, passing through or near Saint Mary's University, College of Notre Dame, Loyola College, and finally Johns Hopkins University, plus the Baltimore Museum of Art and the Bryn Mawr, Gilman Country and Friends Schools.

GWYNNS FALLS

Gwynns Falls rises in Reistertown and flows southeast for 25 miles to the Middle Branch of the Patapsco estuary. It is tiny for its first 7 miles, through Owings Mills, until it is nearly doubled in size (to 17 sq. mi.) by Red Run. It then roughly parallels I-795 and later I-695 for its next 7 miles, with a gradient of 10 ft/mile, to Villa Nova (section 1 put in), where it gradually begins its descent of the fall line. Below section 1 are 2 weirs, a half mile of backwater, and a half mile of class I, until Gwynn Oak Avenue (section 2).

> **Richard Gwin**, a Welshman, settled between what became Gwinns Falls (originally Ferry Branch) and Gwinns Run. In 1669 he was given exclusive trading rights with the local Indians. His son-in-law, Peter Bond, built a mill along Gwynns Falls in 1719. Gneiss for buildings was quarried along the creek, and in 1723 a blast furnace for pig iron was built at the mouth. Starting in 1776, the Owings family built four mills, a quarter mile apart, with a 2-mile long millrace (to get enough of a head, given the low gradient on the upper part of the stream).
> **Gwynns Falls Park,** established in 1906, was a popular retreat for Baltimoreans, but the area gradually deteriorated. Now it is being restored. The 14-mile, paved **Gwynns Falls Trail** follows the creek from Windsor Mill Road to the Patapsco estuary.

Section 1: Buckingham Road (Villa Nova) to Woodlawn Drive

Gradient	Difficulty	Distance	Area	Scenery	Strainers	Rating
22 (55)	II	2.5	32	C+	<1/mi.	**

USGS Quad – Baltimore West; Source – Personal descent 12/04
N39 21.11, W76 44.18 to N39 19.41, W76 43.50

The put in is a little north of Liberty Road (Md. 26) and half a mile above the USGS Villa Nova gauge at Essex Road. The initial mile has good current, with the first serious riffle just above Liberty Road. After a little more flat water, there are five long class II- and II rock gardens, spread over three-fourths of a mile, with the final one (in high water, beware of its hole) as you approach the bridge in Woodlawn Cemetery, where you meet the backwater from the first weir. Take out about 200 yards thereafter, after paddling between tombstones and then exiting the cemetery. The alternative is to portage or run a 3-foot weir and paddle a further half mile of backwater to the 8-foot weir, which you must portage. A half mile of class I water then brings you to the start of section 2.

GAUGE: The gauge on Gwynns Falls at Villa Nova needs 150 cfs. You can check the final rapid by driving into the cemetery, to the bridge. Fullerton and Randallstown (Baltimore Co.) are the nearest rain gauges.

The first person who stopped was from the **local Gwynns Falls organization**, dedicated to keeping the creek clean. She warned us that the water was high and therefore treacherous. Then came a **curious Kenyan family**, who noted that paddling was a lot safer here, with no crocodiles and hippos. We didn't encounter any of those, but a family of beavers splashed into the creek as we passed by, and scores of Canada geese and mallards greeted us near the takeout. At the Villa Nova gauge, a lone USGS employee was wading in the creek, recalibrating the gauge level/cfs relationship.

Section 2: Gwynn Oak Avenue (Md. 126) to Wilkens Avenue (US 1)

Gradient	Difficulty	Distance	Area	Scenery	Strainers	Rating
45 (150)	III (IV-)	5.6	39	D	<1/mi.	***

USGS Quad – Baltimore West; Source – Personal descent 6/96 (1st half), 11/04 (2nd)
N39 19.49, W76 42.89 to N39 16.63, W76 39.67

This long and challenging fall-line descent is marred only by poor water quality and trash (including plastic on the trees) which undermine the otherwise pleasant parkland scenery. The first mile starts off class II-, but steepens to class III-. Below Forest Park Ave., by the restored mill town of Dickeysville, a 10-foot dam must be portaged. The class II-III rapids then resume, and 0.7 miles after the dam comes a tricky class III at the bottom of a long rock garden. (This can be scouted from Wetheredsville Road.) Dead Run enters from the right midway through the trip, by a pair of small ledges. Three-fourths of a mile later, at Hilton Street, some untreated sewerage seeps in. Shortly below, the creek braids; the left channel has a class III- ending.

In another half mile, below Edmondson Avenue (US 40), **there is an iron pipe across the creek**, at the end of a short straightaway. Scout from the eddy on the right, well above the pipe. Except in very low water, you must portage on the right. Then, 200 yards below, is Gwynns Falls, a five-foot drop. In low water, you can scout from the rock ledge in the middle. The right channel is precipitous, with shallow rocks just below that make this class IV-, while the left chute is a narrow and twisty class IV. A short portage may be advisable. This is followed immediately by a delightful class III rock garden and then a four-foot, class III ledge (easiest on the right) and a long class II rock garden that continues to West Baltimore St. Below, the gradient eases up, although there are still some easy rapids, including one wave train. Take out by the park on river right upstream of Wilkins Avenue (US 1).

You could continue a mile to the Gwynns Falls Trailhead parking area by the golf course, just off Washington Boulevard, but the gradient is just 20 ft/mile and the scenery is poor. Below there,

Gwynns Falls is tidal for its final two miles, before entering the Middle Branch of the Patapsco River estuary.

GAUGE: You need about 150 cfs on the gauge at Villa Nova, 3 miles upstream of the put in (which gives you the flow that you will encounter 1-2 hours later). Check the Fullerton and Randallstown rain gauges (Baltimore Co.).

RED RUN: Pleasant Hill and Dolfield Roads to Painters Mill Road

Gradient	Difficulty	Distance	Area	Scenery	Strainers	Rating
25	I	3.0	4.6	C-	2-3/mi.	-

USGS Quad – Reisterstown; Source – Personal descent 10/03
N39 24.69, W76 48.69 to N39 24.29, W76 46.75

Red Run, the flattest tributary of Gwynns Falls, meanders east, south, and east again, with lots of riffles and a few tiny ledges. But due to the strainers and limited forward visibility (the creek is twisty and narrow), it is rather dangerous, especially towards the end where a fallen footbridge blocked the right two-thirds of the creek.

Take out by the Owings Mills Station AATA Parking Lot, 200 yards above the confluence. For the shuttle, take Lakeside Blvd. from Painters Mill Rd. to Dolfield Blvd., turn right and go to the end, and then go right again on Dolfield Road. Use new maps.

There are woods (full of deer) all along the creek, but when the foliage is gone, you see commercial development in the background.

GAUGE: Look for at least 45 cfs on Gwynns Falls near Delight. For rainfall, use an average of the gauges at Freeland and Baptist Home.

Near Red Run was the largest **chromite mine** in the world, the Choate Mine. Isaac Tyson, Jr., discovered the chromite in 1827, built a chrome plant in Baltimore in 1845 and then largely controlled the world chromium market for about a decade. Production ceased in 1860, but was resumed on and off through World War I. Several mining sites can be visited in the Soldiers Delight Natural Environment Area, which preserves the serpentine barrens.

SCOTTS LEVEL BRANCH: Old Court Road to Gwynns Falls

Gradient	Difficulty	Distance	Area	Scenery	Strainers	Rating
50 (150)	III	1.7	3.0	D+	3-5/mi.	**

USGS Quad – Ellicott City/Baltimore West; Source – Personal descent 2/03
N39 22.05, W76 45.95 to N39 21.64, W76 44.74

Scotts Level Branch flows east-southeast for five miles, north of and parallel to Liberty Road (Md. 26), steepening as it approaches Gwynns Falls. The last half mile has dynamite rapids along with strainers, partial strainers, overhanging branches and vines.

The first half-mile of the trip, from Old Court Road to North Rolling Road, is twisty and class I. The next quarter mile, to Twin Lakes Court, has some class II and one good surfing hole. Soon after comes the first class III – a 4-foot ledge with a minor hydraulic; go fast, right of center. Then come some minor rapids and a pair of long class III rock gardens, one of which has a 3-foot ledge midway, plus a few tight chutes that demand good boat control. Everything is runnable and great fun if clean. There are enough eddies to boat scout your way down, as the long rapids are fairly straight.

Under I-695 (the Baltimore Beltway), almost all of the water goes through the right culvert. There is an eddy just above the bridge, where you can stop and check. You can take out (with parking available) at the confluence, on Scotts Hill Drive, or continue down an easy part of Gwynns Falls.

The scenery is poor; through the narrow woods, you see first houses, then apartment buildings. There is also lots of trash – one paddler claims he counted a dozen shopping carts. But in the main rapids, you are in a little, steep-sided gorge, and your attention had better not be on the view.

GAUGE: Look for at least 80 cfs on the Scotts Level Branch gauge; more than 250 cfs is probably dangerous. The riffles just above the take out should not be bony. The Fullerton and Randallstown rain gauges in Baltimore County are the nearest ones.

POWDER MILL RUN: Liberty Heights Ave. to Gwynns Falls

Gradient	Difficulty	Distance	Area	Scenery	Strainers	Rating
55	II (II+)	0.8	3.5	D+	0-3/mi.	**

USGS Quad – Ellicott City; Source – Personal descent 5/03
N39 20.17, W76 42.62 to N39 19.49, W76 42.89

The two arms of Powder Mill Branch meet just above Liberty Heights Avenue, at the terminus of Northern Parkway. From Flannery Lane, west of the creek, carry across the field and woods to put in. The stream starts out class I, but then steepens. After some backyards on the right, the creek splits briefly; the right-side is narrower but deeper. When the channels reunite, there is a steep class II+ chute on the left. And then there are frequent class II rock gardens the rest of the way. The confluence is the start of section 2 of Gwynns Falls. The woodland scenery is ruined by the abundant trash along the banks.

GAUGE: You need 65 cfs on the Powder Mill Run gauge below the put in. Use the Pikesville rain gauge in Baltimore Co. The ledge below Liberty Heights Ave. should be cleanly runnable.

DEAD RUN: Little Creek Drive to Gwynns Falls

Gradient	Difficulty	Distance	Area	Scenery	Strainers	Rating
55 (110)	III+	3.2	5.0	C-	1/mi.	***

USGS Quad – Baltimore West; Source – Personal descent 5/01
N39 18.79, W76 43.55 to N39 18.33, W76 41.20

This exciting trip through Dead Run, Leakin and Gwynns Falls parks would earn four stars were it not for the pollution, the trash and later the riprap. The creek was channelized in the building of Dogwood Road and then, in Baltimore City, Franklintown Road, both of which are useful for scouting.

The first mile, at just 20 ft/mile, consists of pools and riffles. You pass Kernan Dr. at 0.6 miles and, as the creek gets a bit steeper, Forest Park and Old Ingleside avenues in Franklintown at 1.2 miles. In low water, paddle right up to the 6-foot dam there on the far right; in higher water, portage on river left starting beneath the first bridge.

Soon, the creek enters Baltimore City, where the gradient averages 75 ft/mile, with class II and then class III rapids. By Franklintown Road, there is a pair of class III+ rapids, ending in steep right and left turns, respectively. Below the hiking trail footbridge (part of the Gwynns Falls Restoration Project), take the right channel. The creek then mellows, until a long class III+ rapid with no eddies, climaxing in a steep, rock-strewn entry to the passage beneath Wetheredsville Rd., at the confluence. This rapid is dangerous in high water; in that case, take out at the park 1/4 mile above it.

You can take out right at the confluence, by climbing the riprap on river left, or continue down Gwynns Falls to any of a number of spots alongside Wetheredsville Road.

GAUGE: The first riffles need 3 inches above minimum. The Dead Run gauge at Franklintown (Kernan Drive) should be over 100 cfs and that at Woodlawn (a half mile above the put in) 45 cfs. Use Fullerton and Westview (Baltimore Co.) rain gauges.

Leakin Park is part of the old "Crimea Estate" of Thomas Winans, who engineered the Moscow-St. Petersburg railway for Czar Nicholas I. He and his Russian wife built the mansion before the Civil War, as a copy of one in Crimea. His son, a Confederate sympathizer, "fortified" it with logs painted to look like cannons; he was arrested when the ruse was discovered. Leakin Park was reputedly used by gangsters to dispose of their victims; hence "Dead Run"? It was shown in the TV series *The Wire* in a similar role.

MAIDENS CHOICE RUN: Frederick Ave. (Md.144) to Gwynns Falls

Gradient	Difficulty	Distance	Area	Scenery	Strainers	Rating
60 (190)	?	2.0	1.0	?	?	?

USGS Quad – Baltimore West; Source – Scouting at street accesses
N39 16.88, W76 41.57 to N39 16.61, W76 39.67

This tiny, hard to scout, polluted and surprisingly wide *"explorers' special"* emerges at Frederick Ave. Put in a quarter mile below, in the park. Below Yale Ave., it crosses the Loundon Park Cemetery and the railroad tracks. It descends 60 feet in the first 1.5 miles and another 60 feet in the last half mile. **Gabion walls make this part dangerous.** The confluence is just below Wilkens Ave (US 1).

GAUGE: Moores Run should be 200 cfs, Powder Mill Run 140 cfs. For rainfall, use Westview and Bannecker in Baltimore Co. and Carroll Park in Baltimore City.

GWYNNS RUN: Wash Water Lake to Gwynns Falls Parkway

Gradient	Difficulty	Distance	Area	Scenery	Strainers	Rating
110	III- (III)	0.4	1.8	C	0-4/mi.	**

USGS Quad – Baltimore West; Source – Personal descent 10/03
N39 19.28, W76 39.92 to N39 18.88, W76 39.92

What little is left of Gwynns Run, as Julius Caesar said of Gaul, is divided into three parts. The first bit, above Liberty Heights Ave., is tiny and fenced. The final piece, after three underground miles, runs for 350 yards through the Carroll Park Golf Course to Gwynns Falls – but it is heavily polluted and requires a half-mile carry to put in.

But the 650-yard middle piece, which emerges from a pipe in Hanlon Park after being dammed to form Wash Water Lake, is a blast, despite being so short and hard to catch. The scenery, strainer and trash situations are not bad for Baltimore. From the put in (off the north end of Dukeland St.), there is a long class III- rock garden, climaxing in a class III boulder patch with a sheer drop on the right and a twisting channel on the left. After that, the stream is class II+. As you near Gwynns Falls Parkway, there is a **drop-dead, not-to-be missed eddy** on river right, just after a pipe. Below the bridge, the creek plunges into the dark intestines of the city.

GAUGE: The Powder Mill Run and Moores Run gauges should both be over 125 cfs, but timing is more critical. The nearest rain gauge is Jones Falls, in Baltimore City.

CAPITAL CANOEING AND KAYAKING

PATAPSCO RIVER BASIN

© Copyright 2005-2011 Undertow Software Corp.

In 1608, as part of his exploration of the Chesapeake Bay, **Captain John Smith** sailed up the Patapsco estuary. (The name means either "at the rocky point" or "tide covered with froth.") It was here that the British launched their attack on Baltimore in the **War of 1812**, to punish that city for its privateers which plundered British shipping, and where the **Star Spangled Banner** (which became the national anthem in 1931) was written about that battle. The huge 30x42 foot flag had been ordered both as a challenge to the British and a symbol for the Americans. The **Fort McHenry** National Monument overlooks the Patapsco.

Chapter 8:

PATAPSCO RIVER BASIN

This chapter covers the flowing Patapsco River and its tributaries, which drain 370 square miles in Carroll, Baltimore, Howard and Anne Arundel counties. (Gwynns and Jones Falls, which enter the Patapsco River estuary of the Chesapeake Bay, are in chapter 7.) While there are no outstanding (4 star) paddles in this basin, there are half a dozen runs to which I give 3 stars, and another five that I think merit 2 stars.

The major towns within the basin are the Baltimore suburbs of Ellicott City (66,000), Catonsville (42,000), Elkridge (16,000), and Lansdowne/Baltimore Highlands (15,000). Westminster (19,000) is on the boundary with the Monocacy basin, while Reisterstown (26,000) is shared with Gwynns Falls. This is a generally prosperous area that is increasingly becoming suburban.

The **Patapsco River**, formed by its North and South branches, heads east-southeast from the Carroll/Howard/Baltimore County junction to tidewater at Elkridge, southwest of Baltimore, and later widens into an inlet of the Chesapeake Bay, where sailboats and yachts replace canoes and kayaks. It starts rather flat (section 1), descends the fall line with some good rapids (section 2) and then calms down again (section 3).

The **North Branch** was dammed in 1954 to create Liberty Lake, to supplement Gunpowder Falls as a water source for Baltimore City and County. Its only good rapids are in its first mile, and it is usually almost dry below the reservoir. The **East** and **West branches,** which form it, are pleasant novice runs. Of its other tributaries, **Morgan Run** has good rapids and scenery en route to Liberty Lake, smaller **Beaver Run** has one exciting stretch and tiny ***Deep Run [north]*** is a steep "explorers' special."

The **South Branch** is a long, enjoyable creek, with the best intermediate part being Gaither Gorge, and the toughest rapid being the class IV McKeldon Falls below there. It has two main tributaries. **Gillis Falls** is ruined by strainers. Section 1 of **Piney Run** is mild, but the short section 2 has the hardest whitewater in the Patapsco basin.

Below the confluence of the branches are three tiny but good tributaries: **Brice Run** (section 1 of which is an "explorers' special"), **Bens Run** and the **West Branch of Herbert Run**, and one rotten one, **Deep Run [south]**.

Patapsco Valley State Park, the oldest and largest state park in Maryland, was initially built largely by the Civilian Conservation Corps in 1933-42, has been further developed recently, and is full of hiking, biking and horse-riding trails, picnic areas, rock climbs, etc. It encompasses 32 river miles of the Patapsco and its North and South branches. Many of the roads into or across it have been closed, giving the park more of a wilderness feel.

The **B&O Railroad** line that parallels the South Branch and the Patapsco has interesting tunnels and culverts, plus the 704-foot Thomas Viaduct, dating from 1835, the oldest stone arch railroad bridge (it crosses the Patapsco) still in use. These B&O tracks were the first ones in the US for public use; on January 7, 1830, the initial passengers were carried, in railcars pulled by horses. In the summer of that year, the first locomotive, **"Tom Thumb,"** was tested here and then raced against horses; it reached 18 mph.

The Patapsco: Baltimore's River of History, by Paul J. Travers (Tidewater Publishers, 1990), gives a detailed story of the interaction between the river and the people nearby.

GAUGES: There are gauges on Beaver Run (14 sq. mi.), Morgan Run (28 sq. mi.), the North Branch (57 sq. mi.), Cranberry Branch of the West Branch (3.3 sq. mi.), and the East Branch of Herbert Run (2.5 sq. mi.). The gauge on the main Patapsco at Hollofield (285 sq. mi.) was deleted in January 2013, and there is no good substitute. The Patuxent at Unity (35 sq. mi.) correlates well for the South Branch and its tributaries. The gauge on Dead Run at Franklintown (5.5 sq. mi.) in the Gwynns Falls basin is good for the small downstream tributaries.

In the table below, the **gauge column refers to Beaver Run**, except that *from Brice Run onward it refers to Dead Run (in bold italics)*. The rainfall gauges at Winfield and Piney Run (Carroll Co.) are good especially for the South Branch and its tributaries.

name	gradient	difficulty	length	area	gauge	rating
Patapsco River - Section 1	4	I (II-)	6.6	258	n.a.	*
- Section 2	20 (55)	II+(III)	5.7	285	n.a.	***
- Section 3	13	I (II-)	3.2	300	n.a.	*
North Branch - Section 1	50	II (III)	0.8	44	40cfs	**
- Section 2	6	I (II+)	3.2	52	25cfs	*
- Section 3	8	I	2.4	164	(15cfs)	*
West Branch	25	II- (II)	4.4	15	75cfs	**
East Branch	23	I (II-)	4.3	19	65cfs	**
Deep Run [north]	50 (130)	?	2.8	5.6	200cfs	?
Beaver Run	30 (70)	III-	3.7	10	110cfs	***
Morgan Run	27	II+(III-)	2.8	23	70cfs	***
South Branch - Section 1	17	I (II)	4.5	32	40cfs	*
- Section 2	32 (50)	III-	2.2	49	40cfs	***
- Section 3	14	II (IV)	5.6	56	40cfs	**
Gillis Falls	25	II-	5.0	8	100cfs	-
Piney Run - Section 1	17	I	3.2	16	65cfs	*
- Section 2	70 (200)	III (IV+)	1.3	19	90cfs	***
Brice Run - *Section 1*	35	?	1.5	5.7	*90cfs*	?
- Section 2	45 (65)	III- (IV)	1.0	10	*80cfs*	**
Bens Run	50	III	2.0	3.8	*100cfs*	***
Deep Run [south]	24	II-	6.8	3.5	*80cfs*	-
West Br., Herbert Run	43	II (II+)	1.5	2.3	*135cfs*	**

PATAPSCO RIVER

The Patapsco River (originally Patapsco Falls) flows 19 miles from the confluence of its North and South branches to tidewater at Elkridge. The first 1.7 miles are paddled after completing the North or South Branch. The next 16 miles are in sections 1-3 below. The final 1.3 miles are flat, and then the tidewater stretches for 7 miles to the Middle Branch inlet of Baltimore Harbor. (Gertler includes this stretch.) The popular intermediate-level section 2 contains the best rapids and none of the dams.

> The Patapsco River **flooded** disastrously in July 1868 and June 1972, rising very rapidly due to rainfall in its headwaters, and taking many residents in Ellicott City by surprise. In 1868, about 50 people drowned, as the river rose by 5 feet in 10 minutes, cresting some 40 feet above normal, following an intense 18-inch rainfall. In 1972, people ignored the danger of Hurricane Agnes because it had been downgraded to a tropical storm. The river reached the 1868 level, wiped out dams and bridges, inundated downtown Ellicott City, killed a dozen people, and led to the creation of an advanced warning system based on rainfall gauges.

Section 1: Woodstock to Old Frederick Road

Gradient	Difficulty	Distance	Area	Scenery	Strainers	Rating
4	I (II-)	6.6	258	C	<1/mi.	*

USGS Quad – Ellicott City; Source – Gertler; scouting by road
N39 19.90, W76 52.21 to N39 18.62, W76 47.57

This is a long, flat paddle, with some riffles in the 4.7 miles between Woodstock and the 15-foot dam at Daniels (carry on the right), and a short class II- rapid just below. The scenery is mostly woodlands, now that the water-powered mills are gone.

GAUGE: Zero level is about ¾ of that needed for section 2 below.

Section 2: Old Frederick Road to Thistle (River Road/Ilchester Road)

Gradient	Difficulty	Distance	Area	Scenery	Strainers	Rating
20 (55)	II+ (III)	5.7	285	C	<1/mi.	***

USGS Quad – Ellicott City; Source – Personal descent often
N39 18.62, W76 47.57 to N39 15.07, W76 45.84

From the put in, it is 1.6 rather flat but pretty miles to US 40 (high above the river) and the site of the former Union Dam (removed in 2010 with economic stimulus funding) immediately below. There used to be a dangerous hydraulic here, but now it is just a lively class II rapid, followed by 1.4 miles of riffles (tiresome in low water), until the old mill (on river left) at Oella. Oella Falls is a class II+ rock garden, deepest on the far left. A quarter mile later, by a house almost over the water on river left, is the class III, 100-yard Suicide Rapids. Most of the water flows center-left on the first three parts and down the middle on the last. This rapid gets harder with more water. In another quarter mile you reach Ellicott City and Md. 144 (Frederick Road). The class II+ Doughnut Bend rapid (the Doughnut Corporation of America operated a factory there from 1926-72; it is now Maryland's only commercial flour mill) begins at the bridge; for the best water, stay left. There are several class II- rapids in the next half-mile, followed by a mile with just riffles and then a final class II- as you approach the take-out bridge at Thistle.

To run only the final 2.2 miles, starting with Suicide Rapids, you can put in just below the old Oella mill (which was converted into luxury apartments, taking advantage of tax credits for preserving the historic shell) after leaving your car just above it.

GAUGE: If the Patapsco gauge at Hollofield gets restored, zero level is 200 cfs. In the meanwhile, when Liberty Lake is full (see North Branch, Patapsco River below), you need about 40 cfs on the North Branch at Cedarhurst. When it is not full, look for 60 cfs on Morgan Run and 70 cfs on the Patuxent at Unity, about 4 hours earlier. Doughnut Bend rapid is a good visual indicator. If the island upstream from the Ellicott City bridge is all under water, watch out!

The Innocents Aboard. I first ran this in 1980, in the bow of my old Grumman, at a level of 1.3 feet. The large waves below Union Dam swamped us. We never capsized, but the boat just sank beneath us (what are air bags?). Later, in Suicide Rapids, Jim Brown suddenly cursed that he had dropped his paddle. Desperate, I tried to steer from the bow. A few seconds later, the paddle snakes returned to him what they had taken.

The **Ellicott brothers** arrived in 1772 and established a flour milling industry that helped shift local farming from tobacco to wheat. Textile mills later developed as well. Children swam in the river at Ellicott City in the early 1900s – but with a lookout to warn them when the Dickey Woolen Mill at Oella (built 1809) started releasing its dye upstream into the river.

Section 3: Thistle (River Road/Ilchester Road) to Gun Road

Gradient	Difficulty	Distance	Area	Scenery	Strainers	Rating
13*	I (II-)	3.2	300	B-	0	*

USGS Quad – Ellicott City/Savage/Relay; Source – Personal descent 4/05
N39 15.07-W76 45.84 to N39 13.63, W76 43.38

*(excluding the dam)

Just below the put in and a railroad bridge, comes an easy, bouncy rapid. In a half mile is the 25-foot Bloede's Dam (which operated from 1906-24, when it became uneconomic, as the first hydropower dam in the US with its turbines inside the hollow core of the dam itself); carry on the right. There are riffles to the end, but gradually they become more widely spaced. The scenery is pretty through the state park. River Road, on the right bank, was wrecked in 1972 by Hurricane Agnes, and not rebuilt.

GAUGE: Zero level is about ¾ of that needed for section 2 above..

Near the takeout was **Elk Ridge Landing**, the main 18th Century port in the area until siltation there and the development of mills along Jones and Gwynns Falls gave Baltimore the advantage. The remains were washed away in the 1868 flood. Elk Ridge Landing was sited at the head of navigation, just below **Great Falls of the Patapsco**, an 8-foot drop that has disappeared. (Did floods or dynamite destroy the rocky barrier? I can't find any historical explanation.) Now, the final 8 feet of drop are spread over a mile.

NORTH BRANCH, PATAPSCO RIVER

The North Branch is formed by the East and West branches at the hamlet of Patapsco, and then flows 4-5 miles (depending upon the reservoir's level) to Liberty Lake. The lake drowns the next 15 miles (including the former town of Oakland Mills), until a final 3.3 miles to the confluence with the South Branch. The North Branch has whitewater only in its first mile. Although it comprises two-thirds of the watershed of the upper Patapsco, it provides little water to the Patapsco except when Liberty Lake is full.

Section 1: Patapsco to Tank Road

Gradient	Difficulty	Distance	Area	Scenery	Strainers	Rating
50	II (III)	0.8	44	C+	0-1/mi.	**

USGS Quad – Westminster; Source – Personal descent 9/99
N39 32.22, W76 53.60 to N39 31.81, W76 52.98

This short delight, with good play spots, is a great way to finish a trip on the East or West Branch, and a partial alternative to those if the water level is too low. With a foot of water, after a few class I-II chutes, there is a nice class II+ chute, followed by a short but steep class III+ boulder garden; at lower levels, those +s are not warranted, but you still have to be very exact on your line in the final drop of the main rapid.

GAUGE: Look for 175 cfs on the gauge at Cedarhurst (the section 2 take out) an hour after you start. There is a painted RC gauge on the bridge at the take out.

> At the **class III rapid**, Jamie Deehan ran first, and got stuck in the Sarah Palin dead-end on the far right. He signaled me to take the far left Dennis Kucinich sneak route, but I decided instead on the Bill Clinton fandango down the center. First I hit the hydraulic, then the boulder, and when my bow was knocked far left to the base of the main drop, I ended up running the second half of the rapid backwards. Still, I had survived Whitewater, and I exited laughing. Ed Evangelidi watched our heroics, and lacking a wetsuit, chose the Colin Powell portage instead.

Section 2: Tank Road to Cedarhurst Road (off Md. 91)

Gradient	Difficulty	Distance	Area	Scenery	Strainers	Rating
6	I (II+)	3.2	52	B-, D-	<1/mi.	*

USGS Quad – Westminster; Source – Personal descent 9/06
N39 31.81, W76 52.98 to N39 29.96, W76 52.94

This novice section runs alongside the Western Maryland Railroad. There are frequent easy riffles, few strainers, and nice scenery. After one mile you reach Lawndale – where the yards are large and as manicured as the golf course.

In the last half mile, you pass through an industrial area, with a variety of bridges overhead. As you near the Congoleum Company water tower and smokestack on the left, and see a horizon line, pull over on the right to scout this **sheer 4-foot drop into a hydraulic**. The only place to run it is about a quarter of the way from the left bank, where a set of steps (a fish ladder?) makes an exciting class II+ chute. However, the spot is not visible from above until the last second, so have someone below giving directions. About 100 yards later, an 18-inch drop is straightforward. Take out on the right just below Md. 91, up a steep, narrow, muddy trail to the dead-end of Cedarhurst Road. Within a mile below there, Liberty Lake swallows up the river.

GAUGE: Look for 100 cfs on the gauge at Cedarhurst. The painted RC gauge on the bridge by the put in refers to section 1; you can run section 2 down to -3 inches.

Section 3: Marriottsville Road to Patapsco River

Gradient	Difficulty	Distance	Area	Scenery	Strainers	Rating
8	I	2.4*	164	B+	<1/mi.	*

USGS Quad – Sykesville/Ellicott City; Source – Personal descent 3/06
N39 21.88, W76 53.07 to N39 19.90, W76 52.21

*(plus 1.7 miles on the Patapsco at 13 ft/mile)

The North Branch here is the border between Carroll and Baltimore counties. The first mile below the Liberty Lake dam is inaccessible, but Marriottsville Road is a good put in for the rest. After the first quarter mile along the road, the scenery is undisturbed woods and hills. There are about a half dozen riffles, some fairly long.

GAUGE: After prolonged wet periods, when Liberty Lake is full, look for at least 65 cfs on the North Branch gauge at Cedarhurst, 15 cfs on Beaver Run (4-5 hours before you start). The rest of the time there will be only a trickle.

WEST BRANCH, PATAPSCO R.: Gorsuch Road to Confluence

Gradient	Difficulty	Distance	Area	Scenery	Strainers	Rating
25	II- (II)	4.4	15	C	1/mi.	**

USGS Quad – Westminster; Source – Personal descent (last 3 miles) 12/96
N39 34.11, W76 56.60 to N39 32.22, W76 53.60

The West and East branches are similar, but the former is the choice for train buffs, as you pass 9 railroad bridges. Gorsuch Road is 3 miles east of Westminster; short on time, we put in at Carrollton (the Carrollton Roller Mills ground flour until 1952), 1.5 miles below. The trip is pleasant, except for some thorny portages around strainers. The only solid class II is a set of ledges just above the confluence with the East Branch. One can take out there, but it's more fun to continue down section 1 of the North Branch.

GAUGE: Look for at least 300 on the Cedarhurst gauge on the North Branch, 75 cfs on Beaver Run, and 20 cfs on Cranberry Branch (which enters at SR 852).

EAST BRANCH, PATAPSCO R.: Coon Club Road to Confluence

Gradient	Difficulty	Distance	Area	Scenery	Strainers	Rating
23	I (II-)	4.3	19	C	2/mi.	**

USGS Quad – Westminster; Source – Personal descent 2/98
N39 34.51, W76 53.68 to N39 32.22, W76 53.60

The East Branch is a mild run, starting after its main tributary, Aspen Run, enters. (Somewhat steeper are the last 0.8 miles of Aspen Run, with 8 sq. mi. and 40 ft/mile, and the mile of the East Branch above the put in, with 9 sq. mi. and 32 ft/mile.) There are lots of riffles, some of which have overhanging bushes. Above Carrollton Road (1.3 miles), the creek is narrow and fast, and has a series of tight bends. The best (class II-) whitewater is just above Patapsco Road (3.4 miles).

GAUGE: At zero level, the final, rocky chute under the take-out bridge (on the North Branch) is bony on river right. The Cedarhurst gauge needs 270 cfs (2 hours after you start), Beaver Run 70 cfs and Cranberry Branch 15 cfs (2 hours before you put in).

DEEP RUN [north]: Lees Mill to North Branch of the Patapsco

Gradient	Difficulty	Distance	Area	Scenery	Strainers	Rating
50 (130)	?	2.8*	5.6	?	?	?

USGS Quad – Hampstead/Westminster; Source – Scouting accesses and confluence
N39 33.26, W76 52.38 to N39 31.17, W76 52.60

*(plus 0.6 miles of class I on the North Branch)

This steep, tiny *"explorers' special"* should have good rapids. The put in is just below a fence, at Carrollton and Lees Mill roads. The first steep part begins in a mile. A mile later, you pass Emory Road. There is a second steep part in the final quarter mile.

The North Branch will be high, but that should not be a problem because you reach it in the rather flat section 2, and can take out in 0.6 miles, at Lawndale.

GAUGE: This creek requires a lot of water – 200 cfs on the Beaver Run gauge (an hour after you start), 50 cfs on Cranberry Branch.

BEAVER RUN: Green Mill Road to Gamber Road (Md. 91)

Gradient	Difficulty	Distance	Area	Scenery	Strainers	Rating
30 (70)	III-	3.7	10	B-	2-4/mi.	***

USGS Quad – Westminster/Finksburg; Source – Personal descent 12/96
N39 30.62, W76 55.60 to N39 29.22, W76 54.05

Beaver Run rises on the southern fringe of Westminster and flows nine miles to Liberty Lake. It becomes runnable midway, once Middle Run enters. After a few houses in the first half mile, the creek flows through relatively pristine woods. Toward the end of the first mile, there is a quarter mile with eight class III- rapids.

When we reached pasture land, 1.5 miles from the end, there was a pair of barbed wire fences (which we easily lifted up) and an "ALL Trespassers Will Be Shot" sign on a tree. But this dangerous living was enjoyable, with good gradient and class II- rapids, as the creek wound between low mud banks. After a few more houses and bridges, the survivors reentered the woods for a final half mile.

Take out on Hughes Road, just upstream from Gamber Road (Md. 91), or at Cold Saturday Drive just below. Beware of errant bullets from Cheney clones at the shooting range just before the take out.

GAUGE: The staff gauge at Hughes Road should read at least 1.8 and the recorded Beaver Run gauge 130 cfs. After a daylong 1.5-inch winter rain, the creek was at zero level (while the East and West branches of the Patapsco still had at least 6 inches.)

MORGAN RUN: End of Jim Bowers Road to London Bridge Road

Gradient	Difficulty	Distance	Area	Scenery	Strainers	Rating
27	II+ (III-)	2.8	23	A-	0-2/mi.	***

USGS Quad – Finksburg; Source – Personal descent 10/03
N39 28.43, W76 59.04 to N39 27.11, W76 57.31

This is a delightful low-intermediate run, with fun rapids and great scenery. Drive to the end of Jim Bowers Road, and carry 150 yards to the creek.

The first two-thirds mile is still drab, narrow and twisty, with some channeling and quite a few trees that must be maneuvered under, over, around or through. But then the creek improves sharply in both scenery and gradient. The best rapids are in the half-mile above and past the ruins of Klee Mill (at 1.3 miles), where there are several class II rapids, a pair of interesting class II+ boulder gardens with a choice of routes (except in low water), and then a class III- rapid through a jumble of boulders. At most levels, you head to the right and then cut back sharply after punching the hole; less-experienced paddlers should scout this drop. At Klee Mill there is a large platform to permit people in wheelchairs to fish for trout (catch and return) – the stream has one of the highest densities of brown and rainbow trout in Maryland.

Below Klee Mill, the creek remains beautiful and has several nice long class II and II+ rapids, as well as many riffles. Take out at London Bridge Road, on the downstream right side. Below there, Morgan Run continues for 0.4 miles of class I to Liberty Lake, where the road access is not as good.

GAUGE: The visual USGS gauge at London Bridge Road, on downstream river right, should read at least 2.2 and the on-line Morgan Run gauge 140 cfs.

> **Roger Morgan** was one of the original Maryland colonists who came over on the Ark and the Dove in 1634, and his descendents became a prominent family in the area.

SOUTH BRANCH, PATAPSCO RIVER

The South Branch starts as a spring on Four Corners Farm near Mt. Airy, where Montgomery, Frederick, Carroll, and Howard counties meet, and flows east (as the Carroll-Howard boundary) for 18 miles to its confluence with the North Branch. It has only half the watershed of the North Branch, but because the Liberty Lake dam blocks the latter, the South Branch is usually the main contributor of flow to the Patapsco. After 6 miles, it picks up Gillis Falls and some other tributaries just before Woodbine.

Section 1: Woodbine (Md. 94) to Gaither

Gradient	Difficulty	Distance	Area	Scenery	Strainers	Rating
17	I (II)	4.5	32	C-	1-2/mi.	*

USGS Quad – Woodbine/Sykesville; Source – Gertler; AW
N39 21.61, W77 03.76 to N39 21.59, W76 59.53

This stretch has indifferent scenery, lots of riffles and just one rapid, at the ruins of an old milldam by Md. 97 (mile 3.1).
    GAUGE: You need 80 cfs on Morgan Run, and 90 cfs on the Patuxent at Unity. Use the Winfield and Piney Run rain gauges in Carroll County.

Section 2: Gaither to Below Sykesville (River Road)

Gradient	Difficulty	Distance	Area	Scenery	Strainers	Rating
32 (50)	III-	2.2	49	C	<1/mi.	***

USGS Quad – Sykesville; Source – Personal descent 5/06
N39 21.59, W76 59.53 to N39 21.43, W76 57.63

This is a delightful short paddle. After half a mile, you enter the Gaither Gorge, which continues past Sykesville, with eight class II to III- rapids, several of which are long and complex. The sixth brings you to the Baldwin Station restaurant; on the next ledge, avoid the far left line. Class I and II rapids continue for the next half mile, as you pass Md. 32 (the old bridge was left standing because of its rare aluminum girder structure circa 1960). Take out where River Road leaves the creek, at 2.2 miles.
    GAUGE: You need 80 cfs on Morgan Run and 90 cfs on the Patuxent at Unity. Use the Piney Run rain gauge in Carroll Co.

Section 3: Below Sykesville (River Road) to Patapsco River

Gradient	Difficulty	Distance	Area	Scenery	Strainers	Rating
14	II (IV)	5.6*	56	B-	<<1/mi.	**

USGS Quad – Sykesville; Source – Personal descent 4/05
N39 21.43, W76 57.63 to N39 19.90, W76 52.21

*(plus 1.7 miles on the Patapsco at 10 ft/mile)

This section is usually run as a continuation of section 2. The first 1.5 miles has only riffles, until a pair of class II rock gardens. After that, all is flat for over 3 miles, past Mariottsville at mile 4.3 and the confluence with Piney Run. Then comes the class IV McKeldon Falls, a 12-foot drop over 20 yards of closely spaced ledges. The route is normally center left, because of small sieves near both shores and a wide, flat rock at dead center near the bottom. Scouting and portage are easiest on the left, where you can pull up close to the brink (at moderate levels). You could take out and carry up the hill on river left. The remaining half mile to the confluence with the North Fork starts out with a short but steep class II, followed by three longer but more gradual rock gardens. Once on the main Patapsco, it is 1.7 miles to Woodstock, with only a few riffles.

GAUGE: You need 80 cfs on Morgan Run and 90 cfs on the Patuxent at Unity. Use the Piney Run rain gauge in Carroll Co.

> We were hosting **a potluck dinner** for my wife's office staff, and had anticipated a 5-mile trip on the Patapsco. Instead, we did 9.5 miles on the South Branch/Patapsco, and by the time we arrived home in our elegant wetsuits, the guests were waiting, perplexed and then bemused.

GILLIS FALLS: Gillis Road to South Branch of the Patapsco

Gradient	Difficulty	Distance	Area	Scenery	Strainers	Rating
25	II-	5.0	8	C	4-6/mi.	-

USGS Quad – Winfield/Woodbine; Source – Personal descent 2/98
N39 24.72, W77 04.41 to N39 21.61, W77 03.76

This, the smallest of Maryland's six "falls," has no major drops, so its name is a mystery (not the first part – Joseph Gillis had a saw mill along the creek). Two hundred years ago, demand for beaver skin hats helped open up this country. Until that fashion returns, avoid this creek. I followed a swimming beaver, but could not get close enough to thank him. At the put in, there is parking for archery hunters (for beavers??). Take out at Woodbine Road (Md. 94), just below the confluence. The scenery is nice for the first three miles, but houses appear with increasing frequency thereafter.

GAUGE: Beaver Run needs 100 cfs. Use the Winfield rain gauge in Carroll Co.

PINEY RUN

Piney Run heads slowly southeast for 13 miles (including 2 miles behind a dam), except for one brief but dramatic stretch shortly before it flows into the South Branch.

Section 1: Slacks Road to Arrington Road

Gradient	Difficulty	Distance	Area	Scenery	Strainers	Rating
17	I	3.2	16	C	2/mi.	*

USGS Quad – Finksburg/Sykesville; Source – Personal descent (final 2 miles) 2/04
N39 22.86, W76 56.67 to N39 21.98, W76 54.70

This is a pleasant trip through the woods, with access also at Brangels Road at 1.2 miles. Towards the end there are more riffles but also a few back yards. Take out on the left immediately below Arrington Road.

GAUGE: About 140 cfs on Morgan Run or 70 cfs on Beaver Run should suffice. For rainfall, there are well-placed gauges at Winfield and Piney Run in Carroll County.

Section 2: Arrington Road to Marriottsville (Confluence)

Gradient	Difficulty	Distance	Area	Scenery	Strainers	Rating
70 (200)	III (IV+)	1.3	19	B-	1-3/mi.	***

USGS Quad – Sykesville; Source – Personal descent 10/03 (first 0.1 + last 1.1 miles)
N39 21.98, W76 54.70 to N39 21.21, W76 53.83

Suddenly, as Piney Run crosses Arrington Rd. and begins to follow Marriottsville Rd. No. 2, it becomes a terror, dropping 60 feet in a third of a mile. Scout from the road, down to the second parking area. The creek accelerates quickly to class II+ and then has a short class III drop followed by a complex class IV+ ledge. One option is to drive hard left into the swirly eddy by the bank, and then run either the middle or the left chute of the main drop. For most paddlers, the best route is a portage. Then come several class III rapids in quick succession. The second of these is tricky on the right, but needs more water to run the left. The creek eases up to class II+, II and finally I. There tend to be strainers just above the confluence, so you might want to take out a little higher up.

GAUGE: Look for at least 180 cfs on Morgan Run and 90 cfs on Beaver Run. The rainfall gauges at Winfield and Piney Run in Carroll Co. are ideally located.

BRICE RUN

This tiny creek flows south, a little west of Daniels (site of a textile mill until Hurricane Agnes in 1972). Nearby was a Nike missile silo during the Cold War.

Section 1: Old Court Road to Granite Branch (Wrights Mill Road)

Gradient	Difficulty	Distance	Area	Scenery	Strainers	Rating
35	?	1.5	5.7	?	?	?

USGS Quad – Ellicott City; Source – Scouting put in and take out
N39 20.65, W76 50.30 to N39 19.78, W76 49.45

I don't know what's in the creek here – hence, it is an *"explorers' special."* But it is obviously small, hard to catch up, and likely to have some strainers, and its gradient suggests nothing more than class II.

GAUGE: The gauge on Dead Run at Franklintown should be at least 90 cfs. Use the Randallstown and Fullerton rain gauges.

Section 2: Granite Branch (Wrights Mill Road) to Patapsco River

Gradient	Difficulty	Distance	Area	Scenery	Strainers	Rating
45(65)	III- (IV)	1.0*	10	B	3-5/mi.	**

USGS Quad – Ellicott City; Source – Personal descent 5/01
N39 19.78, W76 49.45 to N39 18.90, W76 48.98

*(plus 0.8 flat miles on the Patapsco to Daniels)

Granite Branch adds 40% to the flow. The 0.6 miles along Wrights Mill Road has a class III- boulder garden, a set of class III- ledges and some class II chutes. The creek then crosses the road into Patapsco Valley State Park. After some class II, get out on the left to scout the class IV boulder garden. With enough water, you can stay far left, but at lower levels, you enter left and cut hard right. This rapid requires much more water than anywhere else. There is a class II below, and then a railroad bridge before the Patapsco.

GAUGE: Check the class III- rapids from Wrights Mill Road. Dead Run at Franklintown should be at least 80 cfs. Use the Randallstown and Fullerton rain gauges.

BENS RUN: Ridge Road to Patapsco River

Gradient	Difficulty	Distance	Area	Scenery	Strainers	Rating
50	III	2.0	3.8	B-	1-2/mi.	***

USGS Quad – Ellicott City; Source – Personal descent 6/01
N39 20.08, W76 47.38 to N39 18.62, W76 47.57

This tiny but delightful rapid-and-pool creek has rock gardens, chutes, ledges and sharp turns, some complicated by wood. The first class III is 100 yards below the put in. Watch for a pair of fences in calm water after three-quarters of a mile. Half a mile later, right after the ruins of a stone house on the left, there is a long, class III rock garden. In another quarter mile, you leave the wilderness, and houses and private bridges appear. At the paved ford, Dogwood Run enters from the left, and there is a class II+ rapid. Then the creek turns sharp left, and you are into a steep class III rock garden (**which you should scout beforehand** from Dogwood Road). The final 250 yards to the Patapsco is class II-. Take out at Old Frederick Road (the put in for Patapsco section 2) a third of a mile later.

GAUGE: The rapid just below the put in should be cleanly runnable. Dead Run at Franklintown should exceed 100 cfs. Randallstown and Fullerton are the rain gauges.

DEEP RUN [south]: US 1 to Furnace Avenue/Ridge Road

Gradient	Difficulty	Distance	Area	Scenery	Strainers	Rating
24	II-	6.8	3.5	C-	4-6/mi.	-

USGS Quad – Savage/Relay; Source – Personal descent 5/00 (1st 2.5 miles) and 11/97 (last 2 miles); road scouting remainder
N39 10.54, W76 46.54 via N39 10.76, W76 44.73 (mile 2.5) to N39 12.70, W76 42.11

Deep Run starts east of Columbia and flows for 12 miles, in a 180-degree arc, heading south, east and north as the Howard-Anne Arundel County border. It has a few miles of strainer-ridden rapids. Then the rapids disappear but the strainers remain.

From the Deep Run Business Center, slide down the slope next to US 1. The long, easy rapids were ruined by strainers. At 1.5 miles, a small culvert is runnable only at low levels; with more water, you would be in a pickle, as **the portage is blocked by high fences**. The next half mile is through a beautiful valley with continuous riffles and few strainers; alas, you cannot put in below that first culvert, as it is a private road. The next culvert is immense; there must be wild debates among culvert engineers! You then pass Dorsey Road (Md. 176) and railroad tracks to O'Connor Drive (at mile 2.5).

Below O'Connor Drive, the gradient drops in half and the creek is class I. Piney and Shallow runs double the flow, but there are still lots of strainers. The take out is half a mile above the Patapsco.

GAUGE: The East Branch of Herbert Run needs to be over 35 cfs and Dead Run at Franklintown 80 cfs; below O'Connor Drive, half of these figures should suffice. Check the Elkridge, Columbia and Centennial rain gauges.

WEST BR., HERBERT RUN: Shelbourne Road to Herbert Run

Gradient	Difficulty	Distance	Area	Scenery	Strainers	Rating
43	II (II+)	1.5	2.3	D	1-2/mi.	**

USGS Quad – Relay; Source – Personal descent 8/97
N39 15.00, W76 42.30 to N39 14.03, W76 41.58

This flows from Catonsville past the University of Maryland at Baltimore. At Shelbourne Road the creek is tiny, but a tributary adds 50% to the flow 200 yards later, and the best rock garden (class II+) comes shortly thereafter, approaching Sulphur Spring Road. The creek is class I and II the rest of the way. It is almost straight, so blind turns aren't a big problem, although overhanging branches occasionally reduce visibility.

The trip is through working class suburbs just south of Baltimore city, but as the channelized streambed is sunken, you see mainly rooftops, and they don't impinge much on your narrow world of creek, rocks and trees. Take out at the confluence with the East Branch, alongside US 1 (by the Southwestern Professional Building) in Halethorpe.

GAUGE: If the rock garden just below the put in is runnable, everything is. The gauge on the East Branch of Herbert Run should be at least 60 cfs. For rain gauges, use Elkridge in Howard Co., Westview in Baltimore Co., and Carroll Park in Baltimore city.

You could continue a mile down **Herbert Run** to the Patapsco, at 15 ft/mile, and get a fish's-eye view of US 1, the old Penn Central tracks, Alt US 1, the old B&O tracks and the Harbor Tunnel Thruway. And then you would have 1.7 miles of tidal water.

The last mile of the **East Branch** is at 30 ft/mile, but it is cemented in places and is even a little smaller than the West Branch. But who am I to discourage anyone from exploring?!

PATUXENT RIVER BASIN

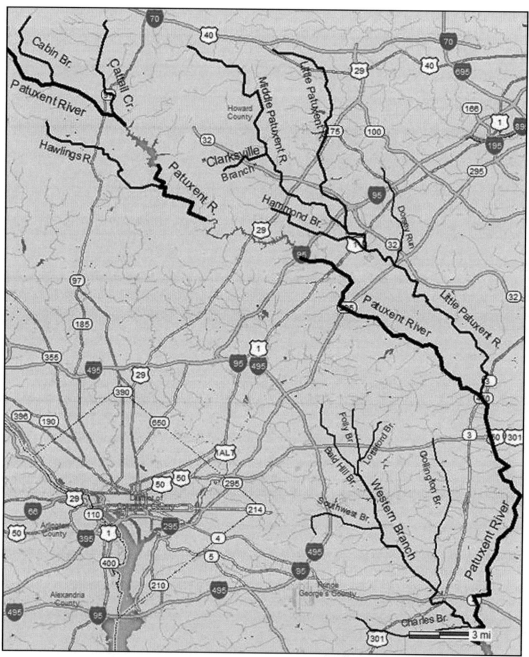

Chapter 9:
PATUXENT RIVER BASIN

The Patuxent River separates the Washington and Baltimore metropolitan areas – or you could say it unites the Washington-Baltimore SMSA. Its 100-mile long, narrow watershed covers some 925 square miles (10% of Maryland) and has a half million people, including in Columbia (100,000 – Maryland's 2nd largest city), Bowie (55,000) and Laurel (25,000). About 30% of its watershed is in the Piedmont, 70% in the coastal plain. And its main rapids, of course, are where those two meet at the fall line.

The **Patuxent's** own fall-line whitewater is mostly buried beneath the Triadelphia and Howard Duckett reservoirs (which combined store 9.1 billion gallons of water, for Prince Georges and Montgomery counties), although there is one decent section with a class III rapid below the latter. The largest upstream tributary, the **Little Patuxent**, is by far the best whitewater creek in this watershed – perhaps the only one worth running. Its fall-line rapids culminate in the class IV Savage Falls, just below the confluence with the **Middle Patuxent**, which has nice scenery but few rapids until the end.

Small upper tributaries are **Cattail Branch**, a placid but strainer-ridden Piedmont stream, and **Cabin Branch**, which is slightly steeper but smaller and even more clogged. Farther down, the **Hawlings River** has some easy whitewater but too many strainers. Aside from the Little Patuxent, the main tributary with fall-line rapids is **Hammond Branch**; unfortunately, it braids badly for a long stretch. An unnamed Middle Patuxent tributary, *"Clarksville Branch,"* is a tiny, short but intriguing "explorers' special."

Below, in the coastal plain, there are few rapids. **Western Branch** is fairly wide and pleasant, but its own tributaries are too strainer prone, as is the Little Patuxent's Dorsey Branch, as well as Mataponi Creek, the final medium-sized Patuxent tributary.

The **Patuxents** were a small tribe in Southern Maryland, between the mouths of the Potomac and Patuxent rivers. In July 1608, Captain John Smith discovered the "river of Pawtuxunt," found "infinit skuls of divers kinds of fish more than elsewhere," and considered the people there "more civill than any." It was from them that Governor Leonard Calvert bought the land for St. Mary's City, the first permanent European settlement in Maryland. The name "Patuxent" apparently meant **"at the falls or rapids."**

Pollution Reduction. Nutrient pollution (mainly from fertilizer), began to decimate the clams, crabs and fish of the lower Patuxent. Southern Maryland counties sued the federal and state governments, and in 1980 won a ruling forcing a cleanup. At a cost of $190 million, nutrient removal systems were installed on all eight major sewage treatment plants. By the mid-1990s, bay grasses were starting to expand and the water was noticeably clearer. However, progress has been erratic, and there has been some slippage in water clarity.

GAUGES: The Patuxent basin is rich in river gauges: the Patuxent at Unity (section 1; 35 sq. mi.), Brighton (section 3; 79 sq. mi.), Laurel (section 4; 132 sq. mi.) and Bowie (348 sq. mi.); the Little Patuxent at Guilford (section 2 put in; 38 sq. mi.) and Savage (section 2 take out; 98 sq. mi.); the Hawlings River near Sandy Spring (section 2; 27 sq. mi.); Cattail Creek at Md. 97 (23 sq. mi.) and Western Branch at Upper Marlboro (near its mouth; 90 sq. mi.). In the table below, **the gauge column refers to the Patuxent at Unity.** The only rainfall gauges are a dozen in the Western Branch area.

name	gradient	difficulty	length	area	gauge	rating
Patuxent River - Section 1	15	I (II-)	4.7	17	120cfs	-
- Section 2	4	I	5.0	85	n.a.	*
- Section 3	20	II- (III)	1.0	132	n.a.	**
Cabin Branch	25	I	0.8	8	250cfs	-
Cattail Creek	20	I	4.3	15	150cfs	*
Hawlings River	18	II-	7.5	8	300cfs	-
Little Patuxent R. - Sec. 1	7	I	4.2	28	90cfs	*
- Sec. 2	40 (140)	III- (IV)	3.0	38	115cfs	****
- Sec. 3	10	I	1.8	98	75cfs	*
Middle Patuxent	13 (45)	II	18.3	10	200cfs	**
"Clarksville Branch"	28 (45)	?	2.5	5	450cfs	?
Hammond Branch	55	II+ (III-)	2.4	6	600cfs	-
Western Branch	8	I	3.8	18	350cfs	*

PATUXENT RIVER

The Patuxent, Maryland's second longest river (after the Potomac), stretches for 100 miles, of which half is tidal. It rises near where Montgomery, Frederick, Carroll and Howard counties meet in their own "four corners." It is the boundary between Howard, Anne Arundel and Calvert Counties on the one side, and Montgomery, PG, Charles and St. Marys Counties on the other. Most of its whitewater is buried behind two dams. Gertler covers 45 miles of its class I water and 44 miles of tidal water, but not the only hard rapid (in section 4 below), which is difficult to get to. He starts 3.2 miles above Hipsley Mill Road (the put in for my section 1), but found the density of strainers high there. There is a gentle (4 ft/mile) 5-mile section 2 between the two reservoirs, until the backwater from the Rocky Gorge Dam. The short section 3 begins right below that dam. After that, the river continues flowing for 25 flat miles, and is then tidal.

> The state capital was moved temporarily to Commissioner Richard Preston's mansion, **Preston-on-the-Patuxent,** in 1653, during Oliver Cromwell's reign in England, because St. Marys City was loyal to Lord Baltimore and the (deposed) Crown. The next year, on orders from Lord Baltimore, Governor Stone attacked that mansion and returned the government records to St. Marys City. Preston-on-the-Patuxent still stands, as a private residence.
>
> The Patuxent River was a major route for commerce, and sections of its banks were cleared to allow horses and men to drag boats up over the rapids.
>
> During the **1814 invasion of Washington,** some 4,000 British soldiers landed along the Patuxent at Benedict, 45 miles from DC, and advanced under the protection of a small British fleet. The Americans scuttled their own, weaker fleet on the river, salvaging only the guns. The British then headed west to Upper Marlboro and eventually Bladensburg, defeated the American troops and crossed the Anacostia into the capital, which they promptly burned.

Much of the Patuxent is protected. The **Patuxent River State Park** on the upper river in Montgomery and Howard counties emphasizes fishing and hunting. **Patuxent River Park** of the MNCPPC on the lower river in PG County has many displays about the 300-year history of the county. That park sponsors ecological tours, bird watching, etc., and contains the rare "walking fern," which propagates by rooting at the tip of its frond.

Section 1: Hipsley Mill Road to Triadelphia Reservoir

Gradient	Difficulty	Distance	Area	Scenery	Strainers	Rating
15	I (II-)	4.7	17	C+	3-5/mi.	-

USGS Quad – Woodbine/Sandy Spring; Source–Personal descent 4/98
N39 15.91, W77 06.89 via N39 14.31, W77 03.36 (Ga. Ave.) to N39 14.03, W77 02.71

This trip through Patuxent River State Park has mainly gravel bars. After 0.7 miles, Cabin Branch enters and the creek widens. Gertler found "the coast … relatively clear" after that, but beavers have since repopulated the area, resulting in many strainers. There are surfing holes at Howard Chapel Road (mile 3.3) and a man-made ledge at Georgia Avenue (mile 4.4). There are many sycamore trees along the river, planted by Trout Unlimited in the late 1980s, to provide shade and thereby lower the water temperature in this popular catch-and-release creek (which has brown trout of up to 24"). You can take out above the Georgia Avenue bridge or continue down to the reservoir.

The 0.3 miles below Georgia Avenue has a pair of class II- rock gardens. When the reservoir is low, there may be another rapid below. You then paddle two-thirds of a mile down the reservoir to a WSSC boat launch off Triadelphia Lake Road; you must first pay $3 for a Daily Watershed Use Permit (available at the store on the corner of Georgia and New Hampshire Avenues).

GAUGE: The USGS gauge at Unity (at Md. 97), should be at least 120 cfs, 2 hours after you start. Look to the Lisbon rain gauge, in Howard County.

Section 2: Brighton Dam Road to Tucker Lane (off Md. 108)

Gradient	Difficulty	Distance	Area	Scenery	Strainers	Rating
4	I	5.0	85	B	<1/mi.	*

USGS Quad – Sandy Spring/Clarksville; Source – Personal descent 3/06
N39 11.58, W77 00.32 to N 39 09.27, W76 58.64

This beginners' run between the reservoirs has fine scenery, a blue heron rookery and occasional riffles. Being dam controlled, it may be up when nothing else is, and vice versa. There is a WSSC parking lot just below the dam; let them know your plans. The WSSC bans launchings from December 15 to March 1, but you can start at Haviland Mill Road, 1.3 miles later. There is no parking at Md. 108, so follow Tucker Lane a half mile to where you can paddle almost to the road. A mile beyond is Brown

Bridge Road. When the water in the T. Howard Duckett Reservoir is low, you could continue to there; however, if you paddle into the reservoir (e.g., when it is full), you must buy a permit.

GAUGE: About 75 cfs on the Patuxent gauge at Brighton is minimal.

Section 3: Rocky Gorge Dam to Laurel

Gradient	Difficulty	Distance	Area	Scenery	Strainers	Rating
20	II- (III)	1.0	132	C	0-2/mi.	**

USGS Quad – Laurel; Source – Personal descent 4/05
N39 06.81, W76 52.39 to N39 06.62, W76 51.45

The main remaining rapids on the Patuxent are shortly below the Rocky Gorge Dam (which you see from I-95). While this section is up often, it is a bit of work to get to the rapids, for a very short run, so the cost/benefit ratio is unappealing.

Take Brooklyn Bridge Road (don't buy it – paddlers will refuse to pay the toll) to Dorset Road, park near the dead end, and go 200 yards down the steep trail. That puts you just below the only hard rapid, so paddle and portage upstream to almost under I-95 (where a sign warns that if you hear a loud whistle, they are about to open a reservoir gate, and you have four minutes to escape). In low water, cut left above the huge boulder, and take the narrow drop; at higher levels there are options on the right.

Below the put in, there are three class II- rapids in the first quarter mile, and a class II- rock garden midway. The rest is flat. Take out alongside the bike path just past the Laurel Public Swimming Pool, or continue on downstream (Gertler's Section 5).

GAUGE: The Patuxent gauge at Laurel should be over 125 cfs. Water need not be flowing over the Rocky Gorge Dam, just being let out sufficiently from under it.

In the latter half of the 19th Century, two large **textiles mills** (Laurel and Avondale) utilized power from the river and employed up to 800 workers. The remains of the 20-foot high mill dam are near the take out. It was breached in the 1950s, to allow fish to spawn upstream. The factory ruins were erased by the construction of a swimming pool.

CABIN BRANCH: Hipsley Mill Road to Patuxent River

Gradient	Difficulty	Distance	Area	Scenery	Strainers	Rating
25	I	0.8*	8	C-	8-12/mi.	-

USGS Quad – Woodbine/SandySpring; Source – Personal descent 4/98
N39 16.58, W77 06.31 to N39 14.99, W77 03.94

*(plus 2.4 miles on the Patuxent)

Cabin Branch (site of the last Indian home in the area) is stocked with rainbow trout and has a breeding population of brown trout. Leave it for the fishermen. The trip begins with lots of riffles in a narrow but clear streambed, but soon beavers begin to make their presence felt, and a cable fence doesn't help. From the confluence, it is 2.4 miles on the Patuxent to Howard Chapel Road, which gives two sets of strainers for one shuttle.

You could start 1.8 miles higher up, at Md. 94, with 4.5 sq. mi. at 30 ft/mile. (There is a class III+ rapid on the upstream side of Md. 94; ask at the nearby house for permission.) But as the USGS quad indicates braiding, expect to do a lot of portaging.

GAUGE: Look for at least 250 cfs on the Patuxent at Unity, 3 hours after you put in. The Lisbon gauge in Howard Co. is the best rainfall measure.

CATTAIL CREEK: Union Chapel Road to Triadelphia Reservoir

Gradient	Difficulty	Distance	Area	Scenery	Strainers	Rating
20	I	4.3*	15	C	1-3/mi.	*

USGS Quad – Woodbine/Sandy Spring; Source – Gertler
N39 17.55, W77 03.59 to N39 14.03, W77 02.71

*(plus one mile on the reservoir)

This novice run past farms and houses has lots of riffles and a few very easy rock gardens, as well as fences and other strainers. After 3 miles, you can take out at Md. 97 (site of the gauge). Below, there are 1.3 miles of flowing river and then a mile on the Triadelphia Reservoir. The take out is the same as for section 2 of the Patuxent.

GAUGE: Look for at least 100 cfs on the Cattail Creek gauge. Lisbon in Howard Co. is the best rain gauge. The staff gauge on the right abutment at Md. 97 should read at least 1.9.

HAWLINGS RIVER: Zion Road to Patuxent River

Gradient	Difficulty	Distance	Area	Scenery	Strainers	Rating
18	II-	7.5	8	C	3-5/mi.	-

USGS Quad – SandySpring; Source – Personal descent 8/95 first 2 miles; trip report (Tom Gray) last 5.5 miles.
N39 12.89, W77 05.41 via N39 12.56, W77 03.76 (Ga. Ave) to N39 10.56, W77 00.46

The Hawlings is the smallest "river" in Maryland. The first 2 miles, to Georgia Avenue, are the steepest part, averaging 30 ft/mile and reaching 40 ft/mile, but strainers ruin it – we encountered about 30 downed trees across the creek, of which maybe 10 required portages, while the rest could be squeezed under. It took two hours to run the two miles. On the positive side, a footbridge was the only sign of civilization.

Below Georgia Avenue, the Hawlings keeps getting flatter; the next 2 miles average 20 ft/mile, the last 3.5 miles only 10 ft/mile. Strainers become less frequent, as the creek is enlarged by Reddy Branch and James Creek, but there is nothing more than riffles in these 5.5 miles. There is access at Brighton Dam Rd. (mile 4), Gold Mine Rd. (mile 5.7) and New Hampshire Ave. (miles 6.5; site of the on-line gauge). Take out at Haviland Mill Road, 200 yards above the Patuxent.

GAUGE: You will need at least 225 cfs on the Hawlings River gauge near Sandy Spring, 3 hours after you put in. The closest rain gauge is Lisbon (Howard Co.)

> The Hollands were early settlers; a 1794 map shows this as "**Hollands River**." The name was corrupted to Hollings and then to Hawlings. Hawleywood could make a movie about this.

LITTLE PATUXENT RIVER

The Little Patuxent flows 37 miles, past Ellicott City, Columbia, Laurel and Fort Meade, into the Patuxent near Bowie. It is rather lazy except where it approaches and crosses the fall line near Savage, culminating in a class IV set of ledges. A reasonable first put in is the one in Gertler, off US 29 in Columbia, as a dam just above backs the water up for almost a mile.

Below section 3, the river continues 16 miles to the Patuxent, but the gradient is only 5 ft/mile.

Section 1: Columbia (Entrance Rd.) to old RR bridge (off Guilford Road)

Gradient	Difficulty	Distance	Area	Scenery	Strainers	Rating
7	I	4.2	28	C	0-2/mi.	*

USGS Quad – Savage; Source – Gertler
N39 12.50, 76 51.42 to N39 10.03, W76 50.64

The put in is just upstream of US 29 (to avoid that major road). The creek flows gently through the woods, with Columbia housing visible not far off.

GAUGE: The gauge on the Little Patuxent at Guilford should exceed 100 cfs. For rainfall, look to the Centennial and Columbia gauges in Howard County.

Section 2: Old RR bridge (off Guilford Road) to Savage (Foundry Street)

Gradient	Difficulty	Distance	Area	Scenery	Strainers	Rating
40 (140)	III- (IV)	3.0	38	B	0-2/mi.	****

USGS Quad – Savage; Source – Personal descent often
N39 10.03, W76 50.64 to N39 08.09, W76 49.49

Put in off Guilford Rd., by the trailhead at the old railroad bridge. The first 1.5 miles is easy, while the next mile, to the Middle Patuxent, is almost continuous class II. Below the confluence rapid, there is a left bending class II rock garden and then the class II+ rock garden leading to the class IV Savage Falls. Catch an eddy on the left to scout.

Savage Falls consists of three ledges, of 6, 4 and 5 feet, respectively. At the first ledge, each of the two main channels has a nasty rock just below the drop. Some paddlers bump down to the left of the left channel. The main route down the second ledge is a twisting class III chute in the middle, which can be reached by ferrying from shore. With more water, there are also chutes near both shores. The final ledge is easiest (class III) far right in low water and far left at higher levels; there is also a bumpy route down the middle. The far right drop is steep and has a hole at its base and a cliff wall 20 feet ahead. The far left route is complicated by ill-placed rocks. Shortly below Savage Falls, a long class III- rock garden bends left, and the final class II water is past (or beneath) Savage Mill. Take out on river right just downstream of the two bridges.

GAUGE: On the USGS gauge on the river left, downstream side of Guilford Road, zero level is 3.5 feet (125 cfs on-line). For Savage Falls itself, you need at least 225 cfs on the Savage gauge; above 500 cfs the falls gets very dangerous. (Some 125 cfs at Guilford Road correlates with 260 cfs at Savage.)

Section 3: Savage (Foundry Street) to Brock Bridge Road

Gradient	Difficulty	Distance	Area	Scenery	Strainers	Rating
10	I	1.8	98	C	<<1/mi.	*

USGS Quad – Savage/Laurel; Source – Personal descent 5/06
N39 08.09, W76 49.49 to N39 07.25, W76 48.70

This section has good current and a fair number of riffles; it can make a mellow finish to a trip down section 2. The riffles are liveliest in the first half mile, to US 1.

GAUGE: On the Internet gauge at Savage, 200 cfs is minimal.

John Savage lent the four Williams brothers $20,000 to build a textile mill there in 1820. Savage Mill's durable, lightweight cotton was used as sails for clipper ships and backdrops for silent movies. From 1947-50, the building was a one-ring circus. In 1984 began a $12 million renovation into a crafts and home design retail center.

The **Bollman Bridge** nearby, built in the 1860s (now for pedestrians), is the only iron truss railroad bridge left of its kind (there were once about 100). It is a National Historic Landmark and one of the few bridges in the area to survive the floods of Hurricane Agnes in June 1972.

MIDDLE PATUXENT R.: Md. 32 (Sykesville Rd.) to Little Patuxent

Gradient	Difficulty	Distance	Area	Scenery	Strainers	Rating
13 (45)	II	18.3*	10	C+	1-2/mi.	**

USGS Quad – Sykesville/Clarksville/Savage; Source – Personal descent 1/85 (last 6 miles); Gertler; AW site
N39 17.26, W76 57.50 via N39 10.09, W76 52.99 (mi. 12.4) to N39 08.00, W76 49.99

*(plus optional 0.6 miles on the Little Patuxent, including the class IV Savage Falls)

The Middle Patuxent meanders southeast for 23 miles across Howard County, between the Patuxent and Little Patuxent, until it meets the latter just above Savage Falls. It can be paddled for a long distance, but it has little gradient until the final half mile. There is a class II broken dam just above Guilford Road/Cedar Lane at mile 10.7. Other access points are Old Columbia Road (off US 29; mile 12.4), and Murray Hill Road (mile 15.5; 45 sq. mi.). From the latter, the creek makes a beeline for the confluence, except for a detour known as The Horseshoe, after crossing I-95. Then it finally wakes up, and has three class II rapids and a 45 ft/mile gradient. The last of these rapids continues into the Little Patuxent, and then, after one more class II, be alert for the rock garden leading into the class IV Savage Falls (see the Little Patuxent write-up). If you don't like hard rapids, take out just below the confluence on river right, and carry 0.3 miles down a trail to Gorman Road (this is the GPS reference).

GAUGE: To start at Sykesville Road, you need 200 cfs on the Patuxent at Unity and 225 cfs on the Little Patuxent at Guilford. By Old Columbia Road, the requirements are 80 cfs and 90 cfs, respectively. Lisbon and Centennial (Howard County) are the rain gauges.

> **Sun shower.** I ran this creek the day after a freezing rain. The overhanging trees were coated in ice, which melted rapidly in the bright sunlight. We had the experience, unique in my paddling career, of needing raingear on a cloudless day.

"CLARKSVILLE BRANCH": Guilford Road to Middle Patuxent R.

Gradient	Difficulty	Distance	Area	Scenery	Strainers	Rating
28 (45)	?	2.5*	5	?	?	?

USGS Quad – Clarksville; Source – Scouting access points
N39 11.68, W76 56.15 to N39 11.30, W76 53.64

*(plus 1.5 miles on the Middle Patuxent to Cedar Lane)

This intriguing tiny *"explorers' special"* has a decent gradient, especially in the final half mile after you cross Md. 32 and Trotter Road. The 1.5 miles on the Middle Patuxent will be class I until the class II remains of a broken dam just above the take out.

GAUGE: You need 450 cfs on the Patuxent at Unity and 500 cfs on the Little Patuxent at Guilford, projected 2-3 hours forward. The rain gauges are Columbia, Simpsonville and Lisbon.

HAMMOND BRANCH: Stephens Road to Little Patuxent River

Gradient	Difficulty	Distance*	Area	Scenery	Strainers	Rating
55	II+ (III-)	2.4	6	D+	5-8/mi.	-

USGS Quad – Savage/Laurel; Source – Personal descent 3/92
(except last 1/2 mile) N39 07.84, W76 50.71 to N39 07.25, W76 48.71

*(plus one-third mile on Little Patuxent to Brock Bridge Road)

Hammond Branch flows 10 miles down a narrow valley between the Middle Patuxent and Rocky Gorge Reservoir, past US 29, I-95 and US 1, before entering the Little Patuxent below Savage.

The put in is half a mile east of the Md. 216 interchange on I-95. After a half mile through tall grass by a high-voltage line, the creek enters the woods and a 50-yard, class III- rock garden raises expectations. But a quarter mile later began a small stream nightmare – braiding. For the next mile, the creek was divided into 2 or 3 strainer-filled channel, requiring many portages. Finally, above US 1, the channels reunited for the final mile.

In December 2012, when I scouted the creek from the road, the braiding was no longer in evidence, perhaps because the construction of a planned community had been completed.

GAUGE: Look for 600 cfs on the Patuxent at Unity, 480 on the Hawlings River and 650 cfs on the Little Patuxent at Guilford, all projected 2-3 hours after you begin. Columbia and Simpsonville (Howard County) are the rain gauges.

John **Hammond** wrote *Leah and Rachel* (London, 1656), on behalf of Maryland Governor Stone, to stimulate immigration into the colony. Thomas Hammond received 190 acres in Maryland in 1664. Major John Hammond was one of the first commissioners for Annapolis, when the state capital moved there from St. Marys City in 1694. His titles included Judge of the Vice-Admiralty, Manager-General of the Western Shore, and Member of Their Majesties' Council. Charles Hammond obtained a 1,000-acre Maryland estate ("Hammond's Gift") in 1723. Col. William Hammond was one of the original Baltimore Commissioners in 1729. And all this illustrious family got named after them was a little village and this pathetic creek!

WESTERN BRANCH: Lottsford Road to Md. 202

Gradient	Difficulty	Distance	Area	Scenery	Strainers	Rating
8	I	3.8	18	C-	2-4/mi.	*

USGS Quad – Lanham; Source – Personal descent 10/96
N38 55.15, W76 49.05 to N38 52.14, W76 47.92

Western Branch begins in Largo, where Bald Hill, Lottsford and Folly branches meet. It flows south-southeast for 15 miles, past Upper Marlboro, to the Patuxent. The first 4 miles (described here) have the best gradient; it drops to 4-5 ft/mile thereafter. I saw 8 deer, a large beaver and a muskrat. The surrounding area is converting from cornfields to suburbs with names like Rocky Gorge. Oh well, exaggeration is as American as secret campaign contributions.

The run is through the woods of Western Branch Stream Park and Robert M. Watkins Regional Park. The banks are low, except for some 15-20 ft mud cliffs. Riffles and strainers keep things interesting. Right after Md. 214, the creek flows under an old millhouse with a large waterwheel; duck low under the steel cables at either end. Shortly below, a man-made wave can be surfed.

GAUGE: Look for 350 cfs on Western Branch at Upper Marlboro (6 miles below the take out), 4 hours after you start. For rain, use the PG Co. gauges at Greenbelt, Bowie and Lottsford Road.

The first **PG County seat,** Charles Town, was at the confluence of Western Branch and the Patuxent. In 1721, the county seat was moved 5 miles up Western Branch to Upper Marlboro. Ships exporting tobacco traveled up and down the creek. In 1759, after rubbish and fallen trees became a threat to navigation, Western Branch had its first major **strainer removal**, financed by a lottery; 1,500 tickets, at two "Pieces of eight" apiece, were sold.

Three Western Branch tributaries, all in the coastal plain, are occasionally runnable; about 650 cfs on Western Branch is minimal for each. But none have much whitewater.

Southwest Branch, the Patuxent basin's only inside-the-Beltway incursion (near exit 15), has just a few riffles and small drops over fallen trees. It is beset with strainers, mainly from beavers. It flows mostly through woodlands until the last mile, but there is lots of trash. I have paddled 4.2 miles from Ritchie Road (7 sq. mi; 16 ft/mile) to Western Branch. The first half mile is very twisty. Then, after a small homeless colony and the Home Depot warehouse in Hampton Mall, there is a long, bouncy riffle down a paved channel. After one mile, you pass under the Beltway, and 1.5 miles later, Harry S. Truman Drive. You can take out at the confluence.

Collington Branch (which I have not run) flows due south for 12 miles from Bowie to Upper Marlboro, through a long valley that it shares with Conrail between Western Branch and the Patuxent. The creek is very narrow. From Hall (9 sq. mi.), on Hall Road off Md. 214, to Leeland Road is 2.7 miles at 10 ft/mile. The remaining 5 miles are at only 5 ft/mile.

I paddled **Charles Branch** for 2 miles from Trumps Road to Croom Station Road, near Upper Marlboro (8 sq. mi; 17 ft/mile), with a dozen strainers and a mess of other vegetation. There are small ledges over fallen trees, and a class II man-made rock garden at the take out. This creek joins Western Branch just before the latter enters the Patuxent.

WILLS CREEK to CATOCTIN CREEK

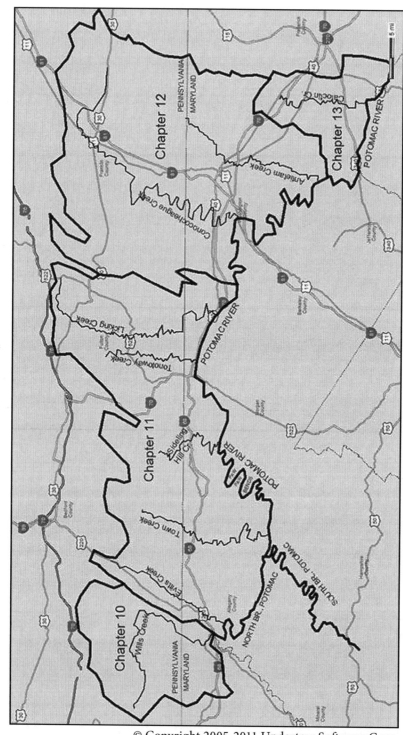

PART III:

WILLS CREEK to CATOCTIN CREEK

Part III covers the watersheds that drain south to the Potomac from Pennsylvania (southern parts of Somerset, Bedford, Fulton and Franklin counties) through Allegany, Washington and western Frederick counties in Maryland. From the air, the most visible feature is a string of north-south ridges, from Wills Mountain to the Catoctin Mountains. This is a mostly rural area, with corn, orchards and cattle in the lowlands, and forested uplands. The population totals some 400,000. Although the distances are comparatively large, I-70/I-68 provides fast access from the Washington and Baltimore areas.

Chapter 10 covers the exciting **Wills Creek basin**; although this is well over 2 hours from the Washington area, its whitewater is too good to omit. In addition to two sections of Wills Creek itself, there are excellent trips on Brush Creek, Jennings Run and its North Branch, Braddock Run and probably some of the "explorers' specials" as well. With 252 square miles, Wills Creek is by far the largest tributary of the North Branch of the Potomac.

Chapter 11 describes a large number of smaller watersheds – **Evitts, Town, Fifteenmile, Sideling Hill, Little Tonoloway [south], Tonoloway, and Licking creeks** – that have less exciting whitewater. The main creeks are written up quite well by Gertler, but, as usual, I add some smaller streams, especially headwaters. Sections of some of the above creeks, plus Flintstone (my favorite), Big Cove and Little Tonoloway [north] creeks, provide quite pleasant and even in places challenging paddling.

Continuing eastward, chapter 12 is on the **Conococheague and Antietam Creek basins**, including tiny Marsh Run between them, which comprise the Hagerstown (or Great) Valley. For its size, the Conococheague basin has remarkably little whitewater, all short, tiny and in its headwaters. The Antietam basin is only somewhat better. Antietam Creek itself is a popular novice run, the top part of its East Branch and of Little Antietam Creek [north] provide challenging albeit dangerous whitewater trips, and there are several other decent but unexciting paddles.

Chapter 13 includes both the **Catoctin Creek basin** and some smaller neighbors. Israel Creek and Little Catoctin Creek [south] are tiny but outstanding high-intermediate paddles, while the upper stretches of Middle Creek are a real catch for advanced and expert paddlers. This is a small chapter but full of punch.

There are **river gauges** on the main stems of most of the principal waterways (Wills, Town, Sideling Hill, Tonoloway, Licking, Conococheague, Antietam and Catoctin creeks), but this area is poorly served with respect to the smaller creeks. The gauge on upper Tonoloway Creek is the key for chapter 11, while all of the chapters benefit from some gauges from neighboring basins. Nevertheless, it is still a challenge to figure out when the small streams are up, especially when the rainfall has been uneven and the gauges to be used are far from the creeks to be paddled.

WILLS CREEK BASIN

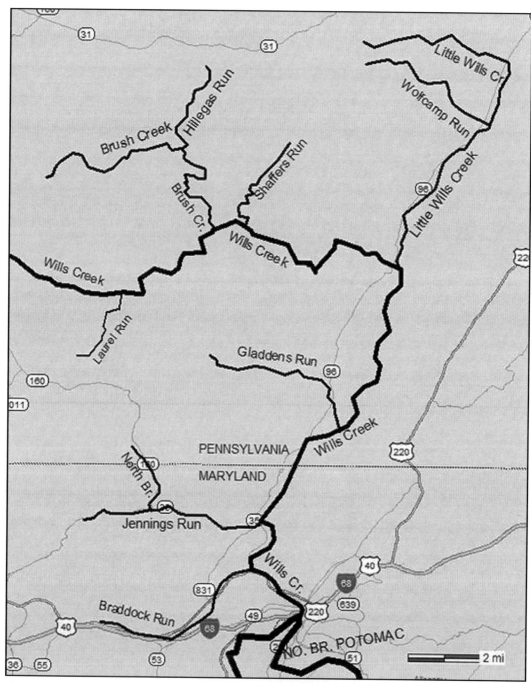

Chapter 10:

WILLS CREEK BASIN

Wills Creek is a very rural watershed that straddles the Maryland/Pennsylvania border, with the only significant town being Cumberland Md. (21,000) at its mouth. On the east, the watershed is separated from Evitts Creek by the imposing bulk of Wills Mountain. Its western border is the sub-continental divide; on the other side is the basin of the Casselman River, whose waters reach the Gulf of Mexico by way of the Youghiogheny, Monongahela, Ohio and Mississippi rivers. The southwest abuts Georges Creek and the north the Susquehanna basin. Wills Creek flows into the North Branch of the Potomac at Cumberland, where it adds about 40% to the latter's flow.

Gertler is enthusiastic about the Wills Creek basin. Although his coverage is limited to most (the lower parts) of **Wills Creek, Brush Creek, Little Wills Creek** and **Jennings Run**, he calls it "the best and closest whitewater package accessible to the Baltimore-Washington area." Adding **Hillegas, Shaffers, Wolf Camp, Gladdens, North Branch Jennings** and **Braddock runs**, and going farther upstream on the four larger creeks, makes this basin even more interesting, as well as hard to complete. I have paddled there nine times, but this chapter still has four "explorers' specials."

GAUGE: The only two gauges in this basin are on Wills Creek itself. In this table, the **reference is Wills Creek below Hyndman** (after the confluence with Little Wills Creek), with 146 sq. mi. The gauge near Cumberland, with 247 sq. mi., has some relevance because it also picks up the water from Gladdens, Jennings and Braddock runs. Sand Spring Run (3.6 sq. mi.) in the upper Georges Creek basin is valuable as a nearby small-creek gauge. For Jennings and Braddock runs, the readings on Georges Creek (72 sq. mi.) and the upper Savage River (49 sq. mi.) are also useful.

name	gradient	difficulty	length	area	gauge	rating
Wills Creek - Section 1	58	III (5.1)	10.8	10	1200cfs	***
- Section 2	70(100)	IV-	6.4	86	350cfs	!!!!
- Section 3	26 (45)	II	5.0	146	250cfs	**
Brush Creek - Sec. 1	55(110)	?	3.3	15	900cfs	?
- Sec. 2	75(130)	III (IV-)	3.2	27	700cfs	****
Hillegas Run	55	?	2.0	9	1200cfs	?
Shaffers Run	95	?	4.6	5	2500cfs	?
Little Wills Cr. - Sec. 1	80	III- (III)	2.0	9	1400cfs	**
- Sec. 2	40	II	2.8	12	1000cfs	-
- Sec. 3	39	II+	6.8	24	600cfs	**
Wolf Camp Run	80	III	3.2	8	1600cfs	**
Gladdens Run - Sec. 1	110(150)	?	2.5	13	1200cfs	?
- Sec. 2	50	II+	2.0	17	900cfs	*
Jennings Run - Sec. 1	115	III+	2.0	12	1200cfs	****
- Sec. 2	77	III+	3.0	31	700cfs	****
No. Br. Jennings Run	100	III	1.9	8	1700cfs	***
Braddock Run	85	III	3.0	10	1200cfs	***

⬙ WILLS CREEK

Wills Creek (Will was an Indian who lived nearby) flows everywhichway in its 34-mile life, and ends up less than 12 miles from where it starts. Section 1 begins where some small tributaries enter, 4 miles above the part written up in Gertler and what I have run. Section 2 is the challenging Fairhope to Hyndman whitewater run through Big Savage and Little Alleghany mountains that strong paddlers associate with Wills Creek. Section 3 is the first and livelier part of the long, easy valley trip that follows. Below section 3, Wills Creek continues for 7.5 miles (at just 15 ft/mile, with some long pools) to Eckhart Junction, where it flows calmly through The Narrows, between Wills and Haystack mountains. Soon thereafter, it is encased in high cement walls (built in the 1950s for flood control) for its final 1.5 miles through Cumberland, until it eases into the North Branch of the Potomac, of which it is the largest tributary.

> **Laurel Run** reaches Wills Creek via a class III+ rapid, 5 miles into section 1. It might be paddled for 4 miles, at 95 ft/mile and 4.7 sq. mi., from T756 (Gomer Hollow Rd) just off Pa. 160. In low water, you can drive a rough road along the creek's first 1.5 miles. Whenever Laurel Run is up, Wills Creek may be too high, so you might need to bushwhack to take out.

Section 1: Mance to above Fairhope (Railroad Cut Falls)

Gradient	Difficulty	Distance	Area	Scenery	Strainers	Rating
58	III (5.0)	10.8	10	C+	<1/mi.	***

USGS Quad – Wittenberg/Fairhope; Source – Personal descent 5/06 (last 6.8 miles); Scouting from road (first 4 miles)
N39 49.97, W78 56.16 via N39 48.62, W78 52.52 (mile 4) and N39 49.20, W78 50.67 (Glencoe) to N39 50.63, W78 47.90

Much of the first 4 miles can be seen from T377, which makes for an easy shuttle (but don't miss the turn where it crosses the railroad tracks). Expect some braiding and strainers, but no major drops.

The next 2.5 miles to Glencoe has an array of fun rapids of up to class III, with no particular problem spots. By Glencoe, the drainage area is up to 30 sq. mi., so the creek is considerably easier to catch. Start counting railroad bridges, because at the 5th one below Glencoe, where the tracks enter a tunnel, there is a ragged 8-foot class 5.0 drop into a hydraulic. Carry on the right.

Soon, Brush Creek enters, and three-fourths mile later (the second time you approach the tracks on your left) are man-made (blasted) ledges that produce the class 5.0 Railroad Cut Falls. Most paddlers carry up over the railroad tracks on the left and take out there (which is what I use for the GPS address), although I have watched some skilled and brave souls run the ledges.

GAUGE: To start at Mance, Wills Creek below Hyndman needs 1,200 cfs (projected 3-4 hours forward) and Sand Spring Run 30 cfs (2 hours before put in). To start at Glencoe, about half these readings will suffice.

Section 2: Fairhope to Hyndman (4th Street)

Gradient	Difficulty	Distance	Area	Scenery	Strainers	Rating
70(100)	IV-	6.4	86	D+	<1/mi.	!!!!

USGS Quad – Fairhope/Hyndman; Source – Personal descent 5/09
N39 50.46, W78 47.57 to N39 48.77, W78 43.00

This is the section that has made Wills Creek famous. The difficulty rises sharply with the water level. Put in at the bridge and ask permission to park at the post office. The trip starts off rather mildly, except for one tricky sloping ledge, but builds in intensity. There is a long rapid that begins with a pair of small ledges, then an even steeper boulder garden, and after about 1.5 miles you reach Yoyo, which culminates in a 5-foot drop. Scout from river right. With enough water, most paddlers take a narrow chute on the right; the middle slot is a sheer drop with a complicated entry, while **the left side may be deadly because of rebar and a fallen concrete slab**. After a few more class III+ rapids (at low levels), you reach the first bridge (at 2.3 miles). Several steep rapids later is Redemption, a 5-foot drop with a powerful curler that pushes you towards the right-side eddy just below. At higher levels, it can be sneaked via a twisty, narrow channel on the far right.

After the second bridge (at 3.5 miles), the creek gradually eases up (and becomes bony in low water), but even past the third bridge (at 5.2 miles), it remains lively, although the scenery deteriorates badly. Instead of taking out at Pa. 96 in Hyndman, continue a mile to the one-lane bridge (4th Street) at the south end of town.

GAUGE: Wills Creek below Hyndman needs at least 350 cfs when you finish.

Section 3: Hyndman (4th Street) to Cooks Mill (SSR 3001)

Gradient	Difficulty	Distance	Area	Scenery	Strainers	Rating
26 (45)	II	5.0	146	C	<<1/mi.	**

USGS Quad – Hyndman/EvittsCreek; Source – Gertler; scouting
N39 48.77, W78 43.00 to N39 44.97, W78 44.27

Below Hyndman, the gradient decreases steadily, so if you want to sample this part, stick to the first 5 miles, where you will have good wave action with enough water. Cooks Mill Road parallels the creek, giving several intermediate take-out options.

GAUGE: The Wills Creek gauge below Hyndman should be at least 250 cfs.

BRUSH CREEK

Section 1: SSR2022 (Leister Road) to T408 – Pack Saddle Road

Gradient	Difficulty	Distance	Area	Scenery	Strainers	Rating
55 (110)	?	3.3	15	?	?	?

USGS Quad – New Baltimore/Fairhope; Source – Scouting put in; Gertler
N39 52.85, W78 51.28 to N39 52.05, W78 49.04

This *"explorers' special"* looks tiny at the start. Ask for permission to put in and park at either house by the bridge. Midway through, Hillegas Run enters. Brush Creek gets steep in the last three-quarters of a mile. Gertler wrote: "The scenery on this section is fine, but the numerous strainers and ill-placed alders ... make this an expedition."

  GAUGE: Wills Creek below Hyndman needs 900 cfs (projected 3 hours later), Sand Spring Run 25 cfs (2 hours earlier).

Section 2: T408 – Pack Saddle Road (Covered Bridge) to Wills Creek

Gradient	Difficulty	Distance	Area	Scenery	Strainers	Rating
75 (130)	III (IV-)	3.2*	27	A	1/mi.	****

USGS Quad – Fairhope; Source – Personal descent 5/02
N39 52.05, W78 49.04 to N39 50.63, W78 47.90

*(plus 0.7 miles on Wills Creek to just above the class 5.0 Railroad Cut Falls)

This paddle has excellent scenery and rapids and an optional class IV+ drop at the put in, right beneath the covered bridge. The class IV- rapid, early in the second mile, is a steep chute with a boulder at bottom left and shallow rocks on the right that try to direct you there. The hardest class III rapid can be seen upstream from the midway bridge, in the steepest overall stretch. Soon after you reach Wills Creek, you need to be alert for the upcoming class 5.0 Railroad Cut Falls (see write up above for Wills Creek section 1.)

  GAUGE: Wills Creek below Hyndman should be at least 700 cfs (in 2 hours).

HILLEGAS RUN: T469(Miller Run Road) to Brush Creek

Gradient	Difficulty	Distance	Area	Scenery	Strainers	Rating
55	?	2.0*	9**	?	?	?

USGS Quad – New Baltimore; Source – Scouting put in
N39 54.23, W78 49.54 to N39 52.05, W78 49.04

*(plus 1.6 miles on Brush Creek at 65(110) ft/mile to T408 – Pack Saddle Road)
**(includes a tributary that enters at 0.2 miles)

The put in area is heavily posted by the North Branch Hunting Club. This *"explorers' special"* is not particularly steep itself, but it continues onto the steepest part of section 1 of Brush Creek (which reaches 110 ft/mile), so Gertler's comments on that will apply here as well.

  GAUGE: Wills Creek below Hyndman needs 1,200 cfs (projected 3-4 hours forward), Sand Spring Run 30 cfs (2 hours earlier).

Michael Hillegas, a wealthy Pennsylvania iron and sugar merchant, became a Co-treasurer of the Continental Congress in 1775 and then the first Treasurer of the US in 1777, serving during the American Revolution and under the Articles of Confederation. He was replaced by Alexander Hamilton (as Secretary of the Treasury) in 1789.

SHAFFERS RUN: Savage and Bruck runs to Wills Creek (Fairhope)

Gradient	Difficulty	Distance	Area	Scenery	Strainers	Rating
95	?	4.6	5	B-	?	?

USGS Quad – Fairhope; Source – Scouting from road
N39 53.13, W78 46.30 via N39 50.95, W78 47.90 to N39 50.46, W78 47.57

SSR 2021 runs alongside almost the whole way. The highest put in is where Savage and Bruck runs enter Shaffers Run, as it crosses SSR 2021 for the first time. Rivulets enter, but even at its mouth, this *"explorers' special"* drains barely 10 sq. mi. No major rapids are visible from the road, but strainers are. There are four road crossings in the final 2 miles, but above that, you must ask for permission to put in. Shaffers Run enters Wills Creek at the railroad bridge just below Railroad Cut Falls, and just one-third mile above the put in for section 3 at Fairhope; however, if Shaffers Run is up, Wills Creek might be too high, so you would need to take out at Fairhope Road (shown as the "via" in the GPS coordinates above), 0.8 miles before Wills Creek.

GAUGE: Wills Creek below Hyndman should be at least 2,500 cfs to start at the top. A more timely reading would be 65 cfs on Sand Spring Run, an hour earlier.

> I happened to scout this creek during a **public fishing competition**. Hundreds of trout anglers lined the banks, while their families picnicked nearby. Hopefully, the landowners who allowed their neighbors this access would be amenable to requests for permission to paddle it.
>
> The large **Shaffer** family began migrating to this area from Germany around 1750.

LITTLE WILLS CREEK

Little Wills Creek, the largest and northernmost tributary of Wills Creek, flows east steeply for 7.5 miles until blocked by Buffalo Mountain, and then south at a lesser gradient for 9.6 miles, to meet Wills Creek at Hyndman. The first reasonable put in is in the hamlet of Straub, at a small tributary; above there, access is across private property.

Section 1: Straub (SSR 3008) to Bard (Pa. 96)

Gradient	Difficulty	Distance	Area	Scenery	Strainers	Rating
80	III- (III)	2.0	9	C+	1-3/mi.	**

USGS Quad – Buffalo Mills; Source – Personal descent 12/07
N39 56.43, W78 41.34 to N39 55.62, W78 39.60

This steep, narrow but fun section has long rapids, few eddies and no major drops. The class III is at mile 1.2, visible upstream from the only road bridge, where the creek bends, braids and tends to catch strainers. There is lots of other wood, usually easy to see in advance. Take out at Pa. 96 in Bard, where the creek turns south and flattens out.

GAUGE: Wills Creek below Hyndman should be over 1,400 cfs (5 hours later), and Sand Spring Creek at least 35 cfs (2 hours earlier).

Section 2: Bard to Madley

Gradient	Difficulty	Distance	Area	Scenery	Strainers	Rating
40	II	2.8	12	C-	2-4/mi.	-

USGS Quad – Buffalo Mills; Source – Personal descent 12/07
N39 55.62, W78 39.60 to N39 53.56, W78 40.25

Skip this part of Little Wills Creek. There are a few nice rapids and some interesting winding stretches, but not nearly enough to compensate for the frequent fences and downed trees. Be especially wary of the former, as some were unmarked strands that were hard to see until the last second. The take out is on a side road, 0.4 miles after Wolf Camp Run enters at Madley.
   GAUGE: Wills Creek below Hyndman should exceed 1,000 cfs.

Section 3: Madley to Hyndman (Wills Creek)

Gradient	Difficulty	Distance	Area	Scenery	Strainers	Rating
39	II+	6.8	24	C	<1/mi.	**

USGS Quad – Buffalo Mills/Hyndman; Source – Personal descent 3/02
N39 53.56, W78 40.25 to N39 48.77, W78 43.00

This, the section in Gertler, is a pleasant run alongside the railroad and Buffalo Mountain/Wills Mountain, with frequent riffles and easy rapids. After the confluence with Wills Creek, continue a half mile to the bridge at the south edge of Hyndman.
   GAUGE: Wills Creek below Hyndman should be at least 600 cfs.

WOLF CAMP RUN: Second SSR 3006 bridge to Little Wills Creek

Gradient	Difficulty	Distance	Area	Scenery	Strainers	Rating
80	III	3.2*	8	C	1-2/mi.	**

USGS Quad – Buffalo Mills; Source – Personal descent (last 2 miles) 3/02
N39 55.19, W78 42.37 to N39 53.56, W78 40.25

*(plus 0.4 miles on Little Wills Creek to take out alongside railroad bridge)

We discovered this stream accidentally, because Gertler's put in for Little Wills Creek is actually on Wolf Camp Run. As there was plenty of water there, we headed upstream for two miles, until some strainers. But as there are no major tributaries or changes in gradient upstream, one might go exploring there. A good put in, for a 3.2-mile trip, is where SSR 3006 crosses the creek for the second time, as you head upstream. The creek is steep for the first 2.2 miles. Then, after crossing SSR 3006 again, it eases up to class II+, with lots of maneuvering but few obstacles. Below Pa. 96 in Madley, it is 0.2 miles to the confluence and then 0.4 miles to the road alongside the railroad bridge.
   GAUGE: Wills Creek below Hyndman should be at least 1,500 cfs, while a timelier indicator would be Sand Spring Creek having been over 35 cfs, 2 hours earlier.

GLADDENS RUN

Gladdens Run lies in the center of the Wills Creek basin. I have divided the creek into two sections, because the gradient drops in half shortly above the private covered bridge (built 1880) at Palo Alto.

Section 1: Kennells Mill to Palo Alto

Gradient	Difficulty	Distance	Area	Scenery	Strainers	Rating
110 (150)	?	2.5	13	?	?	?

USGS Quad – Fairhope; Source – Scouting from road
N39 46.31, W78 47.92 to N39 43.10, W78 45.44

This *"explorers' special"* is one of the steepest runs in the Wills Creek basin. At Kennells Mill, Rush Run adds about 50% to the flow. In very high water, one could start a half mile farther up, where Leapley Run comes in; in lower water, one might put in a half mile below Kennells Mill, at the confluence with Powder Run. Just above Powder Run is what looks like a tough rapid, and the creek gets quite steep again 1.2 miles later.

GAUGE: Wills Creek below Hyndman should be at least 1,200 cfs in 3-4 hours, and Sand Spring Creek 30 cfs 1-2 hours before starting. (Theoretically, the difference between the reading on Wills Creek at Cumberland and the reading three hours earlier at Hyndman – the time it takes for that water to get to Cumberland– should be at least 850 cfs, because that 850 cfs has had to come mainly from Gladdens, Jennings and Braddock runs; however, I have not found this approach usable, because the cfs readings are not sufficiently accurate).

Section 2: Palo Alto to Wills Creek

Gradient	Difficulty	Distance	Area	Scenery	Strainers	Rating
50	II+	2.0*	17	B-	2-4/mi.	*

USGS Quad – Fairhope; Source – Personal descent 6/09
N39 43.10, W78 45.44 to N39 43.10, W78 46.26

*(plus 1.8 flat miles on Wills Creek)

Starting from the covered bridge, you cross roads about every half mile, and finally the railroad. Gladdens Run is full of long, easy rock gardens, but there was a fair bit of wood in the creek, as well as strands of barbed wire at two relatively easy spots early on. After the third bridge, the creek channelizes and runs through the bushes for about 100 yards; the right-side channel seemed best. Soon after the railroad bridge, some of Wills Creek enters and doubles the flow until you reach the main river. Wills Creek is fairly flat here, but the current will move you along nicely whenever Gladdens Run is up. Take out on river right under the bridge at Ellerslie, a half mile after crossing into Maryland.

GAUGE: Wills Creek below Hyndman should be at least 900 cfs in 3 hours, while Sand Spring Run should have been over 25 cfs 2 hours before.

🌊 JENNINGS RUN

I was wary about section 2 because of Gertler's warning: "Jennings Run is 3.4 miles of nonstop terror." Fortunately, however, the creek runs along Md. 36, so we could see that it had been transformed (by dredging) from the strainer-filled nightmare that Gertler encountered to a virtually strainer-free delight. Section 1 (not in Gertler), above the confluence with the North Branch, is steeper and smaller, but equally worthwhile.

Section 1: Mount Savage to Confluence with North Branch

Gradient	Difficulty	Distance	Area	Scenery	Strainers	Rating
115	III+	2.0	12	C-	<1/mi.	****

USGS Quad – Frostburg/Cumberland; Source – Personal descent (2nd half) 3/07; scouting from road
N39 41.70, W78 52.60 to N39 42.04, W78 50.60

Put in just below the Volunteer Fire Department in trendy Mount Savage, 200 yards after the main tributary enters. There are some stone walls along the creek in the town (scout this part for strainers beforehand), but the stream soon returns to a more natural-looking bed. The rapids are continuous and challenging, but there are no major drops. The rock garden visible upstream from the confluence with the North Branch is fairly representative of the creek's difficulty.

GAUGE: Sand Spring Run needs over 30 cfs (2 hours earlier), Georges Creek 600 cfs (3 hours later), the Savage River near Barton 400 cfs (2 hours later) and Wills Creek below Hyndman 1,200 cfs (5 hours later). If they are inconsistent, use an average.

Section 2: Confluence with North Branch to Corriganville

Gradient	Difficulty	Distance	Area	Scenery	Strainers	Rating
77	III+	3.0	31	C-	<1/mi.	****

USGS Quad – Cumberland; Source – Personal descent 3/07
N39 42.04, W78 50.60 to N39 41.57, W78 47.45

This is one of my favorite small streams, in part because there were no strainers on any of my three descents. Three rapids are class III+. The first is visible downstream from the confluence; scout and run far left. The second is a 4-foot drop on a left turn just after a smaller ledge; it often catches one by surprise. The final one, about a mile from the end, is where you see a horizon line after a smaller ledge. Scout from either bank. You can follow the main flow down the middle into a deep hole, take a tight line just to its right, or, in higher water, sneak far right. After that, the creek eases up.

Take out across from the Sheetz gas station in Corriganville. If you continue one-third mile to Wills Creek, you must carry up over the railroad tracks.

GAUGE: Wills Creek below Hyndman should be at least 700 cfs (3 hours later), Georges Creek 350 cfs (2 hours later) and the Savage River near Barton 225 cfs (1 hour later). (In theory, one could utilize the difference between the Hyndman and Cumberland gauges, but the readings are not accurate enough for that.)

NORTH BR., JENNINGS RUN: Witt Hill Road to Jennings Run

Gradient	Difficulty	Distance	Area	Scenery	Strainers	Rating
100	III	1.9	8	C-	0-2/mi.	***

USGS Quad – Cumberland; Source – Personal descent 3/07
N39 43.46, W78 50.86 to N39 42.04, W78 50.60

The North Branch is somewhat smaller and easier than section 1 of Jennings Run. We put in at Witt Hill Road, just north of the Mason-Dixon Line. Both homeowners on river right were amenable when we asked about putting in and parking there. They even informed us (accurately) that there were no fences across the creek. There are no notable rapids, but the trip involves continuous maneuvering in a narrow streambed, and there is always a risk of strainers (although we encountered few).

GAUGE: Sand Spring Run needs 40 cfs (2 hours earlier), Georges Creek 850 cfs (3 hours later), the Savage River near Barton 600 cfs (2 hours later) and Wills Creek below Hyndman 1,700 cfs (5 hours later).

BRADDOCK RUN: Allegany Grove (Lions Park) to Wills Creek

Gradient	Difficulty	Distance	Area	Scenery	Strainers	Rating
85	III	3.0	10	C+	0-2/mi.	***

USGS Quad – Cumberland; Source – Personal descent 6/09
N39 38.39, W78 49.48 to N39 40.22, W78 47.38

Although this creek runs through the suburbs of Allegany Grove and La Vale as it heads northeast, it is surprisingly secluded and attractive. Put in at the Lions Park off Braddock Road, a quarter mile below the I-68 interchange; above that, the creek plays tag with I-68. Take out on Locust Grove Rd., after ferrying across a flat part of Wills Creek.

The first half of the run, to the bridge on US 40A, is quite continuous, averaging almost 100 ft/mile, but with no major drops. The only three strainers we encountered were after about one mile. There is usually good forward visibility, but be careful around several sharp turns to the left. The second half of the trip is not quite as steep, but contains the most exciting rapid, where the creek drops about 6 feet over closely-spaced ledges, immediately after a 90 degree left turn. Here, the right bank is a high cement wall, and you should pull over well above to check for strainers, as once you get close to the rapid it will be too late. There are some more nice ledges shortly below, and then the creek eases up in its final quarter mile.

GAUGE: Georges Creek should be at least 600 cfs (3 hours later), Sand Spring Run 30 cfs (2 hours earlier), Wills Creek below Hyndman 1,200 cfs (4 hours later).

> **General Braddock**, British commander at the start of the French and Indian War, and accompanied by Col. George Washington, strengthened Fort Cumberland as the staging place for his disastrous (and personally fatal) attempt to attack Fort Duquesne (Pittsburgh) in 1755.

EVITTS CREEK to SIDELING HILL CREEK

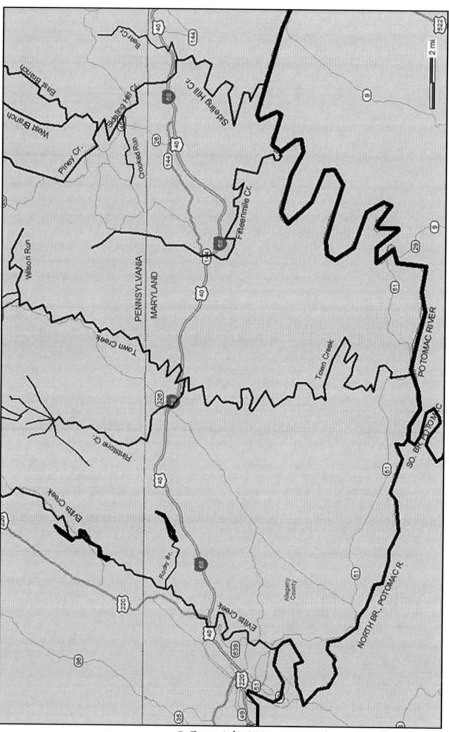

Chapter 11:
EVITTS CREEK to LICKING CREEK

East of Wills Creek are a series of smaller and more mundane watersheds: **Evitts** (93 sq. mi.), **Town** (156 sq. mi.), **Fifteenmile** (62 sq. mi.), **Sideling Hill** (103 sq. mi.), **Little Tonoloway [south]** (25 sq. mi.), **Tonoloway** (112 sq. mi.) and **Licking** (208 sq. mi.) **creeks**. The best for whitewater are relatively short sections of Evitts, **Flintstone, Little Tonoloway [north]** and **Big Cove creeks**. Fifteenmile and lower Sideling Hill Creeks have much longer and somewhat easier paddles in beautiful settings – the latter is very popular and not too difficult to catch. There also are long class I stretches of Evitts, Town, Tonoloway, Licking and Big Cove creeks that I have omitted, as they have no rapids and are well covered by Gertler. As the area is so large, I have two chapter maps.

There are seven "explorers' specials" in this chapter, because I only decided to add it to this book at end-2011; however, I did manage to do three new runs in the area after that. The steepest ones remaining are **Wilson Run** and **upper Evitts Creek**; the other five have gradients of just 17-26 ft/mile.

The main streams begin in Bedford and Fulton counties, Pennsylvania, and flow into Allegany and Washington counties, Maryland. They are the "Folded Appalachian Mountain Section" of the "Ridge and Valley Province." Those in the western part flow south-southwest, but farther east they run due south. Evitts Creek flows into the North Branch of the Potomac, a little east of Cumberland MD, while the other streams enter directly into the Potomac itself, east of where its North and South branches meet near Oldtown Md. and Green Springs WV. The main town servicing this area is Cumberland Md. Its population of 21,000 is barely half what it was in 1940, due to the closure of all its major manufacturing plants. The largest town actually within the area is Hancock Md., on the Potomac; its population is down to 1,500.

Between the mouths of Town and Sideling Hill creeks is the **Paw Paw Bends** section of the Potomac. Here, starting at the village of Paw Paw WV, the river flows northeast through a series of large loops, so that 25 river miles correspond to just 9 air miles.

Farther east, at Hancock, Maryland is less than 2 miles wide, because no one had surveyed the area when the boundaries were set between the Potomac River and what became the Mason-Dixon Line.

GAUGES: There are Maryland downstream gauges on Town (149 sq. mi.), Sideling Hill (102 sq. mi.), Tonoloway (111 sq. mi.) and Licking (193 sq. mi.) creeks. The best gauge for the small streams is upper **Tonoloway Creek near Needmore, PA (10.7 sq. mi.), and this is the reference** in the table below. However, as this gauge is up to 25 miles away from the westernmost streams of this chapter, you often need to use this in combination with the other gauges listed above, plus the one on Wills Creek at Hyndman. And for Fifteenmile Creek and especially Little Tonoloway Creek (Hancock), a gauge from across the Potomac (Warm Springs Run, WV – 6.8 sq. mi.) is helpful.

name	gradient	difficulty	length	area	gauge	rating
Evitts Creek - *Section 1*	32 (75)	?	3.8	24	40cfs	?
- Section 2	45(100)	II+ (III)	2.2	50	30cfs	***
- Section 3	30	II	2.7	53	25cfs	**
Town Creek	15	I	15.0	34	25cfs	*
Wilson Run	50	?	2.0	12	70cfs	?
Flintstone Cr. *– Sec. 1*	28	II	5.7	15	55cfs	*
– Sec. 2	48 (75)	III- (III)	4.3	23	45cfs	****
Fifteenmile Cr. *- Sec. 1*	35	II	2.8	14	60cfs	*
- Sec. 2	28	II+	10.2	28	40cfs	***
Sideling Hill Cr. *- Sec.1*	16	I	14.0	38	25cfs	**
- Sec.2	16	II-	11.6	90	n.a.	***
West Branch	22	?	5.0	14	55cfs	?
East Branch	33	II	5.2	10	75cfs	**
Piney Creek	35	II+	3.4	10	75cfs	-
L. Tonoloway Cr.[south]	23	?	2.8	17	55cfs	?
Tonoloway Creek	23	?	5.6	15	60cfs	?
L. Tonol. Cr.[n.] -Sec.1	48	II+	4.8	10	80cfs	***
-Sec.2	31	II	2.8	30	35cfs	**
Licking Creek	20	II-	4.2	11	75cfs	**
Patterson Run	26	?	4.0	10	75cfs	?
Big Cove Creek	40	III-	2.7	30	45cfs	***
Esther Run	55	III-	0.9	11	85cfs	**
Little Cove Creek	17	?	3.5	20	45cfs	?

EVITTS CREEK

Evitts Creek (named for an early settler who built a mountaintop homestead) drains a 4-5 miles wide valley between Wills and Evitts mountains. It once ran for 30 miles, but is now interrupted by reservoirs that form lakes Koon and Gordon, to provide the water supply for Cumberland. Below section 3, the creek flows for 8 more miles at a gradient of just 15 ft/mile.

Section 1: White Church Lane to Lake Koon

Gradient	Difficulty	Distance	Area	Scenery	Strainers	Rating
32 (75)	?	3.8	24	?	?	?

USGS Quad – Hyndman; Source – Scouting access points
N39 49.61, W78 37.85 to N39 46.63, W78 39.29

This looks like a mostly mild **"explorers' special,"** but just before midway, a little gorge (with the 75 ft/mile gradient) should have some good rapids. The put in is off US 220 a mile east of Centerville, and the take out is alongside the reservoir.

    GAUGE: You need over 40 cfs on Tonoloway Creek near Needmore (1-2 hours earlier) and 550 cfs on Wills Creek at Hyndman and on Town Creek (4 hours later).

Section 2: Below Lake Gordon to Maryland State Line

Gradient	Difficulty	Distance	Area	Scenery	Strainers	Rating
45 (100)	II+ (III)	2.2	50	B+	<1/mi.	***

USGS Quad – Evitts Creek; Source – Personal descent 1/05
N39 44.78, W78 40.59 to N39 43.39, W78 41.29

After 3 miles in the Lake Koon and Lake Gordon reservoirs, Evitts Creek bursts forth at a lively class II pace. Put in where Lake Gordon Road crosses the creek, a quarter mile below the dam. In a little over a mile, you enter an attractive class III gorge, where the gradient briefly reaches 100 ft/mile. There are frequent class II rapids even after that, but a mile after the gorge you cross the state line at Hazen Drive/Bottle Run Road, and the best stuff is over.

GAUGE: After a wet period, when the reservoirs are full, you will need 30 cfs on Tonoloway Cr. near Needmore, with the Wills Cr. at Hyndman and Town Creek gauges projected to 400 cfs, 2-3 hours later. After a dry period, Evitts Creek may not come up.

Section 3: Maryland State Line to Old Mt. Pleasant Road NE

Gradient	Difficulty	Distance	Area	Scenery	Strainers	Rating
30	II	2.7	53	B-	<1/mi.	**

USGS Quad – Evitts Creek; Source – Personal descent 1/05
N39 43.39, W78 41.29 to N39 41.73, W78 42.18

This stretch, while still pleasant and full of riffles and easy rapids, is an anticlimax after section 2. Take out at the third bridge (2.7 miles). You can continue (as we did) another 2.4 miles to the restaurant just below I-68, or even go 6 miles beyond that to West Industrial Boulevard (Md. 51) at the edge of Cumberland, but the gradient for those stretches is down to 18 and 10 ft/mile, respectively.

GAUGE: Look for at least 25 cfs on Tonoloway Creek near Needmore and 350 cfs on Wills and Town Creeks, projected 2 hours later (but see caveat under section 2).

> An Evitts Creek tributary, **Rocky Gap Run** is the steepest stream in the area, averaging 140 ft/mile over its 2.6 mile course. But it is dammed up to create a lake that is the centerpiece of Rocky Gap State Park (which includes a large hotel and resort complex), and may never get enough water to be paddled. In addition, it is hard to get to (the water from the lake goes via a spillway that includes a 20-foot drop back into the original channel) and is full of downed trees at least at the top. There is access to the lower half of the run, but several fences were visible there, and they would be quite dangerous because the gradient hardly eases up at all.

TOWN CREEK: Chaneysville to below I-68 (Md. 144)

Gradient	Difficulty	Distance	Area	Scenery	Strainers	Rating
15	I	15.0	34	B+	<<1/mi.	*

USGS Quad – Beans Cove/Flintstone; Source – Personal descent 11/02; Gertler
N39 49.13, W78 28.96 (Wilson Run) via N39 45.27, W78 30.68 (Covered Bridge Road, mile 7.5) to N39 41.68, W78 32.87

This is a pleasant trip through attractive scenery, but with only riffles. You can put in on Wilson Run (or its tributary Elklick Creek), on Ragged Mountain Road, shortly above the confluence with Sweet Root Creek that forms Town Creek, and take out just below I-68 at Baltimore Pike (Md. 144). There are numerous options to shorten the trip. Below the take out, the gradient averages 9 ft/mile for the final 26 miles.

GAUGE: Some 25 cfs on Tonoloway Creek near Needmore is needed to start near the confluence, while the gauge near the mouth of Town Creek itself should be at least 350 cfs, projected 3 hours later.

WILSON RUN: Grand Rapids Road to Ragged Mountain Road

Gradient	Difficulty	Distance	Area	Scenery	Strainers	Rating
50	?	2.0	12	?	?	?

USGS Quad – Beans Cove; Source – Scouting access points
N39 49.49, W78 27.79 to N39 49.13, W78 28.96

Put in at the confluence with Bushy Run; upstream I saw strainers and braiding. This might be a nice *"explorers' special"* by itself, taking out at Ragged Mountain Road, 0.4 miles above the start of Town Creek, or a lively way to start a trip down upper Town Creek. If you continue down Town Creek, it is 4.7 miles to the first take out option.

GAUGE: Look for at least 70 cfs on Tonoloway Creek at Needmore. The gauge on Town Creek should be above 1,000 cfs, projected 5 hours later.

FLINTSTONE CREEK

Five headwaters meet at Beans Cove to launch Flintstone Creek on its ten mile journey to Town Creek. Section 1 is very narrow in places, has some barbed wire fences, is fairly prone to tree strainers, and has a relatively low gradient. Section 2, starting 0.4 miles above the state line (and 0.7 miles above Gertler's put in), has excellent whitewater and few obstacles.

Section 1: Confluence of branches (Wildcat Run) to Street Road

Gradient	Difficulty	Distance	Area	Scenery	Strainers	Rating
28	II	5.7	15	C	1-3/mi.	*

USGS Quad – Beans Cove; Source – Personal descent (last 2.4 miles) 5/12; scouting
N39 47.46, W78 34.58 via N39 45.18, W78 35.19 (our put in) to N39 43.66, W78 35.46

You can put in just above the confluence on Wildcat Run (or Pigeonroost Run), at the top of Flintstone Creek Road. From that road, the first part looked mild and not too plagued by fences or other strainers, but you would have to investigate that for yourself, especially as the creek is very narrow in places. The next potential put in is in 2.3 miles, and a mile later comes the one which we used (not wanting to paddle the full 10 miles).

We started where the stream comes close to the road (and there is a fine put in without "no trespassing" signs), 1.9 road miles (2.4 creek miles) above the Street Road start of section 2. The trip was pleasant and easy, except for three barbed wire fences by a farm (we ducked under the first one and carried the other two together on river left) and a tree strainer that required a lengthy and thorny portage. Half a mile later, another fence was torn out but might be rebuilt. In high water, at least two bridges would have to be carried, but at a medium level we could just slip under them.

After two miles, the creek divided. The route straight ahead was blocked, so we entered a narrow channel on the left which was twisty class II and good fun, except for one strainer near the end. Soon after the channels reunite, you reach Street Road.

GAUGE: Look for at least 55 cfs on Tonoloway Creek near Needmore (if the rainfall has been even; that gauge is 24 miles east of Beans Cove), with the Town Creek gauge projected 4 hours ahead to be at least 800 cfs.

Section 2: Street Road to Town Creek (Gilpin Road)

Gradient	Difficulty	Distance	Area	Scenery	Strainers	Rating
48 (75)	III- (III)	4.3	23	B-	0-1/mi.	****

USGS Quad – Beans Cove/Flintstone; Source – Personal descent 5/12
N39 43.66, W78 35.46 to N39 41.67, W78 32.85

At Street Road, the gradient picks up and the creek becomes almost continuous class II. In 0.7 miles, at the bridge over Flintstone Creek Road, the really juicy stretch begins, with a drop of 75 feet in the next mile, through long class II+ and III- rapids, with one ledge early on that is a legitimate class III (run it on the far right). There are no completely blind turns, but the creek is pretty twisty and it is sometimes hard to see to the bottom of the rapid until you are in it, so you have to be constantly on guard against strainers. (We were fortunate to encounter none, but this often changes from trip to trip.)

After that mile, the stream slows down gradually, but there are virtually no flat stretches, as riffles and easy rapids move you along all the way, with a few more class IIs near the end. The scenery is excellent at first, but there are more roads and houses visible later. Higher water makes this trip more exciting but the potential of strainers becomes more dangerous, and a bridge or two may need to be portaged.

Take out by the sewage treatment plant, on river left a few yards above the confluence with Town Creek, from where it is a 150 yard, grassy walk up to Gilpin Road.

GAUGE: The Town Creek gauge, projected 3 hours ahead, should be at least 625 cfs. About 45 cfs on Tonoloway Creek near Needmore would be a good advanced indication, but that gauge is 24 miles east of the Flintstone Creek headwaters.

FIFTEENMILE CREEK

Like Flintstone Creek, Fifteenmile Creek starts out heading in the SSW direction of the mountain ridges (section 1), and then swings to ESE (section 2) for the better rapids. Gertler covers section 2 well and does not miss much by skipping section 1.

Section 1: Bear Camp Branch to above US 40

Gradient	Difficulty	Distance	Area	Scenery	Strainers	Rating
35	II	2.5	14	B	2-4/mi.	*

USGS Quad – Artemas; Source – Personal descent 3/10

N39 42.74, W78 26.79 to N39 41.20, W78 27.29

Fifteenmile Creek Road offers many put in options, but above the proposed one (just south of the state line) the creek is too narrow even for my taste. Expect braiding and lots of strainers, for which the limited rapids and moderate scenery are inadequate compensation.

GAUGE: Look for 60 cfs on Tonoloway Creek near Needmore and 40 cfs on Warm Springs Run (WV), with the Sideling Hill gauge over 550 cfs in 4 hours.

Section 2: Above US 40 to Potomac River (Little Orleans)

Gradient	Difficulty	Distance	Area	Scenery	Strainers	Rating
28	II+	10.2	28	A	0-2/mi.	***

USGS Quad – Artemas/Paw Paw; Source – Personal descent 3/10

N39 41.20, W78 27.29 via N39 39.39, W78 23.83 (Mtn. Rd) to N39 37.42, W78 23.11

Put in on Fifteenmile Creek Road, 0.3 miles above US 40, for a long, delightful low intermediate paddle (read Gertler's longer description). To shorten the trip by 3 miles, take out alongside Mountain Road; otherwise, continue to the bridge at Little Orleans or go the final half mile to a boat landing by the Potomac (used for the GPS address).

GAUGE: For timeliness, Tonoloway Creek near Needmore should be 40 cfs and Warm Springs Run (WV) 25 cfs. The Sideling Hill gauge should be 350 cfs (projected 2 hours later) and Town Creek 525 cfs (3 hours after put in).

SIDELING HILL CREEK

Sideling Hill Creek is a lovely beginners' paddle, with section 2 one of the more popular and beautiful trips around, and section 1 an alternative for high water. Both are well described by Gertler. My focus, of course, is on its tributaries. The East and West branches meet by the village of Purcell, while Piney Creek flows in 2.6 miles later.

Section 1: Purcell (confluence of branches) to Old US 40

Gradient	Difficulty	Distance	Area	Scenery	Strainers	Rating
16	I	14.0	38	B	0-2/mi.	**

USGS Quad – Amaranth/Chaneysville/Bellegrove; Source – Gertler

N39 47.17, W78 21.87 via N 39 45.36, W78 21.82 (Silver Mills Road) and N39 44.59, W78 21.55 (Buck Valley Road) to N39 42.01, W78 19.05

While not as remote or interesting as section 2, this is nevertheless an attractive novice paddle when section 2 is running high. Put in at the bridge over the West Branch, or run the first part as a continuation of an East Branch paddle (see below). There is access at Silver Mills Road (mile 4) and Buck Valley Road, SR 484 (mile 7).

GAUGE: The Sideling Hill gauge should be at least 250 cfs (2-3 hours later).

Section 2: Old US 40 to Potomac River

Gradient	Difficulty	Distance	Area	Scenery	Strainers	Rating
16	II-	11.6	90	A	<<1/mi.	***

USGS Quad – Bellegrove; Source – Personal descent 4/93
N39 42.01, W78 19.05 to N39 38.32, W78 19.76

This beautiful, classic Sideling Hill trip is run by many people, especially early in their paddling careers. There are details in Gertler and a map in Cantor. Most of the first half of the run is through a lovely gorge, while the remainder is in more open country, including some farmland. There are about twenty easy rapids, mostly on bends. One can take out after 5 miles on Norris Road, after 10.5 miles on Ziegler Road, or continue the final mile and a bit to the Potomac, and take out at lock 56, off of Pearre Road (used for the GPS coordinates above).

GAUGE: The Sideling Hill gauge should be at least 200 cfs.

Most Sideling Hill paddlers notice **Bear Creek** at the section 2 put in. It might be paddled for 2.6 miles (take Bottenfield Road off Mountain Road) at 55 ft/mile and 8 sq. mi. But there are two problems. First, you need permission from Meadow Valley Farms, which owns the access to the put in – ask for that at their outlet, visible from I-68. Second, you should scout in advance the passage through a long culvert under I-68, shortly above the take out, to check for strainers; unfortunately, this involves trespassing across private land, but a good pair of binoculars might be a compromise. A portage over I-68 is definitely not an advisable Plan B!

An even smaller tributary is **Crooked Run**, which might be run for 1.7 miles from Barnes Road to Sideling Hill Creek at 47 ft/mile and with 7 sq. mi. At 1.3 miles it crosses S. Clear Ridge Road (Pa. 26). Once on Sideling Hill Creek (section 1), the easiest thing might be to attain 375 flat yards to Buck Valley Road (SR 484).

WEST BR., SIDELING HILL CR.: SR 2007/Ward Rd. to Confluence

Gradient	Difficulty	Distance	Area	Scenery	Strainers	Rating
22	?	5.0	14	?	?	?

USGS Quad – Amaranth; Source – Scouting
N39 50.61, W78 20.52 via N39 49.92, W78 20.95 (SR 2008) to N39 47.17, W78 21.87

This *"explorers' special"* does not look particularly interesting from the road (SR 2007) that it parallels, and its gradient suggests relatively few rapids. But it is the larger and therefore slightly easier to catch

Sideling Hill headwater. For the 5-mile run, put in by the confluence with a tributary by SR 2007 and Ward Road. You could shorten this to a 3.7 mile paddle, starting on SR 2008 (off SR 2007). Take out 350 yards above the confluence, at Robinsonville Road in Purcell. The first take out on Sideling Hill Creek itself is 4 miles below the confluence, at Silver Mills Road.

GAUGE: Look for at least 55 cfs on Tonoloway Creek near Needmore, and the Sideling Hill gauge projected to be above 500 cfs some 4 hours later.

⑈ EAST BR., SIDELING HILL CR.: Robinsonville Rd. to Confluence

Gradient	Difficulty	Distance	Area	Scenery	Strainers	Rating
33	II	5.2	10	B+	1-3/mi.	**

USGS Quad – Amaranth; Source – Personal descent 3/12
N39 49.86, W78 19.32 via N39 48.59, W78 20.14 (SR 2006) to N39 46.95, W78 21.60

This is a pleasant paddle through relatively pristine woods, mostly away from the road. There is lots of wood in and overhanging the creek; abundant signs of beavers explain some of the former. There is also a semi-collapsed footbridge near the end, with only marginal head clearance. A few sections are fast and twisty, but there are plenty of eddies so you seldom have to worry about blind turns. There are a few class II drops, but mostly just long riffles and easy rapids throughout the run, with more towards the end.

We put in just above the third bridge, for a 5.2 mile paddle; above there, the creek is very narrow and right along the road. Ask for permission at the house across the road from the tiny paved area just upstream from the bridge and barn. In lower water, you could put in at SR 2006 for a 3-mile paddle to the confluence, or at the first bridge on Robinsonville Road for a 4.2 mile trip.

At the take out bridge, on Sideling Hill Creek Road in Purcell, 100 yards above the confluence, the landowner is not very welcoming, so you might want to continue 4 miles down Sideling Hill Creek to Silver Mills Road (see Sideling Hill Creek section 1 above).

GAUGE: Look for at least 75 cfs on Tonoloway Creek near Needmore, and the Sideling Hill gauge projected to be above 600 cfs some 4 hours later.

⑈ PINEY CREEK: Ridge Road/Clear Ridge Road to Sideling Hill Creek

Gradient	Difficulty	Distance	Area*	Scenery	Strainers	Rating
35	II+	3.4	10	B	4-8/mi.	-

USGS Quad –Chaneysville; Source – Personal descent 11/11 (first 2 miles); scouting
N39 47.26, W78 24.33 via 39 46.13, W78 23.12 (mile 2) to N39 45.76, W78 22.21

*(includes 3 sq. mile from Blackberry Lick Run which enters in 0.3 miles)

This would be a nice little stream if it did not braid so much and have so many strainers – but of course one can say that about many of its brethren. The braiding often led Barb Brown and me into difficult places where we had to portage over logs, cross fast channels or bash through vines and branches. The few nice rapids, including one set of three little ledges, were inadequate compensation. We took out in frustration after 2 miles, at another crossing of Clear Ridge Road (Md. 26), so maybe the final 1.4 miles are better. The take out is at Purcell Road, 100 yards above the confluence.

GAUGE: Look for at least 75 cfs on Tonoloway Creek near Needmore, and the Sideling Hill gauge projected to be above 700 cfs some 4 hours later.

TONOLOWAY & LICKING CREEK BASINS

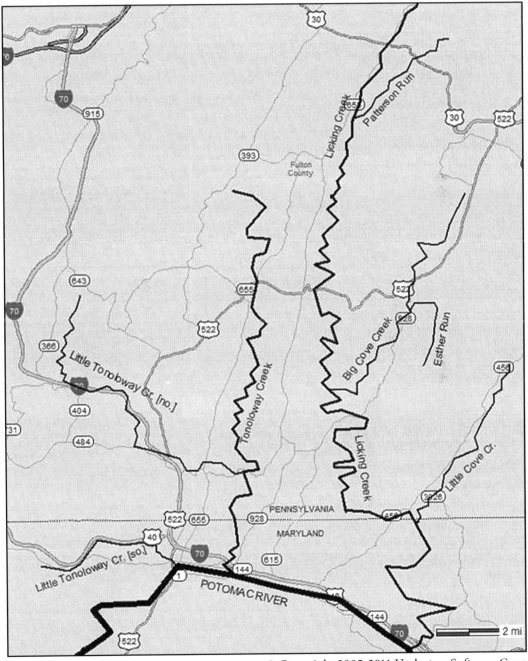

© Copyright 2005-2011 Undertow Software Corp

〰️ LITTLE TONOLOWAY CR. [south]: Minnow Run to Hancock

Gradient	Difficulty	Distance	Area	Scenery	Strainers	Rating
23	?	2.8	17	?	?	?

USGS Quad – Hancock; Source – Scouting
N39 42.75, W78 13.77 to N39 42.08, W78 11.33

The put in is down a steep, trash-strewn slope alongside I-68, just south of where Sandy Mile Road crosses I-68 and Minnow Run enters to almost double the flow. This *"explorers' special"* then parallels I-68 East for 1.5 miles, before twisting to and from Creek Road into Hancock. In Widmyer Park, portage the sheer, 4-foot dam, run the broken, class II+ dam, and take out near Park Road, a half mile above the Potomac.

   GAUGE: Look for at least 35 cfs on Warm Springs Run (WV), 55 cfs on Tonoloway Creek near Needmore and 500 cfs on Sideling Hill 4 hours later.

〰️ TONOLOWAY CREEK: Blairs Hill Road to Needmore (US 522)

Gradient	Difficulty	Distance	Area	Scenery	Strainers	Rating
23	?	5.6	15	?	?	?

USGS Quad – Needmore; Source – Scouting
N39 53.93, W78 07.95 to N39 51.31, W78 08.19

Gertler writes up the 20-mile class I trip on Tonoloway Creek from Needmore to the Potomac, at 10 ft/mile, but this is the *"explorers' special"* above that. Blairs Hill Road is a good place to start, because it is just above the confluence with Foster Creek, which adds over 40% to the flow (and is included in the 15 sq. mi.). Take out at US 522/SR655. Tonoloway was the Shawnee name for the Conoy tribe in the area.

   GAUGE: Look for at least 60 cfs on the Tonoloway gauge at Needmore (at the put in); this will give you over 85 cfs as soon as Foster Creek enters in a quarter mile.

〰️ LITTLE TONOLOWAY CREEK [north]

This Little Tonoloway Creek, a tributary of big Tonoloway Creek, is a steeper and prettier paddle than its namesake above.

Section 1: Moss Road to I-70/SR 3007 (Deneen Gap)

Gradient	Difficulty	Distance	Area	Scenery	Strainers	Rating
48	II+	4.8	10	A-	1-2/mi.	***

USGS Quad – Needmore; Source – Personal descent 4/00
N39 50.13, W78 14.68 to N39 47.93, W78 14.50

This is a very pretty descent through the woods, with few signs of civilization. The rapids are almost continuous but not difficult. The strainers can generally be seen well in advance, and the low banks make portaging easy.

GAUGE: Look for at least 80 cfs on the Tonoloway gauge near Needmore.

Section 2: I-70 (Deneen Gap) to Mill Hill Road

Gradient	Difficulty	Distance	Area	Scenery	Strainers	Rating
31	II	2.8	30	B	0-2/mi.	**

USGS Quad – Needmore; Source – Gertler; scouting
N39 47.93, W78 14.50 to N39 47.23, W78 12.72

Gertler covers the entire 9.6 miles to Tonoloway Creek, but with the gradient dropping steadily over this stretch (to 10 ft/mile for the final 3.5 miles), I propose just the first 2.8 miles down to Mill Hill Road (on the west side of I-70), where you can drive right down to the creek. With section 1, this makes a nice day's trip of 7.6 miles.

GAUGE: Look for over 35 cfs on the Tonoloway gauge near Needmore.

LICKING CREEK: Breezy Point Rd (off US 522) to Mellotts Mill

Gradient	Difficulty	Distance	Area	Scenery	Strainers	Rating
20	II-	4.2	11	B	1-2/mi.	**

USGS Quad – McConnelsburg; Source – Gertler; scouting
N40 00.90, W77 58.85 to N40 01.35, W78 02.37

Based on Gertler and on my scouting trip, this is the liveliest piece of Licking Creek – above it is too small, and below too flat. After a half mile along the road, it enters the woods, interrupted by only one minor road crossing (Cherry Lane). The take out on Mill Road (off Pa. 655) is posted, but access for fishing is permitted.

GAUGE: At least 75 cfs on the Tonoloway gauge near Needmore is needed.

PATTERSON RUN: US 30 to Licking Creek

Gradient	Difficulty	Distance	Area	Scenery	Strainers	Rating
26	?	4.0	10	?	?	?

USGS Quad – McConnelsburg; Source – Scouting
N39 58.80, W78 02.63 to N39 56.81, W78 04.74

This is a tiny *"explorers' special"* from start to finish. You can park along US 30, and Patterson Run Road provides a very direct shuttle. Take out where Patterson Run Road crosses Licking Creek, just below the confluence and just off Pa. 655 (Pleasant Ridge Road). Patterson Run Road also crosses the creek midway in the trip.

GAUGE: Some 75 cfs on the Tonoloway gauge near Needmore is minimal.

BIG COVE CREEK: Ravensburg Road to SR 928/Dutch Ridge Road

Gradient	Difficulty	Distance	Area	Scenery	Strainers	Rating
40	III-	2.7	30	B-	<1/mi.	***

USGS Quad – Big Cove Tannery; Source – Personal descent 3/08
N39 51.97, W78 02.47 to N39 50.31, W78 02.90

Although Big Cove Creek can be run for 12 miles as per Gertler, all of the best whitewater is in this 2.7-mile section. The put in is off US 255 just north of Big Cove Tannery, where Roaring Run races in. (The rapids begin about 50 yards above there, but the price is 3.5 miles of flat water and several fences.) There are long stretches of fun rapids with continuous action. You cross under US 255 and then SR 928. Take out at the parking area soon after returning to SR 928 – this is just below the confluence with Esther Run. If you want a longer paddle, you can go another 5.4 pleasant miles to Laurel Ridge Road, just before Licking Creek, but the gradient averages just 13 ft/mile.

   GAUGE: About 45 cfs on the Tonoloway gauge near Needmore is minimal

ESTHER RUN: Corner Road to Big Cove Creek

Gradient	Difficulty	Distance	Area	Scenery	Strainers	Rating
55	III-	0.9	11	C	1-3/mi.	**

USGS Quad – Big Cove Tannery; Source – Personal descent 3/08
N39 50.54, W78 02.15 to N39 50.31, W78 02.90

Esther Run flows north for 5 miles and then west for almost a mile to Big Cove Creek. It is really hard to catch more than that final mile (the area is just 7 sq. mi. before the stream turns west), but that last bit is a decent descent that you can scout from the road and paddle as an appetizer to a trip on Big Cove Creek. Just make sure to run it first, as it may be too low by the time you finish the latter. There are no big drops, but the stream is narrow, the rapids continuous and wood highly likely, so you need to stay alert. The take out is just below the confluence (at the Big Cove Creek take out.)

   GAUGE: Some 85 cfs on the Tonoloway gauge near Needmore is minimal.

LITTLE COVE CREEK: Sylvan to Licking Creek

Gradient	Difficulty	Distance	Area	Scenery	Strainers	Rating
17	?	3.5*	20	?	?	?

USGS Quad – Big Cove Tannery/Cherry Run; Source – Scouting
N39 45.23, W78 01.39 via N39 44.04, W78 02.18 (Yeakle) to N39 41.67, W78 03.15
*(plus 2.3 miles on Licking Creek at 4 ft/mile, to Slabtown Road)

This mild *"explorers' special"* rises on Cove Mountain and enters Licking Creek just below the Mason-Dixon line. There is access at Yeakle Mill, halfway.

   GAUGE: Look for at least 45 cfs on Tonoloway Creek at Needmore.

CONOCOCHEAGUE & ANTIETAM CREEK BASINS

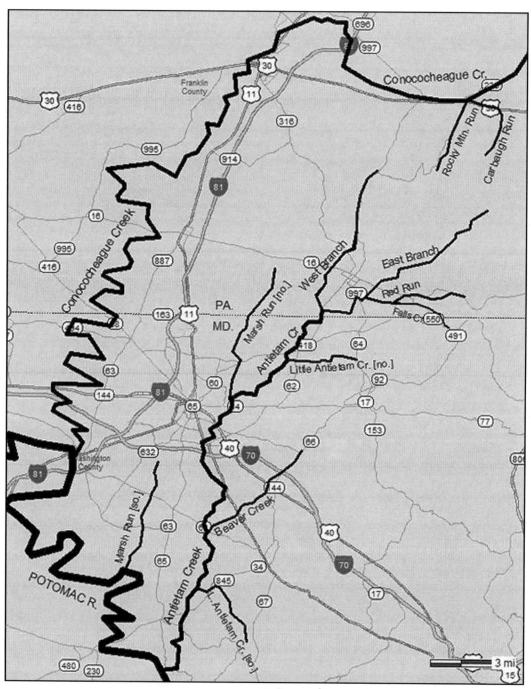

Chapter 12:

CONOCOCHEAGUE & ANTIETAM CREEK BASINS

This chapter covers two large basins with little whitewater, which together comprise the Hagerstown Valley, a northern extension of the Great (Shenandoah) Valley of Virginia. **Conococheague Creek** (more a river than a creek, and pronounced Conocojig) drains 566 sq. mi. as the seventh largest direct Potomac tributary (after the Shenandoah, the South and North branches of the Potomac, and the Monocacy, Cacapon and Occoquan rivers). Its West Branch is the northernmost extension of the Potomac basin, and is separated from Licking Creek by Tuscarora Mountain. Yet the only runnable whitewater in the basin is in Conococheague Creek's extreme headwaters, including tiny **Carbaugh** and **Rocky Mountain runs**. The main town in the basin, Chambersburg Pa., has 20,000 people in the city and 55,000 in the metropolitan area.

The Antietam basin stretches for 35 miles; Hagerstown, Md. (40,000) and Waynesboro, Pa. (10,000) are its main centers. To the west and north it is separated only by low hills from the Conococheague basin, but its eastern boundary is first the Blue Ridge (to the south), which peters out soon, and then South Mountain, along which run the Appalachian Trail. Therefore, the only steep tributaries are on the eastern side of the valley; unfortunately, most are too small and/or strainer-filled to paddle.

Antietam Creek itself, the Potomac's tenth largest direct tributary (290 sq. mi.), contains two popular novice sections, of 12.3 and 23.4 miles, respectively, both of which may be split into trips of almost any length. Being partially spring fed, it tends to stay up and cool longer than most other creeks. There are numerous write-ups of these trips.

Its tributaries are a disappointment. The best is section 1 of the **East Branch**, which is steep and scenic; however, it is short and its pleasures are lessened by strainers. Section 1 of **Little Antietam Creek [north]** is exciting but dangerous as it tumbles westward off of South Mountain; we encountered only a few strainers, but paddlers need to be very wary of them. This section is also extremely difficult to catch up. The other creeks racing down from South Mountain (Red Run, Falls Creek, Sharmans Branch) are even smaller, with watersheds of only a few square miles, and quite a few strainers visible from the road, so I have not included them – except the lower, mellow part of **Red Run**.

On the other hand, down in the valley are some flatter and easier-to-catch streams. Gertler gives the **West Branch** a very poor review, and I found section 2 of the East Branch to be equally bad. **Marsh Run [north]** has one decent mile, before succumbing to an incredible density of strainers. **Beaver Creek**, section 3 of the East Branch and section 2 of Little Antietam Creek (North) are moderately worthwhile novice trips, as is **Little Antietam Creek [south]**, which also has one man-made runnable waterfall.

> The early settlers, starting in the mid-18th Century, were mostly German immigrants. Jonathan and Elizabeth Hager founded two nearby communities, which they called Hager's Delight and Elizabethtown; eventually they were merged into **Hagerstown**.

In between the two large basins is an "explorers' special," **Marsh Run [south]**. It has an on-line gauge and an interesting rapid at the end, but is rarely up.

GAUGES: The gauge on Conococheague Creek (494 sq. mi.) near Fairview Md. (just south of the Mason-Dixon Line) is not of much use for its headwaters. For those, use Bermudian Creek, Pa. (in the West Conewago Basin; 10.2 sq. mi.), 15-20 miles to the east northeast) and Tonoloway Creek near Needmore (10.7 sq. mi.), 35 miles to the west. The historic Antietam Creek gauge is near Sharpsburg (281 sq. mi.), but the one at **Waynesboro (94 sq. mi.)**, at the confluence of the East and West branches, is far better for the tributaries, and is **the zero-level gauge reference below**. Also useful are the gauges on Catoctin Creek (67 sq. mi.), which parallels Antietam Creek about 10 miles to the east and Bermudian Creek. Marsh Run [south], a small watershed just west of Antietam Creek, has its own gauge (19 sq. mi.). Rain gauge data are not reported.

name	gradient	difficulty	length	area	gauge	rating
Conococheague Cr. - Sec.1	65	?	2.8	12	550cfs	?
- Sec.2	37	II+	4.3	36	315cfs	*
Rocky Mountain Run	80	?	1.8	6	1100cfs	?
Carbaugh Run	78	?	1.2	10	700cfs	?
Marsh Run [south]	35 (80)	II+	2.2	19	400cfs	?
Antietam Creek - Section 1	6	I (II+)	12.3	93	175cfs	*
- Section 2	7	II	23.4	182	140cfs	**
West Branch	16	I	5.2	34	225cfs	-
East Branch - Section 1	90 (120)	III-	1.5	12	600cfs	***
- Section 2	40	II	2.3	16	400cfs	-
- Section 3	18	II- (III+)	5.2	27	275cfs	**
Red Run	30	II-	1.5	11	500cfs	*
L. Ant. Cr.[north] -Sec.1	90 (150)	III	1.5	6	1200cfs	**
-Sec.2	25 (65)	II	5.2	8	850cfs	**
Marsh Run [north]	35	II (III)	1.0	30	265cfs	*
Beaver Creek	15	II- (II)	8.5	20	400cfs	**
L. Antietam Cr. [south]	20	II (III+)	2.8	17	500cfs	**

CONOCOCHEAGUE CREEK

Conococheague ("water of many turns") Creek flows for 80 sinuous miles, northwest for the first 20 and then south-southwest to Williamsport Md. (pop. 2,100), only 34 air miles from its start. The gradient keeps decreasing, averaging only 6 ft/mile over the last 65 miles. Section 1 is exploratory. Section 2 is the start of Gertler's coverage, but he reports strainers and braiding galore in this stretch. At the start of section 2, Rocky Mountain and Carbaugh runs enter; these are also described below.

Section 1: Long Pine Run to Caledonia State Park

Gradient	Difficulty	Distance	Area	Scenery	Strainers	Rating
65	?	1.8	12	?	?	?

USGS Quad – Fayetteville; Source – Scouting
N39 55.82, W77 26.37 to N39 54.89, W77 28.03

Long Pine Run and Conococheague Creek cross Pa.233 (Pine Grove Road) 150 yards apart, and meet a quarter mile later to form a runnable *"explorers' special."*. But they start out overgrown with rhododendrons, so you need to carry a quarter mile down a trail alongside Long Pine Run to put in at the confluence. Soon the creek enters the surreal world of what used to be the Chambersburg Reservoir (which collapsed and was replaced by the Long Pine Run Reservoir). After almost a mile through the ex-reservoir, the creek reenters the woods. As it approaches Pa. 233 again, it appears to braid through the rhododendron woods – be careful here. It is probably wise to do this run in the winter or early spring, before the vegetation blocks your view too much.

Carry across the road, and put back in below the fenced Chambersburg Water Intake Station (where you will lose some of the flow). A mile later, it meets its main upstream tributaries in Caledonia State Park. It is likely to pass through additional rhododendron thickets, and a dangerous strainer was visible just upstream of the bridge in the Park. The gradient in this last mile is a bit lower (55 ft/mile vs. 72 ft/mile above), but still lively. On warm days, the final stretch may be filled with people wading and swimming, as this is a popular park (with a pool, water slides, etc.).

GAUGE: Minimum would be about 60 cfs on Tonoloway and Bermudian creeks.

Section 2: Caledonia State Park (Rocky Mtn. Run) to Mt. Pleasant Road

Gradient	Difficulty	Distance	Area	Scenery	Strainers	Rating
37	II+	4.3	36	C+	1-3/mi.	*

USGS Quad – Fayetteville; Source – Gertler; scouting
N39 54.54, W77 28.83 to N39 55.13, W77 33.39

In Caledonia State Park, Carbaugh and Rocky Mountain runs enter, to form a much more frequently available waterway. But according to Gertler, strainers and braiding are serious problems for the next few miles. And after these few miles of section 2, the gradient drops sharply and there is little whitewater.

GAUGE: You need 35 cfs on Tonoloway (Needmore) and Bermudian creeks.

> Caledonia State Park was the site of the iron furnace built and owned by **Thaddeus Stevens** (who came from Caledonia County, Vermont), the leader of the Radical Republicans around the time of the Civil War. The furnace was destroyed by the Confederate forces under General Jubal Early, probably because of Thaddeus Stevens' strong anti-slavery position. The Appalachian Trail passes through the Park.

ROCKY MOUNTAIN RUN: Raccoon Run to Conococheague Creek

Gradient	Difficulty	Distance	Area	Scenery	Strainers	Rating
80	?	1.8	6	?	?	?

USGS Quad – Fayetteville; Source – Scouting
N39 53.08, W77 29.26 to N39 54.54, W77 28.83

This *"explorers' special"* is the smallest of the Conococheague Creek headwaters. It is narrow, braids in at least one spot, and can be expected to have lots of strainers. But it has a nice gradient and runs along the road, so you can take out whenever you want to.

GAUGE: You need 125 cfs on Tonoloway (Needmore) and Bermudian creeks.

CARBAUGH RUN: Coleman's Cr. Campground to Conococheague Cr.

Gradient	Difficulty	Distance	Area	Scenery	Strainers	Rating
78	?	1.2	10	?	?	?

USGS Quad – Fayetteville; Source – Scouting
N39 54.01, W77 27.46 to N39 54.54, W77 28.83

This *"explorers' special"* follows US 30 for its final 1.5 miles, and then joins Rocky Mountain Run for 0.2 miles to the confluence with Conococheague Creek. But access to a put in is a constraint. It is a 1.5 mile paddle from the sign to "El Waho," but the area is posted. The same is true at Coleman's Creek Campground, 0.3 miles later, but there is more likely to be someone there to give permission. A final option is after another 0.3 miles, where there is a large cleared area just where the creek bends left into the Caledonia Public Golf Course. All of these options offer only short trips on Carbaugh Run, but you could then continue onto section 2 of Conococheague Creek.

GAUGE: Look for 80 cfs on Tonoloway (Needmore) and Bermudian creeks.

MARSH RUN [south]: Grimes (Houser Road) to Potomac River

Gradient	Difficulty	Distance	Area	Scenery	Strainers	Rating
35 (80)	II+	2.2	19	?	?	?

USGS Quad – Williamsport; Source – Scouting access points and last rapid on foot
N39 31.23, W77 46.27 to N39 30.09, W77 46.76

This *"explorers' special"* runs parallel to and 3-4 miles west of Antietam Creek, south of Hagerstown. It has its own online gauge, but for some reason that gauge is up even less often than would be expected for its drainage area.

At Grimes, put in at the lower bridge. At 0.6 miles, you pass the gauging station and enter the grounds of a religious camp. At 2.1 miles, portage Taylors Landing Road, where the water pours through a pipe. The final 150 yards to the large culvert beneath the C&O Canal looks like continuous class II+. Scout for strainers, including at the steep entrance to the culvert. Below the culvert, take out on the left and carry to the towpath.

GAUGE: Look for at least 85 cfs on the Marsh Run gauge at Grimes.

ANTIETAM CREEK

Antietam (allegedly "swift water," although paddlers are skeptical) Creek begins just north of the Mason-Dixon Line, where its East and West branches meet. Its many beautiful stone arch bridges, from 1823-63, were built next to factories – mills (for grain, wood, tanning, paper and textiles), iron foundries, distilleries, breweries, wagon makers etc. Springs from the underlying limestone help the flow during dry periods.

Between sections 1 and 2 is an ugly, trashy and even-flatter (4 ft/mile) stretch of 5.8 miles through the outskirts of Hagerstown.

Section 1: Confluence of Branches (Waynesboro) to Security (Md.)

Gradient	Difficulty	Distance	Area	Scenery	Strainers	Rating
6	I (II+)	12.3	93	B	<1/mi.	*

USGS Quad – Smithsburg/Hagerstown; Source – Gertler; running the second weir

N39 43.45, W77 36.29 via N39 39.18, W77 39.65 (mile 8) to N39 38.79, W77 41.32

The first put in is on the East Branch at Pa. 316, just above the confluence, and the last take out is where Antietam Drive comes alongside the creek at Security, but there are numerous ways to shorten the trip. The scenery is attractive, and there are frequent riffles. There are two 3-4 foot weirs (class II+) that you can portage: at 8 miles, right after Trovinger Mill Road comes alongside, and just before the final take out.

GAUGE: Look for 175 cfs on Antietam Creek at Waynesboro.

Section 2: Funkstown (Oak Ridge Rd.) to Potomac R. (Harpers Ferry Rd.)

Gradient	Difficulty	Distance	Area	Scenery	Strainers	Rating
7	II	23.4	182	B-	<<1/mi.	**

USGS Quad – Funkstown/Keedysville; Source – Personal descent 6/96 and 5/98

N39 36.58, W77 42.74 via N39 22.25, W77 42.61 (Md. 68) to N39 25.02, W77 44.53

This pleasant novice section is usually divided at mile 10.1, at Devils Backbone Park, Md. 68 (200 sq. mi.; 6-foot dam), into two trips. The upper trip has class II rapids at crumbled dams under Poffenberger, Wagaman and Roxbury Roads, which often collect strainers. The lower trip, through the Antietam National Battlefield, is easier to catch but is only class I, except for Furnace Rapid at the takeout. In high water, you can start this lower trip at Barnes Road, 1.3 miles up Beaver Creek (see below).

Because the gradient is low, a 10-12 mile trip becomes tedious in low water. There are many shorter trips, but access spots get closed from time to time. For example, rude behavior by some tubers and rafters at the hamlet of Antietam got the National Park Service to close that access. Check with the Paddlers Access Network (PAN) for news.

GAUGE: On the Sharpsburg gauge, minimum is 3.2 (380 cfs) for the upper part, 2.7 (190 cfs) around Devils Backbone, and 2.5 (150 cfs) below Md. 34. As an earlier indicator, look for 140 cfs at Waynesboro to put in at Funkstown.

> Greg Mallet-Prevost's **Antietam Creek Canoe Company** (301-582-1469) is situated at Devil's Backbone Mill. He'll rent you canoes, with or without guide service and/or instruction.

> **Battle of Antietam.** Antietam Creek is best known for the inconclusive contest there on September 17, 1962 – 23,000 killed and wounded in the bloodiest one-day battle of the Civil War. The Confederates on the west bank beat back repeated attacks by Union forces twice their size. Crossing the creek, especially at what became known as Burnside Bridge, was a major challenge. The South failed in its objectives (getting Maryland to secede; convincing the European powers to recognize the Confederacy; making northerners bear as much of the brunt of the war as southerners), but General McClellan missed a golden opportunity to crush the Army of Northern Virginia and thereby win the war.

> **Braddock's Crossing.** In 1755, General William Braddock, commanding 1,400 redcoats plus local militia under Lt. Col. George Washington, issued an order to his advance officer to "go immediately to that part of the Antietam ... and press such Boats or Canoes as you shall meet with upon the river...." There were no boats, but with the creek so shallow, none were needed. Given his knowledge of the area, how could Braddock's attack on the French have failed?!

WEST BRANCH, ANTIETAM CR.: Pa. 316 to Antietam Creek

Gradient	Difficulty	Distance	Area	Scenery	Strainers	Rating
16	I	5.2	34	D+	2-3/mi.	-

USGS Quad – Waynesboro/Smithsburg; Source – Gertler
N39 46.63, W77 35.13 to N 39 43.49, W77 36.33

The West Branch descends steeply from South Mountain for 3.5 miles to Mont Alto, but is too small to paddle there. It then heads south alongside SR 997 for 5 miles and west for a mile until its main (and unnamed) tributary just below Pa. 316. The 6 miles above Pa. 316 are twice as steep as those below, but are full of fences (as is the unnamed tributary, which is about the same size). Below the confluence, the West Branch is more runnable, but it is a dull trip, complicated by fences and downed trees. At least the shuttle is easy, as Pa. 316 goes from confluence to confluence.

GAUGE: About 225 cfs on Antietam Creek at Waynesboro is needed.

EAST BRANCH, ANTIETAM CREEK

This challenging Antietam Creek headwater is not without problems. It flows for 15 miles, from Michaux State Forest to Waynesboro. After 5 miles, near Old Forge, section 1 begins. Where the creek leaves the forest, section 2 starts. There is a 1.4 mile break before section 3, because of low footbridges in a golf course and a weir below it.

Section 1: Rattlesnake Run Road to Leaf Road

Gradient	Difficulty	Distance	Area	Scenery	Strainers	Rating
90 (120)	III-	1.5	12	B+	3-5/mi.	***

USGS Quad – Iron Springs; Source – Personal descent 6/06 (second half); hiking
N39 47.69, W77 28.76 to N39 46.82, W77 29.80

This is a fine short trip except for strainers that would be very dangerous in high water, due to the scarcity of eddies. The woodland scenery is delightful and the rapids continuous but not particularly difficult. After a quarter mile, you pass a picnic area, the Antietam shelter and the Appalachian Trail footbridge. Midway, you cross Old Forge Road; by then, the gradient is down to 80 ft/mile. The creek braids three or four times; the left channel always has the most water. Take out at Leaf Road (the second bridge).

   GAUGE: Minimum is 600 cfs on Antietam Creek at Waynesboro (3 hours later), 400 cfs on Catoctin Creek, and 60 cfs on Bermudian Creek (West Conewago basin, Pa.).

Section 2: Leaf Road to Mentzer Gap Road

Gradient	Difficulty	Distance	Area	Scenery	Strainers	Rating
40	II	2.3	16	D	4-6/mi.	-

USGS Quad – Iron Springs/Waynesboro; Source – Personal descent 6/06
N39 46.82, W77 29.80 to N39 45.89, W77 31.46

This section has mediocre rapids, few eddies, and many strainers, which are often dangerous or require unpleasant portages. After half a mile you leave the state forest and the scenery deteriorates badly. Furthermore, although the gradient has dropped, the danger is higher, because the creek is narrower, deeper and twistier. On one portage, the vegetation was so dense and thorny that we could barely get back to the creek. At another spot, there was a low cable beneath a footbridge around a blind turn.

   The creek crosses Mentzer Gap Road in two channels, 150 yards apart. We took the river-left one – for the last mile. So if you ever wish to plead temporary insanity, and you therefore run this section, please take the right channel and report on what is in there.

   GAUGE: Minimum is 400 cfs at Waynesboro, 275 cfs on Catoctin Creek.

Section 3: Robert E. Stum Soccer Complex to Antietam Creek

Gradient	Difficulty	Distance	Area	Scenery	Strainers	Rating
18	II- (III+)	5.2	27	B-	1/mi.	**

USGS Quad – Waynesboro/Smithsburg; Source – Personal descent 5/04
N39 45.30, W77 32.60 to N39 43.45, W77 36.29

Below the Waynesboro Country Club is an unrunnable 5-foot weir and no parking or rapids for a mile, until the Soccer Complex, off Country Club Road. Soon you face "Wildlife Reserve:

No Trespassing" signs; proceed at your own risk. In the middle of this riffle-filled half mile is a short man-made boulder garden (class III+), with a drop of 5 feet, that requires high water. Soon afterwards, in the outskirts of Waynesboro, is Pa.16 – an alternative put in (at 1.2 miles). Next comes a half-mile of class II- through the Renfrew Museum Park, followed by a short channelized stretch. At 2.1-miles, Red Run enters. The only rapid after that is a class II ledge at SR 997, complicated by a cable (duck under on the right). The final half of the trip is class I and problem free, except for a downed tree or two. The scenery ranges from rock cliffs to commercial sprawl.

GAUGE: Look for 275 cfs on Antietam Creek at Waynesboro, 2 hours later. If the riffle at the put in has a clean channel, everything (except the class III+) will be runnable.

RED RUN: Amsterdam Road to East Branch, Antietam Cr. (Welty Rd.)

Gradient	Difficulty	Distance	Area	Scenery	Strainers	Rating
30	II-	1.5	11*	C	2-4/mi.	*

USGS Quad – Smithsburg; Source – Personal descent 5/04
N39 44.01, W77 32.52 to N39 44.26, W77 34.13

*(including Falls Creek, which enters after 100 yards)

Red Run is class IV as it races down the Hanging Valley, with a drainage area of just 3-4 sq. mi. and many strainers. Near Rouzerville, it is joined by Falls Creek, and can occasionally be paddled. This short trip, one mile north of the Mason-Dixon Line, can be extended by continuing 3.1 miles down the East Branch, to Antietam Creek.

We put in where Red Run pools alongside Amsterdam Road, and then turns left 90 degrees over a paved, 3-foot sloping ledge. For 100 yards, the creek is narrow and strainer strewn, but then Falls Creek enters from the left. In higher water, put in on Falls Creek at Midvale Road (SR 418), 300 yards above the confluence.

The remainder of the run has lots of long riffles, several class II- ledges, and a few strainers. Up to a level of about six inches, there is enough clearance under all four bridges. Below the second bridge, there was a wire strand that we could pass under, followed by a cable with loose filaments hanging down; a little later, this was repeated in reverse. The third road crossing is a private covered bridge.

GAUGE: Minima would be 500 cfs at Waynesboro, 350 cfs on Catoctin Creek and 50 cfs on Bermudian Creek. Check the level near the take out.

In the Falls Creek watershed are two historic sites. **Fort Ritchie** was the Military Intelligence Training Center (MITC) – nicknamed the Mythical Institute for Total Confusion – during World War II. A few miles north of there, straddling the Mason-Dixon Line, **Pen Mar** was developed in the 1870s by the Western Maryland Railway as a summer resort for Baltimoreans. At one point it had seven hotels, and its heyday lasted into the 1920s, before the advent of the automobile increased vacation options. Its great views and cool breezes now attract hang gliders.

🛶 LITTLE ANTIETAM CREEK [north]

The main tributaries in this basin have such imaginative names as East Branch, West Branch and Little Antietam Creek (the last used twice). This Little Antietam Creek runs just north of Smithsburg and south of the Mason-Dixon Line. Its headwaters flow westward through gaps in South Mountain (now as for those mountain namers ...), past the Appalachian Trail. The southern branch is dammed to form Hagerstown's Edgemont Reservoir, while the northern branch tears down Raven Rock Hollow at over 200 ft/mile. Just below the dam, the two tiny branches meet, and section 1 begins.

Section 1: Greensburg Road to Md. 64 (Smithsburg Pike)

Gradient	Difficulty	Distance	Area	Scenery	Strainers	Rating
90 (150)	III	1.5	6	C	1-3/mi.	**

USGS Quad – Smithsburg; Source – Personal descent 6/96
N39 40.11, W77 33.16 to N39 40.71, W77 34.36

This section is dangerous but so hard to catch that few ever need worry about that. It is steep and continuous, but was once channelized and has no big drops. The stream is so narrow that we drove over it the first time without noticing. We put in at Greensburg and Old Raven Rock Roads, just north of Md. 491 and Md. 92, and only 3 miles from the first trickles. Bushes grow in the streambed, but there was a clear channel for the first 10 yards, so off we went, Ed Evangelidi eschewing his double-bladed paddle (which wouldn't fit between the bushes). The friendly landowners saw us off and drove down to watch at each bridge, until we took so long that they probably gave us up for drowned.

Fortunately, we had scouted the first low-water bridge, and knew the eddy where we had to start our portage. We even had permission from the homeowner there to cross her property, although, upon hearing that we came from Lawyer City, she asked for our assurance that we would not sue her in case of a mishap. (Of course we agreed; after all, it wasn't in writing.) Just after that came the first of the two 150-ft/mile sections, and we were fortunate that one of the rare eddies was at hand when we spotted a fallen tree. As we hiked down there, we saw a wooden-board fence a bit further down. Jamie Deehan cut out the tree trunk and propped up the fence with strong poles, so that we could just zoom beneath it; the portage looked particularly unappealing.

GAUGE: We ran this after a 4-inch rainfall. Catoctin Creek needs 850 cfs and Antietam Creek at Waynesboro 1,200 cfs (both projected to 3 hours after put in).

Section 2: Md. 64 to Md. 62

Gradient	Difficulty	Distance	Area	Scenery	Strainers	Rating
25 (65)	II	5.2	8	B	1/mi.	**

USGS Quad – Smithsburg; Source – Personal descent (except last 1.5 mi.) 6/96
N39 40.71, W77 34.36 to N39 40.95, W77 37.73

The gradient and strainers diminish steadily, but the frequent easy rapids keep the water interesting. After 2 miles, the creek leaves the woods and passes through several ranches, with stone mansions and plentiful cattle, ducks, geese and horses. Bowmans Mill, at 3.7 miles, is quite scenic, but complicated slightly by a cattle fence under the bridge. A sign warning of the fence suggested that this was not a first descent.

Below Bowmans Mill (20 sq. mi.), the creek reenters the woods for a mile; we were told to expect strainers there. The gradient averages 25 ft/mile for that first mile, but then drops off sharply. Md. 62, a half mile later, is a good take out. Below that, it is a flat half-mile to Antietam Creek, and then three-fourths mile to Clopper Road.

GAUGE: Look for at least 600 cfs on Catoctin Creek and 850 cfs on Antietam Creek at Waynesboro (both 2 hours after put in).

MARSH RUN [north]: Paramount (Spring Creek Rd.) to below Md. 60

Gradient	Difficulty	Distance	Area	Scenery	Strainers	Rating
35	II (III)	1.0	30	C	3-5/mi.	*

USGS Quad – Hagerstown; Source – Personal descent 3/97
N39 41.23, W77 41.12 to N39 40.68, W77 40.78

When outgoing (both an antonym and synonym of "retiring") President Eisenhower was asked to name a contribution of his Vice President Nixon to policy formation, he replied: "Give me a week, and I'll think of something." I've had much longer to find positive aspects of my paddle on Marsh Run, and here they are:

a) I paddled alone, so I didn't lose any buddies by bringing them here.

b) All of the barbed wire fences were single strands that I could paddle under.

c) The howling winds were at my back (but on my bike shuttle, they were in my face).

d) I saw lots of wildlife – a groundhog, a muskrat, three great blue herons and scores of mallards and Canada geese.

e) The first mile is rather nice, and includes a class III rock garden and a pair of tight class II chutes; **paddlers should definitely limit their trip to that one mile**.

f) Early in the final mile there is a class III+ rock garden (which I half ran).

g) This may have been a first descent – and, for the final two miles, should be a last descent as well!

Well, that's not such a bad list. In fact, the creek started out flat but fine. I found a nice put in at the confluence with the West Branch, in the Paramount neighborhood. After a quarter mile, I slipped under a strand of barbed wire, and a quarter mile later exited the farm the same way. A couple of strainers didn't bother me much. Then came a short class II rapid followed by a class III (with three closely-spaced drops). As I passed under Md. 60 and down a twisty class II rapid, I considered the creek a good discovery. There is a side road a quarter mile below Md. 60, and paddlers should take out there.

GAUGE: You need 265 cfs on Antietam Cr. at Waynesboro (2 hours after put in).

> **Two Miles of Strainer Hell.** But how was I to know to take out after one mile? Over the remaining two miles (and two hours), I had to portage 25-30 trees, mostly along the edge of a pasture full of cows. The barbed wire fences were less of a problem, but made me worry about irate farmers. The creek was a straight, flat channel, until a short rapid and a sharp right turn led into a steep, rocky, 10-yard long drop of about 8 feet. The left channel (class III) was blocked by a fallen tree, while the right channel (class III+) required a 90-degree turn in turbulent water. I started down the right, carried the biggest drop and ran the bottom one.
>
> At 1.4-miles, the creek left the farmland, flowed under Fiddlesburg Road, and began passing through backyards. I foolishly decided to give the creek a second chance, in the hope that homeowners would keep the stream clean. Indeed, the density of fallen trees wasn't quite as great, but fences and footbridges compensated.
>
> I did not feel safe until the Hagerstown suburb of Security, where Marsh Run joins Antietam Creek just at the top of a 4-foot weir (class II+). I took in a bit of water, bounced through the waves below, and took out on river right. And then it was four miles of cycling into the wind.

BEAVER CREEK: Beaver Creek Village to Antietam Cr. (Md. 68)

Gradient	Difficulty	Distance	Area	Scenery	Strainers	Rating
15	II- (II)	8.5	20	C	1/mi.	**

USGS Quad – Funkstown; Source – Personal descent (last 3.6 miles) 11/97; Trip reports (Tom Gray, RC Forney); AW site.
N39 35.01, W77 38.56 via N39 32.37, W77 41.97 (Barnes) to N39 32.09, W77 42.55

You can put in just below I-70, by the Park and Ride in Beaver Creek Village, where Black Rock Creek enters. The stream flows through pastures and beaver meadows, and while the wires across the creek are generally high enough to duck under, there is a smattering of fences and downed trees. After 1.5 miles, you reach Doubs Mill. Portage the dam on the right (or run the far right channel, if there is enough water). Most of the water splits into two channels that both run through the old mill house; **the family has requested that paddlers not boat through their house**. There is a low-water bridge to portage shortly below, and you then pass under US 40.

From there, the creek becomes prettier as it meanders southwest, with many riffles, past historic-looking buildings, cattle and backyards. In 1.5 miles there is a series of ledges (class II) best run on the left. About a mile later, beware of possible fences near Toms Road. Half a mile after that, you reach Kline Mill, at Alt. US 40. Below there, several fences may require tricky maneuvers, have hard put-ins below, or be dangerous in high water. The final mile has the prettiest scenery, passing through woods between high cliffs, and has a long class II- rapid as well as other riffles; you can put in at Barnes Road, and make this a nice start to a trip down Antietam Creek, when there is enough water.

GAUGE: You need about 285 cfs on Catoctin Creek and 400 cfs at Waynesboro to start at the top, and two thirds of those figures to put in at Kline Mill. The staff gauge by the old farm bridge across from the put-in should be at least 1.3.

On Beaver Creek, above the put in, is Cavetown, once the site of the **largest known cave** in Maryland. The cave, first described in 1745, was badly damaged by 19th Century souvenir hunters, and finally destroyed by quarrying in the 1920s.

Beaver Creek is partially spring fed. One spring's 5-10 cfs, 50-degree water is used for rainbow trout in the A.M.Powell state **fish hatchery**. It also keeps the creek from freezing over, and enables it to be used for trout fishing even in mid-winter and mid-summer.

Beavers returned to the creek around 1986, after more than a century's absence.

Doubs Mill was built in 1811-21, by Samuel Funk. The creek was dammed to get a 9-foot head, which produced 12 horsepower from a pair of overshot water wheels. The reservoir refilled at night. The mill operated commercially until 1930 and for friends and family of Frank Doub until 1945. The runnable sluice gate with a 5-foot drop dates from 1908. The water that is diverted into the old mill is audible and visible from the living room.

Beaver Creek's largest tributary, **Little Beaver Creek**, might be run for its final two miles at 35-ft/mile and 7 sq. mi., but it had several visible fences.

As the Confederates retreated from **Gettysburg**, JEB Stuart's cavalry screened their route, while Union cavalry tried in vain to capture their supply train. The cavalries clashed along and near Beaver Creek, but the main Union forces moved too slowly to prevent the Confederates from escaping via pontoon bridges across the Potomac.

LITTLE ANTIETAM CREEK [south]: Dog Street Road to Antietam Creek

Gradient	Difficulty	Distance	Area	Scenery	Strainers	Rating
20	II (III+)	2.8*	17	B	0-2/mi.	**

USGS Quad – Keedysville; Source – Personal descent 3/97
N39 28.61, W77 41.31 via N39 29.22, W77 41.98 (dam) to N39 27.91, W77 43.54

*(plus 2.2 miles on Antietam Creek to Md. 34)

This Little Antietam Creek is too doggone small and dogged by fences until Dog Creek enters at Dog Street Road. The put in is the Felfoot Bridge, a double stone arch built in 1854. All of the land from there to Keedysville is part of Felfoot Farm (surveyed in 1734 and owned by only three families), so ask permission at the house by the put in.

The stream heads northwest for a mile, past fields, moss-covered rocky hills and a pair of wrecked railroad bridges, with frequent class II- rapids. It is narrow and intimate. The only two fences were broken down – the farm's 200 dairy cattle had been sold because, as the owner told me, "I wasn't going to put diapers on all my cattle!"

After the creek turns west into Keedysville, there is 600 yards of backwater of a 6-foot dam. It is class III+ at moderate levels, but scout first. You can portage on the right. For a short trip, you might put in here. Two hundred yards later is Hess's Mill Bridge, built 1832; its double stone arch is unique in that one arch is much bigger than the other. The next 0.7 miles has just a few class II- drops, until you pass beneath Keedysville Road.

This final half-mile has the best whitewater. After several class II and II- ledges and rock gardens, the creek heads towards the 5-story Pry's Mill, which served as a Union hospital at the Battle of Antietam. The longest and best rapid, a class II+, is just as you pass the mill. The take out at the Hitt Bridge, a quarter mile upstream on Antietam Creek (built in 1830 at the ford used by General Braddock's army in 1755 en route west to disaster during the French and Indian War) is now closed, so you must continue 2.2 miles downstream to Md. 34 (Shepherdstown Pike).

GAUGE: The rapid below Keedysville Road should be cleanly runnable. Look for 350 cfs on Catoctin Creek and 500 cfs at Waynesboro.

The **Hitt Bridge** is named after three brothers, Martin, Daniel and Samuel, who moved to the area because they were in love with three sisters, Sarah, Margaret and Ann Smith, whose house overlooked Antietam Creek. The story ended up two-thirds happy – Sarah died young, but Margaret and Ann married Daniel and Samuel, respectively.

Prys Mill operated from the mid-18th Century until 1926. It is now a private residence. A 22-foot dam, some 100 yards upstream, enabled the generation of 24 horsepower. The dam was wiped out by flooding from Hurricane Hazel in 1956, thereby restoring the good rapids.

A mile and a half northeast of Keedysville is the **Crystal Grottoes**, Maryland's only commercial show cave. It is kept natural, with only white floodlights added.

Until 1852, the town was named Cent**re**ville, but there was public dissatisfaction, because much of their mail was mistakenly delivered to Cent**er**ville, Md. The petition to change the name was signed by so many Keedys, that the Post Office selected the name **Keedysville**.

At the **Battle of Antietam**, Little Antietam Creek marked the northern edge of the Union position. After the battle, over 1,000 wounded Union soldiers were treated in Keedysville.

CATOCTIN CREEK AREA

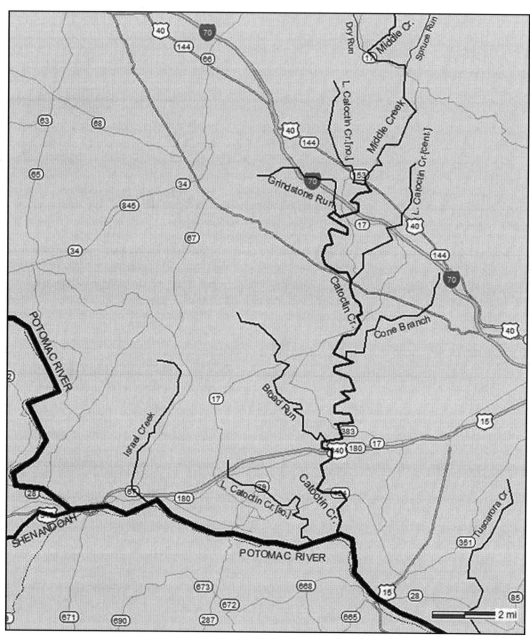

Chapter 13:

CATOCTIN CREEK AREA

Between Antietam Creek and the Monocacy River is **Catoctin Creek** (118 sq. mi. basin), a popular novice stream that coasts gently to the Potomac. But nearby are some whitewater wonders. Until recently, few people knew of **Middle Creek,** the main headwater of Catoctin Creek, which contains up to class IV+ rapids. Now, it has been popularized on the Monocacy Canoe Club message board, and is run often when it is up. For those who can't quite handle that difficulty level, there are two other delights: **Israel Creek**, and **Little Catoctin Creek [south]**, which have the most attractive and challenging runnable gorges that enter the Potomac from its north bank anywhere in that big river's 160-mile journey from Old Town/Green Spring to tidewater. There is also a pair of quite steep and tiny "explorers' specials" – *Little Catoctin Creek [north]* and *Grindstone Run*. And there is a trio of easier Catoctin Creek tributaries – **Broad Run, Cone Branch** and **Little Catoctin Creek [central]** – plus a final, strainer-filled class I, direct Potomac tributary, **Tuscarora Creek**. It's not a bad mixture for this small area.

Each of three Little Catoctin Creeks has a different relationship to Catoctin Creek itself. The southern one near Brunswick never meets Catoctin Creek. The northern and smallest one, near Myersville, is a headwater (Catoctin Creek is formed at the confluence of Middle Creek and this Little Catoctin Creek). The third and largest (but still very small), in the center of the watershed near Middletown, is a side stream of Catoctin Creek.

The area was settled in the 1730s, mainly by German immigrants. It is still rural, with Brunswick (6,000) the largest town and Middletown (4,000) the most historic. It is separated on the east from the Monocacy basin by the Catoctin Mountains and on the west from Antietam Creek by the Blue Ridge and South Mountain, with Israel Creek hiding in a narrow valley between the two.

> Catoctin Creek is named after the Catoctin Mountains. The probable meaning of Catoctin is **"speckled mountain,"** after the patterns on the local rocks, although others think it just means "big mountain." Alas, no one used any "alternative interrogation techniques" to get the Indians to explain better.

> Now if you are looking for something really small and steep, some locals have paddled part of "**Dargan Run**" (a.K.A. "Death Run") which flows into the Potomac near Shinham's Landing on Dargan's Bend (a put in for trips down the Needles section of the Potomac). It's only half a mile, with a drainage area of 1.3 sq. mi. and a 250-ft/mile gradient.

GAUGES: The only river gauge in this area is on **Catoctin Creek** at Middletown (Md.17), with 67 sq. mi. drainage; it is the **zero-level reference** in the table below. The gauge on Piney Run (14 sq. mi.), across the Potomac, is useful especially for Israel Creek, Little Catoctin Creek [south], Broad Run and Tuscarora Creek. Your chances for all the little streams are best when the gauge on Catoctin Creek is still rising. There are no rain gauges reported.

name	gradient	difficulty	length	area	gauge	rating
Israel Creek	67 (100)	III (III+)	2.9	8	700cfs	****
L. Catoc. Cr. [south] – Sec. 1	28	II	4.1	4	950cfs	**
–Sec. 2	31 (70)	III (IV-)	2.6	9	700cfs	****
Catoctin Creek	13	II-	24.5	35	200cfs	**
Little Catoctin Cr. [north]	68 (130)	?	2.8	5	800cfs	?
Middle Creek – Section 1	85 (170)	IV-(IV+)	3.3	12	600cfs	!!!!
– Section 2	45	II+	3.8	21	300cfs	***
Grindstone Run	70 (95)	?	1.6	5	800cfs	?
Little Catoc. Cr. [central]	40	II	3.0	13	400cfs	**
Cone Branch	40	II	1.4	6	600cfs	**
Broad Run	25	I	2.8	13	325cfs	*
Tuscarora Creek	13	I	5.3	13	325cfs	-

⏵⏵⏵ ISRAEL CREEK: Frog Eye Road to Keep Tryst Road (Md. 180)

Gradient	Difficulty	Distance	Area	Scenery	Strainers	Rating
67 (100)	III (III+)	2.9	8	A-	0-2/mi.	****

USGS Quad – Harpers Ferry; Source – Personal descent 5/98
N39 21.64, W77 40.71 to N39 19.74, W77 41.05

North of the Potomac, the Blue Ridge and South Mountain are straight (north-northwest) and parallel, only two miles apart. In between is the Pleasant Valley, down which, for 8 miles, runs Israel Creek. The Appalachian Trail follows the C&O Canal across the mouth of Israel Creek, before ascending South Mountain. Israel Creek can be seen at spots from the Appalachian Trail and even better from a valley trail along the abandoned B&O Railroad tracks (which might become part of a rails-to-trails route).

But the best way to see this creek is from the water, and what a delightful trip it is. Put in at Frog Eye Road (a dead-end spur off Md. 67, which parallels the stream). The water is class II- past Garretts Mill Road and Valley Road (at 1.2 miles). Gradually the gorge deepens, the gradient increases (from 45 ft/mile the first mile, to 95 ft/mile the last mile) and the rapids lengthen. By the time you pass under Md. 67 (at 2.3 miles), the rock gardens cum ledges are class III and the scenery is class A. The old B&O tracks are more picturesque than obtrusive, even as one paddles around or between their stone pillars.

When you can hardly see the next rapid because of vegetation in the water, get out on the steep right bank and scout. The water filters through the trees and funnels to the right, to a narrow, 4-foot ledge. The ledge itself is straightforward but the approach is not, as the main current flows strongly to the right and bounces off the wall. The rapid is class III+, and less-experienced paddlers should portage on river left.

Below, the rapids continue past US 340. The final drop, a short but steep class III down almost to the level of the Potomac, is a fitting end to a glorious trip. Take out just below the bridge on river left, where a narrow trail climbs up to a small parking area.

GAUGE: At zero level, the river-left cement shelf beneath Garretts Mill Road is one foot above the water. Adequate flow at Frog Eye Road is not enough, as the creek gets much wider below. The Catoctin Creek gauge should reach 700 cfs (3-4 hours later), and Piney Run (Va.) 150 cfs (1-2 hours later).

> Although the original source of the creek's name is obvious, it may have come via a local surname. A **Midshipman Israel** from this area died heroically in Tripoli Harbor in 1804, during the Barbary Wars ("… to the shores of Tripoli"). How's that for esoteria!
>
> Near the put in is the hamlet of **Yarrowsburg**, one of the few towns named for an African-American woman, "Aunt Polly" Yarrow, a freed slave, who first settled the area.
>
> In September 1862, during the invasion of the North that ended at Antietam, southern troops passed through the area. McClellan lucked onto a copy of Lee's battle plan, including the risky decision to split the Confederate forces in order to capture Harpers Ferry, but still moved too slowly to take advantage of this. At Crampton's Gap, near the source of Israel Creek, at the **Battle of South Mountain**, a 5,000-man Confederate division under General D.H.Hill blocked for a day the advance of the entire Union army, until it was too late to save the 12,000-man Union garrison at Harpers Ferry.

LITTLE CATOCTIN CREEK [south]

Almost all of the water between South Mountain and Catoctin Mountain makes it into Catoctin Creek, except for the bit in this stream, which flows southeast towards its larger neighbor, but is still a mile away when they empty into the Potomac. It is a delightful creek, especially where it cuts down to the Potomac through a dramatic gorge. One word of warning; we came across 8 fences or remnants thereof. Only 4 of these were still functional, and all could be slipped under without difficulty; however, fences get rebuilt.

Section 1: Jefferson Pike (Md. 180) to Point of Rocks Road (Md. 464)

Gradient	Difficulty	Distance	Area	Scenery	Strainers	Rating
28	II	4.1	4	B-	1/mi.	**

USGS Quad – Harpers Ferry/Point of Rocks; Source – Personal descent 3/98
N39 20.46, W77 38.06 to N39 19.40, W77 35.57

Phil Dimodica called the first 1.5 miles, to Md. 79, "the best of pasture paddling." The cows were merely curious, the fence strands easily avoided, the countryside pretty, the strainers few and uncomplicated, the rapids many and uncomplicated. The last 200 yards of this stretch is the best – a long class II rock garden through a mini-gorge.

Below Md. 79, the creek flows mainly through the woods, with attractive low hills and cliffs. The rapids remain class II, strainers are surprisingly few and wildlife is abundant – we saw two gray foxes plus a herd of deer.

GAUGE: Catoctin Creek should be at least 950 cfs (4 hours afterward), and Piney Run (Va.) 200 cfs (2 hours after you put in).

Section 2: Point of Rocks Road (Md. 464) to Potomac River

Gradient	Difficulty	Distance	Area	Scenery	Strainers	Rating
31 (70)	III (IV-)	2.6*	9	A	0-2/mi.	****

USGS Quad – Point of Rocks; Source – Personal descent 3/98

N39 19.40, W77 35.57 to N39 18.31, W77 33.62

*(plus 1.5 miles on the Potomac to Lander)

The first two miles are like section 1 – pretty scenery, class II rapids and few strainers. Then you reach the fall line, which consists of five rock gardens, each about 100 yards long, with only short pools between them. First comes a class II+ rapid, followed by three class IIIs, the second of them with a tricky hydraulic on an angled ledge at the end. And finally there is a long class IV- rapid, which culminates in a ledge with a strong hole below, on a sharp left-hand turn. You can sneak the first half of this rapid on the far right, and then carry the main drop.

Shortly below are a high railroad bridge and then a low passage under the C&O Canal. (If the Potomac at Harpers Ferry or Point of Rocks is above 14 feet, you will have to carry over the Canal.) There is no access there, so you must paddle 1.5 miles down the Potomac to a boat ramp at Lander, passing the mouth of (big) Catoctin Creek two-thirds of the way down. This is flat water, but it will usually move along fast whenever Little Catoctin Creek [south] is up.

GAUGE: Look for at least 700 cfs on Catoctin Creek (projected to 3 hours after you put in) and 150 cfs on Piney Run (Va.) (1 hour after you start).

CATOCTIN CREEK: Myersville (Brethren Church Rd) to Potomac R

Gradient	Difficulty	Distance	Area	Scenery	Strainers	Rating
13	II-	24.5	35	C+	<1/mi.	**

USGS Quad – Myersville/Middletown/Point of Rocks; Source – Personal descents 5/79 (below Alt US 40) and 4/04 (above Alt US 40); Gertler

N39 30.10, W77 33.14 via N39 27.02, W77 33.77 (Alt US 40) and N39 22.89, W77 34.28 (Poffenberger Road) to N39 18.31, W77 33.62

This long and popular novice run has 14 access points, as the creek winds (it is 13 miles as the crow flies vs. 25 miles as the carp swims) through a pretty valley. The first put in, on Brethren Church Road, is a mile below the confluence of Middle Creek and Little Catoctin Creek [north]. The initial two miles are affected by the sprawl of Myersville and the noise of I-70, but the environment improves after Md. 17. The first 8 miles, to Alt US 40 near Middletown, average 16 ft/mile and include frequent gravel-bar riffles, pretty rock cliffs and a pair of mini-gorges with enough boulders, twists, small drops and play spots to rate class II-. There are a few fences, but two contained sections of loose, orange plastic (a wonderful idea that I have not seen elsewhere), and the others had enough clearance.

The creek widens a bit after Alt US 40, with the addition of Little Catoctin Creek [central], and is somewhat easier to catch (60 sq. mi.). The average gradient of the remaining 17 miles is down to 11 ft/mile, but this is still a bit more than Antietam Creek. It is also more likely to have strainers than Antietam Creek. At mile 10 you pass Md. 17 again; the gauge is downstream of the bridge. Six miles later you pass Poffenberger Road and 1.5 miles after that the Lewis Mill is on river right. The gradient picks up briefly starting at Poffenberger Road, with some of the rapids class II-, so this would be a good put in (85 sq. mi.) for a short paddle down to Md. 160 (3.5 miles) or Md. 464 (5.5 miles), which has a class II- drop under the bridge. The final 3 miles below Md. 464 are flat, and then you must paddle the Potomac half a mile down to the boat ramp at Lander.

GAUGE: Zero level is 2.5 (200 cfs) on the USGS Catoctin Creek (Md.) gauge just downstream of Md. 17. You need a bit less (2.35 or 150 cfs) to put in at Md. 17.

The Missing Catoctin Creek Rapids. The USGS Middletown Quad shows a stretch of 300 yards (above Alt US 40) with a 130-ft/mile gradient. How had past write-ups missed those bodacious rapids? I found some long riffles, up to class II-, with a gradient of perhaps 30 ft/mile.

Probably the most famous Revolutionary War factory was the **Catoctin Furnace**, built in 1774 near a hematite ore deposit and beyond the reach of the British, which used the energy of the creek to produce guns and ammunition for the Continental Army. Afterwards, trees were harvested for charcoal on a 30-year cycle; a few were left to reseed each clear-cut area. The furnace was converted to coal fuel in the 1880s and dismantled in 1905.

LITTLE CATOCTIN CR. [north]: Easterday Rd. to Catoctin Cr.

Gradient	Difficulty	Distance	Area	Scenery	Strainers	Rating
68 (130)	?	2.8*	5	?	?	?

USGS Quad – Myersville; Source – Scouting road access points
N39-32.36, W77 34.57 to N39 30.10, W77 33.14

*(plus 1 mile on Catoctin Creek to Brethren Church Road)

This "*explorers' special*" is the smaller (by far) of the two headwaters of Catoctin Creek, as well as the smallest of the three Little Catoctin creeks. It flows east off of South Mountain for a mile, and then south for five miles to the confluence with Middle Creek. Hike down from Easterday Road to see the waterfall 200 yards above the put in.

There is a good put in at Easterday Road, and in a fifth of a mile, you pass Ward Kline Road. The creek is very narrow and steep here; the first half mile averages 130 ft/mile. The gradient drops over the next mile, until you are alongside US 40, and then picks up a bit approaching a pair of private roads that probably need to be portaged. There are also likely to be fences in this stretch through cattle country.

At 2.2 miles, you cross Church Hill Road and the gradient drops to 30-35 ft/mi. You then pass under US 40 and Md. 17, before merging with Middle Creek to form Catoctin Creek. Take out a flat mile later, at Brethren Church Road.

GAUGE: Look for the Catoctin Creek gauge to reach at least 800 cfs (projected for 5 hours after you start).

MIDDLE CREEK

Middle Creek, and its tributaries Dry Run to the west and Spruce Run to the east, drain the northern Catoctin Valley. Middle Creek (the middle one of these three), in a more rational nomenclature, would be the upstream section of Catoctin Creek itself, as it carries about 80 % of the water that becomes Catoctin Creek at the confluence with Little Catoctin Creek [north]. In very, very high water, Middle Creek becomes paddleable at its confluence with Dry Run, near Wolfsville (section 1). In plain old very high water, and for those who don't want to face the daunting rapids or long portages of section 1, Md. 17 just above Grossnickle Church is the place to start (section 2).

> Don't confuse this stream with the much-smaller **Middle Creek** that flows into Catoctin Creek below Middletown, the Middle Creek in the Monocacy headwaters, or any of the other Middle creeks in Maryland.

Section 1: Wolfsville (Stottlemeyer Road) to Grossnickle Church (Md. 17)

Gradient	Difficulty	Distance	Area	Scenery	Strainers	Rating
85 (170)	IV-(IV+)	3.3	12	B+	1-3/mi.	!!!!

USGS Quad – Myersville; Source – Personal descent 6/06
N39 34.51, W77 33.03 via 39 34.24, W77 31.96 (mile 1.1) to N39 32.77, W77 31.56

For advanced paddlers, this challenging section makes a fine run. It begins at the first reasonable put in on Middle Creek, shortly below Dry Run. After a mild half mile, a string of class III rock gardens brings the stream alongside Md. 17, where there is a pair of class IV- rock gardens that need more water than above. The creek then returns to class II, until a class IV- drop just above Spruce Run, where the left two-thirds of the creek slam into a huge undercut boulder. The scenery is nice, except where the creek is too close to the road.

After Spruce Run adds about 30% to the flow, there is a fantastic half mile of tight, twisty class III and III+ rapids through a lovely gorge. The creek then eases off to class II, and passes a low-water bridge (where a kayaker once got sucked into one of the tubes and needed urgent rescue). After another class III comes the long class IV+ "Little Surprise," with a total drop of over 15 feet, half of it in one ledge. Here, for example, is Steve Revier's report: *"James [Tabor] was next. That man can boat. Perfect placement, right on the line ... until a hidden rock tapped him in the side in the middle of his boof. Landing on his side in an aerated pool ... next drop about a gnat's hair away. He commits to rolling, head just clearing the waterline as his boat hits the next drop, keeping his cool, landing upright like he planned the whole thing."*

After a mellower half mile, there is a class III+ rapid and then the 100-yard class IV+ "S-Turn," with big drops totaling at least 20 feet, curving left and then right. That is followed by a class IV ledge,

"The Fold," that reminds some paddlers of Heizerling and Zinger on the Upper Yough. And then you are out of the gorge and near the take out.

GAUGE: Catoctin Creek should be over 600 cfs (4 hours after you put in).

Section 2: Grossnickle Church (Md. 17) to Catoctin Creek (Myersville)

Gradient	Difficulty	Distance	Area	Scenery	Strainers	Rating
45	II+	3.8*	21	C+	<1/mi.	***

USGS Quad – Myersville; Source – Personal descent 6/06
N39 32.77, W77 31.56 to N39 30.10, W77 33.14

*(plus 1 mile on Catoctin Creek to Brethren Church Road)

This section has a consistent gradient until near the end, and lots of long, fun class II and II+ rock gardens, separated by short pools. If you run this after section 2, you will have plenty of water and waves, with only limited maneuvering required. On the other hand, at zero level, this section is quite technical, with a number of tight turns. There is one low-water bridge, three miles into the trip, divided by an island, with a 3-foot drop that can be paddled over in high water or scraped over/portaged in dryer times.

The scenery alongside Md.17, from which much of the trip can be scouted, is of well-tended homes and gardens. Even in summer, the downstream visibility is pretty good, but in a few spots, especially at islands, you should check for strainers around the bend.

A quarter mile below US 40 (not a good access) is the confluence with Little Catoctin Creek [north], and from there it is a mile of Class I on Catoctin Creek to the take out at Brethren Church Road.

GAUGE: Catoctin Creek should be at least 300 cfs. The river right shelf at Harp Hill Road in Ellerton starts to get dry on top at zero level.

GRINDSTONE RUN: Grindstone Run Park to Catoctin Creek

Gradient	Difficulty	Distance	Area	Scenery	Strainers	Rating
70 (95)	?	1.6*	5	?	?	?

USGS Quad – Myersville/Middletown; Source – Scouting access points
N39 30.49, W77 34.60 to N39 28.36, W77 34.34

*(plus 2.6 miles on Catoctin Creek, at 15 feet/mile, to Station Road)

This tiny *"explorers' special"* is just west of Myersville. Start in Grindstone Run Park, along Monument Road. (One could put in half a mile higher up, at Mt. Tabor Road, but that bit is very steep and narrow; scout from Monument Road before choosing this option.) In a half mile, the stream enters a horse farm, and slows down a bit; be alert for fences. After I-70, there is access at Mill Summers Road, and a quarter mile later you reach Catoctin Creek. Take out 2.6 miles later at Mt. Tabor Road (with an easy shuttle).

GAUGE: Look for 800 cfs on Catoctin Creek (4 hours after you put in).

LITTLE CATOCTIN CR. [central]: Md. 17 to Catoctin Cr.

Gradient	Difficulty	Distance	Area	Scenery	Strainers	Rating
40	II	3.0	13	C	0-2/mi.	**

USGS Quad – Middletown; Source – Personal descent 5/98
N39 28.79, W77 32.46 to N39 27.03, W77 33.77

This trip starts just below I-70, and soon enters cattle country – Ernie Katz had to abort one move when a cow mistook his mottled kayak for a relative. The creek winds between high banks and requires sharp turns in the middle of class II gravel bars with nice waves. Below Pete Wiles Road, almost midway, the creek reenters the woods for most of the remainder. The confluence with Catoctin Creek is just after crossing Old Hagerstown Road and just before the take out on Alt US 40. We had only a few fallen trees and no fences to deal with, but the pair of washed-away fences might get replaced.

    GAUGE: Catoctin Creek should be projected over 400 cfs, 2 hours after put in.

CONE BRANCH: Roy Shafer Road to Catoctin Creek

Gradient	Difficulty	Distance	Area	Scenery	Strainers	Rating
40	II	1.4	6	C	0-2/mi.	**

USGS Quad – Middletown; Source – Personal descent 6/04
N39 25.00, W77 33.32 to N39 24.53, W77 33.92

Cone Branch merges with Hollow Road Creek just south of Middletown. In the next mile, there were two fences in fast water and a 5-foot weir, so a safer put in is the bridge on Roy Shafer Road. The trip follows that road south for a half mile of continuous class I-II whitewater, to where the creek passes some houses, picks up an unnamed tributary, and flows beneath Roy Shafer Road again. In the remaining 0.9 miles, along Bennies Hill Road, the gradient picks up and the creek becomes class II. There are a few boulders and overhanging branches, but the main hazard is the low-water bridge near the end. Follow the main current to the right of the small island, but then cut hard left and catch the eddy just above the bridge. You can take out there, or portage and then paddle 200 yards to the confluence, and take out just upstream on Catoctin Creek.

    GAUGE: Look for 600 cfs on Catoctin Creek (3 hours after put in) and 120 cfs on Piney Run (Va.). This creek fell from 2 feet down to 6 inches in 90 minutes.

BROAD RUN: Gapland Road to Catoctin Creek

Gradient	Difficulty	Distance	Area	Scenery	Strainers	Rating
25	I	2.8*	13	C	1-2/mi.	*

USGS Quad – Middletown/Pt. of Rocks; Source – Personal descent (last half) 2/03
N39 22.78, W77 35.63 to N39 21.44, W77 34.38

*(plus 0.6 miles on Catoctin Creek to Md. 180)

I have run only the bottom half, but expect that it is representative. There are frequent riffles and a good current, through ranch and farmland, with a wooded margin and occasional scenic rock outcroppings. Be careful of barbed wire fences at Gapland Road and the halfway bridge at St. Marks Road (on the upstream side), and of the occasional downed tree. There might also be other fences in the first half of the trip.

GAUGE: Zero level would be 325 cfs on Catoctin Creek (2 hours after you put in) and 70 cfs on Piney Run.

TUSCARORA CREEK: Doubs to New Design Road (C & O Canal)

Gradient	Difficulty	Distance	Area	Scenery	Strainers	Rating
13	I	5.3	13	D+	4-6/mi.	-

USGS Quad – Buckeystown; Source –Personal descent 3/08 (first 3.5 miles); 3/98 (last 1.5 miles).
N39 18.03, W77 29.40 to N39 15.11, W77 28.81

Tuscarora Creek drains the eastern side of Catoctin Mountain, running parallel to and 2-3 miles west of the Monocacy. It once hosted many paper mills. Put in at the bridge in Doubs (site of Charles Carroll's 1812 flourmill), and be prepared for many strainers. The first 1.8 miles to Pleasantview Road are mostly through the woods, with lots of downed trees, often one right after the other. Then you enter ranch country, and will face cattle (one bull blocked us in mid-stream for about 10 minutes) and several fences, as well as more downed trees, until Md. 28 at 3.7 miles. There are lots of little riffles, but no real rapids. Be discreet as you pass near the farmhouses.

Below Md. 28, the creek flows through the woods, with little whitewater and several strainers and/or logjams. When the Potomac is high, the latter part of the run will be backwater, and the greatest challenge will be finding the creek's channel.

GAUGE: The Catoctin Creek gauge needs 325 cfs (projected forward to 2 hours after you put in) and Piney Run (Va.) 70 cfs.

MONOCACY BASIN

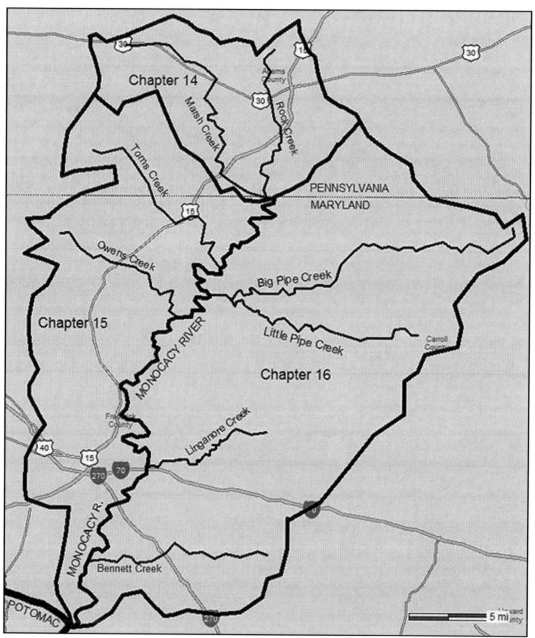

PART IV: MONOCACY BASIN

The Monocacy basin extends for almost 50 miles north-south, with a maximum 32-mile width, an area of 970 sq. mi. (the fourth largest Potomac tributary, after the Shenandoah and the South and North branches) and some 300,000 inhabitants. Frederick Md. (65,000) is its main city, followed by Gettysburg Pa. (7,000). The Maryland portion (77%) occupies the eastern three-quarters of Frederick County and the northwestern half of Carroll County. It is mostly rural, with some 3,500 farms averaging 150 acres apiece, primarily dairy, poultry, hogs, horses and orchards. The Pennsylvania part, all in Adams County, is similar. At its eastern end, the watershed juts into Montgomery County, the start of the Washington D.C. suburbs (Part V). To the north is the Susquehanna basin.

Monocacy sounds like a cross between monarchy and democracy – perhaps an "imperial presidency" – but later I thought of it as a misspelled **"rule by thong-wearing White House interns."** It is actually a Shawnee word (first written by the English as Monnockkesey) meaning either "fortified, fenced, or a garden," or "river of many bends." Native Americans paddled it, and there are remains visible of their fish weirs/traps. But because it is twisty (its 58 miles are only 36.6 as the crow flies), its use for long distance transportation was limited to heavy cargo.

English settlers arrived in the 1720s from both Maryland and Pennsylvania, and established plantations along the river. As the state boundary had not yet been surveyed, there was jockeying for control between those two colonies, and even a touch of violence. Starting in the 1730s, **German immigrants** settled in the uplands, which were similar to their former homes, and started many of the apple and peach orchards that now dot the area.

The **Monocacy River** itself is the flattest (3 ft/mile) major Potomac tributary, and its navigability (by shallow barges called *batteaus*) made Pennsylvania a supporter of the C&O Canal (the Potowmack Co. did some work on the Monocacy as well) as a shipping route for the south-central part of the state. It is formed at the Pennsylvania-Maryland state line by the confluence of Marsh Creek from the northwest and Rock Creek from the north. It is a pleasant but slow beginner run, not to mention being an official state "scenic river." If you want to sample the river, the 2.4 miles from Lilypons (the mouth of Bennett Creek) to Park Mill Road has good access and ends with a long set of riffles.

A Monocacy tributary's gradient depends mainly on its general location. The **Monocacy East** streams (chapter 16) are rather flat, as only slightly higher ground (Parrs Ridge) separates them from the Patapsco and Patuxent basins. In contrast, the **Monocacy West** creeks (chapter 15) are steep as they flow off Catoctin and South mountains. The **Monocacy North** headwaters (chapter 14) are intermediate in gradient; some have a few strong rapids amidst quieter stretches, while others have more constant riffles.

Of the six **river gauges** in the basin, three are quite useful: the Monocacy at Bridgeport for the northern headwaters, Big Pipe Creek for the northern part of Monocacy East, and Bennett Creek for the southern part of Monocacy East. (There are also two downstream gauges on the Monocacy and one on a miniscule tributary of Little Bennett Creek.) The gauges on Bermudian Creek (Pa.) to the north and Grave Run and Beaver Run to the east are also helpful. For the challenging Monocacy West streams, the essential gauge is on Catoctin Creek, Md.

MONOCACY NORTH

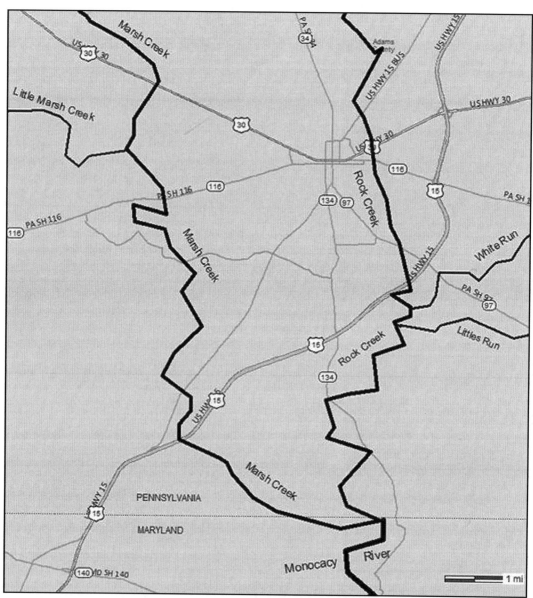

Chapter 14:

MONOCACY NORTH

The Marsh Creek and Rock Creek basins, which are the northern headwaters, cover 82 and 63 square miles, respectively. Gertler covers most of **Marsh Creek,** including the delightful intermediate section 3. Its only runnable tributary, **Little Marsh Creek**, is a novice trip except for one challenging rapid. Gertler also alerted me to the excellent rapids on section 1 of **Rock Creek**, which is followed by a much longer and easier section 2. Rock Creek has a pair of easy but entertaining tiny tributaries; **White Run** is my favorite, while its neighbor **Littles Run** is short but also fun. There are no "explorers' specials" in this chapter (despite my efforts to find one). Because they are short, one can often paddle the good whitewater sections of Marsh Creek and Rock Creek in the same day, or combine one with a small tributary or with Middle Creek (chapter 15).

> **Gettysburg** was called Marsh Creek Settlement, until General James Gettys laid out a proper township in the 1790s. The headwaters of the Monocacy were the site of the bloodiest and most important battle of the Civil War, on July 1-3, 1863, as well as of President Lincoln's famous Gettysburg Address. Right next to the Gettysburg National Military Park is the **Eisenhower National Historic Site**, which served as his presidential retreat.

GAUGES: The standard gauge for this area is **Bridgeport on the upper Monocacy (173 sq. mi.), and that is the zero-level reference** in the table below. But as all these creeks rise and fall faster than the Monocacy, you must look at the trend, not just the current level. The nearest small-creek gauge is Bermudian Creek (10.2 sq. mi.) in the West Conewago Creek (Pa.) basin, 10-15 miles north. Grave Run (7.7 sq. mi.) in the Gunpowder basin and Beaver Run (14 sq. mi.) in the Patapsco basin are about twice as far away, both to the southeast, but still useful. No rainfall gauges are reported.

name	gradient	difficulty	length	area	gauge	rating
Marsh Creek - Section 1	33	II-	3.3	11	1100cfs	-
- Section 2	10	I (III-)	10.6	21	750cfs	**
- Section 3	20 (50)	III	2.7	75	400cfs	****
Little Marsh Creek	25	II (III)	4.7	14	1000cfs	**
Rock Creek - Section 1	20 (60)	III	2.2	18	800cfs	***
- Section 2	7	I	10.0	23	600cfs	*
White Run	22	II-	2.7	8	1500cfs	***
Littles Run	30	II-	1.2	8	1500cfs	**

〰️ MARSH CREEK

Marsh Creek starts 12 miles west-northwest of Gettysburg, flows for 26 miles through Adams County, PA, and meets Rock Creek at the Mason-Dixon Line to form the Monocacy. Section 1 is ruined by fences, section 2 has one good rapid and section 3 has excellent whitewater.

Section 1: Flohrs Church Road to Crooked Creek Road

Gradient	Difficulty	Distance	Area	Scenery	Strainers	Rating
33	II-	3.3	11	C-	2-4/mi.	-

USGS Quad – Arendtsville/Fairfield; Source – Personal descent 5/98
N39 53.35, W77 20.09 to N39 51.76, W77 17.62

Marsh Creek becomes runnable east of Hilltown and Cashtown (where General Lee planned to fight, with South Mountain protecting his rear, before stumbling into the Union forces at Gettysburg). The first 1.3 miles, to Fairview Fruit Road, are busy but not unpleasant, with the 40 ft/mile gradient divided among numerous riffles, several on sharp turns. But the next 2 miles, to Crooked Creek Road at 28 ft/mile, had 6 cattle fences, all with high, barbed-wire constructions extending onto the land. Yuck!

GAUGE: Bridgeport needs 1,100 cfs (5 hours later), Bermudian Creek (Pa.) 65 cfs.

Section 2: Crooked Creek Road to Marsh Creek Road (off BR 15)

Gradient	Difficulty	Distance	Area	Scenery	Strainers	Rating
10	I (III-)	10.4	21*	B	<<1/mi.	**

USGS Quad – Fairfield; Source – Personal Descent 5/98 (first 2 miles); Gertler
N39 51.76, W77 17.62 via N39 50.41, W77 17.79 (mile 1.9) to N39 45.02, W77 16.59

*(including tributaries which enter 0.4 miles below the put in)

This is a novice run, except for one 70-yard class III- rock garden, just upstream from Knoxlyn Road (at 1.9 miles). For better paddlers, this rapid will be the highlight of the trip; at low levels, start down the middle and then cut sharply left.

There is a 2-foot weir below the covered bridge downstream of Pumping Station Road (SR 3005); carry this to avoid the hydraulic below.

Paddlers who want a shorter trip have many alternatives, as seven bridges cross this section. (The first of these, at 0.8 miles, is the US 30 put in mentioned by Gertler.)

GAUGE: The class III- rock garden needs about 750 cfs on the Bridgeport gauge (4 hours after you put in), but 500 cfs suffices for the rest of the trip. Timelier readings would be 45 cfs and 30 cfs, respectively, on Bermudian Creek (Pa.).

Section 3: Marsh Creek Road (off BR 15) to Natural Dam Road

Gradient	Difficulty	Distance	Area	Scenery	Strainers	Rating
20 (50)	III	2.0	75	C+	<1/mi.	****

USGS Quad – Fairfield/Emmitsburg; Source – Personal descent 9/11
N39 45.02, W77 16.59 to N 39 44.09, W77 15.78

Gertler calls this "by far the best piece of whitewater in the Monocacy Basin," and while I would vote for Owens Creek or Friends Creek, this is certainly the best commonly run whitewater – and it is a lot easier to catch than any of the other fine runs.

Now that the private park just below BR 15 is restricted, put in by a large cleared area off Marsh Creek Road (river left), downstream of the 2-foot weir (whose hydraulic is dangerous at high levels). The long, wide class II- rapid just below the weir often has strainers. After another class II rock garden, you pass US 15 (not a good put in), and come upon four delightful rock gardens, the first two of which are class III, the third class II+, and the last a long class II, as the creek slices through Harpers Hill. The rapids are full of boulders and the routes are complex, so you should be good at reading and running. The first rapid culminates in a 3-foot drop into a hole. After these rapids, there is a long eddy that is the backwater of a natural but masonry-capped dam. This is sometimes run via a sheer 5-foot drop on the far right, an extremely tight and undercut chute in the middle for kamikaze types, or a multi-step alternative on the far left. All require more than minimal flows.

Take out by the dam, alongside Natural Dam Road. If you prefer, you can continue 0.6 miles to better parking at Mason-Dixon Road or even a further 2.9 miles to Harney Road, half a mile down the Monocacy. The gradient for all this is just 6 ft/mile.

GAUGE: Look for at least 400 cfs at Bridgeport, projected for 2-3 hours later.

> It took half an hour to get a C-1 out of the **hydraulic below the 2-foot weir**. We walked out on the weir, but every time we pushed the boat out of the strongest part of the hydraulic, it got sucked back in. We got a throw rope under the boat, but it had nothing to hold onto. Finally, I used a large branch with a short stub on it to snag the cockpit and pull the boat to shore

LITTLE MARSH CREEK: Orrtanna to Marsh Creek

Gradient	Difficulty	Distance	Area	Scenery	Strainers	Rating
25	II (III)	4.7	14	C	2/mi.	**

USGS Quad – Fairfield; Source – Personal descent 1/98
N39 51.11, W77 21.20 via N39 50.70, W77 19.32 (mile 2) to N39 49.82, W77 17.60

Little Marsh Creek rises on South Mountain, between Marsh and Middle creeks, 10 miles west of Gettysburg. Five miles later, at Orrtanna, it picks up a pair of tributaries. Put in at Orrtanna Road, at the northeast edge of town. (Park at the first dead end on the left, off the road to town.)

The first 3 miles are class I, winding through the woods, with some braiding. When the creek steepens to include several class II- rapids, and then splits around a large island, you are approaching the main drop. You can scout this by walking up from the Knoxlyn Road bridge. To run it, catch the eddy on river right just above the pair of huge boulders, and then ferry hard across towards the tree standing in the water. Cut back sharply to the right for the first drop, and run the second drop close to the right-hand rock wall, to avoid a hidden boulder at left-center. Just below the bridge is a 100-yard, class II rock garden, ending in a drop where you cut left to avoid a pair of pourovers. The creek then quiets down again for its final 1.3 miles, with just a few more class II- rapids.

Take out alongside Blackhorse Tavern Road, half a mile below the confluence; find an area that is not posted. If you continue another mile to Pa. 116, the take out is much steeper.

To shorten the trip but still run the good rapids, you could put in on Meadowbrook Lane at mile 2 and take out shortly below Knoxlyn, for just a 1.4 mile paddle.

GAUGE: Bridgeport needs at least 1,000 cfs (4-5 hours after you put in), Bermudian Creek 60 cfs, Beaver Run 80 cfs. The rapid just below Knoxlyn Road should be cleanly runnable.

ROCK CREEK

Rock Creek, one of the two streams that form the Monocacy, flows south for 19 miles as it drains Gettysburg and the land east of it. It gets exciting for a half mile as it passes Culps Hill with some challenging rapids (section 1), but soon returns to its somnolent ways (section 2).

Section 1: West Hanover St. (Pa. 116) to Baltimore Pike (Pa. 97)

Gradient	Difficulty	Distance	Area	Scenery	Strainers	Rating
20 (60)	III	2.2	18	C+	0-2/mi.	***

USGS Quad – Gettysburg; Source – Personal descent 9/11
N39 49.85, W77 13.10 to N39 48.32, W77 12.72

There are only riffles and one class II rapid in the first 1.5 miles, as the creek swings around the east side of Culps Hill, but this trip ends with an exciting half mile of class III boulder gardens. The first hard rapid (scouting recommended) ends in a 3-foot drop over a sloping ledge; approach from right of center. Then comes a long rapid, with limited visibility and tight maneuvering. The final ledge (also worth scouting) is just visible (when the trees are bare) from the take out; start left and angle sharp right. The take out, a steep climb on upstream river right, is the main negative of the trip.

Unload your boats in the Gettysburg National Military Park, across from a sewage treatment plant; to be safe, park outside the gate. Later, war monuments are sometimes visible high above along East Confederate Avenue on the right, which runs between the creek and Culps Hill. After this run, Marsh or Middle Creek would be a good chaser.

GAUGE: The Bridgeport gauge needs at least 800 cfs, 4-5 hours after you start; timelier would be 60 cfs on Bermudian Creek (Pa). At the put in, zero level is when the rock next to the piling on downstream river left is just covered.

> **Culps Hill**, which towers 150 feet above Rock Creek, saw major action on days 1 and 2 of the Battle of Gettysburg. Ewell's corps crossed the creek and captured the lowest string of Federal earthworks, but failed to capture the hill itself, and was eventually thrown off it. This failure, along with that at Little Round Top at the other end of the battlefield, set the stage for the South's desperate and disastrous attempt to turn the tide with Pickett's Charge.

Section 2: Baltimore Pike (Pa. 97) to Monocacy River (Harney Rd.)

Gradient	Difficulty	Distance	Area	Scenery	Strainers	Rating
7	I	10.0*	23	C	<1/mi.	*

USGS Quad – Gettysburg/Taneytown; Source – Gertler
N39 48.32, W77 12.72, to N39 42.84, W77 12.94

*(plus 0.5 miles on the Monocacy, including a class II- rapid, to Harney Road)

The section starts off small, but its catchment area is doubled within 3 miles by the addition of White and Littles runs. There are several intermediate access points.

GAUGE: You will need about 600 cfs on the Bridgeport gauge (3-4 hours after you begin) to start at Pa. 97, and 400 cfs once White and Littles runs enter.

WHITE RUN: Low Dutch Road to Rock Creek

Gradient	Difficulty	Distance	Area	Scenery	Strainers	Rating
22	II-	2.7	8	B+	<1/mi.	***

USGS Quad – Gettysburg; Source – Personal descent 2/04
N39-48.13, W77-10.71 to N39-46.96, W77-12.40

This creek has long stretches of bouncy class II- waves, lovely rock cliffs, a remote feel and good wildlife. It is wide for its drainage area, which results in few strainers but makes it harder to catch up. The fun starts right at the put in, where you can run either culvert, with a steep drop. After Pa. 97 (at 1.6 miles), the gradient drops in half and the riffles become intermittent. After you pass a sewage treatment plant, there is a low-water bridge with an 18-inch drop-off. From the confluence, it is 300 yards to Sachs/Goulden Road (site of a Civil War Union hospital for Gettysburg wounded).

GAUGE: The Bridgeport gauge would need to be 1,500 cfs about 5 hours after you start; timelier would be 90 cfs on Bermudian Creek (Pa.) and 70 cfs on Grave Run.

LITTLES RUN: White Church Road to Rock Creek

Gradient	Difficulty	Distance*	Area	Scenery	Strainers	Rating
30	II-	1.2	8	C	1-3/mi.	**

USGS Quad – Gettysburg; Source – Personal descent 2/04
N39 46.92, W77 11.72 to N39 46.34, W77 12.52

*(plus 0.6 flat miles on Rock Creek to Solomon Road)

It's too bad this run is so short; there is access 2 miles upstream, also at 30 ft/mile, but with only 4.5 sq. mi. The riffles are continuous, and the creek is so narrow that you often need to avoid overhanging bushes and branches on turns. In the first quarter mile there are three private bridges (all high enough), but then the scenery become more rustic.

GAUGE: Bridgeport gauge needs to be 1,500 cfs about 5 hours after you start; timelier readings would be 90 cfs on Bermudian Creek (Pa.) and 70 cfs on Grave Run.

MONOCACY WEST

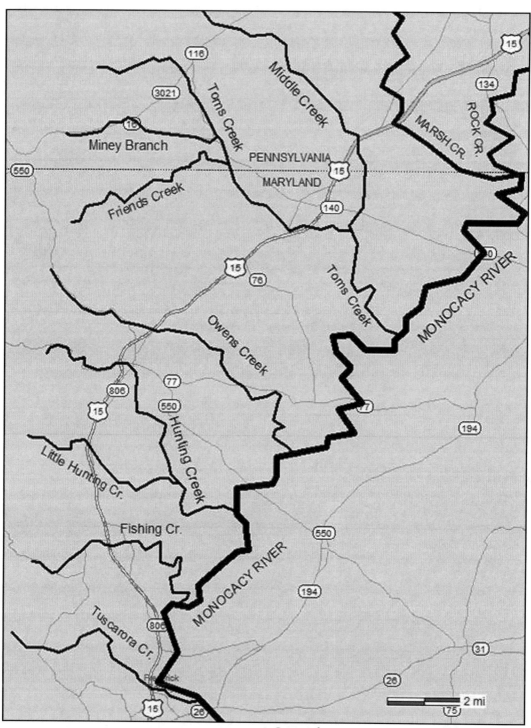

Chapter 15:

MONOCACY WEST

This chapter covers the side streams that enter the Monocacy River from the west, draining some 300 square miles in total. These creeks are generally quite steep as they drop off of Catoctin and South mountains, before mellowing. The best of them are starting to become better known. Not only do they have challenging rapids, but they are close together (so you can do several in a day), their scenery is generally nice (including several covered bridges) and they have few fences in the steep parts, although fallen trees are a danger. These streams are hard to catch – but worth the wait.

Gertler covers only **lower Middle** and **lower Toms** creeks, but there is a lot more whitewater here; in fact, this may still be the most under-appreciated watershed in the area. Starting at the north end, **upper Middle Creek** has a short stretch of exciting rapids. **Upper Toms Creek** includes an "explorers' special" followed by a moderate stretch. **Miney Branch** has a tiny watershed but is quite nice. **Friends** and **Owens creeks** are my favorites, each with an outstanding high-intermediate section, as well as a short, harder piece. **Hunting** and **Little Hunting creeks** have some decent intermediate water, but Hunting Creek is of greater interest to expert paddlers for its very steep part. **Upper Fishing creek** is problematic, while the lower part is an easier "explorers' special." **Tuscarora Creek** is not worth paddling.

Flat Run could be paddled for 4.2 miles, through Emmitsburg to the confluence with Toms Creek, with 7 sq. mi. and at 20 ft/mile – not quite as dull as its name suggests, but it needs a lot of rain, as it has no mountain springs to feed it.

Carroll Creek, which flows through Frederick city, is runnable for less than a mile after it picks up its main arms, through manicured Baker Park (11 sq. mi., 10 ft/mile), before entering subterranean passages; it is a marginally better prospect after it emerges (see box below).

The only whitewater on **Ballenger Creek**, the southernmost western tributary, is 0.7 mild, twisty miles through Ballenger Creek Park (10 sq. mi., 35 ft/mile).

GAUGES: Catching these many fine small creeks was easier when there was a gauge on Fishing Creek near Lewistown (7.3 sq. mi.), in the southern part of the basin, but that gauge stopped reporting in October 2011. That leaves the gauge on **Catoctin Creek, Md. (67 sq. mi.) in the next basin to the west as the most relevant one, and it is the zero-level gauge reference** in the table below. (Don't confuse this gauge with the one on Catoctin Creek in Virginia.) For the northernmost streams, the Bridgeport gauge on the upper Monocacy (173 sq. mi.) is useful for an indication of rainfall to the north. When using the Bridgeport and Catoctin Creek gauges, remember that all the small creeks will rise and fall faster than those gauges, so look at the trend, not just the levels. In most cases, you will want to project the Bridgeport gauge readings forward by about 5 hours and Catoctin Creek by 3 hours, in order to get the appropriate figures. No rainfall gauges are reported from this watershed, so you need to keep checking the rainfall maps.

name	gradient	difficulty	length	area	gauge	rating
Toms Creek - *Section 1*	80 (150)	?	2.9	8	650cfs	?
- Section 2	36	II- (III)	2.3	13	375cfs	**
- Section 3	17	II-	4.6	23	150cfs	**
Miney Branch	62	III-	2.6	5	900cfs	***
Friends Creek - *Sec. 1*	60	II+	1.3	10	500cfs	**
- Sec. 2	170	IV (5.0)	0.5	11	650cfs	!!!
- Sec. 3	65 (130)	III+	3.0	12	550cfs	****
Middle Creek - *Sec. 1*	50 (110)	III (IV-)	1.2	15	450cfs	***
- Sec. 2	12	I (II-)	4.2	16	300cfs	*
- Sec. 3	30	II (II+)	2.0	21	300cfs	***
Owens Creek - *Section 1*	70 (110)	III- (IV-)	2.4	5	1000cfs	***
- Section 2	190	IV	0.4	10	650cfs	!!!!
- Section 3	100 (160)	III+	2.5	11	550cfs	****
- Section 4	40	II-	1.6	13	400cfs	**
Hunting Creek - *Section 1*	90	III	1.2	8	800cfs	***
- Section 2	190 (260)	IV+ (5.0)	1.2	9	900cfs	!!!!
- Section 3	70 (110)	III	3.0	11	600cfs	**
Little Hunting Cr.-*Sec. 1*	160	III+	1.1	6	1000cfs	**
- Sec. 2	110 (180)	III+	1.3	7	875cfs	**
Fishing Creek - *Section 1*	95	III	1.5	10	600cfs	*
- Section 2	23	?	3.3	11	400cfs	?
Tuscarora Creek	33	I	2.0	9	750cfs	-

For relatively short, easy trips, generally smaller than the traditional runs in the next chapter (Monocacy East) and flatter than the new additions there, try the bottom sections of the following creeks, listed here from north to south, with their zero-level gauge readings. All these trips (except Tuscarora Creek) end at the last takeout before the Monocacy.

- **Toms Creek** – Creamery Rd. to Sixes Road – 84 sq. mi. (including Flat Run and Middle Creek, which enter about 1 mile later) – 5.8 miles @ 7 ft/mile; Bridgeport 200 cfs. This trip is in Gertler. N39 41.45, W77 19.04 to N39 38.38, W77 16.90
- **Owens Creek** – Apples Church Rd. to Longs Mill Rd. – 22 sq. mi., 5.6 miles @ 15 ft/mile; Catoctin Creek 225 cfs. N39 37.84, W77 22.23 to N39 35.12, W77 20.11
- **Hunting Creek** – Wilhide Rd. to end of Shyrock Rd. –35 sq. mi., 3.2 miles @ 13 ft/mile; Catoctin Creek 180 cfs. N39 33.88, W77 23.26 to N39 33.02, W77 21.53
- **Tuscarora Creek** – Willowbrook Rd. to Liberty Rd. (Md. 26) –17 sq. mi., 2.8 mi. @ 13 ft/mile; Catoctin Creek 275 cfs. N39 28.28, W77 24.75 to N39-27.15, W77 22.25
- **Carroll Creek** – Highland St. (where it re-emerges) to Disposal Plant Rd. –15 sq. mi., 1.2 miles @ 15 ft/mile; Catoctin Creek 275 cfs. N39 24.94, W77 23.87 to N39 25.64, W77 22.92
- **Ballenger Creek** – New Design R. to Buckeystown Pike (Md. 85) –17 sq. mi., 1.6 miles @ 12 ft/mile; Catoctin Creek 275 cfs. N39 22.66, W77 25.31 to N39 21.87, W77 25.01

⭐ TOMS CREEK

Like other western Monocacy tributaries, Toms Creek races off the Catoctin range (South Mountain, in this case, north of Catoctin Mountain). It is still tiny when it leaves the hills, but it is by far the largest western tributary (88 sq. mi.) by the time it enters the Monocacy, having picked up Miney Branch, Friends Creek, Flat Run and Middle Creek. Of its 20-mile course, it is too small for 4 miles, the next 10 miles are in sections 1 to 3, and the final 6 miles (in the box above and in Gertler) have only a 7-ft/mile gradient.

> Just east of Toms Creek, near the section 2 put in, is **Ski Liberty**, the nearest slopes to the DC area. Visible from the stream is a **game park**, with llamas, monkeys etc. There is iron ore in the vicinity, and around 1770, **Bruce's Iron Furnace** was established alongside the creek.

> **Emmitsburg**, just off of Toms Creek, has long been a center of Catholic education – Mount St. Mary's College was founded there in 1808 and St. Joseph's Academy for girls, the cradle of parochial education, was started by **Mother Elizabeth Ann Seton** (the first American-born saint) in 1810 on the banks of the creek just south of town. In 1809, Mother Seton founded the Sisters of Charity near Emmitsburg; this is now a nationwide order of nuns. Emmitsburg also contains the Seton Shrine Center and the National Shrine Grotto of Lourdes, a replica of the famous pilgrimage site in France.

Section 1: Iron Springs Road to Valley View Trail

Gradient	Difficulty	Distance	Area	Scenery	Strainers	Rating
80 (150)	?	2.9	8	C-	?	?

USGS Quad – Iron Springs; Source – Substantial scouting from road
N39 46.12, W77 25.10 to N39 45.61, W77 23.02

This *"explorers' special"* may occasionally be runnable at the confluence with Copper Run, but there were lots of strainers plus braiding during the next two-thirds mile, so wait until the creek runs next to the road, half a mile upstream of the railroad bridge. The first 1.4 miles to Iron Springs averages 100 ft/mile and looks pretty continuous with no major drops. There are lots of houses along the creek, but all the footbridges looked high enough to paddle under. At Iron Springs, the creek swings southeast through the foothills down to Carroll Valley and the gradient drops to 65 ft/mile. There is a covered bridge on Jacks Mountain Road, half a mile before the take out. **Take out well above the 6-foot, man-made drop** onto boulders at Valley View Trail – scout this in advance.

GAUGE: Look for 650 cfs on Catoctin Creek and 1,700 cfs at Bridgeport.

Section 2: Valley View Trail to Pa. 16

Gradient	Difficulty	Distance	Area	Scenery	Strainers	Rating
36	II- (III)	2.3	13	B-	0-2/mi.	**

USGS Quad – Iron Springs/Blue Ridge Summit/Emmitsburg; Source – Personal descent 3/03

N39 45.61, W77 23.02 to N39 43.90, W77 21.97

This is a milder and prettier part of Toms Creek, with few strainers and only one significant rapid. Put in just below the 6-foot, man-made drop. The first third of a mile is continuous riffles, to Pa. 116. The next half mile is through a golf course, where you pass under four bridges; in high water, you must portage the third of these. This stretch has lots of riffles and a few minor ledges. Then the creek runs alongside a steep wooded slope, with first the golf course and then a lake on your right. After a high footbridge, there is a 2-foot ledge that is scrapey in low water. Soon thereafter, the horizon line disappears, and you should catch the eddy on the left. This is a steep class III drop of about 5 feet, where you angle right. It is hard to portage (thorn bushes on the left, riprap on the right), and the creek calms down immediately below, so you might as well run it.

From there, it is an easy half mile down to the mouth of Miney Branch, and another half mile to the take out. There is good parking at both the put in and take out, but I don't know how golfers would react (it was too rainy for them the day I paddled this).

GAUGE: Look for 375 cfs on Catoctin Creek (projecting 3 hours ahead) and 1,000 cfs at Bridgeport (projecting 4-5 hours ahead). At the put in, the immediate run-out below the drop may be bony, but it needs to be clean very soon thereafter.

Section 3: Pa. 16 to Creamery Road

Gradient	Difficulty	Distance	Area	Scenery	Strainers	Rating
17	II-	4.6	23	C	1/mi.	**

USGS Quad – Emmitsburg; Source – Personal descent (first 2.7 miles) 10/05; Gertler; Trip report (Evangelidi)

N39 43.90, W77 21.97 to N39 41.46, W77 19.03

There are lots of riffles on this run, plus a few small ledges and swift chutes, but also several longish pools. In half a mile, you pass the mouth of Friends Creek. Half a mile later, watch out for a possible barbed-wire strand. At 2.7 miles you reach Annandale Road (a good access). A mile after that you cross BR 15, which adjoins the US Fire Institute; the guards there sometimes discourage cars from parking. Another half mile brings you to the backwater of a dam; have someone in the pool at the bottom to catch the empty boats shoved down the left side. Continue past US 15, and take out at Creamery Road. (This lower stretch passes through a FEMA firefighter training ground, and the US Government closed it briefly after 9/11/01, but now they reportedly no longer object if you paddle through without stopping.) For a half-mile longer run, you can put in on Miney Branch, just above the confluence.

GAUGE: The staff gauge on upstream river left at the put in, on an abandoned stone bridge abutment, should be at least 1.6. Look for 400 cfs at Bridgeport and 150 cfs on Catoctin Creek (projecting 2 hours ahead).

🌊 MINEY BRANCH: Old Waynesboro Road to Pa. 16/Pa. 116

Gradient	Difficulty	Distance	Area	Scenery	Strainers	Rating
62	III-	2.6	5	C+	1-3/mi.	★★★

USGS Quad – Blue Ridge Summit/Emmitsburg; Source – Personal descent 6/06
N39 44.59, W77 24.71 to N39 44.12, W77 22.35

This stream has a steady gradient as it flows east alongside Pa. 16, just above the Mason-Dixon Line. Given its tiny catchment, it was surprisingly clear of obstacles. Put in just east of Jacks Mountain Road, on Old Waynesboro Road. For the first two-thirds of the trip, the rapids are up to class II+ and strainers are likely. But then the creek improves markedly, with longer, more interesting and slightly harder rapids, and fewer strainers. The take out is by the Pa. 16 bridge, just above the intersection with Pa. 116, and 300 yards above Toms Creek; that final 300 yards is often strainer strewn.

GAUGE: Catoctin Creek (Md.) should reach over 900 cfs, 3 hours later.

🌊 FRIENDS CREEK

The Harbaugh Valley (Dr. Henry Harbaugh, 1817-67, was a Pennsylvania-German author, theologian and educator) lies between South and Catoctin mountains. Friends Creek drains this valley and then flows northeast to Toms Creek, as one of the few streams to cross the Mason-Dixon Line in that direction. (Maybe there's some wonderful story about how the Society of Friends used it in the Underground Railroad.) Within 3 miles from their start, the main branches join at the northeast end of the valley, and the hills begin to close in to form a narrow gorge with outstanding whitewater.

> Near the creek's headwaters, Indians quarried **rhyolite rock**, which was better than quartz for arrowheads, spearheads and knives. Large blocks of this rock were carried to the Monocacy by trail and then to the Potomac by canoe. Caches of rhyolite have been found along the route.

Section 1: Sunshine Trail to Start of Gorge (Friends Creek Road)

Gradient	Difficulty	Distance	Area	Scenery	Strainers	Rating
60	II+	1.3	10	B	2-4/mi.	★★

USGS Quad – Blue Ridge Summit; Source – Personal descent 9/03
N39 42.60, W77 25.49 to N39 42.57, W77 24.63

Put in at the bridge where the main branches meet. The creek parallels Sunshine Trail and then Friends Cr. Rd., but there are houses and fields in between. As of 2007, there were three electrified fences, single strands that could be lifted up easily, but none visible much in advance. And yes, I did experience the tingly but not painful shock. All were in the middle part of the trip, upstream of and within sight of the first private bridge.

The first half of the trip is class II, with frequent short rapids. Then the gradient picks up a bit and the rapids get longer and reach class II+. Shortly after the creek comes back alongside the road, there is a pool caused by large boulders. The resultant ledge can be run via a sheer class II+ drop on the far left, or, with a bit more water, a twisty class III- chute on the far right. Below this, the water flows around huge boulders, but the low gradient limits this to class II. The take out is 175 yards below the ledge, where a car-sized rock blocks the left half of the creek, and there is good parking alongside. (The put in and take out are private property, but there are signs granting permission to fishermen.)

GAUGE: Zero level would be 500 cfs on Catoctin Creek (Md.), 3 hours later.

Section 2: Start of Gorge to Friends Creek Church

Gradient	Difficulty	Distance	Area	Scenery	Strainers	Rating
170	IV (5.0)	0.5	11	A	2-8/mi.	!!!

USGS Quad – Blue Ridge Summit; Source – Trip Report (Bobby Miller) 3/00
N39 42.57, W77 24.63 to N39 42.90, W77 24.15

Immediately below the car-sized boulder, the creek gets serious, with two long class IV rapids. The tough quarter mile ends with a class 5.0 boulder garden that drops about 10 feet in 20 yards, including a 4-foot drop onto a piton rock, followed by a steep slide into a hole. Expect several strainers (sometimes put by fishermen to help them across the water). Non-expert paddlers who run this section as part of a longer trip would need to make some long, rocky portages on river right. The next quarter mile, to the bridge by Friends Creek Church, has only class II+ rock gardens.

GAUGE: Because of the steepness, you need a little more water than for sections 1 or 3 – some 650 cfs on Catoctin Creek (Md.), 3 hours later.

Section 3: Friends Creek Church to Toms Creek

Gradient	Difficulty	Distance	Area	Scenery	Strainers	Rating
65 (130)	III+	3.0*	12	A	0-2/mi.	****

USGS Quad – BlueRidgeSummit/Emmitsburg; Source – Personal descent 9/03
N39 42.90, W77 24.15 via N39 43.49, W77 22.25 (Ranch Tr) to N39 42.23, W77 20.67

*(plus 2 miles on Toms Creek at 9 ft/mile to Annandale Road)

This is a wonderful pool-and-rapids trip for intermediate/advanced paddlers. Friends Creek Road runs alongside for the first 0.6 miles, and there are two low-water bridges in that stretch, but both have good eddies above them. You can run up onto the first bridge, but will need to portage the second. The creek then enters a remote-feeling gorge with beautiful rock formations. Expect a few strainers, but the situation was pretty good both times I was here. The creek is mostly wide open and straight enough for boat scouting; however, scout by foot in a few rapids, where you can't see to the bottom.

Right below the second low-water bridge, the creek divides into three channels, at the top of a class III+ rapid. At low levels, stay left. After two more strong rapids, the gradient eases up to class II. When the creek divides again, you are at the top of the hardest rapid, which ends in a steep, rocky drop. You can pull over on the left mid-way down to scout. In low water, the exposed boulders at the bottom make this harder.

The good rapids and scenery continue almost to the end. You can take out at Ranch Trail, 0.4 miles before the confluence, to avoid 2 miles of fast flat water on section 3 of Toms Creek to Annandale Road, but then you would have a longer shuttle.

GAUGE: Catoctin Creek should still be over 550 cfs, 3 hours later. At zero level, there is 2 inches of water flowing over the first low-water bridge.

MIDDLE CREEK

Middle Creek flows for 16 miles, through alternating steep and flat sections, from South Mountain to Toms Creek, southeast of Emmitsburg. After 2 miles it picks up Swamp Creek, to reach 4.5 sq. mi. The next 2 miles, to Virginia Mills, at 100 ft/mile, parallels Mt. Hope Road; the rapids looked good but the strainers looked dangerous. The following 1.4 miles, to Fairfield (Pa. 116), is through farmland, at 50 ft/mile. Then, after 2 miles at just 20 ft/mile, comes the tough section 1. Section 2, in Gertler, is again suitable for novices. Section 3 is a popular intermediate paddle, often run in conjunction with Marsh Creek. And then comes a final flat piece, to the confluence.

Section 1: Bullfrog Road to McGlaughlin Road (T318; east of Fairfield)

Gradient	Difficulty	Distance	Area	Scenery	Strainers	Rating
50 (110)	III (IV-)	1.2	15	B	1-3/mi.	***

USGS Quad – Fairfield; Source – Personal descent (the rapids) 9/03; scouting
N39 47.07, W77 20.23 to N39 46.46, W77 19.97

You can park where Bullfrog Road crosses just below the start of the rapids, and carry 50 yards upstream. (Bullfrog Road also crosses a mile upstream, but Middle Creek is smaller there.) That puts you at the top of a short class II+ stretch, followed, just below the bridge by a 70-yard class III rock garden, ending in a class IV- drop among huge boulders. Hike down on river left to scout the main drop. Catch the eddy on river right to set up for the final drop, which is run by cutting to the right and then sharply to the left.

After a short pool, most of the water goes left over a steep, 30-yard class III rock garden that needs a lot of water. Below that is a 100-yard, narrow but more gradual class III rapid. The rapids conclude just 0.4 miles below the put in, with a pair of class II rock gardens that often have strainers. You can either carry up to Bullfrog Road after the first of these, or continue 0.8 flat miles (with some braiding) down to McGlaughlin Road.

GAUGE: Look for 1,200 cfs at Bridgeport (5 hours later), 450 cfs on Catoctin Creek (Md.) (projected 3 hours later).

Section 2: McGlaughlin Road to Shorbs Mill Road

Gradient	Difficulty	Distance	Area	Scenery	Strainers	Rating
12	I (II-)	4.2	16	B-	1-2/mi.	*

USGS Quad – Fairfield/Emmitsburg; Source – Personal descent (last 3 miles) 1/10; Gertler; Bing Garthright 2/98
N39 46.46, W77 19.97 to N39 44.05, W77 17.78

This mediocre section between two much better ones is a slalom course around boulders and trees and over minor ledges, through woods with a few cattle fences. The gradient picks up in the final mile, including one class II- ledge. There is a paved ford with a hydraulic below, late in the trip, with a brown house visible ahead; run it on the far right.

GAUGE: Minimums are 800 cfs at Bridgeport (4 hours later) and 300 cfs on Catoctin Creek (Md.) (2-3 hours later).

Section 3: Shorbs Mill Road to Harney Road

Gradient	Difficulty	Distance	Area	Scenery	Strainers	Rating
30	II (II+)	2.0	21	B	0-2/mi.	***

USGS Quad – Emmitsburg; Source – Personal descent 1/10
N39 44.05, W77 17.78 to N39 42.42, W77 17.73

This popular trip starts off class I along the road, with fallen trees the main issue. In a half mile you reach Maryland and enter a shallow class II gorge, climaxing in a long class II+ rock garden that ends above an unrunnable 10-foot dam. Carry to Harney Road.

If you continue, you start with a low dam that can be clunked over. The 1.7 miles to Toms Creek are at 12 ft/mile, with minor ledges and riffles. The mile on Toms Creek to Keysville Road, while just 7 ft/mile, will be swift whenever Middle Creek is up.

GAUGE: Bridgeport should be at least 800 cfs (3 hours later), Catoctin Creek (Md.) 300 cfs (in 1-2 hours). At the Harney Road take-out bridge, on downstream river right, 3 inches below the groove in the cement is minimal.

Richard Owen, the first American-born Methodist preacher, was a disciple of Robert Strawbridge, who established the first Methodist society in America in 1760, across the Monocacy from Owens Creek.

Section 1 was all once part of a single estate, "**Arnold's Delight**," acquired in 1744 by Arnold Livers, the most prominent Catholic in the area. He used his estate for surreptitious Catholic worship, which was not then allowed in public. The Catholic population expanded northwards to Emmitsburg, which later became a religious center.

Little Owens Creek (2 sq. mi.) flows past the non-denominational, one-room, non-electrified **Eylers Valley Chapel,** built in 1857, whose candlelight services have become chic.

OWENS CREEK

Owens Creek shares Catoctin Mountain Park with Hunting Creek. Md. 550 and the railroad tracks parallel Owens Creek down to Thurmont. The branches meet a mile west of Lantz, for a 14-mile trip to the Monocacy. The first mile is full of overhanging bushes and fences. The final 6.3 miles average just 15 ft/mile. But in between are 5.3 miles of delightful whitewater (sections 1-3), plus 1.6 miles with easy rapids (section 4).

Section 1: Lantz to Railroad Bridge (Md. 550)

Gradient	Difficulty	Distance	Area	Scenery	Strainers	Rating
70 (110)	III- (IV-)	2.4	5	B+	1-3/mi.	***

USGS Quad – Blue Ridge Summit; Source – Personal descent 6/96
N39 40.52, W77 27.48 to N39 39.05, W77 26.10

Put in by the church, 300 yards west of Lantz (Deerfield Station). The first half mile is mellow, through a farm (whose owners, when they saw us at the put in, came by to warn us about barbed wire). The creek then enters the woods, and after a low-water bridge, the few man-made strainers give way to natural ones, as the gradient gradually picks up. After another quarter mile is a steep, class IV- boulder garden. Get out and scout, and portage if you have concerns.

Below that, there are long class III- rapids, plus few strainers. This mountain gorge is not too badly affected by the presence of the railroad on river left or the road on the other side of it (useful if you have to bail out). At the 1.7-mile mark, you pass the stationmaster's house at Flint. Don't miss the eddy just above the railroad bridge, 0.7 miles later, unless you are prepared to tackle section 2.

GAUGE: Catoctin Creek should still be at least 1000 cfs, 4 hours later.

When I saw that **class IV- rapid**, I was as scared as a senior citizen facing social security privatization, but I managed to ground my boat on some rocks. Ed Evangelidi began to run the drop, but his long canoe could not turn as sharply as Mitt Romney did on "social issues," and he capsized. I dragged my boat down over a few rocks into a tiny eddy, and then pinballed down off boulders. The dead tree trunk Jamie Deehan had been holding broke off, and he got swept into the maelstrom. He then ran the toughest part of the rapid, before flipping on a bottom rock.

Light was fading, especially with the overcast sky and canopied gorge. Ed's glasses kept getting fogged, and Jamie claimed that his distance vision was poor. Guess who had to be probe!

Section 2: Md. 550 – Railroad Bridge to Roadside Parking Area

Gradient	Difficulty	Distance	Area	Scenery	Strainers	Rating
190	IV	0.4	10	B+	0-5/mi.	!!!!

USGS Quad – Blue Ridge Summit; Source – Complete scouting 2/98
N39 39.05, W77 26.10 to N39 38.95, W77 25.58

Scout this from the road. After 100 yards comes a 5-foot drop, followed by a difficult stretch alongside the railroad tracks. Then the creek divides, with more water going left. If you go left, take a shallow, rocky chute 50 yards later to the right channel, to avoid a tough left hand turn where the channels reunite just above the start of section 3.

GAUGE: You will need at least 650 cfs on Catoctin Creek, 3 hours later.

Section 3: Md. 550 Roadside Parking Area to Roddy Covered Bridge

Gradient	Difficulty	Distance	Area	Scenery	Strainers	Rating
100 (160)	III+	2.5	11	B	0-2/mi.	****

USGS Quad – Blue Ridge Summit; Source – Personal descent 9/03
N39 38.95, W77 25.58 to N39 38.43, W77 23.64

This outstanding run has continuous whitewater with few strainers, and is mostly scoutable from the road. Put in where there is parking for many trout fishermen. While the whole trip is exciting, four places stand out. The first is a steep drop at the base of the railroad bridge, where you have to cut sharp right and then left. The second is where a series of large boulders require intricate maneuvering. The third is away from the road, where the creek turns hard left by a cliff. Stay left to avoid pourovers, and then punch the hole where the creek narrows down to 10 feet. The final challenge is a long set of small ledges just past US 15. Shortly below, the Roddy Covered Bridge (built in 1856) is a scenic take out. Watch out for plank footbridges behind a row of houses, a mile before the take out.

GAUGE: Look for at least 550 cfs on Catoctin Creek, projected 3 hours ahead.

As a pack of children ran alongside, we zoomed past backyards and under a makeshift footbridge. As we ran the ledges below US 15, John Lentz was ebullient: "I could do 100 miles of this!" he yelled, just 100 yards above where the good whitewater ended.

Section 4: Roddy Covered Bridge to Apples Church Road

Gradient	Difficulty	Distance	Area	Scenery	Strainers	Rating
40	II-	1.6	13	C	2-3/mi.	**

USGS Quad – Blue Ridge Summit/Emmitsburg; Source – Personal descent 4/93
N39 38.43, W77 23.64 to N39 37.84, W77 22.23

Below the covered bridge, the gradient drops sharply, and there is braiding and more strainers now that the creek has left the gorge, but the trip is still lively. After Apples Church Road (the take out), the creek is just 15 ft/mile for its final 6.3 miles.

GAUGE: Look for 400 cfs on Catoctin Creek, projected 2 hours later.

HUNTING CREEK

Hunting Creek flows 11 miles from Cunningham Falls Park to the Monocacy. Those falls (renamed McAfee Falls after the landowners), on a branch, can be visited from Md. 77. The creek is dammed at the confluence. Shortly below begin 5.4 miles of fun, in three sections, with the middle one the hardest (as on Friends and Owens creeks).

Below section 3, the gradient is 20 ft/mile for a mile and 7 ft/mile for the next 3.5 miles, before rising to 25 ft/mile for its final mile. This is a popular trout catch-and-release stream; controlled hunting is also permitted, so try not to surprise anyone in camouflage.

> Somewhere on Catoctin Mountain ("I could tell you where, but then I'd have to kill you"), between Hunting and Owens creeks, is **Camp David**, the retreat selected by FDR in 1942 (he named it Shangri-la) and used by every president since. Eisenhower renamed it for his grandson, while Jimmy Carter made history with the Camp David accords between Egypt and Israel.
>
> **Thurmont** ("Gateway to the Mountains") was settled in 1751, when the Jacob Weller family abandoned a wagon train headed west. The scenery, altitude and Western Maryland Railroad turned this into a recreational center. Just south of town is the Catoctin Mountain Zoo.
>
> North of Hunting Creek, the **Catoctin Recreation Demonstration Area** was replanted and developed by the Civilian Conservation Corps. Nearby are Hightop, a popular take-off for **hang gliders**, who use the thermals and slope updrafts of the area, and **Blue Blazes Still**, a genuine (if relocated) moonshine maker, now run by the National Park Service as an interpretive program.
>
> Hunting Creek was the first Maryland **catch-and-release trout stream**. For more than 50 years, it has been home to the Brotherhood of the Jungle Cock, a group that teaches fly-fishing to children. The Friends of Big Hunting Creek have built log structures to aid trout during low flow in summer. Rainbow and brook trout are stocked each year, while brown trout reproduce here.

Section 1: Catoctin Hollow Road to Md. 77 Bridge

Gradient	Difficulty	Distance	Area	Scenery	Strainers	Rating
90	III	1.2	8	B+	2-4/mi.	***

USGS Quad – Blue Ridge Summit; Source – Personal descent 3/10
N39 37.89, W77 27.25 to N39 37.57, W77 26.45

Put in at the bridge on Catoctin Hollow Road, just off Md. 77. The rapids start off class II, but get more interesting and continuous, reaching class III in the final one-third mile. Check for strainers from Md. 77, and scout beforehand the passage under Md. 77 into the take out pool, as there is a long rock garden and no eddy right above the bridge.

GAUGE: Look for 800 cfs on Catoctin Cr., 10" on the painted take-out gauge.

> In March 2000, Bobby Miller ran the dam's **spillway**: "This is a long slide that cascades probably 60 feet to the pool at the bottom. I started down the slide, scraping a bunch. As I reached the steep part, I started bouncing over various rock shelves, skipping along. It gets real steep and falls 40 feet in about 25 yards, at a 75 degree angle [sic]. At this point, the boat had passed the skipping speed and was flying over the shelves like they weren't even there. I plunged into the pool at the bottom, surprised at how much the hole slowed me down."

Section 2: Md. 77 (Camp Peniel) Bridge to Frank Bentz Lake

Gradient	Difficulty	Distance	Area	Scenery	Strainers	Rating
190	IV+ (5.0)	1.2	9	A-	2-3/mi.	!!!!

USGS Quad – Blue Ridge Summit/Catoctin Furnace; Source – Trip report (Bobby Miller) 3/00; AW web site   N39 37.57, W77 26.45 to N39 37.25, W77 25.45

This section, "the Canyon," has continuous rapids, narrow chutes and big ledges. Scout for strainers beforehand. Very early on, after a pair of blind 4-foot drops, get out on the right to scout the class 5.0 "20 MPH" rapid (at a 20 MPH bend in the road). Below there, cut right of an island, where you duck a tree as you go down a sloping ledge. The next half mile is continuous class III+, full of man-made ledges (for trout). When you see some small rock formations on your left, there is a slide that ends in a 4-foot drop through a narrow slot, followed by another slide into a 5-foot sloping drop. Soon, the creek turns left over a 6-foot, class IV+ ledge. Most of the water goes left through a wild and narrow notch, but you can sneak down the shallower middle. From there to the lake is class II+. The scenery is beautiful until the mobile homes in the last quarter mile.

GAUGE: Minimum would be 900 cfs on Catoctin Creek, projected 3 hours later. The painted gauge at the put in should read 1-1.5'.

Section 3: Frank Bentz Lake to Jimtown (Hessons Bridge Road)

Gradient	Difficulty	Distance	Area	Scenery	Strainers	Rating
70 (110)	III	3.0	11	C+	1-2/mi.	**

USGS Quad – Catoctin Furnace; Source – Personal descent 3/11
N39 37.25, W77 25.45 to N39 35.62, W77 23.81

Put in at the base of the 8-foot man-made waterfall into a shallow pool. The creek starts off continuous class III. In 50 yards it splits into two channels, which reunite shortly above the road bridge at 0.2 miles. The difficulty remains class III- through the outskirts of Thurmont, where the stream is channelized and therefore much deeper. There are long stretches of continuous bouncy whitewater with few eddies and several blind turns, so you need to be very cautious about strainers; when in doubt, scout.

About midway, the stream enters a swampy area with many routes amongst the vegetation and fallen wood. The rivulets empty into two main channels; we ended up in the left one, which turned out to carry only about 40% of the flow. The first low-water bridge of a golf course might be a good place to carry to the right side channel (which we didn't do). Below that bridge, the left channel contains another low-water bridge (hard to see far in advance), a low pipe and a steep stretch with 3 trees growing in the middle of the stream. After the two channels meet, the final half mile is a welcome anti-climax.

GAUGE: Look for 600cfs on Catoctin Creek (Md), projected 2 hours ahead.

LITTLE HUNTING CREEK

Little Hunting Creek races off of Catoctin Mountain and becomes runnable when its size is doubled by Buzzard Branch. Section 1 is along the road. The creek then passes for almost a mile through private land linked to Cunningham Falls State Park. That stretch is class IV+ (250 ft/mile), and includes lots of 2-4 foot ledges and even a 75-yard long slide, but the police have stopped people from putting on, because the owner objects (and reportedly patrols his private fishing stream with a shotgun). After this gap, section 2 is another short, advanced paddle. The creek is hard to catch up, has lots of strainers and slows down only very gradually.

Section 1: Along Catoctin Hollow Road

Gradient	Difficulty	Distance	Area	Scenery	Strainers	Rating
160	III+	1.1	6	B-	3-5/mi.	**

USGS Quad – Catoctin Furnace; Source – Trip Report (Bobby Miller) 3/00
N39 35.25, W77 27.84 to N39 34.88, W77 26.97

From the confluence with Buzzard Branch, Catoctin Hollow Road remains alongside for 1.1 miles, so you can scout this fairly easily. It is continuous and steep, but not blind. The rapids are mainly just class III, but the strainers add difficulty and danger.

GAUGE: Look for at least 1000 cfs on Catoctin Creek, 3-4 hours after put in.

Section 2: Cunningham Falls State Park parking lot to Blacks Mill Road

Gradient	Difficulty	Distance	Area	Scenery	Strainers	Rating
110 (180)	III+	1.3	7	C	3-5/mi.	**

USGS Quad – Catoctin Furnace; Source – Personal descent 9/99
N39 35.18, W77 26.19 to N39 34.35, W77 25.52

Alongside the parking lot, the gradient drops to a mere 180 ft/mile. This section is class III at zero level but harder above that. Scout the first quarter mile on foot, to US 15. Take the left channel where the creek divides; the braids reunite just before US 15. The creek remains continuous class III as it passes SR 806. If you've had enough, or don't like strainers, you can take out there after just an exciting one-third mile.

The next mile is less steep (90 ft/mile) but more dangerous because of strainers on blind turns. There is another island – again, stay left. The rapids are still excellent, but you must stop to scout frequently. At 1.3 miles the stream flows over Blacks Mill Road, where we took out, because we saw more strainers down below, including a fence just upstream of Hessons Bridge Road a mile later. That mile has a 50 ft/mile gradient. For the final two miles to big Hunting Creek, the gradient is down to 10-15 ft/mile.

GAUGE: Look for 875 cfs on Catoctin Creek, projected 3 hours after you put in.

FISHING CREEK

Fishing Creek, the southernmost steep western tributary of the Monocacy, rises on Catoctin Mountain and then fills the Frederick reservoir. Below the dam, it flows for 10 miles. The gradient averages 145 ft/mile (and reaches 200 ft/mile) for the first 0.9 miles; the only legal access is a bridge after a half mile, and there are wires and low footbridges just below there. Section 1, after that, is still quite dangerous. Section 2 is a flatter "explorers' special." Below that, the creek is even milder for most of the final 4 miles.

Section 1: Mountaindale to Bethel Road

Gradient	Difficulty	Distance	Area	Scenery	Strainers	Rating
95	III	1.5	10	C-	2-4/mi.	*

USGS Quad – Catoctin Furnace; Source – Personal descent 3/07
N39 31.16, W77 27.06 to N39 32.13, W77 25.97

This is my least favorite of the steep Monocacy tributaries, because of the three-quarters mile where we had to bash through over-hanging branches and briars. And that was in the winter, before the vegetation thickens and reduces the visibility even more.

From the bridge at Mountaindale and Putnam roads, the narrow creek makes a beeline northeast. The rapids are continuous but with no major drops, and only a few spots require fairly precise handling. The first and last quarters of the trip are fun, with small but usable eddies, and one barbed-wire fence and one footbridge in the latter part, which can both be slipped under at low water. But the middle half of the trip is no fun at all. Small branches, shrubs and briars hang over the water, in places forcing you to lower your head, close your eyes and bash through. The only eddies are among the branches, which makes them virtually unusable. Definitely stay away in high water.

GAUGE: You need at least 600 cfs on the Catoctin Creek gauge, projected forward to 2-3 hours after put in.

The creek passes ponds of the former **Lewistown State Fish Hatchery**, Maryland's first fish hatchery, from 1918 until the early 1950s. The facility, now in disrepair, is why section 1 is so unappealing; the woods were cleared for it, and the small trees, bushes and briars that have grown back along the narrow stream hang over it far more than do more mature woods.

At the put in, everyone was friendly. The store let us park there. The family across the road came to photograph our launch and phoned to find out whether there were any fences across the creek. While we were portaging some nasty overhangs, a local landowner in his ATV asked whether we had permission to be there, but he seemed satisfied by our response that we had gotten permission at the put in, and didn't know who to ask downstream.

Section 2: Bethel Road to Covered Bridge (Utica Road)

Gradient	Difficulty	Distance	Area	Scenery	Strainers	Rating
23	?	3.3	11	?	?	?

USGS Quad – Catoctin Furnace; Source – Trip Report (Ed Gertler) 3/00; scouting
N39 32.13, W77 25.97 to N39 31.52, W77 23.86

As Fishing Creek crosses Bethel Road and turns east, its gradient drops by 75%. It crosses US 15 (the 4-foot dam there can be run anywhere), Hessong Bridge Road and Lewistown Road, before reaching the covered bridge at Utica Road. Take out at the upstream side of this bridge, for this 3.3-mile *"explorers' special."*

Below, the gradient remains 23 ft/mile for a mile, but there are fences. It drops to 10 ft/mile for the two miles to Devilbliss Road, before increasing to 35 ft/mile in the final half mile to the Monocacy.

However, the price for running just that steeper half mile is a difficult put in at Devilbliss Road and 2 very flat miles (at 3 ft/mile) on the Monocacy.

GAUGE: The Catoctin Creek gauge should be over 400 cfs, 2 hours later.

TUSCARORA CREEK: Sundays Lane to Bloomfield Road

Gradient	Difficulty	Distance	Area	Scenery	Strainers	Rating
33	I	2.0	9	B	3-6/mi.	-

USGS Quad – Frederick; Source – Personal descent 3/10
N39 25.45, W77 25.68 to N39 28.60, W77 25.26

By the time it is big enough, this stream no longer has much gradient. The put in is just off of Opossumtown Pike, where an unnamed tributary from Gambrill State Park triples the flow. The run is through narrow, deer-filled woods, with farms and a few houses visible. There are only riffles but class II skills are needed to maneuver around the wood. The first mile was nice; despite some braiding, there were few strainers, and the two old wire fences were no obstacle. But the second mile was full of downed trees, several of which required thorny portages. The take out was therefore a welcome sight.

Below the take out, the gradient drops in half. It is 0.7 miles to the confluence with Little Tuscarora Creek, and a further 2.8 miles to the Monocacy River, at 13 ft/mile.

GAUGE: Catoctin Creek gauge should be 750 cfs, projected forward 3 hours.

MONOCACY EAST

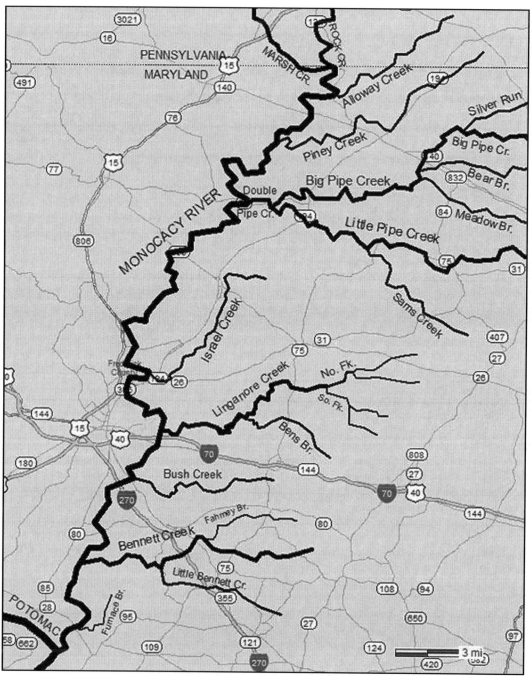

© Copyright 2005-2011 Undertow Software Corp.

Chapter 16:

MONOCACY EAST

This is the largest (525 square miles) and by far the tamest part of the Monocacy basin, of interest mainly to beginner and novice paddlers. Few of these streams get more than one * in my rating system, but if you prefer calmer water, some are quite appealing. Gertler covers the five largest: **Big Pipe, Little Pipe, Double Pipe, Linganore** and **Bennett creeks,** all of which have average gradients of just 7-11 ft/mile. What I have seen of these confirms Gertler's judgments on them (summarized under each creek).

I have added eleven smaller and mostly steeper creeks – but there is nothing very steep on this side of the watershed. There are some class II rapids on **Bush** and **Little Bennett creeks**, which are near to Washington and Baltimore. Farther north, **Piney Creek** is a pleasant beginner run that is easy to catch, while **Alloway Creek** provides a long, scenic and slightly steeper trip. **Silver Run,** the **North Fork of Linganore Creek,** and **Sams Creek** have little to recommend them, although the last has some unusual scenery. *Bear Branch, Meadow Branch* (with the highest gradient in this chapter), *Israel Creek* and *Bens Branch* are waiting for you as "explorers' specials."

Well, it's not entirely true that there are no steep creeks on the east side of the Monocacy. **Furnace Branch** races off of Sugarloaf Mountain, and enters the Monocacy 2 miles above its mouth. It drops 90 feet in its final mile, with a drainage area of 4 sq. mi., but there is no public access to a put in. In the early 19th Century it was the center of an industrial complex that included an iron furnace, lime kiln, gristmill, and quartz and sandstone quarry.

Sugarloaf Mountain, named for its resemblance to an old form of carbs, is an isolated outcropping of the Appalachians that is owned by the non-profit Stronghold Corporation, established by the late Gordon Strong of Chicago, to promote appreciation of nature. It receives over 100,000 visitors annually. You can drive to and picnic at the top of the mountain. Nearby were the **Amelung Glass Works**, the earliest glass factory in the country.

GAUGES: In the 1990s, paddlers had only the Frederick (Jug Bridge) gauge on the lower Monocacy, with 817 sq. mi. drainage. Then came the Bridgeport gauge on the upper Monocacy, which has 173 sq. mi. drainage, and usually peaks 8 to 12 hours before Frederick. Since 2006, gauges have been added on Bennett Creek (62 sq. mi.) and Big Pipe Creek at Bruceville (102 sq. mi.). There is also a gauge on tiny Soper Branch of Little Bennett Creek (1.2 sq. mi.), which can serve as an advanced indicator (almost like a rainfall gauge). For the small streams, the gauge on Grave Run (7.7 sq. mi.) in the upper Gunpowder basin is the best for the north, Beaver Run (14 sq. mi.) in the North Branch of Patapsco watershed is ideal for the central area, and the Patuxent at Unity (35 sq. mi.) correlates well in the south. These three gauges are east of the Monocacy, and their own watersheds abut those of creeks in this chapter.

In the first part of the table below, **the gauge column summarizes the Big Pipe Creek readings that approximate zero level,** while in the lower part of the table, *the bold italics reference is to Bennett Creek.* But as most of the smaller creeks will rise and fall faster than those gauges, you must look at the trends, not just the gauge levels. No rainfall gauges are reported from this watershed.

name	gradient	difficulty	length	area	gauge	rating
Alloway Creek	19	I	6.7	13	500cfs	**
Piney Creek	12	I	9.0	20	375cfs	*
Double Pipe Creek	6	I	1.4	182	100cfs	*
Big Pipe Creek	9	I	16.4	50	175cfs	*
Silver Run	20	I	1.2	9	625cfs	-
Bear Branch	24	?	2.0	11	525cfs	?
Meadow Branch	27	?	2.1	15	450cfs	?
Little Pipe Creek	8	I	9.3	60	175cfs	*
Sams Creek	13	I (II)	4.5	13	500cfs	-
Israel Creek	10	?	4.7	23	225cfs	?
Linganore Cr. - Sec. 1	11	I	5.2	49	125cfs	*
- Sec. 2	11	I	2.5	83	(80cfs)	*
North Fk, Linganore	15	I	0.8	21	225cfs	-
Bens Branch	20	?	2.9	10	350cfs	?
Bush Creek	18	II (II+)	5.3	21	300cfs	**
Bennett Creek	11	I	8.5	27	140cfs	*
Little Bennett Creek	25	II	4.0	12	450cfs	**

ALLOWAY CREEK: Harney Road to Monocacy R. (Baptist Road)

Gradient	Difficulty	Distance	Area	Scenery	Strainers	Rating
19	I	6.7	13	B-	<1/mi.	**

USGS Quad – Taneytown; Source – Personal descent 2/98
N39 43.84, W77 09.25 to N39 41.86, W77 12.93

Alloway ("beautiful tail," in reference to the fox) Creek, the first large side stream to enter the Monocacy, starts flat (at 8 ft/mile above the put in), but gradually steepens; the first 3.7 miles of the trip are at 16 ft/mile, while the last 3 average 23 ft/mile. The riffles become bouncier and more frequent, although they never quite become real rapids.

This nice novice trip is pretty and has few strainers. The creek divides around several islands in the last mile, leaving some narrow passages; one of these, on the far right, may have low-hanging branches. At 6.7 miles, it is a relatively long run for a small creek, but even at zero level the trip took us only two hours. There is a narrow wooded margin alongside, but farms and houses can be seen through it until the leaves come out. There are several nice rock cliffs. The start is in Pennsylvania, the rest in Maryland.

Alloway Creek enters the Monocacy just above Starners Dam, a 3-foot drop into a hydraulic, which is the only dangerous place on that long river. Even more dangerous is the millrace along the near (left) shore, where you would get decapitated by a bridge. So take out on the rocks between the top of the millrace and the main dam. You can park nearby at the bridge over the Monocacy (for $5/day, to the owners of Starners Dam).

GAUGE: The USGS gauge on river left under the second Harney Road bridge (1.4 miles above the Monocacy) needs 2.3 for the bottom section and 2.6 for the top. Look for Big Pipe Creek to be over 500 cfs and Grave Run 40 cfs.

⋙ PINEY CREEK: Taneytown (Fringer Road) to Monocacy River

Gradient	Difficulty	Distance	Area	Scenery	Strainers	Rating
12	I	9.0	20	B-	<<1/mi.	*

USGS Quad – Taneytown/Emmitsburg; Source -Personal descent (last 6 miles) 5/02
N39 40.11, W77 09.97 to N39 39.35, W77 15.89

Piney Creek flows southwest for 18 miles to the Monocacy, through farm land with a wooded margin of "protected forest land." A good put in is Fringer Road, midway on the water's journey. The creek is gentle and wide, with only riffles. Kingfishers, Canada geese, mallards and blue herons are plentiful, as are scenic shale cliffs. A doe and two fawns crossed the creek just in front of me.

GAUGE: Some 375 cfs on the Big Pipe Creek gauge (projected to 2 hours after put in) should suffice. On Grave Run look for at least 30 cfs.

> On June 30, 1863, **General Meade** moved his Army of the Potomac headquarters to Taneytown (near the Piney Creek put in), as he maneuvered to ensure that his forces could block any Confederate movement towards Washington or Baltimore. Late the next day, he began moving towards Gettysburg, in response to reports of the first clashes there.

⋙ DOUBLE PIPE CREEK: Detour to Monocacy R. (Millers Bridge)

Gradient	Difficulty	Distance	Area	Scenery	Strainers	Rating
6	I	1.4	182	C	0	*

USGS Quad –Woodsboro; Source – Personal descent 3/07
N39 36.22, W77 16.17 to N39 36.19, W77 17.59

This is both the largest and the shortest sizable Monocacy tributary, as it combines the waters of Big and Little Pipe creeks shortly before the confluence with the Monocacy. After a few easy riffles, the rest is flat water. It adds about 60% to the flow in the Monocacy.

GAUGE: The Big Pipe Creek gauge should be over 100 cfs.

> One version of the creek's name is that the Indians smoked **peace pipes** nearby to resolve disputes. Or perhaps the clay was good for making pipes.
> Barges once carried **pig iron** from Double Pipe Creek all the way to the Potomac. To improve navigation, wing dams were built on Double Pipe Creek and the Monocacy.

⋙ BIG PIPE CREEK: Mayberry Road to Detour (Md. 77)

Gradient	Difficulty	Distance	Area	Scenery	Strainers	Rating
9	I	16.4	50	B-	<<1/mi.	*

USGS Quad –Littlestown/Taneyt./UnionBr/Woodsboro; Source – Personal descent (first 1.5 miles) 3/03; Gertler.
N39 39.96, W77 06.32 via N39 37.52, W77 08.47 (mile 7) to N39 36.22, W77 16.17

Big Pipe Creek runs for 30 miles from near the Pennsylvania line until it meets Little Pipe Creek at Detour, to form Double Pipe Creek. There are many access points, but Gertler recommends Mayberry Road, the confluence with Silver Run, because there are more fences and other strainers up above. There is one low water bridge and one dam to carry. Below Trevanion Road (mile 7), *Bear and Meadow branches* add considerable water.

GAUGE: About 175 cfs on the Big Pipe Creek gauge is needed to start at Mayberry Road, and 115 cfs to start at Trevanion Road for a 9.5 mile paddle.

> Before to the **battle of Gettysburg**, the main Union forces camped along Parr's Ridge and Big Pipe Creek, to shield Baltimore and Washington from any attack by Lee's forces (whose location was then not accurately known). Stuart's cavalry briefly disturbed the Union forces there, but was driven off. General Meade fortified the **"Pipe Creek Line"** as his preferred position from which to fight, and then after both sides stumbled into battle at Gettysburg, he maintained it as a position to withdraw to in case the North lost at Gettysburg.

SILVER RUN: Kump Station Road to Big Pipe Creek

Gradient	Difficulty	Distance	Area	Scenery	Strainers	Rating
20	I	1.2*	9	C	2-3/mi.	-

USGS Quad –Littlestown; Source – Personal descent 3/03
N39 40.67, W77 05.57 to N39 39.43, W77 07.29

*(plus 1.5 miles on Big Pipe Creek, at 15 ft/mile, to Hyser Road–Wolfs Mill)

The stream twists through the woods, with fast current and occasional riffles and strainers. I saw several fences just upstream (which is why I only ran this short stretch). In high water, you must portage Stone Road. The 1.5 miles on Big Pipe Creek will pass quickly, with long riffles.

GAUGE: You need at least 625 cfs on Big Pipe Creek (2-3 hours after put in), but more timely measures would be 45 cfs on Grave Run and 85 cfs on Beaver Run.

BEAR BRANCH: Bear Branch Road to Big Pipe Creek

Gradient	Difficulty	Distance	Area	Scenery	Strainers	Rating
24	?	2.0*	11	?	?	?

USGS Quad –Littlestown/Taneytown; Source – Scouting accesses
N39 38.36, W77 06.81 to N39 37.52, W77 08.48

*(plus 0.7 miles on Big Pipe Creek to Trevanion Road)

This *"explorers' special"* flows west through cattle country in a valley between Big Pipe Creek and Meadow Branch. Ask permission to put in through the board fence at Bear Branch Road. The alternative is at the end of Runnymeade Road, 0.7 miles later.

GAUGE: You need 40 cfs on Grave Run and 75 cfs on Beaver Run.

MEADOW BRANCH: Md. 84 to Big Pipe Creek (Trevanion Road)

Gradient	Difficulty	Distance	Area	Scenery	Strainers	Rating
27	?	2.1	15	?	?	?

USGS Quad –New Windsor/Union Br./Taneytown; Source – Scouting accesses
N39 36.53, W77 06.83 to N39 37.52, W77 08.48

This *"explorers' special,"* the largest tributary of Big Pipe Creek, flows for ten miles from Westminster, through ranches and cornfields. There are fences at Md. 84, but one can slip beneath the downstream one to put in. The first mile, to Clearview Road, is at 20 ft/mile, and the rest averages 33 ft/mile.

GAUGE: Look for 450 cfs on Big Pipe Creek (4 hours later), 35 cfs on Grave Run and 65 cfs on Beaver Run.

LITTLE PIPE CREEK: Union Bridge (W. Locust St.) to Detour

Gradient	Difficulty	Distance	Area	Scenery	Strainers	Rating
8	I	8.8	60*	C	<1/mi.	*

USGS Quad –Union Br/Woodsboro; Source – Personal descent 3/07 (last 2.8 miles); Gertler
N39 34.13, W77 11.03 via N39 35.00, W77 13.56 to N39 36.22, W77 16.17

*(includes Sams Creek which enters in one-quarter mile)

This is a pleasant but unexciting paddle. Gertler has run it from Wakefield (15 sq. mi.), eight miles above Union Bridge, but the gradient is only slightly higher (12 ft/mile) there, and there are a few fences as well as trees. A quarter mile below Union Bridge, you pick up Sams Creek, and the stream widens and becomes the Frederick/Carroll County line. There is also a good put in 3.3 miles farther downstream, at Simpsons Mill, for a 5.3 mile paddle. Portage the three-foot dam beneath the railroad trestle, visible upstream from Md. 194.

GAUGE: Look for 175 cfs on the Big Pipe Creek gauge.

SAMS CREEK: McKinstrys Mill to Little Pipe Cr. (Good Intent Rd.)

Gradient	Difficulty	Distance	Area	Scenery	Strainers	Rating
13	I (II)	4.5	13	D	1-2/mi.	-

USGS Quad – Union Bridge; Source – Personal descent 2/06
N39 31.98, W77 09.42 to N39 34.11, W77 11.35

Sams Creek meanders northwest, as the Carroll/Frederick Co. line. McKinstrys Mill (1767 to 1950) is a good put in. Soon the creek winds between mud banks, as cattle watch. Expect several fences as well as a private bridge to portage. Half a mile after Lehigh Road (a poor access), there is a mile of straight channels between dirt berms, where the creek was moved by the quarry. A large, capsized motor boat was a surprise.

As the creek turns left into a more natural streambed, there are some long riffles. Up ahead you see the impressive facilities of the Union Bridge Cement Plant, the largest and most modern in the US, producing 1.8 million tons of Portland cement annually. (Their environmental specialist said it was OK to paddle through.) Half a mile later comes a doglegged 150-yard tunnel, through three dark culverts. Take the middle one, if it is clear. Soon afterwards, scout a 2-foot drop over a weir.

You soon cross Md. 75 just south of Union Bridge and reenter ranchland; watch for fences behind the barn. When you reach Little Pipe Creek, you are near Good Intent Road. Take out there with permission, or continue 3.3 miles to Simpsons Mill.

GAUGE: Look for 500 cfs on Big Pipe Creek, 275 cfs on the North Branch of the Patapsco, and 70 cfs on Beaver Run.

ISRAEL CREEK: Daysville Road to Monocacy River (Liberty Road)

Gradient	Difficulty	Distance	Area	Scenery	Strainers	Rating
10	?	4.7	23	?	?	?

USGS Quad – Walkersville; Source – Scouting access points
N39 29.58, W77 19.46 to N39 27.15, W77 22.24

This *"explorers' special"* flows for 14 lazy miles through farm and ranch country. One could run the last 8 miles, from the east edge of Woodsboro, but by Daysville Road the catchment area has almost doubled and the scenery is a bit better. When you reach the Monocacy, it is just 0.2 miles upstream to Md. 26 (Liberty Road).

GAUGE: The Beaver Run gauge needs 50 cfs, Bennett Creek 225 cfs.

LINGANORE CREEK

Linganore ("it melts copiously in springtime") Creek was dammed to form 3-mile long Lake Linganore, for a subdivision. This leaves two runnable sections of the creek.

Section 1: Timmons Road to Gas House Pike

Gradient	Difficulty	Distance	Area	Scenery	Strainers	Rating
11	I	5.2	44	C	1/mi.	*

USGS Quad –Walkersville/Libertytown; Source – Personal descent (first half-mile) 12/03; Gertler; scouting
N39 26.75, W77 14.32 to N39 25.63, W77 16.93

Timmons Road is the first access below the confluence of the North and South branches, and is a half-mile above Gertler's put in. That first half mile has several riffles, including a lively one just above Md. 75, where you bash through small branches. Based on Gertler, the rest sounds similar. There is one more access, midway, at Old Annapolis Road. From Gas House Pike, it is less than a mile to Lake Linganore.

GAUGE: About 125 cfs on the Bennett Creek gauge would be minimal.

Section 2: Lake Linganore (Woodridge Road) to Linganore Road

Gradient	Difficulty	Distance	Area	Scenery	Strainers	Rating
11	I	2.5	83	C+	<1/mi.	*

USGS Quad –Walkersville; Source – Gertler and scouting put in and takeout
N39 25.03, W77 19.60 to N39 25.57, W77 21.63

This stretch below the dam can be paddled only when (a) Lake Linganore is full and overflows from rain or snowmelt, or (b) they release water from the lake. The put in is a dramatic sight – water pouring over the dam and down a steep rock pile, while half a dozen fountains spout like geysers (aerating water released from below). You can climb and run the man-made class II- chutes, or use an easier put in just downstream. And then it is 2.5 miles of riffles and flat water to Linganore Road (0.4 miles above the Monocacy).

Warning: non-residents will be subject to $100 fines and towing for leaving their cars at the dam, unless they get guest passes from a Lake Linganore Association resident.

GAUGE: When Lake Linganore is full, about 75 cfs on Bennett Creek is all that is needed; at other times, there will be just a trickle.

NORTH FORK, LINGANORE CR.: Dollyhyde Rd. to Confluence

Gradient	Difficulty	Distance	Area	Scenery	Strainers	Rating
15	I	0.8*	21	C-	0-2/mi.	-

USGS Quad –Libertytown; Source – Personal descent 12/03
N39 27.10, W77 12.61 to N39 26.75, W77 14.32

*(plus 1.2 miles on Linganore Creek to Timmons Road)

The North Fork is formed by Weldon Creek and Talbot Branch, and the one access, Dollyhyde Road, is 1.2 miles below there. The creek looks wild at the put in, but it soon becomes clear that you are paddling through a catle pasture. The stream is twisty, with many riffles.

The addition of the South Fork widens the streambed, but does not change much else. If there is still a logjam above a riffle, portage on river right; I went left, and had a barbed wire fence and a steep, muddy bank. You can continue down Linganore Creek, section 1.

GAUGE: The Beaver Run gauge needs 50 cfs, Bennett Creek 225 cfs.

BENS BRANCH: Green Valley Road (Md. 75) to St. Andrew Drive

Gradient	Difficulty	Distance	Area	Scenery	Strainers	Rating
20	?	2.9	10	?	?	?

USGS Quad – Walkersville; Source – Scouting first half mile and take out
N39 25.17, W77 15.20 to N39 25.24, W77 17.04

This *"explorers' special"* flows west into Lake Linganore. The put in is off of a busy road, but there is no place to park along Gas House Pike, which follows the creek through the fields for the first half mile.

After that, the stream burrows off into the woods. Finding the take out by road is a challenge – I failed twice. Take Pinehurst Drive off Boyers Mill Rd., turn right on E. Lakeridge Rd., left on Edgewood Rd., left back onto E. Lakeridge Rd., right on Hemlock Point Rd. and continue on St. Andrew Dr., to a bridge by a swimming hole – 300 yards above where the creek enters the lake.

GAUGE: The Beaver Run gauge should be 80 cfs, Bennett Creek 350 cfs.

BUSH CREEK: Ijamsville to Monocacy River

Gradient	Difficulty	Distance	Area	Scenery	Strainers	Rating
18	II (II+)	5.3	21	B-	1-2/mi.	**

USGS Quad – Urbana/Buckeystown; Source – Personal descent 3/97
N39 21.54, W77 19.43 to N39 22.13, W77 23.40

Bush Creek rises near Mount Airy and flows west for 15 miles to the Monocacy. Because of braiding upstream, wait until Ijamsville Road to start. The first half of the trip has up to class II- rapids, the better ones at some of the six railroad crossings. At mile 3, after Ball Road comes alongside, there is a tight class II+ chute on the right. A mile later is a long class II rock garden. Intermittent class II- rapids continue to the confluence. The scenery is mostly woods, with some steep hills on river left.

The Md. 355 take-out bridge over the Monocacy is 300 yards below the confluence. Take out on river left just before the bridge.

GAUGE: If you can get past the first riffles without scraping, there will be enough water. Bennett Creek should exceed 300 cfs.

"The Battle that Saved Washington." Near the take out, is the Monocacy National Battlefield. Here, on July 9, 1864, 5,800 Union troops under Major General Lew Wallace (who after the war wrote *Ben Hur*), held up for a day the advance of Lieutenant General Jubal Early's 15,000 Confederates. The mouth of Bush Creek lay between the two Monocacy River crossings the Union was trying to protect: the B&O Railroad which led to Baltimore, and the Georgetown Pike (now Md. 355) which led to Washington. Eventually, the southerners crossed the Monocacy further south, and outflanked the Yankees, who retreated in good order towards Baltimore, while Early's troops advanced on Washington. While this battle was technically a Confederate victory, the day they lost allowed reinforcements from Grant to arrive just in time to save the capital.

BENNETT CREEK: Big Woods Rd. to Monocacy (So. Criss Ford Rd.)

Gradient	Difficulty	Distance	Area	Scenery	Strainers	Rating
11	I	9.2	27	C+	<<1/mi.	*

USGS Quad – Urbana/Buckeyst.; Source – Personal descent 11/06 (last 3.7 miles); Gertler
N39 19.08, W77 19.59 via N39 18.27, W77 23.58 (Peters Road) to N39 17.61, W77 26.28

Bennett Creek, the southernmost major Monocacy tributary, is pleasant and relaxing. At Thurston Road, after 3.3 miles, Little Bennett Creek almost doubles the flow. Two miles later, alongside Peters Road, there is a low water bridge (to a Korean religious retreat) to portage. There is lovely scenery and lots of riffles in the 1.8 miles from there to Mt. Ephraim Road. Half a mile after you cross Park Mills Road, a 5-foot dam should be scouted from the left; portage or run the class IV- chute on the far right. Approaching the confluence, the route gets sketchy; stay left initially but look for passages on your right to the Monocacy. Take out just below the Lilypons Road bridge, on river right.

GAUGE: You will need about 125 cfs on the Bennett Creek gauge – this corresponds to the staff gauge at Mt. Ephraim Road reading 2.1.

Richard Bennett was one of the Parliamentary Commissioners sent to govern Maryland in 1654-57, during Oliver Cromwell's rule. In the 1720s, when this area was settled, his grandson, also a Richard Bennett, was reputedly the richest person in British North America.

The final mile is alongside the **Lily Pons** fishponds and water gardens, one of the largest suppliers for ornamental fishponds. Its name, after a once-famous actress, is a play on words.

LITTLE BENNETT CREEK: Prescott Road to Bennett Creek

Gradient	Difficulty	Distance	Area	Scenery	Strainers	Rating
25	II	4.0	12	C	0-2/mi.	**

USGS Quad – Urbana; Source – Personal descent 11/96
N39 16.57, W77 18.13 to N39 17.67, W77 21.76

Little Bennett Creek, the southernmost runnable Monocacy tributary, is the only decent Bennett Creek headwaters, as upper Bennett Creek (above Big Woods Road) and Fahrney Branch are both fence infested. We put in at Clarksburg Road (7 sq. mi., 38 ft/mile), 1.7 miles above Prescott Road, but the density of strainers in the first mile was painful.

Half a mile below Prescott Road, the creek passes Md. 355, and in another half mile comes I-270, with two good surfing spots right below. It is 2 more miles to Thurston, and a final mile, along the base of Sugarloaf Mountain, to the confluence. There were two fences in the final mile. There are lots of riffles and small ledges (formed by sunken tree trunks), plus narrow chutes and tight turns around fallen trees. The take out is an easy 100-yard upstream paddle on (big) Bennett Creek.

GAUGE: Bennett Creek should be over 450 cfs, the Patuxent at Unity 225 cfs, and Soper Branch should have been over 7 cfs for several hours.

The **Hyattstown Mill**, a gristmill and sawmill built around 1790 on Little Bennett Creek, just above Md. 355, operated until it burned in 1918. It was then rebuilt, operated until 1940 and restored in 1996. Further upstream was a gristmill as part of a distillery, which operated until 1907. Nearby, at the end of the Froggy Hollow Schoolhouse Trail, are the one-room **Kingsley Schoolhouse**, which was used from 1893 to 1935, and a nearby swinging bridge over the creek that must have been a big hit with the students.

In 1966, **Little Bennett Regional Park** was the site of the first controlled deer hunt in Montgomery County, with the objective of halving the 1,000-animal herd.

WASHINGTON D.C. & MARYLAND SUBURBS

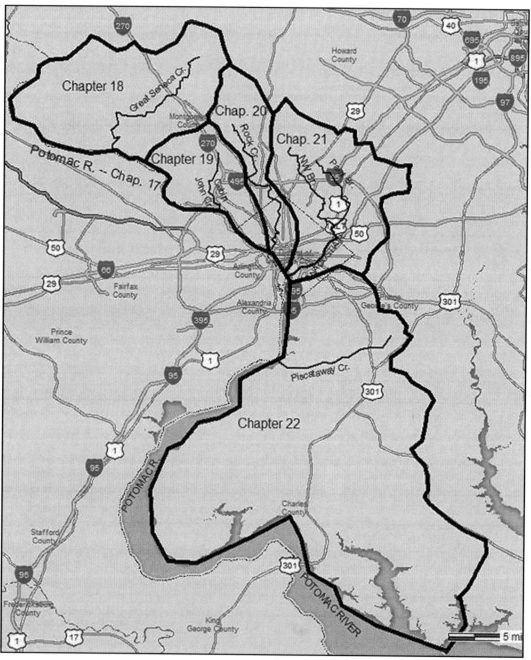

© Copyright 2005-2011 Undertow Software Corp.

PART V: WASHINGTON D.C. & MARYLAND SUBURBS

This part covers Washington D.C. and most of Montgomery, Prince Georges (PG) and Charles counties – the inner core of the metropolitan area from the Potomac River northward, with a population of some 2.4 million. It begins with the **Potomac River** (chapter 17), followed by **Western Montgomery County** (chapter 18), the more-urbanized **Southern Montgomery County** (chapter 19), the **Rock Creek** (chapter 20) and **Anacostia River basins** (chapter 21), and finally **Southern Maryland** (chapter 22).

> The difference between these two parts of Montgomery County is more than just location. **Western Montgomery County** is mainly agricultural, and half of that has been legally preserved by the county buying easements along the edge of this area. In contrast, **southern Montgomery County** is primarily residential or commercial.

The high density of runnable creeks in this compact area covers the whole range of difficulties. The streams in the outer suburbs and the eastern part of the Anacostia basin (which is in western PG County) are rather easy – western Montgomery County is still Piedmont, while PG County is on the coastal plain. On the other hand, there are some steep little creeks in the Rock Creek basin, southern Montgomery County, and the western part of the Anacostia basin, especially where they tumble down the fall line. However, as with other fall-line streams, the stretches of rapids are relatively short.

Urbanization is a mixed blessing here in terms of paddling potential. The main negative effect is water pollution, and sometimes scenery pollution as well. However, many of the creeks run through urban parks and are quite pretty, as the Maryland National Capital Park and Planning Commission (MNCPPC) and the National Park Service (which manages Rock Creek Park) have done well at protecting the immediate surroundings. Also on the positive side, in addition to proximity, is the absence of farmers' fences and of hassles about trespassing on private property.

The flash-flooding nature of urban streams also has both positive and negative aspects. It means that even the tiniest tributaries are occasionally paddleable – you will see catchment areas here far below those that would be runnable in rural areas. On the other hand, even the largest streams like Seneca Creek and Rock Creek hold their water only briefly, and the flash flooding itself is detrimental to water quality. So if you hope to run many of the creeks in this area, you need to fit your schedule and agenda to theirs, and be willing to accept the smells and health risks of their water.

Of the 22 **river gauges** in this area (as of early 2012), 11 provide good coverage of the Anacostia and Southern Maryland. The Little Falls gauge (plus upstream ones) is fine for the Potomac, as are the Rock Creek and Turkey Branch gauges for the Rock Creek basin. The two Montgomery County chapters are not quite as well served, because 4 of their 6 gauges have drainage areas of less than 1.4 sq. mi., and a fifth drains 101 sq. mi., but a new (October 2010) gauge on Ten Mile Creek with 4.5 sq. mi. is very helpful. Several gauges from Virginia and the Patuxent River basin are also worth checking.

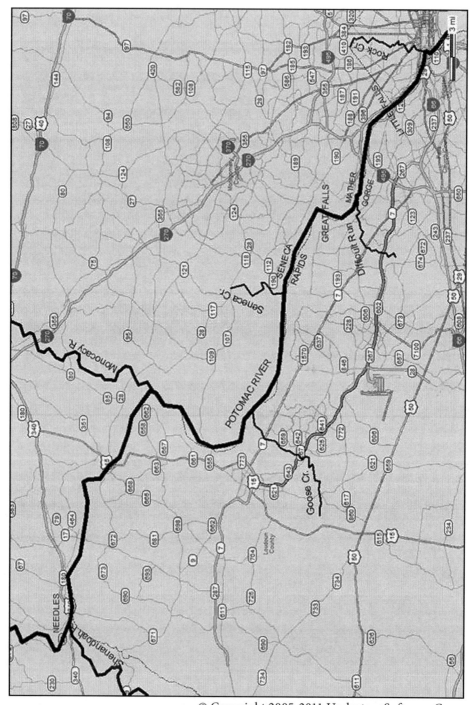

Chapter 17:

POTOMAC RIVER

Because of its importance, the Potomac River gets its own chapter. And because sections 2-5 are in the Maryland suburbs (the entire river belongs to Maryland, based on the original English colonial grants), the chapter fits best here. Although its water quality has been improving, in 2012 the Potomac was named by American Rivers as our "most endangered river," should Congress roll back protections in the Clean Water Act.

The main stem of the Potomac is formed at the confluence of its North (1,350 sq. mi.) and South (1,480 sq. mi.) branches at an uncelebrated spot (inaccessible by road) 1.5 miles east of the hamlets of Green Spring, WV, and Oldtown, Md. A series of small towns are located at river crossings along it – Hancock, Md. (1,700), Williamsport, Md. (1,900), Shepherdstown, WV (800) and Brunswick, Md. (4,900) – but there are no major centers until tidewater at Washington DC. This reflects the limited role that the non-tidal Potomac ever had in transportation, and the fact that the C&O Canal that was built alongside it had been made obsolete by railroads even before it was completed.

The Potomac has only riffles for its first 113 miles, and much of the 3 ft/mile gradient is expended through three dams. It then forms the popular **Needles** trip (section 1), where it breaks through the Blue Ridge at Harpers Ferry, which is followed by 35 miles of even flatter water (1 ft/mile) until the **Seneca Rapids** area (section 2) starting at Violets Lock and ending above Great Falls. **Great Falls** itself (section 3) is a very dangerous class 5.0 rapid that has become the local testing ground for an elite group of experts. Starting shortly below the base of the falls, there is a delightful run through **Mather Gorge** and beyond (section 4), followed by the last section of the fall line, culminating in **Little Falls** (section 5). After that, the Potomac is tidal for some 110 miles to its mouth. It is hard to contemplate an "explorers' special" for this chapter.

Although, consistent with the rest of this book, the Potomac is described here as a number of downriver trips, for a large and growing share of paddlers, it is more a series of play spots. The Potomac Paddlers website, http://www.potomacpaddlers.com, gives you the best water levels for the play spots in sections 4 and 5.

GAUGES: The **Potomac gauge at Little Falls** (11,560 sq. miles) is used for sections 2-5, and is the **zero-level reference below**, except that the *gauge at Hancock (4,090 sq mi. –bold italics) is used for section 1*. It is also useful to keep track of the gauge at Point of Rocks (9,651 sq. miles). For section 1, one should look also at the Shenandoah gauge at Millville (3,022 sq. miles), because the trip finishes below the confluence. At low summer levels, Bloomington dam releases take 4.5 days to reach the Needles, another 1.5 days to get to Seneca Rapids, and about 6 more hours until the water is at Little Falls – so a weekend release gets there starting the following Friday afternoon.

name	gradient	difficulty	length	area	gauge	rating
Section 1 – Needles	9	II	5.0	6,311	*500cfs*	**
Section 2 – Seneca Rapids	4 (10)	II-	6.1	11,385	500cfs	**
Section 3 – Great Falls	300	5.0	0.2	11,450	varies	!!!!
Section 4 – Mather Gorge	5 (15)	II (III)	8.0	11,450	500cfs	***
Section 5 – Little Falls	20 (100)	III	1.0	11,560	250cfs	****

Section 1: Needles – Dam #3 to Knoxville

Gradient	Difficulty	Distance	Area	Scenery	Strainers	Rating
9	II	5.0	6,311	B-	0	**

USGS Quad – Charles Town/Harpers Ferry; Source – Personal descent (often)
N39 19.97, W77 45.08 (Dam #3, WV); N39 21.84, W77 44.44 (Shinham Ramp) to N39 19.22, W77 42.71 (Potoma Wayside); N39 19.68, W77 40.02 (Knoxville)

This is a very popular run, for tubers as well as paddlers, around scenic Harpers Ferry. Shinham Ramp at Dargans Bend (Maryland) has ample parking, but this means starting with 2.5 miles of slack water before Dam #3. This can be good training for beginners, but otherwise I prefer starting at Dam #3 in West Virginia, which you can get to from Harpers Ferry by turning right from US 340 on Bakerton St. (a left turn goes to the Staircase put in) and right again after the one-lane underpass, and driving to the end. The put in is now owned by River Runners – they sell season passes (currently $10 for WV residents and $25 for others) or charge for daily parking (currently $5).

There are many routes through the class II- remains of Dam #3, but strainers are a danger for the unskilled. The next half mile is the class II- Needles per se, a network of rocks and small ledges. After a flat half mile, there is a class II rock garden and then another a half mile later, almost to the confluence with the Shenandoah.

In the following half mile you pass through two easy rock gardens with a wide choice of routes, and then get to White Horse Rapids. The main channel is a lively wave train (class II up to moderate levels, harder in high water), while more adventurous paddlers often prefer a route through the boulders on the right, leading to a tight 4-foot, class III drop. At higher levels, more routes on the right open up. Before reaching US 340, there are popular take outs on the right (Potoma Wayside) and left (Sandy Hook), after paddling just 2.5 miles. Potoma Wayside requires a steep carry, while Sandy Hook involves crossing the railroad tracks illegally.

If you continue, staying to the right of (or going between) the long islands for a mile takes you past a blue heron rookery. Another half mile brings you to a take out on river left (park at the end of Keep Tryst Road). Just below this is Weverton Rapids, followed soon by File Factory Rapids and Knoxville Rapids, all sets of river-wide ledges of up to class II difficulty. After the Knoxville Rapids, stay left and look for the sign to a take out – which also requires crossing the railroad tracks illegally – on the western edge of Knoxville (reached from the first parking area on SR 478, off of US 340). One can also continue 2.5 flat miles farther to an easy and legal take out at Brunswick.

GAUGE: The gauge at Hancock should read at least 2.8 (500 cfs). Above 5, this is a class III trip, and by 7 it is class IV. Novices have gotten in trouble by not paying attention to the river level. Starting at the confluence, the Millville gauge on the Shenandoah is relevant as well; however, the river is quite wide here, and the difficulty increases only very slowly with the water level.

> Near the put in is **John Brown's Cave**, where the abolitionist hid before seizing the federal arsenal at Harpers Ferry. The cave is extensive, but not open to the public.

Section 2: Seneca Rapids – Violets Lock (Dam #2) to Swains Lock

Gradient	Difficulty	Distance	Area	Scenery	Strainers	Rating
4 (10)	II-	6.1-6.8	11,385	B	0	**

USGS Quad – Seneca/Rockville; Source – Personal descent 11/06
N39 04.07, W77 19.74 to N39 01.89, W77 14.63

This is a relatively long trip, but most paddlers go just the first mile downriver, ferry across to the Maryland shore (just below Blockhouse Point State Park, where imposing cliffs come down almost to the river), carry up to the C&O Canal and return to Violets Lock. The downriver mile can be done either in the main river (the Seneca Rapids, starting with the remains of Dam #2) or, generally more interestingly except at higher levels, by running the Potowmack (George Washington) Canal along the Virginia shore, reached by ferrying half a mile across from Maryland just above Dam #2, and entering the channel directly ahead (this produces the 6.8-mile paddle listed above).

The George Washington Canal is more like a creek, with a few rapids of up to class II-, including an excellent surfing ledge, and the possibility of partial strainers. It is a popular place for whitewater and safety training. To run just the first mile, keep alert for an arrow directing you back into the main river. From there, you can ferry across to where you see a trail up to the C&O Canal, or attain back up over the Seneca Rapids (with a short drag or two, depending on water level and your skill).

Below the Seneca Rapids, the river is pretty but rather flat. Stay left at the top of 3-mile long Watkins Island. After another mile, you can paddle up Muddy Branch to a boat ramp off Pennyfield Lock Road. The following 2.5 miles are also flat, but then come some easy riffles at a pair of pipeline crossings. You can take the far left channel and run a little chute by the WSSC facility. After some more riffles, head left to a little cove that brings you close to Swains Lock. If you stay to the right of Watkins Island, you can still reach Swains Lock by ferrying left just below the end of the island, or go another three-fourths mile to Riverbend Park in Virginia.

From Swains Lock, it is two flat miles to the last take out (in Maryland) above Great Falls.

GAUGE: For the George Washington Canal, the minimum is as low as 500 cfs on the Little Falls gauge; Seneca Rapids itself is bony below 1,500 cfs.

Violets Lock (Ab Violette was the last lock keeper) is at **Rowsers Ford**. Dam #2 was built there by the C&O Canal Company in 1828, to channel water into the canal. On the night of June 27-28, 1863, Jeb Stuart's 5,000-strong **Confederate cavalry** crossed the Potomac there en route to Gettysburg. Their tactically brilliant but strategically misguided campaign left Lee without his "eyes and ears" and brought Stuart to Gettysburg too late to be of much assistance.

George Washington promoted the **Potowmack Canal**, in part perhaps to benefit his land holdings out west. Maryland blocked the plans before the Revolution, but not once Washington had become the national hero. The Canal, built along the Virginia shore to bypass the various rapids, was strictly for one-way trips downstream; the boats were broken up for timber in Georgetown. It operated from 1802-1828, and carried as many as 1,300 boats per year. Some of the original stonework can be seen here and at Great Falls Park, Virginia. Later, the more versatile C&O Canal, on which boats could travel upstream as well, replaced it.

Section 3: Great Falls

Gradient	Difficulty	Distance	Area	Scenery	Strainers	Rating
300	5.0	0.2	11,450	A	0	!!!!

USGS Quad – Vienna/Falls Church; Source – Trip reports (many); AW web site
N38 59.62, W77 15.20 (Virginia); N39 00.09, W77 14.81 (Maryland)

Great Falls, first run in 1976, is one of the leading "hair runs" in the East for those few paddlers able to handle it. There are many routes, depending largely upon the water level, but all are dangerous and at least class 5.0. Along the Virginia shore, The Spout ends in a 25-foot drop. The harder middle line starts with Grace under Pressure and ends with the Middle Finger drop. On the Maryland side are lines beginning with Pummel and finishing with Horseshoe. And finally, close to the C&O Canal, there is the man-made Fishladder (which never fulfilled that objective). It is essential to go with paddlers who are familiar with the route, as mistakes about exactly what line to take can be deadly. The AWA web site gives much more information about Great Falls.

The annual race over Great Falls, as part of the Potomac Whitewater Festival in July, draws several hundred spectators.

GAUGE: Varies by route, and small differences can have enormous impact.

National Park Service facilities, on both the Maryland and Virginia sides of Great Falls, provide facts about the falls, fauna, flora, floods etc. This area has high biodiversity, including a number of rare plants.

Paddler access to Great Falls has been negotiated between the National Park Service and paddler organizations. The rules have progressively become less restrictive, as paddlers have by and large demonstrated good judgment. Please keep it that way.

Section 4: Mather Gorge – Below Great Falls to Sycamore Island

Gradient	Difficulty	Distance	Area	Scenery	Strainers	Rating
5 (15)	II (III)	8.0	11,450	A	0	***

USGS Quad – Vienna/Falls Church; Source – Personal descent (often)
N38 59.62, W77 15.20 (Va.); N39 00.09, W77 14.81 (Md.) to N38 57.50, W77 07.92

This is an extremely popular area because of its nice rapids, great scenery, almost year-round availability and close-in location. You can start in Virginia or Maryland. The former involves a shorter carry and gives you some additional rapids, but these are harder than anything else on this trip, and their difficulty rises steeply with the water level. The Virginia put in is down a steep and rocky path to Fisherman's Eddy. From there, one generally ferries across the river, runs squirrelly Fishladder Rapids (by the mouth of the Fishladder), and then enters the S Turn.

For the Maryland put in, you must carry 500 yards down the C&O Canal towpath to Sandy Beach. From there, you can head right, into the main channel at the top of the S Turn. At levels above 3.9, you can also proceed down the Maryland Narrows (to your left), and above 4.1, down the Middle Narrows (straight ahead), thereby avoiding S Turn (which reaches class III+ at around 4.0) and the subsequent big waves of Rocky Island Rapids (which are ideal for surfing at around 4.0). At higher levels (5.5 or more), all of the routes from Sandy Beach are class IV, and paddlers not comfortable with that difficulty should put in down at Rocky Cove, where the channels reunite.

Some 200 yards below Rocky Cove is the class II Wet Bottom Chute. The next mile, through Mather Gorge, is moving flat water (with moving whirlpools at high water). When the river widens out, you are approaching Difficult Run Rapids (just above the mouth of Difficult Run), where you can choose between the Maryland Chute, the wide Middle Chute and the Virginia Chute – all are class II. Many boaters paddle up half a mile from the Maryland access near Old Anglers Inn in order to play in these chutes.

Half a mile below Old Anglers, you should take the left channel (except at levels below about 3, when there is too little water there) to get to the class II Offutt Island Rapid, another popular play spot. From there, most paddlers cross the river to run class II Yellow Falls, three-quarters mile below, on the Virginia shore. In high water Yellow Falls approaches class III, and some paddlers therefore prefer the easier Calico Falls on the left side of Turkey Island.

In another three-quarters mile there is a Maryland take out near the Carderock picnic area, and a quarter mile after that is the last rapid – class II Stubblefield Falls. The final 4.5 miles have nothing more than riffles, and there are additional take outs at Locks 10, 8 and 7 of the C&O Canal. Most of the take outs require carries of 100-200 yards.

GAUGE: This section gets bony only below 500 cfs, but most of the rapids lose their appeal as the Little Falls gauge drops below about 1,000 cfs.

Section 5: Little Falls – Lock 6 to Tidewater (above Chain Bridge)

Gradient	Difficulty	Distance	Area	Scenery	Strainers	Rating
20 (100)	III	1.0	11,560	B	0	****

USGS Quad – Falls Church/Washington West; Source – Personal descent often
N38 56.70, W77 07.42 (Lock 6) to N38 55.12, W77 06.13 (Fletchers boathouse)

This wonderful, short trip is often the only place around worth paddling (except for those few who can handle Great Falls) when water levels everywhere are low. The usual put in is at the feeder canal by Lock 6, and there are then two ways to get to the main river. The more popular one, the Z-channel, starts just downstream of the put in and ends in a tight, twisty class II+ rapid (bony below 800 cfs). The other way is to paddle up the feeder canal, fight (or carry) your way into the water below the Little Falls Dam, and then take the class III- chute down the rubble dam (bony below 3,000 cfs).

After either, you pick your way through the rocks to the Virginia side, and run several sets of waves, with good play options. At levels above 2.8 (2,000 cfs), where a shallow channel drops in from the left, you can get out and carry up the rise and over to a large eddy, and then run the short, steep, rocky, class III Beaver Rapid – start right and, at low levels, cut hard left at the end. A pair of additional easy rapids brings you to Little Falls, where you should get out and scout either from the rocks below the mouth of Little Falls Branch (river left) or, if you are considering running any of the five narrow channels near the Virginia shore, up the rocks on river right.

At Little Falls itself, there are many routes, depending upon the river level, tide, and your abilities. The difficulty of the rapid, especially on the Virginia side, increases greatly with the water level. In addition, high tides make the Virginia side much easier, by keeping the water from trying to ram you into the Eddy of Doom or the cliff wall on the right when you ferry out of the Virginia eddy through fast, turbulent water (this is often harder than running the drops into the Virginia eddy). Very high tides also weaken the hole between the Cleaver and the island, and make it possible to paddle back up into the Virginia eddy. On the Maryland side, high tides shorten the rapid and thereby make it easier but less interesting.

At low to moderate levels (below, say, 3.36 = 5,000 cfs), there are about ten routes – these descriptions will of course make more sense to you when you are at Little Falls itself:

- ▶ The easiest route is the Maryland side, which you can approach right along the Maryland shore or from the center, ferrying hard left below the first hole, so that the water does not push you to the right between the Cleaver and the island (route [d]);
- ▶ There are three sneak routes into the Virginia eddy – by staying along the shoreline (above 4,000 cfs), by catching the first chute below the scouting rocks (above 3,000 cfs) or by taking the steeper second chute (above 2,000 cfs), where the key is to take the drop straight, aiming for the right edge of the rock ahead of you, rather than veering right too early;
- ▶ You can run the main channel to the Virginia side, either by ferrying across from an eddy on the Maryland side, staying in the main current but angling right into the Virginia eddy (much harder than it looks), or starting in the large moving eddy below the scouting rocks and cutting left on either side of the double-headed rock next to the small rocky island (the right side of it is steeper and narrower, and needs at least 1,800 cfs). Whichever route you take, you should normally catch the large Virginia eddy; and

- At low levels or very high tide, you can run between the Cleaver and the island, either straight through or clipping the strong hole on either edge.

There are also various play opportunities. At high tide and low levels, you can paddle back up the Virginia side of the long island, up the "elevator" and all the way into the Virginia eddy. At low levels, you can also do the Hairy Ferry back and forth above the Cleaver, and you can catch the Eddy of Doom.

After running Little Falls, most kayakers carry up over the concrete structure on the left (at high tide, the easiest way is by starting in the downstream channel), and then carry 300 yards to the canal. They then paddle up to Lock 5, and either portage and paddle or walk back to Lock 6. To avoid the carry, I usually paddle a mile down to Fletchers Boathouse; for this option you need a shuttle.

GAUGE: Only once in the past 25 years has this gotten too low to paddle (below 250 cfs on the Little Falls gauge) – and that was corrected within a few days, by the release of water from upstream dams. I have paddled it from 250 cfs (scrapey class II) up to 5,000 cfs (pushy class III even along the Maryland shore). It is often paddled much higher, but the difficulty and danger increase rapidly with the level, because the river is so confined. At high levels, the rapid is a huge wave train, but you must avoid the holes, including the ones around the footings of I-495, and have a bombproof roll.

WESTERN MONTGOMERY COUNTY

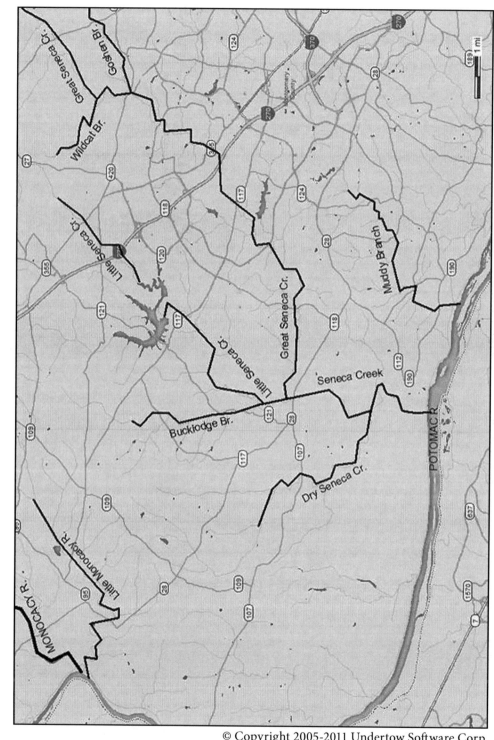

Chapter 18:
WESTERN MONTGOMERY COUNTY

Western Montgomery County is an area of gently rolling hills with little exciting whitewater. Most of the area is in the **Seneca Creek** basin (130 sq. mi.), which stretches from outer suburbs (Germantown – 86,000; Gaithersburg – 60,000) to highly rural areas in the northwest. The main tributaries are **Great Seneca**, **Little Seneca** (which join to form Seneca Creek) and **Dry Seneca creeks**; three others – **Bucklodge**, **Wildcat** and **Goshen branches** – are much smaller. Bucklodge Branch and section 1 of Dry Seneca Creek are the "explorers' specials." Other branches have been dammed to make the lakes for Montgomery Village (32,000) and surrounding communities. Little Seneca Creek has the best rapids of this group, and is very occasionally up during droughts because of dam releases (to ensure the agreed minimum flow in the lower Potomac), but these generally occur only when there has been a miscalculation.

Western Montgomery County also contains, near its northwestern border with Frederick County, the **Little Monocacy River**, which is parallel rather than tributary to the nearby (big) Monocacy. That would be an enjoyable creek, were it not for its strainers. East of the Seneca Creek basin, **Muddy Branch** can be run for a considerable distance, but was also full of strainers until its final two miles. Beyond that are the creeks covered in the next chapter (Southern Montgomery County).

> **General Richard Montgomery**, a 39-year old Irishman, was killed December 31, 1775, as he commanded the ill-fated American attack on Quebec City.

GAUGES: There are gauges on Seneca Creek at Md. 28 near Dawsonville (101 sq. mi.) and Ten Mile Creek near Boyds (4.5 sq. mi.). The gauges on the Hawlings River (27 sq. mi.) in the Patuxent basin, Limestone Branch (8 sq. mi.) in Virginia and Turkey Branch of Rock Creek (2.7 sq. mi.) are also useful. There are no rain gauges; however, river gauges on three miniscule Little Seneca Creek tributaries (drainages of up to 1.35 sq. mi.) serve the same purpose. In the table below, the normal font **zero-level references are to Seneca Creek**, while the *bold italicized figures refer to Ten Mile Creek.*

name	gradient	difficulty	length	area	gauge	rating
Little Monocacy River	22	II-	6.8	6	*45cfs*	*
Seneca Creek	5 (16)	I	5.7	101	85cfs	*
Great Seneca Creek	10	I (II-)	13.9	25	250cfs	*
Wildcat Branch	45	II- (II)	0.5	3.4	*70cfs*	**
Goshen Branch	20	I (II)	1.5	3.8	*60cfs*	-
Little Seneca Creek	17 (40)	II (II+)	5.2	21	400cfs	***
Bucklodge Br.	34	?	3.4	6	*50cfs*	?
Dry Seneca Cr. - *Sec. 1*	25	?	3.0	4.6	*55cfs*	?
- *Sec. 2*	17	I (II-)	4.0	12	*25cfs*	**
Muddy Branch		I	5.5	11	*25cfs*	*

LITTLE MONOCACY RIVER: W. Harris Road to C&O Canal

Gradient	Difficulty	Distance	Area	Scenery	Strainers	Rating
22	II-	6.8	6	C+	2-4/mi.	*

USGS Quad – Poolesville; Source – Personal descent 1/96 (upper), 3/98 (lower)
N39 14.17, W77 23.69 via N39 12.51, W77 25.96 (Md. 28) to N39 14.45, W77 27.00

The Little Monocacy flows through sparsely populated northwest Montgomery County and enters the Potomac a quarter mile south of the mouth of the Monocacy. Most of the run is through woods, except near the four bridges. Although there is generally a well-defined streambed, several short, flat stretches go through flooded woodlands. There are a few 2-3 foot ledges and some gravel bars that produce nice waves. The main challenges are standing and fallen trees. The former, usually on the outsides of sharp bends, require hard paddling and good boat control. The latter were densest between Barnesville Road (mile 1.0) and Big Woods Road (mile 2.5), while the next 1.3 miles, down to Md. 28, is very twisty, resulting in shorter visibility.

By Md. 28, the catchment area has tripled (to 18 sq. mi.), but there is no parking nearby. The next mile had two massive logjams. But then, in the final 2 miles, the trip improves as the rapids get more interesting, the scenery prettier (shale-rock walls and high ridges), the strainers fewer and the wildlife more extensive (I saw deer and beaver).

When the Potomac is high, you reach its backwater before the C&O Canal. Take out on the right, and carry 300 yards to the Monocacy Aqueduct parking. When the Potomac is low, you can paddle beneath the Canal, and then continue 0.4 miles to the Potomac, 0.3 miles upstream on the Potomac and 0.2 miles upstream on the Monocacy.

GAUGE: You need at least 45 cfs on Ten Mile Creek, 1,000 cfs (projected 3 hours forward) on Seneca Creek (Dawsonville), 270 cfs on the Hawlings River and 80 cfs on Limestone Branch (Va.) for the upper portion, but only half that for the lower part.

Alongside the Little Monocacy, **George Washington** owned a 519-acre farm, given to him in 1794 by Francis Mercer (Governor of Maryland, 1801-3) in settlement of a debt.

Between Seneca Creek and the Little Monocacy, **Broad Run** (8 sq. mi.) would be canoeable for 3.6 miles, at 12 ft/mile, if it did not flow through the National Institutes of Health's securely-fenced Animal Center (which has been the target of animal-rights demonstrations).

SENECA CREEK: Md. 28 to Potomac River (Rileys Lock)

Gradient	Difficulty	Distance	Area	Scenery	Strainers	Rating
5 (16)	I	5.7	101	C	<1/mi.	*

USGS Quad – Germantown/Seneca; Source – Personal descent 4/03
N39 07.68, W77 20.11 to N39 04.17, W77 20.46

This easy-to-catch beginner run is mostly through the woods of Seneca Creek State Park. Put in at the confluence of Great Seneca and Little Seneca creeks, on river left. Beneath Md. 28, the sill for the gauging station produces a surfable roller. After a flat first mile, occasional riffles appear, especially once Dry Seneca Creek enters midway. The last 0.7 miles, below River Road (Md. 112), is Potomac backwater, so you may want to take out by a small parking area early in this stretch.

GAUGE: At least 85 cfs on the Seneca Creek gauge at Dawsonville is needed.

> The **Seneca**, southernmost of the Iroquois Federation, often clashed with colonists and other tribes. In 1661-74, they fought the Susquehannock, and finally won when smallpox decimated the latter. Ironically, when the Seneca killed a few white farmers in 1674, the Susquehannock got blamed, and the Virginia militia then crushed their pitiful remnants.
>
> The area was once a major quarrying site for **Seneca red sandstone**, which was used to build the locks for the Patowmack canal and later for the original Smithsonian building. Remains of the main quarry are near the mouth of Seneca Creek, on river right.

GREAT SENECA CREEK: Brink Road to Seneca Creek (Md. 28)

Gradient	Difficulty	Distance	Area	Scenery	Strainers	Rating
10	I (II-)	13.9	25	C+	2/mi.	*

USGS Quad – Gaithersburg/Germantown; Source – Personal descent 2/87 (last 2.6 miles); Gertler.
N39 12.07, W77 12.24 via N39 11.23, W77 12.91 (Md. 118) to N39 07.68, W77 20.11

This is a popular novice trip through Seneca Creek State Park, with a biking/horse trail alongside and lots of deer. Its only real drawback, other than the lack of rapids, is strainers. Paddlers have removed them on numerous occasions, yet somehow, like support for the flat tax or the gold standard, they keep reappearing.

You could start at Md. 124 (8 sq. mi.), from where it is 3 miles, at 20 ft/mile, to Huntmaster Road (the Wildcat Branch take out). But for most paddlers, there is little reason to start above Brink Road (Gertler's put in), 0.8 miles later, after the confluence with Goshen Branch. The best of this creek is the final 2.6 miles from Germantown Road (Md. 118; 60 sq. mi.), which includes the long, bouncy class II- rapid at Blackrock Mill.

GAUGE: You need 250 cfs on the Seneca Creek gauge at Dawsonville and 65 cfs on the Hawlings River gauge to start at Brink Road, but 100 cfs at Dawsonville and 25 cfs on the Hawlings River are enough below Germantown/Watkins Mill Road.

WILDCAT BRANCH: Wildcat Road to Great Seneca Creek

Gradient	Difficulty	Distance	Area	Scenery	Strainers	Rating
45	II- (II)	0.5*	3.4	C	2-6/mi.	**

USGS Quad – Gaithersburg; Source – Personal descent 6/98
N39 13.32, W77 13.08 to N39 12.64, W77 12.33

*(plus 0.5 miles on Great Seneca Creek to Huntmaster Road)

This is the steepest run in the Seneca basin; it can be scouted from the road, and you don't need a shuttle. Wildcat Branch's three little arms meet alongside Wildcat Road. Dump your boats and then park a quarter mile downstream at Davis Mill Road.

The trip starts off with short class II- rapids, some on sharp turns. Approaching the midway bridge, there is a long class II- rock garden. Just below the bridge are a right-hand turn and a short, class II ledge cum rock garden. After that, Wildcat Branch returns to its earlier disposition, with fallen trees and branches the main concern. The confluence is soon reached, and then it is a half mile to the take out at Huntmaster Road.

GAUGE: By the time you get gauge readings, it may be too late, but 70 cfs on Ten Mile Creek, 400 cfs on the Hawlings River, 125 cfs on Limestone Branch (Va.) and 40 cfs on Turkey Branch would be good indications.

GOSHEN BRANCH: Huntmaster Road to Great Seneca Creek

Gradient	Difficulty	Distance	Area	Scenery	Strainers	Rating
20	I (II)	1.5	3.8	C-	3-7/mi.	-

USGS Quad – Gaithersburg; Source – Personal descent 6/98
N39 12.57, W77 11.01 to N39 12.07, W77 12.24

This little creek north of Gaithersburg flows only 4.5 miles, in the northeast corner of the Seneca watershed, up against the headwaters of Rock Creek and the Patuxent basin. It is tiny and twisty, flowing mainly through open fields, lined in some sections with trees. It is far more dangerous than difficult, because one can often see only a few boat lengths ahead, and there is a high density of strainers and partial strainers, usually around blind turns. I also encountered a pair of class II ledges, the first of which was the spillway around a beaver dam. (The beaver itself swam just ahead of my boat for a long while, perhaps trying to guide me into the next strainer it had made.) There are several islands in mid-stream, always where the creek is twisty. Given all the obstacles, the confluence with Great Seneca Creek, just 200 yards before the take out at Brink Road, will be a welcome sight.

GAUGE: About 60 cfs on Ten Mile Creek, 350 cfs on the Hawlings River, 110 cfs on Limestone Branch (Va.) and 35 cfs on Turkey Branch would be minimal.

LITTLE SENECA CREEK: Md. 117 (Clopper Rd.) to Seneca Cr.

Gradient	Difficulty	Distance	Area	Scenery	Strainers	Rating
17 (40)	II (II+)	5.2	21	B	1-2/mi.	***

USGS Quad – Germantown; Source – Personal descent 9/05
N39 10.48, W77 17.99 to N39 07.68, W77 20.11

Little Seneca Creek heads southwest for 13 miles. After 5 miles it reaches the backwater of Little Seneca Lake, where 2 miles of the creek are drowned. The Black Hills Regional Park around the lake belongs to the MNCPPC, which allows boating only on lakes. To avoid (a) breaking MNCPPC rules and (b) lots of strainers, put in less than a mile below the dam, at Clopper Road, at the edge of the MNCPPC jurisdiction; park at the Seneca Lodge (downstream river right) and follow the track down to the creek.

The first 1.6 miles to the gravel ford on Hoyles Mill Road (the foundations of the old mill are on river left, a half mile downstream) are class I, with good current, several riffles and many partial strainers. Around midway there, the creek starts to braid, and some channels get very tight. There is an 18-inch ledge on one leftmost channel. Approaching Hoyles Mill Road, the gradient increases and there are long riffles and even a pair of small side-surfing holes. Hoyles Mill Road itself is now closed to vehicles.

In the next 1.7 miles, to Schaeffer Road, there are two sets of good rapids (plus an excellent play hole). The first is a pair of class II rock gardens, which are more technical and therefore somewhat harder at very low levels. Half a mile after that, as you reach the power line, there is another class II (starting just below a huge boulder on the right), followed by a class II+, where you enter on the far right and then cut back hard. Scout this on the right for strainers, as it is a blind drop. The final 1.9 miles to the confluence with Great Seneca Creek at Md. 28 has only a few riffles.

There are virtually no signs of civilization on this trip, and deer are plentiful. So also are beaver (we saw three on my last trip), but few of their dams block the entire creek. The water is muddy after a hard rain, but clear and refreshingly cool during a dam release, when it produces a romantic light mist on hot days.

GAUGE: About 400 cfs on Seneca Creek at Dawsonville is normally needed (because 20% of that water will come from Little Seneca); however, during droughts, if you see the Seneca Creek reading jump by at least 80 cfs, it means you have enough water from the release from Little Seneca Lake.

> **Little Seneca Lake** holds 4 billion gallons (enough, when full, to release at 80 cfs for 11 weeks) and has flat-water canoeing. It is owned by the three major water utilities of the Washington area, and reserved for droughts. Its proximity (about 12 hours' flow) to the Potomac River water intakes around Great Falls enables this reservoir to fine-tune the larger releases from the Jennings Randolph Reservoir on the North Branch of the Potomac. The release levels vary widely, and can be up to 200 cfs or way below the 80 cfs needed for paddling. Call WSSC at (301) 206-8416 or 206-8861 for release information; unfortunately, they usually don't know in advance, and it is easy to get skunked by sudden reductions in the discharges.

BUCKLODGE BR.: Bucklodge Rd. (Md. 117) to Little Seneca Creek

Gradient	Difficulty	Distance	Area	Scenery	Strainers	Rating
36	?	3.4*	6**	?	?	?

USGS Quad – Germantown; Source – Personal descent (last 0.8 miles) 5/96; Scouting put in and last third of trip
N39 11.28, W77 20.52 via N39 09.20, W77 20.41 (Md. 121) to N39 07.68, W77 20.11

*(plus 1.2 miles on Little Seneca Creek to Md. 28)
**(including a tributary that enters in a half mile)

Bucklodge Branch heads south for 7 miles, past the village of Bucklodge.

The catchment area of this *"explorers' special"* is just 3 sq. mi. at the put in, but a tributary doubles it in half a mile. White Ground Road (Md. 121) comes alongside 1.5 miles after that, and there is access at a bridge half a mile later. The final 0.8 miles (which I have paddled) has frequent riffles and a few easy class II- rapids, as it flows through the woods. The 1.2 miles on lower Little Seneca Creek are flat.

GAUGE: Look for 50 cfs on Ten Mile Creek and 30 cfs on Turkey Branch.

DRY SENECA CREEK

The creek runs for 11 miles, starting north of Poolesville (a small town that has been struggling with how to deal with the threats and allures of the nearby Big City).

Section 1: Poolesville (Cattail Road) to Whites Ferry Road (Md. 107)

Gradient	Difficulty	Distance	Area	Scenery	Strainers	Rating
25	?	3.0	4.6	?	?	?

USGS Quad – Poolesville/Germantown/Seneca; Source – Scouting
N39 08.85, W77 24.13 to N39 07.44, W77 22.10

This is a mild and tiny *"explorers' special"* through the outer suburbs. One could start a mile higher up at Jerusalem road, with a similar gradient.

GAUGE: Look for 55 cfs on Ten Mile Creek, 30 cfs on Turkey Branch.

Section 2: Whites Ferry Road (Md. 107) to Seneca Creek

Gradient	Difficulty	Distance	Area	Scenery	Strainers	Rating
17	I (II-)	4.0*	12	C+	0-2/mi.	**

USGS Quad – Seneca; Source – Personal descent 2/87
N39 07.44, W77 22.10 to N39 04.66, W77 20.46

*(plus 2.3 miles on Seneca Creek to Rileys Lock Road)

Starting at Md.107, this is a mellow trip through woods and fields, with lots of riffles and a long, class II- rock garden towards the end. You can take out at Montevideo Road, 0.3 miles above the confluence, but then you miss much of this rock garden. If you continue onto Seneca Creek, it is 2.3 miles to the takeout alongside Rileys Lock Road.

GAUGE: Look for 550 cfs on Seneca Creek, 25 cfs on Ten Mile Creek.

⑾ MUDDY BRANCH: Quince Orchard Road to Pennyfield Lock Road

Gradient	Difficulty	Distance	Area	Scenery	Strainers	Rating
16	I	5.5	11	B	3-5/mi.	*

USGS Quad – Seneca; Source – Personal descent 6/98
N39 05.59, W77 14.96 via N39 04.44, W77 17.22 (mile 3.5) to N39 03.40, W77 17.59

This stream rises near Gaithersburg and meanders southwest for ten miles through Muddy Branch Park, at 15-20 ft/mile. Fancy subdivisions are springing up nearby, with names like Potomac Chase Estates, and horseback riding is starting to vie with cycling on the rolling, low-traffic roads. Its upper branches are dammed to form lakes with names like Placid, Halcyon, Varuna (Hindu guardian of cosmic order), Nirvana, Inspiration and Elysium (paradise) – a far cry from "Muddy."

True to its name, the water is a rich brown color whenever there is enough runoff for paddling. The low banks, wooded surroundings and beaver population also mean that Muddy Branch has more than its share of strainers, especially between Pennyfoot Road (mile 1.5) and Esworthy Road (mile 3.5), although eventually it becomes wide enough so that most of the fallen trees and branches do not block the entire stream.

The woods are quite pretty, with nice rock formations. There are long riffles as well as 1-foot drops over fallen trees. The riffle just below Esworthy Road is typical of what you will find, and a good gauge of the water level. Take out just before the creek flows under the C&O Canal, off Pennyfield Lock Road (once the destination of President Grover Cleveland's weekend fishing expeditions).

Overall, this is a good creek for a placid, halcyon day, with some small drops to add spice to Varuna's cosmic order. But if nirvana for you is exciting rapids, you must seek your inspiration instead from some of the Elysian streams in the next chapter.

GAUGE: Some 550 cfs at Dawsonville on Seneca Creek (projected to 2 hours after put in), 25 cfs on Ten Mile Creek, 150 cfs on the Hawlings River and 45 cfs on Limestone Branch (Va.) are minimal to start at Quince Orchard Road, and 70% of those figures for the final two miles from Esworthy Road.

CAPITAL CANOEING AND KAYAKING

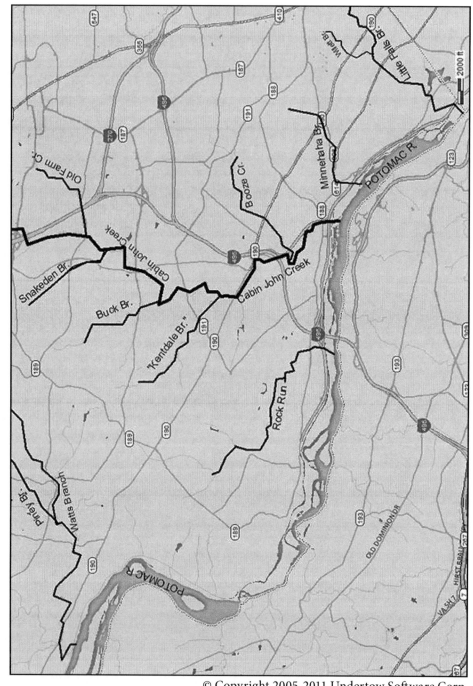

SOUTHERN MONTGOMERY COUNTY

© Copyright 2005-2011 Undertow Software Corp.

Chapter 19:

SOUTHERN MONTGOMERY COUNTY

West of the Rock Creek basin, in populous and prosperous southern Montgomery County, several small watersheds offer surprisingly good paddling, over the full range of difficulty. The creeks are generally quite pretty, as they flow mostly through wooded parkland, a benefit of upscale communities (Potomac – 45,000; North Potomac – 25,000; Bethesda – 61,000; North Bethesda – 44,000). While all are small streams, Watts Branch and Cabin John Creek may hold water after a good rain for the better part of a day.

Section 2 of **Cabin John Creek** is the only somewhat popular trip, and it is a gem. Also very good (but likely to have more strainers), on the alternate blue moons when they can be caught, are some smaller streams: **Rock Run** (section 1), **Buck Branch** and lower **Little Falls Branch**. The hardest and most dangerous runs (both "explorers' specials") are *Minnehaha Branch* and section 2 of Rock Run. And even **Watts Branch, Piney Branch, Old Farm Creek, Snakeden Branch, Booze Creek, "Kentdale Branch"** and the first sections of Cabin John Creek and Little Falls Branch have their positive sides, although strainers can be a big nuisance.

In the table below are drainage areas much smaller than those in more rural chapters. The rapid runoff from impervious surfaces brings these creeks to high levels for very brief periods during and immediately after heavy downpours.

GAUGES: There are no Internet river or rainfall gauges in this area. Useful nearby river gauges are the Hawlings River (27 sq. mi.) to the north Rock Creek (62 sq. mi.) to the east, Fourmile Run (Va.) (14 sq. mi.) to the south, Ten Mile Creek (4.5 sq. mi.) to the northwest and **Turkey Branch** of Rock Creek (2.7 sq. mi.) to the east; the last is **the gauge reference** in the table below. There are also river gauges on three tiny Little Seneca Creek tributaries to the west, which work like rain gauges. But the key for the smaller creeks is to head out during intense rainfall, before gauge readings are available.

name	gradient	difficulty	length	area	gauge	rating
Watts Branch	25 (40)	II-	3.2	9.5	20cfs	**
Piney Branch	55 (100)	III	1.1	2.5	75cfs	*
Rock Run - Section 1	65 (165)	III (III+)	2.6	3.2	60cfs	***
- Section 2	150	III (5.0)	0.5	4.8	60cfs	?
Cabin John Cr. - Sec. 1	19 (50)	II	4.1	7.7	25cfs	*
- Sec. 2	37 (80)	III- (III)	2.6	18	15cfs	****
Old Farm Creek	35	II-	1.8	1.3	100cfs	*
Snakeden Branch	65 (110)	III	0.3	1.0	150cfs	**
Buck Branch	60 (150)	III	1.5	1.0	150cfs	***
"Kentdale Branch"	30	II- (II)	1.1	1.6	80cfs	*
Booze Creek	45 (70)	II+	1.5	2.0	75cfs	**
Minnehaha Branch	125 (200)	IV+	0.8	1.2	150cfs	?
Little Falls Br. - Section 1	35 (70)	II- (III)	1.1	2.1	75cfs	**
- Section 2	80 (200)	III (III+)	0.6	4.2	50cfs	***

🛶 WATTS BRANCH: Glen Mill Road to Potomac R. (Swains Lock)

Gradient	Difficulty	Distance	Area	Scenery	Strainers	Rating
25 (40)	II-	3.2*	9.5	C+	1-3/mi.	**

USGS Quad – Rockville/Seneca; Source – Personal descent 12/96 (upper), 1/93
N39 02.77, W77 13.06 to N39 01.90, W77 14.63

*(plus 1 mile on the Potomac to Swains Lock)

Watts Branch rises west of Rockville and zigzags southwest for ten miles to the Potomac. Put in on North Glen Road, 50 yards above Glen Mill Road. The first half mile has frequent class II- rapids and is 40 ft/mile. After Piney Branch enters at 0.6 miles, there are fewer strainers or rapids. By River Road (mile 2.8), the creek is flat and enlarged by Sandy Branch. One can take out there or go a mile down the Potomac to Swains Lock.

GAUGE: The Ten Mile Creek gauge should be over 35 cfs, Hawlings River 200 cfs, Fourmile Run at Alexandria (Va.) 100 cfs and Turkey Branch 20 cfs.

> **Jubal Early's Retreat.** On July 12, 1864, after the arrival of Union reinforcements ended Jubal Early's raid on Washington, Massachusetts cavalry pursued the retreating rebels and came upon their rear guard at Watts Branch, where there was a brief skirmish. But the Confederates got away and were able to cross the Potomac virtually unhindered.
>
> **Sanders Watts** arrived in Maryland in 1657 and went about getting creeks named after him.

🛶 PINEY BRANCH: Glen Mill Road (lower) to Watts Branch

Gradient	Difficulty	Distance	Area	Scenery	Strainers	Rating
55 (100)	III-	1.1*	2.5	D+	6-10/mi.	*

USGS Quad – Rockville; Source – Personal descent 10/96
N39 03.23, W77 13.03 to N39 02.40, W77 14.06

*(plus 0.5 miles on Watts Branch to Piney Meetinghouse Road, at 22 ft/mile)

Piney Branch flows southwest for 4.5 miles. Glen Mill Road crosses it twice, 2.3 and 1.1 miles above the confluence. Put in at the lower crossing, as the creek is too small even for me at the upper one. The first half mile is narrow and twisting class II-, with lots of wood. Then come three class III- rock gardens. I ran the first one, but strainers ruined the next two drops. Below them, the creek is class II+, down past Glen Road to the confluence. So if you catch this run when Piney Branch is pretty clean, it might rate three stars. When Piney Branch is up, Watts Branch should be moving along quite well.

The area is rich in wildlife. Three deer bounded away as I entered the creek, and I watched a red fox as it probed the riverbank i.s.o. small animals and capsized paddlers.

GAUGE: Turkey Branch should be over 75 cfs and Ten Mile Creek 125 cfs.

> **Autumn 1996.** Every small-stream paddler is used to finding the targeted creek too low, and having to "bail out" onto some larger one. But in September/October 1996, I experienced the opposite three times in a row. Heading off during prolonged heavy rains, I found first Cabin John Creek, later the North Branch of Rock Creek and finally Watts Branch too high, and "bailed out" onto Rock Run, Bel Pre Creek and Piney Branch, respectively.

ROCK RUN

Rock Run, a tiny, well hidden but delightful stream, rises in Potomac Village and flows five miles southeast to the Potomac. Section 1 is class III, but short section 2 is only for experts.

> A **pair of large dogs** from a nearby house first barked loudly and then chased me when I was scouting beforehand. I had to grab a heavy stick, retreat across the almost-dry streambed, and face them down, adrenaline pumping. Fortunately, the dogs did not attempt to cross the creek, either because they saw it as the boundary of their territory or because they felt vulnerable in attacking up a steep muddy bank. Eventually they quieted down, and I backed away slowly.
>
> In 1864, Union soldiers from California and Oregon, billeted here, discovered flakes of alluvial **gold** and later quartz outcrops that had potential for gold. After the war, in 1867, one of those soldiers established the small Maryland Mine, a little west of Rock Run. This mine was periodically worked, when gold prices were high, as late as the 1940s. In 1874, a prospector found specks of gold in Rock Run itself. He opened the Montgomery Mine, but it operated for only a few years. A geologist's report in 1890 identified eight separate gold-bearing quartz veins in the Rock Run valley. Three other small gold mines were established, but no fortunes appear to have been made. As late as the 1970s, one could go deep into a horizontal mine shaft near the put in, on river left. This shaft was filled in when the golf course was built, but several mining trenches are still in evidence.
>
> Until the late 1980s, Rock Run was entirely in the woods, but then Rock Run Ltd. built the luxurious 1,066-acre, 899-home **Avenel community** on the hilltops back from both banks. In addition, the Players Club Golf Course at Avenel, along the left bank, has been the site of PGA tournaments. In 1996, Avenel received the national Award for Excellence for Large Scale Residential Development from the Urban Land Institute. And, indeed, of all the residential neighborhoods that I have paddled through, this is probably the most attractive. Wildlife is still common; I saw deer when scouting, a beaver in the creek while paddling, and a fox as I left.

Section 1: Brickyard Road to below MacArthur Boulevard

Gradient	Difficulty	Distance	Area	Scenery	Strainers	Rating
65 (165)	III (III+)	2.6	3.2	B-	2-4/mi.	***

USGS Quad – Falls Church; Source – Personal descent 9/96
N38 59.51, W77 12.62 to N38 58.54, W77 10.95

The put in is a 70-yard scramble down an obscure trail where Brickyard Road makes a 90-degree bend. There are frequent class II drops, punctuated by two series of class III rock gardens, toward the end of the first half mile, which should be scouted for strainers, as the streambed is narrow and winding.

Soon afterwards, the creek leaves the woods and runs for ¾ mile alongside the golf course. The stream has been channelized here and the only strainers likely are among the eight footbridges; in low water, half of these can be slipped under. The creek reenters the woods and is class II for a half mile, until the whitewater climax: three class III rapids, followed by a class III+ marked by a pool just above an island, with most of the water going right. The creek then widens and returns to class II, leading to a tunnel under MacArthur Boulevard.

Take-out 150 yards past the tunnel at a small bridge by the David Taylor Naval Ship Research and Development Center (whose model basin is used by the US whitewater team for winter training). A sign prohibits entry of unauthorized vehicles, but the creek is outside of the Center's fence.

GAUGE: Turkey Branch should exceed 60 cfs, Ten Mile Creek 100 cfs.

Section 2: Below MacArthur Boulevard to Potomac River

Gradient	Difficulty	Distance	Area	Scenery	Strainers	Rating
150	III (5.0)	0.5*	4.8	C	2-8/mi.	?

USGS Quad – Falls Church; Source – Scouting by foot
N38 58.54, W77 10.95 to N38 58.36, W77 10.10

*(plus 1 mile on the Potomac to Lock 10)

Below the small bridge, this **"explorers' special"** starts off class III and is then class II for a quarter mile. It passes below Clara Barton Parkway and the C&O Canal in two huge, straight, 100-yard long culverts. (There is no place to park nearby, but you can scout from a trail off the towpath.) At its end, the left culvert drops 4 feet over a concrete lip and then hits natural rock where it slides 6 feet at about 60 degrees into a small pool. This looks like class 5.0, and the right culvert looks even tougher. Ten yards later there is a 5-foot natural ledge, and the creek then calms down to class II for a quarter mile, before a final class III that drops 5 feet to the Potomac.

The creek enters the Potomac between Stubblefield Falls and the Beltway, so you would then head down a mile to Lock 10.

GAUGE: I don't know how much water you need or want for the class 5.0 drop. For the rest, 60 cfs on Turkey Branch or 100 cfs on Ten Mile Creek should suffice.

CABIN JOHN CREEK

Cabin John Creek rises in southern Rockville and heads south for ten miles. Section 2 stays up for several hours after a heavy rain, flows through a pretty park, and has good whitewater. Section 1 is also pleasant, but not challenging. Above that, the creek is narrow, much harder to catch and full of strainers.

In 1857-63, the **Union Arch Bridge**, at 220 feet the world's longest stone arch then, was built over Cabin John Creek, near the C&O Canal, to carry the Washington Aqueduct – which is still in operation, currently piping 185 million gallons of water daily from above Great Falls to the Dalecarlia Reservoir.

In the 1870s, the Bobinger brothers built the grandiose, wooden gingerbread **Cabin John Bridge Hotel** nearby. They served wine from vineyards along the creek and kept their bass fresh in a pen in the creek. The hotel closed in 1926 and burned down in 1931, despite the efforts of 7 volunteer fire companies' 33 fire engines.

During the late 19th and early 20th centuries, there were **mills** and **stone quarries** along the creek. The Gilbert Quarry alone provided over 1.5 million cubic feet of granite, which was transported to Washington via the C&O Canal. When the quarries closed they became swimming holes. The millrace for Boones Mill is still visible near Montrose Road.

Don't bother looking for John's cabin. The name is actually a corruption of **Captain John**, probably meaning John Smith, who explored the lower Potomac in 1608.

Virtually the entire creek and its tributaries are protected within **Cabin John Regional Park** of the MNCPPC. Deer are common. A trail parallels the creek, so you can enjoy the scenery even in low water; use a trail map, as you have to exit at both Democracy Boulevard and Tuckerman Lane, and find the new entrances some distance away.

Section 1: Tuckerman Lane to River Road

Gradient	Difficulty	Distance	Area	Scenery	Strainers	Rating
19 (50)	II	4.1	7.7	C	1-3/mi.	*

USGS Quad – Rockville/Falls Church; Source – Personal descent 3/07
N39 02.24, W77 09.24 to N38 59.81, W77 10.15

The put in is at the confluence with Old Farm Creek. The only real hazard, other than strainers, is a 4-foot drop early on, through a rat's nest of broken concrete. After 1.4 miles, you pass Democracy Boulevard, where there are some lively riffles, followed by a flatter mile down to Bradley Boulevard (mile 2.9), with lots of wood in the creek. The next mile has alternating pools and riffles, until the wide floodplain gives way to a narrow valley, the gradient rises to 50 ft/mile and the difficulty to class II for the last quarter mile down to River Road.

GAUGE: If there is adequate water for the riffle just upstream of River Road, you should be OK. Look for 600 cfs on Rock Creek, 40 cfs on Ten Mile Creek and 25 cfs on Turkey Branch. At the put in, the main stem and Old Farm Creek should be runnable.

Section 2: River Road to C&O Canal

Gradient	Difficulty	Distance	Area	Scenery	Strainers	Rating
37 (80)	III- (III)	2.6	18	B-	0-2/mi.	****

USGS Quad – Falls Church; Source – Personal descent 3/07
N38 59.81, W77 10.15 to N38 58.24, W77 08.82

The first half mile has frequent class II rapids. At the island shortly below River Road, the left channel has more water. Where the creek turns sharply left and passes below Seven Locks Road, just past the pipe waterfall, there is a short, bouncy class II+ drop, best run on the far left. The rapids then ease up to class II- for the middle third of the trip. After the Beltway, Booze Creek enters through a garishly-grafittied tunnel under Cabin John Parkway. Then, as Cabin John Creek enters an attractive semi-gorge, the gradient picks up. For a half mile there is one long class II+ or III- rock garden after another, with one solid class III. And there are lots of good surfing waves and holes. The occasional strainers tend to concentrate at the bridges.

Take out on river left just before the culvert under the C&O Canal, after paddling beneath MacArthur Boulevard, Cabin John Parkway and Clara Barton Parkway, and follow the wide slope to the small gravel area on the shoulder of Clara Barton Parkway, where you can leave your boat. To shorten the shuttle and avoid a possible parking ticket, leave your car in the large parking area on MacArthur Boulevard just east of the one-lane bridge over Cabin John Creek. From the take out, follow the trail under Clara Barton Parkway a quarter mile, and then go up the stairs to MacArthur Boulevard.

The passage under the C&O Canal is impassable in high water, and has **6 inches less clearance on the downstream side than on the upstream.** If you do continue, it is a class I quarter mile to the Potomac and then a mile to Sycamore Island (and a fairly stiff carry).

GAUGE: Check the riffle just upstream of River Road. Fourmile Run at Alexandria (Va.) should read over 75 cfs, Rock Creek 325 cfs and Ten Mile Creek 25 cfs.

OLD FARM CREEK: Stonewood Lane to Cabin John Creek

Gradient	Difficulty	Distance	Area	Scenery	Strainers	Rating
35	II-	1.8	1.3	C	3-6/mi.	*

USGS Quad – Rockville; Source – Personal descent 4/96
N39 02.94, W77 08.15 to N39 02.24, W77 09.24

This tiny stream's three branches begin southwest of Rockville Pike and join below Montrose Road. Put in at the confluence, at the northern edge of Tilden Park, at the end of Stonewood Lane. The creek heads south, passes under Tilden Lane and then arcs westward alongside Tuckerman Lane. The gradient is steady, as the creek tumbles over class I and II- gravel bars, twisting through a wooded park. Tilden Lane at 0.4 miles is an alternative put-in if you arrive too late to catch the upper section. A pair of tributaries increases the flow, and then at mile 1.0 the creek passes beneath I-270. In the final section, small ledges replace gravel bars; several can be surfed. There is good parking at the confluence with Cabin John Creek (the put in for the latter's section 1).

This would be a nice run were it not for the strainers. The woods screen out most of the nearby housing, and the only major intrusion of civilization is the noise of the traffic along Tuckerman Lane during the second half of the trip.

GAUGE: Turkey Branch should be over 100 cfs, Ten Mile Creek 170 cfs.

SNAKEDEN BRANCH: Tuckerman Lane and Seven Locks Road

Gradient	Difficulty	Distance	Area	Scenery	Strainers	Rating
65 (110)	III	0.3	1.0	D+	0-7/mi.	**

USGS Quad – Rockville; Source – Personal descent 8/02
N39 02.46, W77 09.67 to N39 02.29, W77 09.55

This very short, "quick and dirty" run, at the major intersection of Tuckerman Lane and Seven Locks Road, keeps you on your toes. The first half is a continuous class III rock garden, and the second half is twisty class II+. Check the first part for strainers, from Tuckerman Lane. You can park by Cobble Creek Circle – I wonder why they didn't name that "Snakeden Branch Circle"? Put in from Tuckerman Lane just downstream of the fence, and take out where the creek pulls alongside Seven Locks Road, just before becoming paved.

The rest of Snakeden Branch is not worth much attention. The half mile above Tuckerman Lane, at 30 ft/mile, is very narrow, unattractive and full of strainers. Right below the recommended section, the creek is a concrete channel for 300 yards, and then passes beneath Seven Locks Road **through a deadly culvert**. Below there, it returns to a natural streambed averaging 40 ft/mile, and is class II for 200 yards and then class I for a quarter mile to Cabin John Creek (one mile above Democracy Boulevard).

GAUGE: Turkey Branch should be over 150 cfs, Ten Mile Creek 250 cfs.

BUCK BRANCH: Powder Horn Drive to Democracy Boulevard

Gradient	Difficulty	Distance	Area	Scenery	Strainers	Rating
60 (150)	III	1.5	1.0	B	1-3/mi.	***

USGS Quad – Rockville; Source – Personal descent 7/96 (last 0.9 miles); scouting
N39 02.30, W77 10.82 to N39 01.34, W77 10.33

Catching and enjoying this tiny creek was as unexpected as the Cain boomlet. Not only is the streambed wide enough to paddle, but it has nice whitewater and scenery as it flows through Cabin John Park. Just wait for an intense rain, and then wait not at all.

The most upstream put in is between 11140 and 11144 Powder Horn Drive; there is also access 0.2 miles later, between 11056 and 11060. (Nobody can accuse me of being all fluff and no specifics.) The first 0.6 miles, down to Bells Mill Road, is continuous class II, with fast current and frequent small drops, at 60 ft/mile. Shortly above Bells Mill Road is a class III, two-foot ledge on a left turn. Then watch for strainers as you approach the bridge.

The first 100 yards below Bells Mill Road are not very propitious, as the creek twists between high, eroded banks. But then the valley and streambed open up, pretty rock formations appear, and a series of class II rock gardens begins, soon becoming continuous. After a tiny tributary enters on the right, marked by a collapsed concrete slab and a sharp turn to the left, the gradient soars to 150 ft/mile and there is a class III rock garden for 150 yards. The creek then returns to class II, winding back and forth as it approaches Democracy Boulevard.

There is no parking at Democracy Boulevard, so you must leave your car one-third mile away at Gainsborough Road, or paddle the final half-mile at just 15 ft/mile, and then a mile on Cabin John Creek (10 ft/mile) to Bradley Boulevard.

GAUGE: It took an intense cloudburst, with 1.5" of rain in one hour. Look for 150 cfs on Turkey Branch, 250 cfs on Four Mile Creek, 750 cfs on Fourmile Run.

"KENTDALE BRANCH": Kendale Road to Cabin John Creek

Gradient	Difficulty	Distance	Area	Scenery	Strainers	Rating
30	II- (II)	1.1*	1.6	B-	4-8/mi.	*

USGS Quad – Rockville; Source – Personal descent 6/97
N39 00.58, W77 10.77 to N38 59.81, W77 10.15

*(plus 0.3 miles of class II on Cabin John Creek down to River Road)

As this stream rises just north of Kentsdale Drive and the put is at Kendale Road, I call it "Kentdale Branch." This poor, nameless creek traverses the rich Bradley Farms part of east Potomac, which results in fine scenery – woods bounded by fancy houses with well-tended gardens. The paddle would also be OK, were it not for the strainers.

From Kendale Road, the creek soon flows under a driveway, with adequate clearance. The first half mile is class II-. The Bradley Boulevard culvert tends to get blocked; you can portage from a trickle on river left about 30 yards before the culvert.

The remaining 0.6 miles contains a class II rock garden (visible from the bridge) and a class II broken ledge with a 3-foot drop. The final 200 yards, below a private footbridge (to a gazebo), is backwater from Cabin John Creek, and then it is 0.3 bouncy miles to River Road, the start of section 2 of Cabin John Creek. But if "Kentdale Branch" is runnable, lower Cabin John Creek may be high. On my paddle, Cabin John Creek was running at about 3 feet, and the 0.3 miles was a fast class II+ flush – the best part of my trip. The takeout eddy is on river left just upstream of River Road.

GAUGE: Zero level is when there are two inches of water flowing over Kendale Road. Look for about 80 cfs on Turkey Branch and 135 cfs on Ten Mile Creek.

The day I ran this, Potomac was preoccupied with day 3 of the 1997 **US Open** at Congressional Country Club. The ¾-inch downpour that made my trip possible was a major nuisance for the 25,000 golf fans there, and a minor irritant for the 25 million watching on TV. Tiger Woods was so thrown off his game that he bogeyed 4 of the next 6 holes. Now if only I had assayed instead the next nameless (and even smaller) tributary downstream, which flows right through Congressional, I might have made national TV.

BOOZE CREEK: Burning Tree Road to Cabin John Creek

Gradient	Difficulty	Distance	Area	Scenery	Strainers	Rating
45 (70)	II+	1.5*	2.0	D+	1-3/mi.	**

USGS Quad – Falls Church; Source – Personal descent (1st half) 8/96; scouting N38 59.66, W77 08.53 via N38 59.26, W77 08.88 (River Rd.) to N38 58.24, W77 08.82

*(plus 1.5 miles on Cabin John Creek, which is class III, down to the C&O Canal)

Bulls Run rises near I-495 and Old Georgetown Road, and heads southwest for 1.5 miles until, just below Bradley Boulevard, it picks up an unnamed tributary and becomes Booze Creek. Bulls Run and the start of Booze Creek are concrete channels. Put in 100 yards before it reverts to a natural streambed, where Beech Tree Road makes a 90-degree bend and becomes Burning Tree Road, near Burning Tree Country Club.

The first half of this run is mostly through the Holton Arms School for girls. It is a pleasant class II paddle, with tight turns, small ledges, easy rock gardens and few strainers. In addition to school buildings, a few houses can be seen from a subdivision named Frenchmans Creek – perhaps a play on the Gallic propensity for wine. Booze Creek then passes beneath River Road, with an 18-inch drop that creates a little hydraulic. There is access on river left here, from Helmsdale Road. (This is where I took out.)

Shortly below, there are nice waves where the creek bends to the right. The gradient rises briefly to 70 ft/mile, but the rapids are just steeper class II+ gravel bars. Booze Creek then flows beneath Cabin John Parkway, through a tunnel with garish graffiti, and over a one-foot ledge into Cabin John Creek. As there is no takeout here, you must continue 1.5 miles down the best part of Cabin John Creek to its takeout. So first check the water level there, as it may be very high whenever Booze Creek is up, and **missing the final eddy above the C&O Canal culvert could be fatal.** One option is to wait at the confluence until Cabin John Creek drops; another is to go before it rises much.

All in all, Booze Creek is one of the nicer little tributaries around. It has moderate but interesting rapids, few strainers and decent water quality. The scenery is poor, mainly because the streambed is lined in places with boulders dumped to limit erosion.

GAUGE: You will want 75 cfs on Turkey Branch, 125 cfs on Ten Mile Creek.

The creek's name is a corruption of the original **Bowie's Run**, named (like the town of Bowie) after the prominent Maryland family that later included Governor Oden Bowie (1867-72).

MINNEHAHA BRANCH: Goldleaf Drive to Clara Barton Parkway

Gradient	Difficulty	Distance	Area	Scenery	Strainers	Rating
125 (200)	IV+	0.8	1.2	D, B-	1-4/mi.	?

USGS Quad – Falls Church; Source – Complete scouting on foot
N38 58.29, W77 10.33 to N38 58.03, W77 08.41

This tiny **"explorers' special"** has serious rapids plus other hazards. It becomes (very rarely) runnable below the intersection of River and Goldsboro Roads. It parallels the latter for a mile, before its final quarter mile through Glen Echo Park, beneath the C&O Canal and into the Potomac near Lock 7.

The first one-third mile is a mess, so put in at Goldleaf Drive. The 0.3 miles to Rannoch Road is continuous class II+. The culvert there may be impassable, but there is a good eddy on river right. After a further 100 yards of class II+, to the high culvert under Goldsboro Road (by the "FLOOD AREA" sign), the serious stuff begins. First, a pair of 2-ft ledges creates a class III rapid, and then a 6-foot drop through narrow chutes looks class IV+. There is no eddy above this, so scout from the road. Some 130 yards later, a live tree creates a quasi-permanent strainer; portage on the left. Then comes a 3-ft sloping ledge. Near MacArthur Blvd., the gradient begins to grow again. In the final 30 yards, the creek drops 10 feet in a second class IV+ rapid, complicated by the entry into the large, 50-yard long culvert. Again, there is no eddy above the rapid, so check beforehand.

Below MacArthur Blvd., the narrow streambed squeezed between a road and a wall is replaced by an open valley. The rock-strewn creek is class III+ for 250 yards and class IV- the final 100 yards to the culvert under Clara Barton Parkway and the C&O Canal. But the graffiti-filled **culvert is a death trap**, with a 6-foot-high entrance but a low exit! Unless the Potomac is in flood and its backwater fills the culvert (the safest time to run this), you must catch the last eddy, 100 yards above the culvert, or get swept down the final rapid and into oblivion.

GAUGE: You need 150 cfs on Turkey Branch and 250 cfs on Ten Mile Creek.

The name was changed from **Naylor's Run** to Minnehaha Branch (from Longfellow's *Song of Hiawatha*) in 1891, when the land near its mouth was bought by the Chautauqua Institution, whose goal was to unify and uplift Protestant churches through adult education. That same year, the 8,000-seat **Chautauqua Amphitheatre** was built over the creek, which flowed along a lighted walkway and powered the organ and speaker system above. After an initial season that drew over 100,000 people, the Amphitheatre was closed (until 1911) due to fear of malaria.

In 1899 the **Glen Echo Amusement Park** was opened alongside, and its increasing popularity led to the amphitheatre being torn down to extend the parking lot in 1956, with the creek in a culvert beneath. In 1989, nature had its revenge, when a flood collapsed the culvert and part of the parking lot, damaging 68 cars, a dozen of which got carried all the way to the Potomac. Two years later, the National Park Service began restoring the streambed by clearing out debris, bringing in large boulders and revegetating the slopes.

Nearby, the **Clara Barton National Historic Site** contains the last home (1897-1912) of the founder of the American Red Cross, who died there at age 90.

🌊 LITTLE FALLS BRANCH

Little Falls Branch rises in the upscale Bethesda/Somerset area. Both the main stem and its tributary, Willett Branch, are soon cemented, flow beneath River Road and meet at Little Falls Parkway, for section 1. After Dalecarlia Reservoir and MacArthur Boulevard, there is a brief but exciting section 2 that leads to Little Falls of the Potomac.

> The **danger of these cemented sections** became evident on September 7, 1996, when Hurricane Fran dumped 4 inches of rain. As the *Washington Post* reported, a 7-year old boy *"fell into the rushing waters of a storm-engorged creek [Little Falls Branch] that runs near his house while trying to measure the surging stream with a stick."* He got washed down over three-quarters of a mile through the cement channels, until the creek regained its natural bed alongside Little Falls Parkway. Then, as he reported: *"The rock hit me, and so I started to stand up on it. Then, I climbed up on it."* He escaped *"with only a few nicks and scrapes and a slight concussion."*

Section 1: Little Falls Parkway to above Dalecarlia Reservoir

Gradient	Difficulty	Distance	Area	Scenery	Strainers	Rating
35 (70)	II- (III)	1.1	2.1	C	0-2/mi.	**

USGS Quad – Washington West; Source – Personal descent 7/92
N38 57.58, W77 06.27 to N38 56.93, W77 06.66

Put-in at the confluence of the two streams. Looking upstream, Willett Branch is steep and tempting, but there are only 100 yards of natural streambed, and you must carry up.

From the confluence, there is an exciting quarter-mile at 70 ft/mile to Massachusetts Ave., highlighted by a short, tight class III rapid 100 yards below the put in, where the water divides around a large boulder (probably the one the little boy climbed onto). In high water, this becomes class IV. Scout this rapid before putting in.

Below Massachusetts Ave., the gradient drops fast, as the creek winds through Little Falls Park toward the chain link fence of Dalecarlia Reservoir. Take-out about 100 yards above the fence, from where it is a 100-yard carry to the dead end of Albemarle Street.

GAUGE: You need at least 75 cfs on Turkey Branch, 125 cfs on Ten Mile Creek

> **Iconoclasm Loves Company.** In July 1992, as I was scouting the class III and preparing to put in, I was amazed to find another paddler with the same idea – kayaker Steve Elder, with a rubber ducky. This is the only micro-stream where I had the pleasure of unplanned company.
> **Dalecarlia Reservoir** is part of the DC drinking water storage and purification system. It was fed by Little Falls Branch until that became too polluted, and its water is now pumped up from the Potomac, while Little Falls Branch is diverted underground.

Section 2: Below MacArthur Boulevard to Potomac River

Gradient	Difficulty	Distance	Area	Scenery	Strainers	Rating
80 (200)	III (III+)	0.6*	4.2	B-	0-3/mi.	***

USGS Quad – Washington West; Source – Personal descent 7/05
N38 56.57, W77 07.23 to N38 55.12, W77 06.13 (Fletchers boathouse)

*(plus running Little Falls on the Potomac and proceeding to either of its take outs)

After Dalecarlia Reservoir, Little Falls Branch passes in a long, dark culvert under MacArthur Boulevard, before reemerging for its final dash to the Potomac. Enter the Brookmont neighborhood (full of paddlers because of walking access to Little Falls of the Potomac and the feeder canal), park at Broad and 64th Streets, and carry 100 yards down a rough trail.

The creek starts out class II, punctuated by a class III- ledge. Then the gradient increases, and the continuous rock garden steepens to class III. Approaching the Clara Barton Parkway, the gradient reaches 200 ft/mile and the difficulty class III+ (at low to moderate levels). Start on the right (beneath the footbridge) and cut all the way left for the final drop, especially avoiding the boulder in the middle there. The cement walls on either side add to the risk. But you have to make a quick decision here, because there is no good scouting eddy and no easy way to portage. If this 50-yard rapid looks too tough, beach your boat on the rocks, and carry out (there is a trail on river right) back to Brookmont.

The water calms down just above the C&O Canal culvert; there will be adequate clearance unless you have over 3 feet of water. The rapids below the Canal are mainly class II+, but with overhanging and fallen branches. In low water, take the right channel at the second rapid. The final drop is class III- into the Potomac, at a popular scouting spot for Little Falls.

The scenery is mostly fine in this little gorge, but the water quality is not.

And then, after running this section, you get the Little Falls of the Potomac as a bonus, **so be sure the level on the latter is one you can handle**. If you had no time to set up a shuttle, you can use the canal as if you had run just Little Falls, and then cross the Clara Barton Parkway to Brookmont. Otherwise, you can continue down to Fletchers Boathouse (the GPS coordinate).

GAUGE: Look for 50 cfs on Turkey Branch, 85 cfs on Ten Mile Creek and 250 cfs on Fourmile Run at Alexandria (Va.). The water needs to be fairly deep in the initial class II chutes, because the creek gets wider below. There are occasional unannounced releases from Dalecarlia Reservoir (to flush out chemicals), but these are when Little Falls Branch is already up (so that the chemicals get further diluted, and you might not even realize that it is happening as you paddle).

ROCK CREEK BASIN

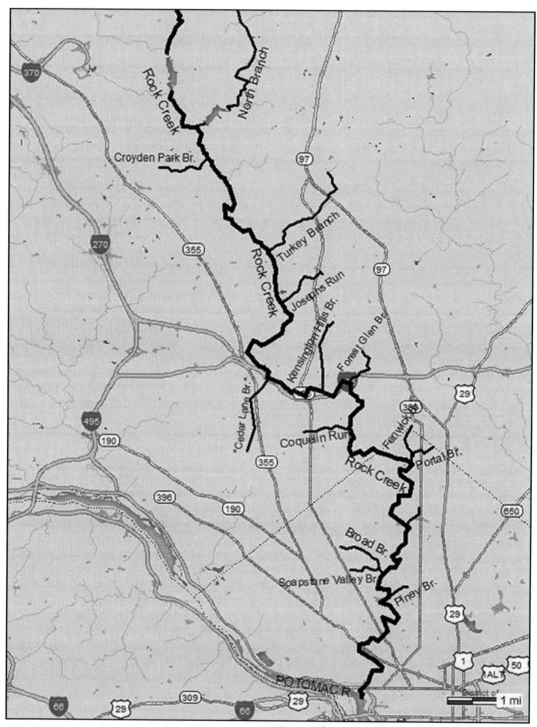

Chapter 20:

ROCK CREEK BASIN

> **Full Disclosure**: I am biased in favor of Rock Creek. I have lived within a mile of it for all my 40 years in the DC area, at 4 locations. It was the first high-intermediate stream I paddled, I have canoed it over 30 times, and its tributaries introduced me to the world of micro-streams.

Rock Creek rises in northern Montgomery County, flows down the middle of that county and northwest DC, and exits the city, as Richard Nixon did, in the shadow of Watergate. Around it is a lovely park, where deer (rare until the early 1990s), foxes (pursued around 1910 by the Chevy Chase Hunt), raccoons and opossums abound. In 1890, Congress created Rock Creek Park, to provide a zoo for the live animals (which were then on the mall) of the Smithsonian Institution, as well as to increase the value of the adjacent acreage of the Chevy Chase Land Company. But whatever the motives, the result was infinitely better than other approaches proposed, such as making the creek a lake or a paved-over sewer. The park provides golf, soccer, cycling, hiking, par courses, playgrounds, picnicking, riding and cross-country skiing (best on 20 miles of horse trails). Other attractions are the National Zoo, Carter Barron Amphitheatre and National Tennis Center. Oh yes, and half a mile of excellent class III rapids (in section 3), plus an unusual way to sightsee DC (section 4). Maryland began buying land along its section of Rock Creek in 1931, and the entire stream is now protected.

The watershed stretches 25 miles from north to south, but averages only 3 miles in width (from Georgia Ave. to Wisconsin Ave./Old Georgetown Rd./Rockville Pike). As a result, except for its **North Branch**, Rock Creek has no major tributaries. Rather, it has numerous small branches that enter at fairly even intervals along both banks. The uppermost ones (Tributary Br., Manor Run, Mill Creek) rise in woodlands, have low gradients (10-30 ft/mi.) and are full of strainers. Further south, the Rock Creek gorge deepens and the tributaries steepen. The final ones (Normanstone, Klingle Valley, Melvin Hazen and Dumbarton Oaks branches) are too steep (gradients over 200 ft/mi.) to paddle safely, given their natural and man-made (low-water bridges and pipes) strainers.

> During April - October 1944, the **Dumbarton Oaks** mansion (where Dumbarton Oaks Branch rises) was the site for the preparatory discussions between the US, UK, USSR and China which led up to the San Francisco Conference which founded the United Nations.

But in between, remarkably, some 13 tributaries can be paddled because the run-off from impervious surfaces is so fast that these tiny streams briefly reach high levels. All have interesting gradients, averaging 35-135 ft/mi, and there are a few exciting rapids. Flowing within the park, most have pretty scenery and no fences or access hassles. The best are **Broad, Turkey, Kensington Hills, Soapstone Valley and Croyden Park branches** – the last two being "explorers' specials." **"Forest Glen"** and

Luzon branches each have one challenging drop, while **"Cedar Lane," Fenwick** and **Piney** branches and **Coquelin Run** also have their good spots. **Josephs Run** and **Portal Branch** are forgettable. Of course, the runs are short, ranging from only a few hundred yards up to 2.4 miles, and stay up only minutes, during and immediately after intense rain.

A major problem, as all but the olfactorily challenged will notice, is poor water quality due to the urban waste that gets washed off the streets. The problem is far worse from Piney Branch (the last runnable tributary) downstream, where the old-style, dual-use conduits carry sewerage and storm water side by side, separated by a concrete divider. In a heavy rain, the storm water rises above the divider and mixes with the sewerage, and part of the combined flow gets dumped into Rock Creek and its tributaries. As Rock Creek flows within a mile of the White House, the smells could sometimes even be a problem for anyone there who inhales. The DC Government periodically posts a "Health Advisory," warning against the dangers of swimming in and eating fish from Rock Creek.

> Not all the pollution is from street run-off or dual-use conduits. For example, the runnable section of **Southlawn Branch** is just downstream of an industrial area that includes Montgomery Concrete, Lafarge Concrete, Southlawn Auto Recyclers, Montgomery Scrap Corporation and Rockville Fuel and Feed.

GAUGES: In March 2007, the gauge at Sherrill Drive on Rock Creek (62 sq. mi.) came on line. Most tributaries rise and fall too rapidly to wait for gauge reports, but the gauge on **Turkey Branch** (2.7 sq. mi.) is the most useful and is the **zero-level reference** in the table below, except that the one on **Rock Creek** is used for most of that creek itself, and is in ***bold italics***. There are no reported rainfall gauges. If the Turkey Branch gauge is not available, use the one on Watts Branch (3.3 sq. mi.) in Anacostia DC (by adding 20% to the zero-level figures for Turkey Branch). The gauge on the Hawlings River (Patuxent basin) is worth checking for the most upstream tributaries.

name	gradient	difficulty	length	area	gauge	rating
Rock Creek - Section 1	25	II- (II)	2.0	5.8	30cfs	-
- Section 2	9	I	17.5	32	*185cfs*	*
- Section 3	40 (100)	III	2.2	67	*185cfs*	***
- Section 4	11	II-	4.6	70	*100cfs*	**
North Branch	28 (75)	II (III-)	2.3	9.4	25cfs	**
Croyden Park Branch	80 (300)	III-(IV+)	1.3	0.6	250cfs	?
Turkey Branch - Sec. 1	50 (100)	?	0.5	1.1	145cfs	?
- Sec. 2	33	II	1.9	1.3	100cfs	**
Josephs Run	40	II-	1.2	2.0	80cfs	-
"Cedar Lane Branch"	50	II (III)	0.5	1.4	125cfs	*
Kensington Hills Br.	50	II (III-)	1.3	1.2	90cfs	**
"Forest Glen Branch"	100	II (III)	0.3	1.1	125cfs	**
Coquelin Run	50	II+(5.0)	0.7	1.3	115cfs	**
Fenwick Branch	70	II (III+)	0.8	0.5	165cfs	*
Portal Branch	70	II+ (III)	0.3	0.4	250cfs	*
Luzon Branch	80	II+ (III)	0.3	0.9	150cfs	**
Broad Branch	75	III	1.2	1.3	115cfs	***
Soapstone Valley Br.	135	IV	0.8	0.3	400cfs	?
Piney Branch	80	II+	0.5	1.3	100cfs	*

ROCK CREEK

Rock Creek flows for 31 miles, from a spring (once tapped in a springhouse) northeast of Gaithersburg, down to Needwood Lake (section 1), across the lake, through 18 miles of class I water (section 2), down the excellent and popular class III whitewater below Military Road (section 3) and through calmer stretches to the Potomac (section 4). For its first 4 miles, it traverses a wooded area with no roads. The first access is in the Agricultural History Farm Park, but a better choice is half a mile later, at the bridge on Muncaster Road.

> Indians quarried flint for arrowheads at numerous sites along the creek. In the 1680s, English settlement began, and Col. John Addison built a fort at the mouth, from which the Rangers sallied forth to battle the Seneca and Susquehannock. Georgetown was originally called Rock Creek Landing, and in 1747 Maryland put a tobacco inspection station there, to ensure sufficient tar and nicotine content. There was navigation at least two miles up the creek, but by the 1790s, the mouth of Rock Creek was silting up because of upstream deforestation.
>
> **Twenty-six mills** once operated along Rock Creek. Pierce Mill (a 19th century grain mill) has been reconstructed, and there are signposts at the other seven mill sites within DC. The Chesapeake and Ohio Canal begins off of Rock Creek, in Georgetown.
>
> In the original creation of DC, the land between Rock Creek and the Anacostia River, up to 1.5 miles from the Potomac, was to be for public buildings; Rock Creek thus formed a **boundary** between the public and private parts of the District. Much later it became the unofficial boundary between the predominantly white areas to the west and a string of racially integrated neighborhoods just to the east (Shepherd Park, Crestwood, Mt. Pleasant, Adams Morgan, Dupont Circle), giving way to virtually all-black communities farther to the east. Prices of comparable houses drop by 20-30% as one crosses Rock Creek heading east.
>
> On August 24-25, 1814, when the British occupied Washington, the flooding of Rock Creek from a hurricane prevented them from reaching and destroying the Foxhall foundry that was the chief source of weapons for the United States Army. In July 1864, Union forts overlooking Rock Creek blocked the advance of General Jubal Early's Confederate forces in their attempted raid on Washington. Presidents Jackson, Lincoln and Theodore Roosevelt used to go horseback riding along the creek, and TR would also lead hiking, wading and climbing trips up into the wilder upstream stretches – invitations to join him were considered a mixed blessing.
>
> In the creek's upper reaches, a dam built in the 1960s created **Needwood Lake**, to reduce flooding and ensure at least a minimal volume during droughts. Needwood Lake is a popular picnicking and recreation center (including canoe rental on the lake), as well as the northern terminus of the Rock Creek Bicycle Trail.

The U.S. Park Police ask that paddlers stay off of sections 2-4 during rush hour, lest they be an "attractive nuisance" and cause accidents. Poor water quality is another problem, which worsens as the creek moves deeper into the urban core.

Section 1: Muncaster Road to Muncaster Mill Rd. (above Needwood Lake)

Gradient	Difficulty	Distance	Area	Scenery	Strainers	Rating
25	II- (II)	2.0	5.8	C-	4-6/mi.	-

USGS Quad – Gaithersburg; Source – Personal descent 3/96
N39 09.25, W77 07.91 to N39 08.25, W77 07.75

At the put in, Rock Creek is small, sluggish and straight. The straightness disappears soon, the sluggishness diminishes as the gradient increases, but the size stays about the same. There are many class II- ledges and gravel bars; the best sequence is towards the end – a 2-ft ledge followed by a 50-yd, class II rock garden. The countryside is lightly wooded, remote and full of deer. The creek winds between 2-4 foot high mud banks; it is never straight for more than 50 yards. The main nuisance, as you might guess, is fallen trees, many due to beavers. There was also a steel mesh fence across the creek – unexpected, as the entire run is within a park. Overall, the paddling is not very good; however, for those of us who love Rock Creek, this is a chance to see its baby album.

GAUGE: Look for 30 cfs on Turkey Branch, 300 cfs on the Hawlings River.

Below Muncaster Mill Road, the creek flows for up to half a mile, depending upon the water level in **Needwood Lake**, and then it is at least a further mile across the lake. Needwood Lake is the only place in its entire system where the Maryland National Capitol Park and Planning Commission (MNCPPC) officially permits canoeing.

Section 2: Southlawn Lane to Military Road

Gradient	Difficulty	Distance	Area	Scenery	Strainers	Rating
9	I	17.5	32*	C+	3/mi.	*

USGS Quad – Rockville/Kensington/Washington West; Source – Personal descent (last 4 miles) 5/92; Gertler; scouting from bicycle path
N39 06.37, W77 07.51 via N39 01.91, W77 05.24 (Knowles Ave) and N38 59.19, W77 03.17 (Md./DC line) to N38 57.78, W77 02.73

*(including the North Branch, which enters after one mile)

This is a long, flattish paddle with many access points and even more strainers, especially in the early part, but it gives you a nice tour of scenic Rock Creek Park. You could carry down a steep 150 yards from the Needwood dam itself, but it is much easier to start half a mile later at Southlawn Lane. In another half mile, the North Branch enters, adding about 80% to the catchment area; how much it adds to the flow is quite variable, as both branches are dam controlled. There are many riffles, most frequently at the start, but no real rapids. Bring a flashlight for the dark, curving passage under the railroad tracks above Knowles Avenue (mile 8). Once in DC, the creek enters an attractive steep-sided valley for the last 3 miles to Military Road. Beach Drive parallels the creek, but is not too intrusive except at rush hour (when the Park Police don't want you on the creek). Take out at the parking lot just above Military Road, unless you can handle section 3.

GAUGE: Scout from the road. Look for 185 cfs on the Rock Creek gauge for the upper parts and 120 cfs by the end.

> **War is Not Good for Flowers and Other Living Things.** The strainers in this section are nothing compared to what it was like during the Civil War, when whole sections of trees were felled to slow any Confederate attack and to give the defenders in Fort DeRussey (in Rock Creek Park, just north of Military Road) a clear line of fire.

Section 3: Military Road to Pierce Mill

Gradient	Difficulty	Distance	Area	Scenery	Strainers	Rating
40 (100)	III	2.2	67	B	<1/mi.	***

USGS Quad – Washington West; Source – Personal descent often
N38 57.78, W77 02.73 to N38 56.41, W77 03.10

This wonderful short trip through the middle of Washington D.C. would get four stars if not for its poor water quality. Start at the parking area just north of Military Road, for a brief warm up. In the 0.4 miles from the Park Police Station to the footbridge, the creek drops 40 feet, through four class III rock gardens and several more class II-III ones. Scout for strainers beforehand from Beach Drive. In low water, there tends to be only one route per rapid, mostly Democratic (left of center). In high water, the rapids run together and a swimmer might be in for a long, bumpy ride. Below the footbridge, the creek is class II for a half mile until the road bridge, and class I after that until Pierce Mill.

Pierce Mill is a 6-foot drop that has often been run, but the Park Police discourage this because of the strong hydraulic below, especially at higher levels, and the miserable quality of the water that will splash in your face. If you do run it, stay near either edge for easier rescue. (A fish ladder was built in 2007 at Pierce Mill, to enable spawning river herring and other species to move upstream.)

GAUGE: The USGS staff gauge on river right at Joyce Road (just above the rapids) should read at least 2.7, and the on-line gauge at Sherrill Drive (1.2 miles above the start of the rapids) 185 cfs. The difficulty starts to increase as the staff gauge reaches 4 and the on-line gauge 500 cfs. The creek drops by about an inch per hour at moderate levels. Some 30-40 cfs on Turkey Branch for several hours is a good leading indicator.

Section 4: Pierce Mill to Potomac River

Gradient	Difficulty	Distance	Area	Scenery	Strainers	Rating
11	II-	4.6	70	B-	<1/mi.	**

USGS Quad – Washington West; Source – Personal descent often
N38 56.41, W77 03.10 to N38 54.08, W77 03.45

This section is best appreciated as a tour of downtown Washington. In addition to many statuesque bridges, you pass the National Zoo, historic Mt. Zion cemetery, an old lime kiln, the first lock of the C&O Canal, Watergate and the Kennedy Center, not to mention homeless people living under some of the bridges. A one-foot drop almost under Connecticut Ave. puts you on top of the Metro's Red Line. Turn right on the Potomac, and take out at the Thompson Boat Center. There is a big parking lot at the end of Virginia Avenue, across from the Watergate, but the meters are good for only 3 hours. Stay out of the water, which includes a very unhealthy mix of raw sewerage.

Despite being in the middle of the city, this section is popular with mallards and wood ducks, which you can often see with their young in the spring.

GAUGE: This stretch needs 3-4 inches less water than section 3, which means 2.4 on the USGS staff gauge and 100 cfs on the on-line gauge at Sherrill Drive.

NORTH BRANCH: Cherry Valley Drive to Lake Bernard Frank

Gradient	Difficulty	Distance	Area	Scenery	Strainers	Rating
28 (75)	II (III-)	2.3	9.4	B-	1-3/mi.	**

USGS Quad – Sandy Spring/Kensington; Source – Personal descent 3/97
N39 07.90, W77 05.90 to N39 06.81, W77 06.38

From Mt. Zion, Rock Creek's largest tributary flows south for 7 miles into Lake Bernard Frank. The first access is Bowie Mill Road at mile 3, but the prospects for finding enough water are minimal until Cherry Valley Drive, after Tributary Branch enters. The Inter-County Connector crosses just below the put in.

It is 70 yards from the small parking area to the creek, along a trail. The first mile is twisty and flat, except for one long class II rock garden. Nearing Muncaster Mill Road (where the last gristmill in the Rock Creek basin operated from 1820 to 1925), is a 50-yard, class III- rock garden. There is a nice surfing wave under the Muncaster Mill bridge (mile 1.4), and then the creek widens out. After several class II- rock gardens, Manor Run enters on the left, and there is a long class II rapid and a final small ledge; from there on it is flat water. There are hiking trails on both sides below Muncaster Mill Road.

The take out is awkward. I took out on river right just after the final small ledge, and climbed 50 vertical feet up a very steep quasi-trail to the Meadowside Nature Center. To avoid this, one could paddle two-thirds mile down Lake Frank, for a short carry to the end of Trailway Drive; however, Lake Frank is closed to boating (presumably to prevent motorboats). Just 200 yards below Lake Frank is the confluence with Rock Creek.

GAUGE: North Branch stays up much longer than any other Rock Creek tributary (which is not saying much). I put in over 3 hours after the rain stopped, and still found just enough water. Look for 25 cfs on Turkey Branch and 250 cfs on the Hawlings River.

> **Lake Frank** is silting up due to soil erosion from construction sites and cultivated fields. At low water, one can see a gully up to 10-feet deep carved by the North Branch through the accumulated silt. Like Needwood Lake on the main stem, Lake Frank was created in the 1960s for storm water management (and named after the man who designed the innovative system).

> On the short road to the Meadowside Nature Center is the **Lathrop E. Smith Outdoor Education Center**, where elementary school children learn how to measure stream water quality by seeing what invertebrates are living there. They collect their samples in the North Branch or, when the water is high, its tributaries.

CROYDEN PARK BRANCH: Norbeck Road to Rock Creek

Gradient	Difficulty	Distance	Area	Scenery	Strainers	Rating
80 (300)	III- (IV+)	1.3	0.6	B-	2-5/mi.	?

USGS Quad – Rockville/Kensington; Source – Complete scouting by foot
N39 05.27, W77 08.15 to N39 05.40, W77 06.91

This *"explorers' special"* emerges in a small park behind the Maryvale School (after an underground trip from the Croyden Park area of east Rockville), where it tumbles over a few man-made ledges. A good put-in is where it leaves the park and returns to a more natural streambed. After the tunnel under Norbeck Road, there is a class III- rock garden, followed by a 2-ft drop at an old weir. By this point, the backyards have been replaced by the manicured lawn of the Rockville Mansion, now part of the city's Civic Center. Soon, the creek enters Rock Creek Park, picks up a small tributary and flows under a steel footbridge. Get ready! The gradient picks up gradually. After a sharp left turn, catch an eddy from which to scout the impressive rapid just up ahead.

Croyden Park Falls, class IV+, the most complex rapid in the Rock Creek basin, can be portaged along a trail on river right. The lead-in drop, just after the turn, is only 3 feet, but is very tight and twisty. Then come 50 yards of class II water, followed by a steep 5-foot drop, best run in the center. Below are a small pool and then a sloping 7-foot drop. I don't know whether there are any bad hydraulics. There is also a 4-foot wide channel on the far right, which looks more dangerous than the drops in the middle.

Below the falls, the creek is class II-, with a few strainers, before it flattens out as it enters the floodplain. The take out is 100 yards down Rock Creek, at Baltimore Road.

> Most of the creek is part of the **Shapiro Tract,** an Urban Wildlife Sanctuary administered by the city of Rockville. If you are thinking of running this creek (or even if you are not), hike a quarter-mile down the Woodland Trail from the end of Avery Road to see the falls.

GAUGE: You need some 250 cfs on Turkey Branch (300 cfs on Watts Branch) for this to be runnable, but you can't usually afford to wait to get the gauge readings.

TURKEY BRANCH

Turkey Branch, Rock Creek's second largest tributary, rises in Aspen Hill, flows under Georgia and Connecticut Avenues, picks up its "West Fork," and then passes beneath Viers Mill Road shortly before reaching Rock Creek. Short as it is, I have divided it into two sections because of the difference is gradient and because I did not have enough water to run the top part. In late 2006, a gauge 1.2 miles above its mouth became available, making this a much easier creek to catch.

Section 1: Beret Lane (in Hermitage Park) to Dauphine Street

Gradient	Difficulty	Distance	Area	Scenery	Strainers	Rating
50 (100)	?	0.5	1.1	?	?	?

USGS Quad – Kensington; Source – Scouting put in and take out
N39 04.92, W77 04.10 to N39 04.51, W77 04.43

The put-in off Beret Lane in Hermitage Park is in the middle of a steep, rocky and narrow stretch where the gradient briefly reaches 100 ft/mi. This *"explorers' special"* appears to be class III for about 200 yards, before calming down. Take out on the right soon after passing Georgia Avenue.

GAUGE: About 145 cfs on the Turkey Branch gauge is minimal.

Section 2: Dauphine Street (off Georgia Avenue) to Rock Creek

Gradient	Difficulty	Distance	Area	Scenery	Strainers	Rating
33	II	1.9	1.3	C	0-2/mi.	**

USGS Quad – Kensington; Source – Personal descent 8/92
N39 04.51, W77 04.43 to N39 03.49, W77 05.56

You can put in on the west side of Georgia Avenue, down a steep bank, but there is an easier spot (used for the GPS coordinates) in 0.2 miles, in Harmony Hills, alongside Dauphine Street. A final choice is off Littleton St. in Stoney Brook Estates, where you get the added flow from the "West Fork," for a 1.2 mile trip.

The paved Matthew Henson (bicycle) Trail runs alongside for most of the way. This is a pretty run for such an urbanized area, with relatively few strainers. The gradient is evenly distributed. There is a nice class II drop and waves under Viers Mill Road. The creek is often deepest close to one bank or the other; in low water, watch out for bushes or small branches hanging over the creek along the banks.

The take out is at a park/playground at the confluence with Rock Creek. There is a nice surfing spot here, where one can put on a demonstration for the local children.

This is the best novice trip among the Rock Creek tributaries. It is relatively long, with a moderate gradient, few strainers, pleasant scenery, easy access and its own gauge.

GAUGE: About 100 cfs on Turkey Branch is minimal.

JOSEPHS RUN: Adams Rd. (off Conn. Ave.) to Beach Drive

Gradient	Difficulty	Distance	Area	Scenery	Strainers	Rating
40	II-	1.2	2.0	D-	3-5/mi.	-

USGS Quad – Kensington; Source – Personal descent 7/91
N39 02.97, W77 04.49 to N39 02.39, W77 05.28

This stream flows at a steady gradient through Connecticut Avenue Hills. Although in a wooded area, it is ugly due to riprap, trash along the banks, tangles of fallen branches and thorn bushes. In low water, the only route winds back and forth between the two banks, under low-hanging bushes and branches. In higher water, the run would be much better. There were also a number of strainers when I ran it.

The put in is in Connecticut Gardens, on Huggins Drive off Adams Road, underneath the northbound lane of Connecticut Avenue and a little south of Viers Mill Road. Just upstream is the confluence of the two main branches – concrete-lined channels that flow mainly underground from where they begin near Wheaton High School. The concrete continues under Connecticut Avenue, but then the stream reverts to a natural bed. The take out is at Beach Drive, just a few yards above Rock Creek. There is parking at both put in and take out, and good access for scouting along Charles Road.

GAUGE: About 80 cfs on Turkey Branch would be minimal.

"CEDAR LANE BRANCH": Above Wisconsin Ave. to Rock Creek

Gradient	Difficulty	Distance	Area	Scenery	Strainers	Rating
50	II (III)	0.5	1.4	D	0-4/mi.	*

USGS Quad – Kensington; Source – Personal descent 6/91
N39 00.38, W77 05.89 to N39 00.72, W77 05.46

The creek rises on the grounds of the National Institutes of Health (NIH), in Bethesda, where several headwaters meet, and then heads north alongside Wisconsin Avenue. At Cedar Lane, another tributary joins, and the creek then flows beneath Wisconsin Avenue and into Locust Hill Estates. It alternates between natural streambed and concrete channels until it reaches the Beltway, where two large pipes carry the water the final 50 yards to Rock Creek. The take out is across Rock Creek, by the intersection of Cedar Lane and Beach Drive.

I put in at the NIH parking lot close to Wisconsin Avenue, for a 0.65 mile run; however, since 9/11/2001, the first 0.15 miles is no longer accessible. The remaining trip is continuous class II, except for an initial 50-yard class III stretch along Cedar Lane. After the culvert under Wisconsin Avenue, there is a pair of bouncy concrete rapids. Catch the eddy just above the Beltway culvert, to check for clearance and strainers.

GAUGE: Notionally, you need about 125 cfs on Turkey Branch.

I ran this stream under the gaze of **Tom Ricks of the *Wall Street Journal*,** and it made page 1, on July 2, 1991. It was the first unnamed creek I paddled and the first where the USGS topo map shows only a broken line (meaning it's sometimes completely dry). Afterwards, I got numerous phone calls and even a few radio interviews, mainly enquiring what it was like to paddle through a dark sewer. The distinction between a "storm drain" and a "sewer" must be as difficult for many to discern as that between an economic stimulus program and profligate spending.

------ ------------------------- ------------------------ --------------------

"Bethesda, Md. The drivers snarled in rain-battered rush-hour traffic in this Washington suburb don't know it, but a small bit of canoeing history is taking place below them.

'Steve Ettinger is making the first recorded descent of what he calls 'Cedar Lane Run' – and what most everyone else calls a storm drain. He drives past the subway station at the National Institutes of Health, stops at the edge of a parking lot and hurls his battered yellow Blue Hole canoe down the grassy bank into the water below. Normally a tranquil trickle, the stream, engorged by an afternoon thunderstorm, is now a rushing rapid. He hops in his canoe and shoots under Wisconsin Avenue.

'The first big rain of the summer has brought more than Mr. Ettinger to the stream. Swirling around his canoe in the chocolate-colored water are a Budweiser beer can, a 7-Eleven coffee cup, cigarette butts and animal droppings.

> **Following the Mainstream**
> 'But Mr. Ettinger, fending off low-hanging branches while racing down concrete rapids, has little time to notice. Soon he is at the spot where the stream passes under the eight lanes of Washington's Beltway, and he is surprised to find the water divide into two narrow, metal pipes. He pauses in an eddy, peers into one dark culvert where most of the water is flowing, sees daylight 50 yards distant – and paddles into the gloom.
> 'Welcome to the new sport of urban canoeing."

Tom Ricks, reporter, Wall Street Journal,
Said he'd like to write up the kernel
Of urban canoeing,
If I'd show him what's doing
In paddling that's Beltway-internal.

So when heavy rains started to fall,
I gave him a most urgent call,
"Hurry up, here's your chance,
Rush to Cedar Lane Branch",
(Though it's real name I don't know at all).

I put in NIH parking lot,
Surely the first to paddle that spot,
Down Wisconsin's storm drain,
Then along Cedar Lane,
Boulders, branches made the going hot.

Down cemented ledges I did glide,
Like a giant's massive water slide,
Then 'neath 495,
Feeling buried alive,
Into Rock Creek, which seemed a mile wide.

But a strange thing was happening that day,
All the rainfall would not go away,
So I said "for more thrills,
I'll try Kensington Hills,
For two runs will the Journal *not* pay?"

Kensington Branch runs 1.3 miles,
And it gave me continuous smiles,
Gradient fifty feet,
With class II drops replete,
And through a pretty park all the while.

'Twas the first time I'd managed this way,
Two Rock Creek tributaries, same day,
And I got a free shuttle,
Though I'll get no rebuttal,
To what Tom writes up on page 1A.

But suppose it gets clipped from the Journal,
No page 1 to give me fame eternal,
Still I won't be a loser,
(Long as this makes The Cruiser),
The main joy of paddling is internal.

KENSINGTON HILLS BRANCH: Kensington to Beach Drive

Gradient	Difficulty	Distance	Area	Scenery	Strainers	Rating
50	II (III-)	1.3	1.2	B-	0-2/mi.	**

USGS Quad – Kensington; Source – Personal descent 6/91
N39 01.49, W77 04.25 to N39 00.60, W77 04.41

This delightful stream flows through a narrow urban park, parallel to and 1-2 blocks east of Connecticut Ave. It rises in North Kensington and flows under the B&O tracks in a concrete culvert. The put-in is just south of the tracks in a Japanese garden, next to the small shopping area that is downtown Kensington. You start with a man-made class III- drop out of the culvert, over large boulders, into the natural streambed. From there it is almost continuous class II, with the hardest spot being a z-turn between large concrete slabs. Although the stream is lined with trees, there are few strainers or overhangs, due to good park maintenance.

There are numerous access points, as Kensington Parkway runs alongside most of the way. The five bridges have sufficient clearance, until Beach Drive just before Rock Creek. I remember getting temporarily stuck there, and having to move forward and back in my canoe to maneuver it free. But it is hardly worth going under Beach Drive, because the remaining 100 yards to Rock Creek are virtually impassable due to vegetation growing in the streambed.

GAUGE: About 90 cfs on Turkey Branch would be a minimum.

Thirty Minutes of Fame. This was the second creek that Tom Ricks watched me paddle, and here continues his write up from the *Wall Street Journal* of July 2, 1991:

"Urban canoeists compete for 'first descents.' In Washington, Mr. Ettinger leads the pack, with four firsts on the Washington tributaries of Rock Creek, and is now moving upstream to Maryland. 'Anything that's wide enough, and not obstructed, is canoeable at some point,' he theorizes.

He proves the point just downstream from a 7-Eleven in Kensington, Md., catching Rock Creek's Kensington Branch during its 15 rainy minutes of navigability. He rides the swollen stream through lush weeds and candy wrappers, hunching under an overhanging pipe and twisting his boat through an S-turn formed by two crumbling blocks of concrete. Dennis Waldroff, a mechanic passing by in his pick-up, jumps out to watch. "This is so freaking cool," he says, 'I've never seen anyone do this before.'

A few blocks later, a man walking a Scottish terrier watches nonplused as Mr. Ettinger zooms through the culvert at East Bexhill Drive. Then he walks away in silence, as if he hadn't just seen someone in a yellow canoe float under his feet.

Mr. Ettinger doesn't know it, but the next culvert contains a trap: it narrows in the middle, leaving just 18 inches of clearance; his canoe needs 20. The boat snags dangerously in the dark pipe, the foul water rushing underneath and around. Loud grunts bellow out from the bridge – 'Oooh! Oooh! Oooooooh!' – as Mr. Ettinger crawls forward and pushes his bow down into the water, popping the canoe free.

He emerges ashen-faced but smiling. Even with the nasty culvert, he says, 'that was the most civilized branch I've ever run.'"

"FOREST GLEN BRANCH": Beltway to Rock Creek

Gradient	Difficulty	Distance	Area	Scenery	Strainers	Rating
100	II (III)	0.3	1.1	C-	0-3/mi.	**

USGS Quad – Kensington; Source – Personal descent 8/94
N39 00.82, W77 03.63 to N39 00.65, W77 03.78

This unnamed creek rises in the Forest Glen part of Kensington, but, alas, there is no public access there. After passing under the Beltway, it picks up its main tributary, and begins its final dash to Rock Creek. It is continuous class II, through a streambed lined by crumbling concrete. And then, just before

Jones Mill Road, it goes over a broken, 6-foot drop between large boulders, one of the nicer rapids in the Rock Creek watershed. Below is calm water, and one can carry back up and run the falls again.

The put in, just below the Beltway culvert, is reached by parking in the first of the dirt areas off the shoulder of Newcastle Ave, and descending 30 yards through the woods. You can scout the falls from Jones Mill Road (park under the Beltway). You can take out just below the falls, or proceed a short distance down Rock Creek to an easier spot.

GAUGE: Some 125 cfs on Turkey Branch would generally be enough.

Forest Glen was started as a summer resort on the B&O Railroad. Near the stream are the National Audubon Society's headquarters and 40-acre nature preserve, and the Mormon Temple.

COQUELIN RUN: Chevy Chase Lake Drive to Rock Creek

Gradient	Difficulty	Distance	Area	Scenery	Strainers	Rating
50	II+ (5.0)	0.7	1.3	D+	0-3/mi.	**

USGS Quad – Washington West; Source – Personal descent 7/93
N38 59.70, W77 04.40 to N38 59.58, W77 03.72

Coquelin Run, in Chevy Chase Md., flows through Columbia Country Club and under Connecticut Avenue. One could put in at a private bridge just below, were it not for "Coquelin Falls" 0.2 miles downstream. There is no good eddy just above the falls, a portage around it would be difficult, and that 0.2 miles has little of merit.

Running "Coquelin Falls" is more dangerous than trying to privatize Social Security. It is a twisting 10-ft drop, with a difficult entrance and a serious pinning risk. The falls can be seen from Chevy Chase Lake Drive; when the water is high, it is impressive. **So start at the base of the falls.**

Below the falls, the action is continuous. The first class II+ comes on a sharp left turn past a large concrete post, where Chevy Chase Lake Drive ends. Below Jones Beach Road, the creek is like a covered passageway between large, overhanging trees. Visibility is limited, but there are no difficulties until a twisting class II+ just before the confluence. Take out on Rock Creek about a hundred yards downstream, at East-West Highway.

GAUGE: Perhaps 115 cfs on Turkey Branch would be needed.

In the 1890s, Coquelin Run was dammed just east of Connecticut Ave., to supply water for the boilers and condensers of the Connecticut Ave. trolley line. The **Chevy Chase Lake** that it created became a popular destination for picnickers and rowers, and the center of an amusement park with a carousel, bowling alleys, a shooting gallery and a dance pavilion. There were vaudeville and circus acts, as well as Marine Band concerts. Fish, turtles, snakes and frogs abounded; at night, kids used flashlights to catch the frogs, and sold them for frogs' legs to the Columbia Country Club. In winter, the lake was used for ice-skating, until several people drowned. The powerhouse was abandoned in 1920 and the dance pavilion burned in 1925. A few years later the dam collapsed, leaving a street name as the only reminder.

FENWICK BRANCH: East Beach Drive to Rock Creek

Gradient	Difficulty	Distance	Area	Scenery	Strainers	Rating
70	II (III+)	0.8	0.5	D	3-5/mi.	*

USGS Quad – Washington West; Source – Personal descent 5/88
N38 59.57, W77 02.62 to N38 59.05, W77 02.57

Fenwick Branch rises at the northernmost tip of DC, in Colonial Village (formerly called Fenwick; Cuthbert Fenwick, friend and Councilor to Lord Thomas Cornwallis, arrived in 1634). It flows south between East Beach and West Beach drives, in a narrow streambed with 5-8 foot high mud sides, in an arm of Rock Creek Park. After it picks up its main tributary, Portal Branch, it flows under Kalmia Road and into Rock Creek.

The stream emerges from a large tunnel/pipe beneath East-West Highway. The first 350 yards is class II, but tends to be blocked by fallen trees. The creek then goes down a 7-foot, class III+ drop over a sloping gabion. Put-in above or below the falls, accessed from East Beach Drive just north of Redbud Road. After a small pool at the base of the falls, the class II action resumes. The fallen trees tend to be high enough to pass under, but vines and bushes growing down from them may create a dense thicket. (Before I ran the creek, I had to cut a passage through this.) The creek then winds back and forth through a more open area. Just below the confluence with Portal Branch, there is a fun class II+ passage under Kalmia Road; check for strainers beforehand. The steep culvert has standing waves in it and a 2-foot drop at the end. Then the streambed widens, the gradient eases up, and a footbridge just before Rock Creek provides a good take out.

GAUGE: Notionally, some 165 cfs on Turkey Branch would be zero level

PORTAL BRANCH: Sixteenth Street to Birch Drive

Gradient	Difficulty	Distance	Area	Scenery	Strainers	Rating
70	II+ (III)	0.3	0.4	D	0-6/mi.	*

USGS Quad – Washington West; Source – Personal descent 5/92
N38 59.50, W77 02.18 to N38 59.37, W77 02.40

Portal Branch (named for the nearby Blair Portal, entrance to DC), a tributary of a tributary of Rock Creek, runs through the narrow woods between East and West Portal drives. From the bus stop on 16th St., next to a large tree, a barely-discernible trail descends steeply to the creek. The put in is a pool just below the pipe from which the water emerges. You start out with a two-step falls totaling 4 feet (class III), over a concrete streambed. Right afterwards is a class II+ rapid, where the stream cuts left. And then there is non-stop class II-II+ action. At low water, you may be forced under overhanging vines and thorns. At higher levels the trip is better, but the take-out footbridge below Birch Drive becomes hazardous, as there are no good eddies close above it. After the footbridge, the strainer density grows exponentially, so don't bother hacking your way through the final 0.2 miles to Fenwick Branch.

GAUGE: Go with a storm that brings Turkey Branch to 250 cfs.

LUZON BRANCH: Military Road to Rock Creek

Gradient	Difficulty	Distance	Area	Scenery	Strainers	Rating
80	II+ (III)	0.3	0.9	D	0-3/mi.	**

USGS Quad – Washington West; Source – Personal descent 4/91
N38 57.80, W77 02.32 to N38 57.63, W77 02.53

This stream once flowed along Luzon Avenue, east of 16th Street, but that part was paved over. Luzon Branch now surfaces just west of 16th Street, alongside the road to the Rock Creek Golf Course, but the class II- quarter mile ends in a dangerous collapsed bridge. So put in just below, a few yards north of Military Road.

The run starts off class II+. After a sharp left turn, you have some calmer water to set up for a sloping, class III, 6-foot drop. You run it like a Democratic candidate; take the left side for the primary drop and then cut back to the middle. Just below, a large rock can be passed on either side; decide early. And then there is a class II rock garden, the paved passage under Beach Drive, and more class II to Rock Creek.

This puts you right at the entrance to Rock Creek's half mile of class III rapids. Paradoxically, however, when Luzon Branch is running, Rock Creek usually isn't, and vice versa, because Luzon Branch rises and falls so much faster.

GAUGE: Some 150 cfs on Turkey Branch would be needed.

Has a world record been broken?
Will I make the Guiness book?
Has a paddler ever spoken
Of running a smaller brook?

'twas hard to even learn its name,
Few know it does exist,
So I'd bet I'm the first to claim
Luzon Branch on his list.

The strainers I had cut away,
The rapids I had scouted,
So when a flash storm came that day,
Toward Luzon I was routed.

I set out while the rain poured down,
There was no time to waste,
If you would run storm drains in town,
You must get there in haste.

Starting 'neath Military Road,
The creek had scarce an eddy,
Over a class III ledge it flowed,
Then it was class II, steady.

My trip just ten minutes did last,
I walked back to the main rapid,
But the water's crest had passed
The creek was low and vapid.

Since at storm drains I do not blanch,
This brief trip left me merry,
After Broad, Piney and Fenwick Branch,
My fourth Rock Creek tributary.

Luzon Branch runs just one-third mile,
Then flows into Rock Creek,
Its 80 feet per mile will make you smile,
If it's quick thrills that you seek.

BROAD BRANCH: Culvert under Broad Branch Road to Rock Creek

Gradient	Difficulty	Distance	Area	Scenery	Strainers	Rating
75	III	1.2	1.3	C+	0-2/mi.	***

USGS Quad – Washington West; Source – Personal descent 7/85 (last 0.8 mi.)
N38 57.46, W77 03.57 to N38 56.62, W77 03.00

Broad Branch rises near the intersection of Connecticut and Nebraska avenues, in Chevy Chase DC, passes through a long culvert under Broad Branch Road and begins its descent to Rock Creek. It can be scouted from the eponymous parkway. It is very narrow – its name is as misleading as the "Clear Skies Act." The trip is continuous class II, with five class III- and III rapids. The first comes in 300 yards, after the creek turns right and passes under 27th Street. The second is directly under Grant Road; check this beforehand for logs. The biggest drop, about 6 feet, comes midway, on a left turn, where the stream runs up against the road. Then, an exciting 3-foot drop, at 0.8 miles, involves a tight chute on the left and a rock just below. About 100 yards from the end, after Soapstone Valley Branch enters from the right, you pass under two bridges; check for fallen trees. A final, man-made class III is a 3-foot drop over large boulders. Continue down Rock Creek to Pierce Mill, where Rock Creek section 3, Broad Branch and Soapstone Valley Branch have a common takeout.

GAUGE: About 115 cfs on Turkey Branch is minimal.

> This was not only **my first Rock Creek tributary**, but also the first creek I ran that was not in a guidebook. The deluge was just ending when I arrived, so I quickly unloaded, topped up my airbag, and ... it was too late! The water had fallen so fast. I left my canoe and drove around. The rainfall began again. Back at the boat, I watched the water rise, crest ... and I shoved off.

SOAPSTONE VALLEY BRANCH: Albemarle St. to Broad Br.

Gradient	Difficulty	Distance	Area	Scenery	Strainers	Rating
135	IV	0.8	0.3	B+	3-5/mi.	?

USGS Quad – Washington West; Source – Complete scouting on foot
N38 56.87, W77 03.91 to N38 56.62, W77 03.00

Short and tiny as it is, this scenic **"explorers' special"** may be the *crème de la crème* of the Rock Creek basin. Eddies are scarce, the narrowness of the stream leaves little room for maneuver, and strainers are a danger. And given the infrequency and brevity of this creek being up, organizing a trip on it is not easy.

From Albemarle Street, just east of Connecticut Avenue, walk 90 yards down the Soapstone Valley Park trail, to where the trail bends left at a large tree, and follow a faint track downhill. The trip starts out class II. After a long straightaway and a sweeping left turn, there is a class III rock garden where the creek swings back to the right. After another straightaway, stop to scout a class IV, Z-turn.

In high water, this is extremely turbulent, while at a low level the turns may be too tight. You can portage on river right.

Then the stream narrows and becomes continuous class III and then IV, dropping steeply between large boulders. A long portage on the left is an option. After that it is mostly class II+, with one class III chute. Approaching Broad Branch Road, the stream cuts left and then right against a stone wall (by the Italian Ambassador's residence), before going through a culvert (check for clearance and strainers) into Broad Branch.

The class IV rapids are on both sides of the eastern end of Audubon Terrace (off 29th St, a block south of Albemarle St.). Before running this little terror, scout at least those drops. A trail follows the creek, but the crossings are impassable in high water.

GAUGE: Forget it! The 400 cfs on Turkey Branch is purely notional.

Soapstone Valley is a wooded, rocky and steep gorge, almost invisible to the commuters who cross its mouth on Broad Branch Parkway. (I once set a Hash House Harriers jogging route along it, and it took the group fifteen minutes to find the trail.) Across Connecticut Ave. (on the current site of UDC), Soapstone Hill was cut down in 1891-2 and used as fill for the trolley line.

The **soapstone** along this creek was quarried by Native Americans, primarily to make pots. Soapstone, an impure form of talc rock, can be cut with a knife and has a soapy feeling. During the 19th Century, it was used for sinks, tubs, firebricks and hearthstones.

PINEY BRANCH: Seventeenth Street to Rock Creek

Gradient	Difficulty	Distance	Area	Scenery	Strainers	Rating
80	II+	0.5	1.3	D+	0-2/mi.	*

USGS Quad – Washington West; Source – Personal descent 6/87
N38 56.24, W77 02.32 to N38 56.12, W77 02.85

Thousands of commuters drive along Piney Branch Parkway each day, never dreaming that this dry streambed could ever be paddled. Indeed, the vegetation shows that it seldom carries water. But when a downpour fills the underground storm drain, a **highly-polluted** mixture of street run-off and raw sewerage bursts from a large tunnel that is usually closed. The water rushes for 50 yards over a wide cement area, drops over large boulders, and enters the natural bed.

If you've had all your shots, have no open cuts and don't mind the smell, put in at the tiny eddy below the boulders. There are no really distinct drops, and the wide streambed allows for maneuvering. The middle part is the steepest, and one hole there requires caution. The stream flattens out approaching Rock Creek, and one can take out on river left before Beach Drive (used for the GPS coordinates), or paddle Rock Creek to the zoo parking lot.

GAUGE: About 100 cfs on Turkey Branch correlates to zero level.

Ironically, given the present pollution, the creek was surveyed in 1918 as a **potential water supply** for Montgomery County. In those days, Piney Branch had a much longer aboveground course; Piney Branch Road, which extends to Takoma Park, is a reminder of this.

Just upstream from the put in was the largest known **Indian quartz quarry** and workshop on the East Coast. Discovered in 1889 by Smithsonian scientists, it had been worked to a depth of 28 feet, and included many discarded axe heads, arrowheads, spear points and tools.

Now here's a trip that was odd fun,
A creek that's surely ne'er been run,
And not too far away, you see,
In fact, right here, Northwest DC.

When my gutters were overflowing,
I reckoned 'twas time to be going,
And drove a total of three blocks,
To a small eddy, 'neath some rocks.

With slope of 80 feet per mile,
It kept me busy all the while,

Continuous class II to III,
But lousy water quality.

In fact, one could say it did reek,
The whole half mile down to Rock Creek.
But I'm not one of your complainers,
At least this short run had no strainers.

From leaving home, to post-run shower,
The trip took me just half an hour.
So if sewerage you do not shun,
Give Piney Branch its second run.

ANACOSTIA RIVER BASIN

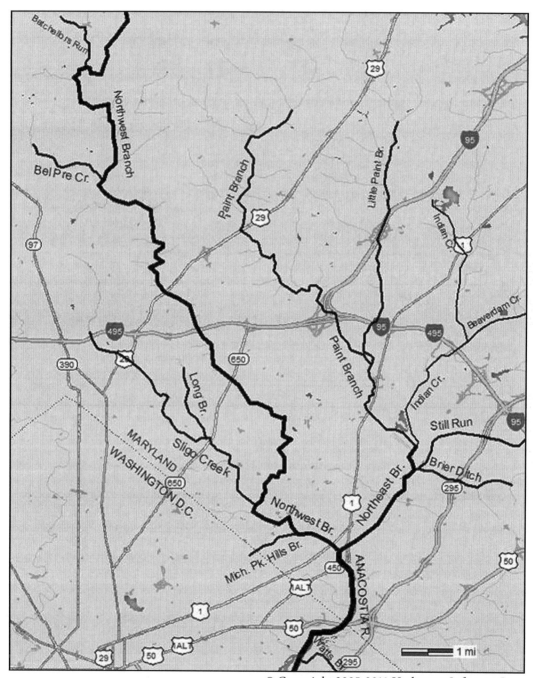

Chapter 21:

ANACOSTIA RIVER BASIN

The Anacostia is Washington DC's "other river." Land degradation and pollution mar much of its basin. The part of DC called Anacostia is the city's poorest. But there are nice things too. The Kenilworth Aquatic Gardens have a wonderful collection of water lilies and lotuses. The Anacostia Watershed Society sponsors trash clean-ups and educational activities. There are paved biking trails along the main tributaries. And, most relevant for our purposes, some of those tributaries have nice fall-line rapids.

Under the 1987 Anacostia Watershed Restoration Agreement, DC, Maryland and its affected counties, Montgomery and Prince Georges (PG), committed to improve basin-wide water quality, protect aquatic life, reduce erosion and expand recreational facilities. With substantial volunteer support, much has been accomplished; however, record levels of tumors in fish, as well as the 20,000 tons of trash that still get washed downstream annually, indicate that serious environmental problems remain. Now, the DC government, with federal support, has started to upgrade the Anacostia waterfront.

The Anacostia basin covers 170 sq. miles (85 in PG Co., 60 in Montgomery Co. and 25 in DC). The Anacostia River itself, formed at the confluence of its Northwest and Northeast branches in Bladensburg, is entirely tidal. The main western tributaries, **Northwest Branch**, **Sligo Creek** and **Paint Branch**, rise in the Piedmont area of Montgomery County, flow southeast, and have attractive fall-line rapids shortly before they enter PG County. The larger eastern tributaries, **Little Paint Branch** and **Northeast Branch**, lie entirely in the coastal plain in PG County, and tend to be flatter, less scenic, and more choked with strainers. The tiny streams – **Long Branch of Sligo Creek, Batchellors Run, Bel Pre Creek, "Michigan Park Hills Branch", Still Run, Brier Ditch** and *Watts Branch* (the "explorers' special") – are a mixed bag, but none of them earn more than one * in my rating system.

Anacostia is a variation of **Nacostine**, who were the early inhabitants of the area. The word itself meant "a town of traders," which reflected their large settlement at the time of Captain John Smith's arrival in 1608. In early maps, the river was called the **Eastern Branch of the Potomac**, but Major Andrew Ellicott, who was surveying land for DC, found "Anna Kastia" on old surveys, and Secretary of State Thomas Jefferson then had the name changed.

Indian Creek runs for 8 miles from Laurel to its confluence with Paint Branch (to form Northeast Branch) at College Park. It becomes large enough to canoe after 3 miles, in Beltsville. But this fourth mile is mostly paved, down to Powder Mill Road. For the fifth mile, to Sunnyside Avenue, the gradient is a decent 20 ft/mile, but I had to portage 12 fallen trees. It was also the most trash-filled creek I have ever paddled. Below Sunnyside Avenue, the gradient drops off rapidly. In the sixth mile, Upper Beaverdam Creek doubles the flow. But in the seventh mile, Indian Creek braids repeatedly, and in its final mile it is a concrete channel.

Other streams that could be run also have little to recommend them. **Upper Beaverdam Creek** has many strainers and a gradient of only 7 ft/mile. **Lower Beaverdam Creek** is steeper (15 ft/mile) but flows alongside railroad tracks through an ugly industrial area. Its tributaries, **Cabin** and **Cattail branches**, are much harder to catch and only marginally steeper.

CAPITAL CANOEING AND KAYAKING

GAUGES: This basin is well served by gauges on Northwest Branch near Colesville (21 sq. mi.) and Hyattsville (49 sq. mi.), Northeast Branch (73 sq. mi.), Paint Branch (13 sq. mi.), Sligo Creek (6.5 sq. mi.), Watts Branch (3.3 sq. mi.) and a Paint Branch tributary (1 sq. mi.). In addition, the AFWS site for PG County includes stream gauges for Northwest, Northeast, Paint and Little Paint branches, and Sligo Creek; for these, you need about a one foot rise for the creek to be up.

In the table below, the **gauge column refers to Sligo Creek**, except that it *refers to Northwest Branch near Colesville if it is in bold italics.* There are several PG County rain gauges for the Northeast Branch basin, but the Northwest Branch headwaters are in Montgomery Co., where rain gauges are not on-line.

The only two medium-sized watersheds extant in DC are the Anacostia River to the southeast and Rock Creek to the northwest. (Oxon Creek drains a small area southeast of the Anacostia, while Foundry, Battery Kemble and Little Falls branches cover the westernmost corner of DC.) But originally, the central 43% of what became DC was drained by Goose Creek, whose name was changed to **Tiber Creek** because Francis Pope wanted to call his estate "Rome on the Tiber." Eventually, that entire watershed was paved over. When new offices are built in downtown Washington, they sometimes expose the casement enclosing Tiber Creek.

Bladensburg once vied with Georgetown and Alexandria for preeminence in tobacco and other exports. In the August 1814 **Battle of Bladensburg**, the invading British routed a larger but ill-trained American force, thereby enabling the capture and burning of Washington. Overlooking the Anacostia and its tiny tributary Dueling Branch, were unofficial **dueling grounds** (dueling was always illegal). There, Stephen Decatur, the naval commander, was killed in 1820 by James Barron, over whose court-martial he had presided.

---

name	gradient	difficulty	length	area	gauge	rating
Northwest Branch - Sec. 1	12	II-	9.6	5.0	*250cfs*	*
- Sec. 2	25	III-(5.1)	3.5	23	*100cfs*	***
Batchellors Run	25	II (II+)	1.6	2.7	140cfs	-
Bel Pre Creek	28	II-	1.4	3.4	110cfs	*
Sligo Creek	35 (150)	III-(III+)	6.3	3.4	140cfs	***
Long Branch, Sligo Cr.	75 (100)	III (III+)	1.4	0.6	600cfs	*
"Michigan Park Hills Br."	40	II- (II)	0.7	0.9	300cfs	*
Northeast Branch	9	A (II)	3.2	62	*90cfs*	-
Paint Branch - Section 1	35 (70)	II (III)	2.4	7.6	70cfs	***
- Section 2	20 (50)	II- (II+)	5.4	15	40cfs	*
Little Paint Br. - Sec. 1	35	II- (III-)	1.3	3.0	140cfs	-
- Sec. 2	18 (40)	II-	2.9	9.1	50cfs	*
Still Run	25	II+	1.6	1.6	200cfs	*
Brier Ditch	25	II-	0.7	3.0	120cfs	*
Watts Branch - Section 1	25	?	1.0	2.0	160cfs	?
- Section 2	25	?	1.0	3.0	120cfs	?

NORTHWEST BRANCH

Northwest Branch flows south-southeast for 21.5 miles from the old Quaker settlement of Sandy Spring until it meets the Northeast Branch at tidewater to form the Anacostia. There is a trail on river left the whole way. In the final 6 miles, below section 2, the creek leaves its pretty gorge, and the gradient drops to 9 ft/mile. After 3.6 miles of this, just past the confluence with Sligo Creek, **a broken 6-foot dam has a deadly hydraulic**. The remaining 2.4 miles to the confluence have been mostly cemented.

Section 1: Norwood Road to Burnt Mills Dam (US 29/Colesville Road)

Gradient	Difficulty	Distance	Area	Scenery	Strainers	Rating
12	II-	9.6	5.0	C+	2/mi.	*

USGS Quad – Kensington; Source – Personal descent (last 4 miles) 10/96 and (upper 1 mile) 3/97; scouting
N39 07.14, W77 01.28 via N39 03.94, W77 01.75 (100 yards below Randolph Road) to N39 01.88, W77 00.30

This trip is mostly through pretty wooded parkland, where deer, beaver and other wildlife abound. The creek soon enters the Northwest Branch Park Golf Course, and 1.6 miles later is doubled in flow by Batchellors Run. A mile below that is Bonifant Road, site of the National Capital Trolley Museum and on the route of the Inter-County Connector. From there, the creek flows 3 miles through Northwest Branch Park to Randolph Road. The gradient averages 17 ft/mile above Bonifant Road, 12 ft/mile from there to Randolph Road, and 9 ft/mile for the final 4 miles.

By Randolph Road, the area is up to 21 sq. mi., and there is good access in 100 yards, down a short staircase alongside a closed bridge, by the Colesville gauge. Two miles later you enter an attractive gorge with three long class II- rock gardens (the last one of which is called Wading Rapids). The trip ends with a half mile on the Burnt Mills Reservoir (denoting the dénouement of an early grain mill there). Carry around the left end of the 15-foot dam to the parking area.

GAUGE: To start at Norwood Road, you need 250 cfs on the Northwest Branch gauge near Colesville, and as an earlier indicator, 75 cfs on Sligo Creek. By Randolph Road, you need only some 100 cfs on the Northwest Branch near Colesville gauge there.

The **Gilbert mica mine**, located 2 miles before the end of this trip, operated for 18 months in the mid-1880s. Large mica sheets were dug out of a 60-foot deep pit, for use as stove windows.

The **Burnt Mills Reservoir** has been a source of drinking water for Montgomery County since 1920, when the newly-formed Washington Suburban Sanitary Commission (WSSC) discovered that DC was unwilling to share its Potomac River water, and found an idle World War I filter plant in Culpeper, Virginia, which it hauled up to Burnt Mills. The present dam was built in 1930, after the old mill was torn down. The Reservoir used to be a nice canoeing spot as well, but WSSC now bans boating on it. However, paddlers sometimes run the dam, which has been called **"the world's easiest 20-foot high drop"** because a lip at the bottom kicks you out of the hydraulic and sends you skidding across the pool.

Section 2: Burnt Mills Dam (US 29) to Adelphi Mills (Riggs Road)

Gradient	Difficulty	Distance	Area	Scenery	Strainers	Rating
25	III- (5.1)	3.5	26	B	<1/mi.	***

USGS Quad – Kensington/Beltsville/WashEast; Source – Personal descent 9/87; AW web site
N39 01.88, W77 00.30 to N38 59.55, W76 58.32

Gertler calls this trip "the aesthetically redeeming silver lining in the dismal cloud of the Anacostia Basin." It starts with a long class III- rapid. Then eddy out on river left, 50 yards below US 29, to portage the class 5.1 Great Falls of the Anacostia (aka the "Colesville Cruncher"), of which Theodore Roosevelt wrote: "Excepting Great Falls, it is the most beautiful place around here." Climb carefully on the rocks to see the water cascade through the boulders, in four drops totaling 20 feet. (Those who run this take the first 6-foot drop on the left. The main rapid, 100 yards later, has two small ledges and a 10-foot drop through a narrow slot; even a perfect line involves bouncing off of rocks.) There is a 100-yard portage trail high on river left.

Depending on water and skill level, you can put back in above or below the final 5-foot (class IV-) boof; the drop itself is not as hard as the ferry to line up for it. A long class II+ rapid follows, and the water then calms down until the class III- Beltway Rapids. After that, there are occasional class II ledges all the way to Riggs Road at Adelphi Mills.

GAUGE: Look for at least 100 cfs on the Northwest Branch gauge near Colesville and 1.9 on the Adelphi Mills gauge (9573) on the AFWS site.

Northwest Branch once powered several gristmills. The one at **Adelphi Mills** dates from 1796; ocean-going ships could sail there until the early 19th Century. It had a 300-yd millrace, and operated until 1916. It was restored and opened to visitors by the MNCPPC in 1954.

"Approval" is required (but unobtainable) to paddle through **MNCPPC parkland** such as this. This is the only creek where a policeman ever stopped me from putting in.

BATCHELLORS RUN: Norbeck Rd. (Md. 28) to Northwest Branch

Gradient	Difficulty	Distance	Area	Scenery	Strainers	Rating
25	II (II+)	1.6*	2.7	D+	4-8/mi.	-

USGS Quad – Kensington; Source – Personal descent 3/97
N39 07.17, W77 02.72 to N39 05.63, W77 02.06
*(plus one mile on Northwest Branch to Bonifant Road)

Batchellors Run (named after an early settler family) has decent rapids but far too many strainers. The first quarter mile is continuous class II past backyards, until the Northwest Branch Park Golf Course, where there are several ledges below footbridges and a long class II rock garden. The last rapid is a class II+ double-S turn, on the right side of an island just above the confluence. Below the confluence, Northwest Branch is much wider but still tends to have strainers in the mile down to Bonifant Road.

GAUGE: You need an intense rainfall and about 140 cfs on Sligo Creek.

BEL PRE CREEK: Layhill Road to Northwest Branch

Gradient	Difficulty	Distance	Area	Scenery	Strainers	Rating
28	II-	1.4	3.4	C-	1-3/mi.	*

USGS Quad – Kensington; Source – Personal descent 9/96
N39 01.53, W77 02.75, to N39 03.75, W77 01.70

This tiny tributary twists southeast from Norbeck through Aspen Hill. It is full of easy gravel-bar rapids and a few ledges. The first half is through the woods, but then the stream borders the Indian Creek Country Club and has a boulder-enhanced left bank, until Northwest Branch. Take out at the small bridge 200 yards below Randolph Road.

GAUGE: Look for 110 cfs on Sligo Creek. I ran this right after a 2-inch rainfall.

SLIGO CREEK: Sligo Creek Golf Course to Northwest Branch

Gradient	Difficulty	Distance	Area	Scenery	Strainers	Rating
35 (150)	III- (III+)	6.3	3.4	D+	<1/mi.	***

USGS Quad – Kensington/Wash.West/Wash.East; Source – Personal descent 5/90
N39 00.84, W77 01.84 via N38 58.26, W76 58.85 (RiggsRd) to N38 57.48, W76 58.35

Sligo Creek is a challenging whitewater trip on those brief occasions when it is up. It is much more "urban" than Northwest and Paint branches, as it is closer to the city, in a narrower and more developed park, and paralleled by a road. It feels as natural as a politician's "conversation" with voters; it is full of pipeline crossings, foot bridges (all normally high enough) and playgrounds, and the banks are reinforced with boulders. The many parking areas along Sligo Creek Parkway enable one to tailor the trip length.

The creek rises in Wheaton and flows over nine miles, through Silver Spring and Takoma Park, before entering Northwest Branch near Hyattsville. You can put in just below the Beltway, opposite the Sligo Creek Golf Course. The creek is class II past Colesville Road (mile 0.6). Just below Piney Branch Road (mile 2) is a class III- rock garden. A little above Maple Avenue (mile 3) is a 3-ft pipeline ledge with a hydraulic in high water. Shortly below Maple Avenue is the main action: a steep (150 ft/mile) and narrow class III+ rock garden, complicated by large concrete pipes almost parallel to the flow. Scout this in advance. Class II rapids continue past New Hampshire Avenue (mile 4.1) and down to Riggs Road (mile 5.2), a popular take out. In the final 1.1 miles, the gradient of 20 ft/mile is primarily in the form of man-made 2-3 foot sloping ledges.

When you reach Northwest Branch, take out almost immediately on your left, and cross the grass to Nicholson St. About 100 yards downstream, just before a footbridge, is a broken 6-ft dam (class 5.0) into a **keeper hydraulic**.

GAUGE: The Sligo Creek gauge (located just above Maple Ave.) needs 140 cfs.

The summer was so hot and dry, a nasty June to August drought,
The rivers so low one could cry, we were impatient to get out.
At last fell one inch; it would do in a pinch.

Now Sligo Creek (Northwest Branch daughter), is very, very seldom run,
But when it (rarely) fills with water, it is excellent paddling fun.
As best we could tell, it was running quite well.

From scout to start, just one hour passed, but the rain had all gone away,
Being so small, the creek fell fast; we could not afford to delay.
Ron Knipling and I, knew we'd have to fly.

We put in above Maple Ave, where the Sligo gorge really starts,
So class III+ was what we'd have, to quicken the beat of our hearts.
Though it was steep and tight, the low flow eased our fright.

Twixt the rock and cement, there was only one cleft,
Our route twisted and bent, then we cut to the left.
With one scrape, OK two, we made it safely through.

The rapids went on a mile, then two, the current eased up but stayed quick,
As the creek widened we had to scrape through, finding a clean route was the trick.
With a Grumman a mess, thank God for ABS.

Rock gardens make Sligo a treasure; this urban gem earned one more shot,
And now we've learned that we should measure, its level at some wider spot.
The next time we seek, to run Sligo Creek.

Night Comes to Sligo Creek. But the next time we had even more problems. It was late afternoon when we launched just below Colesville Road, and we began running out of both water and light, particularly as a tandem open boat kept getting stuck. Finally, I went ahead alone, to locate any strainers before it got too dark. That seemed like an unnecessary precaution, until 100 yards above our take out, where the black shape I could dimly make out turned out to be a tree trunk blocking the creek. During the 20 minutes that I waited there, dusk turned to moonless night, so only by sound could I discern and then warn the approaching paddlers.

Sligo is a county in Connaught, Ireland. Silver Spring was originally called Sligo P.O. Until 1930, Sligo Creek was a source of drinking water. More recently, under the Anacostia Watershed Restoration Program, leaky pipes were removed and trees, native shrubs and wildflowers planted. The hiker-biker trail was also extended to meet up with the one alongside Northwest Branch.

Wounded chief Powhatan allegedly sought the healing waters of **Takoma Spring**, which drains into Sligo Creek. In 1879, the Takoma Springs Water Company bottled and sold it, and later the Washington Sanitarium used it as tonic for patients. As late as 1932, people came to the spring for water. Now, it is paved over.

🌊 LONG BRANCH, SLIGO CREEK: Domer Avenue (off Garland Avenue) to Sligo Creek (just above NH Avenue)

Gradient	Difficulty	Distance	Area	Scenery	Strainers	Rating
75 (100)	III (III+)	1.4	0.6	C-	3-7/mi.	*

USGS Quad – Washington East; Source – Personal descent 6/03
N38 59.81, W76 59.91 to N38 58.84, W76 59.39

This tiny, steep, polluted and dangerous little run through Takoma Park is for the hard-core urban boater who can get there while it is still pouring. Turn south off Piney Branch Road onto Garland Avenue, and take the first left (Domer Avenue). If the water is too high, wait a few minutes.

The first quarter mile is class I. Then the creek bends left and becomes class II, leading into a class III rock garden, as it passes under a footbridge. Scout this in advance, as it is hard to stop once in the rapid. The creek narrows alongside Long Branch Parkway, and at 0.8 miles it passes beneath Carroll Avenue, with a steep class II+ rapid above and a class III- below the bridge.

The creek is more natural but also more problematical below Carroll Avenue (it was channelized and is kept somewhat clear by the local community above there). It is wider, twistier and steeper (average gradient rises from 60 ft/mile to 100 ft/mile), with frequent class II rapids and more strainers, including large trees to portage. There is a class II+ ledge, but fallen trees usually block it. The creek then widens out, and unless you have lots of water, will be bony for 100 yards, as you pass a playground on the left. Toward the end of the playground, get out and scout. Up ahead is a long, narrow class III+ boulder garden, which begins with a tricky 3-foot drop through a slot, with pinning possibilities. You can carry this initial drop on the left. The class III+ continues for 50 yards down to the footbridge, and there is then a final 100 yards of class II+ into Sligo Creek.

It is a 100 yards of class II on Sligo Creek to New Hampshire Ave., where you can take out above the bridge on river right and drive back up to run Sligo Creek itself.

Anyone contemplating this run might want to scout on foot beforehand. Above Carroll Avenue, a paved trail parallels the creek; below it, there is a narrow and rough dirt trail along the stream.

GAUGE: The Sligo Creek gauge should be over 600 cfs. Check the level from the put in. This creek rises and falls extremely fast, so focus more on rainfall.

Between Piney Branch Road and Carroll Ave., the paved hiker/biker path along the creek used to be called the Sri Chinmoy Peace Mile. (Now, a sign advises that the Sri Chinmoy Peace Mile is a round trip on just the northern half mile; I guess it depends upon what the meaning of "mile" is.) As further proof that you're in the **Takoma Park Nuclear-Free Zone**, note the street signs that have "Eating Meat", "War" or "Wearing Fur" written in below the word "STOP." Republicans might prefer to paddle elsewhere.

⫴ "MICHIGAN PARK HILLS BR.": Eastern Ave. to NW Branch

Gradient	Difficulty	Distance	Area	Scenery	Strainers	Rating
40	II- (II)	0.7*	0.9	D	1-5/mi.	*

USGS Quad – Washington East; Source – Personal descent 7/94
N38 57.40, W76 59.46 to N38 57.16, W76 57.98

*(plus 0.6 miles on Northwest Branch to Queens Chapel Road – site of the gauge)

This micro-stream emerges near the DC line, and flows northeast. From Eastern Ave. and Galloway St., carry 50 yards to an easy put-in. The first half of the trip is straight and narrow, with frequent class II- drops. At Chillum Road, there is a 20-yard class II rock garden, with a total drop of 4 feet. The remainder has fast current and a few strainers. At the confluence, look upstream on Northwest Branch at the class 5.0 man-made drop into a deadly hydraulic. It is then 0.6 miles of fast water and small waves to the take-out at Queens Chapel Road, on river right. To shorten your shuttle, you can catch a bus along Queens Chapel Road to Eastern Avenue – if you don't mind stares.

GAUGE: Watts Branch should reach 150 cfs, Sligo Creek 300 cfs.

In the Northwest Branch streambed near the take out are 120-million year old **carbonized logs** from a cypress-like species of the Cretaceous period, which were washed in from the coastal plain as driftwood and exposed when the Northwest Branch cut its present channel. This form of petrified wood falls apart when exposed to air.

⫴ NORTHEAST BRANCH: Below Confluence to Below Confluence

Gradient	Difficulty	Distance	Area	Scenery	Strainers	Rating
9	A (II)	3.2	62	D-	0	-

USGS Quad – Washington East; Source – Personal descent (partial) 6/91; scouting
N38 58.54, W76 55.09 to N38 56.33, W76 56.57

Northeast Branch runs from the confluence of Indian Creek and Paint Branch in College Park to where it meets Northwest Branch at Bladensburg to form the Anacostia. It drains 75 sq. mi., about twice that of Northwest Branch. It was widened and channelized between flood-control levees during the late 1950s. Despite the poor water quality, yellow and white perch, river catfish and striped bass are commonly caught here. But would you eat them?

The one rapid, a 10-yard, class II boulder garden, at mile 1.5 and just below East-West Highway, has decent play. The rest of the trip has just a few slight riffles. There is no access at the confluence of Paint Branch and Indian Creek, but you can put in a quarter mile below at Paint Branch Community Park (entered from Campus Drive or Old Calvert Road). You can take out just below the rapid, continue a mile to Decatur Street or go past the confluence to Bladensburg Road. There is a paved biking trail along the creek.

GAUGE: The Northeast Branch gauge should reach about 150 cfs. The relevant rainfall gauges are Greenbelt and Indian Creek 2 and 3, of PG County.

PAINT BRANCH

Paint Branch (Indians used pigments from its ocher clay soil) is the one decent tributary of the Northeast Branch for paddling, fishing or viewing. It descends the fall line through a 3-mile gorge; however, 1.7 miles (at 40 ft/mile gradient) in the middle of this is in a fenced off Government preserve (formerly the Naval Surface Weapons Research Center and now the White Oak Federal Research Center). As a result, there are two separated trips, with the best part of each being its half mile of the fall line.

> Upper Paint Branch has managed to avoid the pollution of other Anacostia tributaries, and as a result has the only **self-sustaining trout population** in metropolitan Washington. Stocking had ended in 1943, but the breeding population of brown trout was not discovered until 1974. There is catch-and-release fishing upstream of Fairland Road. Good Hope Branch (where the gauge is located) is the main spawning area, because of its cold springs, shaded banks, silt-free bottom and excellent water quality. Gum Springs Branch and the Right Fork are secondary spawning tributaries. The Inter-County Connector was sited not to damage this resource; we shall see. A community group, the Eyes of Paint Branch, is helping protect the creek.

Section 1: Fairland Road to Montgomery Paint Branch Apartments

Gradient	Difficulty	Distance	Area	Scenery	Strainers	Rating
35 (70)	II (III)	2.4	7.6	B	1-3/mi.	***

USGS Quad – Beltsville; Source – Personal descent 11/93
N39 04.64, W76 58.58 to N39 02.80, W76 58.54

This trip is within Paint Branch Park, so it is very pretty and relatively unspoiled. From Fairland Road, it is a mile to the Colesville-Beltsville Road, and a further 0.8 miles to where Hollywood Branch enters. These 1.8 miles are fast flat water with numerous 1-2 foot ledges and occasional strainers. Then, approaching US 29, the creek reaches its fall line and the gradient increases to 70 ft/mile. This gorge is continuous class II for 300 yards, culminating in a class III drop. It is also beautiful, with steep slopes, big rocks, and few signs of human intrusion (except for two bridges high overhead).

A quarter mile below is the take out, recognized by a 15-ft wide clearing down to the creek on both banks (for a buried fiber-optic cable). Finding the take-out from land is more challenging. From US 29, take Stewart Lane to April Street, continue straight into the Montgomery Paint Branch garden apartments, and park in the back at the far right, by the little playground. From behind the last building, 1714 January Drive, it is a steep but straight and wide 200-yard trail to the creek.

In high water, one could start another 1.2 miles upstream, at Briggs Chaney Road, with 4 sq. mi. and at 38 ft/mile, shortly below the confluence of the Left and Right forks. I have not explored this area. You would pass under the Inter-County Connector early in the run.

GAUGE: The Paint Branch gauge (located shortly above the section 2 put in) should be at least 140 cfs. The rainfall gauges are Indian Creek 2 and 3, of PG County.

> **Surface Warfare.** This take out is the last access point before a high chain-link fence. After the Navy pulled out in October 1997, the main part of the 600-acre facility became the Food and Drug Administration headquarters, while the Army and the Air Force occupied other parts. Although consideration was given to opening up the undeveloped land along the creek as parkland under the MNCPPC, the local community felt that this would increase the risk of crime. Consequently, the entire facility remains a fenced campus, under the overall management of the General Services Administration (GSA), and this portion of the creek is not open for paddling.
>
> But it apparently was open for purchasing or leasing. According to the *Washington Post*, E-mails show that **Jack Abramoff** strategized with GSA Chief of Staff David Safavian about how Abramoff could obtain part of this property for a school he supported.

Section 2: Bond Road to Northeast Branch

Gradient	Difficulty	Distance	Area	Scenery	Strainers	Rating
20 (50)	II- (II+)	5.4	15	C+	<1/mi.	*

USGS Quad – Beltsville/Washington East; Source – Personal descent 5/97
N39 01.84, W76 57.52 to N38 58.54, W76 55.09

On this pleasant run to the confluence with Indian Creek, many small ledges produce good surfing waves and holes. The put in is from Bond Road, off of Powder Mill Road; between the houses, a steep 100-yard trail leads to the creek. A sign there, warning of sewage outflow, suggest this is not a good place to practice rolls, and costs this section a **. The first mile, through the woods, is the nicest. It starts off class II-, followed by a long class II+ rock garden approaching Powder Mill Road. The easiest way to run this is like George W. Bush's career – start in the center and then move far right.

Class II- rapids continue below, and the creek then spends 0.7 miles in the I-95/I-495 cloverleaf, passing under five high bridges. At the fifth, the leftmost culvert ends with a pair of 2-foot drops through narrow chutes in cement ledges. The next mile is channelized through the National Agricultural Research Center, followed by a mile through the Paint Branch Golf Course and Paint Branch Park, with the creek flowing below University Boulevard and Greenbelt Road. Little Paint Branch then adds about 60% to the flow, its lighter water gradually mixing with the darker Paint Branch, in a way that would not have been acceptable at Pat Robertson's Liberty University. In its final mile and a half, Paint Branch is wider and flatter, and passes beneath US 1 and alongside the University of Maryland and the College Park Airport, before its confluence with Indian Creek. It is then just a quarter mile to the take out, on river left as you approach Campus Drive, in Paint Branch Community Park.

GAUGE: About 80 cfs on the Paint Branch gauge should suffice. The rainfall gauges are Indian Creek 1 and 2, of PG County. If the class II+ rapid at Powder Mill Road (look from the bridge) has enough water, the rest will too.

> The **College Park Airport** is the oldest continuously operating airport in the nation. It is where the Wright brothers taught military officers to fly in 1909, where airmail began and where the first helicopter flew. A museum there shows this history.
>
> I knew this was not a first descent, but I was surprised to find two **abandoned canoes**, one with a shoe keel and a squared off end (for an outboard motor), and the other a whitewater boat.

LITTLE PAINT BRANCH

Little Paint Branch has one terrible section and one half-decent one, sandwiched around a mandatory portage. The Inter-County Connector crosses section 1.

Section 1: Greencastle Road to Masters Lane (below Briggs Chaney Rd.)

Gradient	Difficulty	Distance	Area	Scenery	Strainers	Rating
35	II- (III-)	1.3	3.0	D	4-8/mi.	-

USGS Quad – Beltsville; Source – Personal descent 4/96
N39 04.58, W76 55.62 to N39 03.57, W76 55.69

This section flows through Little Paint Branch Park, but the enticing view from the put in is soon replaced by the reality of portaging strainers through thorn bushes and poison ivy. Then trash begins appearing alongside and in the creek. The only good rapid is a man-made class III- rock garden, right after Briggs Chaney Road; it requires more water than elsewhere. Take-out on river right just below, and carry up the riprap to where Masters Lane dead-ends at the creek.

Below, the creek is confined to a concrete channel, as it approaches the cloverleaf interchange of I-95 and Powder Mill Road. It then **goes underground for a few hundred yards**, so don't miss your take out!

GAUGE: You will want 20 cfs on the Paint Branch tributary, 280 cfs on Paint Branch and 2.5 on the Briggs Chaney AFWS gauge (9643). The rainfall gauges are Indian Creek 1 and 2, of PG County.

Section 2: Beltsville Neighborhood Park to Paint Branch

Gradient	Difficulty	Distance	Area	Scenery	Strainers	Rating
18 (40)	II-	2.9	9.1	C-	0-2/mi.	*

USGS Quad – Beltsville; Source – Personal descent 6/99
N39 02.75, W76 55.75 to N39 00.09, W76 55.96

Upon reemerging, the creek has fewer strainers. The put in is reached by driving north on Montgomery Road and turning left into Beltsville Park. For the first 100 yards, the right bank is cemented, but then the stream becomes more natural. The first 0.8 miles, to Sellman Road, is full of class II- ledges. The creek then enters the USDA Plant Industry Station, and the ledges become less frequent. At high water, a 2-foot weir just below a bridge could develop a strong hydraulic. You then pass beneath the Beltway, via a bouncy but uncomplicated tunnel, to Cherry Hill Road (mile 2.0), the confluence with Paint Branch (mile 2.9), and the take out a third of a mile later at University Boulevard.

Although you pass through Beltsville and College Park, there is little evidence of them except for the road and bicycle-path bridges. The banks are wooded the entire way, no buildings are visible, and wildlife abounds.

GAUGE: Look for 100 cfs on Paint Branch. On the AFWS site, look for 1.7 on the Briggs Chaney gauge. The rainfall gauges are Indian Creek 1 and 2, of PG County.

STILL RUN: Greenbelt Park to Northeast Branch (River Road)

Gradient	Difficulty	Distance	Area	Scenery	Strainers	Rating
25	II+	1.6	1.6	C	3-7/mi.	*

USGS Quad – Washington East; Source – Personal descent 4/98
N38 58.96, W76 53.71 to N38 58.06, W76 55.21

After its tiny branches meet in Greenbelt Park, Still Run heads west to Kenilworth Ave. and then south alongside it to the confluence with Brier Ditch and Northeast Branch. Put in at the main Park road; the nearest legal parking is 0.4 miles away (either direction).

The first mile is class I, with strainers that require portaging over high mud banks and through briars and poison ivy. Once alongside Kenilworth Ave., the creek improves dramatically. It has fewer strainers and there are three nice rapids: (a) a short but steep class II+ rock garden, with a 3-foot total drop; (b) a longer class II+ rock garden, dropping 5 feet; and (c) a long, bouncy class II- gravel bar. These rapids need much more water than the earlier stretches. Then there is a straight passage under Kenilworth Avenue, a curved passage under Calvert Road, and the two confluences. Take out at the MNCPPC building, a quarter mile down Northeast Branch, or at River Road just beyond.

GAUGE: The Watts Branch gauge should be at least 100 cfs and the Paint Branch tributary 30 cfs. For rainfall, use the Greenbelt gauge of PG County.

Greenbelt Park was established by the Federal Government during the Depression as a buffer between the new model community of Greenbelt and the congestion of Washington DC, and as an example of how depleted tobacco farms could be converted to parkland. Greenbelt itself was one of only three such Government-built model towns in the country, and was the forerunner of the privately developed communities of Reston and Columbia.

BRIER DITCH: Parkview Gardens to Northeast Branch (River Road)

Gradient	Difficulty	Distance	Area	Scenery	Strainers	Rating
25	II-	0.7	3.0	D	3-6/mi.	*

USGS Quad – Wash. E; Source –Personal descent (2nd half) 3/95 and full scouting
N38 58.03, W76 54.37 to N38 58.06, W76 55.21

Where else can you paddle a "ditch"? (Devils Ditch, the only namesake around, is a 600-ft/mile tributary of the Conway.) Brier Ditch starts in New Carrollton, but is paved until the Baltimore-Washington Parkway. Below, there is access at Parkview Gardens. (This townhouse community has a "No Trespassing" sign and a [usually unmanned] guard post on 64th Ave.). Or, you can miss a few strainers by parking at the end of 63rd Place, by Wirt Middle School, and carrying 200 yards. The "ditch" flows west past Kenilworth Ave. to Still Run, and 70 yards later into Northeast Branch. There is a class II- rock garden early on and a pair of class II- drops and a surfing wave toward the end. Take out a quarter mile down Northeast Branch, behind the MNCPPC building.

GAUGE: The Watts Branch gauge should be at least 60 cfs, the Paint Branch tributary 20 cfs. For rainfall, use the Greenbelt gauge of PG County.

WATTS BRANCH

Watts Branch, an *"explorers' special"* (with an on-line gauge) just north of East Capitol St., flows west-northwest for 2.7 miles, to the Anacostia River near Kenilworth Aquatic Gardens. It is divided by an underground stretch into two short sections.

> Although Lady Bird Johnson made **Watts Branch Park** part of her Keep America Beautiful campaign, the area deteriorated after the National Park Service handed it over to the DC Government, leaving the narrow park debris-strewn and crime infested. In 1997, when Washington Parks and People sought out the DC park most desperately in need, they were directed here. The result was a major program to rehabilitate Watts Branch Park (more recently renamed Marvin Gaye Park; the singer composed alongside the stream, before he headed to Motown), including construction of a community center, greenhouse, and recreation facilities. Over 5 years, according to the *Washington Post* (4/2/06), some 24,000 volunteers pulled 2.5 million pounds of trash, 6,000 hypodermic needles and 78 abandoned cars from the stream and surrounding area, and planted 1,000 native trees. So surely someone should add paddling to the park's list of attractions.

Section 1: 61st Street NE to Grant Street NE

Gradient	Difficulty	Distance	Area	Scenery	Strainers	Rating
25	?	1.0	2.0	C-	?	?

USGS Quad – Washington East; Source – Extensive scouting
N38 53.49, W76 54.82 to N38 53.90, W76 56.16

At 61st Street NE, just north of East Capitol Street and just inside DC, put in where Watts Branch is formed by a pair of unnamed headwaters. Expect some strainers and trash. After crossing Division Avenue, take out alongside Grant Street, where you see the stream disappearing underground.

GAUGE: The Watts Branch gauge should read over 80 cfs.

Section 2: 49th Street NE to Jay Street or Deane Avenue NE

Gradient	Difficulty	Distance	Area	Scenery	Strainers	Rating
25	?	1.0	3.0	D	?	?

USGS Quad – Washington East; Source – Extensive scouting
N38 53.90, W76 55.91 to N38 54.20, W76 56.79

The creek is underground for less than a quarter mile. Put in where it reappears, at 49th Street and Burroughs Avenue.

In 0.8 miles you pass Minnesota Avenue, followed by railroad tracks and Kenilworth Ave. Take out soon thereafter, from either Jay Street NE (used for the GPS coordinates) or Deane Avenue NE (which parallel the creek on the other side). You could also continue a final 0.8 flat miles to the (tidal) Anacostia, and then paddle upstream or downstream to any of various access points.

GAUGE: The Watts Branch gauge should be at least 60 cfs.

SOUTHERN MARYLAND

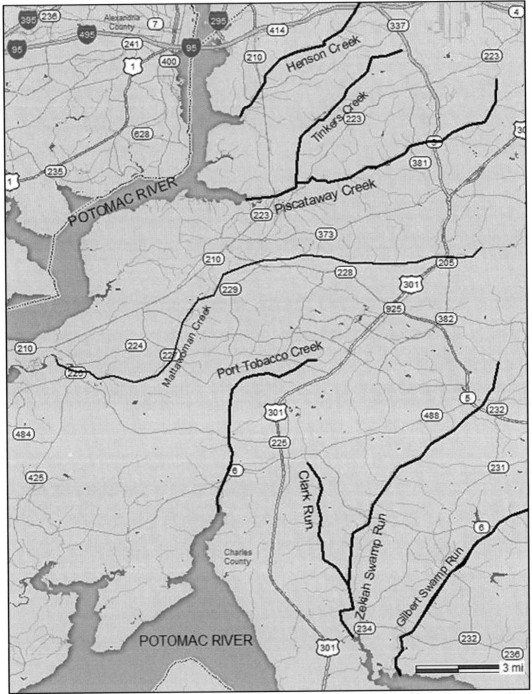

Chapter 22:
SOUTHERN MARYLAND

A long peninsula, known as Southern Maryland, extends south and southeast from Washington between the Potomac River and the Chesapeake Bay. This old agricultural region of low hills and valleys is being slowly suburbanized. The eastern third belongs to the Patuxent River basin (chapter 9), but all of the larger tributaries are in the western two-thirds, which drains to the Potomac, and comprises parts of Prince Georges (PG), Charles and St. Marys counties. Its larger towns are closer to DC – Clinton (36,000), Waldorf (68,000), Camp Springs (19,000) – while the main centers in the southern part are small – La Plata (7,000) and Accokeek (11,000). Geologically, this is all part of the coastal plain, southeast of the fall line – in fact, this is the only chapter in this book limited to that region.

The peninsula is not large enough to spawn any major rivers and not hilly or rocky enough to have much whitewater, but it does contain numerous creeks. The two largest, Mattawoman Creek and Zekiah Swamp Run, are panned by Gertler. Of the former he wrote: "It is small, winding, tangled and choked; a classic coastal plain obstacle course." Zekiah Swamp Run, while more scenic, was called "probably the most uncanoeable stream for its size in the state." Eleven miles on Mattawoman Creek took Gertler (known as a fast paddler) 10 hours, and the same distance on Zekiah Swamp Run took him 14 hours. The main culprits were fallen trees and braiding on the former, beaver dams, vines and braiding on the latter.

Thus forewarned, I approached my initial task, exploring four smaller creeks in the area, with some trepidation. Over four days in April/May 1996, I paddled 18 miles on **Henson, Tinkers** and **Piscataway creeks** in PG County, and **Port Tobacco Creek** in Charles County. I was always thinking about where I could abort the run if the creek became too choked. All of Piscataway Creek and the lower part of Tinkers Creek were shown as swamps on the USGS quads. Visions of becoming trapped in a snake- and alligator-infested hell crossed my mind. OK, forget the alligators, but this had all the appeal of Newt Gingrich at a MoveOn.org convention.

To my pleasant surprise, however, I found these streams all far more navigable than Mattawoman Creek or Zekiah Swamp Run. As the single best indicator of this, my total time to paddle 18 miles was 10 hours, which works out to almost twice the average pace of Gertler's travels/travails. While strainers were a constant nuisance, few were particularly difficult to circumvent, and braiding was significant only in the final quarter mile of Port Tobacco Creek. Although not wild whitewater wonders, these creeks have decent gradients and can be caught a day or, in the case of Piscataway Creek, even two days after a good rain.

Later, I scouted the rest of Southern Maryland for potential paddles. **Gilbert Swamp Run** turned out to be unnatural and dull, but strainer free. I also determined that by starting with 2 miles of "explorer's special" on **Clark Run,** one could get to just the final 2.8 miles of **Zekiah Swamp Run,** and Gertler had reported that in "the last few miles, [Zekiah Swamp Run] … gushes its healthy volume down only a few channels, at least one of which is usually unobstructed."

So why are these creeks so unknown? In part, it is because 95% of the DC area's paddlers (based on Canoe Cruisers Association members' addresses) live in Northern Virginia, Montgomery County or DC, and many of them are only vaguely aware that Southern Maryland exists. But, of course, in greater part, it is because these creeks have little if any whitewater. And as you will quickly see from the table below, nothing in this chapter earns more than one star in my own subjective rating system.

> I had hoped to include **Oxon Run** (originally Oxen Run), which straddles the Southeast DC-PG County line. I found a stream in the Oxon Run Neighborhood Park, off Oxon Run Drive, across from Oxon Run Lane in Oxon Run Hills. Must be the right place! But downstream, most of the creek was confined between sloping concrete walls, and the remainder was full of strainers. Even more disconcerting were signs and fences indicating that a large section of Oxon Run Park in DC was "off limits until the Corps of Engineers locates and removes buried ammunition" left over from Camp Simms.
>
> The other streams in Southern Maryland are very narrow and hence especially likely to have many strainers. Still, if you want to go exploring, you might try **McIntosh Run** (near Leonardtown), at 10 ft/mile for 2.8 miles from McIntosh Road to Md. 5; it is very strainer prone for the first half mile (I saw two from the road in the first 50 yards), but then Burnt Mill Creek almost doubles the catchment area to 22 sq. mi., so it should be considerably
>
> Like nearby Calvert Cliffs and Scientist Cliffs, creeks in this area are good sites for **fossil collecting**, as they cut through layers of what was once the bottom of the ocean. Best known are the "Nanjemoy fossils," from a hillside just below Md. 425.

GAUGES: There are gauges on Piscataway Creek, Md. (39.5 sq. mi. – do not confuse this with the gauge on Piscataway Creek, Va.), Zekiah Swamp Run (80 sq. mi.), Mattawoman Creek (58 sq. mi.) and St. Clements Creek (18.5 sq. mi. – 10 miles southeast of Gilbert Swamp Run). The **Piscataway Creek gauge is used in the "gauge" column below**; however, it rises and falls a little more slowly than the other creeks covered here. The PG County rainfall gauges are only in the Anacostia and Patuxent watersheds, but the ones at District Heights, Marlboro Road and County Justice Center are not too far from the Henson Creek headwaters. There are no rainfall gauges for Charles and St. Marys counties.

name	gradient	difficulty	length	area	gauge	rating
Henson Creek - Section 1	21	I (II-)	2.5	10	250cfs	*
- Section 2	22	II-	3.3	17	200cfs	-
Piscataway Creek	13	I	7.1	23	150cfs	-
Tinkers Creek	25	II- (II)	3.5	9	300cfs	*
Port Tobacco Creek	20	I	2.3	15	175cfs	-
Clark/Zekiah Swamp Run	9	?	4.8	12	200cfs	?
Gilbert Swamp Run	9	A (II)	5.8	15	150cfs	-

HENSON CREEK

Henson Creek rises alongside the Beltway, by Andrews Air Force Base, and flows southwest for 10 miles, at a steady 20 ft/mile, until its name changes to Broad Creek shortly before reaching the Potomac. The run is through Henson Creek Park, part of the MNCPPC system, which is replete with sporting facilities: ball fields, basketball and tennis courts, ice-skating rink, archery range, golf course, etc. A bike path parallels the creek; when the creek is up, short stretches are muddy and/or under a few inches of water. The alternative shuttle route is on hilly, roundabout and heavily traveled roads. The creek is divided into two sections because of the density of strainers in the latter part.

> **Josiah Henson** was the best-known African-American in the Washington area in the mid-19th Century, and is widely considered the model for Uncle Tom. Near Henson Creek is the **Mathew Henson** elementary school, named after the African-American explorer who was in the first party to reach the North Pole. But Henson Creek is not named after either of them, of course, but instead comes from a prominent white Maryland family founded by **Thomas Hinson,** who arrived in 1650. The name was first changed to Hynson, and the district (set large enough to support 100 families) between Oxon and Piscataway was named "Hynson's Hundred."
>
> **Broad Creek** was surveyed for settlement as early as 1662. The town of Aire at Broad Creek was established in 1706 as a tobacco shipping port. The remaining structures and archeological ruins are now protected within the Broad Creek Historic District.

Section 1: Temple Hills Road to Bock Road

Gradient	Difficulty	Distance	Area	Scenery	Strainers	Rating
21	I (II-)	2.5	10	D+	1-3/mi.	*

USGS Quad – Anacostia; Source – Personal descent 4/96
N38 48.53, W76 56.22 to N38 47.42, W76 58.28

This is a pleasant run through Henson Creek Park, past middle-class suburbs, with only a few strainers. From just upstream of the bridge, it is 100 yards through a cement channel, until the creek regains its original bed via a man-made, class II- rock garden. After that there are only gravel bars and tiny ledges, the latter sometimes over submerged logs. After 0.7 miles, you pass Brinkley Road, and soon your nose becomes aware of the Rosecroft Raceway stables; you may see some of the trotters on the practice track close to the creek, while the raceway stadium itself is visible in the distance. Unless you have strong masochistic tendencies, take out at Bock Road.

GAUGE: Look for at least 250 cfs on the Piscataway Creek (Md.) gauge. District Heights (PG County) is the nearest rainfall gauge.

Section 2: Bock Road to St. Johns Church (Broad Creek)

Gradient	Difficulty	Distance	Area	Scenery	Strainers	Rating
20	II-	3.3	17	D	5-10/mi.	-

USGS Quad – Anacostia/Alexandria; Source – Personal descent 4/96
N38 47.42, W76 58.28 to N38 45.37, W77 00.01

This starts like a continuation of section 1, but then you enter beaver territory. A large beaver dam needed to be portaged about a quarter mile below Bock Road; two other beaver-felled strainers followed. After 0.4 miles, you pass Tucker Road and a beehive-shaped gauging station. The Henson Creek Golf Course is now on both sides, so you are traversing a water hazard. Still, the view, though unnatural, is pleasant, and the footbridges are high enough to pass under. The golf course also provides almost a mile respite from the beavers, so you may be lulled into thinking that you are home free.

But you are not. In the next mile, unless conditions have changed, you will encounter more beaver-felled obstacles than there were Republican filibusters against Obama legislation. While the rapids themselves are no more than class II-, maneuvering through them requires class III skills.

When a row of apartment blocks appears on river right, you are finally out of the woods (as it were) and close to Indian Head Highway (Md. 210). There is good access off Livingstone Road, behind a small shopping area just below the Highway.

The final mile, below Indian Head Highway, is pleasant and stress free – class I, with few strainers. The current eases up and the creek widens out (hence "Broad Creek") after Hunters Mill Branch enters midway. The scenery is a mixed bag of woodlands and commercial development, and I saw both deer and abandoned cars alongside the creek.

GAUGE: About 200 cfs on the Piscataway Creek gauge would be zero level.

Damn Builders. In a one-mile stretch, I encountered ten strainers that required exiting my boat, plus numerous more that I managed to maneuver around, under, over or through. Nor were these ten strainers all so easily negotiated. Most consisted of several trees, and the riverbank was often high and choked with vegetation. To avoid portages, I increasingly tried to thread my way through, even where the current was strong and the passages tenuous. At one point, I had to cross the creek on a narrow tree trunk to retrieve a dropped paddle; at another, I had to struggle to keep the canoe from getting pinned.

The hills bordering Henson Creek rise 150-200 feet and are filled with subdivisions. This is one of the steepest places in the coastal plain. Tiny unnamed brooks cascade down at 100-150 ft/mile. **Hunters Mill Branch** is the one tributary that might have a large enough watershed to be paddleable, because it comes in at an angle. The put in is by a residential area off of Palmer Road. Walk past the little marsh full of cattails along Little Stone Drive, to the creek. The run is 1.5 miles at 50 ft/mile, and with a drainage area 1.3 sq. mi. You pass through the Hunter Mill Recreation Area, and then go under Indian Head Highway and Livingston Road. A quarter mile later, you meet Henson Creek, and from there it is 0.4 miles down Broad Creek (the new name) to the St. Johns Church take out. Look for 125 cfs on the Watts Branch gauge.

PISCATAWAY CREEK: Brandywine Road to Indian Head Highway

Gradient	Difficulty	Distance	Area	Scenery	Strainers	Rating
13	I	7.1	23	C+	5-7/mi.	-

USGS Quad – Piscataway; Source – Personal descent 4/96 (first 5.7 miles)
N38 43.68, W76 53.77 via N38 42.40, W76 57.81 (Md. 223) to N38 41.97, W76 59.20

Like Henson and Tinkers Creeks, Piscataway Creek (the one in Maryland, not Virginia) rises on the fringes of Andrews Air Force Base (which is, as you might expect, located on high ground). It has gathered enough tributaries to be runnable by Branch Avenue (Md. 5), but that is a busy road, so use Brandywine Road instead, a mile below.

In the first 3.7 miles, to Windbrook Drive, there were some 30 river-wide strainers, about half of which required short portages – including one long trunk that crossed the winding creek twice. Other than the strainers, the creek is fine. There is little trash and many birds and riffles, the latter mostly in the middle third of the trip. Only once does the creek braid, half a mile above Windbrook Drive; go right.

Between Windbrook Drive and Piscataway Road – Md. 223 (my take out), the strainers were fewer, but the gradient drops from 15 ft/mile to 11 ft/mile. There is relatively unspoiled scenery and clear water. Despite the swamp symbols on the USGS map, the streambed is well-defined. Below Piscataway Road, there is an even flatter 1.4 miles to Indian Head Highway (Md. 210), where there is a good take out on river right. You can even go a further 1.7 miles (mostly tidal) to the end, to a public access at the bottom of Wharf Road.

GAUGE: Some 150 cfs on the Piscataway Creek gauge would give you about 90 cfs at the put in, which should suffice, although it will be slow going. For rainfall, look to the Marlboro Road and County Justice Center gauges of PG County.

The **Piscataway** (aka Conoy) dominated the area, as part of the Powhatan Confederacy. When John Smith visited their town, Moyaone, at the mouth of Piscataway Creek, in 1608, it was said to be already 300 years old; archeologists have found that the site had been inhabited for over 5,000 years. Henry Fleet (later a member of first the Maryland and then the Virginia legislature) lived with them for two years, and in 1634 was visited in a village along Piscataway Creek by Leonard Calvert, first governor of Maryland, who obtained from the Emperor of the Piscataway permission to build a permanent settlement. In 1639, Father Andrew White converted the new Emperor, Tayac, to Christianity, at a celebration attended by Governor Calvert. The Piscataway pursued good relations with the colonists largely as protection against the Susquehannock, Seneca and other northern tribes, who sometimes raided them. In 1669, land between the Piscataway and Mattawoman Creeks was set aside as an Indian reservation, but smallpox and other diseases, warfare and liquor gradually killed off most of the Piscataway and related tribes. In May 1697, after some Piscataway were accused of a murder, the tribe fled to Virginia, where it was decimated by smallpox in 1705. A few descendents have since returned to their ancestral area, and a recent Piscataway chief was buried at the site of Moyaone. In their language, Piscataway apparently meant **"the branch of a stream."**

Below Indian Head Highway, Piscataway Creek is tidal and opens out into a mile-wide bay. On the north side is **Fort Washington** Park. The original fort, built to protect the capital from attack by water, proved worthless, and was blown up by its garrison when the British sailed up the Potomac in August 1814 en route to burning Washington. A new fort, completed in 1824, was the main defense against any Confederate naval attack (none came) on the capital. New gun emplacements were built in the 1890s, and Fort Washington remained in service until 1921. The National Park Service now administers it. On the south side is **Piscataway Park**, which includes the National Colonial Farm and provides a lovely view of Mount Vernon across the Potomac.

TINKERS CREEK: Potomac Airpark to Gallahan Road

Gradient	Difficulty	Distance	Area	Scenery	Strainers	Rating
25	II- (II)	3.5	9	D	2-4/mi.	*

USGS Quad – Piscataway; Source – Personal descent 4/96
N38 45.12, W76 57.22 via N38 43.98, W76 58.27 (mile 2) to N38 42.86, W76 58.27

This creek begins southwest of Andrews Air Force Base and becomes runnable when its largest tributary, Pea Hill Branch, enters at Steed Road. But the next mile was full of strainers, so a better put in is next to the Potomac Airpark, via a 250-yard carry from the end of Rose Valley Drive, just past the northeast end of the runway. The Airpark provides rather drab and unnatural scenery (treeless mud banks interspersed with chunks of gravel) for 0.7 miles, but has the compensating benefit of few strainers. When the creek reenters the woods, beaver-felled trees return, although not in the same density as earlier. For the first two miles, it is best to have a good deal of water, both for scraping over the low strainers and because the creek widens out in many places, becoming quite bony despite what seemed like sufficient water at the put in. At low levels, one often has to go right under the bushes against the riverbanks, especially on the many gravel bars and the class II- ledge towards the end of the Airpark stretch.

At mile 2, there is good access (100 yards across a football field) from the Valley View Community Park, reached by taking Trafalgar Drive to Rosalie Drive, in the town of Friendly. The final 1.5 miles below this is alongside Gallahan Road. The scenery is varied: woods, fancy estates, orchards, and open fields beneath the power line that crosses back and forth overhead. Two memorable spots are an undercut high stone bank on river left, and a class II slalom course between power-line pylons. Watch out for the low bridge at the well-named Rickety Bridge Farm and for fallen trees below there.

From the Gallahan Road take out, it is 0.6 flat miles to the confluence with Piscataway Creek, and then 0.2 miles to an alternative take out on Livingston Road.

GAUGE: You will need at least 300 cfs on the Piscataway Creek gauge. For rainfall, look to the District Heights and Marlboro Road gauges in PG County.

> A mile south of Pea Hill Branch, in Clinton, is the **Mary Surratt House and Tavern,** where John Wilkes Booth and accomplices plotted the Lincoln assassination and hid weapons. Implicated in the plot, Mary Surratt was the first woman ever executed by the Federal Government. The house is open to visitors March-December, Thursdays to Sundays.

PORT TOBACCO CREEK: Md. 225 (Hawthorne Road) to Md. 6

Gradient	Difficulty	Distance	Area	Scenery	Strainers	Rating
20	I	2.3	15	C	4-6/mi.	-

USGS Quad – Port Tobacco; Source – Personal descent 5/96
N38 32.56, W77 01.05 to N38 30.86, W77 01.33

Four things were memorable about this run. First, it was a *Perils of Pauline*-type creek, always looking like there was some horrible strainer around the next bend, but somehow providing an escape route; I had to actually exit my boat only 3 times in the first two miles. Second, the final quarter mile is totally different. There, the creek braids into channels as narrow and twisty as a gerrymandered district, and I feared that I was lost in a swamp worse than health care reform. But fortunately, some of those 4-6 foot wide channels could be run with only a few portages, and the sound and then sight of cars on the highway showed that *terra firma* was near. So if you want to just dip your toe into paddling a swamp, this is a good choice for you. Third, there is lots of wildlife – a groundhog tried to hide alongside the riverbank, frogs hopped into the water and in one case into my canoe (and under my airbag, where it stayed until it jumped out while I was driving home), and I saw a small black water snake at the takeout and several blue herons and their nests. And finally, I had one moment of sheer terror, at a strainer, when I found myself face to face and half surrounded by triads of shiny green leaves, transmogrified in my imagination into a nest of vipers waiting to strike. (I must stop watching those political campaign ads and other horror movies!)

The trip can be started almost a mile further upstream, by driving through the campus of Charles County Community College, past the water tower and the ball field, and down to the wastewater treatment facility, but I cannot vouch for this stretch.

GAUGE: Look for at least 175 cfs on Piscataway Creek and 85 cfs on St. Clements Creek. There are no rainfall gauges nearby. At the take out, you see considerably less flow (into a pool) than at the put in, because only one of several channels entering the pool is visible from the road.

Given that tobacco was the main export here, the source of the creek's name seems obvious. But it is actually a corruption of the name of the Indian village of **Potopaco** ("an inland jutting of the water"), visited by Captain John Smith in 1610.

The English town, at tidewater near the take out, was started in 1634, and is one of the oldest continually inhabited communities in America. It was a frequent destination of George Washington and a major center for the production and export of a popular carcinogen. By the late-18th Century, however, the economy was failing, as soil depletion and siltation of the port drove the industry further south. In 1819, the Charles County courthouse in Port Tobacco burned down, and the county seat was moved three miles east to La Plata. Only a few tobacco farms remain now amongst the vegetable, wheat and soybean growers, but the area is having some resurgence by attracting Washingtonians seeking a less frenetic lifestyle. As for Port Tobacco itself, the local population was down to 16 people as of 2006, making this the smallest incorporated town in Maryland.

During the **Civil War**, Port Tobacco's location and the prevalence of Southern sentiment in this plantation region made it the crossing point for smuggled goods, escaped POWs and Confederate army volunteers from Maryland to Virginia, and Confederate spies in the other direction. After assassinating President Lincoln, John Wilkes Booth (and conspirator David Edgar Herold) spent several nights in the woods near Port Tobacco Creek, waiting for a Confederate agent to transport them across the Potomac.

Near Charles County Community College is the former site of the first **Carmelite monastery** in the US, founded in 1790. Up Rose Hill Road from the take out is Habre de Venture, the **Thomas Stone National Historic Site**, home of one of Maryland's four signers of the Declaration of Independence, who later was an author of the Articles of Confederation.

CLARK RUN / ZEKIAH SWAMP RUN: Bel Alton-Newtown Road to Allens Fresh (Md. 234)

Gradient	Difficulty	Distance	Area	Scenery	Strainers	Rating
9	?	4.8	12	?	?	?

USGS Quad – Popes Creek; Source – Scouting put in/Gertler (for Zekiah portion)
N38 28.36, W76 57.36 to N38 24.92, W76 56.32

The gradient is 15 ft/mile for the 2 *"explorers' special"* miles on Clark Run, and then just 5 ft/mile for the 2.8 miles on Zekiah Swamp Run. Zekiah Swamp Run (a biblically-inspired spelling of the Indian name meaning "dense thicket") is an ecologically important wetland that is covered in considerable detail by Gertler; read that before undertaking this trip. Where Zekiah Swamp Run becomes tidal, at Allens Fresh, the name changes to Allens Fresh Run, and the Maryland Department of Natural Resources manages the Zekiah Swamp Natural Environment Area. In another 2 miles, Allens Fresh Run widens into the Wicomico River estuary of the Chesapeake Bay.

GAUGE: Look for at least 200 cfs on Piscataway Creek and 100 cfs on St. Clements Creek for the Clark Run stretch. If that is up, you will have plenty of water later (the drainage area just below the confluence is 105 sq. mi.); 100 cfs on the Zekiah Swamp Run gauge will suffice. There are no rainfall gauges nearby.

GILBERT SWAMP RUN: Md. 6 to Stines Store Road (by Md. 234)

Gradient	Difficulty	Distance	Area	Scenery	Strainers	Rating
9	A (II)	5.8	15	D	<1/mi.	-

USGS Quad – CharlotteH./PopesCr; Source – Personal descent (last 3.2 miles) 4/06

N38-29.03, W76-50.61 via N38-27.30, W76-52.36 (mile 2.6) to N38-24.98, W76-54.10

I had overlooked this waterway, because on a USGS topographical map it is simply entitled "ditch"; this is fairly apt. At Md. 6, the name changes from Gilbert Creek to Gilbert Swamp Run (now an anachronism, because the swamp was drained and a lake created to stop the creek from flooding). I have not run the 2.6 miles from there to Trinity Church Road, but from the topo map, a park ranger and what can be seen from the start and end of this stretch, it is similar to the 3.2 miles that Alf Cooley and I paddled.

Just below Trinity Church Road, there is a long class II rapid through boulders that were dumped there; enjoy it, because this is all the whitewater you will get. The rest is a straight channel, with occasional slight bends, between dirt berms. The streambed itself has been dredged, giving a deeper channel in the middle in most places. While the scenery is rather drab, the offsetting benefit is the paucity of strainers.

Below Md. 234, the creek becomes tidal, widens out and is called Newport Run, as it ebbs and flows through marsh land to the Wicomico River estuary of the Potomac. Because Md. 234 has considerable traffic, take out just upstream at Stines Store Road.

GAUGE: You need 150 cfs on Mattawoman Creek and 75 cfs on St. Clements Creek. If the rapid at Trinity Church Road is runnable, you will have plenty of water.

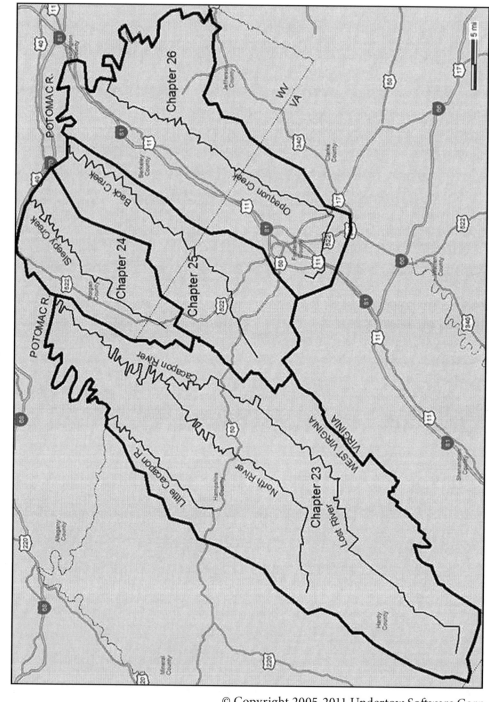
© Copyright 2005-2011 Undertow Software Corp.

PART VI: CACAPON & WEST VIRGINIA PANHANDLE BASINS

Between the South Branch of the Potomac and the Shenandoah are 5 significant Potomac tributaries, all of which flow to the north-northeast: the **Little Cacapon** (107 sq. mi.) **and Cacapon rivers** (680 sq. mi. – both in chapter 23), **Sleepy Creek** (146 sq. mi. –chapter 24), **Back Creek** (271 sq. mi. – chapter 25) and **Opequon Creek** (318 sq. mi. –chapter 26). The Cacapons drain mainly Hardy and Hampshire counties in West Virginia, while the others start in Frederick County, Virginia, and flow into West Virginia's "Eastern Panhandle" – Morgan, Berkeley and Jefferson counties. (The sliver sticking up next to Ohio is the "Western Panhandle.") Cacapon Mountain lies to the west of Sleepy Creek, the Sleepy and Back Creek basins are separated by Third Hill Mountain, while North Mountain lies between Back and Opequon creeks.

This is a rural area, full of small caves and traversed by the Tuscarora Trail and the new 2,000 mile Great Eastern Trail. The main towns are Winchester Va. (26,000) and Martinsburg WV (17,000), both in the Opequon Creek basin. The population of these basins totals some 160,000, about 70% of whom live in West Virginia.

The Cacapon River basin is full of exciting whitewater, with the Lost River and Trout Run being famous high-intermediate paddles, Tearcoat Creek and the North River being somewhat easier and tiny Waites Run containing the stiffest challenge. The Little Cacapon basin's whitewater is mainly in its North Fork. On the other hand, despite the steepness of the mountain ridges between them, the three main Panhandle creeks are rather flat. Back Creek starts off with five miles of good whitewater, but except for one 6-foot drop on Sleepy Creek, that is about all of the excitement you can expect on them, and after their first runnable miles, their gradients are down to 6-10 ft/mile. Most of their tributaries are also rather tame, with the main exception being Sleepy Creek's Meadow Branch. Little Isaacs Creek, in the Back Creek basin, has some good rapids, and Opequon's Mill Creek tributary has a steep but strainer-infested mile.

Aside from these three main creeks and their tributaries, five other runnable streams flow directly into the Potomac from the Panhandle. Of these, tiny Sir Johns Run, just east of the Cacapon, is the most exciting, while Elks Run gets steep briefly.

I have run only a minority of these creeks, mainly in the Cacapon basins, while the others chapters rely heavily on Ed Evangelidi, Roger Corbett's *Virginia Whitewater* (which includes a number of tributaries) and Paul Davidson et al's *A Canoeing and Kayaking Guide to West Virginia* (which covers just the three main streams). Hence there are many *"explorers' specials."*

There are 9 on-line **river gauges** in these watersheds. Three of the 6 in West Virginia have large drainage areas: the Cacapon near Great Cacapon (675 sq. mi.), Opequon Creek near Martinsburg (273 sq. mi.) and Back Creek near Jones Springs (235 sq. mi.). For the smaller streams, Hogue Creek (15.9 sq. mi.) and Opequon Creek near Berryville (58 sq. mi.) in Virginia and Waites Run (12.6 sq. mi.) and Tuscarora Creek (11.3 sq. mi.) in WV are the keys. Dry Marsh Run (11 sq. mi.) in Virginia and Rockymarsh Run (10 sq. mi.) in WV come up surprisingly seldom. There are on-line rainfall gauges in the Panhandle and in Hampshire and Hardy counties, WV.

CACAPON RIVER BASINS

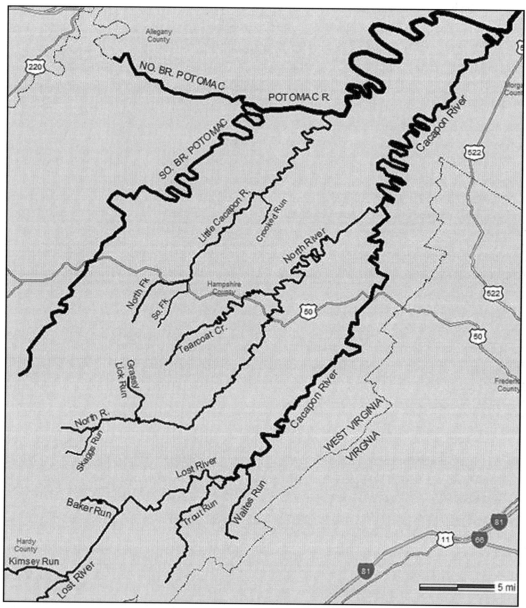

Chapter 23:
CACAPON RIVER BASINS

This chapter covers the whitewater in the West Virginia basins of the Cacapon ("medicinal/healing waters") and Little Cacapon rivers. This rural area, comprising the eastern third of Hardy Co., the eastern two-thirds of Hampshire Co. and the western third of Morgan Co., has about 25,000 residents but no sizable towns. The **Cacapon** begins as the **Lost River** and flows a total of 113 miles north-northeast to the Potomac at Great Cacapon. After 28 miles, some of its water (all of it during dry periods) seeps underground in an area known as "the sinks"; when it reemerges 3 miles later (after the Dry Gorge), the name changes to the Cacapon. The **Little Cacapon** flows 24 miles (class I, 20 ft/mile) from the confluence of its North and South forks at Frenchburg to the Potomac 3 miles southwest of Paw Paw. It is the first tributary to enter the Potomac from the south after that river is formed by the joining of its North and South branches.

There are very popular whitewater runs on the Cacapon and Lost rivers, and when the water is high enough, paddlers can occasionally be found on **Trout Run**, the **North River** at Rio and **Tearcoat Creek**. In addition to these, I have paddled **Baker Run**, lower **Waites Run** and the **North Fork of the Little Cacapon**. The remaining five trips described in this chapter are based on scouting and maps. Accordingly, **Kimsey** and **Grassy Lick runs** are "explorers' specials," as are the top parts of Waites Run, the North River and Tearcoat Creek. Some other North Run tributaries (especially Pot Lick and Skaggs runs) might also be paddled for short distances.

> A number of other creeks looked interesting from the maps until I checked them out more closely. **Moores Run** continues for 4.4 miles at 75 ft/mile (10 sq. mi.) below Warden Lake, but is almost never up because of the dam forming the lake, and flows through cattle and fences country. **Dillons Run** looked like it had a 6 mile trip at 30 ft/mile (16 sq. mi.) down to Capon Bridge, but two dams interrupt that. **Mill Branch** runs for 2.3 miles from US 50 to Capon Bridge at 50 ft/mile (9 sq. mi.), but the only put in access has no parking and heavy traffic. **Sperry Run** flows for 2 miles at 45 ft/mile (12 sq. mi.) to Rio, but had fences and low bridges across it. **Trout Pond Run** intrigued me from the map (13 sq. mi. and 60 ft/mile for 2.5 miles to Trout Run), but one look showed why its other name is Thorny Bottom.

GAUGES: There are only two gauges in these basins – one on the Cacapon near Great Cacapon (675 sq. mi.), a few miles above the Potomac, and the other about halfway down **Waites Run (12.6 sq. mi.), which is the reference** in the table below. For the Lost River Dry Gorge (177 sq. mi.), which holds its water much longer than Waites Run, look also at gauges in the neighboring watersheds – the South Fork, South Branch Potomac (Moorefield) River at Brandywine (103 sq. mi.), the North Fork Shenandoah at Cootes Store (210 sq. mi.) and Cedar Creek near Winchester (102 sq. mi.).

There are rainfall gauges in both Hardy and Hampshire counties that are useful for the small creeks in this chapter. Rainfall in this basin averages about 36 inches/year, which is among the lowest in the areas covered by this book.

name	gradient	difficulty	length	area	gauge	rating
North Fk., Little Cacapon	60	II+	3.7	8	135cfs	***
Cacapon River - Section 1	17	II	3.1	182	15cfs	**
- Section 2	10	II	9.3	330	n.a.	***
Lost River	35	III (IV-)	4.1	177	20cfs	****
Kimsey Run	55	?	2.6	15	95cfs	?
Baker Run	50	II	1.0	20	70cfs	**
Trout Run - Section 1	80	III	2.5	16	125cfs	***
- Section 2	70(110)	III (III+)	4.2	34	85cfs	****
Waites Run - *Section 1*	125	IV(?)	3.8	7	250cfs	?
- *Section 2*	80	III	2.5	13	125cfs	****
North River - *Section 1*	50	?	3.3	18	90cfs	?
- *Section 2*	48	II+ (III)	4.0	50	40cfs	***
Grassy Lick Run	70	?	3.0	5	200cfs	?
Tearcoat Cr.- *Sec. 1*	28	?	7.0	16	85cfs	?
- *Sec. 2*	45	II+	3.6	33	50cfs	***

NORTH FORK, LITTLE CACAPON: CR 10 to Little Cacapon R.

Gradient	Difficulty	Distance	Area	Scenery	Strainers	Rating
60	II+	3.7	8	B	0-2/mi.	***

USGS Quad – Augusta; Source – Personal descent 4/88
N39 17.81, W78 42.64 to N39 18.91, W78 39.43

This is by far the best whitewater run in the Little Cacapon basin. The first mile is through the woods, then Allen Hill Road comes alongside for 0.8 miles, and the remainder is parallel to US 50 down to Frenchburg, where the South Fork joins to form the Little Cacapon. Take out at CR 19 right at the confluence (or continue down the mild Little Cacapon). There are no major rapids, but lots of continuous action. At several blind turns, I stopped to scout for wood around the bend, but the creek was generally clean. In very high water, you could put in 0.8 miles higher up along CR 10, at a slightly steeper gradient (75 ft/mile) but with the drainage area down to 6 sq. mi.

GAUGE: Look for at least 135 cfs on Waites Run. The nearest rain gauge is Romney in Hampshire Co.

> Two other Little Cacapon tributaries could occasionally be run for short distances. I have paddled the class II final 0.9 miles of the **South Fork**, at 60 ft/mile (13 sq. mi.), but above that it flows through cattle pastures. And just before halfway on the Little Cacapon, **Crooked Run** enters from the right, at 90 ft/mi, but runnable only for its final 1.4 miles (9.5 sq. mi.).

CACAPON RIVER

With a drainage area of 680 square miles, the Cacapon is the 5th largest direct tributary of the Potomac (after the Shenandoah, South and North branches and Monocacy). The eastern edge of the Cacapon basin, Great North Mountain, forms the boundary between Hardy and Hampshire counties in West Virginia and Shenandoah and Frederick counties in Virginia.

Although the Cacapon flows for 82 miles (after emerging from the Lost River, Dry Gorge), there are only two sections of interest to whitewater paddlers. The first is the initial 3.1 miles, which is usually run as a continuation of the Lost. The second is a beautiful 9.3 miles from below US 50 down to Forks of Cacapon (where the North River joins). In between are 29 miles of flat water, and below section 2 is a 40-mile stretch with only occasional riffles or very easy rapids (but it makes a nice family camper and/or fishing trip).

Section 1: Remnants of low-water bridge to WV 259

Gradient	Difficulty	Distance	Area	Scenery	Strainers	Rating
17	II	3.1	182	B-	<<1/mi.	**

USGS Quad – Wardensville; Source – Personal descent 4/10
N39 04.94, W78 36.16 to N39 05.54, W78 35.15

After completing the Lost River, Dry Gorge, the paddler has the choice of taking out near the low-water bridge of a private residence (see below) or continuing 3.1 miles, on what is now the Cacapon section 1, to WV 259. There are some class II rapids at the start, but the river soon calms down. You pass downtown Wardensville, and those pretty waterfalls on river right turn out to be coming out of pipes. At one private bridge, your head clearance may be marginal at high water. The take out is on downstream river left, where you can drive down to the water.

GAUGE: You need about 25% less water to run this stretch than to paddle the Lost.

Section 2: Edwards Run to Forks of Cacapon

Gradient	Difficulty	Distance	Area	Scenery	Strainers	Rating
10	II	9.3	330	A-	0	***

USGS Quad – many; Source – Personal descent 3/12
N39-20.14, W78-25.60 to N39-24.20, W78-25.04

This popular novice run is not hard to catch and has fairly frequent easy rapids. The best ones are class II ledges – Darby's Nose, Chapel Rock and Caudy's Castle that are easiest on the far right, left, and center angling right respectively. The take out is on WV 127 – the bridge to the east (the other is on the North River).

Some paddlers put in at US 50 for a 12.6-mile trip. To shorten the run and avoid the flattish first three miles below Capon Bridge, most paddlers pay a small fee (at the red brick house) and put in opposite a 2-story purple house off a service road 0.6 miles north of the Edwards Run W.M.A. parking lot. As this has changed from time to time, go to the Paddlers Access Network (PAN) site (under the Monocacy Canoe Club) for updates.

GAUGE: Zero level is about 250 cfs on the Cacapon River gauge at Great Cacapon (40 miles downstream of the take out). Most paddlers prefer 500-1,000 cfs, which provides better current without creating dangerous hydraulics at the ledges.

> Caudy's Castle is a dramatic and climbable rock formation, downstream on river left from its eponymous ledge; pull over 200 yards below the ledge, take the horse trail to the base of the cliffs, and follow a rough trail around the Castle to the left for the most gradual ascent to the very top. Allow an hour for the round trip.

LOST RIVER: (Dry Gorge): Old WV 55 to low-water bridge

Gradient	Difficulty	Distance	Area	Scenery	Strainers	Rating
35	III (IV-)	4.1	177	A-	<<1/mi.	****

USGS Quad - Wardensville; Source – Personal descent often
N39 03.91, W78 39.30 to N39 04.94, W78 36.16

The Lost River flows gently (15-20 ft/mile) through an agricultural valley until it reaches the Dry Gorge and becomes a very popular trip – indeed, when I have managed to catch it for one of my Thursday paddles, we get an extraordinary turnout.

The first 1.7 miles is class II, until a long class II+ rapid just past a left bend. Soon thereafter comes a solid class III (class III+ above around 1.5 feet), where you can catch an eddy mid-way on the left or run through some holes on the right. The rapid ends in a steep drop right of center where a strong brace really helps. Half a mile later, after another class II, comes the Giant's Staircase, a class III with a choice of routes (usually run right of center). At the bottom, get out on the right (a common lunch spot) to scout and/or carry a man-made ledge with a hydraulic below. There is a tricky class III just below – you might want to pick your line while on shore. Look for water reentering the river from the right below here; henceforth, you are technically on the Cacapon.

After another class II rapid, pull over on the left to scout the class IV- Landslide. The steep entry chute has a large boulder just below. This is not a good place to swim, as the remainder of the rapid is full of rocks and holes. Many paddlers carry the first part on the left and put back in to run the lower half.

After a final class II, by the remains of a low-water bridge, you can take out on the right, where a tolerant family (the 5th house after Old WV 55 joins WV 55) allows cars to drive down a track to the river. Please don't abuse their courtesy or park in their potato field (park alongside the river). Alternatively, you can continue down the Cacapon River, section 1 (see above).

GAUGE: Look for an average of 175 cfs at Brandywine (South Fork, South Branch, Potomac in WV, to the west) and Winchester (Cedar Creek in Va., to the east) and 350 cfs at Cootes Store (North Fork, Shenandoah in Va., to the south). The gauge on Waites Run should have averaged at least 20 cfs for a half day. The relevant rain gauges are Devils Hole, Bald Knob and High Rocks, all in Hardy County. The painted RC gauge on the bridge at the put in is reliable, and even zero level is fine. The difficulty starts to rise as that gauge approaches 2 feet.

KIMSEY RUN: CR 14 bridge to Kimsey Run Lake

Gradient	Difficulty	Distance	Area	Scenery	Strainers	Rating
55	?	2.6	15	B	?	?

USGS Quad – Lost City; Source – Scouting from road
N38 57.98, W78 51.60 to N38 57.60, W78 48.93

This *"explorers' special"* almost doubles in size at the confluence with Dove Hollow (where CR 14/1 meets CR 14), but there are fences at all corners there, so start 0.7 miles lower down at the bridge (unless you have enough water to start higher up). Tributaries almost double the drainage area again in the next mile, but soon you reach the backwater of the dam that forms Kimsey Run Lake (built for the WV Department of Natural Resources to attract fishermen.) Cross perhaps a quarter mile of the lake on the right, to a track down to the water. Below the dam, it is a dry half mile to the Lost.

GAUGE: Waites Run should be at least 95 cfs. Bald Knob is the rain gauge.

BAKER RUN: Needmore (CR 8) to Baker Church (along Old US 55)

Gradient	Difficulty	Distance	Area	Scenery	Strainers	Rating
50	II	1.0	20	B-	1-2/mi.	**

USGS Quad – Needmore; Source – Personal descent 5/11
N39 03.16, W78 46.86 to N39 02.79, W78 46.02

In unincorporated Needmore, along Old US 55, Bears Hell Run and Parker Hollow Run merge to form Baker Run (Confederate soldier Andrew J. Baker was killed there in 1863), and one-third mile later, Long Lick Run joins them from the north. From there, Baker Run flows 3.4 miles (at 47 ft/mile) to join the Lost River at the unincorporated hamlet of Baker, 9 river miles upstream of the put in for the Dry Gorge.

The first mile, down to Baker Church, is a tiny but pleasant class II paddle, much of which is visible from Old US 55. The rapids start out short, but approaching Baker Church the class II is continuous. Take out in the eddy at the bridge to the church. Below, the first quarter mile remains a class II delight, but after a sharp left that takes you away from the road, there are four major fences in a row, on a cattle ranch. We could not find a safe way over, under or around even the first fence, and so had to turn back.

You could put back in to run the last half mile alongside CR 55/2, but why?

GAUGE: Look for 70 cfs on Waites Run. The nearest rain gauge is High Rocks.

TROUT RUN

Trout Run is a delightful alternative to the Lost River when the latter is too high – as a rule of thumb, if the Lost is over 3 feet, Trout Run is up. It enters the Cacapon right in Wardensville. The final 3 miles, below section 2, average just 20 ft/mile and are prone to fences, but there are 6.7 miles of challenging whitewater above that to run.

Section 1: Halfmoon Run (alongside Trout Run Road) to CR 1/6

Gradient	Difficulty	Distance	Area	Scenery	Strainers	Rating
80	III	2.5	16	B-	1-3/mi.	***

USGS Quad – Wolf Gap/Baker; Source – Personal descent 4/87
N38 59.81, W78 39.34 to N39 01.43, W78 40.03

This Halfmoon Run (another one enters Trout Run near the end of section 2 from the other side of Halfmoon Mountain) is probably as far upstream as one should start, as the creek is flatter, smaller

(Halfmoon Run contributes 5 sq. mi.) and more developed up above. The rapids are frequent and challenging, but it is the danger of wood that especially keeps one on his or her toes; in some years, the creek has been virtually unrunnable, but at other times it has been almost clean. Midway down this section, Trout Run Road (CR 23/10) crosses over the stream, and people sometimes put in there.

GAUGE: Waites Run needs at least 125 cfs. Devils Hole is the rain gauge.

Section 2: CR 1/6 to low-water bridge on Trout Run Cutoff Road

Gradient	Difficulty	Distance	Area	Scenery	Strainers	Rating
70(110)	III (III+)	4.2	34	B+	0-2/mi.	****

USGS Quad – Baker; Source – Personal descent 5/08
N39 01.43, W78 40.03 to N39 03.78, W78 37.73

This is an excellent paddle when not full of strainers. The first mile and half is fairly easy, but then you enter the 1.2-mile long gorge and the rapids become increasingly steep and congested. The gorge culminates in a class III+ rapid, where you ferry to the far left for a steep drop into a hydraulic. You exit the gorge on a right turn at Camp Hemlock, and the final mile and a half parallels first Trout Run Road and then Trout Run Cutoff Road (CR 23/12) and is much easier. Take out at the first of two low water bridges, after a left turn and at the end of a large eddy.

GAUGE: Waites Run should be over 85 cfs. The rain gauge is Devils Hole.

WAITES RUN

This tiny creek runs 7.5 miles from Wilson Cove down to the Cacapon. Many paddlers see it as they enter Wardensville en route to the Lost River. Section 1 is an advanced paddle, but section 2 is suitable for high intermediates. The mile below section 2 is class II (45 ft/mile) down to WV55, but the take out and parking are difficult there. Below that, it is just a quarter mile to the Cacapon, but you would then have to paddle 9 miles on that river to the first road access.

> **Wilson Cove** is a center for deer and bear hunting. I happened to be scouting during the 3-day September bear hunting season, and found a half dozen groups of camouflaged hunters, with hounds still in their customized pickups, waiting to get going. There was also an official using an antenna to track collared bears. Coincidentally, I saw a half-grown black bear cub running along the gravel road in front of me, until it panicked and dashed off into the brush.

Section 1: Wilson Cove to Greenery Drive (both along Waites Run Road)

Gradient	Difficulty	Distance	Area	Scenery	Strainers	Rating
125(150)	IV(?)	3.8	7	B+	?	?

USGS Quad – Wardensville; Source – Scouting from road
N39 00.41, W78 35.59 to N39 02.74, W78 35.65

Wilson Cove is almost the end of Waites Run Road. The creek is actually named Cove Run for the first mile, until Pond Run joins from the left. You can scout the first 1.5 miles of this *"explorers' special"* from the road, but then the two separate a bit, and the map shows some braiding. (This section has been run, but the trip reports were rather sketchy.) Half a mile below the first bridge is a 4-foot, two-step ledge close to the road. This is the end of the steeper section, and where we put in to run section 2. On the road, look for the Greenery Drive sign.

GAUGE: The Waites Run gauge, near that bridge, needs at least 250 cfs – perhaps more to start at the top.

Section 2: Greenery Drive to public park (both along Waites Run Road)

Gradient	Difficulty	Distance	Area	Scenery	Strainers	Rating
80	III	2.5	13	B+	0-1/mi.	****

USGS Quad – Wardensville; Source – Personal descent 5/11
N39 02.74, W78 35.65 to N39 04.61, W78 34.75

This delightful paddle is a good choice when the Lost and even Trout Run gorge are too high. There are no memorable rapids but almost continuous class III action until the final half mile, where the gradient eases up. The put in on Waites Run Road is across from a private road with a Greenery Drive sign. Follow a tiny tributary down to the creek, and start in a large eddy just below a 4-foot ledge (that will be very bony at moderate levels for section 2). Scout from the road near the only bridge you cross (after 1.5 miles), as the creek is especially narrow here. Expect some wood in the stream. Take out by a picnic area by following the sign to a public park.

GAUGE: Waites Run gauge should be over 125 cfs; 200 cfs is an excellent level.

NORTH RIVER

The North River is the largest tributary of the Cacapon (even if you count the Lost River as a tributary) – it covers 207 sq. mi., or 30% of the total Cacapon basin. It flows east for 13 miles to Rio and then northeast for 41 sinuous miles to Forks of Cacapon (by the take out for section 2 of the Cacapon). Those first 13 miles are mainly around 50 ft/mile, while the remainder is a class 1 float averaging just 11 ft/mile, and includes a popular final stretch past Ice Mountain (where melting comes very late). The final 4 miles to Rio (section 2) is a well-known if seldom paddled trip, and I have added a 3.3 mile upstream *"explorers' special,"* because the creek looked interesting and is just as steep up there.

Section 1: Skaggs Run to Grassy Lick Run (both along CR1)

Gradient	Difficulty	Distance	Area	Scenery	Strainers	Rating
50	?	3.3	18	?	?	?

USGS Quad – Sector/Rio; Source – Scouting
N39 08.27, W78 46.10 to N39 08.86, W78 43.20

The North River is quite tiny until Skaggs Run almost doubles its size. (At the confluence, there are tempting rapids on both branches, but upstream both run out of water soon.) A series of small tributaries flow in over the next 3.3 miles. (Pot Lick Run, the largest of these, could be run for its final 0.7

miles, from its confluence with Hog Camp Run, at 50 ft/mile with an area of 11 sq. mi.) The gradient of this *"explorers' special"* remains moderately steep, so there should be some long rapids, but I saw no major drops. There are several intermediate access points.

GAUGE: Look for at least 90 cfs on Waites Run. The nearest rain gauges are Delray (Hampshire Co.) and High Rocks (Hardy Co.).

Section 2: Grassy Lick Run (Ford Hill Rd.) to Rio (WV 29)

Gradient	Difficulty	Distance	Area	Scenery	Strainers	Rating
48	II+ (III)	4.0	50	B	0-1/mi.	***

USGS Quad – Rio; Source – Personal descent 5/88
N39 08.86, W78 43.20 to N39 08.29, W78 39.74

This is the well known trip down the North River to Rio (rhymes with Ohio). It is pretty continuous class II and II+ until the hamlet of Rio, where there is a steep class III ledge into a grabby hole that can be partially skirted.

The put in is by the junction of Ford Hill Road (which comes from Rio and then follows Grassy Lick Run) and Rock Oak Road (which follows the North River upstream). The take out is half a mile east of Rio, on North River Road (WV 29).

GAUGE: You will need at least 40 cfs on Waites Run. The nearest rain gauges are Delray (Hampshire Co.) and High Rocks (Hardy Co.).

GRASSY LICK RUN: Kirby to North River

Gradient	Difficulty	Distance	Area	Scenery	Strainers	Rating
70	?	3.0	5	?	?	?

USGS Quad – Rio; Source – Scouting
N39 10.95, W78 43.57 to N39 08.86, W78 43.20

This *"explorers' special"* could be an exciting way to begin a trip down section 2 of the North River; however, when Grassy Lick Run is up, the North River might be raging. The creek follows CR 10 and then CR 7 (Ford Hill Road). It is often visible from Ford Hill Road, and you could put in at the bridge there to run just the final 1.2 miles (7 sq. mi.) through the woods (the land above is cleared and could have fences).

GAUGE: You need about 200 cfs on Waites Run. The rain gauge is Delray.

TEARCOAT CREEK

Tearcoat Creek, the largest tributary of the North River, flows northeast for 18 miles. Section 2 is a beautiful and popular low-intermediate run, while the lower gradient of section 1 suggests that it is relatively easy. The name allegedly is due to tearing of the coats of British soldiers on thorny branches alongside the creek.

Section 1: CR7/1 to Pleasantdale (just below US50)

Gradient	Difficulty	Distance	Area	Scenery	Strainers	Rating
28	?	7.0	16	?	?	?

USGS Quad – Augusta/Hanging Rock; Source – Scouting access points
N39 15.67, W78 38.38 via N39 16.49, W78 36.75 (3.3 mi.) and N39 19.96, W78 36.19 (4.5 mi.) and N39 17.12, W78 35.74 (6.1 miles) to N39 17.74, W78 35.32

This *"explorers' special"* looks like a mild run through remote countryside. Put in is on CR 7/1 (N. Texas Rd.) just off CR 7/5 (Mack Rd.). The stream makes a series of loops; the distance as the crow flies is half that as the trout swims. The access points are CR 50/28 at 3.3 miles and Tearcoat Church Road (CR 50/17) at 4.5 and 6.1 miles, so you could do a shortened version of section 1 and then continue down section 2. Take out at the end of the service road on river right, 150 yards after crossing US 50.

GAUGE: The Waites Run gauge should be over 85 cfs. Delray is the rain gauge.

Section 2: Pleasantdale (just below US50) to the North River

Gradient	Difficulty	Distance	Area	Scenery	Strainers	Rating
45	II+	3.6	33	A	<<1/mi.	***

USGS Quad – Hanging Rock; Source – Personal descent 5/88
N39 17.74, W78 35.32 to N39 17.95, W78 33.21

Lower Tearcoat Creek is a delightful run; we enjoyed it so much that we ran in again immediately – something I very seldom do. (Section 2 of the North River made a fine third run of the day.) The put in is at the end of a service road on river right, 150 yards downstream of US 50. The stream soon enters the woods and begins winding its way through a shallow gorge over innumerable small ledges through a fern-covered wilderness. There are no notable rapids, but the continuous action keeps you entertained and busy. Take out just above the confluence on CR 50/19, which provides a direct route back to US 50.

GAUGE: The Waites Run gauge should be over 50 cfs. Delray (Hampshire Co.) is the nearest rain gauge.

SLEEPY CREEK AREA

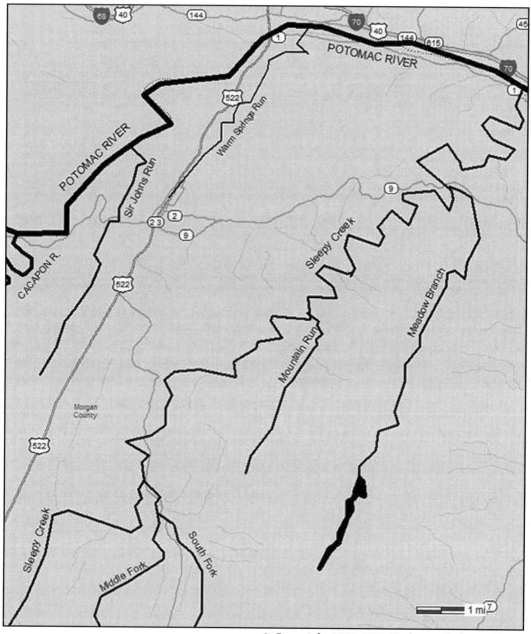

Chapter 24:

SLEEPY CREEK AREA

This chapter covers the area between the Cacapon and Back Creek basins, which means the eastern two-thirds of Morgan County, the western fringe of Berkeley County (both in the western part of the Eastern Panhandle of WV), and the northern tip of Frederick County (Va.). It is a highly rural area, the main town being the tourist spa of Berkeley Springs, WV (700 inhabitants). The ridges all run from south-southwest to north-northeast, and the streams, of course, follow suit.

Sleepy Creek drains most of this area; as its name suggests, this is not a very energetic waterway. What makes it worth paddling is the scenery. Its largest tributary, the **Middle Fork** is somewhat steeper (20 vs. 10 ft/mile) but still rather somnolent, while the **South Fork** has pretty continuous but probably not difficult rapids (these two are both "explorers' specials." Further north, **Mountain Run** is somewhat livelier, while **Meadow Branch** is a long whitewater trip, with one mile that is extremely tough. **Sir Johns Run**, another "explorers' special," tiny and steep, nestled in a small valley to the west of Sleepy Creek, is likely to be an exciting trip on those rare and brief occasions when it is runnable. So overall, this is not such a sleepy chapter.

> **Warm Springs Run** is where the mineral waters of Berkeley Springs mix with rain, treated sewerage and sand mining runoff. And it's the only creek where I've ever had to abort a trip and attain back to the put in. The Burnt Factory Road put in wasn't bad (except for the US Silica "No Trespassing" sign), but soon came a downed tree, then a pipe from the sand mine, then another pipe that was blocking lots of wood and had a 3-foot drop-off, with many more downed trees visible in the rapid below. We had gone barely a quarter mile, and had four miles left to go. What would "The Decider" do? Ed Evangelidi and I cut and ran.

GAUGES: The gauge on Warm Springs Run (6.8 sq. mi.) is good for Sir Johns Run and Mountain Run. For Sleepy Creek and its other tributaries, the best gauges to use are **Hogue Creek** (15.9 sq. mi.), a Back Creek tributary some 15-25 miles south of the creeks in this chapter (the one **used in the table below**) and Tuscarora Creek (11.3 sq. mi., near Martinsburg), an Opequon Creek tributary some 10-15 miles east of the creeks in this chapter. For lower Sleepy Creek itself, one can also look to Back Creek (235 sq. mi.). As for rainfall, the three Morgan County gauges and one in Berkeley County (Sleepy Creek East) cover the area pretty well.

name	gradient	difficulty	length	area	gauge	rating
Sir Johns Run	83 (120)	III+ (?)	2.4	6	200cfs	?
Sleepy Creek	10	I (III)	29	31	35cfs	*
Middle Fork	20	?	4.7	22	65cfs	?
South Fork	40	?	1.1	11	100cfs	?
Mountain Run	50	II (II+)	1.5	7	160cfs	**
Meadow Branch	55 (240)	IV	9.8	10	150cfs	!!!

⬙ SIR JOHNS RUN: CR 9/18 (above WV 9) to CR 3/1

Gradient	Difficulty	Distance	Area	Scenery	Strainers	Rating
83 (120)	III+(?)	2.4	6	C	?	?

USGS Quad – Hancock; Source – Scouting from road
N39 37.19, W78 14.97 to N39 38.95, W78 14.13

This tiny, steep and narrow *"explorers' special,"* which drains the western side of the Coolfont hot springs resort, should be exciting for anyone who manages to catch it. Put in on CR 9/18, 0.4 miles upstream of WV 9. The first mile will not be too hard, but the gradient is pretty steep the rest of the way. Take out at the second bridge, a quarter mile above the Potomac, to avoid a long shuttle for little benefit.

GAUGE: You can check the level at the take out. You need at least 85 cfs on Warm Springs Run. Average the three rainfall gauges in Morgan County (Hospital, Luttrel and Cacapon).

Sir John St. Clair was the deputy quartermaster in Braddock's army when they camped along this creek in 1755 en route to disaster during the French and Indian War.

Steamboat inventor, James Rumsey, and his brother-in-law, Joseph Barnes owned a mill on Sir Johns Run. In May 1785, Rumsey hired Barnes to build a boat near Sir Johns Run which they tested either where the stream enters the Potomac or downstream near Shepherdstown.

⬙ SLEEPY CREEK: CR 28/1 to Potomac River

Gradient	Difficulty	Distance	Area	Scenery	Strainers	Rating
10	I (III)	29	31	A	<<1/mi.	*

USGS Quad – Ridge/GreatCacapon/StotlersCrossroads/Hancock/CherryRun; Source – Davidson et al
N39 30.50, W78 16.20 via N39 34.03, W78 13.56 (Smith Crossroads, mile 6) and N39 37.22, W78 09.35 (mile 15) to N39 40.15, W78 05.33

Sleepy Creek is born in Frederick Co., Va., crosses into WV in 7 miles and then twists another 36 miles to the Potomac. As its name suggests, this creek never really awakens. Even before it is large enough to run, the gradient averages only 25 ft/mile. Ed Gertler has run it from US 522 (7 sq. mi.), or it can be started at SR 697 (13 sq. mi.) just before the creek crosses into WV, but there are fences and no rapids there, so you'd might as well wait at least another 7 miles, to where the creek pulls alongside CR28/1.

This trip is run mainly for its wonderful scenery. After 4 miles, the stream is substantially enlarged by the addition of the Middle Fork. At 6 miles, you reach Smith Crossroads, a popular alternative put in (85 sq. mi.). The only real rapid is a 6-foot drop into a pool with a hydraulic, below the low-water bridge at Johnsons Mill, 1.5 miles later. Paddlers should scout that and carry on the left if necessary. The last take out before the Potomac is on CR 1 (River Road), where there is limited shoulder parking only.

GAUGE: Best would be 35 cfs on Hogue Creek, 600 cfs on Back Creek; you could start below the Middle Fork with as little as 20 cfs on Hogue Creek.

MIDDLE FORK: Oakland (CR 13/8) to CR 13 (above Sleepy Cr.)

Gradient	Difficulty	Distance	Area	Scenery	Strainers	Rating
20	?	4.7	22	?	?	?

USGS Quad – Ridge/Glengary/Stotlers Crossroads; Source – Scouting access points

N39 28.87, W78 15.05 via N39 30.07, W78 13.59 (CR 8) to N39 31.64, W78 13.87

Oakland is a good put in for this *"explorers' special,"* or you could start 3.2 miles upstream on CR 11 (11 sq. mi.), with only a slightly steeper gradient (23 ft/mi.), or 2.1 miles downstream, on CR 8. There is nice scenery and at least one class II+ rapid. Take out on CR 13 (Winchester Grade Road), 0.3 miles above the confluence (or continue 1.8 miles down Sleepy Creek, at 10 ft/mile, to the same road).

GAUGE: Look for at least 65 cfs on Hogue Creek and 45 cfs on Tuscarora Creek. The Luttrel rain gauge (Morgan County) is the nearest one.

SOUTH FORK: CR 8 (near Stotlers Crossroads) to Middle Fork

Gradient	Difficulty	Distance	Area	Scenery	Strainers	Rating
40	?	1.1*	11	?	?	?

USGS Quad – Stotlers Crossroads; Source – Scouting access points

N39 30.43, W78 13.01 to N39 31.64, W78 13.87

*(plus 0.5 miles on the Middle Fork to CR 13/CR 8/6)

This *"explorers' special"* enters the Middle Fork 1.3 miles above Sleepy Creek. Fences are likely. If you start higher up, you lose 30% of the drainage.

GAUGE: Look for at least 100 cfs on Hogue Creek and 75 cfs on Tuscarora Creek. The Luttrel rain gauge (Morgan County) is the nearest one.

MOUNTAIN RUN: CR 8/1 to Sleepy Creek

Gradient	Difficulty	Distance	Area	Scenery	Strainers	Rating
60	II (II+)	1.5*	7	B-	1-3/mi.	**

USGS Quad – Stotlers Crossroads; Source – Personal descent 3/10

N39 34.58, W78 10.21 to N39 35.85, W78 10.24

*(plus 0.5 miles on Sleepy Creek, to CR 8/1 near New Hope)

Flowing between Sleepy Creek and Meadow Branch, Mountain Run has an intermediate gradient. It is, of course, very small and hard to catch. The shuttle is easy, entirely along CR 8/1, and you can scout in places from the road. At the next upstream access (CR 8/2), 1.3 miles higher up, the drainage is just 4.5 sq. mi.

The creek is busy but not difficult, with frequent class II rapids and one rock garden, on a left turn around midway, which merits II+. I encountered a few downed trees (all visible from the road) but no fences. A culvert in the second half of the trip is easily portaged. Right after that, a 15-foot waterfall tumbles in from the right. Otherwise, the scenery is undramatic but pleasant, except when passing backyards. Whenever Mountain Run is up, the half mile on Sleepy Creek will move quickly.

GAUGE: Look for 70 cfs on Warm Springs Run, 160 cfs on Hogue Creek and 120 cfs on Tuscarora Creek. The Luttrel rain gauge (Morgan Co.) is the nearest one.

MEADOW BRANCH: Sleepy Creek Lake to WV 9 Roadside

Gradient	Difficulty	Distance	Area	Scenery	Strainers	Rating
55 (240)	IV	9.8	10	B	1-2/mi.	!!!

USGS Quad – Stotlers Crossroads/Big Pool/Cherry Run; Source – Canter; Evangelidi
N39 31.91, W78 08.88 to N39 37.90, W78 06.50

This is the crème de la crème of this whole area. Meadow Branch drains an isolated, high valley between Sleepy Creek and Third Hill mountains. But its charms do not come cheaply. There is lots of wood in the creek, most dangerously in the section of hard rapids, and you have to either paddle a lot of fairly easy water or do a long carry to get to the hard rapids. So be sure you have enough time as well as skill for this run.

To get to the put in, follow the Sleepy Creek Public Hunting and Fishing Area signs on CR 7, just south of Jones Springs, five miles to the lake, turn right and go another mile and half north to the creek's outlet – where the culvert needs to be at least half full. There are three class III rapids in the first mile – The Tunnel (through overhanging bushes), Beatgrinder (a 7-foot sloping falls) and Dead End (with a dangerous undercut rock). The next mile, to the power line, is class II-III. The following five miles are class I-II. When the gradient picks up, some class III rapids appear, the creek makes a decisive turn to the right and you see the overhanging cliff called Devils Nose ahead, you are approaching the main action.

The steepest part of the run starts when you round the tip of Devils Nose, and start heading north again. Names like Log Rapids, Devils Chute, Devils Cauldron and Suicide Alley characterize the next two-thirds mile, where the gradient averages 150 ft/mile and reaches 240 ft/mile. This section is continuous class IV, complicated by wood in most rapids. The creek then eases up to class III for the next half mile and is mainly class II for the final mile after that, except for a few harder drops, especially the class IV Double Falls soon after another power line crossing. Take out at the trail from the Spruce Pine Park picnic area; if you run an addition three-quarters mile of class II down to Sleepy Creek and then WV 9, the take out and parking are not as good.

There is an alternative way to get to the rapids around Devils Nose, and skip the first 6.5 miles of the paddle – by hiking in about half a mile from Maverick Trail road at the The Woods resort. Go to www.thewoodsresort.com/hikingmap.html for details. These are public access points that they have graciously allowed, so don't abuse their generosity (e.g. abide by their slow speed limit).

GAUGE: Look for at least 150 cfs on Hogue Creek and 110 cfs on Tuscarora Creek. Sleepy Creek East (Berkeley Co.) is the nearest rain gauge. But you first need substantial rain or snowmelt to fill Sleepy Creek Lake before it will begin overflowing.

BACK CREEK BASIN

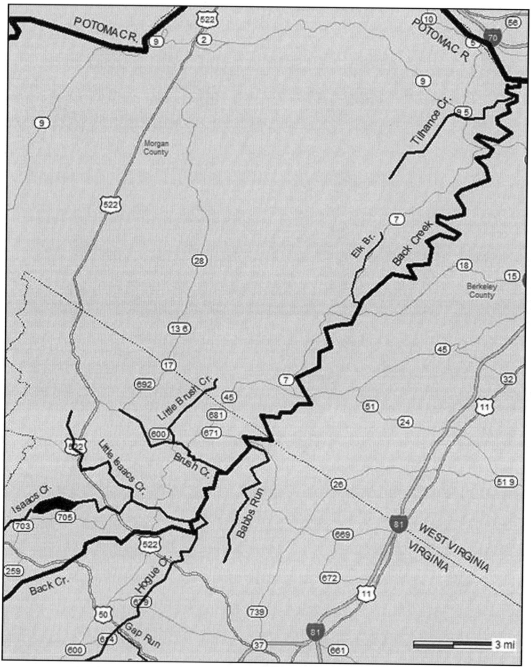

© Copyright 2005-2011 Undertow Software Corp.

Chapter 25:

BACK CREEK BASIN

Back Creek winds north-northeast from western Frederick County (Va.) through western Berkeley County (WV) to the Potomac. It flows through a very rural area, with nothing more than a few villages. It starts off much steeper than Sleepy and Opequon creeks, and the 5 mile section 1 is a fine whitewater trip; however, it soon calms down.

Another gem is tiny **Little Isaacs Creek**. By far the steepest creek in the chapter is *Little Brush Creek* (an "explorers' special"), so it should have some exciting whitewater. Section 1 of **Brush Creek** (another "explorers' special") is also promising, and its section 2 as well as **Tilhance Creek** are moderately enjoyable runs. The remaining tributaries – **Isaacs Creek, Hogue Creek** and **Babbs Run** are rather undistinguished in terms of whitewater, but they all traverse remote areas. You will see from the table below that the best runs and the most promising ones all have drainage areas of less than 10 sq. mi. – so catching them is a challenge as well as a treat.

GAUGES: The gauge on Back Creek (235 sq. mi.), near Jones Springs, is useful mainly for Back Creek section 2. For Back Creek section 1 and the upstream tributaries, the relevant gauge is **Hogue Creek** (15.9 sq. mi.), which is what is **used in this table**. For the downstream tributaries, the gauges on Mill Creek (18.4 sq. mi.) and Tuscarora Creek (11.3 sq. mi.) are closer. For rainfall, use the three gauges for Berkeley County, WV (there are none for Frederick County, Va.).

Elk Branch may occasionally have enough water for a float along CR 7 and then down a class II gorge to Back Creek. You can start at any of a number of spots along CR 7. For a 2 mile run, you have 10 sq. mi. at 30 ft/mile. I was going to include this creek until I scouted it and found it very narrow, unattractive and with fences likely. Take out at the last bridge (CR 7/12) above Back Creek, or you must paddle 5.5 miles down flat Back Creek.

Willa Cather's 1940 novel *Sapphira and the Slave Girl* tells the story of life around a fictional grain mill on upper Back Creek during the antebellum 1850s, from the point of view of both the white and black residents.

---

name	*gradient*	*difficulty*	*length*	*area*	*gauge*	*rating*
Back Creek - Section 1	41	II+	5.0	9	200cfs	***
– Section 2	6	I (II)	44	27	40cfs	*
Isaacs Creek - Section 1	38	II	2.4	5	180cfs	*
– Section 2	22	I	4.5	16	60cfs	*
Little Isaacs Creek	45	II+	4.5	7	120cfs	***
Hogue Creek	13	I	6.5	28	40cfs	*
Brush Creek - *Section 1*	40	?	2.3	8	120cfs	?
– Section 2	33	II	3.2	18	60cfs	**
Little Brush Creek	75	?	1.6	6	180cfs	?
Babbs Run	26	I (II)	5.7	11	120cfs	*
Tilhance Creek	15	I (II+)	2.9	18	60cfs	**

BACK CREEK

Back Creek flows for 60 miles – 25 in Virginia, 35 in West Virginia – and is runnable after about the first 5. Corbett and Davidson together cover all the rest, except for the 6-mile stretch that crosses the state line. I have divided the creek into two sections, based on gradient and difficulty.

Section 1: Laurel Run (along SR 704) to Gore (Mine Spring Lane)

Gradient	Difficulty	Distance	Area	Scenery	Strainers	Rating
41	II+	5.0	9	B	0-2/mi.	***

USGS Quad – Capon Springs/Hayfield/Gore; Source – Personal descent 3/10
N39 12.95, W78 23.52 via N39 13.88, W78 22.50 (mile 1.5) to N39 15.64, W78 19.98

SR 704 runs alongside Back Creek, so you can partially scout from the road. The confluence with Laurel Run, a little past the second bridge, is a good put in. (In lower water, you could start 1.5 miles later, at the first bridge over SR 704, where White Pine Branch brings the catchment area up to 13 sq. mi.) The many small ledges, long rock gardens and nice scenery make this trip enjoyable. Watch out for a collapsed private bridge (visible on the shuttle) to portage. We encountered no fences.

The best take out is the second bridge just south of Gore, where you can drive right down to the creek. Just below is a railroad abutment that may trap debris.

GAUGE: Look for at least 200 cfs on Hogue Creek. Round Top (Berkeley Co.) is the rain gauge.

Section 2: Gore to Allensville Rd. (CR 3/2 – 2.5 mi. above Potomac R.)

Gradient	Difficulty	Distance	Area	Scenery	Strainers	Rating
6	I (II)	44	27	B	<1/mi.	*

USGS Quad – Gore/Whitehall/Glengary/TablersSt'n/BigPool/Hedgesville; Source – Davidson, Evangelidi
N39 15.64, W78 19.98 via N39 21.19, W78 11.53 (Va. SR 671) and N39 22.94, W78 08.66 (WV 45) to N39 35.38, W78 00.16

This is a very long stretch of variable scenery but relatively constant gradient (after the 20 ft/mile for the first 3 miles), with many access points. It is mostly class I, but Ed Evangelidi reports a few class II rapids in the 6-miles between SR 671 in Virginia (mile 14; 170 sq. mi.; just below Babbs Run) and WV 45 – the bit not in the existing guidebooks. There is no parking at WV 45 (Glengary), but you can take out a mile earlier alongside CR 22. The final 7 miles, from WV 9 to CR 3/2, are also quite nice, with good scenery and long riffles. Watch out for a nasty fence under SR 608 and a low water bridge/hydraulic above SR 671.

GAUGE: Look for at least 40 cfs on Hogue Creek and 600 cfs on the Back Creek gauge for the top stretch, 100 cfs on Back Creek to put in at SR 671, 70 cfs to start at WV 9. The Round Top rain gauge (Berkeley County) is the one nearest the start.

ISAACS CREEK

A private lake community divides Isaacs Creek into two mediocre trips, with a 4.6 mile gap in between (including 2 miles across the lake and 2.3 miles below it).

Section 1: US 50 to SR 703

Gradient	Difficulty	Distance	Area	Scenery	Strainers	Rating
38	II	2.4	5	C	3-5/mi.	*

USGS Quad – Gore; Source – Personal descent 4/04
N39 16.81, W78 22.39 to N39 18.06, W78 20.60

This is the one of the few bits of this chapter that I have paddled, even though (some would say "especially because") it has the smallest watershed. Until the last quarter mile, there were lots of strainers, no interesting rapids and mediocre scenery. Finally, alongside SR 703, the stream becomes continuous class II, and you leave it with better memories than it deserves.

   GAUGE: You will need at least 180 cfs on the Hogue Creek gauge. The Round Top rain gauge (Berkeley County) is the nearest one.

Section 2: US 522 to SR 681 (just above Back Creek)

Gradient	Difficulty	Distance	Area	Scenery	Strainers	Rating
22	I	4.5	16	C	1/mi.	*

USGS Quad – Gore/White Hall; Source – Corbett
N39 18.91, W78 16.78 to N39 17.79, W78 13.73

This is a mild, pleasant, fast-moving paddle, except for the fallen trees in the first mile. Soon after that, the stream is widened by the addition of Little Isaacs Creek.

   GAUGE: Look for over 60 cfs on the Hogue Creek gauge. Round Top (Berkeley County) is the nearest rain gauge.

LITTLE ISAACS CREEK: US 522/Va. 127 to Isaacs Creek

Gradient	Difficulty	Distance	Area	Scenery	Strainers	Rating
45	II+	4.5*	7	B	0-2/mi.	***

USGS Quad – Gore; Source – Evangelidi
N39 20.44, W78 18.45 to N39 18.34, W78 15.17

*(plus 1.2 flat miles on Isaacs Creek)

Put in for this little gem on Crockett Run, near the confluence, to get your car off of US 522. You soon paddle between the north and south lanes, with sporting underpasses – the second set has a twisty rapid entering and a nice drop exiting the tunnel. Soon you leave US 522, and thereafter see just a little civilization (along SR 693). There are numerous small gorges with class II or II+ rapids. The scenery is nice and the strainers few. Take out at SR 600 on Isaacs Creek.

GAUGE: Look for at least 120 cfs on the Hogue Creek gauge.

HOGUE CREEK: US 50/SR614 (on Gap Run) to Back Creek

Gradient	Difficulty	Distance	Area	Scenery	Strainers	Rating
13	I	6.5*	28	C	1/mi.	*

USGS Quad – Hayfield/Gore/White Hall; Source – Corbett; Evangelidi trip report; Scouting put in

N39 12.29, W78 16.64 to N39 19.24, W78 12.56

*(plus 2 miles on Back Creek to SR 608)

Put in on Gap Run, on SR 614 just off US 50, and 0.2 miles above Hogue Creek (pronounced "hog," and named after William Hoge who moved here in the 1730s). Gap Run might be bony (just 9 sq. mi.), but it will be short; with more water you could start with 0.9 miles on Gap Run, with a gradient of 35 ft/mile. Below US 50, Hogue Creek is pleasant, except for occasional downed trees, some braiding and one low-water bridge to portage.

GAUGE: Look for at least 40 cfs on the Hogue Creek gauge. The Round Top rain gauge (Berkeley County) is the nearest one.

BRUSH CREEK

This creek tries to match the rapids entertainment of its neighbor, Little Isaacs Creek, and may come close. Section 2 is in Corbett and section 1 is worth exploring.

Section 1: Little Mountain Run (SR 600) to Siler (SR 600)

Gradient	Difficulty	Distance	Area	Scenery	Strainers	Rating
40	?	2.3	8	?	?	?

USGS Quad – Gore/White Hall; Source – Evangelidi

N39 21.85, W78 15.91 to N39 21.01, W78 14.39

The put in for this *"explorer's special"* is the confluence with Little Mountain Run, and the shuttle is straight along SR 600. You cross SR 689 around midway.

GAUGE: Look for at least 120 cfs on Hogue Creek and 140 cfs on Mill Creek.

Section 2: Siler (SR 600) to Back Creek

Gradient	Difficulty	Distance	Area	Scenery	Strainers	Rating
33	II	3.2*	18	C	1-3/mi.	**

USGS Quad – White Hall; Source – Corbett; Evangelidi

N39 21.01, W78 14.39 to N39 21.19, W78 11.53

*(plus 2 miles on Back Cr. to SR 671; but check at 0.4 miles on Baileys Ford off SR608)

The put in is at the confluence with Little Brush Creek. The first rapid provides a good visual on whether the creek is up. The rapids do not exceed class II. The best part is some short gorges. There are three low-water bridges, all connected with SR 681..

GAUGE: Look for at least 60 cfs on the Hogue Creek gauge, 70 cfs on Mill Creek. The Round Top rain gauge (Berkeley County) is the nearest one.

LITTLE BRUSH CR.: Shockeysville Rd. (SR 671) to Brush Cr. (Siler)

Gradient	Difficulty	Distance	Area	Scenery	Strainers	Rating
75	?	1.6	6	?	?	?

USGS Quad – White Hall; Source – Scouting put in and take out

N39 22.07, W78 14.24 to N39 21.01, W78 14.39

This looks like a tiny, steep, wilderness stream, with lots of strainers likely.

GAUGE: Look for at least 180 cfs on Hogue Creek, 200 cfs on Mill Creek.

BABBS RUN: Va. 731 (Cattail Road) to Back Creek

Gradient	Difficulty	Distance	Area	Scenery	Strainers	Rating
26	I (II-)	5.7*	11	C	1-3/mi.	*

USGS Quad – White Hall; Source – Corbett

N39 17.78, W78 11.77 to N39 21.19, W78 11.53

*(plus 0.5 miles on Back Creek to SR 671)

Babbs Run (Thomas Babb, Jr. settled here in the 1730s) is an easy trip through back country, with one 18" class II- ledge and lots of riffles and chutes, including over beaver dams, as well as a low-water bridge, several fences and plenty of tree strainers. You can take out on SR 741 at De Haven, shortly above the confluence, or continue down to SR 671 half a mile below (and 1.6 miles before Back Creek enters WV).

GAUGE: Look for at least 120 cfs on the Hogue Creek gauge and 140 cfs on Mill Creek.

🌊 TILHANCE CREEK: Johnsontown (WV 9) to Back Creek (CR 3/2)

Gradient	Difficulty	Distance	Area	Scenery	Strainers	Rating
15	I (II+)	2.9	18	B	1-3/mi.	**

USGS Quad – Big Pool; Source – Trip report (Ed Evangelidi) 10/06
N39 34.46, W78 02.24 to N39 35.38, W78 00.16

The first mile is unattractive and strainer prone, with one nasty river wide wire, but then the creek goes into a pair of beautiful gorges with just about every kind of water, land and air animal that you would expect or rarely expect. It is class I except for one spot in the second gorge where the creek splits, with about 2/3 of the water going right. The left is short and has a pair of class II+ rapids, while the longer right channel has many riffles. The take out is the same as for Back Creek, section 2. One could start 2 miles higher up, at CR 9/6 (15 sq. mi.), but that section has braiding, strainers, poor scenery and no whitewater.

    GAUGE: Look for at least 45 cfs on Tuscarora Creek, 70 cfs on Mill Creek and 60 cfs on Hogue Creek. The Round Top rain gauge (Berkeley County) is the nearest one.

    This creek is best known for the local 4-man **country and western group** Tilhance, and their theme song, *Tilhance Creek,* about growing up and finding love in a simpler time and place.

OPEQUON CREEK AREA

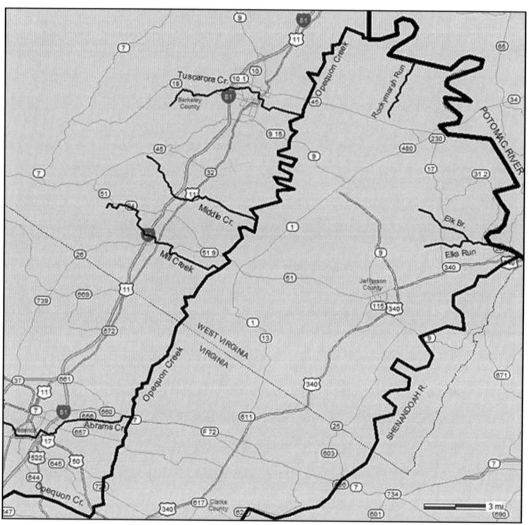

© Copyright 2005-2011 Undertow Software Corp.

Chapter 26:
OPEQUON CREEK AREA

This chapter's coverage is the lightly-paddled territory between Back Creek and the lower Shenandoah River, which includes eastern Frederick County (Va.), the northwestern corner of Clarke County (Va.), eastern Berkeley County (WV) and the northwestern half of Jefferson County (WV). Winchester Va. (26,000) and Martinsburg WV (17,000) are in this area.

The dominant waterway is **Opequon Creek**, the Potomac's ninth largest direct tributary (318 sq. mi). It flows a long way, but even in its uppermost reaches ("explorers' special" section 1) is not very swift. Neither, alas, are its tributaries **Abrams, Middle** and **Tuscarora creeks** – all also "explorers' specials." Some of the liveliest water is a mile of Opequon Creek's largest tributary, **Mill Creek**; unfortunately, that stretch tends to have fences and other strainers. There is also some brief, challenging gradient on two tiny "explorers' specials" to the east of Opequon Creek: **Rockymarsh Run** and especially **Elk Branch/Elks Run**. As you can tell from all the "explorers' specials," this chapter is not ready for prime time – but I did not want to hold up the rest of the book because of that.

Harlan Run (13 sq. mi.) could be paddled 2.3 miles from Spring Mills (WV901) to the Potomac at 15 ft/mi., but shortly above the Potomac, at Little Georgetown, there is a fence and no parking, so one must continue onto the river. There is a good take out at the Four Locks area in Maryland, 2.5 miles downstream, but that requires a 17.5-mile shuttle each way.

Hopewell Run (10 sq. mi.) might be paddled from Leetown to Opequon Creek, just south of Martinsburg, for 1.6 miles at 30 ft/mile; however, this would require putting in at the National Fish Hatchery and Research Station, and this is not permitted.

GAUGES: There are gauges on Opequon Creek at Berryville (58 sq. mi.) and Martinsburg (273 sq. mi.). The best gauge for most of the smaller creeks is **Tuscarora Creek** near Martinsburg (11.3 sq. mi.) and it is the one **used in the table below.** In 2012, a gauge appeared for Mill Creek at Bunker Hill (18.4 sq. mi.). There are also gauges on Dry Marsh Run near Berryville (11 sq. mi.) and Rockymarsh Run near Scrabble (10 sq. mi.), but these come less than one would expect; perhaps the marshes absorb much of the rainfall. In some cases, it also pays to check the gauges on Hogue Creek (15.9 sq. mi.) and on Piney Run (13.7 sq. mi., just southeast of Harpers Ferry).

name	gradient	difficulty	length	area	gauge	rating
Opequon Creek - Sec. 1	17	?	8.3	13	55cfs	?
- Sec. 2	5	I	50	37	25cfs	*
Abrams Creek	24	?	4.3	12	75cfs	?
Mill Creek	45 (70)	III	2.5	14	60cfs	*
Middle Creek	31	?	4.7	11	90cfs	?
Tuscarora Creek	20	I (II+)	2.0	25	35cfs	?
Rockymarsh Run	22 (45)	?	3.3	13	60cfs	?
Elk Branch/Elks Run	67 (100)	?	1.6	7	100cfs	?

OPEQUON CREEK

Opequon Creek's 68 miles are divided almost equally between Virginia and West Virginia. The creek flows east-southeast for its first 14 miles, as it swings south of Winchester, before turning 90 degrees and heading north-northeast for the remainder, through a series of small meanderings (e.g. the 35 miles in WV are only 20 miles as the crow flies). Section 2 is covered by Corbett and Davidson (in Virginia and West Virginia, respectively), while I have added a smaller and somewhat steeper section 1.

Section 1: Bartonsville (SR 649) to SR 644/Parkins Mill Rd. (off US 17/50)

Gradient	Difficulty	Distance	Area	Scenery	Strainers	Rating
17	?	8.3	13	?	?	?

USGS Quad – Stephens City/Boyce; Source – Scouting access points
N39 06.73, W78 12.96 to N39 06.38, W78 06.13

This is as high up as you might want to start on Opequon Creek, especially as the gradient is even less above Bartonsville. You pass the remains of an old dam, cross US 11 and I-81, and enter what looks like a pretty mini-gorge, down to Parkins Mill at US 522 and SR 644. This *"explorers' special"* slows down a bit below there (it averages 23 ft/mile these first 4.3 miles), but gets really sluggish only in the final two miles, after Wrights Run enters and you start following the Frederick/Clarke County line.

US 17/50 is not a very good take out, due to limited parking and a steep, long climb, so continue a further 1.2 miles to the ford on SR 644.

GAUGE: Look for at least 75 cfs on Hogue Creek and 275 cfs on Opequon Creek at Berryville (3 hours after put in). Round Top (Berkeley County) and Summit Point (Jefferson County) are the nearest rain gauges.

Section 2: SR 644 to CR 12 (two miles before Potomac River)

Gradient	Difficulty	Distance	Area	Scenery	Strainers	Rating
5	I	50	37	B	<<1/mi.	*

USGS Quad –Boyce/Stephenson/Inwood/Middleway/Martinsburg/Hedgesville/Williamsport; Source – Personal descent (5.8 miles) 9/06; Evangelidi
N39 06.38, W78 06.13 via N39 19.17, W77 59.33 (WV 51) to N39 31.06, W77 53.38

This pretty but rather flat section can be divided into many trips. Another good access is 8 miles below SR 644, at the ford downstream of Va. 7, shortly below the Berryville gauge. The gradient drops slowly. The 20.5 miles in Virginia average 7 ft/mile, the first 11 miles (to Sulphur Spring Road) in West Virginia 5 ft/mile, the final 20 miles a mere (and unscenic) 3 ft/mile. The 5.8 miles in WV from Middleway (WV 51; 200 sq. mi.) to Sulphur Springs Road is the most downstream stretch that still has at least a moderate (6 ft/mile) gradient. Strainers are now rare; Ed Evangelidi reports just 1 in the 40 miles he has paddled, although Corbett reported many more in the initial miles.

GAUGE: Look for 125 cfs on the Opequon Creek gauge at Berryville to start at SR 644; by Middleway, 250 cfs at Martinsburg and 50 cfs at Berryville will suffice.

ABRAMS CREEK: Winchester (Senseny Rd.) to Opequon Cr. (SR 664)

Gradient	Difficulty	Distance	Area	Scenery	Strainers	Rating
24	?	4.3*	12	?	?	?

USGS Quad – Winchester/Stephenson; Source – Scouting put in and take out
N39 10.29, W78 08.50 to N39 11.58, W78 04.43

*(plus 1 mile on Opequon Creek)

Abrams Creek is fed by springs west of Winchester, flows through that city, and continues east to Opequon Creek. If you put in at the city park, where Town Run and overflow from the lake enter, you would face at least half a dozen footbridges of the Winchester Country Club. It is therefore best to start this *"explorers' special"* 1.3 miles downstream, at Senseny Road (SR 657) (you can see the final two footbridges from there). Take out on river left, at a muddy ford on SR 664, a mile down Opequon Creek (or if that is closed, on Abrams Creek at Va. 7, half a mile before the confluence).

GAUGE: Look for at least 100 cfs on Hogue Creek, 115 cfs on Mill Creek. The Round Top rain gauge (Berkeley County) is the nearest one.

MILL CREEK: Mish Road (CR 24/3) to Runny Meade Road (CR 26)

Gradient	Difficulty	Distance	Area	Scenery	Strainers	Rating
45 (70)	III	2.5	14	D	2-3/mi.	*

USGS Quad – Inwood; Source – Personal descent 11/05
N39 20.72, W78 04.03 to N39 19.75, W78 02.43

Mill Creek can be run for 9.3 miles from near Gerrardstown to Opequon Creek. However, the first 3.5 miles starts out very narrow, and part of its 20 ft/mile gradient is expended behind at least two weirs. In addition, there are likely to be fences, as it passes through farmland. The final 3.3 miles are at only 13 ft/mile, and include at least one major fence, a quarter mile above the confluence. I have therefore paddled and included only the steeper middle section.

The put in is on a quiet back road, but in 3/4 mile you pass beneath I-81, and in another 3/4 mile, beneath US 11. This first 1.5 miles is at 28 ft/mile and is class I except for a short class II stretch before I-81 and a set of class II ledges approaching US 11.

The next mile would be the best whitewater in the Opequon basin, were it not for strainers, as Mill Creek drops off Bunker Hill at 70 ft/mile. The action begins with a 3-foot ledge leading into a long class III rock garden. Then, after some straightforward class II water, the creek divides, with most of the water making a sharp left turn followed by a right turn into a narrow channel. Alas, both of these turns tend to catch tree trunks, and the latter is in fast water. That channel contains three 2-3 foot ledges in quick succession, producing another fun class III rapid. When the channels reunite (another strainer-prone spot), there is another long class III rapid, ending in a pool that was blocked by a swinging board fence. With some effort, we slipped under the fence on the far right. The next set of class III ledges was notable for the waterfall dripping in below on river left and the strand of barbed wire at water level just above the first drop. Soon thereafter, there is a ford with a 6-foot precipitous drop; the water below is deep enough to run this. At higher levels, there is a more gradual descent on the far right. The final quarter mile, below the ford, is again mellow, with just a few short class II drops. Take out on the upstream river right side of the CR 26 bridge (there is a fence beneath it), as the gradient soon disappears; you can park across the road by the old mill wheel.

GAUGE: Look for at least 100 cfs on the Mill Creek gauge (at US 11) and 60 cfs on Tuscarora Creek. The Round Top rain gauge (Berkeley County) is the nearest one.

MIDDLE CREEK: Nollville Rd. (CR 30) to Nadenbousch Rd. (CR 34)

Gradient	Difficulty	Distance	Area	Scenery	Strainers	Rating
31	?	4.7	11	?	?	?

USGS Quad – Tablers Station/Inwood/Middleway; Source – Scouting access points
N39 22.55, W78 02.45 to N39 21.37, W77 58.22

This *"explorer's special"* has less water than expected, probably due to the absence of springs. It also attracts a lot of strainers. Within the first mile, you cross I-81, the Penn Central Railroad and US 11 at Darkesville (not a good put in because of heavy traffic and lack of parking). The stream wanders around for the next mile, but then gets into a shallow gorge, and makes a south-southeast beeline for Opequon Creek. At 2.9 miles, it crosses Middle Creek Road (CR 34/2), a potential put in for a 1.8-mile paddle without many strainers. Take out at Nadenbousch Road (CR 34), one-fifth mile before Opequon Creek.

GAUGE: Look for at least 90 cfs on Tuscarora Creek, 145 cfs on Mill Creek. The Round Top rain gauge (Berkeley County) is the nearest one.

TUSCARORA CREEK: Martinsburg (Oak St.) to Opequon Creek

Gradient	Difficulty	Distance	Area	Scenery	Strainers	Rating
20	I (II+)	2.0	25	?	?	?

USGS Quad – Martinsburg; Source – Evangelidi (by train); scouting by road
N39 27.18, W77 57.56 to N39 26.76, W77 55.59

This *"explorers' special"* flows through the industrial heart of Martinsburg and has numerous pipes across it there, some in spots where there are no eddies. So put in as the creek departs town, at the unrunnable low-water bridge on Oak Street. Below there, the main annoyances are passing trains and occasional strainers. Be careful just below Flaggs Crossing (CR 36), where a sharp man-made drop with many rocks creates a class II+ rapid. Take out just downstream of the confluence on river right (Blairton Road).

GAUGE: Look for at least 35 cfs on the Tuscarora Creek gauge (upstream of Martinsburg). Round Top (Berkeley County) is the nearest rain gauge.

ROCKYMARSH RUN: Swan Pond Road (CR 5/3) to Potomac River

Gradient	Difficulty	Distance	Area	Scenery	Strainers	Rating
22 (45)	?	3.3	13	?	?	?

USGS Quad – Shepherdstown; Source – Scouting from road
N39 27.15, W77 50.77 to N39 29.60, W77 49.53

This *"explorers' special,"*, less than three miles west of Shepherdstown, makes a beeline north from WV 45 to the Potomac, and forms the border between Berkeley and Jefferson counties. There are quite a few fences, but even more serious are the culverts at road crossings, especially the final one just above the Potomac, which is in fast water. Scout this one in advance to see whether you have enough clearance or where to begin your portage. The steepest section is the final three-quarters of a mile from Scrabble (CR 5) to the Potomac. The take out is a lovely spot just below Dam No. 4 on the Potomac

GAUGE: Look for at least 90 cfs on the Rockymarsh Run gauge near Scrabble. It may not come up for months, but during very wet periods it may flow for days as the water is released by springs. Bardane (Jefferson County) is the nearest rain gauge.

ELK BRANCH / ELKS RUN: Engle (CR 29 & CR 3/1) to Potomac R.

Gradient	Difficulty	Distance	Area	Scenery	Strainers	Rating
67 (100)	?	1.6	7	?	?	?

USGS Quad – Charles Town; Source – Evangelidi (scouting from train)
N39 20.60, W77 46.82 to N39 20.09, W77 45.47

Elks Run and its main tributary, Elk Branch, meet 1.1 miles above the Potomac, a bit west of Harpers Ferry. As there is no road access to the confluence, one must go 1.8 miles upstream to Shepherdstown Pike in order to start on Elks Run, but there are likely to be farm fences and other strainers in this first part. To avoid this, begin the trip with a half mile on Elk Branch, at 40 ft/mile, starting a bit downstream of the CR 3/1 bridge by the old furnace, just below where the creek gets squeezed between CR 29 and the railroad tracks.

Below the confluence, this *"explorers' special"* is much more navigable, which is good because its gradient averages 80 ft/mile and briefly reaches 100 ft/mile, including some good ledges. The stream follows the rail line from the confluence, until it turns sharply left just before the Potomac (at the Bakerton put in for the Needles section, just above Dam #3). Just east of the creek is the (closed) cave where John Brown sheltered just prior to his raid on Harpers Ferry. The rafting company that owns the land by the take out charges for parking ($5/vehicle, as of 2012).

GAUGE: Look for at least 125 cfs on Piney Run (Va.) and 100 cfs on Tuscarora Creek (WV). Bardane (Jefferson County) is the nearest rain gauge.

SHENANDOAH BASIN

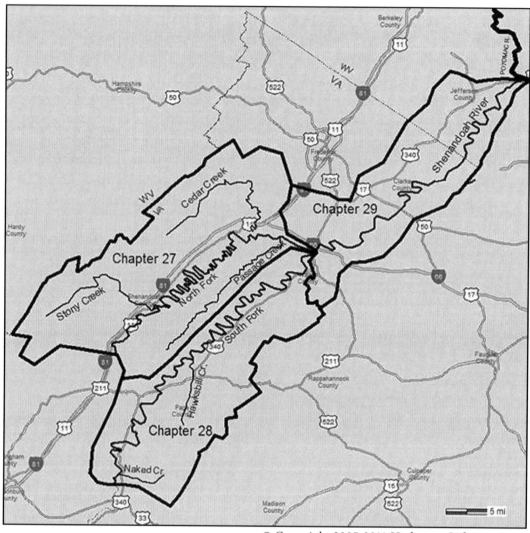

© Copyright 2005-2011 Undertow Software Corp.

The Shenandoah Valley, being underlain by limestone from its time as an inland sea, is full of underground **caves**, quite a few of which are open to the public. The most popular are Shenandoah and Endless caverns in the North Fork basin and Grand, Luray and Skyline caverns in the South Fork watershed. The limestone also counteracts acid rain and thereby keeps the rivers healthy for fish and other aquatic life – except when overwhelmed by pollution.

PART VII: SHENANDOAH BASIN

With a drainage area of 3,055 square miles, the Shenandoah is by far the largest tributary of the Potomac – even its South Fork is itself larger than any other one. And it stretches too far from the DC area (158 road miles past the Beltway, 10 miles further than even the end of the Wills Creek basin) to be included in its entirety in this book.

The basin divides naturally into three chapters – the **North Fork** (chapter 27), the **South Fork** (chapter 28), and the **Main Stem** (chapter 29) below the confluence. Within my two-hour limit, I go only as far upstream as Mill Creek on the North Fork and Naked Creek on the South Fork, but there is still a lot of whitewater in that range. In the North Fork basin, lower Passage Creek is a popular and outstanding run, but I also give **** to short trips down Pughs and Paddy runs. Gooney Run is the most outstanding South Fork tributary, but Naked Creek and its South, East and West branches are delightful paddles as well. The Shenandoah Staircase is the one really popular trip down the main stem, but two small main stem tributaries (both near Front Royal), Manassas Run and Happy Creek, are worth a lot of attention on the rare occasions when they are up.

The Shenandoah River's Indian name, "Daughter of the Stars," conjures up nostalgia and romance, as does the old refrain "Oh Shenandoah, I long to hear you." Its rich soils and abundant water have long made the Shenandoah Valley the breadbasket of Virginia. George Washington kept the valley safe from Native American attacks during the French and Indian War. During the Civil War, the struggle for control of the Shenandoah Valley was of critical importance, because of both its economic value and its strategic location near the two capitals. Stonewall Jackson's success in gaining control over the area, via a brilliant campaign against Union forces that in total outnumbered him three to one, enabled the South to endure for years and to launch its incursions into the North, whereas the eventual capture and destruction of the valley by Philip Sheridan was the beginning of the end for the Confederacy.

There are many towns but no major cities in the Shenandoah Valley. The main ones – Harrisonburg (40,000), Staunton (24,000) and Waynesboro (20,000) - are in the upper valley (i.e. southern part) and outside the scope of this book. Front Royal (14,000), at the confluence of the North and South forks, is the largest town in the lower valley. Most of the valley is still agricultural, including cattle ranches, chicken farms, orchards, vineyards and wheat fields. The total population of the lower valley is only about 140,000, in Virginia (Shenandoah, Page, Warren, Clarke and southern Frederick counties) and West Virginia (Jefferson County).

There are **river gauges** on the Shenandoah, its 2 forks, the 3 main headwaters of the South Fork (the North, Middle and South rivers – all of which are beyond this book's coverage) and 6 smaller tributaries – Muddy Creek, Linville Creek, Smith Creek (these 3 are also outside of this book's scope), Cedar Creek, Passage Creek and Spout Run. Even so, this is not good coverage for the small creeks, so one often has to rely on gauges on Waites Run in the Cacapon watershed to the northwest and Battle Run, the Robinson River and the Rapidan River in the Rappahannock basin to the southeast.

Shenandoah National Park. Unlike most national parks, Shenandoah was not an effort to protect pristine land, but rather to reclaim it. The upland forests of the Blue Ridge had been harvested extensively since the late 18th Century. Chestnut oaks were cut down for their bark, which was used in tanning leather. American chestnuts, once the most common trees in the area, were used for shingles and barrel staves, until blight wiped them out in the early 20th Century. Other hardwoods, such as ash, hickory and oak, were harvested down to 5-inch diameter.

Stephen Mather (as in Mather gorge), the first director of the National Park Service, considered eastern parks essential for building public support for the system. In 1924, the Secretary of the Interior established a committee to select sites. George Pollock, owner of the Skyland resort, mobilized his influential guests in favor of Shenandoah Park. Political and business leaders in Virginia considered that the park would be a boon for the state. In May 1926, Congress passed the Shenandoah-Smoky bill, authorizing the establishment of both parks once enough land had been obtained.

Funds had to be raised privately and from the Virginia state government to buy the private land, as Congress would not finance this. As most of the 1,300 landowners were unwilling to sell at the prices being offered, condemnation processes were required; as a result, the "Feds" are still unpopular with old-timers there. Will Carson, Chairman of the Virginia State Commission on Conservation and Development, was the moving force behind the land acquisition. He also attracted President Hoover to the Rapidan headwaters for fishing, and got him to authorize building the Skyline Drive. President Roosevelt chose the area for the first Civilian Conservation Corps (CCC) sites in 1933, and the CCC did large-scale tree planting and other landscaping. Finally, by the end of 1935, sufficient land (302 square miles) had been acquired to establish the Shenandoah National Park.

Paddling within the Park itself is minimal, because of both steepness and the closing of most roads at the Park boundary, but the Park's 311 square miles protect the headwaters of the Rappahannock (112 sq. mi.) and northern James (33 sq. mi.) rivers, as well as many tributaries of the Shenandoah (166 sq. mi.), almost all in the South Fork watershed (plus Happy Creek which joins the Shenandoah at the confluence of the North and South forks).

The Blue Ridge Parkway winds the full length of the Park, starting at the southern edge of Front Royal and continuing way beyond the Park to the south. It is crossed many times by the Appalachian Trail, which also links up with a plethora of hiking trails coming up from both sides (but especially from the east, as that is more convenient to the population centers). Only two roads cross the Park east-west – through Thornton Gap between the Thornton River and Pass Run in the north, and through Swift Run Gap in the south (just beyond the scope of this book).

The **Friends of the Shenandoah**, and a sister group, the **Friends of the North Fork,** were established in response to the damage done in the 1960s by industrial dumping of mercury and PCB into the rivers. Now the main pollution issue is from cattle and poultry; Virginia is moving slowly to establish controls on this. Fish kills, believed to be due to the rapid expansion of poultry production, have reduced the smallmouth bass population in both forks by about 80% Largely as a result of this, in 2006 American Rivers named the Shenandoah to its "America's Most Endangered Rivers" list.

NORTH FORK SHENANDOAH BASIN

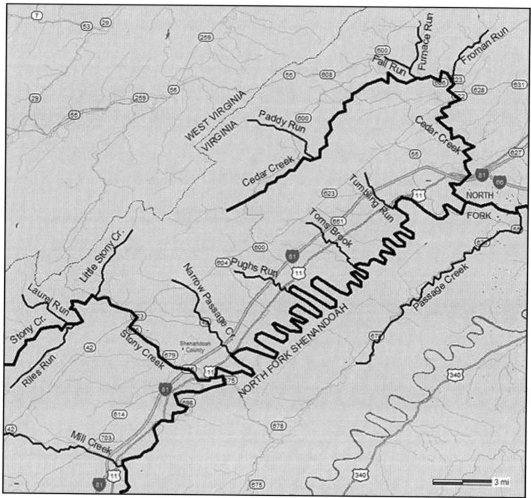

© Copyright 2005-2011 Undertow Software Corp.

The North Fork basin was the scene of most of the Civil War action in the two main **Shenandoah Valley campaigns**: Stonewall Jackson's March-June 1862 victories (primarily upstream of this book's coverage) that gave the Confederacy control of the Valley, and Philip Sheridan's successful effort in August 1864-March 1865 to secure control for the Union. The two most decisive battles of the latter were fought along Cedar Creek and Tumbling Run.

Chapter 27:
NORTH FORK SHENANDOAH BASIN

The **North Fork, Shenandoah River** drains 1,038 square miles. It runs northeast for 106 sinuous miles (42 miles as the crow flies), from the confluence of the German River and Crab Run near Bergton, to Front Royal/Riverton. Its gradient does not exceed 10 ft/mile for the last 90 of these, and the short whitewater section above that, at Brocks Gap, is almost three hours from Washington and hence outside the scope of this book; however, I have included the best nearer bit. Also too far away are the German River (6 miles, 18 sq. mi., 55 ft/mile from Snake Hollow), Crab Run (2.3 miles, 15 sq. mi., 35 ft/mile from Sirks Run), the Little Dry River, (4.4 miles, 25 sq. mi., 50 ft/mile from Bible Run), the Shoemaker River (5.3 miles, 22 sq. mi., 30 ft/mile from Slate Lick Run), Runion Creek (2.5 miles, 19 sq. mi., 30 ft/mile from Sours Run), and the flattish Smith and Linville creeks. But that still leaves a lot of fine whitewater for this book, covering about 60% of the basin.

Three North Fork tributaries – Stony, Cedar and Passage creeks – are popular novice or intermediate runs, and provide the basis for informally dividing the tributaries into 4 sub-chapters. The farthest upstream are **Mill Creek, Stony Creek,** and three of the latter's tributaries (all three "explorers' specials"): the very steep **Laurel Run** and **Little Stony Creek,** and the moderate **Riles Run.** For Stony Creek itself, I have added two sections, totaling 6 miles, upstream of those written up elsewhere.

The second sub-chapter is 4 small streams between Stony and Cedar creeks, all of which have their source on Little North Mountain. These short runs are within a 12-mile stretch of US 11, so several can be paddled the same day. **Tumbling Run** (an "explorers' special") has the most difficult rapids, while lower **Pughs Run** is the most continuous. **Narrow Passage Creek** has two good sections, separated by an avoidable mile full of fences. **Toms Brook** is a moderate descent over many small ledges.

The third sub-chapter is **Cedar Creek** and four of its tributaries. Cedar Creek starts off steeply and slows down steadily. I have covered 13 upstream miles, in addition to the well known beautiful novice parts. **Paddy Run** flattens out very little, and remains an attractive class III stream almost all the way. **Furnace Run** and **Fall Run** are basically class I, with a bit of class II, and "explorers' special" **Froman Run** looks similar.

The final sub-chapter, **Passage Creek,** has two excellent intermediate sections – a virtually unknown 3.4 miles at the top and the famous 6.8-mile trip through the gorge to the confluence – which sandwich 21.3 novice miles.

This chapter covers mainly Shenandoah County, a rich and diversified agricultural area. It has a string of small towns close to the North Fork – Mt. Jackson, Edinburg (the county seat), Woodstock, Maurertown, Toms Brook and Strasburg – but no major center.

GAUGES: The Cootes Store gauge, on the upper North Fork, was once used for this basin; however, its drainage area is 210 sq. mi., and it is 15-50 miles away (to the southwest). There is a more useful gauge not far from it, on Linville Creek (46 sq. mi.), and another on Smith Creek (94 sq. mi.); these are both a little upstream of the creeks covered in this book. The gauge on Cedar Creek near Winchester (102 sq. mi.) is helpful for the downstream tributaries, while the one on lower Passage Creek (87 sq. mi.) works for that stream. For the smaller creeks, the best gauges are in nearby watersheds – Hogue Creek (Back Creek basin; 15.9 sq. mi.) to the north, Waites Run WV (Cacapon basin; 12.6 sq. mi.) to the west and Muddy Creek at Mt. Clinton (South Fork basin; 14.3 sq. mi.) to the south. On the lower North Fork, there are gauges at Mt. Jackson (508 sq. mi.) and Strasburg (770 sq. mi.). There are also ten relevant AFWS rainfall gauges in Shenandoah Co. The table below shows the **Waites Run correlation to zero-level paddling,** except that the figures in **bold italics** for Mill and Stony creeks refer to **Linville Creek.** For downstream sections of the North Fork, Cedar Creek and Passage Creek, the relevant gauges are on those streams themselves.

name	gradient	difficulty	length	area	gauge	rating
North Fork, Shenandoah	8	I (II-)	6.6	520	n.a.	**
Mill Creek - Section 1	23	II	6.6	19	*200cfs*	**
- Section 2	70	III (5.0)	0.4	47	*220cfs*	**
Stony Creek - Section 1	18	II-	2.7	22	*220cfs*	*
- Section 2	25	II	3.2	30	*170cfs*	***
- Section 3	23	II+	6.4	54	*100cfs*	***
- Section 4	22	II (II+)	7.6	75	*70cfs*	**
Laurel Run	100	III+ (?)	1.2	7	150cfs	?
Riles Run	38	?	2.7	7	120cfs	?
Little Stony Creek	115	IV- (?)	1.2	7	165cfs	?
Narrow Passage Cr-Sec.1	42	II+	1.2	15	70cfs	**
- Sec.2	44	II+(III)	1.4	17	85cfs	***
Pughs Run	75 (130)	III	1.6	12	85cfs	****
Toms Brook	47 (80)	III	1.9	10	105cfs	**
Tumbling Run	110 (200)	IV+	1.3	11	130cfs	?
Cedar Creek - Section 1	85 (135)	III	2.0	7	145cfs	***
- Section 2	41	II+	5.6	12	80cfs	*
- Section 3	18	II	4.9	39	35cfs	**
- Section 4	12	II (III-)	23.0	56	n.a.	**
Paddy Run	105	III	1.7	10	105cfs	****
Fall Run	40	II-	0.6	17	50cfs	**
Furnace Run	35	II	2.7	10	65cfs	**
Froman Run	35	?	3.1	9	95cfs	?
Passage Creek - Section 1	53 (90)	III-	3.4	13	80cfs	***
- Section 2	13	II	21.3	25	45cfs	**
- Section 3	40 (70)	III	6.8	83	n.a.	****

NO. FK., SHENANDOAH: Mt. Jackson (SR698) to Edinburg (SR675)

Gradient	Difficulty	Distance	Area	Scenery	Strainers	Rating
8	I (II-)	6.6	520	C	0	**

USGS Quad – Edinburg; Source – Personal descent 2/07 (first 5 miles)
N38 46.90, W78 35.77 to N38 49.39, W78 32.95

There are long write-ups of the North Fork in both Grove and Corbett, and I will not triplicate that, especially as I have not paddled most of it. But I picked out what looked like the nicest bit in the 68 miles below the confluence with Mill Creek. As SR 698 runs alongside the river in places, you can vary the trip length easily.

This pleasant run through mostly woods begins near Mt. Jackson and ends near Edinburg. A good put in is a quarter mile below Red Banks Road (SR 707), on SR 698. There are several long riffles, one of which, at three miles, ends in a 2-foot, class II- ledge. A mile later, you pass beneath SR 698. In 0.8 miles, SR 695 comes alongside, at an excellent takeout). Shortly below, portage the SR 695 low water bridge. The 1.5 miles below there has good riffles, but the price is a 100-yard, steep carry to the takeout on SR 675, just below the confluence with Stony Creek. A potential side benefit is Club Dub, a nudist beach on river left near the take out, with its Tiki bar.

And what is wrong with the stretches below this? The next 15 miles, from Edinburg to Burnside Bridge (SR 758), is interrupted by three dams. And for the final 42 miles after that, the gradient averages just 4.5 ft/mile. So if you want a longer trip than 6.6 miles, start 4 miles upstream at Mt. Jackson, or even another 4 miles above that at SR 730.

GAUGE: About 300 cfs on the North Fork at Mt. Jackson or 125 cfs at Cootes Store is needed for a pleasant run, although you could scrape down with a bit less.

MILL CREEK

Mill Creek rises on Supin Lick Mountain and heads northeast for eight miles, until it meets Straight Run, just above Va. 42, the put in for section 1. There it turns east-southeast, and for the next 6.6 miles is a mild stream, until its dramatic fall line at Mt. Jackson (section 2). Above Va. 42, numerous strainers were visible from the road.

Section 1: Va. 42 to Just Above I-81 (alongside Va. 263)

Gradient	Difficulty	Distance	Area	Scenery	Strainers	Rating
23	II	6.6	19	C	1-2/mi.	**

USGS Quad – Conicville/New Market; Source – Personal descent 2/04 (last 1.5 miles); scouting a few spots from road; Corbett
N38 46.20, W78 44.73 via N38 45.49, W78 40.44 (Va. 263) to N38 44.91, W78 39.19

There is a nice set of Class II mini-ledges just above Rinkerton, and then nothing more than class I, but with a good current. The scenery is relatively poor, because you are next to the road. The scenery should be better upstream, and the gradient is similar, as is the whitewater (according to Corbett); however, there are likely to be fences and downed trees. This section ends when you see I-81 appear and the horizon disappear. You can easily climb up to Va. 263 and park on its shoulder.

GAUGE: You will need at 200 cfs on Linville Creek, 55 cfs on Waites Run and 60 cfs on Muddy Creek (Mt. Clinton) to start at Va. 42, and 60% of these figures for the final 1.5 miles.

Section 2: Just Above I-81 (alongside Va. 263) to SR 698

Gradient	Difficulty	Distance	Area	Scenery	Strainers	Rating
70	III (5.0)	0.4	47	D	<1/mile	**

USGS Quad –New Market; Source – Personal descent 2/04
N38 44.91, W78 39.19 to N38 44.74, W78 38.87

This brief section is the plunge of Mill Creek down to the North Fork. It begins with the class III Mill Rapid, a long, wide sloping ledge with several steps and many possible routes, which requires much more water than the lower part of section 1. You can pull over on either side to scout and select your line. In the final bit, most of the water goes to the left.

After you pass I-81, riffles carry you swiftly to the next horizon line, where most of the water channels to the far left. Stay right and land on the rock ledge in the middle. This is an **extremely dangerous drop** of about 15 feet, at least class 5.0, through a 6 to 8-foot wide mill-race cleft in the rock, with a complicated entry, an undercut left side, a large pillow midway and a keeper hydraulic. Portage over the rock ledge.

Shortly below, pull over on the left to scout the final two drops. Most of the water goes left over a diagonal ledge (class IV) with a serious hydraulic on the far left (where the current will try to push you), apparently the result of blasting. To avoid this hydraulic, take a class III sneak route on the far right. Whichever route you take, stay on the right side of the wave train below and blast through the strong hydraulic of the final drop, within sight of the take-out bridge.

You can also continue one-third mile down to Va. 11 (after portaging an 8-foot dam on the left), another one-third mile to the confluence, and a final one-third mile on the North Fork down to SR 698 (again), but this mile has nothing but a few riffles.

GAUGE: About 220 cfs on Linville Creek, 60 cfs on Waites Run and 65 cfs on Muddy Creek are needed to run Mill Rapid and the class III right side further down.

STONY CREEK

Only lower Stony Creek (sections 3 and 4) is in previous guidebooks, but upper Stony Creek is just as nice. The gradient and scenery in section 2 is comparable to that immediately following; section 1 is a little flatter and has more strainers, but is also pretty. And while the many bridges in all four sections detract a bit from the scenery, they do give a lot of options for designing a trip of exactly the length you want.

Three other Stony Creek tributaries have drainage areas of 6-8 sq. mi. **Swover Creek** has lots of fences. **Painter Run** and **"Garlic Hollow Run"** are rather flat until their final half miles, and look surprisingly tiny; much of their water probably gets drained off for irrigation.

Section 1: SR 720 (Barb Run) to SR 703 (Jerome)

Gradient	Difficulty	Distance	Area	Scenery	Strainers	Rating
18	II-	2.7	22	B	1-3/mi.	*

USGS Quad – Orkney Springs/Conicville; Source – Personal descent 3/98
N38 49.83, W78 45.15 to N38 51.27, W78 43.63

This is as far upstream as you should start; above, the creek braids through the Bryce golf course. The best aspect is the scenery, with rock cliffs, tiny waterfalls and good views of Great North Mountain. A dog, literally nipping at its heels, chased a deer into the creek just ahead of me; the deer swam a quarter mile downstream before exiting.

GAUGE: About 220 cfs on Linville Creek, 60 cfs on Waites Run and 65 cfs on Muddy Creek near Mt. Clinton are needed.

> **Bryce Resort** is a year-round sports-oriented attraction that includes a golf course, a lake, and the area's smallest downhill ski area, which is also used for grass skiing in summer.

Section 2: SR 703 (Jerome) to SR 691

Gradient	Difficulty	Distance	Area	Scenery	Strainers	Rating
25	II	3.2	30	B+	<1/mi.	***

USGS Quad – Conicville; Source – Personal descent 3/98
N38 51.27, W78 43.63 to N38 52.21, W78 41.03

On the right bank, rock cliffs with cedar groves extend down to the creek. On the left, Great North Mountain looms in the distance. A few houses are visible and one farm is close to the water – but most signs of civilization are blocked out by foliage.

The rapids are frequent and moderate. The good ones produce big waves along the cliffs on the right bank, usually on sharp left-hand turns. The best and longest rapids are in the final half mile, so you leave with good feelings for the creek.

There are two low-water bridges; the first one has a strong hydraulic. There were two barbed-wire fences alongside the large farm after the second bridge, but we could slip beneath if someone held the fences up.

GAUGE: About 170 cfs on Linville Creek, 45 cfs on Waites Run and 50 cfs on Muddy Creek at Mt. Clinton are needed. At the put in, the water should be at least up to the bottom of the drainpipes. Check the rainfall gauges at Bryce Mountain, Jerome Gap and Woodstock Reservoir.

Section 3: SR 691 to Columbia Furnace (SR 675, just off Va. 42)

Gradient	Difficulty	Distance	Area	Scenery	Strainers	Rating
23	II+	6.4	54	B	<1/mi.	***

USGS Quad – Conicville/WolfGap; Source – Personal descent 6/97
N38 52.21, W78 41.03 to N38 52.60, W78 37.53

This is the beginning of the popular Stony Creek trip, written up by Randy Carter, Roger Corbett, Ed Grove et al. The scenery is best near the start, before one gets too close to civilization, but there are class II and II+ chutes and rock gardens, some with boulders and good waves, scattered throughout. There are also three dams and one low water bridge, in varying stages of collapse, which should be approached carefully.

The remains of the historic Columbia Furnace are on river right by the take out. Just downstream is a large pool that is popular for fishing and swimming.

GAUGE: You'll want at least 500 cfs at Cootes Store, 250 cfs on Cedar Creek and 100 cfs on Linville Creek. If the start of this trip has enough water, the rest will too.

Section 4: Columbia Furnace to North Fork, Shenandoah (near Edinburg)

Gradient	Difficulty	Distance	Area	Scenery	Strainers	Rating
22	II (II+)	7.6	75	C	<<1/mi.	**

USGS Quad – Conicville/Edinburg; Source – Personal descent 5/96
N38 52.60, W78 37.53 to N38 49.39, W78 32.95

This section is similar to the preceding in gradient, but less scenic. The six low water bridges provide a choice of put ins and take outs, but can become annoying if you want to keep going. A 5-foot dam is the most challenging drop (class II+); scout before running. You have a choice of take-outs; SR 675 over the North Fork is the easiest.

GAUGE: About 340 cfs on Cootes Store, 160 cfs on Cedar Creek and 70 cfs on Linville Creek should suffice.

LAUREL RUN: Liberty Furnace to private bridge above Stony Creek

Gradient	Difficulty	Distance	Area	Scenery	Strainers	Rating
100	III+(?)	1.2	7	B	?	?

USGS Quad – Wolf Gap/Conicville; Source – Almost complete scouting
N38 52.97, W78 42.42 to N38 52.38, W78 41.51

Much of this *"explorers' special"* marks the boundary of the George Washington National Forest, so there won't be fences there; however, the bottom part runs through private land. Virtually the entire short trip can be scouted from SR 691.

Put in at Liberty Furnace, alongside SR 691, at the SR 717 bridge. (SR 691 crosses Laurel Run 0.4 miles upstream, but the gradient is 200 ft/mile and a class IV rapid comes soon.)

At Liberty Furnace, you can see the former iron furnace, as well as an old mill with a waterwheel. Take out at the bridge 0.2 miles above Stony Creek, to avoid a 4-foot man-made drop at a low water bridge, plus a pair of fences, as the creek traverses a farm. (You can check this area from the road to see if the fences are gone. If you continue down to Stony Creek, it is then only 0.4 miles to SR 691 (the start of section 3).

GAUGE: The Waites Run gauge should be over 150 cfs. The Jerome Gap and Woodstock Reservoir rain gauges (Shenandoah Co.) need heavy downpours.

RILES RUN: SR 703 to Stony Creek (Dellinger Acres Rd. – SR 691)

Gradient	Difficulty	Distance	Area	Scenery	Strainers	Rating
38	?	2.7	7	?	?	?

USGS Quad – Conicville; Source – Scouting put in and take out
N38 50.65, W78 42.45 to N38 52.13, W78 41.07

Riles Run rises on the back side of Bryce Mountain, and flows northeast, parallel to Stony Creek. The confluence is 200 yards from the Stony Creek section 3 put in. This *"explorers' special"* starts on private land but ends in the George Washington National Forest.

GAUGE: The Waites Run gauge should be over 120 cfs and Muddy Creek at Mt. Clinton 135 cfs. Jerome Gap and Woodstock Reservoir are the rain gauges.

LITTLE STONY CREEK: Woodstock Reservoir to SR 749

Gradient	Difficulty	Distance	Area	Scenery	Strainers	Rating
115	IV-(?)	1.2	7	C	?	?

USGS Quad – Wolf Gap; Source – Considerable scouting from road
N38 55.05, W78 39.47 to N38 54.02, W78 39.66

Hikers know this *"explorers' special"* far better than paddlers do, as the Stony Creek Trail goes along it for 4 miles. But the only regular road access is to the bottom 1.7 miles, starting about 100 yards below the Woodstock Reservoir. Take SR 749 until it ends 1.1 miles above SR 675, and continue another half mile up the private road, past all the summer cabins, to the entrance to the National Forest, where there is a small parking area for hikers before the locked gate. The creek is very steep here, and likely to have strainers. All of the bridges (to cabins) appear to have adequate head clearance, but there are some 2-3 foot drops below the low-water ones. The creek continues steep but more natural after the first half mile. It can be seen intermittently from the road. Take out at the bridge on SR 749 (unless conditions have changed below – see next paragraph).

The creek continues another half mile, but beware of that stretch. The gradient reaches 165 ft/mile, on a blind left turn early on. More dangerously, there is a sturdy fence just upstream of SR 675, in an eddyless rapid, shortly above the confluence with Stony Creek. With high fences all around, the portage would be a bear.

GAUGE: Look for 165 cfs on Waites Run. Woodstock Reservoir is the rainfall gauge.

NARROW PASSAGE CREEK

Narrow Passage Creek rises between Little North and Little Sluice mountains, and flows 12 miles to the North Fork. It is steeper and shorter than its upstream neighbor to the south,

Stony Creek, but flatter and longer than its downstream neighbors to the north – Pughs Run, Toms Brook and Tumbling Run.

It is 3.6 miles from the section 1 put in, just above Va. 42, to the North Fork. Alas, this should not be done as a continuous trip (as Ed Evangelidi and I learned to our pain), because getting through a one-mile section in the middle was as difficult as getting a tax increase through Congress. It contained 8 fences, 6 of which were major. This *milus horribilus* will only be of interest to masochists, fence engineers and tire-recycling experts who might want to study the wonderful variety of obstructions concocted by the local farmers – barbed wire, wooden boards, steel sheets and 3 different ways to recycle used tires. So our strong advice to paddlers is to shuttle their boats by car between sections 1 and 2.

> One-third mile above its mouth, the creek swings very close to the North Fork, allowing only a **"narrow passage"** on the road (named, in turn, the Indian Road, the Great Wagon Road, the Stage Road, the Valley Turnpike and US 11) between Woodstock and Edinburg. This was reportedly a popular ambush site, first for Native Americans and later for highwaymen.
>
> The Willow Grove Tavern, built around 1800 at Narrow Passage, was **Stonewall Jackson's headquarters** in the spring of 1862. (The current name is the Inn at Narrow Passage.) The wooden trestle on the **Narrow Passage Railroad Bridge** of the Manassas Gap Railroad collapsed on the night of March 6-7, 1876. The entire train fell into the gorge, killing 11 people and 25 carloads of livestock.

Section 1: SR 680 (just above Va. 42) to SR 605

Gradient	Difficulty	Distance	Area	Scenery	Strainers	Rating
42	II+	1.2	15	C	2-4/mi.	**

USGS Quad – Edinburg; Source – Personal descent 6/97
N38 52.47, W78 33.52 to N38 51.59, W78 33.01

This is a pleasant trip, mostly through woods, with only one fence when we ran it (on the downstream side of Va. 42, in calm water), plus a pair of low water bridges along SR 605 (from which road you can scout the second half of the run) and a 4-foot dam to portage. There is a nice variety of rapids.

Put in at SR 680, 200 yards above Va. 42, and less than a half mile after the largest tributary enters. Take out where SR 605 turns sharply away from the creek, just above or at a third low water bridge (on a private driveway), and set up a new shuttle for section 2, so as to avoid the intervening mile of fences.

GAUGE: The gauge on Waites Run (WV) needs 70 cfs.

Section 2: SR 686 (just above I-81) to North Fork, Shenandoah River

Gradient	Difficulty	Distance	Area	Scenery	Strainers	Rating
44	II+ (III)	1.4	17	B	1-3/mi.	***

USGS Quad – Edinburg; Source – Personal descent 6/97
N38 51.08, W78 32.73 to N38 50.75, W78 31.75

This is prettier and somewhat more challenging than section 1. After a swift passage below I-81, you come to a 12-foot milldam. Portage on river right. You can put back in at the large eddy, for a dramatic peel out, or just below it.

Most of the next mile is through woods, where we saw beaver and muskrat in the creek, with no fences but a few fallen trees. Approaching the railroad bridge is a long series of ledges (class III), which will be bony unless you had extra water up above. There are nice class II+ drops above and below this. Take out at Chapman Landing at the confluence with the North Fork, just below US 11.

GAUGE: This needs a bit more water than section 1 – say 85 cfs on Waites Run.

> Near the take out is the site of the last **clash with Native Americans** in the Valley, in 1766. Two settlers, Sheetz and Taylor, were killed as they tried to escape with their families to the nearby fort at Woodstock. However, their wives drove off the attackers with axes, and they and their children survived. The Sheetz family remains prominent in the area, with Sheetz Mill Road and a service-station chain to remind us of them.

PUGHS RUN: Swartz Rd (SR 642) to North Fork, Shenandoah River

Gradient	Difficulty	Distance	Area	Scenery	Strainers	Rating
75 (130)	III	1.6	12	C	2-4/mi.	****

USGS Quad – Toms Brook; Source –Personal descent 09/03 (2nd half); 03/01
N38 54.43, W78 29.73 via N38 54.17, W 78 29.31 (US 11) to N38 54.13, W78 28.88

Putting in at SR 642 enables you to run the nice rapids just above US 11, at a moderate price. (Don't start 1.3 miles higher up, at SR 676, where you would face many fences and downed trees, for just one good rapid.) The first half-mile is pretty flat, with a few fences and trees, but then the gradient picks up, and the creek becomes class II. Beneath the railway bridge, 200 yards upstream of (and visible from) US 11, the best part begins dramatically with a 6-foot drop (class III) over three steps, best run with the tongue right down the middle. Then comes a class II+ boulder garden which continues all the way to US 11.

The 0.7 miles below US 11 averages 95-ft/mile, has a wonderful variety of rapids, and can be scouted from SR 663. It starts with a class III- rock garden, changes to a series of tight class III chutes and drops (of up to four feet), continues with a series of class II ledges (to a low water bridge that must be portaged, on the left), and ends with a 5-foot vertical man-made plunge. (These difficulty ratings are for low flow; this trip would be harder with more water.) There were no strainers in this part when we ran it, but we saw evidence that at least one had been cut out. You can take out alongside the road after the nice ledge below the low-water bridge, or continue over the man-made ledge to the backwater of the North Fork. At the North Fork, run down some bouncy waves in the center, and then cut left of the island. Take out upstream of the low water bridge (which could be a hazard).

GAUGE: Look for the Waites Run gauge to be over 85 cfs. The Woodstock Reservoir and Fetzer Gap rainfall gauges (Shenandoah County) bracket the Pughs Run headwaters. If the boulder garden upstream of US 11 is runnable, everything is.

TOMS BROOK: Toms Brook (Miller Rd.) to SR 747 (Riverview Dr.)

Gradient	Difficulty	Distance	Area	Scenery	Strainers	Rating
47 (80)	III	1.9	10	C	2-4/mi.	**

USGS Quad – Toms Brook; Source – Personal descent 6/97
N38 56.70, W78 26.44 to N38 55.59, W78 25.46

Here is your chance to paddle a "brook." From a series of cascades off of Little North Mountain, Toms Brook runs 9 miles to the North Fork. Fences and other strainers bedevil it above the town of Toms Brook on US 11, but you can see some tantalizing rapids if you drive up SR 653.

Put in 200 yards below US 11, on Miller Road; otherwise that road would be a major hazard. The beginning is trashy, but soon the brook enters a mixture of woods and farms. There are four low-water bridges, including the take out; none are particularly dangerous, but scout beforehand to identify the last eddies. We encountered only one fence. Much of this section can be scouted from Creek Road (SR 653).

The steepest and toughest part is the rock gardens and chutes of the first half mile. After that, there are lots of nice ledges, a few of which are bony at zero level. Take out at the last low-water bridge (SR 747) above the North Fork. This misses the final half-mile, but at high water much of that will be backwater from the North Fork. If you continue to the North Fork, you must paddle seven miles on it, at 5 ft/mile.

GAUGE: Waites Run needs 100 cfs and Cedar Creek 850 cfs (2-3 hours later). At zero level, the water is even with the upstream, river right cement ledge at the put in.

Tom was an early drifter who built a cabin on the stream. It was originally called Toms Creek, but when the nearby town was established, the founder decided that Toms Brook would be a catchier name. But the street alongside the brook is still called Creek Road, while nearby is an attempt to square the circle – Brook Creek Road! The Big Blue Trail runs along Creek Road, so Toms Brook is better known to hikers than to paddlers.

On October 9, 1864, two weeks after the Union triumph at Fisher's Hill, Sheridan's Union **cavalry** won a minor but decisive victory over Jubal Early's cavalry, which had foolishly camped at Toms Brook, 26 miles north of the rest of its army. The Confederates fled south, with Union cavalry in pursuit, in what became known as **"the Woodstock Races"** (after the nearby town). Union losses were 57 and Confederate losses (mostly captured) 350, plus 11 cannons and all their supplies. The Union General Torbert had been egged on by Sheridan: "Either whip the enemy or get whipped yourself."

TUMBLING RUN: *Fisher's Hill to North Fork, Shenandoah River*

Gradient	Difficulty	Distance	Area	Scenery	Strainers	Rating
110 (200)	IV+	1.3	11	C	1-3/mi.	?

USGS Quad – Toms Brook; Source – Complete scouting; personal descent last half mile

N38 59.20, W78 24.08 to N38 59.18, W78 22.91

This *"explorers' special"* is not for the faint of heart or the short of skill. Tumbling Run and its equal-sized South Fork both tumble down from Little North Mountain, pass through farmland and under I-81, and meet at the Civil War battlefield town of Fishers Hill, for a short, dramatic trip to the North Fork. You can put in on Tumbling Run about 30 yards above the confluence – there was parking across from the post office. Just below the confluence is a beautiful set of limestone ledges (class III+), right in the middle of town. Most of the water starts on the left and then cuts back sharply to the right, before making a hard left turn. But this stretch needs more water than that below, and you must figure out in advance how you are going to deal with the SR 601 road crossing (in high water you can paddle right onto the road). Note the water wheel and mill remains on river left.

Below the bridge is a short class II stretch, ending in a man-made ledge alongside SR 601 and under the railroad tracks, and then comes the 150-yard backwater of a 15-foot dam. Carry on the left. There is a 6-foot double ledge immediately below (class IV+), which can also be carried. This is followed by 6 other closely spaced ledges (class III+), and after a brief period to relax in class II+ water, come more class III+ ledges on a right hand turn. Below the high bridge on SR 601 and a class III rapid on a sharp left turn, catch an eddy on the left and scout the 6-foot class III+ drop into a hydraulic (visible from the road). Below that, the creek splits around an island. The right looks like a slightly more gradual descent than the 10-foot double ledge (class IV+) on the left, complicated by an undercut rock on the approach. Scout the right side route on foot from the island; there were two strainers there when I last looked. Once the two channels reunite, you are home free, provided you can catch the eddy on the left just above the low-water bridge coming up.

The final half-mile (the only bit I've actually run) is class II, passing under US 11. Where the creek turns left away from the road, you reach the backwater from the North Fork. A half-mile of fast flat water on the North Fork brings you to a US 11 wayside access.

GAUGE: Look for 130 cfs on Waites Run and 1,000 cfs on Cedar Creek (3 hours later).

At **Fishers Hill**, on September 22, 1864, Lt. Gen. Jubal Early's forces, reeling from their defeat in the 3rd battle of Winchester, tried to stop Maj. Gen. Philip Sheridan's Union troops from overrunning the Shenandoah Valley. The Valley had been both the breadbasket of the Confederacy and the route by which Southern forces had thrice invaded the North (Antietam, Gettysburg and Jubal Early's raid on Washington). Fishers Hill was called "the Gibraltar of the Shenandoah," as the armies faced each other across Tumbling Run. The southerners' dug-in position on the hillside was strong, but their 11,000 troops were outnumbered three to one, and were stretched especially thin on their left flank in the foothills. After probing for weaknesses most of the day, Union forces broke through there, capturing over 1,000 prisoners and fourteen artillery pieces, and driving the enemy 60 miles south. (The heart of the battlefield, just north of I-81, is preserved and can be visited.) Sheridan then carried out the second part of his task, which was, in Grant's instructions, to turn "the Shenandoah Valley into a barren waste ... so that crows flying over it for the balance of this season will have to carry their provender with them." This burning of the valley, remembered as "Red October," included the destruction of over 70 mills. The South later made one final attempt to reclaim the Valley, ending in the Battle of Cedar Creek (see below).

CEDAR CREEK

Cedar Creek, the largest North Fork tributary, is one of the prettiest and most popular. Its final 23 miles, section 4, from Star Tannery (Va. 55) to the North Fork, is described in several books. Much less well known are the first runnable 12.5 miles, as the creek flows northeastward on the far side of Little North Mountain. There are several access points and a steadily falling gradient, so you can put in as far upstream as skill, time and water allow. While section 1 is a challenge for both catching and running, sections 3 and 4 are OK for shepherded novices.

> In December 2005, the Potomac Conservancy unveiled its report entitled *Cedar Creek Revealed: A Study of the Ecological and Historic Context of Cedar Creek.*
>
> A few other Cedar Creek tributaries are conceivably runnable, but only for very short distances or with too many strainers. **Buffalo Marsh Run** (9 sq. mi.) could be paddled for its final 0.8 miles (there are fences above that), followed by 4.2 miles on Cedar Creek. **Turkey Run** (7 sq. mi.) escapes fences only in its last quarter mile. **Duck Run** (6.5 sq. mi.) is so narrow that I saw 3 strainers in just its last 200 yards. **Mulberry Run** (5.5 sq. mi.) starts off tiny and fenced. **Meadow Brook** (7 sq. mi.) goes through backyards.

Section 1: Upstream SR 713 bridge to SR 600 (0.3 mi. below bridge)

Gradient	Difficulty	Distance	Area	Scenery	Strainers	Rating
85 (135)	III	2.0	7	B	1-3/mi.	***

USGS Quad – Woodstock; Source – Personal descent 9/03 (last 1.3 miles)
N38 58.56, W78 33.01 to N38 59.20, W78 31.19

This is as high up Cedar Creek as one should consider starting, as the half-mile above it (to the ruins of Van Buren Furnace) was full of strainers. Even this section will usually have some strainers (although we encountered only one in the 1.3 miles we ran), plus a pair of low-water bridges to contend with. Fortunately, after the first half mile, you can see this stretch pretty well from the road.

When Cedar Creek is high, the downstream SR 713 bridge will be dangerous to cross – or to run. We put in just below that bridge, and had a delightful paddle, full of class II and III rapids. The creek is so narrow that there is usually only one route. Fortunately, the stream is also pretty straight, with only a few blind turns where you might find unanticipated strainers. Take out below the private bridge after SR 600.

GAUGE: Check the level from the roadside. The Cedar Creek gauge at Middletown should reach at least 1,200 cfs, 4 hours later; more timely, the gauge on Waites Run (WV) should be over 145 cfs. A key indicator will be heavy rainfall at the Zepp and Fetzer Gap rain gauges, Shenandoah Co.

Section 2: SR 600 (0.3 mi. below bridge) to SR 621 (Cedar Creek Road)

Gradient	Difficulty	Distance	Area	Scenery	Strainers	Rating
41	II+	5.6	12	C	2-4/mi.	*

USGS Quad – Woodstock/Mountain Falls; Source – Personal descent 9/03
N38 59.20, W78 31.19 to N39 01.79, W78 27.23

This otherwise-pleasant trip is largely ruined by fences (we encountered 6) and downed trees, mainly in the first and third miles. The creek is quite twisty in places, and you need to approach all blind turns with caution. There are no important tributaries until Shell and Cold Spring runs near the end, but the volume keeps increasing gradually and the gradient decreasing proportionately. At SR 759, after four miles, there is a low-water bridge with a 3-foot drop into a hydraulic; the owner of the land around this bridge views launching, taking out or parking here as trespassing, so move quickly across the bridge. The remaining 1.6 miles is class II, with the best rapid being a long rock garden toward the end, after Paddy Run enters on the left. The 2 low-water bridges in this stretch were no problem when we ran them at low water, but could have hydraulics at higher levels.

GAUGE: Look for at least 80 cfs on the Waites Run gauge in WV, with the Cedar Creek gauge heading for 700 cfs, 3 hours after you start.

Section 3: SR 621 (Cedar Creek Road) bridge to Star Tannery (Va. 55)

Gradient	Difficulty	Distance	Area	Scenery	Strainers	Rating
18	II	4.9	39	B	<1/mi.	**

USGS Quad – Mountain Falls; Source – Personal descent 1/99
N39 01.79, W78 27.23 to N39 04.92, W78 25.47

This has a better gradient than the well-known section 4 and is almost as pretty. It normally has only a few complete strainers but perhaps a dozen partial strainers, so caution and good boat control are necessary.

This run is alternately through the woods, with frequent beautiful cliff walls, and farmland. It's one of the only two places I ever saw a river otter. SR 621 runs parallel for most of the way, with pretty views of the creek down below, but the land is heavily posted so there are actually few legal access points. Even the normal take out at Star Tannery is now posted. Rusty Dowling and I ran this as our way back from Paddy Run to our car at Star Tannery, so it was pleasant but anticlimactic. We were in a big rush, the water was high, we encountered only one strainer, and we did this section in 75 minutes. On a later trip, Kevin Cleaver, John Lentz and I had to portage two fallen trees, and just managed to scrape over a barbed-wire fence. The best surfing wave is within sight of the take-out bridge.

GAUGE: You will want at least 35 cfs on Waites Run (two hours earlier), and 270 cfs on the Cedar Creek gauge (an hour after put in).

> Frank and Bridget Fico had set up their bicycle shuttle, when a policeman told them that it was illegal to paddle this section because it went through private property. They explained that common law provided an exception for navigable rivers. The policeman countered that since this was Cedar **Creek**, the exception did not apply. I hope I can find that same policeman if I get stopped on the far smaller Covington, Rush or upper Thornton **rivers**.

Section 4: Star Tannery to North Fork, Shenandoah (SR 611)

Gradient	Difficulty	Distance	Area	Scenery	Strainers	Rating
12	II (III-)	23.0	56	A	0	**

USGS Quad – Mountain Falls/Middletown/Strasburg ; Source – Personal descent 5/96, 3/84 and 10/95 (for the top, middle and lower parts, respectively)
N39 04.92, W78 25.47 via N39 04.66, W78 19.54 (SR 622) and N39 00.35, W78 19.15 (US 11) to N38 59.04, W78 18.97

This part of Cedar Creek has been written up extensively and is normally divided into three trips. The first is 9.5 miles down to Stephens Fort (SR 622), the second is 10.5 miles from there to US 11, and the last is 3 miles down to the North Fork. Towards the end of the first stretch, you can paddle through a small cave on river left. Stephens Fort is an interesting historic structure, and just upstream from it is a pretty waterfall created by an old millrace. The second trip is particularly known for its scenic beauty, and contains one tricky class II+ rock garden, where the best route is between the two large boulders near the top. The class III- rapid is just one mile above the North Fork, visible upstream from the SR 635 low-water bridge.

GAUGE: The gauge on Cedar Creek near Winchester should be at least 200 cfs.

Cedar Creek was the base for Union General David Hunter's operations further south in the Valley in May-June 1864, while Grant and Lee were battling in the Wilderness. Additional Union troops returned in August 1864, when Sheridan replaced Hunter.

The **Battle of Cedar Creek** was the final Confederate attempt to regain the Valley. At dawn on October 19, 1864, four weeks after his defeat at Fishers Hill, General Early, having been reinforced to 21,000 men and having observed the 32,000-man Union encampment from nearby Signal Knob, at the northern end of Massanutten Mountain, surprised and routed four Union divisions camped along Cedar Creek. But the hungry southerners stopped to forage among the Union supplies, and Sheridan, returning from meetings in Washington, personally rallied his forces for a counterattack that devastated Early's army. A Union captain wrote: "Never since the world was created was such a crushing defeat turned into such a splendid victory as at Cedar Creek." Sheridan's conquest of the Valley helped ensure Lincoln's reelection the following month, and Sheridan's personal role has been held up as a model at West Point ever since. The weekend closest to October 19 has an annual battle reenactment. Belle Grove Plantation, the Union headquarters, was reportedly designed in part by Thomas Jefferson; James and Dolley Madison honeymooned there. Some 3,500 acres of the battlefield are the **Cedar Creek and Belle Grove National Historic Park**.

Near the confluence with the North Fork, close to Middletown, is an **old stone fort** built circa 1755 for defense against the Indians.

PADDY RUN: SR 600 (Zepp Road) to SR 602 (Paddy Run Road)

Gradient	Difficulty	Distance	Area	Scenery	Strainers	Rating
105	III	1.7	10	A	0-2/mi.	****

USGS Quad – Mountain Falls; Source – Personal descent 12/92
N39 02.72, W78 29.90 to N39 01.64, W78 28.01

Paddy Run starts on the Virginia-WV border, between Great North and Paddy mountains. It flows northeast for 3 miles to Vances Cove, where it picks up its only major tributary, and then southeast for 4.5 miles to Cedar Creek. About a mile below Vances Cove it passes through Paddy Gap, where the 800 ft high Half Moon stands guard. A mile later, it crosses SR 600, the put in, and its gradient drops from 180 to 120 ft/mile; below there, the gradient declines more slowly. (Ambitious paddlers could follow Paddys Cove Lane one-third mile upstream from SR 600.)

The creek (until SR 602) is a typical mountain brawler – no big drops, but a continuous class III rock garden, with few strainers, through mountain wilderness, with steep, rocky slopes on river left and a more gradual rise on the right. The creek flows pretty straight, so there is good visibility. Unless you plan to continue on down Cedar Creek, take out at SR 602, 0.7 miles above the confluence.

Below SR 602, Paddy Run emerges into the Cedar Creek valley, and the strainers begin to multiply – when we ran it, there were 7 or 8 in the last half mile, plus lots of partial ones. Skip this final stretch and preserve your fine memories of Paddy Run.

GAUGE: The nearby gauge on Waites Run (WV) should be at least 105 cfs.

Until the night before, I had never even heard of Paddy Run. But when the evening gauge reading had Cootes Store at 7.3, from rain and snowmelt, it was time to go exploring.

To Rusty Dowling, I must confess, I only mentioned upper Cedar Creek, taking out at Star Tannery (Va. 55), but I knew the shuttle drive would cross Paddy Run. The fisherman we met at Star Tannery was heading for Paddy Run. "Is it canoeable?" "No, it's just a tiny creek" he responded. "Well, Rusty, you wouldn't mind stopping just to look, would you?" With Cedar Creek running at over two feet, there was a glint in my eye.

Paddy Run was wider (30-40 ft) and steeper than I'd expected, but it looked runnable. Rusty was dubious, but I wasn't going to pass up easily a chance like this. "It would probably be a first descent, Rusty, and I'm sure it flattens out just beyond the bend." She was still skeptical, but game. Eventually she forgave me (I hope).

FALL RUN: Alongside SR 606

Gradient	Difficulty	Distance	Area	Scenery	Strainers	Rating
40	II-	0.6*	17	C	2-5/mi.	**

USGS Quad – Middletown; Source – Personal descent 4/04
N39 06.09, W78 22.25 to N39 05.85, W78 21.31

* (plus 0.4 miles on Cedar Creek)

This trip is best done as a continuation of a paddle down Furnace Run. Fall Run is just a tiny creek (5 sq. mi.) flowing southeast from Mountain Falls, until its confluence with Furnace Run, 0.8 miles before Cedar Creek, which almost triples its flow. Some 0.2 miles below the confluence, Fall Run flows beneath SR 606 – and from there to Cedar Creek is this Fall Run trip. The creek runs pretty straight, with good gradient, continuous riffles, easy rapids and a few play spots. Access at the confluence is difficult, so continue 0.4 miles down Cedar Creek to where SR 606 crosses on a paved ford (that is impossible whenever Cedar Creek is up). Be careful driving to the takeout, as you have to cross Fall Run on a low water bridge that will be under water.

GAUGE: You will want some 65 cfs on Hogue Creek, 50 cfs on Waites Run.

FURNACE RUN: SR 608 (Wardensville Grade) to Fall Run

Gradient	Difficulty	Distance	Area	Scenery	Strainers	Rating
35	II	2.7	10	B	2-5/mi.	**

USGS Quad – Hayfield/Middletown; Source – Personal descent 4/04
N39 08.16, W78 21.84 to N39 06.09, W78 22.25

This little creek flows south between Great and Little North mountains, and maintains its moderate gradient throughout. It starts out extremely narrow with overhanging bushes, but widens considerably in a quarter mile when a tributary enters. It is full of long riffles, with the only class II spots being a pair of small weirs early on, a slightly larger drop on the right-hand channel about midway, and a tricky turn amidst partial strainers just below the confluence with Fall Run. The creek channelizes only once; most of the water flows to the right, down a class II ledge.

The scenery is delightful, including several high cliffs on river left. In the last half mile, a few houses appear. There are quite a few downed trees, but the only evidence of fences was a cable we could pass beneath and the remains of a wooden fence. You can take out at SR 606, 0.2 miles below the confluence with Fall Run, or continue a further 0.6 miles down the latter plus 0.4 miles on Cedar Creek (see immediately above).

This is one of only two sixth-level creeks (i.e. tributary of a tributary of a tributary etc.) in this book – Furnace Run/Fall Run/Cedar Creek/North Fork/Shenandoah/Potomac.

GAUGE: The gauge on Hogue Creek should be above 85 cfs, and Waites Run 65 cfs. Where the creek (now Fall Run) crosses SR 606, zero level is 6 inches on the gauge on river left and zero on the gauge on river right.

The man who pulled up behind us was friendly, but told us that we had been trespassing by paddling the creek, and should not do it again. He pointed out that the creek was not "navigable," and that most of the land along it, including at the put in, was posted. He himself canoed, and was therefore sympathetic, but most of the landowners were very protective of their property, and wouldn't even allow neighbors to fish or gather mushrooms. He said that the people who owned the land by the put in would probably have called the police, except that it was a weekday and they were working. Much of the land had been bought up by new people, who were less neighborly than their predecessors.

FROMAN RUN: SR 629 (Laurel Grove Road) to SR 623 (Fromans Rd.)

Gradient	Difficulty	Distance	Area	Scenery	Strainers	Rating
35	?	3.1	9	?	?	?

USGS Quad – Hayfield/Middletown; Source – Scouting put in and take out
N39 07.64, W78 18.71 to N39 05.66, W78 19.85

This *"explorers' special,"* cuts through Little North Mountain. Put in at Fawcett Gap, a few yards above the confluence with Preffitt Run (the creek to the west). The take out is 300 yards above Cedar Creek – or you could continue 1.7 miles to Stephens Fort. This creek is likely to be a slightly smaller version of nearby Furnace Run.

GAUGE: Look for at least 120 cfs on Hogue Creek, 95 cfs on Waites Run.

⑾ PASSAGE CREEK

Passage Creek, a geographic oddity, flows northeast for 38 miles through the 4-mile wide Fort Valley (where George Washington planned to retreat for a final stand against the British, if necessary) in the middle of Massanutten Mountain (a contender to be the site of what became Shenandoah National Park, but beaten out by the larger and higher Blue Ridge). There is no room for major side streams; the largest ones, Little Passage Creek and Peters Mill Run, are too steep (over 200 ft/mile) and small (about 5 sq. mi.) even for this book.

Section 1 begins seven miles from the creek's source, where Passage Creek is joined by two tributaries, Mountain Run (coming down Little Fort Valley) and Duncan Hollow Run, which together almost double the volume. It is steep, hard to catch and seldom paddled, but definitely worth doing. Section 2 is much flatter, and has been paddled extensively. The Passage Creek gorge (section 3) is a very popular intermediate whitewater trip.

Section 1: Camp Roosevelt (SR 730) to Kings Crossing/Joppa Church (Stone Pillar Road, off St. David's Church Road - SR 769)

Gradient	Difficulty	Distance	Area	Scenery	Strainers	Rating
53 (90)	III-	3.4	13	B	2-3/mi.	***

USGS Quad – Hamburg/Edinburg/Rileyville; Source – Personal descent 4/02
N38 44.11, W78 31.14 to N38 45.95, W78 29.18

This delightful trip begins right at the confluence with Duncan Hollow Run. With enough water, Passage Creek looks tempting upstream as well, but the next good access is in 1.4 miles, with a drainage area of only 6 sq. mi. and a gradient of 105(200) ft/mile. Still, if you have the water and the skills, go exploring.

After a class II start, the creek braids a bit, with the attendant strainers and one very tricky drop as a result. Try to stay in the main channel, as the smaller ones get easily blocked. After about a quarter mile, the problems are over, and the fun begins. There are some long class III- rapids, starting at the footbridge, decent forward visibility, and only a few strainers. The drop in the first mile is 80 feet.

After 1.1 miles, you pass below SR 675. The remaining 2.3 miles are less challenging but just as continuous and enjoyable, and have a lower density of strainers. The class II+ rapids are long and varied (rock gardens, chutes, ledges), with numerous play spots. The scenery is remote and beautiful in places, but you also pass several houses. From the take out, the creek downstream looks lively as well, but the rapids end sooner than do the fences.

I only encountered one problem fence – a steel gate, visible upstream from the take out, which I could just squeeze through, after catching an eddy on the right. The earlier fences were of a rare type: a single cable, high enough to pass under, with flexible metal filaments hanging down. If those stop livestock from wandering, it is an ideal type of river fence, because boats just push the filaments aside.

GAUGE: Passage Creek at Buckton should be over 575 cfs (projected 4 hours ahead), Muddy Creek at Mt. Clinton 95 cfs, Waites Run 80 cfs. The rapid at the put in is a good indicator. The Camp Roosevelt rainfall gauge should register heavy rain.

Section 2: Kings Crossing (Joppa Church) to Elizabeth Furnace

Gradient	Difficulty	Distance	Area	Scenery	Strainers	Rating
13	II	21.3	25	B	1/mi.	**

USGS Quad – Rileyville/TomsBrook/Strasburg; Source – Grove, Corbett
N38 45.95, W78 29.18 via N38 48.73, W 78 27.00 (SR 775) and N38 51.29, W78 24.26 (SR 758) and N38 53.53, W78 22.23 (SR 772) to N38 55.76, W78 19.73

The creek is slowing down by the time it reaches Joppa Church, and is much easier to catch. The drainage area grows slowly but steadily, and the final part of section 2 is actually up more often than section 3 (because of its lower gradient). The rapids are mostly small ledges.

The prettiest section is the 6 miles from St. Davids Church (SR 775 – at the 5-mile mark) to Seven Fountains (SR 758). At higher levels, scout the SR 769 bridge, 1.5 miles below St. Davids Church, and portage left if necessary. Within the next mile, another bridge and a pair of farm fences may also require portages. If you don't take out at the second SR 758 bridge, you will have to portage it and a pair of cattle fences just downstream, on the left. Another good alternative is the final 5.5 miles of this section, from SR 772 to the Elizabeth Furnace picnic area, as that is both scenic and easier to catch up. Just watch out for the wrecked bridge a mile below the put in. And be wary of this stretch in high water, because of low bridges and other strainers.

GAUGE: Look for about 315 cfs on Passage Creek at Buckton or 45 cfs on Waites Run to put in at Kings Crossing, 180 cfs at Buckton or 25 cfs on Waites Run (or 4 foot vertical clearance under SR 775, at the 5-mile mark) for the lower section.

Section 3: Elizabeth Furnace to North Fork, Shenandoah River

Gradient	Difficulty	Distance	Area	Scenery	Strainers	Rating
40 (70)	III	6.8	83	B	<1/mi.	****

USGS Quad – Strasburg; Source – Personal descent often
N38 55.76, W78 19.73 via N38 57.08, W78 17.64 (SR 619) to N38 58.57, W78 16.20

This popular and delightful trip is not too hard to catch in wet years. The put in is from the Elizabeth Furnace parking area, a reminder of the days when these creeks were economic engines. The first mile and a half is rather quiet, but then you enter the gorge between Richardson Knob and Buzzard Rock, and the class III rapids come one after another. The best known are Z-Turn, below a rock shelf alongside the road on river left, and Out-of-Sight rapids, below a high rock wall on the right. Shortly below that comes another big drop, and then the creek swings back to the roadside. This is the first good takeout (with parking), for a 2.8-mile trip, which includes all of the class III drops.

The creek calms down for awhile, until a class II+ shortly before the 4-foot dam above the fish hatchery. Portage on the left or, with more than 350 cfs, run a sneak route there. Some paddlers run the dam on the left at the right levels. There are more long class II and II+ rapids down to and beyond SR 619 (Fish Hatchery Road) at the 3.6-mile mark. You can take out here, but it gets tricky at high levels, when the rapids before, under and below the bridge run together.

Below SR 619, there are some beautiful sloping shale cliffs on river right, with nice rapids leading to them. At the second of these cliffs, take the side channel on the left (whose entrance is often blocked by fallen trees), even though most of the water continues straight ahead. The reason for that choice becomes clear when you see a series of much narrower channels flowing back in from the right. The water reunites for awhile, but there are two briefer stretches of braiding below. Be very careful there, especially in high water, as strainers easily block these narrow routes. Class II rapids continue down to Va. 55 (5.4 miles), with a popular take out on upstream river right, but one that is sometimes contested by the local landowners. So the safer strategy is to continue down to the North Fork.

The remaining 1.4 miles down to the North Fork start off flat and between buildings, and there have also been occasional problems with the landowner here. But soon you reenter the woods, and some long riffles move you along quickly and pleasantly to the SR 610 low-water bridge. You can take out there or portage it and continue the final 200 yards to the North Fork, where there is better parking right at the confluence.

GAUGE: There are RC gauges at the put in and at Va. 55 (upstream river right), which have been adjusted from time to time as the river has changed after heavy floods. The on-line gauge on Passage Creek near Buckton (just above Va. 55) should be at least 140 cfs; 250 cfs equals 6 inches on the RC take-out gauge.

The **fish hatchery** here was one of the first in Virginia, established in 1933 for smallmouth bass and other species for stocking the public waters of Virginia.

SOUTH FORK SHENANDOAH BASIN

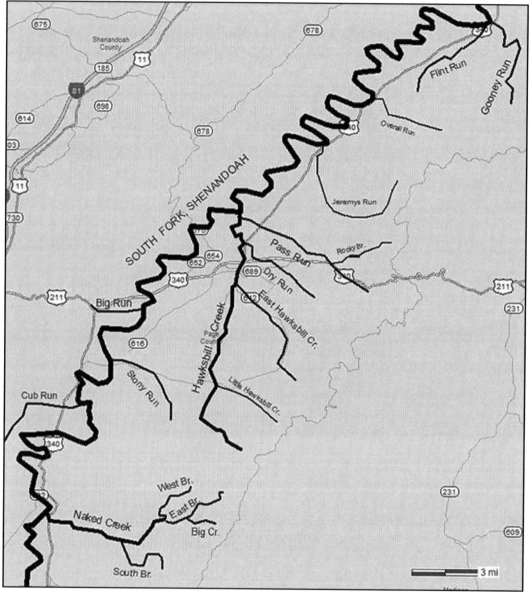

© Copyright 2005-2011 Undertow Software Corp.

> In 1716, Virginia Governor Spotswood crossed the Blue Ridge to the South Fork, which he named the **Euphrates River**. The early settlers, starting in the 1720s, were mostly German and Swiss farmers, who raised cattle and grain. They moved there from both the Virginia Piedmont and Pennsylvania, in order to get their own land. They were soon joined by "Scotch-Irish" – Scots who had been pushed off their land and had moved to Ireland in the 17th Century, but then found the American prospect more appealing.

Chapter 28:
SOUTH FORK SHENANDOAH BASIN

The basin of the South Fork, Shenandoah River covers 1,670 square miles and is popular with paddlers, from beginners to experts. The South Fork itself flows north-northeast for 100 miles (66 miles as the crow flies) from Port Republic (the confluence of the North and South rivers) to Front Royal (the confluence with the North Fork). It is the chief river for beginners (its average gradient is 5.5 ft/mile), with 8 canoe liveries totaling 400 boats catering to them.

Amongst its headwaters, the South River has some good novice sections, Back Creek is fun for low intermediates, and the North River gorge is one of the better high intermediate trips around. Other interesting upstream tributaries include the Dry and Little rivers and Briery and Jennings branches. But all of these streams are in the Staunton/Harrisonburg/Waynesboro area, well over two hours from Washington DC, and hence outside the geographic scope of this book – which includes the tributaries which enter during the final 75 miles.

Much closer to home **Gooney Run**, south of Front Royal, has become the first choice in small creeks among advanced paddlers from the Washington area. Gooney Run is described in detail in Grove and is summarized in this chapter as well.

Less well known to paddlers are a string of other creeks that flow down from the Blue Ridge to the South Fork. Driving southwest on US 340 (Stonewall Jackson Memorial Highway) from Front Royal to Luray, after passing Gooney Run, one crosses successively, *inter alia*, **Flint Run, Pass Run, Dry Run** and **Hawksbill Creek**. South of Luray lie **East Hawksbill Creek, Stony Run** (an "explorers' special") and **Naked Creek**. All of these, and **Naked Creek's East, West** and **South branches**, along with the East Branch's own headwater, **Big Creek**, are described below. Hawksbill Creek is by far the easiest to catch up, the only novice trip, and one of the most scenic, but has landowner problems. The longest intermediate run is on Naked Creek, where a trip of over 8 or 9 miles is feasible, starting on the East or West Branch; this small basin gives you a lot of options.

On the west side of the South Fork is Massanutten Mountain, and there is not enough space between them for major tributaries. The largest one, **Cub Run**, which drains an interior valley in the Massanutten chain, and the smaller **Big Run** are both "explorers' specials."

Most of the creeks in this chapter are small and steep (gradients above 70 ft/mile) until they reach the valley floor. If you go to paddle them, beware of the duplication of names. For example, upstream/south of Naked Creek (the southernmost tributary in this book), the South Fork has other tributaries named Cub Run, Stony Run, Dry Run and Hawksbill Creek.

This chapter covers Page and southern Warren Counties, and is centered on Luray. Because there is relatively little flat, fertile land between Massanutten Mountain and the Blue Ridge, the population density is low, and cattle (which, alas, mean fences) rather than crops predominate.

GAUGES: For the South Fork itself, the gauge near Luray (1,372 sq. mi.) is fine, being between the best paddling sections. For the smaller creeks, the situation is much more complicated and less satisfactory. The gauges on the South Fork headwaters, the North, South and Middle rivers, are too far away upstream. To the west, the nearest gauge is on Smith Creek (a North Fork tributary), but it is 94 sq. mi. A little farther is Linville Creek (also a North Fork tributary) with 46 sq. mi., while beyond that is Muddy Creek at Mt. Clinton (a North River tributary), with 14.3 sq. mi. To the east, across the Blue Ridge, are gauges at Ruckersville (Rapidan R., 115 sq. mi.), Locust Dale (Robinson R., 150 sq. mi.), Rixeyville (Hazel R., 283 sq. mi.) and Battle Run (26 sq mi), all in the Rappahannock Basin, but except for Battle Run (which is far from most of the South Fork tributaries), their catchments areas are large. Some combination of these gauges needs to be used to balance size with proximity, and rainfall to the east with that to the west.

In the table below, I use the **gauge on Muddy Creek at Mt. Clinton**, except that I use *Luray for the South Fork itself (in bold italics)* and Battle Run for Flint and Gooney runs (in bold, non-italic). In addition, both Page and Warren counties are covered by the AFWS, with eight rain gauges in the relevant area, and these are very useful for selecting and catching the smaller tributaries.

name	gradient	difficulty	length	area	gauge	rating
South Fk., Shen. - Sec. 1	7	I (II-)	8.5	1330	*280cfs*	*
- Sec. 2	4	I	11.2	1400	*265cfs*	*
- Sec. 3	5	I (II)	11.3	1530	*250cfs*	*
Naked Creek	50 (100)	III	6.5	18	85cfs	***
East Br., Naked Cr.	90	III+	1.5	8.3	110cfs	***
Big Creek	175	IV-	0.3	3.5	300cfs	!!!
West Br., Naked Cr.	110 (135)	III+	2.8	4.3	235cfs	***
South Br, Naked Cr.	75	III- (III)	1.6	9.1	150cfs	***
Cub Run	110 (150)	IV-(?)	2.3	15	100cfs	?
Stony Run	100 (175)	IV-(?)	2.2	5.5	225cfs	?
Big Run	75 (130)	?	2.0	8.4	150cfs	?
Hawksbill Creek	15	II	6.0	45	35cfs	**
East Hawksbill Cr.	100 (140)	III	3.4	4.4	250cfs	*
Dry Run - Section 1	73	III	2.5	11	85cfs	-
- Section 2	35 (60)	II	1.4	14	70cfs	-
Pass Run	75	II+	2.5	12	100cfs	***
Flint Run	37	II	1.6	14	125cfs	*
Gooney Run	75 (150)	IV- (IV+)	4.2	20	125cfs	!!!!

SOUTH FORK, SHENANDOAH RIVER

This popular beginner river has good scenery, frequent riffles and no serious hazards, and is usually runnable all summer. As a result, it is ideal for beginners, and there are canoe-rental companies for them. Included here are the three most popular runs; other sections are either flatter or interrupted by dams.

> The South Fork was a major **freight route** in the 19th Century. Iron, lumber and flour from the Blue Ridge and the Shenandoah Valley were shipped down to Harpers Ferry on flat wooden boats called **gundalows**, propelled by two huge oars. Water flow and economics dictated that these boats only travel downstream; at Harpers Ferry, they were either converted into houses or sold for lumber. Commerce later shifted to the **Shenandoah Valley Railroad**, which was completed in 1882. Building high trestles crossing the South Fork tributaries was the most expensive and time-consuming part of the construction; stop and admire them.

Section 1: Newport (US 340) to White House Landing (US 211)

Gradient	Difficulty	Distance	Area	Scenery	Strainers	Rating
7	I (II-)	8.5	1330	B	0	*

USGS Quad: Stanley/Hamburg; Source – Personal descent 7/02
N38 34.25, W78 35.78 to N38 38.75, W78 32.09

This section has the best gradient on the river (which indicates how flat the rest is) and lots of riffles. You can put in either at the campground (the GPS reference above) across from Kites Store, for a fee) or shortly downstream, where the road comes alongside the river. If you do the former, you get to run the class II- rapid at the remains of the Foltz Mill dam. Thereafter, there are only riffles formed by series of small ledges.

The take out is at an important river crossing, where there was a ferry service and then a covered bridge in the first half of the 19th Century. Stonewall Jackson burned the bridge in 1852, and floods washed away its replacement in 1870. Ferry service resumed until 1910, when a new bridge was built.

GAUGE: Zero level is about 280 cfs (2.2) at the Luray gauge. At high levels, the riffles wash out, but the strong current moves you along.

Section 2: Bixler Bridge (SR 675) to Goods Mill (SR 684)

Gradient	Difficulty	Distance	Area	Scenery	Strainers	Rating
4	1	11.2	1400	B	0	*

USGS Quad: Luray/Rileyville; Source – Personal descent 5/96
N38 42.08, W78 29.54 to N38 46.24, W78 24.36

Bixler Bridge is 3 miles northwest of Luray. This is a relatively long paddle at a low gradient. You could take out at Bealers Ferry after 8 miles (at SR 661), right after a half mile of riffles, but then you would miss the mile of riffles that ends at Goods Mill. The takeout is on private land; ask permission and pay a small fee in advance.

GAUGE: You will need about 265 cfs (2.1) on the Luray gauge.

Section 3: SR 663 (Island Ford Road) to Bentonville (SR 613)

Gradient	Difficulty	Distance	Area	Scenery	Strainers	Rating
5	I (II)	11.3	1530	B	0	*

USGS Quad: Rileyville/Bentonville; Source – Personal descent 7/80
N38 47.14, W78 23.58 to N38 50.49, W78 19.73

The put in is 4 miles after the section 2 takeout. About a mile after you put in, you come to the biggest drop on the entire South Fork, the class II Compton Rapid, recognized by the railroad bridge above a rock cliff on river right. The rapid is fairly steep but straightforward – just point downhill. A few miles later there is a 2-foot ledge near the village of Overall.

GAUGE: Minimum would be 250 cfs (2.0) on the Luray gauge.

NAKED CREEK: Jollett to Verbena (US 340)

Gradient	Difficulty	Distance	Area	Scenery	Strainers	Rating
50 (100)	III	6.5	18	C	0-2/mi.	***

USGS Quad – Elkton East; Source – Personal descent 11/03
N38 27.83, W78 31.39 to N38 27.91, W78 37.04

The first report I read on this creek was by a group of Coastal Canoeists, in an article entitled "I Paddled Naked!" It was long on humor, short on information. So I'll skip the sophomoric jokes and stick to the bare essentials.

Naked Creek is formed at the confluence of its East and West branches at Jollett, the junction of SR 759 and SR 607, and flows seven miles to the South Fork, near Shenandoah town. It is the second largest side stream (after Hawksbill Creek) to enter the South Fork. Its South Branch joins it after 2.5 miles at Furnace. From there to its mouth, Naked Creek forms the boundary between Page and Rockingham counties. Together with its three branches (described below), Naked Creek provides plenty of enjoyable intermediate whitewater after heavy rains.

Both the main stem and the branches have roads alongside; however, not all hazards are visible from them. Floods and subsequent bulldozing in 1995, 1996 and 2003 scoured this watershed. The ledges remain but the rock gardens were mostly replaced by steep cobble bars. The creek got quite wide, which makes it harder to catch.

This is a delightful trip, full of long class II and III rapids, with lots of play spots and virtually no flat water until the later stages. There is a quarter-mile set of class III ledges, about a half mile into the trip. Scout this from the road. A low water bridge two-thirds of a mile above Furnace should be portaged on the right. Shortly below, footbridges near the Naked Creek Baptist Church may require portaging. There is a class III rapid right above the confluence with the South Branch. The chute on the left is tight and steep, while that to the right of the island is more gradual but blind.

The South Branch adds 30-40% to the flow. The gradient drops, but the higher volume of water keeps the rapids lively. A low-water bridge after 2.1 miles is easily portaged. A half-mile later, right after a regular bridge, is the remains of another low-water bridge, with a class II+ chute on the far left. Scout this from the road. In the last mile is a pair of nice class II+ rock gardens. Take out on river left just before US 340.

This is a westward flowing creek, so you paddle into the sun in the afternoon, and the glare off the water makes reading the rapids difficult. Also, beware of several short stretches full of bushes growing in the streambed, as there are not always clear channels between them.

GAUGE: The Rapidan at Ruckersville, just across the Blue Ridge, should be at least 700 cfs (2 hours later). Look also for 85 cfs on Muddy Creek, 280 cfs on Linville Creek and 375 cfs on Smith Creek to the west. For rainfall, average the gauges at Big Meadows, Lewis Mountain Camp (Page Co.), Swift Run (Rockingham Co.) and Fork Mountain (Madison Co.).

A **fallen tree** blocked the right two-thirds of the channel, with its large root ball to the left. From our eddy 40 yards away on river right, it looked easy to get to the clear channel, by cutting left below some vines and hanging branches. Kevin Howe barely made it in his K-1; I assumed he had not bothered to work hard. Jamie Deehan almost made it in his OC-1, but the roots flipped him to the left; as a right-side paddler, he was weak bracing on the left. I saw Jamie swim, and had two choices. The portage past might take too long to be of help. Besides, "forewarned is forearmed," and I figured I would paddle harder and smarter. I thought I had it made, until the powerful left-to-right current hit me in the final seconds. Four days later, I pulled my misshapen boat off the tree with one finger.

The first permanent **European settlers** in the Shenandoah Valley, in the early 18th Century, lived near the mouth of Naked Creek. In 1803, the Verbena Mill was built (near what is now US 340). In 1836, the Forrer brothers constructed an **iron furnace** at what became the town of Shenandoah, and in 1857 built a second one at the confluence of Naked Creek and its South Branch, at a place still named Furnace, with a capacity of 3,000 tons of iron per year. The energy came from charcoal, which was gotten by denuding the forests. (So much for any salacious ideas about the origin of the creek's name!) It took about 8,000 acres to support one furnace, and the easiest access was to those near the creeks. The furnaces were operated until 1905, by which time the forests and iron-ore deposits were largely depleted. Except for limited farm and pastureland along the creeks, most of the land east of Furnace has returned to forest, much of it now within Shenandoah National Park.

EAST BRANCH, NAKED CREEK: Big Creek to Naked Creek

Gradient	Difficulty	Distance	Area	Scenery	Strainers	Rating
90	III+	1.5	8.3	C	1-3/mi.	***

USGS Quad – Elkton East; Source – Personal descent 1/98
N38 27.95, W78 30.11 to N38 27.83, W78 31.39

The East Branch flows for 6 miles, but there is no road access until its confluence with its principal tributary, Big Creek. The remaining 1.5 miles makes a great start to a trip down Naked Creek. This branch was less affected by the floods than its parent, so the scenery is still pretty, except for the pigsties. The rapids are continuous and range from class II+ to III+. Be careful approaching the bridge at 0.5 miles, where you have to catch a narrow chute between pourovers. More dangerous is the steep and narrow chute midway, where the main current flows beneath an undercut bank/tree root; a short portage on the right is the wise course. Just below that is a steep drop into a hole, which you can avoid by staying hard left. Because the water moves so fast and there are so few eddies, check carefully from the roadside for strainers.

GAUGE: This is the easiest of the three branches to catch – it needs only a little more water than the top part of Naked Creek, because its narrowness offsets its smaller drainage. Look for at least 900 cfs on the Rapidan at Ruckersville (3 hours later), 110 cfs on Muddy Creek and 360 cfs on Linville Creek (2 hours later). There are two nearby rainfall gauges: Lewis Mountain Camp (Page Co.) and Fork Mountain (Madison Co.).

BIG CREEK: First Low-Water Bridge to East Branch

Gradient	Difficulty	Distance	Area	Scenery	Strainers	Rating
175	IV-	0.3	3.5	B	0-7/mi.	!!!

USGS Quad – Elkton East/Fletcher; Source – Trip report (1/99) and road scouting
N38 27.74, W78 29.89 to N38 27.95, W78 30.11

This is an exciting way to begin a trip on the East Branch/Naked Creek. Just make sure that there is enough water, you have the skill, reflexes and experience to handle creeks like this, and there are no ill-placed strainers (check from the road).

Higher up, Big Creek's gradient is an even more daunting 265 ft/mile, and it is even tinier as it doesn't yet have the water from Little Creek. Big Creek is one of only two sixth-level creeks (tributary of a tributary of a tributary etc.) in this book (Big Creek/East Branch/Naked Creek/South Fork/Shenandoah/Potomac).

GAUGE: You need at least 300 cfs on Muddy Creek. Check the level from the road. Most relevantly, go right after heavy rainfall recorded on the AFWS gauges at Lewis Mountain Camp (Page Co.) and Fork Mountain (Madison Co.), both only 2-3 miles away.

WEST BRANCH, NAKED CR.: Shenandoah Park to Naked Cr.

Gradient	Difficulty	Distance	Area	Scenery	Strainers	Rating
110 (135)	III+	2.8	4.3	C	2-4/mi.	***

USGS Quad – Elkton East; Source – Personal descent 9/04
N38 29.13, W78 30.08 to N38 27.83, W78 31.39

This is the hardest to catch of the three main Naked Creek tributaries, but you can get the longest run on it. Start at end of the road, where SR 607 is replaced by a hiking trail into Shenandoah National Park. The first mile, at 135 ft/mile, is pretty continuous, with a few spots class III+, especially a steep chute on the left followed by large boulders. Being very narrow, it tends to have strainers, so approach turns with caution.

After a mile, Harris Cove Run adds about 40% to the flow, and the creek widens out and slows to 100 ft/mile. There are fewer strainers and most of the rapids are no more than class III-. But scout one class III drop between large boulders, shortly before the creek leaves the road, where you should stay right. It has a tricky entry and a squeeze between rocks below the main drop. At 2 miles, the creek leaves the road and you get more of a wilderness feel. Soon thereafter the stream drops steeply around an island; the left channel is more straightforward (if it is not blocked by a strainer). A rocky island a bit later also splits a steep rapid – most water goes to the left. Just above the confluence, check in advance for fences (there in 1998 but gone in 2004) and narrow culverts.

GAUGE: Look for 235 cfs on Muddy Creek, 750 cfs on Linville Creek and 1,900 cfs on Rapidan at Ruckersville. Big Meadows (Page Co.) rainfall gauge is two miles north of the headwaters. We had a bony run the day after 8 inches of rain!

SOUTH BRANCH, NAKED CREEK: SR 607 to Furnace

Gradient	Difficulty	Distance	Area	Scenery	Strainers	Rating
75	III- (III)	1.6	9.1	C	0-2/mi.	***

USGS Quad – Elkton East; Source – Personal descent 9/04
N38 25.63, W78 32.99 to N38 26.82, W78 33.77

This delightful stream only flows 5.5 miles, but it contains enough tributaries (including one called Big Ugly Run, which comes out of Shenandoah National Park) to occasionally be up. Despite having a slightly larger drainage area, it is harder to catch than the East Branch because it is wider.

Follow SR 606 up the creek from Furnace, across the bridge and a little past the private bridge, and park on the grass shoulder, shortly before the one creek-side house, where the road turns sharply to the right (and gets promoted to SR 607). The put in is ugly, down a steep, trash-encrusted bank, but the trip is delightful after that.

You start off in a straight class II section, but soon reach a sharp turn to the left, where some side channels meander off through the woods. This marks a steep, class III rapid, ending in a cut back to the right. A quarter mile later is the road bridge. In low or moderate water, you can paddle under it, running the 3-foot ledge at the end, followed by a lively class III- rapid. After that, the creek is pool and drop, with the rapids class II+, except for a class III- after the final bridge, as the South Branch drops into Naked Creek. You can take out a quarter mile later, or continue down Naked Creek.

The South Branch is the border between Page and Rockingham counties, which helps account for the absence of fences across it. We had to portage only one downed tree, but I saw four from the road on an earlier scouting trip.

GAUGE: You will want at least 150 cfs on Muddy Creek, 500 cfs on Linville Creek and 1,300 cfs on the Rapidan at Ruckersville. The rainfall gauges are Lewis Mountain Camp (Page Co.) just to the east and Swift Run (Rockingham Co.) five miles to the southwest.

CUB RUN: Pitt Spring Run (SR 685) to SR 613 (Strole Farm Road)

Gradient	Difficulty	Distance	Area	Scenery	Strainers	Rating
110(150)	IV-(?)	2.3	15*	?	?	?

USGS Quad – Tenth Legion/Stanley; Source – Partial scouting
N38 33.29, W78 38.23 to N38 33.26, W78 35.91

*(including 2.5 from Roaring Run, after one-quarter mile)

This *"explorers' special"* drains a little valley between Massanutten and First Mountain (a ridge southeast of and parallel to Massanutten Mountain). Small as it is, it is the largest tributary to enter the South Fork (which flows for 103 miles) from river left. It flows north-northeast, picks up Pitt Spring Run at the put in, and a quarter mile later Roaring Run, right at Catherine Furnace; together, they almost double its volume.

At Catherine Furnace, Cub Run swings 90-degrees to head due east through a gap in First Mountain, past US 340 and down to the South Fork. The creek looked to me (with minimal water) like class III from Pitt Spring Run to Catherine Furnace, class IV- for the next 100 yards, and then class III again.

Take out at SR 613, one-third mile above the South Fork. If you continue beyond, the alternatives are (a) paddle a mile of dead water behind the Massanutten power dam, plus another three-fourths mile on the South Fork down to Newport, or (b) take out just across from the mouth of Cub Run, which adds 7 miles to the shuttle each way.

Depending on the water level and your derring-do, you can put in higher up along Cub Run Road. The 1.5 miles from the campground (6.5 sq. mi.) to Pitt Spring Run averages 135 ft/mile and reaches 200 ft/mile; above, the creek is even steeper.

GAUGE: Linville Creek should be over 350 cfs and Muddy Creek at Mt. Clinton 100 cfs. You will need a bit more to start above Catherine Furnace.

Catherine Furnace, named for Catherine Forrer (whose family owned several iron works), is one of the best-preserved iron furnaces in the valley. It shipped pig iron downriver by Gundalow, some of it to Speedwell Forge #1 on Hawksbill Creek. Its shot and shell were used in the Mexican War of 1846-48 and later by the Confederacy.

STONY RUN: Twin Valley Church to SR 638 (Honeyville Road)

Gradient	Difficulty	Distance	Area	Scenery	Strainers	Rating
100 (175)	IV-(?)	2.2	5.5	?	?	?

USGS Quad – Stanley; Source – Scouting first 1.2 miles from road
N38 32.59, W78 30.79 to N38 34.20, W78 31.25

The two branches of Stony Run race northward 2.5 miles down Cubbage and Basin Hollows, at gradients of 150-200 ft/mile, to their confluence at the Twin Valley Church, between Roundhead Mountain and Dog Slaughter Ridge. (One day, when everything was in flood, Jamie Deehan and I looked at the Basin Hollow [east] branch; however, it was too steep and narrow, with more strainers than eddies.)

The initial 1.2 miles of this *"exlorers' special"* be seen from SR 621. The creek is narrow and very steep, especially around the half-mile mark where it goes under SR 621. Just before the stream leaves the road, there is a 20-foot waterfall through a broken dam; get out well above and portage (or take out for good) on the left. This waterfall lands on solid rock, and there is a nasty chunk of cement sticking out halfway down.

Below the dam, the gradient remains 100 ft/mile for the next mile, past several farmhouses and under the railway tracks. Expect fallen trees and maybe fences. The take out at SR 638 looks OK, but do not miss the eddy there, as barbed-wire awaits below.

GAUGE: You will need about 225 cfs on Muddy Creek at Mt. Clinton and 1,700 cfs on the Rapidan at Ruckersville (3 hours later).

Below SR 638, it is another 3.5 miles to the South Fork, with a gradient that averages 75 ft/mile and reaches 150 ft/mile. Those data may be appealing, but this stretch begins with barbed wire fences in farming country, has many fallen trees in the middle reaches, and has really trashy scenery down below. Skip it.

BIG RUN: US 340 to SR 615 (Longs Road; 2nd intersection)

Gradient	Difficulty	Distance	Area	Scenery	Strainers	Rating
75 (130)	?	2.0	8.4	?	?	?

USGS Quad – Hamburg; Source – Scouting put in and take out
N38 38.03, W78 34.80 to N38 37.96, W78 32.84

This *"explorers' special"* drops 120 feet in the first mile but only 30 in the second. The put in is a busy spot, where US 340 and US 211 meet, as well as Big Run and its main tributary, Browns Run. You start alongside US 211 and continue east. You cross SR 615 in 0.7 miles and then again at 2 miles; take out there, as it is just a flat quarter mile to the South Fork.

GAUGE: Look for 150 cfs on Muddy Creek and 430 cfs on Linville Creek 2 hours after put in.

HAWKSBILL CREEK: Luray (Linden Ave.) to Pass Run (SR 648)

Gradient	Difficulty	Distance	Area	Scenery	Strainers	Rating
15	II	6.0	45	A-D	<1/mi.	**

USGS Quad – Luray; Source – Personal descent 9/99
N38 39.56, W78 27.71 to N38 42.51, W78 27.37

Hawksbill Creek rises in Big Meadows off the Skyline Drive, drops over Lewis Spring Falls (an 80-foot cascade) and flows north to Luray and the South Fork, a total of almost 20 miles. It is by far the largest creek to enter the South Fork in its entire 103 miles between Port Republic and Front Royal. It becomes occasionally runnable below the confluence with Little Hawksbill Creek (which looks very dangerous; 1.4 miles from Bethlehem Church to SR 626, with 5 sq. mi. and 160 ft/mi.), but flows through farmland and fences. At the southern edge of Luray, after 13 miles, it meets East Hawksbill Creek, backs up behind a farm dam and drops 3 feet over cement to the put in.

The trip starts out with pleasant riffles, and then flows through downtown Luray alongside US Bus 340 and a bicycle trail. There is a class II rapid directly under US 211. The scenery gradually improves, as does the bird life. At 2.3 miles, Dry Run joins. (An alternative put in is SR 718 on Dry Run, 350 class II yards above the confluence; rusty barbed wire hidden in the weeds sent me for a tetanus shot.) Hawksbill Creek then twists everywhichway on its journey north, with high rocky cliffs (some with small caves) first on one side and then the other. Class I gravel bars are frequent, and there is one bouncy class II, as well as a short section of narrow, twisty channels, with partial strainers likely.

The creek then enters ranchland, where you may share the water with cattle. The wire fences were easily paddled over when we were here, but that could change.

Finally, a mile before the South Fork, take out at SR 648, at the confluence with Pass Run, to avoid an unrunnable 10-foot dam, unfriendly landowners and two miles of flat water on the South Fork (or a long shuttle to its other bank).

GAUGE: You will need 110 cfs on Linville Creek, 280 cfs on the Rapidan at Ruckersville, 360 cfs on the Robinson near Locust Dale and 60 cfs on Battle Run.

> **Hawksbill Mountain**, at 4,049 feet the highest point in Shenandoah National Park, when viewed from the east side of New Market Gap, resembles the head and beak of a raptor.
>
> **Luray Caverns**, discovered 1878, is the biggest tourist attraction in the valley. Its stalagmites and stalactites are still growing, at one cubic inch every 120 years. The "Stalacpipe Organ" is particularly unusual.
>
> I had no problems in three trips on Hawksbill Creek, but a land owner informed Roger Corbett that the creek flows through land where ownership of the creek itself was conveyed in the initial title from the British throne (a "**King's Grant**"), and that the land owners near the take out had decided to allow no outside use. So if you don't want to risk being hassled, ask permission at the house by the take out.

EAST HAWKSBILL CR.: Ida (SR 689) to Stony Man (SR 611)

Gradient	Difficulty	Distance	Area	Scenery	Strainers	Rating
100(140)	III	3.4	4.4	C	2-6/mi.	*

USGS Quad – Big Meadows/Luray; Source – Personal descent 6/01
N38 35.35, W78 25.43 to N38 37.79, W78 26.02

This creek is wonderful for whitewater and miserable for fences. It starts off a pure delight, 140 ft/mile for the first mile, continuous class II-III, with just enough visibility that you don't have to stop to scout. But at 0.7 miles, the problems begin: a fence, a low-water bridge, a second fence, some downed trees, another fence and on and on. Altogether, we encountered 7 fences plus almost as many downed trees, as well as 2 low-water bridges, which together ruined a bunch of good rapids. Still, in between was a lot of nice action, including several class IIIs. The creek slows down gradually, and the last mile and a half was class II, with no more downed trees, but still some fences. The scenery is very nice in spots, but deteriorates in the latter half, as it gets into farm and ranch country. In summer, there are lots of bushes growing in the creek, which are entertaining in one sense, but cut down severely on visibility. Also, the creek braids in a few places, with the main flow usually going to the left, and downed trees tend to lurk there. The put in and take out are fine, and the shuttle is quick.

The 0.9 miles above Ida average 220 ft/mile, and looks like continuous class IV, with tree strainers but probably no fences. It requires considerably more water. Below the take-out hamlet of Stony Man, the creek flows through 2.5 miles of farmland, at 45 ft/mile, with frequent fences, down to Hawksbill Creek at Luray; it's a section well worth skipping.

GAUGE: You need heavy rainfall at Ida (Page Co.) Look for 800 cfs on Linville Creek (2 hours later), 250 cfs on Muddy Creek at Mt. Clinton and 2,000 cfs on the Rapidan at Ruckersville (4 hours later). At the take-out bridge, the water should be up to the bottom of the white drainpipe in the upstream river right pillar. At the put in, the creek should be cleanly runnable looking downstream, but need not be so upstream.

> The headwaters of East Hawksbill Creek stretch along the **Blue Ridge** from Skyland to Hawksbill Mountain. From the end of SR 629, one can take the Timber Hollow Trail to the creek's source at the Hawksbill Spring. Nearby are the Appalachian Trail, a side trail that ascends Hawksbill Mountain, and the Cedar Run trail down to the Robinson River. The Pollocks developed Skyland in the early 20th Century as a resort, a little south of Stony Man Mountain. The stone structure they built in 1918 as their home, Massanutten Lodge, still stands as a historic structure. The resort helped popularize the Shenandoah Mountains and build support for a national park there.
>
> The lady who owns the land by the put in (and lives in the house on upstream right), came down to warn us of copperhead snakes in the area; we were therefore quite careful at our many portages. She was quite friendly, being a canoeist herself.

DRY RUN

Dry Run drains the Blue Ridge between Pass Run and East Hawksbill Creek, and heads northwest to Hawksbill Creek. But while it is useful for access to lower Hawksbill Creek, and has some decent rapids, the hazards and nuisances outweigh the joys.

Section 1: SR 611 (Brookstone Road) to Luray (top of Stoney Brook Lane)

Gradient	Difficulty	Distance	Area	Scenery	Strainers	Rating
72	III	2.5	11	D	3-7/mi.	-

USGS Quad – Luray; Source – Personal descent 6/97
N38 39.06, W78 24.43 to N38 40.33, W78 25.85

Put in on SR 611, shortly after the South and North forks enter. Dry Run itself is dammed (to create the Luray Reservoir) a half mile above the confluences, and damned by any paddlers below that for its downed trees and two low-water bridges. SR 667 parallels the creek, so you can scout much of it from your car. The only nice part is the final half mile, after passing US Business 211 and SR 656, which lacked strainers and culminates in a class III broken ledge, best run left of center. Take out just below that ledge, to avoid a stretch with dangerous braiding below.

The scenery is rotten – the backsides of buildings, discarded machinery and lots of downed trees. The creek was channelized after the 1996 floods, and there were banks of piled gravel, and trees that were bulldozed together out of the streambed.

GAUGE: Linville Creek needs 275 cfs, the Rapidan at Ruckersville 700 cfs and the Robinson 900 cfs (both 2 hours later).

Section 2: Luray (end of Stoney Brook Lane) to SR 718 (off US 340)

Gradient	Difficulty	Distance	Area	Scenery	Strainers	Rating
35 (60)	II	1.4	14	C	3-7/mi.	-

USGS Quad – Luray; Source – Personal descent 2/98
N38 40.41, W78 26.23 to N38 41.18, W78 27.09

This is a much calmer section than its predecessor and it requires a little less water, but it has few appeals. Put in by a private bridge at the end of Stoney Brook Lane; don't start a third of a mile upstream at the beginning of Stoney Brook Lane (the section 1 take out), because in between the creek braids in the woods, ending in very dangerous, strainer-blocked drops. But even without that stretch, there are dangers galore – three fences, two low-water bridges near the end, and, except where the creek has been channelized, slalom routes between standing trees. And the rapids are no great shakes either. Take out at SR 718, just before US 340, unless you plan to continue down Hawksbill Creek.

GAUGE: Linville Creek needs 225 cfs, the Rapidan at Ruckersville 570 cfs, the Robinson 750 cfs (the latter two, 1-2 hours later).

PASS RUN: Bethlehem Church to SR 656

Gradient	Difficulty	Distance	Area	Scenery	Strainers	Rating
75	II+	2.5	12	C	1-3/mi.	***

USGS Quad – Luray; Source – Personal descent 10/95
N38 40.43, W78 22.95 to N38 41.57, W78 25.18

US 211 through Thornton Gap is one of only two east-west routes across the 65-mile long Shenandoah National Park. On the east side of the Blue Ridge, the popular Thornton River tumbles down from Thornton Gap; on the west side, it is the virtually unknown Pass Run. (Pass Mountain is two miles north of Thornton Gap.)

Pass Run races for 1.5 miles alongside US 211, past the Park headquarters. Just below Bethlehem Church, it is doubled in size by Rocky Branch, and slows to a gentler pace. At Bethlehem Church, a short spur connects US 211 and SR 658. Pass Run and Rocky Branch cross this spur 70 yards apart, and you can put in on either (they meet in 200 yards). When there is enough water to paddle, both creeks will be up over the road.

From Bethlehem Church, it is almost 5 miles to where Pass Run flows into Hawksbill Creek north of Luray, but only the first half is worth paddling, because the creek moves from woods to ranchland and farmland, with fences and small dams.

GAUGE: Look for at least 300 cfs on Linville Creek, 750 cfs on the Rapidan at Ruckersville, 1,000 cfs on the Robinson (the latter two, 2 hours later).

The first official **road across the Blue Ridge** was built through Thornton Gap and down along Pass Run, starting in 1740. Because wagons kept getting mired in the mud, it was paved with stone starting in 1786 by a private partnership, which charged a 25c toll for wagons and stagecoaches. A major widening (to 18 feet) and relocation (to reduce the maximum grade to 4 degrees) was undertaken in 1849.

In really high water, if you want to go further upstream, try **Rocky Branch** (4.5 sq. mi.) rather than the top part of Pass Run (which exceeds 200 ft/mile within a half mile above Bethlehem Church). You can follow SR 612 upstream for 1.3 miles, with an average gradient of 100 ft/mile. But scout carefully for strainers as well as a hazardous bridge underpass, as the creek is very narrow with only tiny eddies. This is a sixth level creek – Rocky Branch/Pass Run/Hawksbill Creek/South Fork/Shenandoah/Potomac.

Just north of Pass Run, **Jeremys Run** swings for 11 miles in a half arc from the Blue Ridge to the South Fork. The first 7 miles, within Shenandoah National Park, can be seen from the beautiful Jeremys Run Trail, which connects Skyline Drive with Jeremys Run Drive.

Our attempt to canoe this creek is summarized in the doggerel about Pass Run. The landowner had agreed to let us leave our shuttle cars there, until I opened my big mouth and asked whether anyone else had paddled Jeremys Run. "I thought you were going to paddle the South Fork," he said. "I can't let you paddle Jeremys Run; it goes through private property."

In retrospect, we were lucky. Soon after the creek crosses Jeremys Run Drive, there was a massive logjam. Then, the creek was separated from the road by a high, barbed-wire fence, and there were several barbed-wire fences across it, connected to other barbed-wire fences.

The first trip of the day was done, Survival test on Gooney Run,
The finest small stream that I know, Where Washington-based paddlers go,
And it was only half past two, Ron Knipling asked, "What's next to do?"

Now paddling books are all replete, With Rappa tribs, and some are neat,
But you can scarcely find a smidge, On what flows west off the Blue Ridge,
These South Fork trips that most have missed, Can be canoed, I had my list.

Jeremys Run was first in mind, A lovely takeout we did find,
Alas, the owner of that land, Said paddling private land was banned,
Frank Fico said "this creek let's shun," We headed south, down to Pass Run.

Pass Run is not in any book, Like Grove or Corbett, take a look,
Our put in was about halfway, Between Thornton Gap and Luray,
Where Rocky Branch 'longside does flow, 'til it meets Pass Run just below.

With gradient seventy-five, Bob Kimmel said, "This creek's alive,"
Small drops and waves continuous, But class III rapids we did miss,
Because, Ed Gertler soon surmised, The creek had once been channelized.

Barbed wire fences we did fear, After mile one some did appear,
Two needed lifting to pass under, (A high-water trip would be a blunder),
Of other strainers there were few, In fact I counted only two.

The stretch we chose was some 4K, (2.5 miles, the English way),
To Route 656 took one hour, We headed home, to eat and shower,
Pass Run had been a pleasant way, To end a super paddling day.

> **Overall Run**, between Jeremys and Flint Runs, is tiny (5 sq. mi.) and steep (120 ft/mile in its final, flattest mile). It forms the boundary between Warren and Page counties. At 93 feet, Overall Run Falls is the highest waterfall in the Park. The Overall Run Trail follows the stream within the Park, but there is no road access to the creek until near its mouth.
>
> The **Overall family** traces back in England to one Adam de Overhalle (large hall, but not a castle) in the 13th Century. A 17th Century bishop, John Overall, wrote The Convocation Book, setting forth the divine origin of government, which gained such favor with Virginia Governor John Spotswood, that he gave a large land patent to the family, which settled in the Valley in the 1730s, and developed a 40-sq. mi. plantation on the south bank of Overall Run. In 1871, it was divided among descendents, who sold off much of it to other families and lost other parts to squatters. (See Darwin Lambert's *The Undying Past of Shenandoah National Park*, 1989.)

FLINT RUN: Limeton (SR 622 – Buck Mountain Road) to US 340

Gradient	Difficulty	Distance	Area	Scenery	Strainers	Rating
37	II	1.6	14	B	3-5/mi.	*

USGS Quad – Bentonville; Source – Personal descent 6/97
N38 51.00, W78 16.44 to N38 51.74, W78 15.56

Flint Run is the closest creek to Gooney Run, but only geographically. It enters the South Fork less than a half mile upstream of Gooney Run, but it is a pale shadow of its neighbor. Its two main arms come together at the put in near Limeton, just two miles from the South Fork. And the last 0.4 miles is more trouble than it's worth; I encountered three fences in the first half of that stretch, and then soon reached the backwater of the South Fork. So skip this by taking out at US 340 (upstream river right).

The trip starts out with a few class II rapids, visible from the road, and then goes through a cow pasture guarded by board fences (which can be swung up to permit a boat to pass) at both ends. The creek then enters the woods, which continue almost to the take out. There are frequent class II rapids, and in shallow water one has to work hard to keep from being swept under stream-bank branches. There are several strainers and one section where one-third of the water takes a short cut to the left (which paddlers should avoid). The best rapid, a 50-yard class II, is shortly before the take out.

GAUGE: Flint Run has only two-thirds the watershed of Gooney Run, but it is just as easy to catch because it is much less steep. Look for 135 cfs on Battle Run.

> Flint Run was a **major archaeological site**. Early Indians had a jasper quarry and knapping (tool-making by chipping) site here, both before and during the Clovis period (circa 11,500 years ago) when spear points sharp enough to kill large mammals were developed.

GOONEY RUN: Boyds Mill (SR 622) to Campground (US 340)

Gradient	Difficulty	Distance	Area	Scenery	Strainers	Rating
75(150)	IV- (IV+)	4.2	20	A	<1/mi.	!!!!

USGS Quad – Chester Gap/Bentonville; Source – Personal descent 10/95; Grove N38 50.09, W78 13.93 to N38 52.13, W78 15.01

This is **the** small creek for advanced/expert boaters in the Washington D.C. area. A high water, pleasant day in January 1995, for example, found 30 boats at the put-in at the same time, ready to test their skills against its 15 or so class III and above rapids.

The usual put in is Boyds Mill, 1.5 miles below Browntown. This leaves two miles for warm up. SR 649 runs alongside the creek for the first mile, to Glen Echo, where the creek veers left and the road right. The next mile is still mild – 40 ft/mile, but the anticipation grows.

And then ... boom! After just a short lead-in rapid, which you had better recognize, you are at the top of First Falls, the hardest (class IV+) and most dangerous spot on the river, with a heavily undercut boulder in the center. Pull over to scout and/or portage. At low to moderate levels, there is no clean line, but expert closed and open boaters have run this. About 30 yards below is Second Falls, the second hardest rapid (class IV), with several very tight routes. This should also be scouted in advance and/or portaged.

The next two miles are full of long class III to IV- rock gardens. Scouting would take forever, so most advanced paddlers just work their way through them, but you'll want someone up front who knows the creek and can keep an eye out for strainers. This creek produces many strainers – about 10 were found by the first groups to run it in January 1999, for example – but the density of paddlers keeps that of strainers down.

You can take out at the Gooney Creek (sic) Campground ($1/person, payable at the house there), or continue the final third of a mile to Karo Landing on the South Fork; however, there is limited parking at the latter, and when the South Fork is up, Karo Landing is often flooded out.

GAUGE: The Battle Run gauge should read at least 125 cfs (2.6). There are RC gauges at the put in and US 340 bridges; however, the latter, may be distorted by the backwater from the South Fork. There are often postings on the MCC board.

A number of gristmills were built along Gooney Run, and one of these sites grew into **Browntown**, which rivaled Front Royal as a regional center in the late 19th Century. Its largest industry, starting in 1874, was a tannery, which employed over 150 people; but within 30 years, it had drained the area of chestnut oaks, whose bark provided the tannin.

Gooney Run Manor was part of the vast Northern Neck Proprietary, granted in the mid-17th Century to seven court favorites by Kings Charles I and II. (Originally this was limited to the Northern Neck, the peninsula between the lower Potomac and Rappahannock Rivers, but later expanded westward.) By 1670, Lord Culpeper had control of the area, and it passed on to the Fifth Lord Fairfax when he married Lord Culpeper's daughter, Catherine. Their son, the Sixth Lord Fairfax, is believed to have given the creek its current name, when his favorite hunting hound, Gooney, drowned in it. Chief Justice John Marshall and his brother James later purchased 120,000 acres in the area, including Gooney Run Manor.

MAIN STEM SHENANDOAH BASIN

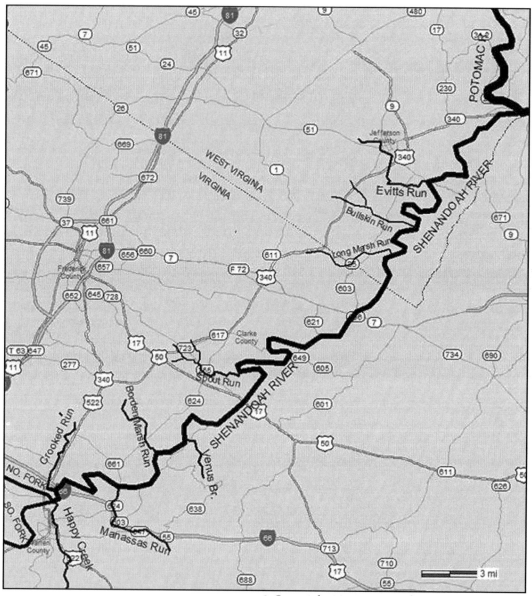

© Copyright 2005-2011 Undertow Software Corp.

Chapter 29:
MAIN STEM SHENANDOAH BASIN

The Shenandoah ("daughter of the stars") River, the Potomac's largest tributary, is formed at Front Royal, at the confluence of its North and South forks, with about two-thirds of the flow from the latter. The main stem then heads north-northeast through a narrow watershed, averaging only 10 miles wide, which is why there are no major tributaries along its 55 miles (the first 35 in Virginia, the rest in West Virginia) as it heads to Harpers Ferry – and hence why this is not a long chapter. The main stem is flat (4 ft/mile) for the first 48 miles, until it begins cutting down to the Potomac at **Snyders Falls** (section 1). Then, after a mile of backwater, comes the 15-foot Snyders Hill Dam, which requires a long portage. There is an almost inaccessible rapid, one more mile of flat water, and then the put in for the **Shenandoah Staircase** (section 2), one of the most popular novice/intermediate trips at low water and advanced trips at high water.

Just 2-4 miles to the southeast of the main stem is the Blue Ridge, with the Appalachian Trail on top. The only place where there is room for sizable tributaries is just south and east of Front Royal, where the valley is about twice as wide. **Happy Creek** and **Manassas Run**, a pair of exciting whitewater trips, are located here. A little further north, **Venus Branch** (an "explorers' special") can be run for almost a mile, at 90 ft/mile, but it drains only 6 sq. mi. Beyond that, the tributaries are even smaller.

On the northwest side of the Shenandoah is rolling farmland, with only a low ridge before the next valley, that of Opequon Creek. Here the basin is 6-8 miles wide, with consequent room for larger tributaries; however, from a whitewater paddling perspective, this is more than offset by the much lower gradient and the frequency of both fences and tree strainers. The largest stream is **Crooked Run**, just north of Front Royal, which is easy to catch, but has minimal whitewater. Tiny **Borden Marsh Run** (an "explorers' special") has a mile-long gorge with a road alongside, a class IV rapid and several strainers. Further north, there are four medium-sized creeks (about 20 sq. mi. apiece) that all have decent but very short (quarter mile on average) final gorges as they cut down to the Shenandoah, and lots of junk up above. Of these, I have run and written up **Spout** and **Evitts runs** – but except for their final bits (which are much too short to justify the trips), I do not recommend them. Bullskin Run, the site of the first land that George Washington bought (1,000 acres, at the age of 18), can be paddled just its last third of a mile (above, it is full of fences), while the only access to Long Marsh Run involves paddling through a mile of farmland to get to its quarter mile of semi-gorge.

GAUGES: The Staircase has its own gauge, at *Millville* – used in the table below, in ***bold italics, just for the Shenandoah***. There is also one on **Spout Run** (21.4 sq. mi.), which is centrally located **and is used for all the other creeks** in the table below. For the steeper trips in the south (especially Happy and Manassas runs) the Rappahannock basin gauge on Battle Run (26 sq. mi.) is also very useful. There are rainfall gauges (Warren County) in the Happy Creek, Manassas Run and Crooked Run headwaters.

name	gradient	difficulty	length	area	gauge	rating
Shenandoah - Section 1	50	II+	0.2	3,050	*1000cfs*	**
- Section 2	12 (20)	II (II+)	4.2	3,058	*1000cfs*	***
Happy Creek - Sec. 1	92(150)	III+ (IV)	4.4	7	200cfs	***
- Sec. 2	40	II-	1.3	15	115cfs	*
Crooked Run	9	I (II-)	2.8	41	45cfs	-
Manassas Run	82	III	2.8	8	190cfs	***
Borden Marsh Run	75	II+(IV)?	0.8	9	190cfs	?
Venus Branch	90	?	0.9	6	300cfs	?
Spout Run	27 (60)	II (5.0)	3.1	19	130cfs	-
Evitts Run	40(100)	II	1.8	18	100cfs	-

SHENANDOAH RIVER

For most whitewater paddlers, the Shenandoah is synonymous with the Staircase (section 2). However, there is also a class II+ rapid above that, called Snyders Falls (section 1); unfortunately, it cannot be run without either paddling a mile of backwater down to the Snyder Hill (power) Dam or carrying/attaining back up. There is also a long class II- rapid below the dam that is rarely run because it washes out at high water, it is dry at low water when the power plant is running, and you have to portage and then paddle upstream to get to the top of it (it is separated from the portage route on river left by the spillway).

Above Snyders Falls there are only occasional riffles, over 48 miles.

Section 1: Snyders Falls

Gradient	Difficulty	Distance	Area	Scenery	Strainers	Rating
50	II+	0.2	3050	B	0	**

USGS Quad – Charles Town; Source – Personal descent 5/04
N39 15.81, W77 47.46 (attain, drag or carry back up)

This 150-yard rapid has many routes. The right side is more gradual and shallower, so it is a good alternative at high water. The left side starts easy, with eddies and surfing spots, and then gets steeper and more continuous towards the end. There are several routes between the boulders on the far left, but the more usual way is down the more open area, left of center. Experienced paddlers can boat-scout on the way down.

This nice rapid is seldom run because of the dilemma of what to do at the end. One option is to paddle almost a mile of dead water towards the spillway, where you park by following signs to "Fishermen Access." (You could also then do a half-mile portage on river left, along a Potomac Edison Company trail, and then paddle another flat mile to the start of section 2.) The better option is to work your way back up, and then do a short shuttle to section 2. There is a trail close to the shore on river left, but beware of poison ivy and sometimes of "No Trespassing" signs; for open boats in warm weather and low water, it is often easier to drag back up through the water along the river left shore.

GAUGE: Similar to section 2 – you want at least 1,000 cfs at Millville.

Section 2: Millville to Potomac River (the Shenandoah Staircase)

Gradient	Difficulty	Distance	Area	Scenery	Strainers	Rating
12 (20)	II (II+)	4.2*	3058	B	0	***

USGS Quad – Charles Town/Harpers Ferry; Source – Personal descent often
N39 17.18, W77 47.41 to N39 19.22, W77 42.71

*(plus 0.8 miles on the Potomac to Potoma Wayside at the mouth of Piney Run)

The Shenandoah Staircase, one of the region's classic paddles, is in numerous guidebooks. It is popular with kayaks and canoes, rafts and inner tubes. The Shenandoah portion is in West Virginia, the Potomac in Maryland, and the best take out in Virginia. And it passes Harpers Ferry National Historical Park, a great place to visit.

To put in, for a small fee ($3/boat), you can park at the River and Trail Outfitters site soon after crossing the railroad tracks at Millville; cars in the public lot beyond that have occasionally been broken into. My preferred take out is at Potoma Wayside, in Virginia, just upstream of the US 340 bridge over the Potomac, although this is a steep carry and there is parking for only 3-4 cars right there (others can park across the road). Alternatives involve continuing a few miles down the Potomac, or taking out on the Maryland side at Sandy Hook, and carrying (illegally) over the railroad tracks.

After a flat mile and half, you come to class II- Little Bull Falls (Entrance Rapid), where most water goes left, and soon see the rock ledge that defines Bull Falls itself. Pull onto the big flat section in the middle to scout. At low levels, there are 4 channels, of which the far left one is easiest (class II) and the third from the left the widest, wettest and most popular (class II+). The safest approach is to go almost parallel to the ledge, and then help the current turn you downstream into the near part of the channel, avoiding the rooster tail from the submerged rock in mid channel. At higher levels, the main channels get harder, but other drops on river right open up, as well as the class II Lagoon Chutes that start on river right well above Little Bull Falls, and offer a lovely creek feeling.

Below Bull Falls, you have a choice of routes down the class II Bulls Tail – the left is the most straightforward and has some good surfing waves, but there are interesting channels to the right between the rock islands. Below that is another class II, Spike Rapids (the spikes are the remnants of a dam that fed the mills on Virginius Island). The most popular lunch spot is on river right, below the waterfall of tiny Stikeys Run.

A half-mile later is the Staircase itself, where it can be a challenge to find a clean route in low water, especially in the first half above the bridge. There are many good play spots at the larger drops in the lower part of the Staircase.

Below the confluence, it is just under a mile down the Potomac to the take out. After the easy Mad Dog Rapids, you end up with the class II White Horse Rapids, where again you have a choice of routes. The biggest waves are in the middle of the river, but there are more technical routes (up to class III) on river right.

GAUGE: You need at least 1,000 cfs (2.1) at Millville to have a clean run down the Staircase, and 1,500 makes it much more enjoyable. (In dry summers, the growth of aquatic grasses distorts this gauge reading.) In high water (above 5 feet), there are big holes on the river right side of the lower Staircase, so less experienced paddlers should stay to the left below the bridge.

> **Harpers Ferry** is one of the most historic towns in the US. Sited at the confluence of the Potomac and Shenandoah Rivers – the view of which, Thomas Jefferson said, was alone worth a trip across the Atlantic – it was selected by George Washington to be the site of a federal armory. This made it a target first for John Brown's raid, and later for a successful Confederate siege, led by Stonewall Jackson, which resulted in the largest number of US troops being taken prisoner until the Korean War.

HAPPY CREEK

Happy Creek flows north from the Blue Ridge for 9 miles, into the Shenandoah right at Front Royal. But it is probably not the reason for the road sign announcing that Front Royal is the "Canoe Capital of Virginia." Section 1 is an exciting and dangerous trip, for high intermediate or advanced paddlers only, due to its continuous steepness and occasional strainers. There is then a 0.7-mile gap between sections 1 and 2, because of a few dangerous man-made obstacles. Section 2 is a much milder and less interesting trip through Front Royal and down to the Shenandoah.

> **Front Royal** was so wild in the mid-1700s that its nickname was Helltown. Today, it is both the western end of the Washington/Baltimore SMSA and the gateway to Shenandoah National Park and the Skyline Drive. **Happy Creek House** was the residence of James Marshall, brother of the first chief justice. It was ruined by fire in 1921. The revitalized downtown includes a Confederate Museum as well as boutiques and antique shops.

Section 1: Harmony Orchard Rd./SR 604 to Happy Creek Rd. (Front Royal)

Gradient	Difficulty	Distance	Area	Scenery	Strainers	Rating
92 (150)	III+ (IV)	4.4	7	D	1-2/mi.	***

USGS Quad – Chester Gap/Front Royal; Source – Personal descent 03/01 (last 2.6 miles); 09/04 (first 1.8 miles)
N38 52.11, W78 10.67 via N38 53.38, W78 10.30 to N38 55.25, W78 11.22

This is a trip that you do for the exciting whitewater, not for the scenery. Much of it can be scouted from SR 604 and US 522. Harmony Orchard Road, 3 miles from the creek's source and shortly after the confluence with Moore Run, is the best place to put in. Above there, the creek is extremely narrow. Below, the landowners object to your putting in at their private bridges (as one of them told us), and the Department of Homeland Security will not be happy if you start on their property (we asked them). But no one objected to our paddling through their territory.

The trip starts out in the woods, and although the rapids are technically no more than class II+, their continuousness, the paucity of eddies and the narrowness of the stream, which makes partial strainers inevitable, result in this stretch being class III in challenge. The creek then flows through open fields, under a private bridge (with adequate headroom) and then through a culvert that requires a portage. This part is easily scouted from the road, but eddy out well above the culvert, as the calm looking water above is actually rather fast flowing. Soon you return to the woods, and then at 0.8 miles, pass the DHS/Customs Service's Canine Enforcement Training Center – those sniffing dogs at airports. A half mile later, the gradient rises to 150 ft/mile, and there are several class III+ rapids in the half-mile approaching Sloan Creek and US 522. There is also one spot, visible from the road (you can pull off to scout it), which is class IV, where most of the water drops steeply towards a boulder on the right, as the stream cuts sharply left. There are eddies above on river left, and you can portage or sneak on the far left. We were lucky enough to encounter only one complete strainer in this first 1.8 miles.

There is good road access 200 yards below the confluence with Sloan Creek (which adds almost 50% to the catchment area, but sometimes less to the flow because of a dam just upstream), below the large grassy area alongside US 522. The gradient is somewhat lower here, but the stream is still tough. Although it has no more strainers than usual for its size, it remains very narrow, with limited visibility, long rapids and few eddies, so you have to paddle defensively. In a few places, the creek braids, and one channel may be clear but the other blocked. Most of this part is class III, becoming class II+ after Criser Road (at 3.3 miles), but three spots are class III+. The first, half a mile above Criser Road, requires a hard cut to the left just below a tree standing in the creek, to avoid a boulder. The second, soon after, is a long, steep section with two large rocks toward the bottom in midstream. And after Criser Road, following some easier rapids, the horizon line disappears and there is a steep boulder patch with a 6-foot drop over about 20 feet. Bounce down it from left to right, or portage on the right. In high water, there may be a strong hydraulic at the bottom.

In this stretch, the view is delightful on river left (where rivulets cascade down from nearby Shenandoah National Park) but horrendous on river right (trash-laden industrial sites off US 522). It is the scenery that keeps this creek from getting four stars.

After you reach Va. 55 and Front Royal proper, there are several long and enjoyable class II+ rock gardens as the creek runs through the narrow Happy Creek Greenway and beneath five more bridges. After passing under a white-painted bridge on a private driveway, take out on river left, before the creek makes a sharp left turn to go under Happy Creek Road, to avoid a dangerous waist-high pipe that crosses the creek beneath the bridge.

GAUGE: Look for at least 235 cfs on Battle Run gauge and 200 cfs on Spout Run. For rainfall, use the Chester Gap reading (Warren County).

Skip the next 0.7 miles down to the Moose Bridge on 8th Street. The most dangerous spot is a **pipe 18 inches above the water** which you don't see until you are already under the Happy Creek Road bridge. Soon afterwards, you have to portage a collapsed bridge and two fences. The final quarter mile is nice, especially the class II+ ledge directly under the railroad bridge, but then the Moose Bridge must also be portaged.

Section 2: Moose Bridge (E. 8th St.) to Shenandoah River

Gradient	Difficulty	Distance	Area	Scenery	Strainers	Rating
40	II-	1.3*	15	C+	2-6/mi.	*

USGS Quad – Front Royal; Source – Personal descent 4/02
N38 55.75, W78 11.40 to N38 57.43, W78 11.02

*(plus 1.1 flat miles on the Shenandoah)

The put in is in a pretty park, 0.7 miles after the section 1 take out. The creek has long sections of riffles and a few places that rate class II- because of the combination of riffles, tight turns and partial strainers. There are also 4 or 5 complete strainers. The scenery is surprisingly pretty, with high cliffs on river left, and few signs of civilization, except for the trash that tends to pile up behind the strainers. Shortly before the Shenandoah, you must portage a low-water bridge leading to a quarry – although at minimal levels, a kayak might squeeze through the right hand culvert. There are sometimes other obstacles as well, when construction is underway.

Happy Creek ends right where the Shenandoah is born at the confluence of its North and South forks. Paddle downstream for 1.1 miles, getting an excellent view of the quarry and its processing works, and passing beneath its conveyor belt. Shortly below I-66, take out at the mouth of Crooked Run, on river left, which you can access from the Front Royal Country Club ("Public Welcome"); this is considerably easier than the half-mile upstream paddle Corbett mentions.

GAUGE: Battle Run should be over 130 cfs and Spout Run 115 cfs. For rainfall, use Chester Gap (Warren County).

⫴ CROOKED RUN: West Run (SR 609) to Shenandoah River

Gradient	Difficulty	Distance	Area	Scenery	Strainers	Rating
9	I (II-)	2.8	41	C	1-2/mi.	-

USGS Quad – Front Royal; Source –Personal descent 10/99
N38 58.67, W78 11.52 to N38 57.43, W78 11.02

This is by far the largest tributary to enter the Shenandoah River after it is formed by the North and South forks. Crooked Run is dammed in its upper reaches, and then flows parallel to and just west of US 340/522, picking up rivulets from the hill country to its west. It could be run at times from the confluence with Stephens Run at Nineveh, but as it is tiny, flat and fence prone for the next 4 miles, it is better to wait for its largest tributary, West Run, at Cedarville, to double the volume.

The easiest put in is actually on West Run, at the SR 609 low-water bridge, 0.2 miles above the confluence. (In higher water, you can put in almost a mile up West Run, at its confluence with Molly Camel Run, with 15 sq. mi. at 15 ft/mile.) The first two miles of the trip are essentially flat, with just a few tiny riffles. Except at high water, you can pass under the private bridge before I-66, but between I-66 and US 340/522 is a pair of fences that you have to stop at. The first is rather unusual, consisting of ten, 44-gallon drums (with their ends cut off) strung over a pair of steel cables. You can climb out onto a drum as if it were a tree trunk, but then be prepared for some acrobatic maneuvering. The second is a board fence, partly broken on the right. Below US 340/522, the creek turns east for its final mile, enters the woods, and starts to descend some nice long riffles (one of which even has a play spot). But soon the sounds and sights of a local quarry interrupt the sylvan setting. Its private bridge is a very tight fit, so avoid the fast water in the middle. Below that comes a class II- gravel bar, the only good wave action on the trip, approaching I-66 again. Take out right at the confluence with the Shenandoah, at the Front Royal Country Club. The "Public Welcome" sign is reassuring, but ask permission before you leave cars there.

GAUGE: You need at least 45 cfs on the Spout Run gauge. The rainfall gauge is Nineveh (Warren Co.).

On August 7, 1864, Grant put **Major Gen. Philip Sheridan** in charge of clearing the Confederates from the Shenandoah Valley. His **first clash with Gen. Jubal Early's forces** came on August 16, at Guard Hill, which separates Crooked Run from the North Fork, just north of Front Royal. The Confederates had scattered the Union pickets at Front Royal, and were chasing them northwards along the Front Royal Pike (now US 340), when they were ambushed by dismounted Union cavalry firing from the scrub along the steep banks of Crooked Run. Union General George Custer joined the fray and extended the Union line along Crooked Run, and 300 southerners were taken prisoner. But Confederate artillery on Guard Hill forced the Federals to withdraw.

MANASSAS RUN: Park & Ride (Dismal Hollow Rd.) to SR 624

Gradient	Difficulty	Distance	Area	Scenery	Strainers	Rating
82	III	2.8	8	C-	<1/mi.	***

USGS Quad – Linden/Front Royal; Source – Personal descent 04/05
N38 54.98, W78 06.63 to N38 56.26, W78 07.76

This little stream was channelized for long stretches when I-66 was built, and has rather unattractive scenery (such as many views of I-66). The put in and take out are both steep. But the whitewater in between is excellent, and RC Forney and I did not encounter a single creek-wide strainer in April 2005. The rapids also seemed considerably more difficult than I remembered from my only previous descent, 16 years earlier. Perhaps floods had affected it, perhaps boulders were dumped there from above, or perhaps memory just plays tricks on you.

The headwaters race down the mountainsides to Linden, just west of Manassas Gap – you can see one cascading down toward I-66 there. Then Manassas Run heads west (Goose Creek heads east on the other side of Manassas Gap) along with I-66 (which crosses it three times) and the Southern Railway, makes a few big bends, and turns north to Morgan Ford on the Shenandoah. At Morgan Ford, there is a low-water bridge over the Shenandoah, which is usually underwater whenever Manassas Run is up. Dismal Hollow Road parallels the creek for the first two miles, providing a quick way to scout.

Put in 200 yards downstream of the Park & Ride, where the creek first comes alongside Dismal Hollow Road; there is room to park between the road and I-66. (The creek is considerably narrower half a mile upstream, where Dismal Hollow Road crosses it, before a major tributary enters.) The trip starts out class II+ (unless you choose to put in above the 4-foot ledge). In one-third mile, you pass beneath a private road; the exit drop is class III, due to boulders just below (and sometimes fallen trees). The gradient picks up a bit, and the creek becomes continuous class III-, as you approach and pass beneath I-66 for the first time, at 0.7 miles.

Below there, the rapids are less continuous, but there are several complicated drops of 3-4 feet that are class III. These can all be boat-scouted. The creek divides around an island at one spot. At 2 miles, you pass beneath I-66 for the third time, and the gradient drops to 60 ft/mile. The rapids become easier, but watch out for (a) a low-water driveway to portage, (b) a brief section of braiding, and (c) a man-made 4-foot drop at a road crossing into a mild hydraulic, which is best run with speed in the middle.

Take out at Happy Creek Road (SR 624). One could continue a further 1.7 miles of class II down to the Shenandoah, at a 50 ft/mile; however, when I ran this stretch in May 1989, there were four fences and even more tree strainers in the final mile.

GAUGE: The Spout Run gauge should read at least 190 cfs and Battle Run 225 cfs. For rainfall, look at the Manassas Gap gauge (Warren Co.).

A paddler's dream, that every day
Was like the past 2nd of May,
The small creeks high, the weather sunny,
To hell with office, job and money!

So since we prefer fun to toil,
That Tuesday found us near Front Royal,
On a Run that's named "Manassas",
O'er it I-66 thrice passes,

Perhaps its sign has caught your eye,
The creek itself deserves a try.
Though it's not found in any book,
Youker and I gave it a look.

Its watershed is very small,
It's hard to catch, winter to fall,
But after rains that would scare Noah,
We ran it to the Shenandoah.

We put in off Dismal Hollow Road,
A dreary name, as boats unload,
But one that bore zero relation,
To our explore-a-creek elation.

Often technical and aerobic
This creek's not for the claustrophobic,
At spots less than a boat's length wide,
You could shore brace on either side!

With gradient near 80 feet,
Finding an eddy was a treat,
Good thing the level was not high,
So from blind turns we needn't shy.

The trip was just 3.8 miles,
The first two-thirds produced wide smiles,
With rapids many and strainers few,
It was delightful, through and through.

The last third, though, was quite a bore,
Its wire fences numbered four,
And fallen trees were even more,
A section paddlers should ignore.

We took out shortly before one,
I phoned my office, just for fun,
Soon the morning's joys they were a-fleeting
As I raced back for a 2:30 meeting.

> **Living Dangerously.** I had a staff job at the World Bank then (1989), and was to attend a meeting on Monday afternoon with the President and Senior Vice President, about environmental policy – the one time I was ever to be in such august company. When the meeting got postponed to Tuesday, I was assured that it would not be until late afternoon, after the Board meeting. The heavy rains of Monday night were too tempting to pass up, and right after taking out, at 1:15, I phoned my secretary to find out if the meeting had been rescheduled yet. To my horror, she said that the Board meeting had been unusually short, and our meeting was set for 2:30. I had a towel and clean clothes, but I was 70 miles from the office. To make a long story short, I changed *everything* while racing back along I-66, and arrived fully dressed at the office just in time.

> The biblical **King Manasseh** was son of the patriarch Joseph of Israel. Manassas Gap, at 950 feet the lowest pass and the route of the first railroad through the Blue Ridge, was named for the creek. The town of Manassas was originally called Tudor Hall, but became Manassas Junction when the Orange and Alexandria and the Manassas Gap Railroads joined there in 1854. It was this railroad junction that led to the area becoming the site of two major Civil War battles.

BORDEN MARSH RUN: Below SR 624 to above Shenandoah R.

Gradient	Difficulty	Distance	Area	Scenery	Strainers	Rating
75	II+ (IV)?	0.8	9	C	5-10/mi.	?

USGS Quad – Linden; Source – Scouting from SR 642 alongside
N39 00.00, W78 05.77 to N38 59.48, W78 05.23

Borden Marsh Run (Benjamin Borden, a New Jersey Quaker, settled here in 1734) is a quasi *"explorers' special,"* as I have road-scouted but not paddled it. Turn off SR 624 onto SR 642, and put in at the bridge. After an easy quarter mile, there is a (class IV?) broken ledge with 9 feet total drop. The right channel seems easier, but both sides drop onto boulders. Below that, there is a lot of action but no major drops. I saw about half a dozen strainers. Take out 250 yards before the Shenandoah, where the creek bends away from the dead-end road; it is a steep climb. If you continue to the river, the next access is in 5 miles.

GAUGE: You will need at least 190 cfs on the Spout Run gauge.

VENUS BRANCH: Oak Lane (Rock Springs Br.) to Shenandoah River

Gradient	Difficulty	Distance	Area	Scenery	Strainers	Rating
90	?	0.9*	6	?	?	?

USGS Quad – Linden/Boyce; Source – Scouting access points
N38 59.96, W78 02.79 to N39 00.40, W78 03.40

*(plus 0.4 flat miles on the Shenandoah)

This little *"explorers' special"* rises on the Blue Ridge and curls around Venus Hill. Put in at the confluence with its main tributary, Rock Spring Branch (unless you have enough water to start at the bridge a quarter mile above). You can scout the first 300 yards from the road. The gradient remains fairly constant. About two-thirds through the trip and 20 yards after you pass under SR 638 through a large culvert, there is a man-made 3-foot drop that could have a hydraulic; scout beforehand.

When you reach the Shenandoah, turn right (downstream). In 300 yards, enter the channel to the right of Treasure Island. Some 400 yards after that, take out at the end of a narrow trail that comes down to the river, just past a pair of trees with some exposed roots. From there, it is a 125-yard carry up to the end of Treasure Island Lane, which turns off of SR 638 across from the church. So even finding your way is a bit of an exploration!

GAUGE: You will need at least 300 cfs on the Spout Run gauge. There is a small dam on upper Venus Run, so it may not be runnable at all after a dry spell.

Just south of Venus Run, **Howellsville Branch** has the same gradient and length, a beautiful gorge (visible from the road) and just a slightly smaller drainage. But it has too many strainers, including 3 dangerous culverts with not quite enough head clearance.

SPOUT RUN: Millwood (SR 255/723) to Shenandoah River (SR 621)

Gradient	Difficulty	Distance	Area	Scenery	Strainers	Rating
27 (60)	II (5.0)	3.4	19	C	3-7/mi.	-

USGS Quad – Boyce; Source – Personal descent 9/04
N39 04.04, W78 02.26 to N39 04.44, W78 00.34

You can skip this creek, because Bob Lucas and I suffered the pain for you. Westbrook Run, Roseville Run and Page Brook join to form Spout Run. You can put in at the bridge at the south end of Millwood, where a class II rapid welcomes you. And then a fence suggests that maybe you are not so welcome after all. For the next 3 miles, the gradient is just 15 ft/mile and the riffles and short class II- rapids are widely spaced, while the strainers are more closely spaced. Most of the trip is through the woods, but you also pass through the backyard of a mansion, and several other impressive homes are visible as well. There are about eight fences, of varying types; all can be crossed, but with pain. Lots of other trees block the creek as well. Towards the end of this part, the creek improves, and the rapids include a 3-foot (class II) and 2-foot ledge (class II-).

When the creek crosses SR 621, the real excitement comes, with a class 5.0, 12-foot double ledge. The left side has a 2-3 foot lead in, and then a sheer 10-foot drop into shallow water. The right side is a bit more gradual, but requires a sharp turn midway, and crashes down onto a protruding rock that may not be visible when the creek is high. Ouch! Fallen trees tend to complicate the spot as well. You can carry up (although the land is heavily posted) to the road at the USGS gauge, and then follow the trail down to the base of the drop. Below Spout Run Falls, the gradient is 60 ft/mile and the water class II, but, alas, this is just for the final quarter mile to the Shenandoah. The river is also posted near the confluence, but there is good access in a quarter mile on river left.

GAUGE: The Spout Run on-line gauge (at SR 621) should be at least 130 cfs.

> By the put in is the restored **Burwell-Morgan Gristmill**, built in 1782-85 by Nathaniel Burwell and General Daniel Morgan. It was one of the longest-operating mills in the country, in continuous use until 1943. Burwell's stone mansion, Carter Hall, built in 1792, is nearby. Stonewall Jackson used is as his headquarters in October 1862.

EVITTS RUN: Kabletown Road to Bloomery

Gradient	Difficulty	Distance	Area	Scenery	Strainers	Rating
40 (100)	II	1.8	18	C	3-7/mi.	-

USGS Quad – Charles Town; Source – Personal descent 6/00
N39 15.04, W77 50.44 to N39 15.45, W77 48.77

Someday, drive 4 miles upstream from the Staircase put in along the river to Bloomery, and check out this tiny tributary and its old water wheel. But don't paddle it!

Evitts Run flows 10 miles, passing by Charles Town. On the upstream side of Clips Mill, on Kabletown Road, is an 8-foot waterfall. Both banks are posted, so to run the drop, you must put in half a mile upstream at a low water bridge on Old Cave Road. Avoid the right side of the waterfall, which lands on rocks.

If you ignore my advice and run the rest of this creek, put in on downstream river left at Kabletown Road. The stream is mostly flat (20 ft/mile) for 1.4 miles, with just a few riffles. But it isn't uneventful. There are simple wire fences, wire mesh fences and barbed wire fences. Some can be slipped under; others must be climbed over. The cattle in the creek add their own drama. While I found only a few tree strainers here, there were long stretches of low branches that had to be ducked and dodged. The two footbridges were just high enough to glide under. I would call this section painful but not dangerous.

The creek then begins its 0.4-mile plunge to the Shenandoah with a pair of short class II rapids that are hard and thorny to portage but likely to be clogged. The walls of the little gorge steepen, but finally there are (or at least were) some clean class II rapids to enjoy, as you pass the ruins of an old bridge and head down to Md. 9. From there, it is 150 yards of class II down to Bloomery Road, where the creek splits into several small (and at least partially blocked) channels for the final twisty riffles down to the river. Take out a quarter mile downstream on the Shenandoah, where Bloomery Road runs close to the bank. Before starting, check for strainers downstream of both bridges in Bloomery.

GAUGE: Judge from the bridges in Bloomery. The Spout Run gauge should exceed 100 cfs, Piney Run 65 cfs.

> This was a **scary trip** in two places. The long portage around the first fence took me right past an open barn door; I heard noise from within, but it was just a cat. Then, after the second strainer-blocked rapid, I could not see to the bottom of the third rapid, and dared not enter it blindly because both banks had steep mud walls. I clawed my way up a steep beaver slide, grabbing bits of vegetation. I was prepared to abandon my boat, scramble out, and hike back up the streambed for it when the level was much lower. Fortunately, that was not necessary.

NORTHERN VIRGINIA

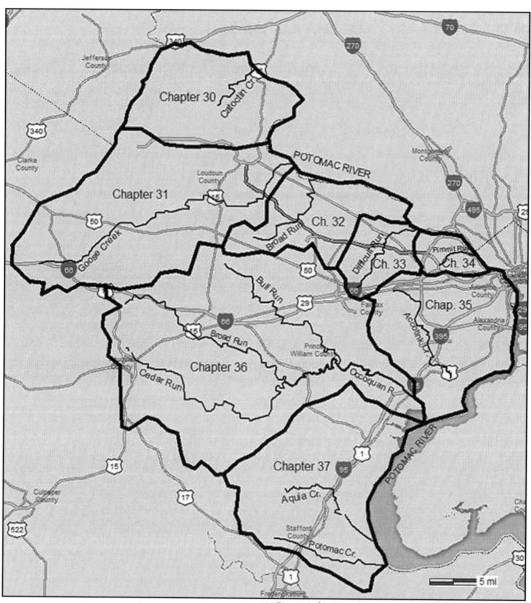

PART VIII : NORTHERN VIRGINIA

Part VIII covers a large swath of territory drained by the Potomac that coincides roughly with what is called Northern Virginia. It ranges from urban areas in Alexandria and Arlington to the still rural parts of Fauquier, Prince William and Stafford Counties. Its 2.3 million people comprise 29% of Virginia's total, although it covers but 5% of the state geographically. It is a mostly prosperous and attractive area of rolling hills, farmlands and sub-divisions, bounded by the Shenandoah basin to the west, the Rappahannock drainage to the south, and the Potomac River to the east and north. The only sub-watersheds of more than 100 square miles are the Occoquan River (600 sq. mi.) and Goose Creek (380 sq. mi.).

Chapter 30 covers Catoctin Creek and its tributaries and neighbors in **Northwest Loudoun County**. The steepest of these are a pair of tiny creeks not far from the Shenandoah: Piney Run and Dutchman Creek. There is also some easy but pleasant whitewater in several Catoctin Creek tributaries, especially "Morrisonville Creek."

Chapter 31 is on the **Goose Creek Basin**, which covers most of the rest of Loudoun Co., as well as northern Fauquier Co. It contains some nice novice runs and a few short intermediate trips, but nothing outstanding. In all of my paddles there, I came across only a single, short class III rapid. The well-known final section of Goose Creek can be paddled again, although there are some administrative hoops to jump through.

Moving southeast, chapter 32, **Above Great Falls**, is on the creeks from Broad Run in eastern Loudoun Co. to Mine Run Branch in northwestern Fairfax Co. Broad Run itself is easy to catch and very mild, but these streams get smaller and steeper to the east.

Chapter 33 covers the small but lively **Difficult Run Basin**. The great challenge here is the final mile of Difficult Run, but Wolftrap Creek and Captain Hickory Run are also somewhat interesting.

Chapter 34 is entitled **Virginia Palisades**, because its tiny creeks all cut down to the Potomac River through high cliffs. Pimmit Run, Scott Run, Little Pimmit Run and Bullneck Run all have good intermediate sections, while most others are for experts only. Almost all have enough water only very briefly after an intense rainfall.

The remainder of the heavily urban area, Alexandria and southeastern Fairfax County, is in chapter 35, **Virginia Suburbs South**, whose streams enter the Potomac below downtown Washington D.C. Pohick and Accotink creeks are fairly well known, but there are good trips on South Run, Holmes Run, Fourmile Run and Pike Branch as well.

The **Occoquan River Basin**, chapter 36, covers the last major Potomac tributary. This watershed is mainly in Fauquier, western Prince William, and southwestern Fairfax counties. The best whitewater trips are short stretches on Broad and Cub runs, while Big Rocky Run offers a fast flush for experts.

Finally, **South of the Occoquan**, chapter 37, picks up the remaining small tributaries in eastern Prince William and Stafford counties, before the Potomac heads east across the coastal plain to the Chesapeake Bay. Aquia Creek is the largest of these, but Quantico and Neabsco creeks are more exciting.

There are lots of **river gauges** in this area – 22 as of early 2013 – making this one of the best covered areas. No rainfall gauges are reported over the Internet, but if you live nearby, you can usually figure out how much rain is falling.

CAPITAL CANOEING AND KAYAKING

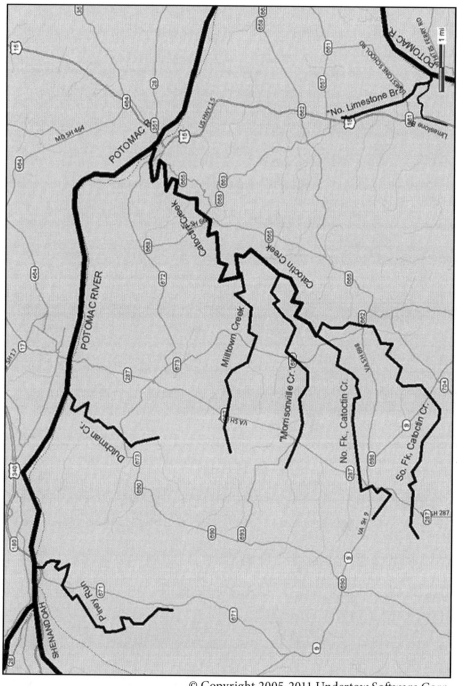

© Copyright 2005-2011 Undertow Software Corp.

Chapter 30:
NORTHWEST LOUDOUN COUNTY

Run, don't walk, to paddle these creeks within the next few years. Although no longer the US geographic center of population, as it was in 1810, Loudoun is one of the fastest growing counties in the nation, with an 84% population increase from 2000 to 2010. Spurred by the hi-tech boom and the convenience of access to Dulles International Airport and the Dulles Toll Road, eastern Loudoun County is already heavily developed, and subdivisions are spreading into the western part as well, especially along the main east-west highway, Va. 7. In a few decades, this county of gentle hills, unpaved side roads, horse farms (the most horses of any county in Virginia), fox hunts, cattle ranches, vineyards and cornfields, will look and feel like the rest of the metropolitan area.

The northwest part of the county is bounded by the Potomac River to the north and east, the Blue Ridge to the west, and (roughly) Va. 7 to the south. Two north-south mountains, Short Hill to the west and Catoctin to the east, divide its watersheds. It is still primarily rural, centered on historic Waterford, although Purcellville, along Va. 7, is now much larger (5,000). The main stream is **Catoctin Creek**. Its **North and South forks** are class I, with the former being delightful. Catoctin Creek also has two smaller, steeper and somewhat more challenging tributaries: **Milltown Creek** and my favorite, an unnamed one which I call "**Morrisonville Creek**" after the hamlet in its headwaters.

In the northwest corner of the northwest, not far from Harpers Ferry WV, are two tiny but steep creeks, which flow directly into the Potomac. **Piney Run**, the larger and steeper of the pair, ends in the waterfall at the Potoma Wayside takeout for Staircase trips, and is a challenging run up above. **Dutchman Creek** is an "explorers' special." A bit further east, another tiny, unnamed stream, "**North Limestone Branch**," flows more gently down to Whites Ferry.

> John Campbell, the fourth **Earl of Loudoun**, was commander-in-chief of the British and American forces during the unsuccessful second part of the French and Indian War (following the defeat and death of General Braddock). The county was settled in the early 18th Century by the mostly Scotch-Irish "**Loudoun pioneers**."
>
> During the **Civil War**, John Mosby's Confederate raiders were active in Loudoun County. To destroy their economic base, Union cavalry entered the county in late 1864, burning barns and capturing livestock (as was done on a larger scale in the Shenandoah Valley). Ironically, the bulk of the damage was inflicted on pro-Union German and Quaker farmers.

GAUGES: Five gauges are currently (early 2012) reported over the Internet, which is a lot for this small area: Piney Run (13.5 sq. mi.), Catoctin Creek at Taylorstown (90 sq. mi.), the North and South forks of Catoctin Creek near Waterford (23 and 32 sq. mi., respectively), and Limestone Branch (8 sq. mi.). Loudoun County is not included in the AFWS gauge reports, so for the latest trends you need to rely on the rainfall maps. In the table below, **the gauge column refers to Piney Run**. Of course, for most of the other creeks you would use their own gauges.

name	gradient	difficulty	length	area	gauge	rating
Piney Run	90 (200)	III+(IV)	1.6	14	100cfs	**
Dutchman Creek	50 (100)	?	3.0	8	150cfs	?
Catoctin Creek	8	I (II)	13.8	58	25cfs	*
North Fork, Catoctin Cr.	16	I	4.3	20	50cfs	**
South Fork, Catoctin Cr.	9	I	3.8	24	45cfs	-
"Morrisonville Creek"	27 (45)	II (II+)	2.3	10	105cfs	***
Milltown Creek	30 (50)	II	2.0	8	140cfs	**
"North Limestone Branch"	27 (60)	I (II)	0.9	7	140cfs	*

PINEY RUN: SR 671 to US 340

Gradient	Difficulty	Distance	Area	Scenery	Strainers	Rating
90 (200)	III+ (IV)	1.6	14	B	1-3/mi.	**

USGS Quad – Harpers Ferry; Source – Personal descent 4/04
N39 18.58, W77 43.45 to N39 19.17, W77 42.75

Piney Run ("Crazy Creek" to local paddlers) flows north for 9 miles through the Loudoun Valley in the northwest corner of the county, between the Blue Ridge and Short Hill Mountain. It is dull for its first 8 miles, but then changes dramatically even before it ends in a 20-foot waterfall at the US 340 Potoma Wayside take out for the Staircase. (Even daredevils run this waterfall only when the Shenandoah is very high; otherwise, it's splat onto the rocks below. Bobby "Zone Dogg" Miller survived it, but his kayak didn't.)

Put in at SR 671, but park just upstream on SR 833. The class I first half mile can be scouted from SR 683. The next quarter mile, down to a private bridge by a house, is twisty class II. Just below that bridge, watch out for barbed wire fences on both channels. The creek picks up gradient, goes over a class III ledge, and you soon reach an island. The left channel is a narrow twisting class IV, best scouted from the island. The right channel is class III+, but needs more water. You can portage on the island or river right. Then come some fun class III and III+ ledges and rock gardens; watch out, of course, for downed trees. When you reach the next island, scout again. At low water, the best route is to start left and then cut right in the narrow channel between the islands; at higher water, you can stay left the whole way. (You can see the bottom of this rapid if you hike upstream a bit from the take out.) Below, the creek reverts to class II, and there is then a big eddy. Take out on river left upstream of US 340, and bushwhack up the slope (to across from the gas station). Below the bridge there are steep walls and only a small pool before the waterfall.

The scenery starts out dull, but the last half of the trip is through a deep gorge. Look for the high cascade on river right above the last island.

GAUGE: There is a painted gauge on downstream river left of the takeout bridge, visible from the end of the Potoma Wayside parking lot – minimum for a clean run is 1.5. The Internet gauge on Piney Run near Lovettsville, located at the put in, should be at least 100 cfs (equivalent to 2.6 on the staff gauge at the put in bridge).

ᛞ DUTCHMAN CREEK: SR 673 to Potomac River

Gradient	Difficulty	Length	Area	Scenery	Strainers	Rating
50 (100)	?	3.0	8	?	?	?

USGS Quad – Harpers Ferry; Source – Scouting road accesses
N39 17.21, W77 39.64 to N39 18.66, W77 37.65

Although the valley just east of Short Hill Mountain is mainly agricultural, a little swath has been left as woodland alongside Dutchman Creek. Most of the tiny headwaters have come together by Georges Mill (George family members still live nearby), but they are less than 3 miles from their sources, so you'd better get to this creek quickly. The stream is so small at SR 673 that I missed it, even though I was looking for it!

Before putting in, ask permission at the house on either river right or river left. They own the land for a good ways down, and will kick you off the creek if you put on without their approval. That is why this is the *"explorers' special"* for this chapter.

The first mile is relatively flat, but the gradient then picks up to almost 100 ft/mile, slows down approaching SR 674 (the only intermediate access, half a mile above the Potomac), increases right after that to 100 ft/mile again, and then slows down in the final quarter mile. It should be an exciting paddle.

Take out on the Maryland side of the Md. 17/Va 287 bridge at Brunswick Md. There is an opening into the C & O Canal just downstream of the bridge, and parking right there (reached by crossing the railroad tracks at the station). When the Potomac is high, you will need a vigorous ferry to cross, but there is no takeout on the Virginia shore.

GAUGE: The Piney Run gauge should be over 150 cfs, Limestone Branch 85 cfs.

Despite the creek's name, the **early settlers** of this area were English Quakers and Germans (*Deutschmann* – the source of the name), who remained loyal to the Union during the Civil War, supplying men and horses to the Loudoun Independent Rangers.

ᛞ CATOCTIN CREEK: North Fork (SR 681) to Potomac River (US 15)

Gradient	Difficulty	Distance	Area	Scenery	Strainers	Rating
8	I (II)	13.8	58	B	0	*

USGS Quad – Waterford/Point of Rocks; Source – Personal descent 5/98 (last 8.5 miles); Grove; Corbett
N39 12.30, W77 37.43 via N39 13.92, W77 35.50 (SR 673) to N39 16.33, W77 32.79

This novice trip is not too difficult to catch. To run all of Catoctin Creek but not much more, put in on the North Fork, 600 yards above the confluence. But watch out for barbed wire there. You can also put in on the South Fork just outside Waterford (the sign just says "Catoctin Creek"), but that adds 1.5 dull miles to a long day.

Five miles below the confluence is SR 673, a good put in except that staff of the Firestone estate there (which raises racing horses, such as Genuine Risk, the 1980 Kentucky Derby winner) have objected on occasion. Enough water on the class I ledge there means enough everywhere. After another 4 miles you reach SR 668 at Taylorstown. About 2 miles below there, the gradient picks up to 15 ft/mile, and there are some long riffles and bigger waves, including the only class II chute. When the current suddenly disappears, you have reached the Potomac's backwater, which often stretches 1.5 miles up Catoctin Creek (which drops only 5 feet in that distance).

The attractive scenery alternates between woodland and estates. You pass the ruins of an old mill on river left above Taylorstown, and beautiful rock formations on river right below.

GAUGE: A reading of 160 cfs on Catoctin Creek at Taylorstown is minimal. If you can run the small ledge just downstream of SR 673, you can run everything.

NORTH FORK, CATOCTIN CREEK: Va. 287 to SR 681

Gradient	Difficulty	Distance	Area	Scenery	Strainers	Rating
16	I	4.3	20	B	<1/mi.	**

USGS Quad – Purcellville/Waterford; Source – Personal descent 2/04
N39 11.53, W77 40.50 to N39 12.30, W77 37.43

What a pleasant surprise this stream was – far nicer than Corbett's "little more than overgrown ditches" reference to the two Catoctin forks would suggest. Although you twist alongside farmers' fields at the beginning, end, and a few spots in between, you are in attractive woods most of the time. The surrounding hills abound with deer (I had 4 separate sightings). The riffles are frequent and the slack water infrequent, and in the second half of the trip, the riffles become quite lively. I had to leave my boat for only one strainer in the entire 4.3 miles – all the other wood in the creek could be maneuvered under, over or around. And the only fence I encountered, about five minutes into the trip, had an opening on the right. The creek is so nice that you might consider putting in 2.9 miles higher up, at SR 611, at the cost of only 3 sq. mi and with the same 16 ft/mile gradient – but that stretch appears to flow mainly through fields rather than woods. A compromise would be to add just 0.6 miles to the trip, by starting at the intersection of Va. 9 and Va. 287.

The take out is a third of a mile above the confluence – if you continue onto Catoctin Creek, it is 5 miles to the next access (see above). The take out was the only negative to my trip (other than the absence of rapids); all four corners were guarded by barbed wire, but I found it low enough to step over on downstream, river left.

The North Fork rises on the Blue Ridge and about four miles later cuts through Short Hill Mountain at Hillsboro. It reaches 40 ft/mile for a mile, with a drainage area of 13 sq. mi., but there are only continuous riffles (as best I could see from the roads), and there are access limitations (you must put in over a mile above the steep section, with a catchment area of only 7 sq. mi., and take out 1.5 miles below (SR 611) after crossing a quarter-mile man-made lake).

GAUGE: About 70 cfs on the North Fork, Catoctin Creek gauge is minimal. On the USGS staff at the takeout, downstream river left, 70 cfs is 2.9.

SOUTH FORK, CATOCTIN CREEK: Va. 9 to SR 698

Gradient	Difficulty	Distance	Area	Scenery	Strainers	Rating
9	I	3.8	24	C	0-2/mi.	-

USGS Quad – Purcellville/Waterford; Source – Corbett
N39 09.83, W77 38.64 to N39 11.46, W77 36.96

The South Fork is slightly larger than the North Fork, but has just over half the latter's gradient and spends much more time in the fields rather than the woods, so it hasn't been high on my priority list. The takeout is just outside historic Waterford.

Below SR 698, it is 1.5 miles to the confluence with the North Fork, and then another 5 miles down Catoctin Creek to the first access at SR 673.

GAUGE: Look for at least 90 cfs on the South Fork, Catoctin Creek gauge (at the takeout). On the USGS staff, 3.25 equals 90 cfs.

"MORRISONVILLE CREEK": SR 681 to Catoctin Creek

Gradient	Difficulty	Distance	Area	Scenery	Strainers	Rating
27 (45)	II (II+)	2.3*	10	B	1-2/mi.	***

USGS Quad – Purcellville/Waterford; Source – Personal descent 5/01
N39 13.04, W77 37.84 to N39 13.93, W77 35.50

*(plus 1 mile on Catoctin Creek to SR 673 – Featherbed Lane)

This unnamed creek flows east from Short Hill Mountain, past Morrisonville. It's a delightful run, initially with farmland on one side and then all through the woods. We encountered no fences and surprisingly few downed trees for such a small creek.

Put in at SR 681, although the access and parking are not great. The first two-thirds of the run are class I, but after high bluffs appear on river right, the gradient rises to 45 ft/mile for the final three-quarters mile. The first class II is on a sharp right turn, and after a few more short rock gardens, there is a 100-yard, class II+ rapid shortly before the confluence. Once on Catoctin Creek, it is a mile to SR 673.

GAUGE: The riffles at the put in need to be at least 6 inches above minimum, because the creek gets wider and steeper down below. The gauge on Piney Run should be at least 105 cfs, Limestone Branch 60 cfs and North Fork, Catoctin Creek 175 cfs.

MILLTOWN CREEK: SR 673 to Catoctin Creek

Gradient	Difficulty	Distance	Area	Scenery	Strainers	Rating
30 (50)	II	2.0*	8	B	1-2/mi.	**

USGS Quad – Waterford; Source – Personal descent 6/01
N39 14.18, W77 36.87 to N39 14.97, W77 35.20

*(plus 2 miles on Catoctin Creek to SR 663 roadside)

The put in is under the fence of a horse ranch; ask permission at the beige house next to the red barn a quarter mile downstream. (They were very agreeable with us.) The first half mile meanders through that ranch. The triple strands of white wire are electrified, but there is enough clearance; however, the board fence below may require a short portage. The creek then enters the woods, but remains class I for the first mile.

Midway, you reach a little gorge, where there are class II rock gardens and ledges, often complicated by partial strainers. All too soon this ends at Catoctin Creek, and it is then two miles to the nearest takeout along Downey Mill Road (SR 663), and another mile to Taylorstown.

GAUGE: This seems to need more rain than "Morrisonville Creek." At the put in, the riffle upstream should be cleanly runnable all the way across. Look for 140 cfs on Piney Run, 80 cfs on Limestone Branch, and 230 cfs on North Fork, Catoctin Creek.

"NORTH LIMESTONE BR.": SR 661 to Potomac R. (Whites Ferry)

Gradient	Difficulty	Distance	Area	Scenery	Strainers	Rating
27 (60)	I (II)	0.9*	7	C+	1-2/mi.	*

USGS Quad – Waterford; Source – Personal descent 4/04
N39 10.45, W77 31.78 to N39 09.33, W77 31.39

*(plus 0.8 miles on the Potomac to Whites Ferry)

Two tiny creeks meet at an inlet of the Potomac, 0.6 miles north of Whites Ferry. One is Limestone Branch, and the other, of almost equal size, is unnamed – as it is the more northerly, I call it "North Limestone Branch." One can paddle 0.2 miles into the flat inlet, to where the creeks meet. Each ends in a long class II rock garden. There was a large cable-and-board fence across the middle of Limestone Branch's rapid, which effectively wrecked the best part of that creek. But "North Limestone Branch" was clean.

From SR 661 to the confluence is a very short trip, but above there are fences and no access. The scenery is pleasant – fields on the left, mainly woods on the right. There was only one creek-wide strainer to portage. The first quarter mile is full of riffles, the second quarter mile is mainly flat, and then the creek becomes a little livelier again and twisty. When you pass some moss-covered boulders on river right, and the stream bends sharply to the right, catch the big eddy on river left to set up for the one real (class II) rapid. There are three distinct drops, but the bottom one gets drowned when the Potomac at Point of Rocks is over 4 feet, and the middle one is probably gone by 5.5 feet.

If you take out on the Virginia side, be careful not to interfere with the ferry landing. There is room for 2-3 cars on the gravel across from where the vehicles line up for the ferry. You could take out on the Maryland side of Whites Ferry (for a $1.50 fee/boat), where there are refreshments and lots of parking.

GAUGE: The Limestone Branch gauge should be at least 80 cfs. The riffle at the put in should be cleanly runnable.

> **Whites Ferry**, crossed by the General Jubal A. Early, is the only remaining ferry across the Potomac. Residents and others have resisted efforts to replace it with a bridge. This was the main ford used on September 4-7, 1862, by General Lee en route to Antietam.

CAPITAL CANOEING AND KAYAKING

GOOSE CREEK BASIN

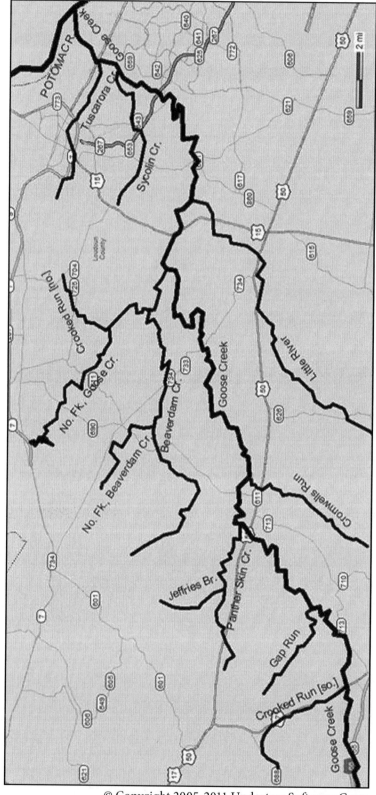

Chapter 31:

GOOSE CREEK BASIN

Goose Creek, the eighth largest direct Potomac tributary, flows 50 miles from southwest to northeast and drains 380 sq. mi. in southern/central Loudoun and northern Fauquier Counties. Its basin abuts those of Catoctin Creek to the north, the Shenandoah to the west (across the Blue Ridge), the Rappahannock to the southwest, the Occoquan to the southeast and Broad Run to the east. Leesburg (28,000) is the main city. There is a good variety of easy whitewater, but little harder stuff, so nothing rates more than **.

Lower **Goose Creek** has long been a popular novice run, but access has been restricted since 9/11/01 because the put in is at the base of a water-supply reservoir. Upper/middle Goose Creek and its three large tributaries, **Little River, Beaverdam Creek** and the **North Fork of Goose Creek** are all pretty flat, except for a brief stretch of the North Fork. There is moderate whitewater on the other nine sizable tributaries: **Gap Run** and **Crooked Run [south]** in the headwaters; **Jeffries Branch, Panther Skin Creek** and **Cromwells Run** (an "explorers' special") in the middle of the basin; **Crooked Run [north]** and the **North Fork of Beaverdam Creek** in the North Fork of Goose Creek catchment; and **Sycolin** and **Tuscarora creeks** near Leesburg, towards the mouth of Goose Creek.

GAUGES: The gauges on Goose Creek near Middleburg (122 sq. mi.) and Leesburg (332 sq. mi.) are good mainly for that waterway. Those on the North Fork of Goose Creek (38 sq. mi.) and Beaverdam Creek (47 sq. mi.) are more widely useful, but for most of the small creeks, the best gauges are in the nearby watersheds of Limestone Branch (8 sq. mi.) to the northeast, Battle Run (26 sq. mi.) to the southwest and Spout Run (21 sq. mi.) to the west. In this table, **the gauge column refers to Limestone Branch**, except that when it is in ***bold italics, it refers to Beaverdam Creek***. No rainfall gauges are reported for this basin, so you have to use the rainfall maps.

name	gradient	difficulty	length	area	gauge	rating
Goose Creek - Section 1	22 (40)	I	5.5	13	45cfs	*
- Section 2	6	I (II)	32.5	45	*90cfs*	*
- Section 3	10	II- (II+)	2.4	340	*45cfs*	**
Crooked Run [south]	36	II+	3.5	10	60cfs	*
Gap Run	38	II-	2.3	14	45cfs	**
Panther Skin Creek	22	II (III)	4.0	19	30cfs	**
Jeffries Branch	30	I	2.5	6	50cfs	-
Cromwells Run	18 (65)	?	5.0	8	50cfs	?
North Fork, Goose Cr.	55	II+	0.5	10	60cfs	**
Crooked Run [north]	18 (35)	I	2.2	10	50cfs	*
Beaverdam Creek	6	I	8.2	41	*100cfs*	*
No. Fork, B'dam Cr.	33 (60)	II	2.4	12	*290cfs*	**
Little River	10	I	5.6	38	*100cfs*	*
Sycolin Creek	26	II+	2.3	14	45cfs	**
Tuscarora Creek	25	II+	4.0	10	60cfs	**

GOOSE CREEK

Goose Creek begins at Manassas Gap in the Blue Ridge near Linden and flows east alongside I-66/Va. 55 and the railroad, before turning northeast after Delaplane. Unfortunately, (a) the creek is pretty flat by the time it is big enough to run, (b) much of the fall line is buried under the 17-foot Fairfax water supply dam, and (c) direct access to the once-popular novice trip (section 3) near Leesburg has become more difficult after 9/11. The headwater section 1 is mediocre, as is the long beginner section 2 (in Corbett). Section 3 is still interesting, and there is also access via Sycolin Run to its bottom half. The low gradient did make it possible for the Goose Creek and Little River Navigation Company to build locks that would promote river commerce and connect up with the C&O Canal, but by the time 12 miles of Goose Creek were navigable (1854), the age of the railroads had begun, and the Company was dissolved three years later.

> The Indians called the Potomac above Great Falls the "**River of Geese**," because of the large populations that rested there during their spring and autumn migrations. (Below Great Falls, it was the "River of Swans.") When the English introduced the name Potomac River, they applied the "Goose" reference instead to the first large tributary above Great Falls.

Section 1: Markham to Delaplane (US 17)

Gradient	Difficulty	Distance	Area	Scenery	Strainers	Rating
22 (40)	I	5.5	13	C	1-2/mi.	*

USGS Quad – Upperville; Source – Personal descent 2/04
N38 54.32, W77 59.59 to N38 54.84, W77 55.30

As Goose Creek spends its first 6.5 miles alongside Va. 55, there are numerous put-in options. We started a quarter mile east of the I-66 Markham interchange. The trip starts out with poor scenery and lots of strainers; beavers are much in evidence. The gradient is expended in frequent riffles. After the creek passes beneath I-66, at 1.5 miles, the scenery improves, with some attractive cliffs on river right, although you paddle for long distances along the railroad, and cross it five times. Whitetails abound. Several small tributaries enter, which widens the creek and reduces the frequency of strainers, but the few narrow, blind turns should be approached with caution. There was also a pair of wire fences; the first required a portage, the second could be paddled under. The gradient decreases gradually, with the riffles becoming more widely spaced, although a few of them are livelier. Take out on river left, immediately after passing beneath US 17.

GAUGE: The Battle Run gauge should be over 150 cfs.

> **Rail Warfare.** On July 19, 1861, at Delaplane (then called Piedmont Station), on upper Goose Creek, Confederate Gen. Joseph E. Johnson's 10,000-man corps boarded freight and cattle cars and traveled by rail to the 1st Battle of Manassas (Bull Run), arriving in time to help turn the tide against the Union. This was the first large-scale use of railroads in war, anywhere in the world, and therefore marked the start of a new era in military transport.

Section 2: Delaplane (US 17) to Evergreen Mills (SR 621)

Gradient	Difficulty	Distance	Area	Scenery	Strainers	Rating
6	I (II)	32.5	45	C	0	*

USGS Quad – Upperville/Rectort./Middleburg/Lincoln/Leesburg; Source – Corbett; personal descent (2 miles) 4/04
N38 54.84, W77 55.30 to N39 01.08, W77 34.56

At Delaplane, the entry of Crooked Run, Goose Creek's first major tributary, adds about 50% to the flow. The creek is quite slow, with the only class II being the remains of a broken dam, below US 15. There are numerous access points. Corbett covers this section in detail, but you should also check the Paddlers Access Network (reached from monocacycanoe.org) to find out about current access. As of now, you must take out at Evergreen Mills, because there is no legal access at Sycolin Road (SR 643) 4.5 miles downstream (near where the reservoir begins).

GAUGE: The Beaverdam Creek gauge should be over 90 cfs to start at Delaplane and 45 cfs to start at Oatlands (US 15) for the final 8 miles.

Section 3: Fairfax Dam to Kephart Bridge Landing

Gradient	Difficulty	Distance	Area	Scenery	Strainers	Rating
10	II- (II+)	2.4	340	C	0	**

USGS Quad – Leesburg; Source – Personal descent 9/00
N39 03.29, W77 31.47 to N39 05.92, W77 29.74

The put in is at the base of the Fairfax Dam, reached from SR 642 off of Belmont Road (SR 659). Access has been restricted since September 2001 to protect the reservoir against poisoning, and the start of this trip was feasible only if you put in 6 miles upstream, at Evergreen Mills, and then paddled 1.5-miles across the reservoir. In 2011, Tim Tilson negotiated limited access with the Fairfax water authority – contact him at hmslydia@msn.com for details. The last half of this trip, including the best rapid, can also be reached during high water from Sycolin Creek – see below.

The first two miles has only riffles and one class II- rock garden, where you thread the needle between boulders on the right. In another half mile, you reach Golf Course Rapid (class II+), by the remains of Cook's Mill on the left bank and a dam/lock on both banks, a large house on the right, and the start of a golf course on the left. The easiest route is down the left, cutting back to the right below a large mid-stream boulder. At higher water, there are slightly tougher routes on the right. From there, it is a flat half-mile to the old take out, on river left, where there is public parking on a golf course access road just upstream of Va. 7.

Below Va. 7, continue 1.3 miles to a new public take out at Kephart Bridge Landing, reached via Riverpoint Drive. You pass under a bridge, over an old mill dam, and 0.6 miles later run a rock garden. Eddy out on the right for the take out. It is a further 2.2 flat miles to the Potomac, but if you paddle that, you will have to ferry a quarter mile directly across the Potomac to the Goose Creek Locks of the C&O Canal at the end of Edwards Ferry Road, and do a 13-mile shuttle (back to Va. 7) via Whites Ferry.

GAUGE: The Goose Creek gauge at Leesburg should read at least 180 cfs.

CROOKED RUN [south]: Alongside US 17 to Delaplane

Gradient	Difficulty	Distance	Area	Scenery	Strainers	Rating
36	II+	3.5	10	C	0-2/mi.	*

USGS Quad – Upperville; Source – Personal descent 2/04
N38 57.34, W77 56.52 to N38 54.84, W77 55.30

This Crooked Run (and it is twisty) rises in Sky Meadows State Park, off the Blue Ridge/Appalachian Trail. One could add 2 miles by putting in at SR 688, with a 7 sq. mi. drainage and 60-ft/mile gradient, but we did not have time to explore that section.

This trip has continuous, moderate whitewater and surprisingly few strainers, as it parallels US 17 south-southeast between Paris and Delaplane. So for 90 % of the time, this trip was pure joy. Unfortunately, the creek passes through about five large estates with fences and low-water bridges, spaced about every three-quarters of a mile.

Larry Lempert and I put in exactly 3 road miles north of Delaplane, just past the driveway to a mansion on the hillside, where a tiny brook has carved a short, straight channel to Crooked Run. (A bit beyond, a fence blocks access to the creek, and farther north, Crooked Run moves away from the road.) In 200 yards, you pass beneath that driveway. At moderate levels, there is just enough headroom, and there is an exciting 2-foot drop right underneath the driveway – line up straight. In another 200 yards, there is a low water bridge with barbed-wire fences above and below. Fortunately, it is calm water just above, and the barbed wire is loose enough that you can easily get under or through. The next obstacle is a heavy metal fence across the creek, beneath a driveway. There is an eddy just above on river right, and from there we could squeeze through an opening in the fence. At SR 724, another fence requires taking out on the right, crossing the bridge, and putting back in on the left, where a gully leaves room beneath the barbed wire. Then the creek passes twice beneath US 17, leading to a wire mesh fence that must be portaged on the left, which would be easy except for the barbed wire fence that you have to climb over. From there, all is clear, until the low-water bridge to portage 100 yards above the confluence. Take out a few yards up Goose Creek, on river left, where there is good parking. Three stars for the paddling, minus two for the fences.

GAUGE: You need readings on Battle Run of 190 cfs, on Spout Run of 165 cfs, and on Limestone Branch of 60 cfs.

GAP RUN: SR 623 to Goose Creek (SR 710 – Rectortown Road)

Gradient	Difficulty	Distance	Area	Scenery	Strainers	Rating
38	II-	2.3	14	B	0-2/mi.	**

USGS Quad – Upperville/Rectortown; Source – Personal descent 2/04
N38 56.62, W77 53.74 to N38 56.26, W77 52.14

I had written this creek off, until Ed Evangelidi told me that paddlers were actually running it. It flows 10 miles from Ashby Gap (hence its name) near Paris, southeast to Goose Creek, but it meanders through cattle pastures until SR 623.

This is a pleasant novice run, with nearly continuous riffles and easy rapids the entire way. The more challenging places are typically on sharp turns and through partial strainers. The surrounding countryside is hilly and full of deer – we saw 40-50, in the largest herd I can recall. We had only two trees and no fences to portage. At the one island, you can go either way. The takeout just below the confluence with Goose Creek, at SR 710, is long, steep and slippery. If you have the time, it might be worthwhile to paddle 1.7 miles farther down Goose Creek to SR 715.

GAUGE: The Battle Run gauge should be over 140 cfs, Spout Run 120 cfs and Limestone Branch 45 cfs.

PANTHER SKIN CREEK: Green Garden Rd (SR 719) to Goose Cr.

Gradient	Difficulty	Distance	Area	Scenery	Strainers	Rating
22	II (III)	4.0*	19**	B	<1/mi.	**

USGS Quad –Rectortown; Source – Personal descent 4/04
N38 59.77, W77 51.75 to N38 59.18, W77 47.73

*(plus 2 miles on Goose Creek to SR 611)
**(including Jeffries Branch, which enters a quarter mile downstream)

Goose Creek's fourth largest tributary, just north of the Fauquier Co. line, is quite narrow at first, but in a quarter mile Jeffries Branch almost doubles the flow. It is a very pleasant trip below there, with the creek wide enough to minimize the problem of downed trees. However, a man who was looking after the downstream property prevented us from putting in at Green Garden Road. As a result, we had to start 2.5 miles upstream on Jeffries Branch (see below); the alternative of putting in 2 miles upstream on Panther Skin Creek (at US 50) was more problematical because of fences beneath and on the upstream side of Green Garden Road.

The first mile below the confluence is class I, until a class III rapid at the remains of an old dam. Angle left on the 3-foot drop at the top, to miss the cement chunk below. Soon after is a long class II and then a dam that you can skirt via a class II rapid on the far right. This brings you to SR 623 (at 1.7 miles). Below, the creek calms down until a beautiful section with some good class II rapids beneath sheer cliffs. After you pass the only houses alongside, the stream reverts to class I.

We encountered one wire fence that could be just slipped under and several other high cables with only the remnants of fences. There is excellent wildlife; we saw lots of deer, a red fox, great blue herons, hawks, mallards, Canada geese and evidence of beavers (but no beaver dams).

From the confluence, it is 2 miles down Goose Creek, at 4 ft/mile, to SR 611 (Saint Louis Road); fortunately, however, whenever Panther Skin Creek is up, Goose Creek will be fast. Take out on downstream river left, outside Notre Dame Academy. The shuttle along US 50 is direct.

GAUGE: Limestone Branch needs 30 cfs, Beaverdam Creek 180 cfs, Goose Creek near Middleburg (the gauge is just above the take out) 500 cfs. Check the level from the riffles at the put in and the class II visible upstream from SR 623.

JEFFRIES BRANCH: Millville Rd. (SR 743) to Panther Skin Creek

Gradient	Difficulty	Distance	Area	Scenery	Strainers	Rating
30	I	2.5*	6	C	3-5/mi.	-

USGS Quad –Bluemont/Rectortown; Source – Personal descent 4/04
N39 01.47, W77 52.26 to N38 59.83, W77 50.44

*(plus 1.5 miles on Panther Skin Creek to SR 623 – Willisville Road)

This trip passes through some of the prime horse and Angus country of Loudoun County. The riffles are nearly continuous, the estates well maintained, and the tree strainers infrequent. So this would not be a bad paddle, except for the ten fences and the consequent surreptitious feeling you get slipping through them. Fortunately, these estate owners can afford to use wooden boards rather than barbed wire for their fences, and there is usually space to pass your boats and climb through between the boards. There is also one low-water bridge to portage, and quite a few partial strainers to work around.

When you paddle through the fence under Green Garden Road, you are just a quarter mile from Panther Skin Creek. But there are fences at all corners of that bridge, and the same caretaker who wouldn't let us put in on Panther Skin Creek itself (see above), would probably have raised objections at the Jeffries Branch bridge as well (which is just 300 yards away).

GAUGE: The Battle Run gauge should be over 155 cfs and Limestone Branch 50 cfs. If the riffle below the put in is cleanly runnable, you will be okay.

Alf Cooley and I were tying up our boats along Goose Creek, after running Jeffries Branch and Panther Skin Creek, when a Loudoun Co. policeman drove up to ask whether that was our Subaru on Millville Road, two creeks and 8.2 river miles away. We were impressed.

CROMWELLS RUN: Carters Mill Road (SR 715) to Goose Creek

Gradient	Difficulty	Distance	Area	Scenery	Strainers	Rating
18 (65)	?	5.2*	8	?	?	?

USGS Quad –Rectortown; Source – Scouting put in and from US 50
N39 55.86, W77 48.58 to N38 59.55, W77 45.08

*(plus 2.7 miles on Goose Creek to SR 626 – Foxcroft Road)

The put in for this *"explorers' special"* is over the horse jump through a high fence on a dirt road. But first, drive a third of a mile east and ask permission at the house. (Training Barn Road, in 300 yards, might be an alternative.) The flow is supplemented by about 50% in 0.7

miles. The first mile drops 25 feet, but the gradient then decreases to below 10 ft/mile. Most of the run is through woods, so the scenery should be nice and fences few. Approaching US 50 (1.1 miles above Goose Creek), the gradient picks up to 65 ft/mile, but there are fences visible and some houses near the creek. From the confluence, it is 2.7 miles to Bentons Bridge at SR 626 (Foxcroft Road).

GAUGE: Battle Run should be over 90 cfs and Limestone Branch 50 cfs.

NORTH FORK, GOOSE CR.: Along SR 762 (below Sleeter Lake)

Gradient	Difficulty	Distance	Area	Scenery	Strainers	Rating
55	II+	0.5	10	B	2-6/mi.	**

USGS Quad – Bluemont; Source – Personal descent 5/98
N39 07.18, W77 45.25 to 39 06.98, W77 45.00

The North Fork, Goose Creek's largest tributary, starts along the Blue Ridge on the Virginia-WV line, only a few miles from the Shenandoah. In 3 miles, it is impounded behind the 40-foot high Sleeter Lake Dam. A quarter mile below the dam, SR 762 dead-ends at the creek, and there is a delightful half-mile long gorge full of class II and II+ rock gardens and ledges – probably the best paddling in the Goose Creek watershed.

The fun ends abruptly at the SR 782 low-water bridge. Below that, the North Fork quickly flattens out (its average gradient for the remaining 12 miles is 10 ft/mile) and enters ranchland. It is also likely to have fences until it enters the woods just above the confluence with Beaverdam Creek; the final 2.2 miles below that confluence is included in the Beaverdam Creek write-up below, as the access to it from the North Fork itself is not nearly as good.

GAUGE: Look for 300 cfs on the downstream gauge on the North Fork, 60 cfs at Limestone Branch and 170 cfs on Spout Run.

Along Goose Creek, two miles below the confluence with the North Fork, is **Oatlands**, a plantation centered on a Greek Revival mansion that dates from the beginning of the 19th Century. It is operated by the National Trust for Historic Preservation, and is open for visitors from April to November. It is the site of the Loudoun Hunt Point-to-Point races in mid-April and a foxhound show in May. Call 703-777-3174 for details.

CROOKED RUN [north]: SR 725 to No. Fork, Goose Cr. (SR 729)

Gradient	Difficulty	Distance	Area	Scenery	Strainers	Rating
18 (35)	I	2.2	10	C	1-3/mi.	*

USGS Quad – Lincoln; Source – Personal descent 5/02
N39 06.04, W77 40.58 to N39 04.34, W77 41.04

This creek rises just east of Purcellville and flows southwest 5 miles to the North Fork – it is the only significant Goose Creek tributary that does not head to the east. SR 725 provides good access below the confluence of the main branches. Riffles are frequent in the first mile to SR 727 and infrequent after that. From the confluence with the North Fork, it is one-third mile to SR 729, where you take out on river left just above the bridge, and climb up the wall to avoid the barbed wire fence.

At the put in, park on river right so as not to interfere with horse trailers entering the driveway on river left; the couple there are friendly, and the husband kayaks.

GAUGE: The North Fork of Goose Creek gauge near Lincoln (the takeout) should be at least 225 cfs, with 50 cfs on Limestone Branch.

BEAVERDAM CREEK/NORTH FORK GOOSE CREEK: SR 746 (Beaverdam Br. Rd.) to Goose Cr. (SR 733 – Lime Kiln Rd.)

Gradient	Difficulty	Distance	Area	Scenery	Strainers	Rating
6	I	8.2	41	B	1-2/mi.	*

USGS Quad – Lincoln; Source – Personal descent (last 6.7 miles) 2/97
N39 02.61, W77 44.74 to N39 02.30, W77 38.99

Beaverdam Creek flows east for 16 miles from the Blue Ridge to the North Fork. By the time it is big enough to paddle, it is flat, so you might as well wait until it picks up its own North Fork; the first access after that is SR 746. The trip consists of 6 miles on Beaverdam Creek and 2.2 miles on the North Fork. There are few traces of civilization and just one intermediate access – SR 734, after 1.5 miles. There are long ridges and attractive rock formations. Canada geese, kingfishers and hawks will keep you company.

Strainers are relatively common but easy to see and deal with. There was one tricky stretch of riffles, where several partial strainers required precise handling in fast water. The best riffle is half a mile below the confluence, just past the only house close to the creek. Except for 3 or 4 riffles, the North Fork is flat, but had no strainers.

GAUGE: You need about 100 cfs on the Beaverdam Creek gauge near the put in.

NO. FORK, BEAVERDAM CR.: SR 719 to SR 734 spur

Gradient	Difficulty	Distance	Area	Scenery	Strainers	Rating
33 (60)	II	2.4	12	B	1-3/mi.	**

USGS Quad – Bluemont; Source – Personal descent 5/98
N39 04.77, W77 47.28 to N39 04.52, W77 45.78

The put in is shortly below the confluence with Butchers Branch. The steepest section is at the beginning and consists of several nice class II rock gardens. The gradient eases up within a half mile, when you pass under SR 700, but riffles and easy rapids are frequent for the entire paddle. The scenic trip starts out in the woods, enters partially wooded, hilly ranchland for a mile, and then reenters the woods, where there are some pretty rock formations. Deer abound; I saw only two, but was told that close to a hundred have been seen together. Take out at the first low-water bridge, on an unnamed and unpaved private road, just off SR 734. The landowner there welcomes paddlers, as he believes natural beauty was put here to be shared.

I encountered one fence early in the trip, and four tree strainers later on. I only saw the top strand of that fence, which left room to slip under, until the lower strand grabbed me; fortunately it was loose and not barbed, and I could shove it over my head.

It is another 2.9 miles to the confluence with Beaverdam Creek and then 0.3 miles more to SR 746; however, at 13 ft/mile, that stretch would be anticlimactic.

GAUGE: Look for 290 cfs on Beaverdam Creek, 50 cfs on Limestone Branch.

LITTLE RIVER: Aldie to Goose Creek

Gradient	Difficulty	Distance	Area	Scenery	Strainers	Rating
10	I	5.6*	38	C	0-2/mi.	*

USGS Quad – Middleburg/Leesburg; Source – Corbett
N38 58.51, W77 38.37 to N39 01.08, W77 34.56

*(plus 1.5 miles on Goose Creek to Evergreen Mills – SR 621))

The Little River rises along I-66 and occupies the southeast portion of the Goose Creek watershed. It winds for 22 miles across Fauquier and Loudoun Counties, with low gradient and no real rapids. So you might as well limit yourself to the final 5.6 miles, which passes through attractive estates – read about it in Corbett. Incidentally, this is the only "river" in this region which is the tributary of a "creek."

GAUGE: You need about 100 cfs on the Beaverdam Creek gauge.

SYCOLIN CREEK: SR 643 to Goose Creek

Gradient	Difficulty	Distance	Area	Scenery	Strainers	Rating
26	II+	2.3*	14	B	<1/mi.	**

USGS Quad – Leesburg; Source – Personal descent 3/04
N39 03.63, W77 33.14 to N39 05.13, W77 30.67

*(plus 1.3 miles on Goose Creek to Golf Club Road, off Va. 7)

Sycolin Creek drains the land just south of Leesburg. It is a pleasant low-intermediate meal in its own right, with the Golf Course Rapid on Goose Creek as dessert. One could start 4 miles above SR 643, at SR 650, with 8 sq. miles and at 22 ft/mile; however, from what can be seen from the road, and from the final half mile of this, which we ran, there are numerous strainers and few if any interesting rapids.

From the low water bridge on SR 643, just off of SR 653, the trip starts off with riffles and class II- rapids, until a pair of class II+ rock gardens enlivens things. Soon we passed over the walkway of a paintball battlefield. The only fence we encountered was just below this, a double strand of barbed wire, in slow water. In a while, the creek leaves the woods and winds through a more open area, full of geese and mallards, and passes beneath the W&OD bicycle trail. It is mainly flat water and riffles here, and remains so as it reenters the woods, where the one disconcerting factor is gunshots, presumably from a shooting range nearby. At one point, the horizon line disappears, and there is a

50-yard, class II+ rock garden. A little more easy water and attractive scenery, including some high cliffs, bring you to Goose Creek.

Whenever Sycolin Creek is up, Goose Creek will be juicy – we did Sycolin close to zero level, but had 1,500 cfs (3.6, about 17 inches above minimum) on Goose Creek. After one easy rapid, you come to Golf Course Rapid. The easiest route (class II) is far left, just avoiding the trees, while it is class II+ on the far right. For more excitement, the middle is class III, with three holes to avoid or punch. You can scout on the right after running the man-made ledge into an eddy, or scout on the left above that.

GAUGE: Look for at least 45 cfs on the Limestone Branch gauge. The creek is narrow at the put in, so check the level at the riffles upstream along the road.

TUSCARORA CREEK: BR US 15 to SR 653

Gradient	Difficulty	Distance	Area	Scenery	Strainers	Rating
25	II+	4.0	10*	C	<1/mi.	**

USGS Quad – Leesburg; Source – Personal descent 3/93
N39 06.14, W77 34.24 to N39 05.07, W77 31.03

*(including Town Branch, which enters in half a mile)

I first read of this creek in the *Voyageur*, as Mike Stinebaugh's favorite in Loudoun Co. So one cold Saturday, after heavy overnight rain, I led a trip there. Goose Creek was in flood (the gauge was 15 feet), and the water was backed up across the Goose Creek Golf Course to our take out. Tuscarora Creek itself was over two feet at the take out, but dropping.

The best put in is on Davis Avenue off BR 15, just north of the Leesburg Bypass on US 15 and US 7, at the Olde Izaak Walton Park. This is just downstream of the Leesburg Country Club and the confluence with **Dry Mill Branch** (which is larger than upstream Tuscarora Creek). A half mile later, the only other sizable tributary, **Town Branch**, adds 20% to the flow. Take out at Cochran Mill Road (SR 653), just above the Goose Creek Golf Course.

If you lack water for the full trip, you can start at South Harrison St. (0.6 miles), Sycolin St. (SR 643; 1.2 miles) or Lawson Road (SR 653; 1.9 miles).

The scenery is unexciting. Some sections have high mud banks, whereas others are more natural looking. The rapids are mostly class II or II+ ledges and rock gardens. The creek flows around the southern edge of Leesburg. President Grover Cleveland liked to fish in Tuscarora Creek.

GAUGE: Look for at least 60 cfs on the gauge on Limestone Branch.

When the British burned Washington in 1814, the **Government fled to Leesburg**, taking along the originals of the Constitution and Declaration of Independence. During the Civil War, it was a key objective, and changed hands several times. At the nearby **1861 Battle of Balls Bluff**, the Confederates drove Union troops over sheer cliffs and into the Potomac, prompting the first Congressional investigation of the conduct of the war.

The **Tuscarora Indians**, ill treated by the settlers in North Carolina, fled north to New York State after losing a war against the colonists in 1711-13. Being part of the Iroquoian language group, they became the sixth member of the Iroquois Federation, in 1722. They passed only briefly through this area, so it must be the music of their name which has resulted in there being four Tuscarora Creeks in this guidebook (of which the one described here is the best).

ABOVE GREAT FALLS

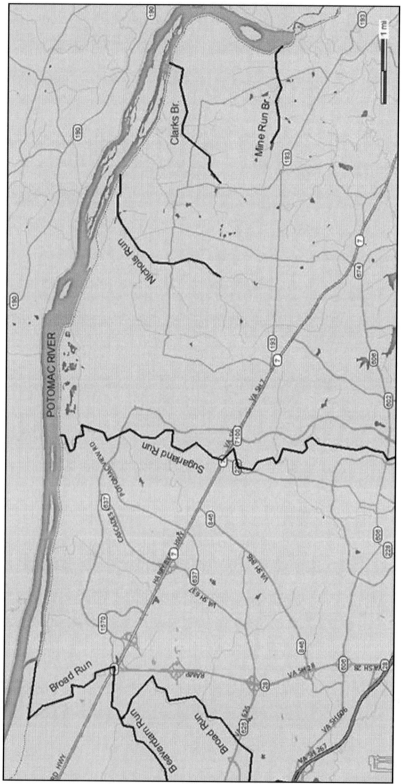

Chapter 32:
ABOVE GREAT FALLS

This chapter covers the streams which flow into a 15-mile stretch of the Potomac, between the Goose Creek and Difficult Run basins, in eastern Loudoun and northwestern Fairfax Counties. In truth, this is not one of the more useful chapters in this book, but it covers some seldom paddled terrain and might satisfy some quirky tastes. **Broad Run**, the only sizable one of these creeks, is a pleasant beginners' trip, with one harder spot. **Beaverdam Run**, the "explorers' special" of the chapter, provides one good drop and a convenient way to access Broad Run. The remaining creeks are all tiny, as you can see from the table below. **Sugarland Run** is a nice little trip. **Nichols Run** is not. **Clarks Branch** has good rapids but too many strainers. **Mine Run Branch** is short but dynamite. Because these creeks enter the Potomac above Great Falls, they do not have the long, steep drops down to the gorge that you will find in the streams in Chapter 34 (Virginia Palisades), but note that the gradients closer to Great Falls are considerably steeper than those further away.

Broad, Beaverdam and Sugarland Runs drain the relatively built-up towns of Sterling, Ashburn and Herndon, respectively, close to the Dulles International Airport. Nichols Run, Clarks Branch and Mine Run Branch, on the other hand, flow through more exclusive residential areas just west of Great Falls.

> Broad Run's largest tributary is not Beaverdam Run but **Horsepen Run**; however, most of that creek is off-limits, within the boundary fence of Dulles International Airport. Only the final third of a mile could ever be run, below the dam at SR 606. It has 25-sq. mi. drainage but not much gradient, and would only flow when the dam overflows.

GAUGES: The one Internet river gauge in this area is on **Broad Run**, near its mouth (76 sq. mi.). The remaining creeks are bracketed between that and the gauges on Difficult Run. For the smaller creeks, there are gauges on Difficult Run above Fox Lake (5.5 sq. mi.) and South Fork, Little Difficult Run (2.7 sq. mi.) – but the readings on the latter can be puzzling. Usually, however, the key strategy is to get to these creeks just as a heavy rain is ending, as time is more critical than river gauge readings. In the table below, **the gauge column reference is to Difficult Run above Fox Lake**, except that the figures *in bold italics are for the Broad Run gauge*.

name	gradient	difficulty	length	area	gauge	rating
Broad Run	5	II- (II+)	5.3	53	*135 cfs*	*
Beaverdam Run	13	I (III-)(?)	0.5	14	*450 cfs*	?
Sugarland Run	20 (40)	II	3.7	3.5	85 cfs	**
Nichols Run	20	II-	2.2	3.3	85 cfs	-
Clarks Branch	58 (100)	II+	1.7	1.4	200 cfs	*
Mine Run Branch	125 (225)	II (IV)	0.4	2.0	200 cfs	**

BROAD RUN: SR 625 (Waxpool Road) to Youngs Cliff Road

Gradient	Difficulty	Distance	Area	Scenery	Strainers	Rating
5	II- (II+)	5.3	53	C	<1/mi.	*

USGS Quad – Sterling; Source – Personal descent 4/97
N39 00.56, W77 27.13 to N39 03.77, W77 26.38

This pleasant, novice creek drains the north side of Dulles International Airport (the south side drains into Cub Run.) The first four miles, to Va. 7, have no rapids, except for three weirs with 2-foot drops into rocky run outs. Then, as the creek makes a sharp left turn, there is a 100-yard, class II+ rapid. The top and bottom parts are wide rock gardens with several routes, while the middle is a 6-foot-wide chute with a wave just below. Check this out in advance for possible strainers by looking upstream from Va. 7. There are a half dozen class I-II rapids over the next mile, until the backwater from the Potomac.

To minimize that backwater, take out 0.7 miles above the confluence, at a set of five metal stairs just upstream of a maple tree, with a house (the first in a half mile) visible beyond it. (Does this sound more like orienteering than paddling?) A narrow trail alongside a fenced yard provides access to the creek – if the trail is still there.

The creek's name is well chosen, for it is 60-100 feet wide. As a result, there are few creek-wide strainers.

If you want to skip most of the flat water and just do the bottom part, you have two alternatives. One is to put in on Beaverdam Run at SR 607 (see below), half a mile above the confluence. The other is to take Va. 7 some 0.4 miles west from Broad Run, turn left into the parking lot behind the Loudoun Square office building, and carry down to Broad Run (if the "no trespassing" signs do not deter you).

Broad Run flows for 12 miles before the put in, and it is over 8 miles from the previous access point (near Arcola, with 9 sq. miles) to SR 625, with a gradient of 8 ft/mile. That's steeper than the section below, but it still doesn't sound like much fun.

GAUGE: The Broad Run gauge (at Va. 7) should read at least 135 cfs. If the class II+ rapid at the upstream side of Va. 7 is runnable, everything is. Even in a dry springtime, a half-inch of rain is likely to bring the creek up.

I ran this creek in mid-April, and was treated to a wonderful display of the famous **Virginia bluebells**, which lined either one bank or the other in great profusion almost the entire way. There was also an interesting array of **wildlife** –two foxes, lots of turtles (including a 2-foot long snapper), an osprey (whose huge nest overhung the creek), and several pairs each of Canada geese and mallards (which accompanied me for much of the way, noisily and quietly, respectively). But if you want to see the wildlife and enjoy the solitude of the woods, you had better come soon; the area is on the cusp of major residential and commercial development.

BEAVERDAM RUN: SR 607 to Broad Run

Gradient	Difficulty	Distance	Area	Scenery	Strainers	Rating
13	I (III-)(?)	0.5*	14	?	?	?

USGS Quad – Sterling; Source – Scouting put in and confluence
N39 02.39, W77 26.97 to N39 03.77, W77 26.38

*(plus 2.2 miles on Broad Run to Youngs Cliff Road)

Beaverdam Run, an *"explorers' special,"* is Broad Run's second largest tributary (after Horsepen Run), and it can be paddled from 3 miles further upstream, starting at SR 641 just south of Ashburn, with 9 sq. mi. at 8 ft/mile. But as that is likely to be all flat water, I just include the final half mile, which has a 3-foot weir with a rocky run out, that looked like class III-, just 100 yards above the confluence. This is a good way to begin a short Broad Run trip, as it gives you all the rapids on both creeks.

GAUGE: The Broad Run gauge should read at least 450 cfs. At that level, the rapid on Broad Run at Va. 7 might also be at least class III-.

SUGARLAND RUN: Queens Row St. to Thomas Ave.

Gradient	Difficulty	Length	Area	Scenery	Strainers	Rating
20 (40)	II	3.7	3.5	C	0-2/mi.	**

USGS Quad – Vienna/Seneca; Source – Trip report (Frank Fico)
N38 58.67, W77 22.14 to N39 01.24, W77 22.09

What I know of this creek, I owe to Mike Stinebaugh, who pioneered this trip, and Frank Fico, who wrote it up in the *Voyageur*. The creek rises a little south of the Dulles Access Road, and then flows between Herndon and Reston.

The uppermost part is debris-choked and multi-channeled, so the first good put in is behind a swim club parking lot off of Queens Row St., near Herndon Parkway in northeast Herndon. The trip starts off through heavy woods, passes subdivisions, follows a bike path, reenters the woods, and finally gets to Va. 228 and Va. 7. There are three class II rapids, plus a variety of good surfing waves. The second of these rapids is formed by a network of beaver dams alongside Va. 228; keep to the left, and aim for a telephone pole standing in the water. (This rapid, of course, is subject to change at the beavers' whim.) The third, not far below Va. 7, provides the best surfing. The first bridge below Va. 7, Thomas Avenue, is a good take out, unless you want to continue on flat water. It is a further 3.8 miles to the Potomac, through a subdivision, at only 8 ft/mile.

GAUGE: About 85 cfs on the gauge on Difficult Run above Fox Lake is minimal; but of course you probably must get to the put in before that reading becomes available.

> The first land grant in Virginia above Great Falls was at the **Sugar Lands**, to Daniel McCarty, who married Ann Lee, daughter of the 2nd Richard Lee, and hence a great aunt once removed (or something like that) to Robert E. Lee.
>
> At the mouth of Sugarland Run is **Lowes Island**, once the site of an Indian village, later the terminal of the Seneca ferry and now the location of two golf courses.
>
> Unfortunately, all the development along Sugarland Run is degrading its water quality, and even dumping so much pollution into the Potomac River that Virginia needed a **new mid-river intake** for its water system because the former intake, shortly below Sugarland Run along the shore, was not getting clean enough water.

NICHOLS RUN: Beach Mill Road (SR 603) to Potomac River

Gradient	Difficulty	Length	Area	Scenery	Strainers	Rating
20	II-	2.2*	3.3	C	7-10/mi.	-

USGS Quad – Seneca; Source – Personal descent 7/04
N39 01.82, W77 18.95 to N39 01.10, W77 14.76

*(plus 3.3 miles on the Potomac to River Bend Park)

This little known stream flows through an upscale residential area near the northernmost tip of Fairfax Co. And, from a paddling standpoint, it deserves to remain little known, for it has tons of negatives but no interesting rapids. The first mile, through hilly woodlands, is full of riffles and very tight turns. Then Jefferson Branch adds up to 50% to the flow, you portage a private low-water bridge, and reach the backwater of a dam. The next quarter mile is across a small lake (with lots of cattails) that appears to be shared by 4 or 5 estates. Stay to the left, past the water intake, and then portage the 8-foot dam. The creek then enters Northern Virginia Regional Park, and conditions really deteriorate. First, the water begins to stink; there must be a sewer outlet nearby. Second, the riffles disappear, and you are left with just flowing flat water, through indifferent scenery. And third, the density of strainers rises.

After three-quarters of a mile of this (it seems much longer), you reach the Potomac (just downstream of Pennyfield Lock on the Maryland side, but on the other side of long Watkins Island). From there, it is 3.3 miles to the Virginia take out at River Bend Park. The current is slow except for a few brief riffles. The most interesting sight is the collection of pipes and valves when you cross the natural gas pipeline.

GAUGE: About 85 cfs on the Difficult Run gauge above Fox Lake is minimal.

CLARKS BRANCH: Beach Mill Road (SR 603) to Potomac River

Gradient	Difficulty	Length	Area	Scenery	Strainers	Rating
57(100)	II+	1.7*	1.4	C	5-10/mi.	*

USGS Quad – Seneca; Source – Personal descent 7/05
N39 01.44, W77 16.92 to N39 01.10, W77 14.76

*(plus 1.3 miles on the Potomac to River Bend Park)

This tiny stream drains the water hazards of River Bend Country Club. It is an interesting adventure, with both variety and fun rapids, but is ruined by a dozen strainers and a dangerous culvert. The first quarter mile is just fast riffles, but then the gradient increases to 100 ft/mile, and there is a 200-yard, twisty, class II+ rapid, which fortunately was free of strainers, as there was not an eddy in sight. Soon the creek jogs sharply right and then left, and goes under a high footbridge. Portage (either side). Ahead, the stream is bound between stone walls, as it rushes steeply towards an unrunnable culvert beneath Carrwood Road.

After that, the creek remains steep and twisty; this limits your advance warning for the frequent strainers. A low water bridge is easily paddled over, and then Clarks Run Road easily paddled under. Below there, the gradient eases up, although there is an interesting rapid through the firebreak, complicated by a cable that you can duck under on the left. Potomac Ridge Road also has an unrunnable culvert. Approaching the Potomac, there is a runnable culvert – except when it is blocked by wood.

From the mouth, it is 1.3 miles, with just a few riffles, down to River Bend Park (Virginia). The Potomac is quite pretty in this section, with many islands. Deer are common throughout the area.

GAUGE: About 200 cfs on the gauge on Difficult Run above Fox Lake is minimal. Timing, of course, is critical, so get there right after a heavy rainfall.

MINE RUN BRANCH: River Bend Road to Patowmack Canal

Gradient	Difficulty	Length	Area	Scenery	Strainers	Rating
125 (225)	II (IV)	0.4	2.0	C	2-5/mi.	**

USGS Quad – Vienna/Seneca; Source – trip report (John Alden) 3/04; full scouting

N38 59.97, W77 15.76 to N38 59.99, W77 15.40

This is the stream that you drive over on the way to the farthest parking areas at Great Falls Park, Virginia. Its little branches, full of small livestock dams, come together at River Bend Road, where there is parking for one car. You can scout almost the entire trip from a hiking trail on river left – and should do so, especially to check for strainers.

The creek starts out twisty and class II, until you approach the private bridge (to a beautifully landscaped house). The next 70 yards is a steep, narrow class IV rock garden – exciting but dangerous. Then comes about 70 yards of class II water, before the stream steepens again for a short class III stretch. Then it slows to class II and finally class I, approaching the road. Take out well above the road, as there is a rapid just above it and not enough head clearance below.

Purists can put back in for the final 100 yards of class II down to the Patowmack Canal. If you do that, note that the water flows down the canal, rather than continuing in the original Mine Run Branch streambed. You could continue down the canal for 300 yards or so, until it is blocked by wood; I don't know if the park rangers would object.

GAUGE: Look for an intense rainfall that leads to at least 200 cfs on the gauge on Difficult Run above Fox Lake.

DIFFICULT RUN BASIN

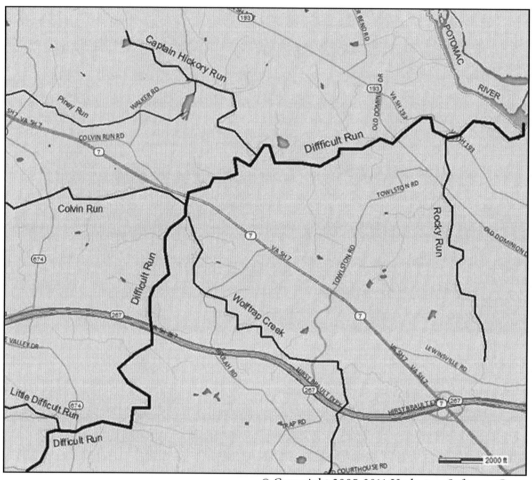

© Copyright 2005-2011 Undertow Software Corp.

Chapter 33:
DIFFICULT RUN BASIN

Difficult Run drains 60 square miles in western Fairfax County, mainly Reston (56,000), Vienna (14,000) and Great Falls (9,000). (Its name is known to paddlers mainly from the Difficult Run Rapids on the Potomac, just above the confluence with Difficult Run itself.) The main stem is rather flat (section 1) until its dramatic final mile (section 2), the *crème de la crème* of this chapter.

It has six moderate-sized tributaries, but several of them have man-made lakes (part of the planned city of Reston) that must generally be full in advance to permit enough flow below them. Snakeden Branch is almost never up, but the other five are included below. **Captain Hickory Run** is the most interesting overall, while short **Rocky Run** has the hardest individual rapid. **Wolftrap Creek** has a decent gorge section. **Colvin Run** (an "explorers' special") is up only when water is pouring over the dam at Lake Fairfax. **Little Difficult Run** (also an "explorers' special") probably has little appeal, and is included only in the interest of completeness.

GAUGES: The Difficult Run near Great Falls gauge (58 sq. mi.) is near the top of section 2. For the tributaries, the gauge on Difficult Run above Fox Lake (5.5 sq. mi.) is more useful. In the table below, the **gauge column refers to Difficult Run above Fox Lake**, except that for Difficult Run itself the gauge near Great Falls is used (in ***bold italics***). There is also a gauge on the South Fork of Little Difficult Run (2.7 sq. mi.), but its readings can be puzzling.

name	gradient	difficulty	length	area	gauge	rating
Difficult Run - Section 1	9	I	7.5	18	***200cfs***	-
- Section 2	80 (300)	IV- (5.1)	1.1	58	***110cfs***	!!!
Little Difficult Run	25	?	0.8	6.2	50cfs	?
Wolftrap Creek	30 (65)	II	2.4	5.3	60cfs	**
Colvin Run	35	?	2.0	3.8	80cfs	?
Captain Hickory Run	40 (75)	III	1.4	5.3	100cfs	**
Rocky Run	40 (100)	I (III+)	0.4	3.3	120cfs	*

DIFFICULT RUN

Almost all local paddlers know Difficult Run Rapids on the Potomac, yet many have never investigated Difficult Run itself. European settlement there began in the 1720s, in the eastern part of the watershed. The width of the main stem prevented easy access to the west, which gave rise to the name "Difficult Run." (And you thought it related to paddling challenges?!) The creek lazes for 13 miles across western Fairfax County, until Georgetown Pike (Va. 193), where it begins to live up to its name (section 2). Section 1, above Georgetown Pike, is a beginners' trip, whose length can be varied. Ron Knipling wrote in the *Voyageur*, regarding the part above Va. 7: "Don't bother with this upper section unless you gain deep personal satisfaction from overcoming all manner of obstacles." But Ed Evangelidi assured me that the strainer situation has improved.

Section 1: Lawyers Road (SR 673) to Va. 193 Parking Area

Gradient	Difficulty	Distance	Area	Scenery	Strainers	Rating
9	I	7.5	18	C	2-4/mi.	-

USGS Quad – Vienna/FallsChurch; Source – Personal descent (last 3 miles) 5/88
N38 55.41, W77 18.75 via N38 57.96, W77 17.25 (Va. 7) to N38 58.66, W77 14.93

There are a variety of put-in and take-out options. Lawyers Road, just below the confluence with Little Difficult Run, is a first reasonable choice. Next come Hunters Mill Road (SR 674) at 1.0 miles (23 sq. mi.), Browns Mill Road at 3.5 miles (30 sq. mi.), Leesburg Pike (Va. 7) at 4.5 miles – just downstream at the sewage treatment plant (45 sq. mi.), Leigh Mill Road at 6 miles and Old Dominion Drive a mile later. The creek then runs alongside Va. 193. Just before it moves away, there is a large parking area. Take out there, because there is no parking at the Va. 193 bridge in a quarter mile.

This rather unexciting paddle has only a few minor ledges and man-made riffles at trail crossings (there is a hiking trail most of the way alongside), but it is scenic, relatively easy to catch up, and feels rather remote considering its suburban location. The gradient diminishes gradually, from 13 ft/mile initially to about half that by the end, while the density of strainers normally decreases as well.

GAUGE: You need 200 cfs on the Difficult Run gauge near Great Falls to start at Lawyers Road, 100 cfs to start at Leesburg Pike. The take out riffle should be runnable.

Section 2: Georgetown Pike (Va. 193) Parking Area to Potomac River

Gradient	Difficulty	Distance	Area	Scenery	Strainers	Rating
80 (300)	IV- (5.1)	1.1	58	A	0-2/mi.	!!!

USGS Quad – Falls Church; Source – Personal descent 5/01
N38 58.66, W77 14.93 to N38 58.92, W77 13.60

This challenging trip is run less than it deserves to be, for two reasons: except for experts, it has a narrow window of suitable water levels, and except for super experts, there is a long, steep portage. But on the positive side, the creek offers six interesting and challenging rapids in a beautiful gorge, only a few miles outside the Washington beltway. It has its own gauge, is not that hard to catch and can be scouted from a hiking trail.

The first quarter mile, to Va. 193, is almost flat, as is the next, but then the excitement begins. The first rapid starts with a 100-yard class II rock garden, which then steepens to end in a class III+ chute. Scout from shore, and then catch an eddy behind a large boulder, just before the hard stuff. At low levels, take the first main drop between the two cone-shaped rocks in midstream, and then stick to the far right of the main tongue. At higher levels, the easiest route is to take the second main drop on the right. After a calm 100 yards, comes a class II+ rock garden, ending in a class III+ double ledge. Eddy out just above the first ledge, on river right. Most of the water flows to the left (class IV-), but you can boof in the middle or try a tight sneak route on the far right. The third rapid starts very soon, class II+ leading up to the final class III chute. Most of the water goes left of the island. About 30 yards after that chute is a 6-foot, class IV- ledge, with a tricky entrance (it pushes you right, against the boulder above) and a grabby hole at the bottom. Catch the eddy below on the right, and ferry across to begin your portage. Just below is the class 5.1 Difficult Run Falls, a complex 10-foot drop with serious pinning possibilities, which has done a lot of damage to paddlers over the years.

Portage up the steep slope on river left, to the main trail, and after that trail peaks, take the side trail with wooden steps back to the creek, with a superb view of the Falls. Before you put in, scout the next rapid, which has a class IV- entrance, unless you have enough water for the sneak on the right. This rapid is harder than it looks, and has pinned some very good paddlers. Then the creek splits around an island. The left side has a very tight entrance (unrunnable at zero level) and is then class III-. The right is a fine class III rock garden (bony at zero level). After the channels meet, there's a short bouncy class II if the Potomac is low, and backwater otherwise. It's then just a flat half-mile to the Old Anglers Inn take out on the Maryland side.

When the Potomac is in flood, with the Little Falls gauge over 10 feet, its backwater into Difficult Run inundates the last two rapids and then starts reducing the drop of Difficult Run Falls. (Paul Schelp ran it during the Hurricane Fran flood of 9/96, when the Potomac was around 15 feet, and faced only a 2-foot drop.) Under those conditions, however, the ferry across the Potomac would be hazardous.

Both the first 4 rapids and the final 2 are often run separately, without a shuttle, the former by carrying back up to the put in, the latter by carrying up from below Difficult Run Rapid on the Potomac.

As the water level rises above zero, the first, third and fourth rapids get harder, the second and fifth easier (because sneak routes open up), and the sixth less bony.

GAUGE: The USGS on-line staff gauge on river right, 70 yards downstream of the Va. 193 bridge, should be at least 3.8 (110 cfs) to run all the rapids. At the put in, the downstream cement footing of the structure at the upstream end of the parking lot should have at least an inch of water flowing over it. However, the drops above the Falls can be run down to about 60 cfs. The creek normally drops around one inch per hour the day after a moderate rain.

At the **second rapid**, when I proposed the sneak route on river right, Ed Grove wondered how I would get past the rock at the bottom of the first drop. I didn't, and came to a screeching halt, with my bow on that rock and my stern in the air. At the **fifth rapid**, just below the main falls, I took the bony sneak route on the right, and Miles Townes, in a kayak, made the extremely tight cut to the left, with the main current. Ed Grove tried that route too, but caught his longer canoe on the rocks and flipped. He carried back up, and repeated his exact performance. In a show of true grit, he tried again. And *deja vu* all over again. When he proposed a fourth attempt, I reminded him of my family commitments that afternoon, and he reluctantly headed downstream.

Unionist Sentiments. At the onset of the Civil War, John Hawxhurst, a Quaker, operated a mill on Difficult Run. While the Virginia legislature was meeting in Richmond to declare secession, the pro-Union residents of Fairfax elected him to represent them at the meeting of the "loyal Virginia government" in Wheeling, on July 2, 1861. The 3-man delegation from Fairfax and Alexandria was the only one from outside of what became West Virginia.

🛶 LITTLE DIFFICULT RUN: Stuart Mill Rd. (SR671) to Difficult Run

Gradient	Difficulty	Distance	Area	Scenery	Strainers	Rating
25	?	0.8	6.2	?	?	?

USGS Quad – Vienna; Source – Scouting put in
N38 55.11, W77 19.54 to N38 55.41, W77 18.75

Little Difficult Run is tiny and flat until it picks up the South Fork of Difficult Run. To avoid some barbed wire, start this *"explorers' special"* at the last crossing of Stuart Mill Road, where it is SR 671. There are horse and mountain bike trails along much of the creek. You can take out at Lawyers Road, a third of a mile below the confluence with Difficult Run, or continue down Difficult Run.

GAUGE: You need at least 25 cfs on the Little Difficult Run gauge.

🛶 WOLFTRAP CREEK: Trap Road (SR 676) to Difficult Run

Gradient	Difficulty	Distance	Area	Scenery	Strainers	Rating
30 (65)	II	2.4	5.3	C	2-4/mi.	**

USGS Quad – Vienna; Source – Personal descent (first 1.5 miles) 11/97
N38 56.47, W77 16.03 to N38 57.95, W77 17.24

Here's an opportunity for you culture vultures to combine a performance at Wolf Trap Farm with a whitewater paddle. And don't complain that any time Wolftrap Creek is up, the grassy slope at the Filene Center will be too wet to sit on; that's what wetsuits and lifejackets are for! Parking at the put in is no problem, as there are about 5,000 spaces (but the lots close at dark on non-performance nights).

After a flat half mile, there is almost a mile of continuous class II rapids, with the gradient reaching 65 feet/mile, down to Beulah Road (Browns Mill), before the creek calms down again. It's another 0.9 miles to the confluence (at 20 ft/mile) and then just a quarter mile down Difficult Run to Va. 7.

We only ran into (as it were – see box below) a few creek-wide strainers above Beulah Road, but there were lots of partial ones that needed to be maneuvered around, plus one footbridge that we could just slip under. We were told there were even more downed trees below Beulah Road.

GAUGE: Difficult Run above Fox Lake should be over 60 cfs.

Wolf Trap Park was the first national park for the performing arts. Established in 1966, it was expanded in 1981 by the addition of The Barns, more intimate 18th century structures, dismantled in upstate New York and reassembled here.

Two miles upstream of the put in is a footbridge under which **FBI mole** Robert Hanssen would place packages of top-secret documents for his Soviet/Russian contacts to collect.

> **Hastening Makes for Chastening.** Frank Fico and I put in with just an hour of daylight left – we had just done Captain Hickory Run, and wanted to take full advantage of the 3-inch rainfall. The creek was high – about two feet. Being in a hurry, we tried not to portage strainers. There was a narrow slot between two big branches, with just a long "twig" in the way, but my boat's stability gave way before that "twig" did, and I had an uncomfortable swim past some other fallen branches and under a low bridge before I could self-rescue. A while later, Frank was about to slip under a fallen tree, when he noticed a branch that was too low. His effort to recover was too late. He managed to get out of the water quickly, but his boat did not come to rest for about 200 yards, and on the opposite side of the creek. By the time it was recovered, dusk had arrived. Luckily, there was just enough light left and no strainers in the steep final quarter mile down to Beulah Road, and a kind motorist drove us down to our car at the take out.

COLVIN RUN: Lake Fairfax to Va. 7/Carpers Farm Way

Gradient	Difficulty	Distance	Area	Scenery	Strainers	Rating
35	?	2.0	3.8	?	?	?

USGS Quad – Vienna; Source – Partial scouting
N38 57.89, W77 19.04 to N38 58.03, W77 17.49

This *"explorer's special,"* is to northern Reston, Northern Virginia's planned city, what the Potomac is to Washington, the nation's planned city. Even more so, because it and its tributaries are dammed 7 times to form lakes that help make Reston so attractive.

Colvin Run itself flows out of one of these, Lake Fairfax, over a sloping spillway with a 15-foot vertical drop; put in below the spillway. For the first 100 yards the streambed is wide, filled with boulders and protected by riprap against the erosive power of water racing down from the spillway. The next quarter mile winds through the developed part of Lake Fairfax Park; this section, and the lake itself, are stocked with trout, and attract lots of local fishermen (for $6/day, with a 6-fish limit). The creek then drops over a 2-foot man-made ledge, and returns to a more natural streambed. There is a mountain-bike trail parallel to the run, but with only occasional views of it. There appear to be no major rapids, but lots of riffles and perhaps an occasional class II. You can also expect a considerable number of strainers.

Take out soon after the creek comes alongside Va. 7 (Leesburg Pike), at Carpers Farm Way – unless you want to continue a channelized quarter mile to Difficult Run.

GAUGE: This creek needs heavy rain that brings Difficult Run above Fox Lake to 80 cfs, when Lake Fairfax is already full.

Near the take out is the restored **Colvin Run Mill**, now a historical landmark, built by Philip Carper in 1794-1810 for milling corn and wheat, much of it for export. Next door is a restored general store, where one can buy flour from the mill. Overlooking the mill, the restored 1820 miller's house is a local arts and crafts museum. The mill is open Wednesday-Sunday from 11:00 to 4:00, from March 15 to December 31. At the put in, **Lake Fairfax Park** is very popular for its water park and soccer fields, as well as for fishing and picnicking. A mile upstream of Lake Fairfax, is an abandoned quarry, once Virginia's only commercial source of **talc**.

CAPTAIN HICKORY RUN: Walker Rd. (SR 681) to Difficult Run

Gradient	Difficulty	Distance	Area	Scenery	Strainers	Rating
40 (75)	III	1.4	5.3	B	3-5/mi.	**

USGS Quad – Vienna; Source – Personal descent 11/97
N38 59.02, W77 17.20 to N38 58.28, W77 16.18

What could be wrong with a creek with a name like this? Not much, except for strainers and brevity. Put in one mile south of Great Falls town center, where the largest tributary, Piney Run (which is much bigger than upstream Captain Hickory Run), enters.

The creek is flat for the first third of a mile, and then there is a class III rapid divided by an island. Scout. Most of the water goes to the right, but we chose the left, as the right was congested with rocks and logs. After another third of a mile comes a steep but straightforward class II+ ledge. I remember thinking that two nice rapids was not really enough payback for the half dozen strainers. But then comes the gorge, and whoopee! There are two class III rock gardens, each at least 200 yards long, with a short pool between them. The trip ends with an easy 200 yards to the confluence, followed by a half mile of fast class I water on Difficult Run to Leigh Mill Road.

GAUGE: The Difficult Run gauge above Fox Lake should be over 100 cfs.

ROCKY RUN: Towlston Road to Difficult Run

Gradient	Difficulty	Distance	Area	Scenery	Strainers	Rating
40 (100)	I (III+)	0.4	3.3	B	5-10/mi.	*

USGS Quad – Falls Church; Source – Personal descent 6/02
N38 58.27, W77 14.82 to N38 58.56, W77 14.77

From near the intersection of Leesburg Pike and the Dulles Access Road, this creek flows north for 3 miles until it meets Difficult Run at Georgetown Pike. It is hardly runnable until it picks up its main tributary, Sharpers Run, just above Old Dominion Drive. But the access is poor there, so put in at Towlston Road, for the one hard rapid.

The creek has continuous riffles for the first 600 yards, with pretty scenery and a few strainers, as it flows through upscale real estate. Watch out for low branches. After a short pool, the creek suddenly becomes class III+ for its final 100 yards. This rapid will almost certainly have at least partial strainers, but it is difficult to scout from shore or to portage because of the steep slopes and heavy vegetation in this little gorge. It begins with a short, narrow chute on the left, which leads into a steep rock garden, followed by a sharp, blind left turn and a final bouncy straightaway. Because it is narrow, blind and prone to strainers, **this rapid is more dangerous** than its class III+ rating suggests.

You flush out just above Va. 193, a quarter mile into Difficult Run section 2. Your choices then are to (a) take on the downstream challenge, (b) load your boat quickly in a no-parking area (which I did), (c) paddle upstream a quarter mile (tough), or (d) ferry across and carry upstream. Choose your poison.

GAUGE: The Difficult Run gauge above Fox Lake should be at least 120 cfs.

CAPITAL CANOEING AND KAYAKING

VIRGINIA PALISADES

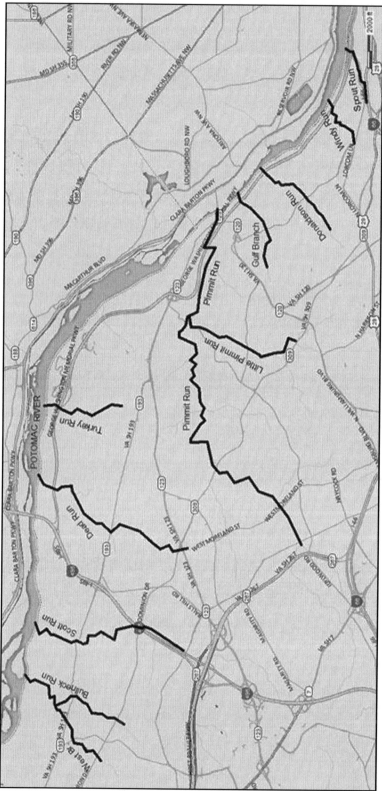

© Copyright 2005-2011 Undertow Software Corp.

Chapter 34:
VIRGINIA PALISADES

This chapter covers the area around McLean and northern Arlington that drains into the Potomac before that river turns due south at Washington National Airport. The main physical characteristic, which distinguishes this area from both the Maryland/DC shore across the Potomac (chapters 18-19) and Virginia Suburbs South (chapter 35), is the impressive cliffs/palisades, averaging about 100 feet high, along the Potomac. These have been carved by the power of the river below Great Falls. They produce beautiful waterfalls and cascades, most of which can be seen from the Potomac River or the Potomac Heritage Trail. From a paddling perspective, however, this makes it extremely difficult to run the creeks all the way to the Potomac. For most paddlers, that means a difficult portage as well as a trans-Potomac shuttle.

While many paddlers know these streams' waterfalls and mouths along the Potomac, several of the creeks in this chapter may never have been paddled, and this is one of the only chapters in this book for which none of the streams are in any other guidebooks (although some are on the web).

There are hiking trails along most of these streams, so it is relatively easy to scout them in advance. **Pimmit Run**, an intermediate trip (section 1), is now paddled fairly regularly. Ron Knipling has been down **Little Pimmit Run** twice, and I have heard of other trips on **Scott Run**. Erik Amason has run **Donaldson, Windy and Dead runs,** and written them up on the AWA site. Other experts have run several of the waterfalls in very high water. Otherwise, this is all virgin territory, as far as I know. Given the tiny size of the watersheds, that is hardly surprising.

Much of it is also extremely difficult and dangerous, because of the steep gradients and frequent strainers. In particular, **Gulf Branch** and Donaldson, Windy and **Spout runs**, which are all close together, have average gradients around 170 ft/mile – excluding the waterfalls. Instead of a waterfall, **Dead Run** has a strainer-filled 700 ft/mile gorge over the last 250 yards. **Turkey Run** (125 ft/mile) and **Bullneck Run** (140 ft/mile) are the only streams in this area that can be paddled to the Potomac without going over a waterfall. So this chapter has quite a few "explorers' specials."

GAUGES: For the larger streams (Pimmit and Scott Runs), the gauge on Fourmile Run at Alexandria (12.6 sq. mi.), a few miles to the southeast is applicable. For the smallest creeks, just get to your put in immediately after (or even during) a heavy downpour; by the time you get any gauge readings, the water has probably drained out to the Potomac. But the new (2011) gauge on Dead Run at Whann Ave (2.05 sq. mi.) should help. **Dead Run is the reference in the gauge column below**, except that *Fourmile Run is used for the readings in bold italics.* Unfortunately, no rainfall gauges are reported for this area.

name	gradient	difficulty	length	area	gauge	rating
Bullneck Run	140	III	0.9	1.0	140cfs	***
"West Branch"	250	II (VI)	0.3	1.0	140cfs	*
Scott Run - Section 1	50	II (II+)	1.3	4.1	200cfs	*
- Section 2	95 (125)	III	0.7	5.0	225cfs	***
- Section 3	250	IV+ (5.0)	0.1	5.6	250cfs	!!!
Dead Run - Section 1	35	II	1.0	0.6	150cfs	-
- Section 2	200 (700)	5.1	0.6	2.3	115cfs	!!!
Turkey Run	125 (175)	III+ (?)	0.8	0.8	160cfs	?
Pimmit Run - Section 1	45 (125)	III	4.0	5.9	200cfs	***
- Section 2	250	5.1	0.1	1.0	400cfs	!!
Little Pimmit Run	60	III-	1.8	2.1	65 cfs	***
Gulf Branch	170 (300)	IV (?)	0.5	0.7	180cfs	?
Donaldson Run	170 (230)	IV (5.0)	0.7	1.0	140cfs	!!
Windy Run	170	III (?)	0.7	0.4	250cfs	?
Spout Run	200 (400)	III+ (IV+)	0.8	1.5	130cfs	?

BULLNECK RUN: Georgetown Pike (Va. 193) to the Potomac

Gradient	Difficulty	Distance	Area	Scenery	Strainers	Rating
140	III	0.9*	1.0	A	3-7/mi.	***

USGS Quad – Falls Church; Source – Personal descent 5/05 (last 0.6 miles)
N38 57.60, W77 13.13 to N38 58.23, W77 11.89

*(plus a mile on the Potomac to Carderock)

I had seen the mouth of this little creek at the entrance to Yellow Falls, but higher up was *aqua incognita*. Georgetown Pike (Va.193) crosses Bullneck Run and its "West Branch" a quarter mile above their confluence. On the main stem, there is barely space to park, so you might want to just unload there and then park at the "West Branch."

The gradient is pretty steep all the way, but there are no major drops. I have not run the first quarter mile (we came down the "West Branch"). Below the confluence, the creek starts off class II with a few class III spots, but the latter soon come to predominate, before the gradient eases up toward the end. It is a continuous rock garden, with a few minor ledges. At low levels, there are enough eddies to boat scout most of the way. It is a lovely gorge, with no signs of civilization other than hiking trails and a No Trespassing sign. We had few creek-wide strainers, but wood complicated several of the drops.

Once you reach the Potomac, you run Yellow Falls and continue almost a mile to the take out at Carderock (on the Maryland side).

GAUGE: Dead Run needs 140 cfs and Fourmile Run should be rising steeply, to about 850 cfs. We had just enough water after 2.5 inches of morning rain.

> Like Rock Run on the other side of the Potomac, Bullneck Run also had its gold rush. The **Kirk Gold Mine**, located 350 yards above the Potomac, included a 25-yard long shaft, and, in 1936-37, a narrow gauge track to haul the ore for processing.

"WEST BR., BULLNECK RUN": Va. 193 to the Potomac

Gradient	Difficulty	Distance	Area	Scenery	Strainers	Rating
250	II(VI)	0.3	1.0	A	3-7/mi.	*

USGS Quad – Falls Church; Source – Personal descent 5/05
N38 57.67, W77 13.31 to N38 58.23, W77 11.89

Alf Cooley, RC Forney and I would never have run this creek, except that a fallen tree blocked access to Bullneck Run. So instead of a quarter mile of class III, we got a play wave at the put in, a quarter mile of class I, a portage around a 35-foot waterfall, and 50 yards of class II to the confluence – so inferior to its sister stream just to the east.

You could double the length of your run on this creek by putting in at Spring Hill Road. The gradient for that section is 60 ft/mile, and I have no idea what is in there.

GAUGE: Dead Run needs 140 cfs and Fourmile Run should be rising steeply to about 850 cfs. We had just enough water after 2.5 inches of morning rain.

SCOTT RUN

Scott Run Falls, visible from the Potomac across from Carderock, may have discouraged trips on this stream. But except for the problem of what to do after you finish, section 2 of Scott Run is a high-intermediate delight. The creek rises alongside I-495, drains Tysons Corner and flows north for 5 miles to the Potomac. It is channelized for 2 miles alongside I-495 until Old Dominion Drive, where it leaves the Beltway and enters its natural streambed. The three short sections differ greatly in difficulty.

Section 1: Old Dominion Drive (Va. 738) to Georgetown Pike (Va. 197)

Gradient	Difficulty	Distance	Area	Scenery	Strainers	Rating
50	II (II+)	1.3	4.1	D	2-4/mi.	*

USGS Quad – Falls Church; Source – Personal descent 9/97
N38 56.73, W77 12.12 to N38 57.57, W77 12.33

The put in is a short, steep descent at the southwest corner of the bridge. The first half mile, under the Beltway and through the woods, is class I. Where the creek takes a sharp right turn alongside a pretty cliff, and begins to parallel Swinks Mill Road, the difficulty increases to class II, but the scenery deteriorates to backyards and riprap. When the stream pulls alongside Swinks Mill Road, there is a dangerous low-water bridge; portage on the right well in advance, as there is no eddy at the bridge. (A tragic accident occurred here; anticipating high water, the owner of the house across the creek had left his car on the Swinks Mill Road side, but he was swept into the creek and drowned when he attempted to return to his car on foot across the bridge.) Soon afterwards, the creek passes beneath Swinks Mill Road, with limited clearance. Check out both of these bridges on your shuttle. Below the second bridge is a class II+ rapid followed by an overhanging bamboo grove, and then Old Georgetown Pike (Va. 193).

GAUGE: Look for 200 cfs on Fourmile Run at Alexandria. The midstream gravel bar on the upstream side of Old Dominion Drive is just under water at zero level.

Section 2: Georgetown Pike (Va. 197) to Above Final Gorge

Gradient	Difficulty	Distance	Area	Scenery	Strainers	Rating
95 (125)	III	0.7	5.0	A	1-5/mi.	***

USGS Quad – Falls Church; Source – Personal descent 9/97
N38 57.57, W77 12.33 to N38 58.03, W77 12.24

Here the best part begins, in a pretty gorge through Scott Run Nature Preserve. There is a hiking trail alongside, which you might use to scout in advance. Take the right side around the first island alongside the parking area. Class III rock gardens and ledges abound. There are likely to be strainers, plus two sets of low cylindrical concrete piles for hikers to keep their feet dry where the trail crosses the stream; at low levels, it will be scrapey crossing these. Shortly below the first set is a steep ledge with a midstream boulder at the bottom – probably the hardest rapid above the falls.

As you approach the hills guarding the Potomac, the creek bends 90-degrees to the right, and begins its dramatic plunge down to the river. Catch the large eddy on the left just at the turn. You now have three alternatives: (a) run section 3, if you have the skills; (b) transport your boat back to Va. 193, along a wide, level trail; (c) drag/carry up the steep trail over the ridge and then down (sort of on a trail) to the Potomac, and ferry almost directly across to Carderock.

GAUGE: The rapid alongside the parking area at Swinks Mill is a good gauge. Fourmile Run at Alexandria should be over 225 cfs. This creek drops 6-12 inches per hour after a heavy summer storm.

Section 3: Above Final Gorge to Potomac River (ferry to Carderock)

Gradient	Difficulty	Distance	Area	Scenery	Strainers	Rating
250	IV+ (5.0)	0.1	5.0	A	0-10/mi.	!!!

USGS Quad – Falls Church; Source – Trip report (John Alden, on AWA site)
N38 58.03, W77 12.24 to N38 58.23, W77 11.89

This is way above my skill level, so I quote from John Alden's trip report on the AW website: *"The creek narrows down to 10-15' as it plummets over boulder piles and ledges …. Eddies abound and the drops can all be boat scouted, but … make sure there are no trees below the drops before committing. The entrance rapid can be entered on the right or left. Either side requires some technical moves to avoid broaching on the numerous rocks. Either way, there are at least two must-make moves …. The entrance [class 5.0] drops about 7 feet in the span of about 15 linear feet. The next rapid is a boulder drop of about 3 feet that can be run anywhere. The run out … brings you to the next ledge, which abruptly drops 4 feet …. The right side is more straightforward, with the left being more technical …. This leads directly into the next broken ledge, which was run on both the left and right. The total drop was about 5 feet. The right side of the drop had plenty of pinning potential and almost flipped me …."*

After a few more tough rapids, they reached *"the only sizable eddy in the gorge, which served as our take-out.... The creek continued through three more rapids in the next 25 feet and dropped another 20 feet.... Then the water rebounded off the right side gorge wall and formed a flume that fed directly into a 15-foot waterfall. The waterfall was runnable, but the landing zone in the Potomac River was shallow and rocky. The Potomac would need over 7 feet on the Little Falls gauge to pad out the landing zone."*

GAUGE: This probably needs a bit more water than section 2; the creek is steeper but narrower here. A minimum would be 250 cfs on Fourmile Run.

In 1969-70, it looked like most of what is now **Scott Run Nature Preserve** was going to become a subdivision. The property had belonged to Edward B. Burling, one of the founders of the Covington and Burling law firm, and had been used for entertaining the Washington elite. After he died, developers bought the land, but strong local opposition, including a petition with 2,300 signatures collected door to door by high school students, convinced Fairfax County to opt for a park instead, once voters approved a special tax for the purchase. And the poor developers, who had paid $2.4 million, were forced to sell for just $3.6 million a few months later!

Alexander Scott acquired 946 acres alongside the creek in 1716.

DEAD RUN

Despite its unappealing name, this is an interesting little stream, through the suburbs of McLean and Langley (better known as the site of the CIA). Perhaps its name comes from the fate of enemy agents who were caught ... but I digress.

Section 1 is an easy paddle mostly through McLean Central Park and Dead Run Park, while section 2 starts off relatively flat but becomes the steepest and probably toughest trip in the area. Before you run section 2, make sure to hike it.

Section 1: McLean Central Park to Georgetown Pike

Gradient	Difficulty	Distance	Area	Scenery	Strainers	Rating
35	II	1.0	0.6	C	1-5/mi.	*

USGS Quad – Falls Church; Source – Personal descent 8/97
N38 58.36, W77 11.22 to N38 57.12, W77 11.00

The put-in is near the intersection of Old Dominion Drive and Dolley Madison Blvd. (Va 123). Take Earnestine St. off Old Dominion for one block and turn right on Martha Jane St. to where it dead ends into the park. The narrow creek twists through the woods, past backyards and beneath overhanging branches. The four footbridges are no problem, nor is Churchill Road, midway. Below that, the gradient picks up, and there are some class II rock gardens. Take out on river right, 50 yards above Georgetown Pike, because the passage under it is a serious hazard, and reentry is very difficult as well.

GAUGE: Look for intense rainfall. The Dead Run gauge needs 150 cfs and the Fourmile Run gauge would probably have to get over 900 cfs.

> The day I ran this creek, National Airport recorded 105 degrees, the hottest in 61 years. This sparked intense early evening **thunderstorms** – 3.23 inches at Dulles and 1.35 at National. Dead Run is in between. Just as a downpour was ending, I dropped off my bicycle at Georgetown Pike, where there was at least a foot of water on Dead Run. But the creek drops so fast that I had zero level at the put in, 10 minutes later. I was passing Churchill Road when the next storm hit. I had to stop twice to dump water, but at least the creek was no longer bony! The bike shuttle was a continuous splash, but I was already soaked and didn't mind the cooling effect.

Section 2: End of Whann Avenue to Potomac River (ferry to Lock 10)

Gradient	Difficulty	Distance	Area	Scenery	Strainers	Rating
200(700)	5.1	0.6	2.3	B	2-6/mi.	!!!

USGS Quad – Falls Church; Source – AW site (Erik Amason)
N38 57.55, W77 10.55 to N38 58.35, W77 10.13

Park at the end of Whann Ave., proceed straight (this is a narrow public access to the Potomac River hiking network) and pass the USGS gauging station. (When the creek is dry, the visual gauge reads 1.3.) The trip consists of an easy three-eighths mile at 40 ft/mile through Langley Forest and down to the GW Parkway, and then an incredibly steep quarter mile (described in detail and with photos on the AW site), where the creek drops 100 feet over 250 yards. There is a final 70-yard, class III+ rock garden to the Potomac.

GAUGE: Look for over 115 cfs on Dead Run and 700 cfs on Fourmile Run.

〰️ TURKEY RUN: Turkey Run Road to Potomac River (ferry to Lock 7)

Gradient	Difficulty	Distance	Area	Scenery	Strainers	Rating
125 (175)	III+(?)	0.8	0.8	B-	6-10/mi.	?

USGS Quad – Falls Church; Source – Complete scouting on foot
N38 57.29, W77 09.51 to N38 57.88, W77 08.33

This *"explorers' special,"* along with Bullneck Run, is one of the only two runs from the Virginia heights to the Potomac without a waterfall. Take the right fork of Turkey Run Road (off Georgetown Pike) to the very end, and then continuing straight on foot for a few yards. The other branch of the creek enters in 150 yards. I suggest you hike the trail along this creek before running it, especially to look for strainers.

The stream starts out mild but twisty and strainer prone. Shortly after the creek crosses the trail for the first time, on a sharp left turn, there is an irregular 6-foot drop (class III+?) that is often blocked by wood. Then the stream becomes continuous class III and strainers less common, especially once you reach the GW Memorial Parkway. Below the Parkway is a steep drop (class III+) marked by a large mid-stream boulder, with a tight channel on the right. Soon you are at the delta, where the stream splits into two channels – the right one has more water and less wood. Ferry across the Potomac to Lock 7 (a mile away).

GAUGE: Dead Run needs 160 cfs and Fourmile Run some 1,000 cfs.

PIMMIT RUN

Pimmit Run has become fairly popular because of its good rapids and in-town location. It even has a web site, http://www.deepwater.org/asa/pimmit. While it does not stay up as long as Rock or Pohick creeks, it is, along with Scott Run, the easiest creek to catch in this chapter. But timing is still critical, as it can drop several inches an hour.

The creek rises near the intersections of I-66, I-495 and Va.7, between Tysons Corner and Falls Church. It flows through upscale neighborhoods and pretty parks, has surprisingly good water quality, but is too narrow, flat and strainer filled until Old Dominion Drive, after 3.5 miles.

> The creek is named after **John Pommett**, who had a plantation there around 1680.
> Just above its mouth, Pimmit Run passes **Fort Marcy**, an earthwork 18-gun fortification built by the Union in late 1861 to guard the Virginia side of Chain Bridge. Civil War rifle pits and breastworks are common alongside lower Pimmit Run. Early in the Clinton administration, Fort Marcy was the site of Vince Foster's suicide.

Section 1: Old Dominion Drive to above Chain Bridge/Glebe Road

Gradient	Difficulty	Distance	Area	Scenery	Strainers	Rating
45 (125)	III	4.0	5.9	C	2-3/mi.	***

USGS Quad – Falls Church/Washington West; Source – Personal descent 6/06
N38 55.79, W77 10.18 to N38 55.74, W77 07.12

After an easy first third of mile, the gradient increases to 80 ft/mile, and there are several class III-rapids over the next third of a mile. The following 1.5 miles have mainly riffles, until the gradient picks up to 60 ft/mile a quarter mile before Ranleigh Road (which comes right after a footbridge). Scout Ranleigh Road; the creek divides into 6 tubes, some of which may be blocked, too high or too low. Next comes Kirby Road, where there is adequate clearance, and then the largest tributary, Little Pimmit Run, enters. The gradient eases up a quarter mile below Kirby Road, as the creek swings alongside the GW Parkway.

But a half mile later, as you pass a stone wall high on the right (reachable from Richmond St., off Glebe Road), it begins its mile-long plunge to the Potomac. The gradient reaches 100 ft/mile beneath the Parkway, and then 125 ft/mile in the approach to Chain Bridge/Glebe Road, in a continuous class III rock garden with only micro eddies. Scout your take out beforehand; my approach is to run aground on river right and carry out along the Potomac Heritage Trail to the parking area.

For an urban stream, Pimmit Run is rather pretty and clean, and the water, while a deep muddy brown, has only the faintest whiff of sewage and according to the EPA has the best quality in Arlington County. No doubt, its location in upscale McLean is of great help, as is the fact that it flows mostly through parkland (Pimmit Bend, Potomac Hills and Fort Marcy parks). Strainers are a drawback, but the creek is generally wide and straight enough that these can be seen in advance.

GAUGE: The Fourmile Run gauge at Alexandria should be at least 200 cfs.

Section 2: Chain Bridge/Glebe Road to Potomac River

Gradient	Difficulty	Distance	Area	Scenery	Strainers	Rating
250	5.1	0.1	11	C	0-20/mi.	!!

USGS Quad – Washington West; Source – John Alden 2/03; watching a run 6/06
N38 55.74, W77 07.12 (carry back up or go a mile to Fletchers Boathouse in Md.)

This short and dangerous plunge to the Potomac River should be scouted carefully from both banks. There is a low-water footbridge (the remains of a gristmill) under Glebe Road, with a pair of 4-foot wide culverts that may be blocked; one can put in below there. In 50 yards, the creek turns left and drops 25 feet over a series of irregular 3-10 foot ledges, with lots of serious dangers. The far left route involves a sharp turn around the remnants of a wall, soon followed by a 10-foot drop. The rest is anticlimactic.
    GAUGE: The Fourmile Run gauge should be at least 400 cfs.

> At **the mouth of Pimmit Run**, a tobacco inspection warehouse was built in 1742, and this area subsequently became an industrial center with a gristmill, paper mill, brewery, distillery, woolen factory, and cooper and blacksmith shops. After floods destroyed early bridges, a chain suspension bridge (Chain Bridge) was built here across the Potomac in 1808. When the British burned Washington in 1814, State Department documents, including the original Declaration of Independence, spent a night at the Patterson gristmill at the mouth of Pimmit Run. In the 1890s, Columbia Power and Light generated electricity from the final rapid on Pimmit Run. Iron rings, that were used to moor scows picking up rocks from nearby quarries, can still be seen in the boulders near the mouth. The current bridge dates from 1936.

LITTLE PIMMIT RUN: Dumbarton St. to Pimmit Run (Kirby Rd.)

Gradient	Difficulty	Distance	Area	Scenery	Strainers	Rating
60	III-	1.8	2.1*	C	1-3/mi.	***

USGS Quad – Falls Church; Source – Trip report (Ron Knipling) 6/91
N38 54.81, W77 08.58 to N38 56.12, W77 08.40

*(including a tributary that enters after 0.15 miles

This stream has continuous action but no major rapids, as it heads north through the Chesterbrook area of McLean (you cross Chesterbrook Road midway). You can take out where the creek leaves Kirby Road, 100 yards above the confluence, or continue down Pimmit Run for its best and final 1.5 miles (if it is not too high). Ron Knipling enjoyed this creek enough to come back. Here is most of his trip report in *The Voyageur*:

    "At 9:30am on a Saturday, I was up on a ladder painting window trim. Then the rain came – 45 minutes of moderate-to-heavy rain. I told Leslie that I couldn't paint in the rain, and ran to get my paddling gear. I'd coveted Little Pimmit Run for years. It had never been paddled, at least not to the knowledge of fellow creek fanciers or incredulous residents along the creek. One little girl (my daughter's friend) who lives next to Little Pimmit told me, 'Mr. Knipling, you can't paddle that creek. You'd hit too many rocks.'

'You don't understand, Adrian,' I replied, 'I'm an expert at hitting rocks!'

When I got to the put-in just off Old Dominion Drive on Dumbarton Street, Little Pimmit was running at about +2 inches. The creek is basically class 2-3 and similar to "Big" Pimmit in its rapids and ambiance, including smell. Little Pimmit has a few blind turns and occasional tree strainers, but fewer obstacles than you'd expect on a stream that's only 10 feet wide. The best parts are at the beginning and then near the end where it parallels Kirby Road for 1/4 mile before joining "Big" Pimmit.

I made the run in my Old Town Otter OC-1, the best shallow creek boat in existence. It's the best because of its narrow, flat-bottom hull and because you know that if you do destroy it, it's no great loss.

The most dangerous part was jogging the shuttle along Kirby Road – no shoulders, steep banks, and blind curves. On the creek, poison ivy was ubiquitous."

GAUGE: Dead Run needs 65 cfs and Fourmile Run at Alexandria 400 cfs.

> **History.** Small as this creek is, it had a mill, owned by William Adams. Reportedly, Dolly Madison passed by there in her flight from the British in 1814. Much of the run goes through the Marie Butler Leven Preserve, an 18-acre arboretum and nature preserve that was a 1962 bequest in her honor by her husband

GULF BRANCH: Military Rd to beneath George Washington Pkwy.

Gradient	Difficulty	Distance	Area	Scenery	Strainers	Rating
170 (300)	IV(?)	0.5	0.7	B	4-8/mi.	?

USGS Quad – Washington West; Source – Complete scouting
N38 55.16, W77 07.19 to N38 55.29, W77 07.06

Scout this tiny *"explorers' special"* on foot – there is a good trail all the way. It flows above ground for only 1.4 miles, in northwestern Arlington County, mostly through Gulf Branch Park. Above Military Road, it is strainer clogged, and there is an unrunnable culvert beneath Military Road. So put in just below Military Road, to savor the widest and steepest part of this little stream.

The first 0.4 miles, at 100 ft/mile but with no major drops, is class III. Then, just past some stone stairs on river right, the stream really gets serious for 0.1 miles, as the gradient soars and the opportunities to stop before any strainers diminish. Right beneath the GW Parkway is the last take-out option; below, in its final 100 yards, the creek drops 60 feet to the Potomac, in a series of cascades. The steep trail down the cliff side is slippery when wet, so instead carry back up a quarter mile to 36th Road N. and Nelson St. That is a long carry for a short run (but I didn't design the creek).

GAUGE: Wait for an intense rainfall, and then judge from the trail. Notionally, Dead Run needs 180 cfs and Fourmile Run should be rising rapidly to 1,100 cfs.

> The **Gulf Branch Nature Center**, on the upstream side of Military Road, is popular for elementary school trips in search of environmental education. They can tell you that the creek was originally called Spring Run, but not why it was changed to Gulf Branch, as there is nothing that you might call a "gulf" nearby.

🏞 DONALDSON RUN: Military Road to above Potomac River

Gradient	Difficulty	Distance	Area	Scenery	Strainers	Rating
170 (230)	IV (5.0)	0.7	1.0	B	3-7/mi.	!!

USGS Quad – Wash. West; Source – Complete scouting; AW website (Eric Amason) N38 54.66, W77 06.81 to N38 55.11, W77 06.14

The two branches join at Military Road. This *"explorers' special"* is class III and IV except for two major drops. The first is the remains of a broken dam, named "Pump House Falls" by Eric Amason, who made the first reported descent (in 2003), where most of the water goes through a narrow, rocky 8-foot drop on the far left. Portage on the right. Soon after there is a 15-foot waterfall ("the George"), consisting of three distinct drops, shortly above the GW Parkway. This is class 5.0 and prone to strainers. You may want to carry a ways below this waterfall, as the creek stays very steep. Fortunately, there is a good (albeit steep in places) trail alongside the stream. Put back in 100 yards above the Potomac, for the final rapids, and then ferry across to Fletchers Boathouse.

GAUGE: Like all the similar creeks around, you must go after intense rainfall. Maybe 140 cfs on Dead Run and 850 cfs on Fourmile Run are the notional equivalents.

This was **Swimming Landing Run** until the Donaldsons bought the land. The foundations of their 1840's barn can still be seen, as can the family cemetery. Their former estate, on the east side of the creek, is now part of Potomac Overlook Regional Park. Remains have also been found of an **Indian camp** used from about 500 BC to 500 AD. The Nature Center has exhibits.

Upstream of the put in is the Donaldson Run community of North Arlington. The **restoration** of the upstream stretch of Donaldson Run, involving clean up, erosion control, removal of invasive species and replanting with native shrubs and trees, has been the main focus of activity by the local civic association, according to a Washington *Post* article of March 11, 2006.

🏞 WINDY RUN: Lorcom Lane to above Potomac R. (ferry to Fletchers)

Gradient	Difficulty	Distance	Area	Scenery	Strainers	Rating
170	III(?)	0.7	0.4	C	4-8/mi.	?

USGS Quad – Washington West; Source – Complete scouting; AW website (Eric Amason) N38 54.03, W77 06.12 to N38 55.11, W77 06.14

This tiny *"explorers' special"* (whose name means blowy, not twisty) is a surprisingly respectable run that you can scout from a trail. But it has problems galore. First, to put in, you scramble down a steep bank near the intersection of Lorcom Lane and Nellie Custis Drive, where the creek emerges from a culvert. Second, expect strainers, some in bad spots. Finally, there is the slide, just past the GW Parkway, where the creek drops 25 feet. You can portage down the staircase on river right, but decide in advance where you will pull out, as a class III rapid leads to the big drop. From the bottom it's only 30 yards of class II to the Potomac and then a mile of flat water up to Fletchers or down to the Key Bridge.

GAUGE: This stream needs 250 cfs on Dead Run, 1,500 cfs on Fourmile Run.

SPOUT RUN: Spout Run Parkway to Potomac River (Georgetown)

Gradient	Difficulty	Distance	Area	Scenery	Strainers	Rating
200 (400)	III+(IV+)	0.8	1.5	C	1-4/mi.	?

USGS Quad – Washington West; Source – Complete scouting on foot
N38 53.83, W77 05.70 to N38 54.22, W77 04.11

Because of Spout Run Parkway, this little *"explorers' special"* is far better known among the driving public than larger nearby creeks like Pimmit Run or Scott Run, but, it is virtually unknown (in the Biblical sense) to the paddling community. Yet it contains the nearest difficult rapids to downtown Washington; yes, I actually measured.

Spout Run emerges just north of US 29 (Lee Highway), and flows 0.8 miles to the Potomac, dropping 160 feet in the process, the final 40 feet in the last 0.1 miles. As is usual when a highway has been built alongside, the creek has been tampered with, to minimize the risk of it undermining or flooding the roadway. In this case, the evident signs of that include large boulders in the streambed, high banks and comparatively few strainers.

You can park at the Spout Run Terrace Apartments or, preferably, at Giant across the street from there, at the top of Spout Run Parkway, and put in just after the creek emerges from underground. The trip starts out mainly class II, with a few drops of up to class III, as you pass beneath I-66, and then runs in a narrow gorge between Spout Run Parkway and a wooded hillside. At the 0.3-mile mark the stream makes a sharp left turn under the eastbound lanes of Spout Run Parkway, and then runs in the median between the eastbound and westbound lanes. It gradually steepens, to 200 feet/mile; there are no major drops, but I rate this class III+ due to its continuity.

As you approach the eastbound lanes of the George Washington Parkway (high above you), and just before cutting under the westbound lane of Spout Run Parkway, the water plunges over a broken 8-foot drop that looks to be class 5.0. Scout this in advance, and be sure you know where the last safe eddy is above it; there is one behind a large boulder on the left, just before the drop, but most paddlers will want to play it safe and take out some 50 yards above that, up the steep left bank and then through the poison ivy to Spout Run Parkway. Below the waterfall, the creek is continuous class IV+ for about 150 yards, as it passes beneath the westbound lanes of both Spout Run and George Washington Memorial Parkway, before it eases into the Potomac. This stretch has been straightened and cleared of strainers and rubble, and it looks like an exciting ride for those who can handle the 400 ft/mile gradient.

If you continue to the Potomac, you can ferry across the tidal water to Georgetown. If you take out before the class 5.0 drop, the easiest shuttle may be to leave your boats, hike back to your put-in car, take Spout Run Parkway to George Washington Parkway east, reverse directions by Key Bridge, pull off onto the grassy area where Spout Run Parkway leaves George Washington Parkway, and load quickly. During rush hour, the traffic on Spout Run Parkway may be too continuous for this.

GAUGE: You need an intense rainfall that brings Dead Run to 130 cfs and Fourmile Run at Alexandria to over 800 cfs. If it looks too high, just wait a few minutes.

VIRGINIA SUBURBS SOUTH

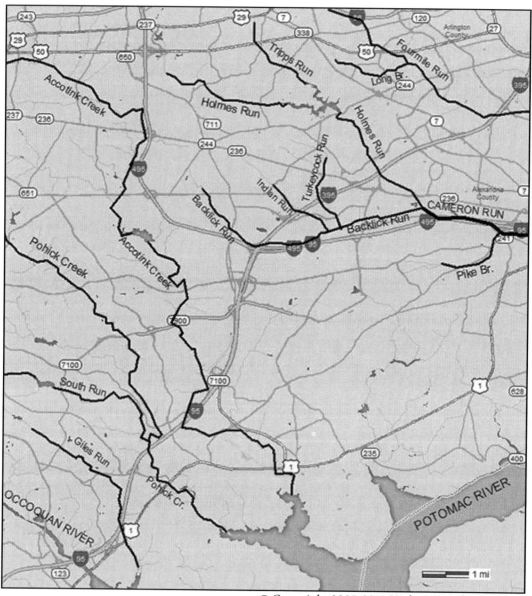

Chapter 35:

VIRGINIA SUBURBS SOUTH

This chapter covers the creeks in Alexandria and southern Fairfax County, or equivalently, those south of I-66 or that enter the Potomac between National Airport and the Occoquan River. This is a densely-populated part of the Washington metropolitan area. Unlike Virginia Palisades streams, none of these creeks have dramatic cascades to the Potomac. But they do have some nice fall line rapids.

The creeks, from north to south, are Fourmile Run, Cameron Run, Accotink Creek, Pohick Creek and Giles Run, plus tributaries. Corbett calls **Fourmile Run** "for looking at - not for paddling." Nevertheless, it is paddled from time to time, and is both exciting and dangerous. **Long Branch** is its short but attractive "explorers' special" tributary. Cameron Run (named after the 6th Lord Fairfax, Baron of Cameron) is almost flat, but the creeks which form it, **Holmes** and **Backlick runs**, have whitewater, as do their tiny tributaries **Tripps** (barely), **Indian** and **Turkeycock runs**, as well as miniscule but interesting **Pike Branch**, which enters farther downstream. **Accotink Creek** is divided into four sections, with the third one having some nice rapids and the others being rather flat. **Pohick Creek** is a popular and outstanding (albeit hard to catch) whitewater trip, and section 2 of its tributary, **South Run**, is perhaps even nicer (and even harder to catch). Finally, **Giles Run** has far too many trees and branches across it, and no decent rapids despite its relatively steep gradient.

> **Cameron Run** is class I for less than a half mile below the confluence of Holmes and Backlick Runs, and then becomes tidal for three miles, with a runnable 3-foot weir in low tide. It is known to paddlers mainly because of its on-line gauge. Where it widens out, its name changes to **Hunting Creek**. The District of Columbia was limited to land "above the mouth of Hunting Creek." The first cornerstone was laid at Jones Point at the northern side of the mouth, and the **boundaries of D.C.** were then defined by straight lines, 10 miles long, at 45 degrees from this point. Fortifications along Hunting Creek were the Union's southernmost **defense line** of Washington D.C., in 1862-65.
>
> East of Accotink Creek, near Mt. Vernon, is **Dogue Creek,** where you could paddle 2 miles from Leaf Road to Va. 235 (Mt. Vernon Memorial Highway) with 9 sq. mi. but only a 7 ft/mile gradient. This stream is infamous for its concentration of invasive snakefish.

GAUGES: The gauge on Fourmile Run in Alexandria (12.6 sq. mi.) is ideal for the northern part of this chapter, and that on Accotink Creek near Annandale (24 sq. mi.) for the southern part. There is a new (end-2011) gauge on Accotink Creek at Fairfax (4 sq. mi.) that helps for the tiny streams. The one on Cameron Run (34 sq. mi.) is also useful, especially when the rainfall is uneven, for its own tributaries. The **gauge column below refers to Fourmile Run**, except the *bold italicized figures are for Accotink Creek near Annandale.* Of course, as all these creeks rise and fall so fast, timing is more important than exact level.

name	gradient	difficulty	length	area	gauge	rating
Fourmile Run - Section 1	50 (100)	III- (III+)	3.7	3.5	250cfs	**
- Section 2	30	II+	2.2	9	135cfs	*
Long Branch	85	III- (?)	0.6	1.0	650cfs	?
Holmes Run - Section 1	22	I (II+)	1.9	5.1	135cfs	*
- Section 2	27	II+ (IV)	2.3	15	90cfs	***
Tripps Run	30	II-	1.2	2.9	200cfs	*
Backlick Run - Section 1	40	II	0.9	1.4	400cfs	**
- Section 2	36	II (III)	3.4	2.2	325cfs	-
Indian Run	60	II (III)	0.5	2.2	325cfs	**
Turkeycock Run	45	II+ (III-)	1.4	2.4	325cfs	**
Pike Branch	55	II+ (III)	1.4	1.5	450cfs	***
Accotink Creek - Sec. 1	14	I	3.7	17	100cfs	-
- Sec. 2	11	I	3.5	29	100cfs	*
- Sec. 3	33 (65)	II	1.4	37	100cfs	***
- Sec. 4	14	I (II)	3.4	39	75cfs	*
Pohick Creek	33 (110)	III (III+)	3.4	21	175cfs	****
South Run - Section 1	20	II-	2.0	6.4	250cfs	**
- Section 2	60	III	1.7	7.7	300cfs	****
Giles Run	35	I	2.6	2.5	425cfs	-

FOURMILE RUN

Fourmile Run rises alongside I-66, near the boundary with Fairfax County and Falls Church, and flows through Arlington County for 8 miles. There is a bike path along most of it. The first 2 miles are seldom runnable and include a dangerous, dark passage under I-66. Because this is an urban stream, there are many access points in the 5.9 miles remaining. I have divided the creek into two sections, based on difficulty and the nature of the dangers. But both share the plus of proximity, the minus of water quality (see box below), and the challenge of getting to the stream while it is still up. The day Alf Cooley and I ran section 1, for example, the gauge fell from 700 cfs at 10 AM, to 230 cfs at noon, despite continuing light rain. Below section 2, the stream is tidal, flows under railroad yards and enters the Potomac as the border with Alexandria, at the southern edge of National Airport.

> Fourmile Run is heavily **polluted**, but the four jurisdictions through which it flows – Arlington and Fairfax counties and the cities of Alexandria and Falls Church – signed an agreement in August 1998 to address this. Pollution problems date back to the Civil War, when train engines that used Fourmile Run water had their boilers sudsing over because thousands of Union soldiers were washing their clothes in the creek.
>
> **Four Miles to Where?** The name does not refer to the length of the creek, but rather to the location of its mouth, four miles north of Hunting Creek (the starting point for the original definition of the District of Columbia).

Section 1: Ohio St. to Barcroft Park

Gradient	Difficulty	Distance	Area	Scenery	Strainers	Rating
50 (100)	III- (III+)	3.7	3.5	C	1-3/mi.	**

USGS Quad – Falls Ch./Annandale/Alexandria; Source – Personal descent 7/02
N38 52.90, W77 08.76 to N38 50.94, W77 06.05

This would be an excellent run were not for the half dozen low-water bridges of the bike path, which can be serious hazards. Those bridges (and overhanging branches, vines and shrubs, especially in summer) are the main reason why you should only paddle Fourmile Run in low water (when you can stop in time) or, if you are good enough, in high water (when you can paddle over the bridges). Some of the hazards mentioned by Corbett (steel debris; steel railings across the stream) are no longer in evidence, but the creek should still be treated with great caution.

Ohio St. is the first suitable put in, shortly below I-66. Just upstream of the bridge is a natural 8-foot slide (class IV), with a complicated entry and a risk of pitoning at the bottom. You can put in above or below this, depending upon the water level and your abilities. The first mile is class I, but complicated by overhanging vegetation. The next mile is class II-, with a few small ledges and a pair of low-water bridges, which you come upon with little warning. The first of these, just after a parking area on the right, is in slow water, but the second, just above US 50 (1.8 miles) is more dangerous. At 2.1 miles, Lubber Run enters from the left, and at 2.5 miles you reach a river-right access point at Glencarlyn Park, by the confluence with Long Branch (see below).

The next 0.7 miles, down to Columbia Pike, contains the fall line, where the creek drops at 100 ft/mile for 1/3 mile. It starts off with some long class II+ rapids. Then, when the horizon line disappears, pull over on the right to scout the 5-foot, class III+ Hoffman Falls (best run in the middle), which is followed immediately by some class III- chutes and then more class II+ ledges and rock gardens. Great stuff, except for the three low-water bridges, which fortunately can be seen well in advance, as they have no eddies immediately above. There is another class III- ledge, at a sharp angle to the flow, just below Columbia Pike (at 3.2 miles).

The creek then reverts to class I-II, but the rapids are frequent. There is a nice chute next to a cement wall on the far left, but don't get too close because of projecting rebar. The sixth and final low-water bridge hazard comes at Barcroft Park (off Fourmile Run Road at the downstream end of the tennis courts), the end of section 1. Be wary of running this bridge, even if the water level permits, as there are sharp boulders below.

GAUGE: The gauge on Fourmile Run (in section 2) should read at least 250 cfs (more if the level is dropping), to start at Ohio St., and 180 cfs for a Glencarlyn Park put in. If the riffles below the Ohio St. falls are runnable, everything should be. A one-inch rainfall usually suffices to give a brief window of opportunity (depending on season, intensity and prior conditions). At somewhat higher levels, the low-water bridges become dangerous, until about 1,000 cfs, at which point you can paddle over them safely.

Section 2: Barcroft Park to Arlington Ridge Road/Mt. Vernon Ave.

Gradient	Difficulty	Distance	Area	Scenery	Strainers	Rating
30	II+	2.2	9	C	<1/mi.	*

USGS Quad – Alexandria; Source – Personal descent 8/02
N38 50.94, W77 06.05 to N38 50.67, W77 03.87

Below Barcroft Park the nature of the trip changes. There are no more low-water bridges on the bicycle trail, and the creek is mostly straight and wide, with few strainers. After the initial long riffle by the put in, the gradient for 1.5 miles is mainly expended in a dozen 1-2 foot weirs (the last of which are in closely spaced pairs). This results in a rather narrow range of suitable water levels. Because the weirs are wide and level, they require more water than section 1. But because they were constructed without regard for their paddling safety, several of them develop serious hydraulics at high water. These should be scouted beforehand, and if run, done so with maximum speed. Some of the weirs are just bores to scrape over, but others have interesting run-outs.

The weirs end by I-395, and there are then some short class II- rapids, followed by riffles. Take out just below Arlington Ridge Road/Mt. Vernon Ave., at the Fourmile Run Park (there is better parking on river right). Below, the creek is tidal.

GAUGE: The water should be no more than level with and no lower than a few inches below the put in bridge. The Fourmile Run gauge should be 135-400 cfs.

⑊ LONG BRANCH: S. Carlin Springs Road to Fourmile Run

Gradient	Difficulty	Distance	Area	Scenery	Strainers	Rating
85	III-(?)	0.6	1.0	B	2-4/mi.	?

USGS Quad – Annandale/Alexandria; Source – Scouting entire run from trail
N38 51.51, W77 07.61 to N38 51.71, W77 07.14

What a delightful little *"explorers' special."* Follow the sign to the Long Branch Nature Center, but put in right after you turn off S. Carlin Springs Road, where the creek exits from a large culvert. Two bicycle path crossings can be paddled over at moderate levels, scraped over at minimum flows. In very high water, the footbridge just before the confluence would be a hazard; wait a few minutes for the level to drop.

The confluence is right at the start of the steepest and best part of Fourmile Run (section 1, mile 2.5), so starting on Long Branch gives you an interesting twofer – just make sure that Fourmile Run is not too high for you to handle, or wait for it to drop.

GAUGE: Fourmile Run needs 650 cfs and Accotink Creek in Fairfax 200 cfs.

> **Lubber Run** and (another) **Long Branch** could each be paddled for 2/3 mile from N. Carlyn Springs Rd. (the former on the north side of Fourmile Run, the latter on the south) with average gradients of 90 ft/mile and 75 ft/mile, respectively, but even smaller drainage areas of about 0.5 sq. mi.

🌊 HOLMES RUN

This creek begins at one of the transport nodes of the region, the intersection of I-66 and the Beltway (I-495) in Dunn Loring. It heads south past Arlington Boulevard and Falls Church High School, and then gradually swings east, until it reaches the section 1 put in at Annandale Road. In Annandale, it is interrupted by Lake Barcroft; section 2 begins immediately below the Lake Barcroft dam. The creek continues for a mile beyond section 2, but is channelized and has only man-made drops.

> The **Lake Barcroft** Dam, originally the site of the Barcroft Mill (built in the 1790s), was constructed in 1915 to supply water to Alexandria. By 1950, the water had become too polluted from upstream development, and the Alexandria Water Company sold it to developers, who built a community of "miniature country estates" (while Alexandria shifted its water supply to the Occoquan River).

Section 1: Annandale Road to Lake Barcroft

Gradient	Difficulty	Distance	Area	Scenery	Strainers	Rating
22	I (II+)	1.9	5.1	B	2-4/mi.	*

USGS Quad – Annandale; Source – Personal descent 9/99
N38 51.20, W77 11.82 to N38 50.84, W77 10.09

Put in at the end of Hockett St., just off Annandale Road. The trip is quite pretty, through Holmes Run Stream Valley II Park, with groves of bamboo at the start and finish. Although there are no real rapids until just before the end, full and (especially) partial strainers are rather common, so good boat control is needed. There is a hike/bike trail alongside much of the way, and in nice weather you can expect spectators.

Tennis courts on the left announce the approach of Sleepy Hollow Road, 1.6 miles into the trip. The creek has been channelized here and is uninteresting, until, within sight of the take out, you come upon a huge wave (class II+), at the bottom of a steep chute. At high levels, this can flip you, so angle hard right to avoid its full impact. Take out at the footbridge at the entrance to Lake Barcroft, for a 50-yard carry to Dearborn Drive; the sign there says "No boat launching, except by residents," but does not explicitly restrict taking out. (Try that one on the authorities if you are apprehended!)

Above Annandale Road, the creek is very narrow, twisty and strainer prone.

GAUGE: Look for 135 cfs on the Fourmile Run gauge at Alexandria, 365 cfs on Cameron Run (projected an hour later) and 45 cfs on Accotink Creek in Fairfax.

Section 2: Columbia Pike to Holmes Run Parkway (past I-395)

Gradient	Difficulty	Distance	Area	Scenery	Strainers	Rating
27	II+ (IV)	2.5	15	B	0-2/mi.	***

USGS Quad – Annandale; Source – Personal descent 1/97
N38 50.55, W77 08.67 to N38 49.10, W77 07.50

This little urban gem combines pretty scenery with nice rapids, near Baileys Crossroads. Park and put in on the south side of Columbia Pike, after checking whether enough water is flowing over the 50-ft dam that creates Lake Barcroft. The creek flows through a pretty gorge, in Holmes Run III Park, where Trout Unlimited does an annual fall trash cleanup, prior to the stream being stocked. There is a hiking trail alongside.

The trip starts off with a long class II rock garden, and there are several other nice rapids in the first quarter mile. The rapids themselves are steeper than the average gradient suggests, because it is a pool-and-rapids creek. As you approach Beauregard St., there are a pair of man-made drops: a smooth 2-footer (class II) and a rocky 3-footer (class II+), followed by a twisty, narrow chute (class II+) and a final bouncy drop (class II). After passing I-395 and N. Van Dorn St., you can take out (on either side) above the man-made 8-foot drop through a boulder pile (class IV, and needing a lot of water to run cleanly), or run that and finish with a final 5-foot, two-part drop (class II+).

You could continue a mile farther, through a stretch which has been widened and channelized. The creek flattens out and crosses Duke Street. At its confluence with Backlick Run (to create Cameron Run), Holmes Run goes over another man-made 8-foot ledge (probably class IV), which is wider than the previous one and therefore needs even more water.

GAUGE: Look for over 90 cfs on Fourmile Run and 240 cfs on Cameron Run.

TRIPPS RUN: Annandale Road to Lake Barcroft

Gradient	Difficulty	Distance	Area	Scenery	Strainers	Rating
30	II-	1.2	2.9	C	0-2/mi.	*

USGS Quad – Annandale; Source – Personal descent 1/98
N38 52.01, W77 10.48 to N38 51.31, W77 09.51

Lake Barcroft has a "Y" shape: the base is Holmes Run below the confluence, the left arm Holmes Run above the confluence, and the right arm Tripps Run. Tripps Run begins in West Falls Church, and flows south-southeast for 1.5 miles along a paved channel to the put in at Annandale Road, and then 1.2 miles down to Lake Barcroft.

The first third of the trip is alongside streets and houses, but the remainder is mostly through parkland. A little after halfway, the creek crosses Sleepy Hollow Road, and the Congressional School is then on river right. Afterwards, some lovely houses can be seen on river left. Take-out on Potterton Drive, just before entering Lake Barcroft (which is closed to non-residents' boats). A heavy chain fence (which traps debris) in calm water will remind you of this.

The run is continuous class I with three class II- spots: a) the rock garden at the put in, if you put in at the upstream side of the bridge, b) an 18 inch ledge, a little before midway, and c) an S-turn in fast water, shortly before the end.

GAUGE: A 2 inch rainfall in January brought this creek just a bit above zero level. Fourmile Run should be above 200 cfs, Accotink Creek at Fairfax 65 cfs.

> Near the take out was the **Tripp quarry**, opened in 1872, which supplied granite-gneiss stone for construction, including of the Falls Church Presbyterian and Catholic churches.

> *The scandal'd come, the rain had too, What was there topical to do?*
> *The **Jordan** River was too far, Cedar Creek's Tannery's not spelled **Starr**,*
> ***Jones** Falls I had already done, In Annandale, I found **Tripps** Run.*
>
> *The trip on Tripps was not great fun, Rather low class, merely class I,*
> *Branches (with wires?) hanging down, The unwary to trap and drown,*
> *The distance just one mile point two, The wildlife? nothing but a shrew.*
>
> *OK, Ok, I have rethunk, I saw no shrew, it was a skunk,*
> *I didn't mean to tell a lie, Or to suborn my sweetie pie,*
> *You'll get no more bad poems from me, 'til I get full immunity!*

BACKLICK RUN

This creek sees it all in its short life: parkland, I-95/395/495 interchange, railroad and commercial center. It grows considerably but maintains a good gradient, and provides an interesting way to see a variety of urban scenery (euphemistically).

Section 1: Braddock Road to Leesville Boulevard

Gradient	Difficulty	Distance	Area	Scenery	Strainers	Rating
40	II	0.9	1.4	C	0-2/mi.	**

USGS Quad – Annandale; Source – Personal descent 4/02
N38 48.70, W77 11.69 to N38 48.08, W77 11.25

This is by far the nicest part of Backlick Run. You need a BIG rain (over an inch within a few hours) and you have to arrive VERY early to run this. Put in by a paved driveway to nowhere, on the north side of Braddock Road, just east of the stream. The creek flows swiftly over class II rapids, with mostly woods but some houses visible, and a few sections hemmed in by riprap. Don't run this in high water, as it would be very difficult to stop if you encounter strainers (we were pretty lucky, with only one); instead, wait a few minutes for the creek to drop. Take out at the first bridge; you could continue another quarter mile to Backlick Road, but we encountered strainers and trash in that stretch.
    GAUGE: You need 125 cfs on Accotink Cr. in Fairfax, 400 cfs on Fourmile Run.

Section 2: Leesville Boulevard to South Van Dorn St.

Gradient	Difficulty	Distance	Area	Scenery	Strainers	Rating
36	II (III)	3.4	2.2	D	5-10/mi.	-

USGS Quad – Annandale; Source – Personal descent 4/02
N38 48.08, W77 11.25 to N38 48.20, W77 08.04

The first quarter mile to Backlick Road is decent, except for strainers and trash. The creek then crosses the railroad tracks (you can see Springfield Station), and half a mile later approaches the I-95/395/495 "Mixing Bowl" intersection. Here the trouble begins; the first (of four) culverts is potentially dangerous because you cannot see through to the end (see box below). The others were no problem when we ran them, but construction may change that.

The creek then runs east between the Beltway and the tracks. Great views of traffic! The first mile of is full of fallen trees. After you re-cross the railroad tracks, the strainers are pretty much gone. Indian Run and Turkeycock Run soon enter in quick succession, doubling the catchment area. There are two steep class III drops through boulders, one above and the other below Indian Run. In the last half mile, you see the backside of a commercial area and encounter two metal weirs (of unclear purpose). There is a channel around the right of the first one, and a break in the second. There is a ledge as you exit the South Van Dorn St. bridge; in high water, take the leftmost culvert, otherwise the one next to it. Take out on river left; you can park in the commercial area.

From the takeout, it is 1.3 miles to the confluence with Holmes Run, but most of this is a straight, paved channel, with low gradient and no rapids.

GAUGE: Look for 100 cfs on Accotink Creek at Fairfax, 325 cfs on Fourmile Run, 850 cfs on Cameron Run (projected an hour later).

The **long culvert** that began the passage beneath the **"Mixing Bowl"** went straight for about 70 yards, and then bent to the right for another 70 yards – too dark to see through. Construction had all the water channeled into the leftmost culvert, where it raced through at over 10 mph. I hiked through the dry middle culvert, and looked back up the left culvert from the exit. Everything seemed OK. But as I paddled through, approaching the bend, an obstruction suddenly loomed vaguely out of the darkness – a 2 by 4 board, obviously anchored to a base, about a foot above the water. Having no better alternative, I smashed my canoe straight into it. The board cracked but held, and I jumped out of my boat. The canoe filled with water, and its added weight forced the board and the wood it was attached to out of the way, and they floated down the culvert. I signaled to Frank Fico, and he paddled into the culvert and past me. I managed to mostly dump out my boat and hop into it (fighting the strong current). Yes, it would have been wiser to just drag the boats through the dry culvert.

INDIAN RUN: Edsall Road to Bren Mar Drive

Gradient	Difficulty	Distance	Area	Scenery	Strainers	Rating
60	II (III)	0.5	2.2	D	0-/mi.	**

USGS Quad – Annandale; Source – Personal descent 1/98
N38 48.26, W77 09.29 to N38 47.98, W77 08.95

This short, tiny creek rises just east of downtown Annandale, alongside Little River Turnpike, and flows for 2.5 miles through a strainer-filled woods past Braddock Road and I-395, down to Edsall Road.

Put in on the upstream, river right side of Edsall Road, to enjoy the triple-drop, class III, man-made rapid under and just below that road; but check first downstream from the bridge for strainers. Then it is 0.4 miles of alternating class I and II, with much of the bank reinforced with boulders or riprap; you can scout from Indian Run Road. Expect some vines and branches, and perhaps also real strainers. The trip ends in another man-made class III rapid, at Bren Mar Drive, with a total drop of 8 feet. No maneuvering is required, but make sure you have enough water, as you don't want to get hung up and/or turned sideways just above the final 3-foot drop into a hydraulic, or to capsize here in shallow water, as the paved bottom is rough.

Take out at the eddy on river right at the bottom of the rapid, or continue the final 0.15 miles, which is class I and narrow, with overhanging branches, and then do the last 0.8 miles of Backlick Run (see above), with another class III rapid and not too many problems, to South Van Dorn Street.

GAUGE: Look for about 100 cfs on Accotink Creek at Fairfax, 325 cfs on Fourmile Run, 850 cfs on Cameron Run (projected an hour later).

TURKEYCOCK RUN: Chowan Ave. to above Backlick Run

Gradient	Difficulty	Distance	Area	Scenery	Strainers	Rating
45	II+ (III-)	1.4	2.4	D	1-5/mi.	**

USGS Quad – Annandale; Source – Personal descent 9/99
N38 48.99, W77 09.15 to N38 48.04, W77 08.57

Put in alongside Chowan Ave., a quarter mile below Braddock Road, shortly after the two branches meet. The first mile winds through parkland, with frequent class II rapids. It would be great fun, were it not for the frequent total and partial strainers, the limited visibility (at least in the summer), and the piles of trash. Watch out for the footbridge, which is a danger to your head if the water level is above about 1 foot.

The 170-yard passage under I-395 is through almost total darkness, and only about midway, where the culvert turns to the left and you must stay right to avoid getting showered by the outflow from a pipe (if you take the left culvert, as we did), do you see the proverbial light at the end of the tunnel. (Before entering in our boats, Jamie Deehan and I hiked up to this point, to make sure there was a way out.)

Just above Edsall Road is a 4-foot man-made drop (class III-), consisting of a ledge followed by boulders, with somewhat more water going on the far right. The final one-third mile below Edsall Road is alongside the parking lot for a commercial area. It has good gradient and class II+ rapids, but is narrow and channelized, with a likelihood of strainers. We took out there. If you continue, the creek ends with a drop on a blind turn into Backlick Run; watch out for a strainer lying in ambush. It is just a half-mile on Backlick Run to the South Van Dorn Street take out.

GAUGE: Minimum is some 100 cfs on Accotink Creek at Fairfax, 325 cfs on Fourmile Run, 850 cfs on Cameron Run (projected an hour later).

PIKE BRANCH: Old Telegraph Road to Burgundy Road

Gradient	Difficulty	Distance	Area	Scenery	Strainers	Rating
55	II+ (III)	1.4	1.5	C	0-2/mi.	***

USGS Quad – Alexandria; Source - Personal descent 4/02
N38 47.12, W77 05.86 to N38 47.88, W77 04.88

This creek parallels Telegraph Road, just south of Alexandria, flowing northeast into Cameron Run. Considering how tiny its watershed is, the stream is relatively wide and unobstructed (we never had to leave our boats for a strainer).

Put in just below the confluence of its arms, by a pullout downstream of the Hope United Church of Christ. In a quarter mile, the creek passes beneath Telegraph Road. Take the left culvert and stay left for the rocky but more gradual 4-foot, class III drop just below – the right culvert or the right side of the left culvert leads to a steeper drop. There are then long stretches of class II, interspersed with calmer water. Six bridges and a mile later, Pike Branch again flows under Telegraph Road, exiting with a class II+ drop; check the exit for strainers. Soon thereafter is the best rapid, a long class II+ rock garden behind some townhouses. As you reach the power line, take out on river left, just by the huge pylon, and carry up to Burgundy Road. Only 30 yards downstream is a sheer 8-foot drop that looks dangerous from the bridge. Some 200 yards below that, the creek slips into Cameron Run, just across from the Telegraph Road (Va. 241) Beltway interchange.

The scenery includes the Browne Academy, walls of riprap and 100 yards of pavement (below the school), which in low water may thin out the bottom of your boat.

GAUGE: Fourmile Run should be over 450 cfs, Accotink Creek at Fairfax 150 cfs. You need six inches above minimum at the put in, because the creek widens below.

ACCOTINK CREEK

Accotink Creek, the largest stream in this chapter, flows for 19 miles between the first possible put in and its mouth at Accotink Bay. But the runnable part is divided first by mile-long Lake Accotink and then by the Engineer Proving Ground (EPG) portion of the Fort Belvoir Military Reservation, where the Army tests equipment. There are no physical barriers to traversing the EPG, but large signs say: "WARNING. It is illegal to enter this area without permission of the installation commander." A few paddlers have reportedly gotten through without being caught, but for 1.5 miles at 20-ft/mile, the risk/reward ratio seems analogous to a president playing around with a White House intern. The final 2 miles also used to be through closed military land, but the boundaries were changed, making this accessible. So there is a lot to paddle, but it is all class I, except for a half mile descending the fall line in section 3. The gauge is on Braddock Road, just above Lake Accotink (near the end of section 1), which gives you advance notice of the level below there – it takes some 2 hours for the "bubble" to cross the lake to section 2, and then an additional 2 hours until it reaches the rapids of section 3. As this gauge is updated hourly, you have no excuse for missing the water when it is there.

> **Lake Accotink.** Accotink Creek was dammed in 1913 to provide drinking water for the Ft. Belvoir army base. But development upstream eventually polluted the water, so the area around the reservoir and creek was converted to parkland.

Accotink Creek's three largest tributaries are all called **Long Branch**:

a) a flattish stream (10 ft/mile) that rises in Merrifield and can be run for its final mile (2 sq. mi.) from Arlington Blvd.;

b) a steeper stream (40 ft/mile) runnable for 2.2 miles from Guinea Road (3 sq. mi.), past Canterbury Woods and across Braddock Road, entering Accotink Creek just above Lake Accotink; it is very narrow and has lots of strainers; and

c) much further south, through Newington, a stream paralleling the railroad tracks and I-95; this also has a decent gradient (38 ft/mile) and could theoretically be run for up to 3.3 miles (4 sq. mi.), but it passes through an unattractive commercial/industrial area, including a quarry which may have serious fences across the creek.

Accotink is an Algonquian word meaning **"at the end of the hill."** The settlers first called it the **Main Branch of Pohick Creek**, with modern-day Pohick Creek being the West or Northwest Branch. It is crossed in the middle of section 1 by the **Little River Turnpike**, the first private turnpike charter in Virginia, built 1796-1806 from Alexandria to Aldie, on the Little River in Loudoun County. It had tollhouses at 5-mile intervals over its 34-mile length.

Section 1: King Arthur Road to above Lake Accotink

Gradient	Difficulty	Distance	Area	Scenery	Strainers	Rating
14	1	3.7	17	D	2-4/mi.	-

USGS Quad – Fairfax/Annandale; Source – Personal descent (last 2.1 miles) 1/97; Trip report (Ed Evangelidi)
N38 50.55, W77 13.84 to N38 48.39, W77 14.04

The true Accotinkphile can put in as high as Barkley Drive, for a 5.7-mile trip to Lake Accotink. However, there are lots of strainers in these upper stretches, so a better put in choice is two miles downstream, at King Arthur Road (in Camelot, of course). This still provides excellent vistas of the Beltway, especially the Little River Turnpike interchange. After 1.6 more miles, you reach American Park, off Accotink Parkway, just below the Little River Turnpike. This put in is not quite as good for Beltway buffs, but will still give you all the best views of the power line and substation.

Once I realized that the rapids would be only class 1, I set staying in my boat, as I passed through the many fallen trees, as my goal. Just in time, I remembered the need to make goals realistic, so I changed mine to avoiding portages, by climbing over the fallen trees when necessary. And thus my trip was a success, in a certain way.

Go 0.4 miles past Braddock Road and 50 yards past a footbridge, and pull into the small tributary on river right, a quarter mile above where the creek enters Lake Accotink. It is then a short carry up the stone stairs to Danbury Forest Drive. My bicycle shuttle along the Accotink Creek trail was more challenging than the paddle, and I had to remind myself that the deep mud was just the flip side of having enough water to paddle.

GAUGE: Look for 20 cfs and 100 cfs on the Accotink Creek gauges at Fairfax and Annandale (Braddock Road), respectively.

Section 2: Lake Accotink to Hooes Road

Gradient	Difficulty	Distance	Area	Scenery	Strainers	Rating
11	I	3.5	29	C+	<1/mi.	*

USGS Quad – Annandale; Source – Personal descent 8/06
N38 47.53, W77 12.98 to N38 45.71, W77 12.40

Put in just below the dam, in Lake Accotink Park. Although you are traversing residential Springfield, you are mostly in parkland, and elsewhere the wooded margin alongside the creek largely conceals the houses and playing fields nearby. The only real intrusions of civilization are two roads. The water is mostly flat, but the riffles and current move you along, and the strainers are few. You could continue a half mile below Hooes Road, but then would have to attain back up to avoid trespassing on restricted military land (slipping below the fence there is no longer recommended).

GAUGE: Look for 100 cfs on the Accotink Creek gauge near Annandale.

Section 3: Ward Park Lane to Alban Road (SR790)

Gradient	Difficulty	Distance	Area	Scenery	Strainers	Rating
33 (65)	II	1.4	37	B, C	0-2/mi.	***

USGS Quad – Fort Belvoir; Source – Personal descent 11/06
N38 44.66, W77 11.95 to N38 43.72, W77 12.19

The first part of this trip, over the fall line, is the only good accessible whitewater on Accotink Creek, but to get to the put in is a challenge. At the end of Ward Park Lane (off Yarwood Ct., off Fullerton Rd.), drive to the back of the trucking company (they were friendly) and unload. After you park in front (ask permission), you must slide your boat down a steep slope that drops 70 feet. Wear gloves, to avoid both thorns and rope burns, and angle upstream where the gradient is somewhat less.

Your reward is a series of rock gardens and ledges in close succession, through a pretty gorge. The best rapids, which are class II, are the rock garden and the ledge just above Fullerton Road. The second one-third mile, below Fullerton Road, is a bit less lively, and after that there are only occasional riffles. Alongside the power line, two small ledges (that mark an old tank road) produce minor hydraulics. The scenery is excellent through the gorge, especially when the wisterias are in bloom in mid-spring, but deteriorates afterwards. If you are interested just in white water, take out at Alban Road.

GAUGE: You will need about 100 cfs on the Accotink gauge near Annandale. It takes about 4 hours for the water to get from the gauge to section 3.

Section 4: Alban Road to US 1 (Richmond Highway)

Gradient	Difficulty	Distance	Area	Scenery	Strainers	Rating
14	I (II)	3.5	39	C	1/mi.	*

USGS Quad – Fort Belvoir; Source – Personal descent 5/05
N38 43.72, W77 12.19 to N38 42.47, W77 10.13

A quarter mile below Alban Road, you pass beneath I-95 (which you can hear from the put in, despite the noise barriers). Don't miss the excellent graffiti painting of a juggler/acrobat. The creek winds between low gravel banks, with some braiding and fallen trees to work your way around and through. You are likely to see blue herons and Canada geese. The gradient to Telegraph Road, at 1.4 miles, is just 7 feet/mile. The class II ledge at the bridge is excellent for surfing. Below there, the gradient picks up to 20 feet/mile, expended through a series of long riffles, before slowing down again. (Corbett warns not to paddle below Telegraph Road, because you would be going through the military's Davison Airfield, but the airfield boundaries have changed and there is no problem anymore.) The take out on upstream river right at US 1 is muddy, but it is only a short carry/drag to a parking area. Below US 1, it is 1.2 flat miles down to Accotink Bay.

GAUGE: If the ledge at Telegraph Road is runnable, then everything will be. Look for at least 75 cfs on the Accotink Creek gauge at Annandale (4 hours earlier).

POHICK CREEK: Near Pleasant Lake Drive to US 1

Gradient	Difficulty	Distance	Area	Scenery	Strainers	Rating
33 (110)	III (III+)	3.4	21	C	<1/mi.	****

USGS Quad – Fort Belvoir; Source – Personal descent 4/02
N38 44.20, W77 13.20 to N38 42.06, W77 12.62

Pohick Creek is formed near Burke, and flows for 13 miles to Pohick Bay. It is flat and braided for its first 5.5 miles, down to Hooes Road (the traditional put in). Because it is pretty flat for the next 2 miles as well, which usually also contain some fallen trees, paddlers found a downstream put in, amongst the new housing developments. Take Rolling Road to Northumberland Road (heading west), and then turn left onto Lake Pleasant Drive. At the bottom of the hill is a sign and paved footpath into the park; about 300 yards carry brings you to the creek.

The trip is a delight, with three memorable rapids. Double Z (class III+) comes less than a mile from the put in, after several class II and II+ rock gardens. You have to make a very sharp left, right, left. With about a foot of water, the rapid is actually easier, because the route widens out and you can bounce through holes instead of crashing into rocks. Pohick Falls (class III) comes soon thereafter and is more straightforward, but it is easy to flip in the turbulence at the bottom, where the creek is funneled into a narrow chute. It too is less technical at higher levels. Lorelei Ledge (class II+), almost at the end of the trip, is wide and often scrapey; at higher levels it becomes class III because of the hole that forms at the bottom (except on a more gradual route on the far left).

The scenery is suburban. Don't miss the graffiti art gallery beneath I-95. If you don't stop to scout or play, this trip takes only about one hour. But after work, allow more time than that for the drive on I-95 from DC. Below US 1, the creek flows for two miles (10 ft/mile) to Pohick Bay, which opens into Gunston Cove and then the Potomac.

GAUGE: Look for 175 cfs on Accotink Creek at Annandale. Although one of the larger creeks in this chapter, Pohick rises and falls rapidly.

The creek's name is a variation of the Indian word for the **hickory tree**. The second **George Mason** settled near the mouth of Pohick Creek in 1690. **Pohick Church** was built in 1769-74, under the guidance of a committee that included George Washington, George Mason (the fourth) and Lord Fairfax. Burke Station, alongside Pohick Creek, was raided in December, 1862, by Confederate General **J.E.B. Stuart**, whose famous telegram to the Union quartermaster general complained of the poor quality of the Union mules he captured.

My first descent of Pohick Creek was on a chilly March day, in low water. An OC-2 paddler, wearing a borrowed and ill-fitting wet suit, kept getting stuck on the rocks and jumping in and out of the icy water. His behavior became irrational; I remember him lying down on a boulder, then suddenly jumping up and saying everything was all right. Fortunately, one paddler recognized the early symptoms of **hypothermia**. He gave the victim hot coffee, took him into his canoe, raced downstream to the take out, and got him into a warm car.

SOUTH RUN

South Run flows into and out of Burke Lake (dammed in 1960 and a big camping site) through South Run Stream Valley Park. Subdivisions have made the view from the creek less pristine.

Section 1: Hooes Road to South Run Road

Gradient	Difficulty	Distance	Area	Scenery	Strainers	Rating
20	II-	2.0	6.4	C	2/mi.	**

USGS Quad – Occoquan/Fort Belvoir; Source – Personal descent 6/89
N38 44.19, W77 15.15 to N38 44.04, W77 13.62

This is a pleasant and easy trip. The gradient is just starting to pick up by the end. To take out, cross under South Run Road and then climb to the parking lot on river left.

GAUGE: You will need at least 40 cfs and 250 cfs on the Accotink Creek gauges at Fairfax and Annandale, respectively.

Section 2: South Run Road to Pohick Creek

Gradient	Difficulty	Distance	Area	Scenery	Strainers	Rating
60	III	1.7*	7.7	B	1-3/mi.	****

USGS Quad – Fort Belvoir; Source – Personal descent 6/89
N38 44.04, W77 13.62 to N38 42.06, W77 12.62

*(plus 2 miles on Pohick Creek, to US 1)

Even with the strainers, this is a delightful intermediate/advanced whitewater trip, entirely within a narrow gorge with 70-100 foot high slopes on either side. There is a succession of class III rapids, mostly broken ledges, with short pools and class II sections in between. And 60 ft/mile is quite steep for a "pool and drop" creek. The stream mostly parallels Pohick Creek, sometimes as close as 200 yards, on the other side of the ridge along which Pohick Road runs. And then it is 2 easier miles on

Pohick Creek, with Lorelei Ledge the most interesting spot, down to US 1. So if you set your shuttle but get to the South Run put too late, just move to Pohick Creek.

GAUGE: You will need over 50 cfs and 300 cfs on the Accotink Creek gauges at Fairfax and Annandale, respectively.

> When I first ran Pohick Creek, which was as small a creek as I could imagine paddling, Sam Chambliss mentioned its tributary South Run. I thought "why would anyone run a creek smaller than Pohick?" Well, as they said in some dumb TV ad: "That was then and this is now."

GILES RUN: Lorton Road (SR 642) to Old Colchester Road (SR 611)

Gradient	Difficulty	Distance	Area	Scenery	Strainers	Rating
35	I	2.6	2.5	D	8-12/mi.	-

USGS Quad – Fort Belvoir; Source – Personal descent 4/01
N38 42.32, W77 14.19 to N38 40.68, W77 13.50

There is a class II rapid just upstream of the put in, but nothing even that interesting below – just riffles and tight turns that bring you under bushes and branches, and strainer after strainer. So while it's only class I, the danger element is much higher.

You start in the woods, enter a residential area, return to the woods and then parallel I-95; great views of the traffic! The passage under I-95 is perverse. The central and left culverts are straight and high, with the outlet easy to see, but carry little water. The right culvert has most of the water but less headroom, and curves into total darkness. After you pass under a railway and US 1, take out upstream at Old Colchester Road.

Below Old Colchester Road, Giles Run flows for 0.7 miles to the Massey Creek estuary, which leads into Belmont and then Occoquan Bay, before reaching the Potomac.

GAUGE: You will need at least 70 cfs on Accotink Creek at Fairfax.

> **Captain Giles Brent** married the daughter of the Piscataway Emperor. When Lord Baltimore rejected his consequent land claims in Maryland, he moved to the wilds near Pohick Creek in 1646, becoming the northernmost English resident of Virginia. His unmarried sister, **Margaret Brent**, had substantial property in Maryland, earning the title "gent." in the real estate records. Governor Leonard Calvert made her administrator of his estate when he died in 1647. She was the earliest advocate in America of political rights for women, but when her efforts to obtain suffrage in Maryland failed, she joined her brother in Virginia.
>
> Ironically, it was by this creek, in the Occoquan Workhouse (later site of the Lorton Penitentiary Youth Center), that scores of **women suffragists** were imprisoned by the D.C. Government from June-December 1917, for picketing the White House for the right to vote. Their courage and dedication during harsh treatment aroused the nation to hasten the passage and ratification of the 19th Amendment in 1920. The struggle for women's suffrage had taken 72 years, not counting the two centuries after Margaret Brent's failed effort.

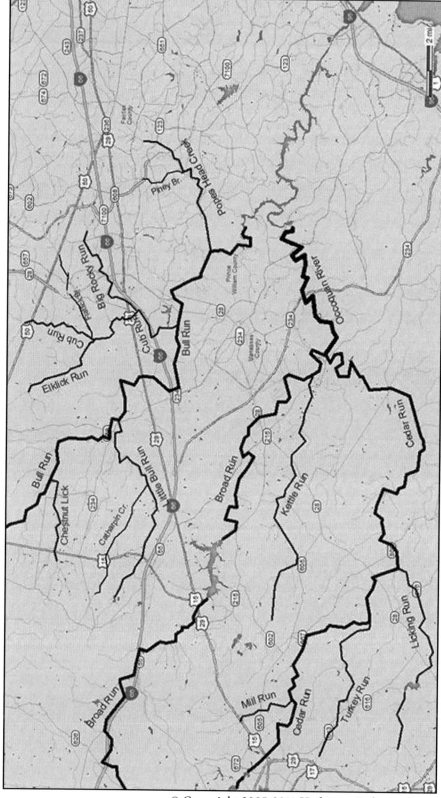

Chapter 36:
OCCOQUAN RIVER BASIN

The **Occoquan River** is the sixth largest tributary of the Potomac, its 600 square mile drainage exceeded only, in order, by the Shenandoah, South and North branches, Monocacy and Cacapon. It is formed at the confluence of Broad and Cedar Runs, and picks up its third main source, Bull Run, 11 miles later. The Occoquan itself is mostly dammed, to store 8.2 billion gallons of water for the Fairfax County Water Authority in Lake Jackson and the Occoquan Reservoir; however, it does have an exciting, but short and difficult-to-access fall line rapids below the dams. After that, it becomes tidal and widens into Belmont Bay and then Occoquan Bay (inlets of the Potomac).

The Occoquan basin covers parts of Fairfax, Loudoun, Fauquier and Prince William counties. It is largely rural, but is gradually being developed. Manassas (38,000) in the middle of the basin and Woodbridge magisterial district (51,000) at the mouth of the Occoquan are the largest towns. This is classic Virginia Piedmont, lacking the steeper terrain of the Blue Ridge, but consisting instead of rolling countryside and small ranges of hills that, in a few spots, produce interesting gradients. Lying directly between Washington and Richmond, it was a center of struggle during the Civil War, climaxing in the two great Confederate victories at Manassas/Bull Run.

There are two very popular, intermediate/advanced one-mile trips in the basin – **Broad Run** and **Cub Run**. Both are close to I-66, make outstanding brief after-work paddles or chasers to trips further west, and are in Grove and Corbett. Also in Corbett are novice trips on **Bull, Cedar** and **Kettle runs**, plus the peaceful lower part of Broad Run. There is considerably more decent canoeing in this basin, but nothing to match the Broad and Cub Run gorges, except for the hard-to-catch and even harder-to-run last 150 yards of **Big Rocky Run**. Paddlers looking for variety on high-water days can try novice trips on **Little Bull Run**, **upper Cub and Broad runs** and **Chestnut Lick**, low-intermediate paddles on **Cedar, Kettle** (in both cases above the sections in Corbett), **Turkey, Licking** and **Elklick runs** and **Popes Head Creek**, or go explore **Mill Run** or the sections of Cedar and Turkey runs that I have not yet been able to get to.

According to Ed Evangelidi, this basin has excellent creek-like, **flat-water paddles**. One is the narrow top part of **Lake Jackson**, between the last bridges on Cedar and Broad Runs. A second, with good wildlife, is the upper Occoquan Reservoir, from **Bull Run Marina** (where there are rental boats) as far up Bull Run as feasible. A third is **Kanes Creek**, which flows through a pristine part of Mason Neck State Park into Belmont Bay. Try to come in and out with the tide in your favor, and don't get trapped upstream at low tide. Both arms of the creek are beautiful as well, with water lilies (late spring bloom) in the beaver ponds, and bald eagle nests (the area is closed at sensitive nesting times). And a fourth, on Occoquan Bay, is the bottom part of **Marumsco Creek**, in the Marumsco National Wildlife Refuge. There is also a flat water **Occoquan Water Trail** that runs from Bull Run Marina to above the two dams, and then resumes from the town of Occoquan down to the Potomac Water Trail

The Occoquan Reservoir is fed directly by several smaller whitewater streams, notably **Sandy**, **Wolf** and **Hooes runs**, but none of them have particular paddling potential (small watersheds, limited access). However, there are crew races and sailing on the reservoir.

GAUGES: There are on-line gauges on Cedar Run near Catlett (4 miles below section 3; 93 sq. mi.) and Flatlick Branch (a tributary of Cub Run; 4.2 sq. mi.). One should complement these with the nearby gauges on the South Fork of Quantico Creek (7.6 sq. mi.) and Aquia Creek (35 sq. mi.) to the south, Fourmile Run (12.6 sq. mi.) and Difficult Run (58 sq. mi.) to the northeast, Broad Run (76 sq. mi.) to the north, and Beaverdam Creek (47 sq. mi.) and Limestone Branch (8 sq. mi.) to the northwest. As for rainfall, none of the four counties are included in the AFWS data, so you have to rely on the rainfall maps. In the table below, the **gauge column relates to Aquia Creek**.

name	gradient	difficulty	length	area	gauge	rating
Occoquan River	80	III (IV)	0.2	595	n.a.	**
Broad Run - Section 1	18	I	3.2	18	125cfs	-
- Section 2	70 (120)	III (III+)	1.1	39	125cfs	****
- Section 3	14	II-	5.0	40	80cfs	*
Kettle Run	17	II-	5.5	9	235cfs	**
Cedar Run - *Section 1*	18	?	3.5	15	175cfs	?
- Section 2	22	II	3.6	21	140cfs	***
- Section 3	12	I (II+)	4.4	35	80cfs	*
Mill Run	30	?	2.0	7	300cfs	?
Turkey Run - Sec. 1	30	II-	2.3	8	285cfs	*
- Sec. 2	17	?	3.5	14	175cfs	?
Licking Run	35	II	1.6	9	275cfs	*
Bull Run	6	I	22.3	25	100cfs	*
Chestnut Lick	20	I (II-)	1.0	11	200cfs	*
Little Bull Run	15	I (II-)	4.0	19	140cfs	*
Cub Run - Section 1	5	I	4.7	12	185cfs	*
- Section 2	42 (100)	III	1.2	39	115cfs	****
Elklick Run	14	II+	1.3	11	250cfs	**
Big Rocky Run	65 (300)	IV+	0.7	7	500cfs	!!!
Popes Head Creek	21	II-(II)	5.6	12	225cfs	**

🎵 OCCOQUAN RIVER: Occoquan Dam to Tidewater

Gradient	Difficulty	Distance	Area	Scenery	Strainers	Rating
80	III (IV)	0.2	595	B	0	**

USGS Quad – Occoquan; Source – Personal descent 5/96
N38 14.13, W77 15.75 (attain/carry and paddle back down)

The Occoquan River stretches 22 miles, from the confluence of Broad and Cedar runs to Belmont Bay below the town of Occoquan. But less than two miles of this is flowing, consisting of a class I bit between Lake Jackson and the Occoquan Reservoir, a brief whitewater stretch between the Fairfax and Lorton dams (at the bottom of the Reservoir) which is not open to the public, and the short, steep rapids below the Lorton Dam, which is the subject here.

From the historic town of Occoquan (Mill St.), paddle 200 yards up to the base of the last rapid, and carry uphill. Below the dam are two rapids, each about 150 yards long, with 100 yards of class I water between them. The first rapid begins with a wide, long class II+ rock garden, and ends with a class IV drop into a huge, sticky-looking hole.

In the second rapid, the water divides around a rock island. The right hand channel is a nice class III rock garden, which you can scout from the shore. The route left of the island looks like class III+.

On weekends, the Fairfax County Water Authority opens a paved, mile-long hiking trail up to the dam, but does not permit vehicular entry. **Since 9/11/01, boaters have not been permitted to carry up to run this section – but this could change.**

GAUGE: You have to scout this one, as there are no relevant gauges. Because of the dams and large catchment area, this is normally up most of the winter and spring.

The town name Occoquan meant **"at the end of the water."** The river was originally called the **Western Branch of the Potomac** (the Anacostia River was the Eastern Branch), until explorers found larger tributaries upstream.

The **town of Occoquan** was first settled around 1734, and received a big boost in 1758 when John Ballendine built his home Rockledge overlooking the creek. By 1765, there were gristmills, a foundry and, most importantly, tobacco warehouses. Rockledge and part of the Merchants Mill, the first automated gristmill in the nation, still stand. In 1804, Occoquan was laid out in streets and lots, and by 1835 had about 50 dwellings. But the estuary soon began silting up, presaging the town's diminishing economic importance.

Early in the **Civil War**, the Confederates used the Occoquan River as the right anchor of their defensive line, and built batteries along the Potomac south of there to blockade Washington. General Wade Hampton had his headquarters in the Hammill Hotel (which also still stands), from which he organized raids on Union wagon trains.

The **early 20th Century** was not kind to Occoquan. A fire destroyed much of the town in 1919, and the new road (US 1) and railroad bypassed the town. Hurricane Agnes in 1972 seemed like the *coup de grace*, but residents and merchants repaired the historic buildings. Nowadays, Historic Occoquan is a restored area with a museum, antique shops and trendy boutiques, and ghost stories to enhance the town's mystique. In the tidal waters downstream are several large yacht basins, and below that a massive new residential development. Just above the rapids are two dams, built in 1950 and 1957 respectively, to provide drinking water for the city of Alexandria. Power from the dams runs the water treatment plant.

Nowadays, the name Occoquan is feared by **commuters**, as in the typical announcement: "Traffic is stop and go on I-95 from the Occoquan to ...."

⫽ BROAD RUN

Broad Run, the smallest of the three main Occoquan tributaries (140 sq. mi.), occupies the center of the basin. It stretches 35 miles (including 3 on Lake Manassas), but only 1 mile (section 2) is good whitewater. Section 1 is drab. Section 2 is a wonderful, challenging short run. Section 3 is a mild trip that ends at Lake Manassas. Broad Run continues for 16 miles below Lake Manassas (in Corbett), at 7 ft/mile, to where the Occoquan River/Lake Jackson begins, at the confluence with Cedar Run; this stretch is dependent upon power releases.

Section 1: Va. 55/SR 698 to SR 628

Gradient	Difficulty	Distance	Area	Scenery	Strainers	Rating
18	I	3.2	18	C	3-4/mi.	-

USGS Quad – Marshall/Thoroughfare Gap; Source – Personal descent 5/02
N38 50.90, W77 45.51 to N38 49.69, W77 43.33

The first excitement is a runnable culvert at 0.8 miles. Below, there are long riffles and a handful of 1-foot ledges (often over fallen trees). The downed trees were a big hassle, and the 5 fences we encountered were even worse, as we usually had to lift our boats over them. On the positive side, there is good current, few signs of civilization and lots of wildlife.

   GAUGE: About 125 cfs on Aquia Creek, 340 cfs on Cedar Run and 165 cfs on Beaverdam Creek would be minimal.

Section 2: SR 628 to Va. 55

Gradient	Difficulty	Distance	Area	Scenery	Strainers	Rating
70 (120)	III (III+)	1.1	39*	C	0-2/mi.	****

USGS Quad – Thoroughfare Gap; Source – Personal descent 7/03
N38 49.69, W77 43.33 to N38 49.40, W77 42.29

*(includes Trapp Branch, which enters after a quarter mile)

Voila! This short but exciting trip through Thoroughfare Gap (between the Bull Run and Pond mountains) has become a "must" for advanced boaters in the Washington area. It starts off mildly, but quickly steepens, right after Trapp Branch enters from the right, in a narrow class II+ rock garden where big boulders and mid-stream trees block the view, and most of the eddies are either behind the boulders or in the woods. You can glimpse this section from I-66 west, and you can hear the traffic even over the sound of the rushing water. The rapid continues for almost a half-mile, and reaches class III at the end, where most of the water heads left under a sometimes-overhanging thorn bush. Watch out for strainers throughout, but especially here and in the final class III rapid below the ledges.

   Catch the eddy on the left just before the first ledge, and climb up to the railroad tracks for a good view of the second ledge as well. The first ledge is class III- and is normally run straight down the middle of the left chute. Eddy out quickly after running this drop, to bail any water and set up for the second ledge. This one is class III+, with a hydraulic on the left side, but it is not really as hard as it looks. Enter the drop on the right edge of the main channel, angling left. Open boats take on a lot of water if they don't enter correctly, and then have to try to stay upright in the steep run-out and avoid the midstream boulder just below and the rock wall further ahead on the left. Above about 1 foot, a sneak route opens up to the right of the island. There is calmer water below, where you can recover before a class II- rapid and then a bouncy class III boulder garden, which is a pretty straight shot after a twisty entrance – a fine finale to the trip.

You can park along the road on the downstream side at the put in. At the take out, park on the field at downstream river right – the owners of the property are very friendly to paddlers, whereas the road shoulder is posted against parking.

GAUGE: There is a painted RC gauge on the downstream end of the bridge at the put in. Look for 125 cfs on Aquia Creek, 340 cfs on Cedar Run and 165 cfs on Beaverdam Creek.

Through **Thoroughfare Gap** in the Bull Run Mountains run I-66, the Manassas Gap Railroad (the first rail line to the Blue Ridge) and Broad Run. Stonewall Jackson's troops moved through on July 19, 1861, en route to the First Battle of Bull Run, in the world's first large-scale movement of troops to battle by train, and again on August 26, 1862, followed by General Longstreet, heading for the Second Battle of Bull Run. In the latter engagement, Jackson destroyed the railroad bridge over Broad Run, 12 miles downstream at Bristow, as well as vast quantities of Union supplies at Manassas.

Just below the two ledges are the remains of **Beverly Mill**. This fine structure was well preserved and being restored in the mid-1990s, when arsonists destroyed it.

Shortly below the put in, **Trapp Branch** enters from the right. It might be run for its final mile with a 9 sq. mi. catchment and a 35 ft/mile gradient, but it flows through farms with fences (the last one visible from Va. 55), and is unlikely to have any real rapids.

Section 3: Va. 55 to Buckland/Lake Manassas (US15/29)

Gradient	Difficulty	Distance	Area	Scenery	Strainers	Rating
14	II-	5.0	40	B	<1/mi.	*

USGS Quad – Thoroughfare Gap; Source – Corbett
N38 49.40, W77 42.29 to N38 46.85, W77 40.34

The rapids are all in the first mile, and the gradient drops considerably towards the end. Shortly below the take out, the creek gets drowned by Lake Manassas.

GAUGE: Look for 80 cfs on Aquia Creek, 225 cfs on Cedar Run, 110 cfs on Beaverdam Run.

KETTLE RUN: SR 604 to SR 646 (Marsteller Road)

Gradient	Difficulty	Distance	Area	Scenery	Strainers	Rating
17	II-	5.5	9	C	1/mi.	**

USGS Quad – Nokesville; Source – Personal descent (middle 3.2 miles) 12/90
N38 42.49, W77 38.17 to N38 42.74, W77 33.68

As Cedar Run and Broad Run spread apart, a little valley develops between them, and here one finds Kettle Run. We put in at SR 652 (2 miles above Corbett's put in), but one could start a mile higher up at SR 604 without losing too much water. There were a few strainers, but overall this is a pleasant trip, through a mixture of woods and pastures, with several nice class II- ledges. The take out is a quarter mile after you pass under Va. 28. Kettle Run continues another 4.3 miles to Broad Run, but the gradient for that stretch is only 8 ft/mile, and Corbett reports nothing more than riffles.

GAUGE: Look for 55 cfs on the South Fork, Quantico Creek, 235 cfs on Aquia Creek, 30 cfs on Flatlick Branch and 640 cfs on Cedar Run (3 hours later).

> In the lead in to the **Second Battle of Bull Run**, Confederate Major General Ewell's division fought a brisk rear-guard action against Major General Joseph Hooker's division, on August 27, 1862, along Kettle Run, and succeeded in keeping the Union forces south of Broad Run. This enabled General Longstreet to arrive at Manassas unimpeded, bringing the Confederates almost up to the same strength as the Union troops.

CEDAR RUN

Cedar Run flows from northwest of Warrenton, only a mile from the source of Broad Run, until its meets that same creek 37 miles later to form the Occoquan River. Its 195 square mile watershed occupies the southern portion of the Occoquan basin. Roger Corbett wrote: "Cedar Run has been voted by a group of very weary paddlers as the flattest, slowest, crookedest stream in the Commonwealth of Virginia.... At no time between its headwaters and where it joins Broad Run to form Occoquan Creek (sic), does Cedar Run cause enjoyment or excitement." Well, that description applies to the lower section, which I have accordingly left out of this book. But upstream, there are 11.5 miles that are quite enjoyable, even if their excitement value is limited.

Four miles below its source, Cedar Run is dammed to form the Warrenton Reservoir, and I have divided the next 11.5 mile into 3 sections. Below section 3, it is a further 11.5 miles at 4 ft/mile to SR 611 (where Corbett's coverage begins), and 10 more miles at 3 ft/mile to the confluence with Broad Run, where the Occoquan River and Lake Jackson start.

> Near Auburn was **George Neavil's Ordinary** (Inn), where George Washington and Lord Fairfax stopped on their way to the Shenandoah Valley in 1748. Six miles downstream, at Catlett, was the site of Union **General Pope's headquarters** on August 22, 1862, a week before the Battle of Second Manassas. General J.E.B. Stuart raided the headquarters, taking 300 prisoners plus Pope's dispatch case, but he had to withdraw after a thunderstorm prevented him from burning the bridge over Cedar Run. Nearby was also the Cedar Run Mine, which operated from 1845 to 1903 and was the first **barite mine** in Virginia and probably in the whole country.
>
> A flood control and water supply **dam** at Auburn has been on the US Army Corps of Engineers' drawing boards since the late 1960s, but local opposition and doubts about its justification have kept it from coming to fruition.
>
> Cedar Run's largest tributary, **Town Run**, has a 37 sq. mi. catchment but its gradient never exceeds 10 ft/mile, and it gets even flatter towards the end.

Section 1: SR 672 (north of Warrenton) to SR 672 (east of Frytown)

Gradient	Difficulty	Distance	Area	Scenery	Strainers	Rating
18	?	3.5	15	?	?	?

USGS Quad – Warrenton; Source – Scouting access points
N38 44.45, W77 47.29 to N38 42.68, W77 45.24

The put in for this *"explorers' special"* is within sight of the Warrenton Reservoir dam, 2 miles north of downtown Warrenton. In a mile, you pass beneath US 15/29/211, and half a mile later you cross a small lake, just before a low-water bridge. There is one additional bridge three-quarters of a mile after that. The put in and take out are on the same road (SR 672), which would make the shuttle straightforward except that the road is interrupted.

GAUGE: Look for 475 cfs on Cedar Run near Catlett (projected to 3 hours later), 175 cfs on Aquia Creek, 20 cfs on Flatlick Branch (an hour earlier).

Section 2: SR 672 (east of Frytown) to Auburn (SR 602)

Gradient	Difficulty	Distance	Area	Scenery	Strainers	Rating
22	II	3.6	21	A-	0-2/mi.	***

USGS Quad – Warrenton/Catlett; Source – Personal descent 12/90
N38 42.68, W77 45.24 to N38 42.14, W77 42.10

This is the steepest section of Cedar Run. The creek is still very small but had few strainers. The rapids are class II ledges and rock gardens, plus lots of riffles. Perhaps best is the scenery – lovely rock outcrops below 100-ft rocky cliffs. Mill Run enters from the left near midway. In the last mile the creek leaves the woods, but the gradient continues right to the end.

More recent maps show a small lake a mile before the take out, so it is likely that the creek has been dammed here and you will need a short portage.

GAUGE: Look for 380 cfs on Cedar Run near Catlett (projected to 2 hours later), 140 cfs on Aquia Creek, 15 cfs on Flatlick Branch (2 hours earlier).

Section 3: Auburn (SR 602) to SR 603 (2 miles west of Catlett)

Gradient	Difficulty	Distance	Area	Scenery	Strainers	Rating
12	I (II+)	4.4	35	C	<1/mi.	*

USGS Quad – Catlett; Source – Personal descent 1/06
N38 42.14, W77 42 10 to N38 39.15, W77 40.68

This is the final piece of Cedar Run worth paddling, as the gradient is down to 6 ft/mile by the end. It is both easier to run (except for one spot, described below) and easier to catch than the preceding sections. There are frequent riffles, no fences and few strainers (despite much evidence of beavers). After about half a mile, the creek splits around an island; the left side is better. The first half of the trip is mainly through woods, and includes some attractive cliffs, but after that you see more fields and houses. Trees are being planted along several sections, and in due course they will provide a nice riparian buffer. We didn't see much wildlife, but a dozen curious llamas came down to watch us pass. Turkey Run enters on the right just above the take out.

About two-thirds of the way through the trip, you enter the backwater of a natural dam. Work your way between the standing trees to the left bank, and get out to scout (or portage) the drop ahead. Most of the creek was blocked by a permanent logjam, leaving a 6-foot wide opening on the left. There, all of the water rushed down a 3-foot drop (class II+ at moderate levels, harder with more water), and then raced between an undercut root ball on the left and a small island on the right.

GAUGE: Look for 225 cfs on Cedar Run near Catlett (4 miles past the take out). At the put in, zero level is when the water is even with the top of the cement foot of the central pier support.

MILL RUN: SR 605 to Cedar Run

Gradient	Difficulty	Distance	Area	Scenery	Strainers	Rating
30	?	2.0*	7	?	?	?

USGS Quad – Catlett; Source – Scouting put in
N38-44.01, W77-44.70 to N38-42.14, W42.10

*(plus 2.4 miles on Cedar Run to Auburn-SR 602)

This tiny *"explorers' special"* joins Cedar Run one-third of the way through section 2, giving a 4.4 mile paddle. Its 30 ft/mile gradient suggests that there are probably some class II rapids; its small catchment area suggests there are strainers too.

GAUGE: Look for 800 cfs on Cedar Run near Catlett (projected to 4 hours later), 300 cfs on Aquia Creek, 65 cfs on So Fork, Quantico Creek, 35 cfs on Flatlick Branch.

TURKEY RUN

This stream begins on the southern outskirts of Warrenton and meanders east-southeast to Cedar Run.

Section 1: SR 779 (Turkey Run Road) to SR 602 (Rogues Road)

Gradient	Difficulty	Distance	Area	Scenery	Strainers	Rating
30	II-	2.3	8	C	1-2/mi.	*

USGS Quad – Catlett; Source – Personal descent 10/05
N38 40.50, W77 44.34 to N38 40.28, W77 42.84

This trip is mostly through Spring Hill Farm, a thoroughbred breeding estate, whose entry fence you encounter in a half mile and whose exit fence comes a half mile before the end; both have eddies above them. The scenery is woodlands and fields, but just out of view on river left during the first half mile is a huge quarry.

At high water (which is what we had), the private bridge shortly before the take out is very dangerous, as you don't see it until late, the current is fast, the nearby eddy tiny and the headroom minimal. You might check out the clearance (with binoculars) from the road. If it is too low, you can catch an eddy on river left about 75 yards above the bridge, just where the creek bends right, and portage from there (although you will be within sight of the house on this property that you are trespassing).

GAUGE: Look for 775 cfs on Cedar Run near Catlett (4 hours later), 285 cfs on Aquia Creek, 60 cfs on So Fork, Quantico Creek and 30 cfs on Flatlick Branch.

Section 2: SR 602 to Cedar Run (SR 603, Casanova, 2 mi. w. of Catlett)

Gradient	Difficulty	Distance	Area	Scenery	Strainers	Rating
17	?	3.5	14*	?	?	?

USGS Quad – Catlett; Source – Scouting put in and take out
N38 40.28, W77 42.84 to N38 39.15, W77 40.68

*(includes Gupton Run which enters after half a mile)

The gradient is lower but still respectable on this *"explorers' special."* Watch out for a private, low-water bridge after a half mile. There are woodlands on the right and fields on the left for most of the trip. The take out bridge, on Cedar Creek, is visible from the confluence.

GAUGE: Look for 475 cfs on Cedar Run (4.5 miles below the confluence with Turkey Run), 175 cfs on Aquia Creek, 40 cfs on So Fork, Quantico Creek and 20 cfs on Flatlick Branch.

LICKING RUN: SR 674 to Balls Mills (SR 663)

Gradient	Difficulty	Distance	Area	Scenery	Strainers	Rating
35	II	1.6	9	B+	2-3/mi.	*

USGS Quad – Warrenton/Catlett; Source – Personal descent 3/11
N38 37.74, W77 45.81 to N38 37.80, W77 44.42

Licking Run rises just south of Warrenton and flows south and then east for 15 miles, to Cedar Run. It is too small for its first 5 miles and quite flat (10 ft/mile) for its last 7. The 1.6 miles from SR 674 to Balls Mill is the steepest runnable stretch and all that I have run. The put in and take out are easy. The scenery is pleasant, consisting mainly of woods but with a few rock outcroppings, while some farmhouses are visible in the background. There are lots of riffles and easy rapids, but the creek braids about a half dozen times, usually at rapids, and strainers tend to block all the channels. Below Balls Mills it is just a half mile (at 20 ft/mi.) to the Germantown Lake reservoir, which stretches for over a mile. After that there is little gradient and no good access.

GAUGE: Look for 750 cfs on Cedar Run near Catlett (a mile below the confluence with Licking Creek), 275 cfs on Aquia Creek, and 60 cfs on So Fork, Quantico Creek.

Alongside Licking Creek, just downstream of Va. 28, is the **birthplace of John Marshall**, the early, pathbreaking Chief Justice of the Supreme Court. He lived there, as the eldest of nine children, for his first 20 years (1755-75), until his family moved northwest to Goose Creek.

🌊 BULL RUN: Sanders Lane (SR 705) to Bull Run Marina

Gradient	Difficulty	Distance	Area	Scenery	Strainers	Rating
6	I	22.3	25	C	<1/mi.	*

USGS Quad – Arcola/Gainesville/Manassas/Indep.Hill; Source – Personal descent (last 4 miles) 7/92, Corbett, Grove
N38 53.38, W77 34.22 to N38 44.54, W77 23.22

Bull Run forms the boundary between Loudoun/Fairfax counties and Prince William County, from the Bull Run Mountains to the Occoquan Reservoir. It can at times be run from the confluence with Black Branch at SR 624, but a better prospect is SR 705, three-quarters of a mile below where Chestnut Lick enters (the starting point in Corbett also). With its low gradient, Bull Run avoids having any real rapids during its entire runnable length.

This long trip can be divided in many ways. The first part has the better scenery but is likely to have more strainers. Little Bull Run (mile 7), Cub Run (mile 12) and Popes Head Creek (mile 18) add a lot of water. The final 1.5 miles is hard work on the Reservoir (which buries the final 3 miles of the stream). The best riffle is the remains of a dam, below Popes Head Creek, that powered the first generating station in Fairfax County.

Look for early spring wildflowers near the confluence with Little Bull Run, many thousands of Virginia bluebells shortly above Cub Run, and a large stand of hemlocks on river right below Popes Head Creek. There are hiking trails along lower Bull Run.

GAUGE: You will want at least 130 cfs on Beaverdam Creek, 215 cfs on Broad Run and 275 cfs on Cedar Creek. At slightly lower levels, put in downstream.

Bull Run is best known, of course, for the **battles** fought there in July 1861 and August 1862. The first battle marked the end of innocence for the North, which had expected a quick and easy victory. General Beauregard deployed his southern forces along Bull Run to protect the Manassas rail junction. The creek itself was not a serious impediment to the attacking Union forces at the onset of the battle (they feigned an attack at the Stone Bridge while crossing at fords upstream), but it became a more significant barrier in their panicky retreat, and many guns and other supplies were abandoned in their rush to ford it.

For an exotic paddle, Ed Evangelidi recommends the unnamed, class I outflow from the regional **water treatment plant** on river left between the mouth of Cub Run and Va. 28. You can access it from Ordway Rd. (SR 616), and run it much of the year for almost half a mile.

🌊 CHESTNUT LICK: Logmill Road (SR 701) to Bull Run

Gradient	Difficulty	Distance	Area	Scenery	Strainers	Rating
20	I (II-)	1.0*	11	B	1-3/mi.	*

USGS Quad – Arcola; Source – Personal descent 2/98
N38 53.29, W77 35.58 to N38 53.38, W77 34.22

*(plus 0.8 miles on Bull Run to Sanders Lane – SR 705, the start of Bull Run write up)

I knew about rivers and creeks, runs and branches, even forks, falls, brooks, streams, prongs and ditches – but a "lick"?!

At Ingram Drive, just east of US 15, the main tributaries come together, but a high, strong fence blocks access, and there might well be a similar obstacle downstream. As there is no access for the next 2.5 miles, only the final mile can be paddled, followed by 0.8 miles down Bull Run to Sanders Lane (SR 705).

That final mile is pleasant, through pretty woods. It is full of riffles and has a 2-foot ledge (class II-). One logjam required a short portage, while I could just slip under two other fallen trees. The probable source of these obstacles showed up in person – a large brown beaver, who, unlike most others I have encountered, was in no hurry to dive into the creek. Soon after the logjam, the creek splits around an island – the right channel has more water and was clean.

At the confluence, Chestnut Lick carries as much water as Bull Run. Halfway through the Bull Run stretch, small channels start going off to the left. These can be ignored, but soon half of the remaining water also heads sharply to the left. I took this channel, had to work past some branches in the water, picked up the flow from the other leftist channels, and then had clear sailing to the SR 705 take out.

GAUGE: Look for 50 cfs on both Limestone Branch and the South Fork, Quantico Creek, 25 cfs on Flatlick Branch and 275 cfs on Beaverdam Creek.

LITTLE BULL RUN: SR 705 (Pageland Lane) to Va. 234

Gradient	Difficulty	Distance	Area	Scenery	Strainers	Rating
15	I (II-)	4.0	19	C	0-2/mi.	*

USGS Quad – Gainesville; Source – Personal descent 12/96
N38 49.62, W77 34.29 to N38 50.55, W77 32.33

If you want to paddle in the headwaters of Bull Run, Little Bull Run is a better choice than its parent, as it is almost the same size and has twice the gradient. It is one of the easier creeks to catch up, because it is compounded behind a lake in its upper stretches, which slows down the runoff. Two days after an inch of rain in early December, I found it low but still passable.

Little Bull Run rises in the Bull Run Mountains and flows southeast and then northeast for 14.5 miles to meet Bull Run at the northern tip of Manassas National Battlefield Park. It starts as a mountain torrent through Hopewell Gap at 200-300 ft/mile. After 3 miles, it is impounded behind Silver Lake. Below, the gradient diminishes sharply, but much of the course is through fenced farmland. Only after the confluence with its main tributary, Catharpin Creek, is Little Bull Run a nice trip, as its size doubles, the fences virtually disappear, and the gradient increases from 10 ft/mile to 15 ft/mile. (Catharpin Creek averages 22 ft/mile for 4 miles and reaching 65 ft/mile, but from the last bridge I saw four strainers, and decided that the gain could not be worth the pain.)

Put in at SR 705. (The first access below the confluence with Catharpin Creek is half a mile upstream, at SR 704, but you won't want to tangle with a nasty-looking fence just above SR 705.) It is a mellow trip, full of riffles and some tight passages around little islands, with relatively few strainers. Around midway the creek emerges briefly from the woods, and there were 3 broken down fences (all easily paddled under) pretending to guard the cattle that watched me from the riverbank. Just above the only intermediate access point, Robin Road (after 3 miles), is a 20-yard class II- rock garden. Below that, the creek braids briefly, with each narrow passage likely to be blocked by a fallen tree; this is one of the two places (the other is beneath the second crossing of the power line, where the stream also braids in swift current) where a novice might get into trouble. Towards the end, the scenery improves, as rocky outcrops appear on river right. Just above the takeout, use the right channel where the creek splits. Take out at Va. 234, some 200 yards above the confluence, unless you want to paddle 3 flat miles (5 ft/mile) on Bull Run. In early spring, the wildflowers are wonderful here.

You can park at the intersection with SR 622 (Featherbed Lane), and carry 100 yards to your car. The trip took me just 75 minutes of steady paddling.

There's lots of **wildlife** in this area. I saw deer (twice), great blue herons, and about 20 hawks congregating on two nearby trees, who began circling low overhead as I approached, as if contemplating this new prey.

GAUGE: Broad Run should be at least 300 cfs, Aquia Creek 140 cfs, Cedar Run 375 cfs, Limestone Branch 30 cfs, Flatlick Branch 15 cfs and Beaverdam Creek 180 cfs.

Don't be misled by the **"Catharpin Run"** sign at Little Bull Run on Va. 234 – it must be some quaint VDOT way of combining Catharpin Creek with Little Bull Run.

This watershed was the target of the **Disney** history theme park; Virginia's Governor Allen supported the proposed development, but Disney eventually withdrew because of strong opposition from local residents and environmental groups.

At the **Battle of Second Manassas**/Bull Run, the Confederate left was anchored at Sudley Springs, the confluence of Bull and Little Bull runs. US Major General Philip Kearney attacked there, and drove the southerners back, but General Pope failed to send him reinforcements, and he had to retreat when General Jubal Early's brigade came to Major General A.P.Hill's support.

CUB RUN

Cub Run begins on the southern fringes of Dulles Airport and flows south for 13 miles into Bull Run. It picks up tributaries quickly, and within 4 miles can be paddled. Section 1 is pleasant but flat. Below that is the short but delightful class III section 2. Section 2 and the remaining 2.7 flat miles (full of Virginia bluebells) down to Bull Run are in Corbett and Grove. There are hiking trails along much of the creek.

During the Union retreat after the **First Battle of Bull Run**, Confederate artillery fire hit a supply wagon crossing the narrow bridge over Cub Run, thereby blocking the route. Panic gripped the retreating troops and civilians (inside-the-beltway types who wanted to watch history being made from the comfort of their own vehicles), many of whom abandoned their wagons, carriages and even ambulances carrying the wounded, in a helter-skelter effort to cross Cub Run and get back to Washington. Although the bridge was eventually cleared, the abandoned vehicles slowed everyone else's progress.

In the headwaters of Cub Run is the **Sully Plantation** of Richard Bland Lee, the first congressman from northern Virginia, who cast the decisive vote that brought the nation's capital to the banks of the Potomac. He was later one of the three commissioners appointed by President Madison to direct the restoration of the federal buildings burned by the British in 1814.

Section 1: Old Lee Road (SR 661) to Lee Highway (US 29)

Gradient	Difficulty	Distance	Area	Scenery	Strainers	Rating
5	I	4.7	12	C	<1/mi.	*

USGS Quad – Herndon/Manassas; Source –Personal descent (last 3 miles) 5/98
N38 52.94, W77 28.19 to N38 49.98, W77 27.82

Upper Cub Run is for the lover of flat water who wants to enjoy a pretty day on a small creek. The initial half mile down to Braddock Road (SR 620) is relatively swift, at 15 ft/mile, but then the creek calms way down. A mile below Braddock Road, Flatlick Branch and then Elklick Run double the flow. From there to US 29 there are only three riffles.

   GAUGE: About 25 cfs on Flatlick Branch, 400 cfs on Broad Run, and 300 cfs on Difficult Run should suffice.

Section 2: Lee Highway (US 29) to Compton Rd (SR 658)

Gradient	Difficulty	Distance	Area	Scenery	Strainers	Rating
42 (100)	III	1.2	39	B	0-2/mi	****

USGS Quad – Manassas; Source –Personal descent 8/10
N38 49.98, W77 27.82 to N38 49.28, W77 27.97

This is a very popular intermediate trip. It is relatively easy to catch (despite having the same drainage area as section 2 of Broad Run, Cub Run is up more often), close to the Washington area, just off I-66, and has half a mile of class III, even in low water. It is a highly symmetric run – flat, class I, class II, class III, class II, class I, flat. The steepest part is approaching the mouth of Big Rocky Run, and there is a good play spot just below, as well as one under the power line. In high water, this is a fast flush, with big waves and holes; in low water, it is tight and technical, with about a half dozen distinct class III drops. Most of the drops have alternative routes, depending on the water level. At moderate levels, go far left for the last ledge before Big Rocky Run. The trip is popular enough that paddlers tend to clean most strainers out.

   Unload and put in downstream river left or right; park on the service road across the highway. For the shortest shuttle, drive through the subdivision of Gates Post Estates (on White Post Rd.), take the third right (Jade Post Rd.) and then the second right (Blue Post Rd.) to the dead end, which is next to the Compton Road bridge.

   GAUGE: Expert kayakers run this at levels like 6 feet (on the RC gauge at the put in, on downstream river right), but I found 3 feet sufficiently daunting in my open boat. Look for at least 250 cfs on Broad Run, 190 cfs on Difficult Run. Some 15 cfs on Flatlick Branch would be an early indicator.

ELKLICK RUN: SR 609 (Pleasant Valley Road) to Cub Run

Gradient	Difficulty	Distance	Area	Scenery	Strainers	Rating
14	II+	1.3*	11	C	2-4/mi.	**

USGS Quad – Manassas; Source –Personal descent 5/98
N38 52.30, W77 29.64 to N38 49.98, W77 27.82

*(plus 3 miles on Cub Run to US 29, at 5 ft/mile)

There are three ways to start a trip down section 1 of Cub Run – Cub Run itself, Flatlick Branch or Elklick Run. For rapids, the last is by far the best.

This creek doesn't squander much of its limited gradient on riffles, but saves it for a pair of class II+ rapids towards the end. The first is a short, 4-foot drop that is best run on the far right, because trees and boulders clog the left side. The second, shortly before Cub Run, is a 50-yard rock garden. At low water, the cleanest route ends up on the left. And then it is three flat miles down Cub Run to US 29, which is the start of the more challenging Cub Run section 2.

GAUGE: The riffle 100 yards below the put in needs to be cleanly runnable. About 30 cfs on the Flatlick Branch gauge is the on-line requirement.

BIG ROCKY RUN: US 29 to Cub Run

Gradient	Difficulty	Distance	Area	Scenery	Strainers	Rating
65(300)	IV+	0.7*	7	C	5/mi.	!!!

USGS Quad – Manassas; Source – Trip report (Pete Rutkowski); scouting on foot
N38 50.18, W77 26.99 (or N38 49.85, W77 27.41 sub-div.) to N38 49.28, W77 27.97

*(plus 0.7 miles on Cub Run to Compton Road)

Many paddlers see this creek tearing down from the left just after the hardest rapids on Cub Run. It is essentially a 150-yard rapid that starts and ends at 200 ft/mile and reaches 300 ft/mile midway. It begins with a Z-turn around huge boulders at the top, and then it's pretty much a straight shot – sort of a longer, narrower, steeper version of Cucumber – except for a tight double-Z between boulders midway. Make sure you avoid the tree trunks lining both banks and the branches hanging over the water. If you run Big Rocky from US 29, the first 0.6 miles is class I with several strainers, until the creek disappears around a bend. But the main rapid is usually paddled with a carry up from Cub Run, along a bike path, or by carrying down from a sub-division parking lot.

Big Rocky Run rises in western Fairfax County and flows 7 miles to Cub Run. Its gradient is as consistent as W's justification for the Iraq war. From 15 ft/mile at Stringfellow Road, it soars to 130 ft/mile, drops to 20, rises again to 80, collapses to 10, and finally rockets up to 300. One could occasionally paddle 2.2 miles from Centreville Road to US 29, with a drainage area of 5 sq. mi. and a gradient of 12 ft/mile. But why?

GAUGE: Look for 60 cfs on Flatlick Branch and 180 cfs on Fourmile Run.

In the headwaters of Big Rocky Run is **Ox Hill (Chantilly) Battlefield Park**, site of a clash on September 1, 1862. Stonewall Jackson, after winning the Second Battle of Bull Run, was attempting to cut off Pope's retreat to Washington. Although two Union generals (Kearny and Stevens) were killed, the smaller Union forces held off the attack, and Pope's Army of Virginia was able to join McClellan's Army of the Potomac. This ended the Second Manassas campaign.

🌊 POPES HEAD CREEK: Fairfax Station Road (SR 660) to Bull Run

Gradient	Difficulty	Distance	Area	Scenery	Strainers	Rating
21	II- (II)	5.6*	12**	C	1-3/mi.	**

USGS Quad – Fairfax/Manassas; Source – Personal descent 7/92

N38 47.89, W77 21.12 via N38 46.88, W77 23.26 (Clifton) to N38 44.95, W77 23.21

*(plus 1-2 miles on Bull Run and 2-3 miles on Occoquan Reservoir to Kinchaloe Rd.)
**(including Piney Branch, which enters in 350 yards)

Put in just above the confluence with Piney Branch. The stream meanders in a broad floodplain, but the tight turns give you little warning of the occasional strainer.

At Main St. in Clifton, after 3.6 miles, the "classic" Popes Head Creek trip begins. (Nathaniel Pope was an early settler in the area (1654), and a promontory is a "head" of land.) There is somewhat more water (17 sq. mi.), which results in a wider but not deeper streambed. Several stretches are right up against the railway tracks, but otherwise there are no intrusions of civilization once you leave Clifton.

The highlight is a long class II rock garden in the second mile. The lowlight is the 2-3 miles (depending on the water level) on the Occoquan Reservoir. In between are 1-2 miles of Bull Run – no rapids, but decent current and small waves. Don't bother looking for Yates Ford on Bull Run; the steep 0.4 mile carry up to you car is worse than the reservoir paddle. Instead of paddling all the way to Bull Run Marina, cut off the last half mile by taking out alongside Kinchaloe Road.

GAUGE: Look for 25 cfs on Flatlick Branch and 80 cfs on Fourmile Run.

SOUTH of the OCCOQUAN

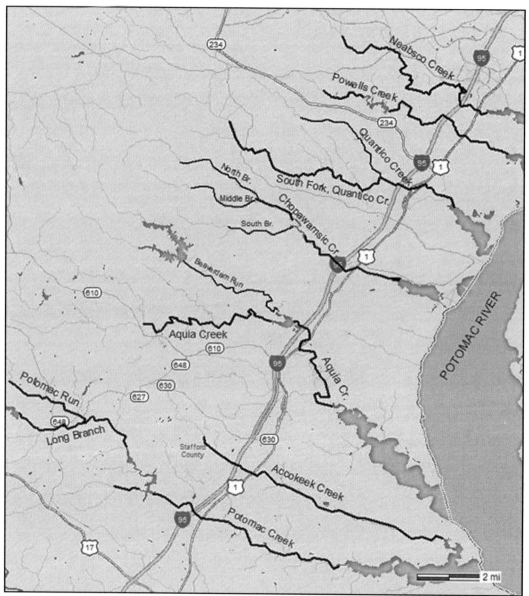

©Copyright 2005-2011 Undertow Software Corp.

Chapter 37:

SOUTH of the OCCOQUAN

Below the Occoquan River, the sub-basins of the Potomac are all small, as they are hemmed in by the Occoquan to the north and west and the Rappahannock to the south. The runnable streams are **Neabsco, Powells, Quantico** and its **South Fork, Chopawamsic, Aquia, Accokeek** (an 'explorer's special") and **Potomac creeks,** plus the **Long Branch** (also an "explorers' special") and **Potomac Run** tributaries of Potomac Creek. What gives them some good whitewater is that they drop over the fall line; unfortunately, reservoirs on all except Neabsco Creek have drowned part of this. The whitewater in this area must have been a whole lot better in pre-Army Corps of Engineers time. For flat water paddlers, the situation is improving, as a Potomac River "trail" is being developed with campsites a day's paddle apart from Washington DC to the Chesapeake Bay, on both shores of the river.

Chopawamsic Creek flows within the sprawling Quantico Marine Corps Development and Education Command Base; it used to be fully accessible when not required for marine training exercises, but since 9/11, the top third is off limits. Quantico Creek, its South Fork, and Aquia Creek (sections 2 and 3) are described in Corbett, and Aquia, in more detail (and very positively), in Grove as well. Gertler writes up the tidal portions of most of these creeks, despite their being on the Virginia side, as they are inlets of the Potomac River (which belongs to Maryland). Quantico and Powells creeks each have a class III+ drop, while Neabsco Creek has a pair of long, fun rapids.

The northern part of this area is suburban, especially Dale City (66,000 people; site of Neabsco Creek and the Potomac Mills shopping complex), but further south it is predominantly rural, except for a row of historic port towns (Dumfries, Triangle, Quantico, Stafford). But fear not, suburbia will rescue them too before long.

Several even-tinier streams are problematical. Upper **Quantico Creek** is in Corbett (he calls it the "North Branch," which is what it should be named), but requires a 3/4-mile carry to get there, and the one major rapid (class IV+) is often strainer-choked. **Cannon Creek,** the largest tributary of Aquia Creek, has no good access.

The most interesting creek that is not an option is **Beaverdam Run**, inside the marine base. It might be run for 4.4 miles from the base of the Lunga Reservoir down to Smith Lake, with a gradient that averages 40 ft/mile and reaches 100 ft/mile, and an 11 sq. mi. catchment. But there are two problems. First, it is virtually never up because it is behind a high dam, from which lots of water is withdrawn. And second, since 9/11/01, access to the area has been restricted.

GAUGES: There are Internet gauges on the South Fork of Quantico Creek and on Aquia Creek. The South Fork gauge has a 7.6 sq. mi. catchment, so it is excellent also for Neabsco and Powells Creeks, while the Aquia gauge's 35 sq. mi. drainage makes it ideal for Potomac Creek. In the table below, **"gauge" refers to the South Fork, Quantico Creek,** except that when it is in ***bold italics, it refers to Aquia Creek.***

name	gradient	difficulty	length	area	gauge	rating
Neabsco Creek	29 (90)	II+	8.0	5	100cfs	***
Powells Creek	28 (40)	II (III+)	4.0	11	70cfs	**
So.Fk/Quantico Cr.- Sec. 1	25 (50)	II+ (?)	5.7	8	75cfs	?
- Sec. 2	27 (110)	III- (III+)	2.6	15	50cfs	***
Chopawamsic Creek	25	II	1.9	18	(35cfs)	*
Aquia Creek - Section 1	14	I	3.0	10	200cfs	-
- Section 2	15 (55)	II- (II+)	8.5	24	100cfs	**
- Section 3	9	II-	1.4	52	70cfs	*
Accokeek Creek	17	?	3.0	9	50cfs	?
Potomac Creek	8	I (II)	4.8	32	90cfs	-
Long Branch – Sec. 1	40	?	1.4	5	90cfs	?
- Sec. 2	17	?	2.5	17	135cfs	?
Potomac Run	18	I	1.5	7	60cfs	-

NEABSCO CREEK: Lindendale Road (SR 610) to US 1

Gradient	Difficulty	Distance	Area	Scenery	Strainers	Rating
29 (90)	II+	8.0	5	A-D	<1/mi.	***

USGS Quad – Occoquan/Quantico; Source – Personal descent 3/94
N38 38.72, W77 21.96 via N38 38.69, W77 20.38 (SR 640) to N38 36.55, W77 17.43

How delightful – a suburban creek with interesting whitewater and few strainers, that can be run for 8 miles! In lower water, one could paddle 6 miles from Minnieville Road (SR 640), with 9 sq. mi., but you would miss one of the two best sections of rapids. This write up is adapted from Larry Gladieux's trip report in *The Voyageur*.

"Our first put in was somewhat speculative. Topo maps were terrific but outdated by suburban development in Dale City. After wandering a couple of neighborhoods, we crossed a stream and asked some locals what it was called. They had no clue, and looked at us like we were nuts. Maybe we were. But we knew things were looking up when the cold drizzle stopped and the sky started to brighten. What the hell, this had to be the right watershed (the Potomac at least) and we were (90%) certain this was Neabsco.

"And it was. We soon floated out of sight of homes into woods. Our first wildlife sighting was a beaver, which disappeared underwater quickly. The stream meandered a mile over a moderate gradient, then steepened for half a mile of continuous class II+, flattened out in a middle section, and finally descended into a deep gorge (also class II+) passing under I-95. Scenery ran the gamut, including golf courses, parks, backs of houses, power lines and auto wrecks. But sections were remarkably pristine and pretty, reminiscent of Sideling Hill Creek. When we reached our take out at US 1, the water level there was a foot lower than it had been 4 hours earlier."

The bridge just below the McDonald's has three tubes, which bend in the middle, so you cannot see through. Portage or check carefully to ensure no mid-tube strainers.

GAUGE: You need at least 100 cfs on the South Fork, Quantico Creek gauge.

> Neabsco means **"at the point of rocks,"** a reference to Freestone Point at the creek's mouth. Confederate artillery there blockaded the Potomac River during the early part of the Civil War. Between the mouths of Neabsco and Powells creeks is **Leesylvania State Park**, with ruins from the plantation of "Light Horse" Harry Lee, father of Robert E. Lee. Iron was mined along the creek before 1738. Nowadays, Dale City is the home of Potomac Mills shopping center.

POWELLS CREEK: Below Lake Montclair to US 1

Gradient	Difficulty	Distance	Area	Scenery	Strainers	Rating
28 (40)	II (III+)	4.0	11	C	0-2/mi.	**

USGS Quad – Quantico; Source – Personal descent 3/94
N38 36.69, W77 20.26 to N38 35.76, W77 17.94

This stream is the same size as Neabsco, but is interrupted by a dam midway that creates the 2-mile long Lake Montclair. Fairly early on comes the one hard rapid – a class III+ boulder garden, just after a right hand turn. Scout and portage, if necessary, on the right. Powells Creek does not have long class II+ rock gardens like Neabsco, but it does have similar mixed suburban scenery. Here continues Larry Gladieux's *Voyageur* write up of our late March day on those two creeks.

"On Powells Creek, shortly before I-95, we encountered an unfriendly 10 ft-high wood-and-chain-link fence stretching from bank to bank and as far as the eye could see on either side, with a sign saying 'Private Property/No Trespassing'. We momentarily wondered how we would get back to our cars. Fortunately, we were able to squeeze through a portion of the fence forced open by the current. Half a mile later we squeezed through their other fence and out of the no trespassing zone, without getting arrested or shot. In late afternoon, when we shuttled back to the put in, the creek was almost gone."

Below US 1, Powells Creek braids for a mile through a marsh, before opening into a wide estuary. The area just south of this was the proposed site of the Legoland theme park in the early 1990s, until local opposition killed the idea.

GAUGE: Because of its dam, Powells Creek tends to rise more slowly and stay up longer than Neabsco Creek. Look for 70 cfs on the South Fork, Quantico Creek.

> **Yosockeccomocoe**. This creek's original name, Yosocomico (with variations), meant "in the middle of the enclosure," suggesting an Indian fort – the predecessor of the "no-trespassing" fence we encountered! The colonists eventually found this a mouthful, and changed the name – but just who the Powells were is a mystery.

SOUTH FORK/QUANTICO CREEK

Quantico Creek and its South Fork flow through Prince William Forest Park and meet at its edge, just 1.5 miles above the town of Dumfries and tidewater. At the confluence, Quantico Creek is less than half the size of its South Fork (7 vs.17 sq. mi.), but then if you were still expecting some logic to the names of streams, you obviously have not paid attention to earlier parts of this book.

A mile above the confluence, Quantico Creek (the smaller branch) goes over the class IV+ Quantico Falls, where it drops 20 feet in 100 yards, around huge boulders. This would be an exciting rapid for experts, except that it (a) is almost never up, (b) requires carrying in three-quarters of a mile (along Quantico Falls and North Valley Trails, from parking area E), and (c) is usually blocked in several places by strainers. Therefore, the only trips discussed below are on the South Fork, with section 2 continuing past the confluence and onto Quantico Creek.

The Park rangers have varied over time in their acceptance of paddlers. Corbett reported that canoeing required advanced permission in writing. When I inquired in 1996, I was told there was no clear policy, but now that I had asked, maybe they would adopt one. Oops! But both times I ran it, rangers spoke to us but did not object.

Prince William Forest Park was developed during the Depression by the Civilian Conservation Corps (CCC), to both restore the environment and create jobs. During World War II, it was a top-secret training area for the OSS (forerunner of the CIA), where spies practiced information-gathering skills in the neighboring towns. It is the largest natural park area in metropolitan Washington, and is run by the National Park Service, with emphasis on hiking and group camping. This had been a tobacco and corn farming area, but the topsoil had been depleted of nutrients and washed down the creek, to silt up Dumfries harbor. There has since been a remarkable ecological recovery; the streams are full of aquatic life, and over 150 bird species have been recorded in the park, as well as deer (which we saw twice) and other mammals. Beavers were reintroduced in the 1950s – the only drawback (for paddlers) in this story, as it helps explain the high density of strainers. There is a $4 per vehicle fee for entering the park. A large public campground is open year round.

History. Land along Quantico Creek was first patented in 1653, divided into 500-3,000 acre estates. A tobacco warehouse was built at Dumfries in 1730. This was the eastern terminus of the first road to the Blue Ridge, via Ashby's Gap, which was opened in 1731 and crossed the mountains by 1759. There were minor clashes in the area during the Civil War, as the Union broke the Confederate blockade of the Potomac; in a daring raid on October 11, 1861, Union sailors burned the *Martha Washington*, which was anchored in Quantico Creek.

Alongside Quantico Creek, a quarter mile above the confluence, is the remains of an **iron pyrite (fools' gold) mine**, which operated from 1889 to 1920. The ore was mined for its sulfur, which was particularly in demand during World War I. Miners were lowered in buckets by 80-foot cables into the three main shafts. By 1920, however, cheaper sources had been developed, and the mine closed. One can still see the foundations of some of the 70 structures that once lined the creek.

Quantico is a native American word possibly meaning **"at the long inlet,"** a reference to the three-mile long, half-mile wide, tidal part of the creek below US 1.

Section 1: SR 619 (Joplin Rd) to Parking Area A (Prince William Park)

Gradient	Difficulty	Distance	Area	Scenery	Strainers	Rating
25 (55)	II+(?)	5.7	8	B	3-5/mi.	?

USGS Quad – Joplin/Quantico; Source – Corbett; scouting on foot
N38 35.22, W77 25.72 to N38 34.11, W77 21.94

This is a quasi-*"explorer's special,"* as I haven't run it but I've hiked most of it. (It's also in Corbett, but his write-up is rather vague, so he may not have run it either.) The put in is at the western edge of Prince William Forest Park. After 1.5 easy miles, you reach the half-mile backwater of a 20-foot dam. Portage on the right. (The lake is used by groups staying in cabins, and is the only part of this creek that is often canoed.) Below the dam is a class II or II+ section. The gradient then eases up, but riffles remain frequent the entire way. A hiking trail follows the creek after the first half mile.

You cross the Prince William Forest Scenic Drive at 4.2 and 4.5 miles; parking area (letter) I is between them. The take-out, parking area A, is just before the third and final bridge. The main problem with this run is strainers (what a surprise!).

GAUGE: On the Internet gauge at the put in, 75 cfs would be minimal.

Section 2: Parking Area A (Prince William Park) to Dumfries (Van Buren Road)

Gradient	Difficulty	Distance	Area	Scenery	Strainers	Rating
27 (110)	III- (III+)	2.6	15	B	1-2/mi.	***

USGS Quad – Quantico; Source – Personal descent 5/03
N38 34.11, W77 21.94 to N38 34.11, W77 20.16

The first 1.5 miles are fast flat water, through pretty woods. After a good rain, a lovely waterfall cascades down at a sharp turn on river right. Below that is a footbridge and then the first rapid – a 4-5 foot ledge (class III-) with a hydraulic, best run left to right. Then the creek becomes continuous class I-II for a quarter mile.

The "main stem" adds about 40% to the flow, and shortly thereafter (you are now on Quantico Creek itself) begins the descent of the fall line, starting with the toughest bit – a complex class III+ rapid with a closely-spaced series of drops totaling about 8 feet. Run the first drop left to right, then cut back sharply left on either side of the pillow, and then cut right again. Portage on either side if you have concerns; if you mess up here, you could be in for a long swim. Some 50 yards below comes another irregular class III- ledge, where most of the water goes to the right into a squirrelly hydraulic, but you can also run left of the island, starting with a 2-foot ledge. Another 50 yards, another class III- drop, with good wave action on the right. Then comes some class I-II water, passing the only house I saw on the trip, ending in a class II+ ledge. The Van Buren Road take out, just before I-95, is soon reached. Watch out for strainers blocking some of the channels in the gorge, below the hardest drop.

GAUGE: The South Fork gauge (at the section 1 put in) should be at least 50 cfs, 2-3 hours before you put in. The flow will be doubled by the time you reach the section 2 put-in, and three times as much by the main rapids below the confluence.

CHOPAWAMSIC CREEK: Breckenridge Reservoir to Russell Rd.

Gradient	Difficulty	Distance	Area	Scenery	Strainers	Rating
25	II	1.9	18	B	3-5/mi.	*

USGS Quad – Joplin/Quantico; Source – Personal descent 2/00
N38 31.89, W77 23.10 (top of what was still open) to N38 31.38, W77 22.43

Chopawamsic Creek, the boundary between Prince William and Stafford counties, is looking for a few good (or even not so good) paddlers. Although it flows through the Quantico Marine Corps Base, all of it was open to fishermen and boaters, except when closed by training exercises. **Since 9/11/01, however, about a half mile on each side of the reservoir has been off limits, to protect the base's water supply.** Also, stay away during the fall hunting season. It is a popular catch-and-release rainbow trout stream. Breckenridge Reservoir sits astride the creek and ends in a 40-ft high dam. A gravel road follows the creek from the reservoir to Russell Road.

The 6 weirs and 8 road crossings on this stream provide much of the action. You used to be able to put in right at the foot of the dam, or to avoid the first 2 weirs by putting in 70 yards downstream. The first weir is easily scrapable, but the second is best portaged on the left (unless you have enough water to run it cleanly). In less than 100 yards comes the third weir, which I portaged on the right, as it was full of debris. The fourth weir can be circumvented by a twisting class II diversion on the far left, and the fifth weir can be run in the middle with a 3-foot drop. The final weir, a much bigger structure than its predecessors, is best portaged on the left, as it is so wide that the water flowing over it is extremely shallow.

Several of the road crossings produce surfing waves and have class I or II rapids just below them. The better rapids are in the first half of the trip; after that there is mainly flat water and riffles. The scenery is very pretty, with rock outcroppings and wild rhododendrons. Great blue herons compete with the fishermen, but do not practice catch and release. There are quite a few strainers, but none were dangerous when I was there.

Whenever the creek is runnable, you would want a pick-up truck, SUV or tank to do the direct shuttle, as a lower-clearance vehicle might suck water into its tailpipe when crossing the creek. For regular cars, it's a roundabout 8-mile shuttle instead (currently closed to the public).

Below Russell Road, one could run an additional flat mile past I-95 and down to US 1, or even 1.6 miles beyond that, all at 10 ft/mile, down to a landing off Russell Road (which would involve driving through a Marine checkpoint). There, Chopawamsic Creek opens into a half-mile wide estuary (which is very attractive and full of bird life, according to Gertler), and finally narrows into a man-made channel at the south end of the Marine Corps Air Station, which leads to the Potomac River. (The original channel, a little north of this, was filled in to help make the Air Station.)

GAUGE: About 90 cfs on the Chopawamsic Creek gauge (if it ever becomes available again over the Internet) is zero level. Because of the dam, this creek rises and falls more slowly than others of comparable size, and it often stays up for most of a day. Look, roughly, for 35 cfs on the South Fork, Quantico Creek.

USMC. Visitors to the Quantico area might also visit the Quantico National Cemetery and the Marine Corps Air-Ground Museum. The Quantico shipyard serviced American vessels during the Revolutionary War, while during the early 20th Century, the Chopawamsic Recreation Area was a tourist escape from the Capital, and then a shipbuilding center again. The Marine Corps purchased 5,300 acres in 1918, as they expanded during WWI. Quantico, a port on the Potomac stretching from Quantico Creek to Chopawamsic Creek, is the only US town completely surrounded by a military base.

The creek's name is a whole phrase, usually interpreted as **"by the separation of the outlet"** (Chopawamsic Island split the creek's former mouth in two).

Chopawamsic Creek is fed by 3 **headwaters** – its North, Middle and South branches. The **South Branch** flows directly into the reservoir, and is rather small (4 sq. mi.), but has an exciting 75 ft/mile for a mile. The **Middle Branch** flows into the somewhat larger **North Branch,** 1.3 miles above the reservoir. To get to the confluence, you could paddle a mile down the upper North Branch (starting with just 5.7 sq. mi.) or a half-mile down the Middle Branch (3.5 sq. mi.). The North Branch trip would have a 50-ft/mile gradient for the first 1.5 miles, but then a flat 0.8 miles to the reservoir. And in all cases, you would have to paddle over a mile across the reservoir to reach the access road. Still, they might be worth exploring, if and when the Marine Corps again relaxes access to the base.

AQUIA CREEK

Aquia Creek flows for 20 miles and has the largest watershed in this chapter. Section 2 is a popular paddle that would be even more so were it not dammed to form Smith Lake (which may be frozen, even when the creek is not). Section 1 is very hard to catch and has too many strainers. A mile below section 3, the stream becomes tidal.

History. Giles Brent (see Giles Run in Chapter 35) built the first house along the creek in 1647, and later established the first Roman Catholic church in Virginia. After the Indian War of 1676, Aquia Creek was for ten years the northern frontier of Virginia. The current Aquia Church was built in 1757; its communion silver was buried in three wars, in 1776, 1812 and 1861.

In an attempt to close the Potomac to Union shipping, the Confederates constructed batteries along the south bank of Aquia Creek. In one of the first **Civil War** engagements, on June 1, 1861, Union ships exchanged fire with those batteries and determined that the Confederate guns did not have the range to stop shipping on the Potomac. The Army of the Potomac, coming from the James, landed here in August 1862, and then used the Aquia Creek railway terminus for a year as its supply base for ineffectual campaigns.

Sandstone from a quarry near the creek was used for the boundary stones demarcating the District of Columbia and for the Capitol Building there.

The Piscataway named the creek, to mean either "muddy," "bush nut" or "seagull"; they stubbornly refused to say which, but most paddlers vote for the first.

Section 1: SR 644 to SR 610 (Garrisonville Road)

Gradient	Difficulty	Distance	Area	Scenery	Strainers	Rating
14	I	3.0	10	C	3-5/mi.	-

USGS Quad – Stafford; Source – Personal descent 5/02

N38 29.24, W77 31.90 to N38 29.11, W77 29.32

The topographic map shows a short, steep stretch, but that is apocryphal. The longest and best riffles are in the final half mile. Above that are only short ones, plus a pair of straightforward 2-foot ledges.

The main problem is the strainers, many of them beaver dams. All along the banks were beavers' mudslides, and I saw two of the miscreants swimming.

GAUGE: Look for at the Aquia Creek gauge to be at least 200 cfs.

Section 2: SR 610 to Smith Lake Dam

Gradient	Difficulty	Distance	Area	Scenery	Strainers	Rating
15 (55)	II- (II+)	8.5	24*	B	1/mi.	**

USGS Quad – Stafford; Source – Personal descent 7/04

N38 29.11, W77 29.32 to N38 29.37, W77 24.32 (SR 639) or N38 29.10, W77 23.98 (SR 659)

*(including Cannon Creek which enters in a quarter mile)

This creek has good scenery and over two miles of low-intermediate rapids, can be canoed a long distance and is not too difficult to catch. But the first 4 miles are pretty flat and tend to collect strainers, and the last 1.5 miles are across a lake; those are rather big caveats. The Quantico Marine Base occupies the left bank, while suburban housing is starting to creep up towards the right shoreline.

The creek is very narrow at the put in, but widens a bit when Cannon Creek, after a quarter mile, adds almost 50% to the flow. In another half mile, you pass under a tank road; strainers often block one or more of the three culverts. The first four miles average only 10 ft/mile. Beaver slides and chewed branches were everywhere. Then the creek enters a little gorge, with some long riffles and a few class II- rapids, culminating in a nice class II+ rock garden. At 5.5 miles, the stream crosses SR 641 and the riffles and easy rapids resume, with another class II+ as the highlight. But in only 1.5 miles you reach the backwater of Smith Lake, the reservoir for Stafford County, under which the second half of the fall line is buried.

You then have three choices. You can cross Smith Lake (1.5 miles) on the left side, carry over the dam and paddle section 3 down to US 1 (as per Corbett); you can cross Smith Lake on the right side and take out at SR 659 (as per Grove); or you can paddle one mile down the lake, to just before the Beaverdam Run and Aquia Creek branches meet, and drag your boat uphill to SR 639. This would shorten your flatwater paddle, but unpaved SR 639 will be muddy after a heavy rain.

GAUGE: There is a gauge, available over the Internet (but not readable on site), at SR 641. About 100 cfs is minimal, and you can also judge by the riffles at SR 641; if the level is dropping you will of course need more when you start.

Section 3: Smith Lake to US 1

Gradient	Difficulty	Distance	Area	Scenery	Strainers	Rating
9	II-	1.4	52	C	<1/mi.	*

USGS Quad – Stafford; Source – Personal descent 7/04
End of section 2 to N38 28.47, W77 23.68

This section is not for doing by itself, but is usually the best alternative after running section 2. To reach it, carry over the dam near the left side (but not so far left that you might get washed over the spillway!). The carry up is short, but it is a much longer way down, and the rough surface is not friendly to dragged boats. The waves just below the spillway make a decent play spot. The run itself starts off class II- through pretty woods, but the gradient, quietude and scenery deteriorate en route to US 1.

GAUGE: Check the flow from the takeout; 70 cfs on the Aquia Creek gauge is minimal. But if the reservoir was not close to full before, you may need instead one of the other takeout options discussed under section 2.

ACCOKEEK CREEK: US 1 to Brooke (SR 608)

Gradient	Difficulty	Distance	Area	Scenery	Strainers	Rating
17	?	3.0	9	?	?	?

USGS Quad – Stafford; Source – Scouting put in and take out
N38 24.16, W77 25.29 to N38 23.05, W77 23.02

Accokeek ("at the edge of the hill") Creek, squeezed between Aquia and Potomac creeks, is too small to run until US 1. You can park by the Stafford Co. offices, on upstream river left. The first half of this *"explorers' special"* is through a flood plain. Then the creek enters a little gorge for a mile, but the gradient increases only marginally. In the final half mile, the countryside opens up again.

Below Brooke, it is another 5 miles to the Potomac, at just 8 ft/mile, and the map shows the creek braiding through a swampy area.

GAUGE: The Aquia gauge is the best for proximity, the South Fork, Quantico gauge for drainage area. Look for 240 cfs on the former, 50 cfs on the latter.

> Nearby were iron mines and a furnace in which **Augustine Washington**, the father of George, began to smelt iron in 1727. Now the main sight along US 1 is an automobile graveyard.

POTOMAC CREEK: SR 627 (Mountain View Road) to SR 626

Gradient	Difficulty	Distance	Area	Scenery	Strainers	Rating
8	I (II)	4.8	32	C	1-3/mi.	-

USGS Quad – Stafford/Fredericksburg; Source – Personal descent 1/98
N38 23.05, W77 28.09 to N38 21.67, W77 25.22

This is the final Potomac tributary that one crosses heading south along I-95, just five miles above Fredericksburg and the Rappahannock (although the tidal Potomac continues east-southeast for another 70 miles). The trip begins three-quarters of a mile below the Able Lake Reservoir, under which the final part of Potomac Creek's fall line lies buried. Because of its relatively large watershed, this is an easy creek to catch up.

But why bother? The scenery is rustic but boring; in winter, everything is gray. The only rapid is a 2-foot ledge (class II) between I-95 and US 1. There are quite a few strainers. A few places would be dangerous for novices, where the water flows swiftly under low branches. But the worst spot I encountered was a 4-strand, barbed-wire fence, after about three-quarters of a mile (when I was not yet disliking the creek), in fast water, just after a hard left turn. Get over to river left, where there is a larger eddy and a low bank. I realized that too late, and had a hard (and wet) time getting through on river right.

Below the take out, it is another 3 miles to tidewater, but half of this is through a swamp, where Canter calls the going "rough."

GAUGE: About 90 cfs on the Aquia Creek gauge should be adequate.

The largest source of water for the Able Lake Reservoir is actually **Long Branch**, which in turn has a main tributary named **Potomac Run**. In the early days, following British usage, "creek" meant a stream which ended up tidal, whereas a "run" flowed its entire length. This terminology was fine for an island like Great Britain, but as the settlers moved inland, they wanted to keep a term for streams intermediate in size between rivers and runs, and so the usage of "creek" was broadened.

In 1608, at the confluence of what are now called Potomac Creek and the Potomac River, Captain Smith found the village of **"Petomek"** ("where something is brought," suggesting tribute), a powerful part of the Powhatan Confederacy. It was here, five years later, that Pocahontas was kidnapped by an Indian chief and sold to the British Captain Argall. During the Civil War, this was the Union transfer point between river and rail.

LONG BRANCH

Long Branch is the largest tributary of Potomac Creek; in fact, when they enter Abel Lake (Stafford County water supply), Long Branch has a drainage area of 30 sq. mi. and Potomac Creek less than 4 sq. mi. Long Branch itself is also dammed, early in its life, and the only access spot, SR 616, is a mile and a half below the dam. Section 2 is run either by continuing down from section 1 or by putting in on Potomac Run, 0.3 miles above the confluence.

Section 1: SR 616 to confluence with Potomac Run

Gradient	Difficulty	Distance	Area	Scenery	Strainers	Rating
40	?	1.4*	5	?	?	?

USGS Quad – Storck; Source – Scouting put in
N38 25.63, W77 32.38 to N38 24.79, W77 29.74

*(plus 2.9 miles down section 2)

This is a very hard *"explorers' special"* to catch up, especially as there will only be a significant flow when the lake was filled beforehand; however, its good gradient suggests that the wait might be worthwhile. After completing these 1.4 miles, you then must paddle section 2.

GAUGE: Look for 90 cfs on the South Fork, Quantico Creek and 400 cfs on Aquia Creek (projected 2 hours later).

Section 2: SR 648 (on Potomac Run) to Abel Lake (SR 651)

Gradient	Difficulty	Distance	Area	Scenery	Strainers	Rating
17 (40)	?	2.5*	17	?	?	?

USGS Quad – Storck/Stafford; Source – Scouting put in and take out
N38 26.04, W77 31.39 to N38 24.79, W77 29.74

*(plus an initial 0.3 miles on Potomac Run and a final 0.4 miles on Abel Lake)

The put in for this *"explorers' special"* is actually on Potomac Run, 0.3 miles above the confluence. You then paddle 2.5 miles on Long Branch, until a final 0.4 miles on Abel Lake. The initial drainage area is 11 sq. mi., and the remaining 6 sq. mi. is picked up from Long Branch at the confluence. The steepest section is the final quarter mile before Abel Lake. There is a good public access to the lake and a parking area on the right, just before SR 651.

GAUGE: Look for 135 cfs on Aquia Creek, although you may need closer to 200 cfs to get down that first 500 yards cleanly.

POTOMAC RUN: SR 616 to SR 648

Gradient	Difficulty	Distance	Area	Scenery	Strainers	Rating
18	I	1.5	7	C	5-10/mi.	-

USGS Quad – Storck; Source – Personal descent 9/06
N38 26.52, W77 32.42 to N38 26.04, W77 31.39

The only reason to paddle this is for exploration, and since I have done that already, don't waste your time here. The strainers visible from the take out should have deterred me, but the word "Potomac" inspired me – although I had already discovered that Potomac Creek was a drag. In any case, expect a few riffles, no rapids and lots of wood. The main skill needed is how to get under, over or around fallen trees. In high water, there would be almost twice as many strainers, given how many tree trunks I was able to just slip under. But then anyone who chooses to paddle this must enjoy strainers.

The take out is one-third mile above the confluence with Long Branch; that final bit is included in the Long Branch write up.

GAUGE: Look for 60 cfs on the South Fork, Quantico Creek and 275 cfs on Aquia Creek (projected 2 hours later).

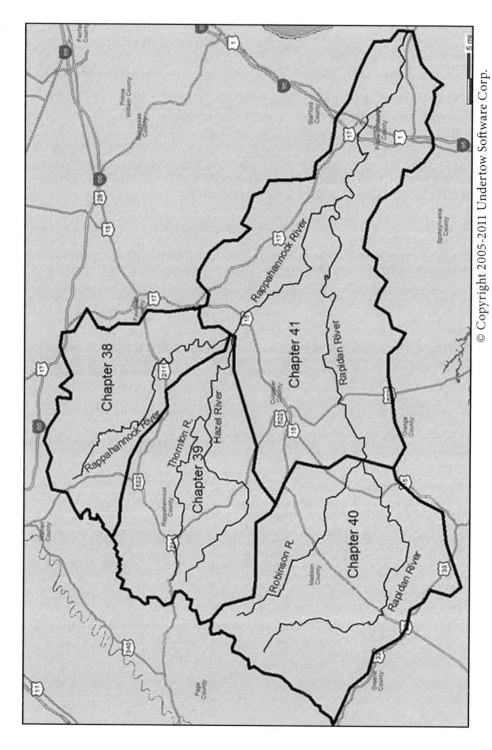

PART IX: RAPPAHANNOCK BASIN

The Rappahannock watershed covers 2,850 square miles (6% of Virginia), of which 1,650 are above the fall line (and therefore prone to rapids) that runs through Fredericksburg, and 1,200 in the coastal plain. The basin is deservedly popular with Washington-area paddlers for its whitewater, scenery and proximity. The lower sections of the **Rappahannock** and **Rapidan rivers** are runnable much of a normal year. The headwaters, which are generally more exciting, have a density of creeks that makes multiple runs in the same day easy, when the water is high.

These creeks rise in Shenandoah National Park, and flow east-southeast off the Blue Ridge. Many are popular trout streams. They have rather similar and simple contours: very steep in the mountains, easing up gradually in the foothills, and flat across the Piedmont. The Rappahannock itself then has a final descent over the fall line at Fredericksburg. South and west of this basin, the watersheds of the York and James rivers are beyond the scope of this book. To the northwest is the Shenandoah drainage.

The Rappahannock headwaters are the smallest "rivers" around. The terms "creek" and "branch" virtually never made it into this area, so after the tiniest "runs" come the only-slightly-larger "rivers." On the other hand, in the Piedmont portion of the basin, even much larger tributaries are "runs."

The most popular trips are in Corbett, Grove and other guidebooks. But I have added steeper sections farther upstream, as well as some additional downstream runs. In addition, as many of the creeks have been changed by flooding and subsequent dredging, or from removal or addition of fences, the information here is significantly updated.

The Rappahannock's two main tributaries, the **Hazel River** (chapter 39) and the **Rapidan River** (chapter 40), provide the basis for dividing the headwaters into chapters. There are outstanding runs on the Covington, Rush, Hughes, Piney, Thornton and North Fork of Thornton rivers in the Hazel River basin, and on the Conway, South, Robinson and Rose rivers in the Rapidan headwaters. Chapter 38 on the **Upper Rappahannock Basin** covers the main stem and its tributaries above the confluence with the Hazel, while chapter 41 describes the downstream **Rappahannock "Tailwaters"** and its tributaries.

The watershed is mostly rural, with the largest towns being Fredericksburg (24,000) at the fall line and Culpeper (16,000) and Warrenton (10,000) in the Piedmont. In the headwaters there are only small, scenic villages. The total population of some 225,000 (3% of Virginia) is growing rapidly, as more people push beyond the near-in suburbs. Located between Washington and Richmond, this basin was the scene of much Civil War fighting, including the decisive Confederate victories at Fredericksburg and Chancellorsville, and the bloody but inconclusive battle of the Wilderness, which marked the beginning of Grant's final campaign toward Richmond.

In 2004, the **river gauges** on the Rappahannock, Rapidan and Hazel rivers were supplemented by others on the Robinson River and Battle Run; for some of the smaller streams, one can also look at readings from neighboring basins. Even so, this is one of the areas with inadequate gauge coverage for the smaller creeks.

UPPER RAPPAHANNOCK BASIN

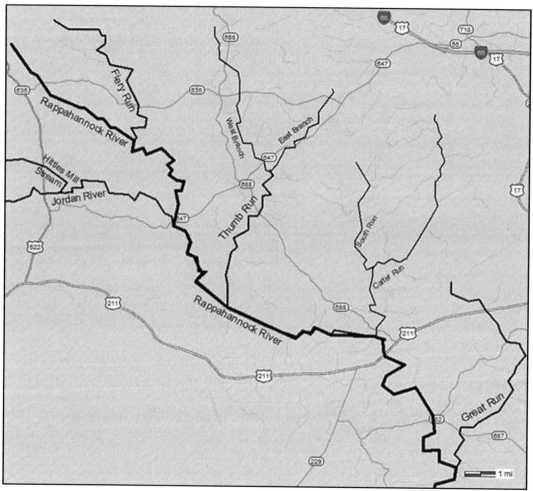

© Copyright 2005-2011 Undertow Software Corp.

Chapter 38:

UPPER RAPPAHANNOCK BASIN

Although the Rappahannock River is very well known, its earliest miles and tributaries are not. And for good reason, as there is no paddling there even remotely comparable to the headwaters of the Hazel and Rapidan rivers. This is because the Blue Ridge is thin at its northern end, and therefore does not provide large enough mountain basins before the creeks enter the flatter and fence-strewn ranchland.

The **Rappahannock** itself occupies the northernmost end of the headwaters, and becomes occasionally runnable (section 1) just 4 miles below its source; this first section, surprisingly for such a well-known river, is an "explorers' special." The next access is in 11.5 miles, where a popular novice trip (section 2) begins. The first large tributary, **Fiery Run**, can be paddled for over five miles, with access midway, but beware of fences. And after completing section 2, one would face 7.4 relatively flat miles on section 1 of the Rappahannock; I therefore leave that as an "explorers' special." The next major tributary, the **Jordan River**, is covered (but not praised) by Corbett. It is joined early on by steep **Hittles Mill Stream** (the only "stream" in this book), which can be paddled for 2 miles down to US 522 (the first mile of that being another "explorers' special"); its final 1.5 miles, from US 522 to the Jordan River, is through pastures with serious cattle gates.

Three major tributaries enter below there from the north (there is not much space between the Rappahannock and the Hazel to the south), but they are mostly rather flat Piedmont streams. **Thumb Run** starts off dull but ends in a nice gorge. **Great Run** stays dull but is pleasant, while I leave out easy-to-catch Carter Run (30 sq. mi. drainage for its final 6 miles) because of its 5 ft/mile gradient. Its main tributary, South Run, could be paddled for its last 3 miles with 12 sq. mi at 12 ft/mile; for some reason, even those numbers failed to inspire me.

GAUGES: While there are no gauges in this area per se, **Battle Run** (26 sq. mi.) in the Hazel River headwaters just to the south, **which is the reference** in the table below, serves pretty well. Cedar Run (93 sq. mi.) in the Occoquan basin to the east is useful for Great Run, and the Hazel River gauge (285 sq. mi.) is relevant for section 2 of the Rappahannock.

name	gradient	difficulty	length	area	gauge	rating
Rappahannock R. - Sec. 1	23 (75)	?	11.5	7	300cfs	?
- Sec. 2	7	I (II-)	13.5	73	45cfs	*
Fiery Run - Section 1	68	II+	2.8	7	330cfs	**
- Section 2	38	?	2.5	10	210cfs	?
Jordan River	18 (40)	I (II)	7.4	7	300cfs	*
Hittles Mill Str.- Sec.1	110 (150)	?	1.1	6	250cfs	?
- Sec. 2	70	II	0.9	7	200cfs	*
Thumb Run	15 (50)	I (II)	3.0	30	75cfs	**
Great Run	15	I	1.8	25	75cfs	*

🎵 RAPPAHANNOCK RIVER (upper)

The Rappahannock River flows southeast for 80 miles, from High Knob on the Blue Ridge, 5 miles southeast of Front Royal, to Fredericksburg, where it becomes tidal and eventually eases into the Chesapeake Bay. The first 4 miles are too small to paddle, and the next 25 miles are in sections 1 and 2 below.

Section 2 is a fairly well known beginners' paddle, but I have never heard of anyone running the "explorers' special" section 1. After section 2 there are 18 miles of flat water (at 3.5 ft/mile) that are in Corbett but not here. The last 33 miles are covered in my final chapter, "Rappahannock Tailwaters."

Section 1: Hume Road (SR 635) to Crest Hill Road (SR 647)

Gradient	Difficulty	Distance	Area	Scenery	Strainers	Rating
23 (75)	?	11.5	7	?	?	?

USGS Quad – Flint Hill; Source – Scouting put in and take out
N38 50.27, W78 06.34 to N38 45.56, W78 01.68

This *"explorers' special"* starts after the confluence with Foot of the Mountain Run, and between the wineries of Oasis Vineyards and Rappahannock Cellars. There is a cattle fence beneath the put in bridge, so put in downstream river left. Hopefully there are not many more fences, but one cannot be sure.

The gradient averages 50 ft/mile for the first 4 miles (to shortly before Fiery Run), 9 ft/mile for the remainder. Many small tributaries flow in, bringing the catchment area to 26 sq. mi. after the addition of Fiery Run, so you will have a strong flow despite the low gradient. There are no intermediate access points, so you are committed to a long paddle; start early in the day, as strainers may slow your progress.

GAUGE: Look for 300 cfs on Battle Run (projected for 2 hours after you put in).

Section 2: Crest Hill Road (SR 647) to US 211

Gradient	Difficulty	Distance	Area	Scenery	Strainers	Rating
7	I (II-)	13.5	73	B	<<1/mile	*

USGS Quad – Flint Hill/Massies Corner/Jeffersonton; Source – Grove and Corbett
N38 45.56, W78 01.68 via N38 43.15, W78 00.41 (SR 645) to N38 41.04, W77 54.20

This is a decent beginners' run, with intermediate accesses at SR 645 (Tapps Ford Road) at 5.5 miles and SR 613 (Waterloo) at 12.5 miles. The two class II- rapids are both in the second half of the trip.

GAUGE: You will need some average of 45 cfs on Battle Run (1 hour before put in) and 425 cfs on the Hazel River (projected to 2 hours after you put in) to start as SR 647, and 30 cfs and 285 cfs, respectively, to start at SR 645.

🎵 FIERY RUN

Fiery Run starts at a spring on the Warren/Fauquier County line, by the Mosby Shelter, and meanders southeast for almost 10 miles to the Rappahannock. Section 1 has good rapids and scenery but bad fences. If you paddle section 2, you are committed to a long day on the Rappahannock itself.

Section 1: Fiery Run Road (SR 726) to Hume Road (SR 635)

Gradient	Difficulty	Distance	Area	Scenery	Strainers	Rating
68	II+	2.8	7	B	4-6/mi.	**

USGS Quad – Flint Hill; Source – Personal descent 7/05
N38 50.92, W78 03.77 to N38 49.51, W78 02.86

The rapids are virtually continuous the, class II- in the first half, with more interesting class II+ rock gardens after that; the one visible from the take out is typical. The scenery is attractive woodlands until some pastures toward the end. About a dozen fallen trees had to be portaged or lifted over, but none were too problematical. Alas, that was not true of the three fences, all near the end, as boards prevented passage down the creek and barbed wire hindered portage. Since our run, another steel fence has been added at the put in.

GAUGE: You will normally need about 330 cfs on Battle Run (projected 2 hours after you put in). At the put in, the mid-stream rock should be almost covered.

Section 2: Hume Road (SR 635) to Rappahannock River

Gradient	Difficulty	Distance	Area	Scenery	Strainers	Rating
38	?	2.5*	10	?	?	?

USGS Quad – Flint Hill; Source – Scouting put in
N38 49.51, W78 02.86 to N38 45.56, W78 01.68

*(plus 7.4 miles on the Rappahannock River at 9 ft/mile)

This *"explorers' special"* is flatter than section 1, but likely to have more fences, as it traverses a cattle ranch. And at the end you would face a flat 7.4-mile paddle on the Rappahannock – so it's probably a better idea to run the Rappahannock all the way, and get a somewhat longer and steeper stretch with rapids, and probably fewer fences.

GAUGE: Look for at least 210 cfs on Battle Run, projected an hour after put in.

JORDAN RIVER: US 522 to Rappahannock River (SR 647)

Gradient	Difficulty	Distance	Area	Scenery	Strainers	Rating
18 (40)	I (II)	7.4	7	C	2-3/mi.	*

USGS Quad – Flint Hill; Source – Corbett
N38 46.58, W78 06.19 to N38 45.56, W78 01.68

The Jordan River (named after a local family, not the Biblical waterway) is tiny at the put in, but within a half mile it picks up Hittles Mill Stream (which earlier merged with Indian Run) and triples its catchment area. The gradient averages 28 ft/mile for the first 3 miles, but just 12 ft/mile for the remainder. After tiny Hickman Run enters from the right about midway, there is a class II, 3-foot ledge, just below an island. Corbett wrote: "the most memorable part of the trip is the numerous ... portages for trees and fences." The first fence is visible from the put in.

You could take out at SR 637, but it is just over a half mile from there to the Rappahannock.

GAUGE: Look for 300 cfs on Battle Run, projected 2 hours after put in.

 HITTLES MILL STREAM

The only "stream" in this book is formed at the confluence of Bearwallow Creek and Bolton Branch, and there is access one-third mile later at SR 631. The next two miles, to US 522, are described below. From there, it is 1.5 miles to the Jordan River, at 50 ft/mile; however, that part is full of fences, and you would then have almost 7 miles to paddle on the Jordan.

Section 1: SR 631 to SR 630 (above SR 628)

Gradient	Difficulty	Distance	Area	Scenery	Strainers	Rating
110 (150)	?	1.1	6	C	?	?

USGS Quad – Chester Gap/Flint Hill; Source – Scouting from road
N38 47.87, W78 08.00 to N38 47.64, W78 07.06

This is a very narrow creek, and long stretches of the bank are covered in poison ivy – which is why we only ran section 2, leaving this as an *"explorers' special."*

GAUGE: Look for 250 cfs on Battle Run (2 hours after put in). Because the creek is narrow, it requires less water than the top of the Rappahannock or Jordan rivers.

Section 2: SR 630 (above SR 628) to US 522

Gradient	Difficulty	Distance	Area	Scenery	Strainers	Rating
70	II	0.9	7	C	1-3/mi.	*

USGS Quad – Flint Hill; Source – Personal descent 7/05
N38 47.64, W78 07.06 to N38 47.42, W78 06.30

"Short but not so sweet" was Gisela Zarkowski's summation. The rapids were easy and continuous, and we had no trees to portage. However, one steel fence midway was a big hassle, and overhanging branches on this narrow creek both reduced visibility and forced us to keep ducking and bashing through. SR 630 closely parallels the creek. We put in a little upstream of SR 628, as it was one of the few spots that did not require crossing a lush patch of poison ivy. The take out at US 522 required pulling our boats up a very narrow, steep slope on upstream river right, to avoid the fences. A large fence just downstream was sufficient discouragement to continuing down to the Jordan River.

GAUGE: Look for 200 cfs on Battle Run, projected 2 hours after put in.

THUMB RUN: Thumb Run Road (SR 736) to Rappahannock River

Gradient	Difficulty	Distance	Area	Scenery	Strainers	Rating
15 (50)	I (II)	3.0*	30	?	?	**

USGS Quad – Jeffersonton; Source – Trip report (Ron Canter); Scouting put in
N38 44.84, W77 59.39 to N38 41.74, W77 54.39 or N38 43.16, W78 00.41

*(plus on the Rappahannock, at 7 ft/mile, 6.2 miles downstream or 0.9 miles upstream)

Thumb Run, formed at the confluence of its East and West branches, flows for 7 miles to the Rappahannock. The first access is after 2 miles (SR 688), but as Ron Canter reported numerous fallen trees, cattle fences and beaver dams in this upper stretch, you should instead start at SR 736, two miles later. This is a great put in, at the end of a dirt road, by a rickety bridge, across from a sign announcing a conservation easement. The stream meanders through indifferent scenery most of the way, but the final three-quarters mile is straight and through a little gorge, with a pair of interesting ledges at the end.

Once you reach the Rappahannock, you can either paddle 6.2 miles downstream on the latter part of section 2 to Waterloo (SR 613) if the water is high, or 0.9 miles upstream to Tapps Ford Road (SR 645) if the water is low. Pick your poison.

GAUGE: Look for 75 cfs on nearby Battle Run.

The **West Branch** is the larger headwater; you could paddle it for 5 miles, with 11 sq. mi. drainage and at 14 ft/mile, through mostly woodlands, to a half mile above the confluence.

GREAT RUN: Opal Road (SR687) to Rappahannock River

Gradient	Difficulty	Distance	Area	Scenery	Strainers	Rating
15	I	1.8*	25	C+	0-2/mi.	*

USGS Quad – Warrenton/Remington; Source – Personal descent 2/07
N38 38.58, W77 51.57 to N38 34.98, W77 52.53

*(plus 4 miles on the Rappahannock, at 4 ft/mile, to Lakota – SR 621)

This stream crosses US 211, west of Warrenton. There is access a half mile downstream, at SR 682 (8 sq. mi.), starting at 45 ft/mile, but fences are likely, including at the put in. Half a mile later, after crossing SR 802, the creek enters some large estates. The gradient averages 14 ft/mile, with no public access points, for 6 miles. Accordingly, this trip begins at the only public access below those estates.

The trip starts off flat but gradually speeds up and gets more riffles. But that's as exciting as it gets. Great Run winds between low mud banks, mostly through the woods but with a few houses visible, and finally eases into the Rappahannock. I encountered no fences and little wood. There is no access near the mouth (the road shown on old maps has been closed), so you must continue four miles down the Rappahannock, at 4 ft/mile, with just two riffles; fortunately, when Great Run is up, the river should be fast. The take-out hamlet, Lakota, consists of one shack, one mansion and one normal home.

GAUGE: Look for 75 cfs on Battle Run and 250 cfs on Cedar Run (2 hours later).

HAZEL RIVER BASIN

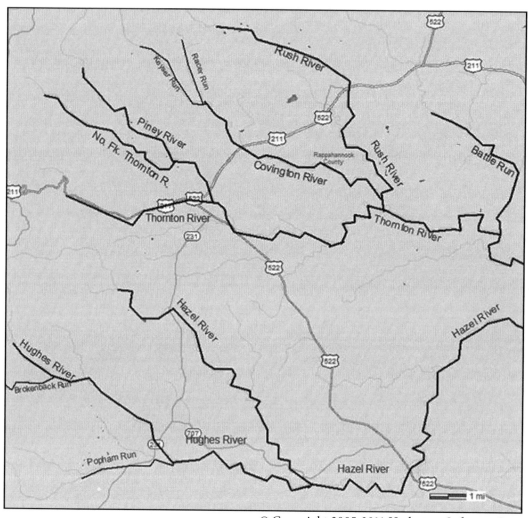

© Copyright 2005-2011 Undertow Software Corp.

There were an estimated **70 mills** in this area during the 19th Century, mostly for grain (gristmills) but also sawmills and woolen mills. There was a gristmill about every two miles along the creeks, so that customers would not have to walk or ride more than a mile each way, with a 56 lb. bushel of un-milled corn or 48 lbs. of cornmeal (the difference being the miller's fee). Even back then there was environmental regulation; the wheat mills were not allowed to dump the bran into the streams, so they learned to market it for animal feed.

Section 2 of the Thornton, Covington and Rush all end at Rock Mills. The land there is so bad for growing crops that it used to be known locally as **"Poison Forks."**

Chapter 39:

HAZEL RIVER BASIN

The 15-mile (as the crow flies) section of the Blue Ridge from Mt. Marshall (the northernmost major peak in Shenandoah National Park) to Stony Man (4,011 ft.; the second highest peak in the Park) spawns a remarkable seven runnable "rivers" on the east side, which form the Hazel River basin and drain Rappahannock County. These streams begin extremely steeply and gradually flatten out, and all provide excellent paddling. The intermediate-level stretches of the **Covington** (section 2), **Thornton** (section 2) and **Hughes** (section 3)/**Hazel rivers** (section 2) are all popular and much written up, as is the **Rush** (section 2) to a lesser extent, but few people have paddled farther upstream. My favorites are three of the latter: the **upper Hughes** (section 1), **North Fork of the Thornton** (sections 1 & 2) and **Piney rivers**. So if you can handle the gradient (which often exceeds 100 ft/mile) and get the opportunity, don't miss them. At the other extreme, there are 14 flat miles of the lower Thornton to its confluence with the Hazel, and 25 flat miles of the lower Hazel until it reaches the Rappahannock, which are described in Corbett but not here, as they have no whitewater. However, I have added **Battle Run** (as the chapter's "explorers' special"), which starts just north of the Rush, and flows through a pretty gorge, though without serious rapids.

None of the creeks in this chapter are up very often, but there is a definite hierarchy; the Hughes/Hazel is the easiest to catch, followed by the Thornton (section 2). The relative catchment areas are a good indication of which trips to do first when water levels are falling, as one can often combine several runs in a single day.

> Several Piedmont tributaries of the lower Hazel are runnable but not too interesting. The largest, **Muddy Run**, could be paddled for 4 miles from SR 630 (just off VA 229) down to SR 625 (5 miles west of Remington), with 20 sq. mi. and at 13 ft/mile.

GAUGES: The Rappahannock at Remington (619 sq. mi.), the traditional gauge for this basin, is too far downstream. In 2002, a gauge on the Hazel River near Rixeyville (285 sq. mi.), 12 miles upstream of Remington, became available. Its watershed is virtually congruent with this chapter. In 2004, came even more useful additions: **Battle Run** (26 sq. mi.), just north of the Rush River, which **is the reference in the table below,** and the Robinson near Locust Dale (179 sq. mi.), a little south of the Hughes.

The AFWS does not cover Rappahannock County, but you can use rainfall data from three neighboring counties. The Nethers gauge, at the northern tip of Madison County, covers the upper Hughes; the Rocky Branch gauge in Page County is just across the Blue Ridge from the Thornton and its North Fork; and the Hogback Mountain gauge in Warren County is near the headwaters of the Rush, Covington and Piney Rivers. You usually need a rainfall of over 2 inches to catch the smaller tributaries (except when the ground was previously saturated), and they will seldom stay up more than a day. On the plus side, this basin is one of the wetter parts of the area.

name	gradient	difficulty	length	area	gauge	rating
Hazel River - Section 1	24 (50)	II	6.5	12	165cfs	**
- Section 2	12	II	5.4	74	50cfs	**
Hughes River - Section 1	63 (100)	III (III+)	3.6	13	210cfs	****
- Section 2	30	II	2.1	20	110cfs	-
- Section 3	20	II	4.1	43	60cfs	***
Thornton River - Sec. 1	68 (100)	III-	3.0	8	250cfs	***
- Sec. 2	25	II (III-)	7.2	35	70cfs	***
No. Fk. Thornton-Sec. 1	105 (130)	III+ (IV-)	2.5	9	260cfs	****
-Sec. 2	55 (70)	III- (III)	2.0	18	140cfs	****
Piney River	100 (125)	III	2.2	7	300cfs	***
Rush River - Section 1	65 (100)	II+	1.8	8	225cfs	***
- Section 2	34 (65)	II	6.5	11	175cfs	***
Covington R. – Sec. 1	50	II+	4.1	10	200cfs	*
- Sec. 2	48 (90)	III (IV-)	3.3	17	150cfs	****
Battle Run	17	?	6.0	10	150cfs	?

HAZEL RIVER

The Hazel is the second largest Rappahannock tributary (after the Rapidan), drains 355 sq. mi., yet most paddlers know it only for the bottom five miles of the Hughes/Hazel trip. Although many paddlers cross the upper Hazel en route between the Thornton and the Hughes, they pay it little heed. Not so for hikers – the Hazel River Trail is part of a popular circuit hike around Hazel Mountain, and the Hazel River falls and a nearby cave are popular.

Five miles after its origin near the Skyline Drive, the Hazel River leaves the Park and intersects SR 600. Its first mile, which can be scouted from SR 600, starts out at 220 ft/mile and drops 150 ft. The next mile, down to Va. 231, averages 100 ft/mile, but passes through fenced fields. Va. 231 (9 sq. mi.) would be a good put in, starting at 65 ft/mile, were it not for the high fence there and the nasty fence under SR 618, two miles later. (Of course, these might disappear over time.) So I used the downstream side of SR 618 as the put in for section 1. Section 2 is the lower half of the popular Hughes/Hazel trip. Below that, the Hazel continues for 25 miles, at 5 ft/mile, to the Rappahannock.

> The original name of this river was Gourdvine, but it was changed to be consistent with **Hazel Mountain** off which it flows. The name probably comes from the Hazell family, early local landowners, rather than the hazelnut tree.

> **Why does the "Hazel River" run so long?** At its confluence with the Hughes, the Hazel is by far the smaller creek (27 vs. 50 sq. mi.), and yet its name sticks to the combined flow. When it meets the Thornton, it is also somewhat smaller (130 vs. 155 sq. mi.), but again its name continues. Ironically, by the time it meets and loses its name to the Rappahannock, the Hazel is the larger of the pair by 40% (350 vs. 250 sq. mi.) – poetic justice, I suppose.

HAZEL RIVER BASIN

Section 1: SR 618 to just above Hughes River (SR 707/644)

Gradient	Difficulty	Distance	Area	Scenery	Strainers	Rating
24 (50)	II	6.5	12	B	1-2/mi.	**

USGS Quad – Woodville; Source – Personal descent 10/99 (top), 7/94 (bottom)
N38 35.01, W78 13.26 via N38 33.01, W78 11.41 (SR 607) to N38 31.59, W78 10.30

This novice trip has lots of easy rapids, good scenery and surfing waves. The gradient is steepest in the first 1.5 miles, but there are gravel bars, ledges and occasional rock gardens throughout. The main negatives were three board fences, a half dozen river-wide downed trees and a barbed-wire fence at the put in (which you can get around by climbing over the wooden fence). Partial strainers added a bit of spice to the run. Although the creek starts out fairly narrow and with overhanging trees, visibility is generally quite good thereafter.

At 4.1 miles you cross SR 607 (with good access). The final 2.4 miles has swift current, a few class II- rapids, good swimming spots and few strainers. You can take out at the low-water bridge a quarter mile above the confluence (near a similar low-water bridge over the Hughes), or continue past the confluence down the Hazel section 2.

GAUGE: At the put in, the rapid upstream should not look bony, and the water should be at least a foot deep at the bridge, because the creek widens out below. At SR 607, zero level is when the water is 6 inches below the top of the narrow cement shelf below the bridge on river right. You will want at least 1,750 cfs on the Hazel gauge at Rixeyville (3 hours after put in), 1,100 cfs on the Robinson (2 hours after) and 165 cfs on Battle Run (1 hour after put in). The rain gauge is Nethers in Madison County.

> The last 2.4 miles of this is the only "exploratory" trip that I **took my family** on. The weather and water were warm, the gradient was mild, there was enough but not too much water, so what could possibly go wrong? My older son (then 9) and I pulled into an eddy across from the only dangerous spot, where a thorny branch blocked half the passage, on the inside of a swift turn. Soon our old Blue Hole appeared, with my wife in the stern, my younger son (5 1/2) amidships and our neighbor Tim (9 1/2) in the bow. As they began their move to avoid the partial strainer, Tim leaped up in panic, nearly capsizing the canoe. Luckily, the bank was low, and my wife managed to run the boat onto the shore above the strainer. The cause of the near disaster? – a frog in the canoe.

Section 2: Just above Hughes River (SR 707/644) to US 522

Gradient	Difficulty	Distance	Area	Scenery	Strainers	Rating
12	II	5.4	74	B	<<1/mi.	**

USGS Quad – Woodville/Castleton; Source – Personal descent 7/94
N38 31.59, W78 10.30 to N38 31.94, W78 07.23

This section is almost always run as a continuation of the popular section 3 of the Hughes River, but it can also be run coming down from the Hazel itself, or by starting on either river shortly above the confluence. It is described in detail in Corbett and Grove.

The best rapids come towards the end of the first mile: four ledges, of which the first is the biggest and is easiest on the left. Surfing opportunities abound. After that, there are mainly only riffles.

GAUGE: Readings of 475 cfs on the Hazel at Rixeyville (projected forward one hour), 300 cfs on the Robinson and 45 cfs on Battle Run are normally sufficient.

 HUGHES RIVER

The Hughes River from SR 603 (the former chicken farm; section 3) down to SR 522 near Boston (by then it is the Hazel) is a classic low-intermediate trip. But the sections upstream are far less often paddled. Many people may have been scared away by Roger Corbett's dramatic *Virginia Whitewater* description: "The upper reaches of the Hughes River are canoed only by the brave, the foolish, the unwitting and those who love pain. The river ... [is] punctuated by a large number of barbed wire fences." Well, that description is more outdated than a booming economy; those fences were all gone by 1996, but the section remained, as Roger also wrote, "exciting, challenging and competitive."

The Hughes ("Hugh's") River rises in Shenandoah National Park near the Skyline Drive, passes the Corbin Cabin and flows southeast through Nicholson Hollow and out of the Park. There it picks up Brokenback Run (originally called the South Fork of the Hughes), which drains the north side of Old Rag Mountain – probably the most popular circuit hike in the Park, because of its rock scrambling and unobstructed views. The road follows Brokenback Run upstream for 0.3 miles, to a gate where the circuit to Old Rag begins. In that brief stretch, Brokenback Run drops at 400 ft/mile and is continuous class 5.0; perhaps its name is no accident. But there is no parking for it, and no access to the first 0.4 miles on the Hughes below the confluence.

> The **Nethers gristmill** operated from 1794 until Tip Nethers closed it in 1945. Declining water flow in the Hughes was a major problem, which was partly addressed by technological improvements to the mill. The mill also served as post office and polling place. In the early 20th Century, Nicholson Hollow was the domain of Aaron **Nicholson**, "the King of Free-State Hollow."Even the sheriff dared not enter without his permission. The preacher in Nicholson Hollow was Warren **Corbin**, whose cousin George Corbin was reputedly a leading moonshiner; any relationship to a Miss Paula Corbin Jones is purely speculative.

Section 1: Old Rag Parking Area to Va. 231

Gradient	Difficulty	Distance	Area	Scenery	Strainers	Rating
63 (100)	III (III+)	3.6	13	C	1-3/mi.	****

USGS Quad – Old Rag Mountain/Woodville; Source – Personal descent 9/96
N38 34.26, W78 17.24 via N38 34.14, W78 16.43 (Nethers) to N38-32.51, W78 14.63

From the Old Rag Parking Area, cross the road and you can see the creek. You could also put in 100 yards upstream, at River Song Lane. The initial gradient is 100 ft/mile, and the creek is only continuous class II+, with a pair of class III+ rapids in the first half mile. One, on a sharp left turn, was like looking down a Metro escalator; the other had huge boulders, a tree growing mid-stream and no clean route.

If you don't want to hazard the first half mile, you can put in at the SR 749 bridge in Nethers (the start of Corbett's first section) by Bethlehem Church, for lots of class II+ action plus three class III rapids. There is a good rapid a quarter mile below Nethers, where the creek cuts back right towards the road, and the final and best one comes shortly below the last bridge. Those three class III rapids can be scouted from SR 600/601/602.

The only negative is the strainers. We had to make 5 portages, for a low-water bridge (check it out as you drive, a half mile below Nethers) and fallen trees, but all were preceded by good eddies.

GAUGE: Minimum would be about 210 cfs on Battle Run, 2,250 cfs at Rixeyville (projected 3 hours forward) and 1,450 cfs on the Robinson (2 hours forward). Look for heavy rain at Nethers in Madison County.

Five boats put in about 30 yards up Brokenback Run, but **paddlers dropped out** faster than presidential candidates after a New Hampshire primary; within 100 yards, we were down to three, as the others, one of whom had already flipped twice, decided that this section was too much for them. I realized that I should have forcefully discouraging that paddler, who was no longer young enough to make the quick moves required. (The first 0.4 miles of our run is no longer accessible, as the former Old Rag parking area that we used has been closed by its private owner.)

My own comeuppance came when I tried to slip beneath a low-hanging branch, but didn't have enough clearance. As my boat flipped, **wood punctured both of my air bags** faster than Lloyd Bentsen punctured Dan Quayle's Kennedyesque pretensions. I managed to unpin the canoe, but water-filled it was too heavy for me to control. I had to let go, and watched it roll over a few times on the shallow rocks and then come to a stop upright, as if just waiting for me to climb in. I felt a little more nervous doing the rest of the run without flotation.

Section 2: Va. 231 to SR 603 (ex-chicken farm)

Gradient	Difficulty	Distance	Area	Scenery	Strainers	Rating
30	II	2.1	20	C	3-7/mi.	-

USGS Quad – Woodville; Source – Personal descent 9/96
N38 32.51, W78 14.63 to N38 32.31, W78 12.98

The first quarter mile is class II with no problems, but then the creek splits. Take the (smaller) right channel, as the left soon braids further. But even on the right, in only 50 yards pull up alongside a collapsed concrete structure to check around the bend. Yuck! For half a mile, you are confined to a small channel, with at least a half dozen portages. Finally, the channels reunite, Popham Run (itself large enough to paddle, but rather flat and full of fences) enters, and it is a pleasant mile and a quarter to the start of section 3. Still, it is preferable to take out at Va. 231, and put back in at SR 603 if you want to paddle all the good parts of the Hughes on the same day.

GAUGE: Minimum levels would be 1,200 cfs on the Hazel River at Rixeyville (2 hours later), 750 cfs on the Robinson (1 hour later) and 110 cfs on Battle Run.

> **Strainered Relationship.** I ran this section tandem with my wife, as novices on a chilly day in May 1979, because I had not noticed Corbett's admonition to put in at the chicken farm. We picked our way through the woods, and then came to a (since-destroyed) bridge on SR 603, which it seemed we could fit under if we were in just the right place. I hopped out, and with a friend, tried to maneuver the boat (with my wife still in it!) below the bridge. But the current swung it sideways, and the rest is history. She still refers to this as "the time Steve tried to drown me." After her swim, as I paddled solo down to the chicken farm, I tried to slip under a fallen tree. The bow caught, the boat swung sideways and filled (*deja vu*); however, I climbed up onto the trunk, warm and dry. But as I watched my Grumman slip under the tree and proceed downstream by itself, I realized that I had been too clever by half!

Section 3: SR 603 to just above Hazel River (SR 607/644)

Gradient	Difficulty	Distance	Area	Scenery	Strainers	Rating
20	II	4.1	43	B	<<1/mi.	***

USGS Quad – Woodville; Source – Personal descent often
N38 32.31, W78 12.98 to N38 31.34, W78 10.28

This is the most popular Rappahannock headwaters trip. It is comparatively easy to catch, has about a dozen nice ledges (with excellent side surfing) and good scenery. There are bridges at the 1.5 and 3-mile marks, and a convenient shuttle. At 4 miles, you reach the SR 644 low water bridge, where you can portage or take out. The confluence with the (much smaller) Hazel River is shortly below, and most paddlers continue down the Hazel River (section 2), making a nice 9.5-mile run.

GAUGE: Look for the Hazel River at Rixeyville to be over 650 cfs (an hour later), the Robinson 425 cfs and Battle Run 60 cfs, but the trip is better with more water.

THORNTON RIVER

There is remarkable symmetry to the Thornton headwaters. Four creeks of similar size cross US 211/522 in the six-mile stretch between Washington Va. and Sperryville: the Rush, Covington, North Fork of the Thornton, and Thornton Rivers. The two forks of the Thornton merge near Sperryville, the Rush and Covington unite, and finally they all meet at Rock Mills. For the Covington and the North Fork of the Thornton, this simple 2x2 multiplication also applies to their own headwaters.

The Thornton River itself comes down from Thornton Gap, alongside US 211 (one of only two roads to cross Shenandoah National Park). There is a popular novice/intermediate trip on the Thornton, from Fletchers Mill to Rock Mills (section 2), and a far less common and more difficult trip starting 3 miles above Fletchers Mill (section 1). The Thornton has been run from the Park boundary, 4.5 miles above Fletchers Mill. But from the road, I saw 5 barbed wire fences within a half-mile stretch (starting at Acornbrook Private Lane, less than a mile from the Park boundary) where the gradient was 100 ft/mile. So unless large ice jams have recently broken out the fences, stay off this part.

Below section 2, the Thornton is class I (7 ft/mile) for 14 miles to the Hazel.

At Sperryville, on June 26, 1862, Major General John Pope's 50,000 man **Union Army of Virginia** was created, from the remaining forces of Generals Banks, Fremont and McDowell (all beaten earlier by Stonewall Jackson in his Shenandoah Valley Campaign). It then moved east to engage Generals Jackson and Longstreet in the Second Battle of Manassas – a Union disaster, in part because Pope's rival, General McClellan, refused to let his Army of the Potomac help.

Contrary to opinion among paddlers, the Thornton was not named after the kayaker and conservation guru Mac Thornton. Rather, it was named after **Francis Thornton** (second cousin by marriage to the Washingtons), who was granted 4,452 acres there in 1750. The area is called the FT Valley after him. George Washington was a frequent visitor to the plantations of Francis' sons.

The **first gristmill** in the Blue Ridge was built in the 1730s near the confluence with the North Fork (originally called Thornton's Mill, later Fletcher's Mill), and operated until 1956, as the last water-powered mill in Rappahannock County. Settlers across the mountain petitioned for better access to the mill; this led to the first highway across the Blue Ridge, through Thornton Gap.

Section 1: One Mile above Sperryville (on US211) to Fletchers Mill

Gradient	Difficulty	Distance	Area	Scenery	Strainers	Rating
68 (100)	III-	3.0	8	D	0-2/mi.	***

USGS Quad – Washington Va.; Source – Personal descent 3/01
N38 39.18, W78 14.85 to N38 38.78, W78 12.38

Put in a little above SR 667 – as of 2012, near the Glassworks Gallery with its brown footbridge would be good. The creek is fast and narrow, continuous class II with a few class III- drops. Low branches grow almost across the creek in places, and visibility is limited when the leaves are out. The trickiest spot is beneath SR 100 entering Sperryville, because of a cement pillar midstream. The half-mile stretch that cannot be scouted from the road is relatively mild. The half mile through Sperryville is very fast with good waves, and the half mile below that alternates pools with relatively steep rapids. In the final mile, below the confluence with the North Fork, the river is much wider and the gradient is half that of the first two miles (40 ft/mile vs. 82 ft/mile), with the main fun being three, 3-foot ledges, all best run right of center. Take out on river right, above the fences at Fletchers Mill.

Check carefully from the road for barbed wire fences; we encountered one, 100 yards above SR 100, which I could just duck under. The other negative is the drab scenery – the backs of shops and houses – until you leave Sperryville.

GAUGE: Zero level is 250 cfs on Battle Run (projected 1 hour forward), 2,750 cfs at Rixeyville (3 hours forward) and 1,800 cfs on the Robinson (2 hours forward). Check the Rocky Branch rainfall gauge in Page County.

Section 2: Fletchers Mill (SR 620) to Rock Mills (SR 626)

Gradient	Difficulty	Distance	Area	Scenery	Strainers	Rating
25	II (III-)	7.2	35	B	<1/mi.	***

USGS Quad – Washington Va.; Source – Personal descent 6/96
N38 38.78, W78 12.38 to N38 39.25, W78 07.85

This pretty and popular trip has a good mix of ledges, rock gardens, cobble bars and chutes. It is much easier to catch than section 1, because of the entry of the North Fork and then, at the put in, Beaverdam Creek. The land owner there is a paddler and quite friendly, but this is King's grant land and he could close the put in.

At 1.2 miles, after a long pool, comes a sharp right hand turn, with a rock cliff on the right, leading to a 4 foot, class III- drop, called Boulder Ledge Rapid. The easiest route is to stay left and take the ledge as a sheer drop, rather than follow the main flow.

After you cross SR 621 at three miles, the creek becomes even more scenic. As of 2011, there were no fences or beaver dams. The take out is at the confluence with the Rush River. Be considerate there (don't block the road, change in public view or litter), as it would be terrible to lose this great take out for the Thornton, Rush and Covington.

GAUGE: Minimum requirements would be 775 cfs at Rixeyville (2 hours later), 70 cfs on Battle Run and 500 cfs on the Robinson (1 hour later).

The Fletcher family maintained a nice **put in** access until October 1999, when the access door was wired shut, and barbed wire fences constructed both under the put in bridge and 100 yards downstream, because cattle had wandered onto the road during the drought. But the family doesn't mind if you carry past the fences on river left. A pair of friendly **river hounds** used to accompany paddlers down the creek; they welcomed lifts back on the shuttle.

NORTH FORK, THORNTON RIVER

This might have become the main stem of the Thornton, with the other branch the South Fork, except that the latter flows down from the Thornton Gap. Mac Thornton wrote the North Fork up in *The Voyageur* as his favorite near-by small stream. At the time, I thought he was just entranced by its name, but after paddling it twice, I concluded that his enthusiasm was well justified.

The North Fork rises between Elkwallow Gap and the Thornton Hollow Overlook. Popular hiking trails crisscross the area, between Fork and Oventop mountains. A fire road parallels the uppermost creek, but access is restricted until 0.7 miles outside the Park. From there, it is 2.5 miles to the Piney River and a further 2 miles to the confluence with the Thornton. SR 612 parallels the creek, which more than compensates in safety for what it costs in terms of scenery; besides, the creek will keep you too busy to worry much about the scenery, and what you see is still rather pleasant.

If you were to proceed up the Rappahannock from Fredericksburg, at each confluence taking the fork with the greater catchment area, you would ignore the Rapidan, take the Hazel, then the Thornton, and end up, as you might have guessed by now, on the North Fork of the Thornton (where you would skip the Piney River).

Section 1: Head of SR 612 to Confluence with Piney River

Gradient	Difficulty	Distance	Area	Scenery	Strainers	Rating
105 (130)	III+ (IV-)	2.5	9	C	0-2/mi.	****

USGS Quad – Thornton Gap/Washington, Va.; Source – Personal descent 6/97

N38 41.29, W78 15.80 to N38 40.68, W78 13.96

This is a wonderful little creek for those who like continuous action. You can scout it from SR 612, especially in winter and early spring when there is little vegetation.

We put in at the low bridge near where the pavement ends and a spur road crosses over to the Piney River. (One could follow the road up to 0.6 miles above that, but we saw several bad strainers there.) There are many long class III stretches where one has to maneuver smartly between the rocks, several steeper class III+ rapids, and, about midway, a class IV- rock garden with large boulders and sharp turns. There are no flat pools, but there are occasional small moving eddies.

There are two low water bridges with mild hydraulics, but one can paddle right up onto the sides of the bridges to stop. And the one other bridge with marginal clearance has eddies on either side.

GAUGE: At the right side of the take-out bridge, zero level is when the water is up to the base of the red upstream rock and the third downstream rock. Battle Run should exceed 260 cfs, Rixeyville 3,000 cfs (3 hours later). The rain gauge is Rocky Branch.

Section 2: Piney River to Thornton River

Gradient	Difficulty	Distance	Area	Scenery	Strainers	Rating
55 (70)	III- (III)	2.0*	18	C	<1/mi.	****

USGS Quad – Washington VA; Source – Personal descent 8/96

N38 40.68, W78 13.96 to N38 38.78, W78 12.38

*(plus 1 mile on the Thornton River to Fletchers Mill)

The entrance of the Piney River almost doubles the flow in the North Fork. Although the gradient (70 ft/mile in the first mile) is less than that of the earlier part, the larger volume produces higher waves and pushier rapids, which are virtually continuous class II+ to III-, with occasional short pools. After the first bridge (near Thornton Gap Church), the creek divides around an island; the clearer passage is to the left. The route becomes steep and narrow, culminating in a class III ledge. Approaching US 211/522, the gradient eases up a bit, and half a mile later comes the confluence with the Thornton. There is no access here, so continue a mile to Fletchers Mill (the put in for section 2), at a gradient of 45 ft/mile, and with three nice class II+ ledges (all best run right of center).

We encountered only one river-wide fallen tree and no fences, but as there had been fences on the Thornton section in previous years, be alert for their resurrection.

GAUGE: This trip is slightly easier to catch than the lower Rush and lower Covington. Battle Run needs 140 cfs, Rixeyville 1,500 cfs (2 hours later). For rainfall, check Rocky Branch (Page Co.).

🚣 PINEY RIVER: SR 653 to North Fork, Thornton River

Gradient	Difficulty	Distance	Area	Scenery	Strainers	Rating
100 (125)	III	2.2	7	C	1-3/mi.	***

USGS Quad – Thornton Gap/Washington, Va.; Source – Personal descent 5/98
N38 41.66, W78 15.54 to N38 40.68, W78 13.96

This, the smallest paddleable "river" in Virginia, is almost the twin of the upper North Fork of the Thornton, which it parallels on the other side of Fork Mountain. Put in at the highest public access, the bridge on SR 612 that links to the North Fork. (Above there, you can hike the beautiful **Piney Branch** (sic) **Trail** northwards for over four miles to the very start of this creek.) The first mile drops 125 ft. SR 600 parallels the creek much of the first mile, but the four strainers we ran into were hidden when we scouted. As you might guess from the gradient, this creek is non-stop action. However, unlike the upper Hughes and upper North Fork, it has no notable drops. But scout blind turns and enjoy going where few have gone before.

GAUGE: Look for 300 cfs on Battle Run and 3,250 cfs at Rixeyville (3 hours later). Hogback Mountain in Warren County is the rainfall gauge.

🚣 RUSH RIVER

This is the first significant Rappahannock tributary as you head down US 211/522 from big Washington to little Washington. Section 2 is paddled from time to time (although less than it deserves), but section 1 is barely known.

The Rush River begins as a series of parallel, southward flowing cascades down 3,368 foot Mt. Marshall. The most spectacular is Big Devil Stairs, along which runs a steep and beautiful trail. (You can no longer access this from SR 622 below and make a circuit, but you can hike down from the Skyline Drive.)

SR 622 parallels the upper Rush for 4.5 miles, giving a choice put ins. Near Big Devil Stairs, and for three-quarters of a mile below it, the gradient averages 150 ft/mile, the streambed is tiny and it is rare to find enough water. A little upstream of the Old School Church and the first bridge (heading upstream) on SR 622, a tributary adds about 30% to the flow, the gradient drops below 100 ft/mile, and an adventuresome paddler might put in (section 1). There is a half-mile break between sections 1 and 2, to avoid three barbed-wire fences.

It would be nice if the **Rush** River were named, as Corbett speculated, "after the fact that its water is in a terrible rush to join the Thornton River," but in fact, like most other Rappahannock tributaries, it was named after a settler family. In the 1960s, the **Skyline Ski Club** operated rope tows, a ski lodge and snowmaking equipment overlooking the river, but the venture failed after nine years, due to several successive warm winters. (Now it would be hopeless!)

Of the **28 Washingtons** in the US, this was the first. It was surveyed and platted by George Washington in 1749, established as a town in 1796 and incorporated in 1894. Several streets are named after GW's mistresses. The Inn at Little Washington is famous for its food. The village also contains a performing arts center, an artists' cooperative, and an assortment of boutiques, galleries, antique shops and inns.

Section 1: Persimmon Private Road to SR 622 Roadside

Gradient	Difficulty	Distance	Area	Scenery	Strainers	Rating
65 (100)	II+	1.8	8	C	2-4/mi.	***

USGS Quad – Washington Va.; Source – Personal descent 11/97

N38 44.02, W78 11.38 to N38 43.37, W78 09.83

From Persimmon Private Road, just above the SR 622 bridge, the rapids are continuous but not difficult, even in the stretch with a 100-ft/mile gradient (a half mile below the put in). Watch out for fallen trees and a low-water bridge with a moderate hydraulic (easily seen and avoided). This section can be scouted from SR 622; however, only 1 of the 5 fallen trees we encountered was visible from the road. The scenery is mediocre – houses, fields, woods and the road.

Take out where SR 622 leaves the river, rather than paddling the half-mile down to section 2. We encountered three barbed wire fences in that short stretch (just outside Washington Va.), which were not easily seen and were a nuisance to crawl under.

GAUGE: You need 225 cfs on Battle Run and 2,500 cfs at Rixeyville (projected 3 hours forward). Hogback Mountain in Warren County is the rainfall gauge.

Section 2: SR 628 to Rock Mills

Gradient	Difficulty	Distance	Area	Scenery	Strainers	Rating
34 (65)	II	6.5	11	B	<1/mi	***

USGS Quad – Washington Va.; Source – Personal descent 11/99

N38 43.16, W78 09.40 via N38 42.59, W78 09.17 (park) to N38 39.25, W78 07.85

This section (except for the first half mile, above SR 623 – old US 211) is in Corbett and makes a great day in conjunction with the more popular and difficult section 2 of the Covington. Still, it does not get nearly the attention it deserves. Corbett is ambivalent about it and Grove does not even include it. Perhaps it was partly the fall colors and the crisp autumn weather, but I found this creek an absolute delight.

Most importantly, it had few strainers, and the only two fences were in calm stretches and could be easily paddled under. This is a vast improvement from Corbett's list of hazards: "Electric wire fence. Three or four barbed/woven wire fences. Two wooden cattle gates. Three or four trees across the stream." However, there has often been a stout fence on a blind left turn, so paddle defensively.

Starting at SR 628 (turn right at The Inn) gives you a nice additional half-mile of class II-. At the traditional put in, SR 623, there is a twisty class II rapid you can scout in advance, and you then pass through a culvert under US 211/522 – the leftmost tube carries the most water. Many paddlers put in at a park on river right just downstream of this. After another half mile full of class II rapids, you pass SR 626 and reach the steepest section. There are some long class II rock gardens and a pair of tight right hand turns where most of the water piles into a tree. After the access midway at SR 621, the pools get longer but the rapids stay interesting, especially one with a tree in midstream. The rock gardens gradually give way to ledges with great playing options. The Covington enters 0.8 miles before the take out, and doubles the flow. This final bit is mostly flat, but has several excellent surfing ledges.

The scenery is very nice, especially in the latter half where there is more woods and less farmland. Scenic rock outcroppings abound, many of them on sharp turns. Deer are plentiful.

GAUGE: Look for 175 cfs on Battle Run and 1,900 cfs on the Hazel River at Rixeyville (projected 2 hours forward). At SR 623, the water should be up to the top of the upstream end of the river right cement footing of the bridge. The rapids seen from the SR 621 bridge should be clearly runnable, as should the riffles just below US 211/522. Hogback Mountain in Warren County is the rain gauge.

COVINGTON RIVER

The Covington River, although originally named the Long River, runs for just 7.5 miles – from where Keyser and Racer runs meet, to the confluence with the Rush. Unlike nearby headwaters, the Covington maintains an almost even gradient. SR 622 parallels the river and can be used to put in and take out for both sections.

Section 2 may be the best intermediate trip in the Rappahannock Basin and, for its size, is one of the most popular. Paddlers have been discouraged from the 2.3-mile stretch below US 211 by the warnings about strainers and overhanging briars in Corbett's and Grove's books, and few have even looked at the 1.8 miles above US 211. Both of those parts (combined into section 1) in fact have good rapids and not too many natural problems, but man-made strainers are a big negative.

> **Keyser and Racer runs,** named after local families, speed down Keyser Mountain at gradients that finally lessen to 100 ft/mile for the last mile. **Little Devil Stairs**, with its spectacular hiking trail, is the main tributary of Keyser Run. (It is not the "stairs" which are smaller than those of Big Devil Stairs, but the "devil.")SR 614 and 622 follow these streams up typical Appalachian "hollows," but there are too many low footbridges to make either runnable.

Section 1: Racer/Keyser Run Confluence to SR 622 (Rock Mills Rd.)

Gradient	Difficulty	Distance	Area	Scenery	Strainers	Rating
50	II+	4.1	10	C	2-4/mi.	*

USGS Quad – Washington Va.; Source – Personal descent 11/99
N38 42.32, W78 13.18 to N38 40.40, W78 10.21

The easy whitewater here is delightful, and there are only a few trees to deal with, but man-made strainers in pastureland mess it up. Above US 211, there are 3 low-water bridges; portage the first two and clunk over the third on river right. We also encountered 3 fences in that stretch. You will probably need to portage the Old US 211 bridge (now Rediviva Private Lane), 100 yards above the present highway, as it had a barbed wire fence and tends to catch logs.

Below US 211, the stream becomes continuous class II, with a few slightly harder spots. But I encountered four board fences, two topped with barbed wire. The "briars and low bushes" reported by Corbett were not a problem – creeks change.

GAUGE: Look for Battle Run to be over 200 cfs and Rixeyville 2,100 cfs (projected 3 hours forward). Hogback Mtn. (Warren Co.) needs to show heavy rainfall.

Section 2: SR 622 (Rock Mills Road) to Rush River

Gradient	Difficulty	Distance	Area	Scenery	Strainers	Rating
48 (90)	III (IV-)	3.3*	17	A	0-2/mi.	****

USGS Quad – Washington Va.; Source – Personal descent often
N38 40.40, W78 10.21 to N38 39.25, W78 07.85

*(plus 0.8 miles on Rush River to confluence with Thornton at Rock Mills)

This popular trip is full of class II and III rapids, play spots and good scenery. About midway, soon after the SR 621 bridge, is Volkswagen Rock, a class IV-, Z-turn following the main current on the left, but with a class III sneak route on the right (above about 6 inches). This rapid tends to catch strainers, so stop above to scout. (It comes right after a cliff on the left, above a blind right turn, which follows a similar cliff and right hand turn.) If you run the "heroes' route," have companions on the rocks at both sharp turns of the "Z," in case you cannot swing your boat around fast enough.

After 3.3 miles comes the confluence with the Rush. The final 0.8 miles on the Rush to the take out at Rock Mills is mild but has several excellent surfing ledges.

GAUGE: There is an RC gauge at the put in. About 150 cfs on Battle Run and 1,650 cfs at Rixeyville (projected 2 hours forward) approximate zero level. Hogback Mountain in Warren County is the nearest rain gauge.

BATTLE RUN: SR 633 to SR 618

Gradient	Difficulty	Distance	Area	Scenery	Strainers	Rating
17	?	6.0	10	?	?	?

USGS Quad – Massies Corner; Source – Scouting access points
N38 42.22, W78 06.76 via N38 40.74, W78 04.43 (SR 749) to N38 38.94, W78 04.53

You cross this *"explorers' special"* (named after the Bataille family) on US 211. Its Internet gauge is very useful; however, the creek is not too exciting, because it rises several miles below the Blue Ridge, and hence does not have enough watershed area while it is still steep.

The put in is 1.5 miles south of Massies Corner. You start out in a scenic semi-gorge; you can scout the first mile from SR 633. The valley then opens up, and you cross SR 729 (an alternative put in, with 18 sq. mi.). The gauging station is at the second SR 729 bridge, and the take out is half a mile beyond. If you continue a final half mile to the Thornton, you would then have to paddle 3 miles at just 5 ft/mile.

GAUGE: Look for 150 cfs on the Battle Run gauge (projected an hour forward) to start at SR 633, 110 cfs for SR 729.

RAPIDAN HEADWATERS

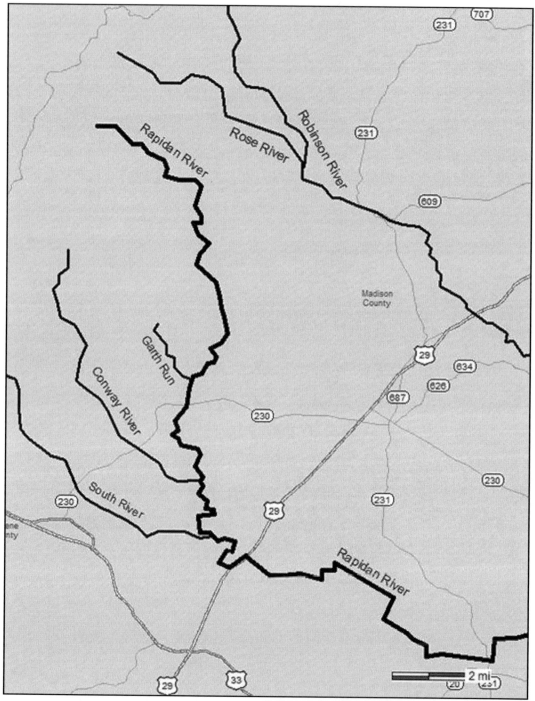

Chapter 40:
RAPIDAN HEADWATERS

The Rapidan is the largest Rappahannock tributary; its 700 square mile basin is almost double that of the Hazel River (355 sq. mi.). It flows for 82 miles – slightly longer than the flowing (above tidewater) section of the Rappahannock itself. This chapter covers only the upper part of the Rapidan and its headwater tributaries; downstream trips are in the next chapter.

Like the seven Hazel River headwaters in the previous chapter, the Rapidan's five main headwaters rise on the Blue Ridge, starting very steep and gradually mellowing. In this case, the rivers spawn along an 18-mile stretch from Stony Man to Hawksbill Mountain, just above Swift Run Gap (where a road traverses the Park). One can get a long run by starting high up on any of these creeks. Section 2 of the **Robinson** is the easiest both to paddle and to catch, and therefore the most popular run in this chapter. The sections 2 of the **Rapidan, Conway** and **South** are also manageable by intermediate paddlers. But the **Rose** and the sections 1 of the other four rivers are a different story. My favorite is the upper Conway, which is steep, fairly wide (because of clearing operations), easily scouted from the road, full of dynamite rapids, and was virtually free of strainers in 2003-4. The top parts of the Robinson and the South rivers are almost as nice, but harder to scout and not quite as challenging. Section 2 of the Rose has some nice rapids, but also a few man-made hazards; section 1 remains an "explorers' special." The incredibly steep section 1 of the Rapidan is in a difficulty class by itself, and is the other "explorers' special." I also include the final mile of **Garth Run,** a tiny but bouncy little tributary. For those seeking calmer water, there are subsequent parts of the Rapidan, Robinson and Conway that I have not covered – they are all in Corbett.

These streams drain most of Madison County and the northern part of Greene County, with Madison and Standardsville the main towns, respectively, in this rural area. While all of these creeks (except Garth Run) are in Corbett, I have added sections higher up (except for the Rose), as well as updated the information (see box below).

In 1995 and 1996, this watershed was thrice blasted by extraordinary precipitation. During June 21-28, 1995, rainfall totaling 20" on the upper Rapidan, 15" on the Rose, and 13" on the Conway produced the devastating "**Madison County Flood.**"Garth Run, for example, the smallest creek in this chapter, was still at flood stage four days after the rain stopped. On January 7, 1996, a blizzard dropped 3-4' of snow in the same area. Then on September 6, 1996, **Hurricane Fran** inundated most of the area with 8-12" of rain, with the greatest amount, 15.6", again on the uppermost Rapidan, just as the cleanup from the earlier flood was in full swing. The flooding was only slightly less severe on the west side of the Blue Ridge, around Naked Creek (chapter 28). The bridges and valley roads were washed out, and enormous amounts of gravel, rock and vegetation were dumped into the streambeds and had to be cleared out to prevent the streams from overrunning their banks with each rain. The creeks had artificial looks, but time heals such wounds. The clearing operations did remove most of the fallen trees. But strainers, like "bimbo eruptions," have a way of re-emerging.

> The **smallest "river" in Virginia** is the **Staunton River**. Barely four miles long and with a total catchment of only 5 sq. mi., it flows entirely within Shenandoah National Park, from a saddle named The Sag to its confluence with the Rapidan, a half mile above the start of section 2. It is too steep to paddle (average gradient 550 ft/mile), but the Staunton River Trail is a popular hike. An 1,100-acre tract on the upper Staunton is one of the only sites in the Park where timber was never cut.
>
> Two medium-sized (30-35 sq. mi.) tributaries, **Blue Run** and **Beautiful Run**, rise in the foothills and enter the Rapidan near its southernmost point. Both are flat until their final descents at 25 ft/mile for less than a mile. And then you would face a long (4 miles for Beautiful Run, 7 miles for Blue Run) flat paddle on the Rapidan to US 15.
>
> If you like the creeks in this chapter, you might want to try also the next watershed to the south, that of the **Rivanna River**. Swift Run, Parker Branch, the Roach River and the Lynch River flow down from the Blue Ridge to the North Fork of the Rivanna, followed by the South Fork tributaries of Buck Mountain Creek, Doyles River and the delightful class III Moormans River (the only one of these that I have paddled).

GAUGES: The gauge on the Rapidan near Culpeper (468 sq. mi.), past which the water from all the creeks in this chapter soon flows, is too far downstream. Somewhat better are upstream gauges on the Rapidan near Ruckersville at US 29 (115 sq. mi.), which includes the contributions of the Conway and South rivers, and the Robinson near Locust Dale (179 sq. mi.) at US 15. The gauge on the North Fork of the Rivanna near Earlysville (108 sq. mi.), in the watershed just to the south of the Rapidan, is worth checking for the southern part of this basin. There are rainfall data on the AFWS for seven spots in Madison County, as well as for points on the Blue Ridge just inside Page County (to the west); this is important, because these creeks drop very fast, leaving a short window between the water being too high and too low.

The table below shows **the approximate minimal gauge readings for the Rapidan near Ruckersville**, when the levels are pretty steady. Usually, of course, the creeks are run when the levels are falling, so you need to project this gauge about 3 hours forward from your put-in time. Fortunately, one can in most cases put in downstream if there is not quite enough water for the steeper sections higher up.

name	gradient	difficulty	length	area	gauge	rating
Rapidan River - *Section 1*	240 (600)	IV+ (?)	5.5	5	3000cfs	?
- *Section 2*	47 (100)	II (III-)	7.0	16	700cfs	***
Garth Run	45	II	1.0	7	1000cfs	**
Conway R. - *Section 1*	110 (165)	IV-	4.0	10	1700cfs	!!!!
- *Section 2*	50	II+(III+)	3.5	18	750cfs	***
South River - *Section 1*	105 (150)	III- (III)	2.8	8	1300cfs	****
- *Section 2*	36	II+(III-)	6.2	16	700cfs	***
Robinson R. - *Section 1*	90 (140)	III (III+)	4.8	10	1000cfs	****
- *Section 2*	23 (45)	II+	8.8	33	375cfs	***
Rose R. - *Section 1*	120 (160)	?	1.2	10	1000cfs	?
- *Section 2*	85	III (III+)	2.7	14	850cfs	***

🌊 RAPIDAN RIVER (upper)

The Rapidan River is created at the confluence of Mill Prong and Laurel Prong at Camp Hoover, the "Summer White House," where the then president could fish for trout while the economy froze. A gate blocks road access to the first mile, in Shenandoah National Park, so section 1 begins just below that, for those few expert steep creekers who can handle it. A road parallels the first 3.5 miles, but the following 2 are wilderness. The Park boundary is the next road access and the start of section 2.

Below the section 2 take out, the 8.5 miles to US 29 is 20 ft/mile for the first 3.3 miles and 12 ft/mile for the last 5.2 miles (below the Conway). Corbett covers that and the even flatter 56 miles below. The final 6 miles, which has some easy rapids, is in the next and last chapter of this book.

> **"Good Queen Anne,** whose mind was as shallow as a lowland river," eldest daughter of King George II and wife of William IV, whom she married in 1734, left her name on Virginia rivers like no one else. There are the North Anna, South Anna, Rivanna (River Anna) and Rapidan (Rapid Anne, because of its fast current).
>
> There were many Civil War skirmishes in this area. On September 22, 1863, at Rochelle, Confederate Major General J.E.B.Stuart's forces were in a **cavalry fight** against General Buford, when they were attacked in the rear by the cavalry of Brigadier General Judson Kilpatrick. Stuart's men managed to break through Kilpatrick's lines and escape across the Rapidan.
>
> Will Carson, Chairman of the Virginia State Commission on Conservation and Development, arranged for setting up **Camp Hoover** as a means of getting the President's support for establishing the national park. The Camp is still available for use by members of Congress and their staffs. The road is gated a mile before Camp Hoover, but this should be no problem for our hardwalking Congress.

Section 1: Gate above Rapidan Camp to Park Boundary (end of SR 662)

Gradient	Difficulty	Distance	Area	Scenery	Strainers	Rating
240 (600)	IV+(?)	5.5	5	A	8-12/mi.	?

USGS Quad –Fletcher; Source – Scouting from road alongside
N38 29.23, W78 24.39 via N38 27.71, W78 21.92 (mile 3.5) to N38 26.22, W78 22.00

Jim Long alerted me to this *"explorers' special,"* which, as you can tell from the data, is difficult to catch and beyond difficult to paddle. Access is by a rough road (used for trout fishing and access to Camp Hoover) that requires 4-wheel drive when wet, e.g whenever the creek is up. The access road starts up Quaker Run from the Robinson River, a little below Syria. It becomes gravel, and twists steeply up into the Park. Continue straight at the intersection.

This is a beautiful mountain creek, with steep, narrow, tortuous rapids. But, alas, it is full of huge logjams. Much of the first 3.5 miles is visible from the road; however, it gets even steeper after that, until the final half mile, after the confluence with the Staunton River. From where the creek leaves the road it is only 2 river miles to the take out, but 25 shuttle miles.

GAUGE: You probably need around 3,000 cfs on the Ruckersville gauge, but of course this section will rise and fall much more rapidly than that gauge reading, so project that gauge 4 hours ahead.

Section 2: Park Boundary (end of SR 662) to Va. 230

Gradient	Difficulty	Distance	Area	Scenery	Strainers	Rating
47 (100)	II (III-)	7.0	16	B+	<1/mi.	***

USGS Quad – Madison/Rochelle; Source – Personal descent 1/98 (top), 10/99 (middle), 9/04 (bottom)

N38 26.22, W78 22.00 via N38 22.22, W78 21.87 (SR 662) to N38 21.23, W78 22.43

Advanced paddlers used to put in at the confluence with the **Staunton River**, starting with a half mile, class III+ stretch inside the Park, with a 125-ft/mile gradient. The floods of 1995 and 1996, however, washed away the access road, and while Virginia repaired the road outside the Park, the National Park Service did not do so inside the Park. As a result, one can run this half mile only by carrying upstream.

The normal run now begins alongside the parking lot where the road ends at the Park boundary. In 1996, tractors cleared the riverbed of trees and boulders that came down in the floods and were causing the stream to overflow onto the road after every heavy rain. As a result, much of the river had a scoured appearance; however, it is transforming itself back towards what it was before, until the next serious floods cause man to interfere again. The scenery rating of "B+" is an average between a "B-" for the immediate environment and an "A" for the background views of the valley.

While not technically difficult, the continuousness of the rapids makes this a very enjoyable paddle. The trip starts off at 100 ft/mile, with a 100-yard, class III- rock garden, culminating in a ledge best run on the far right. Below that, the bulldozers' work is more evident, and while the gradient remains steep, it is mostly expended in long gravel bars. The initial ones have class II waves, but below Graves Mill (at 1.3 miles, the confluence with Kinsey Run) they are gradually replaced by class II- and then class I sections (although above one foot, the creek remains class II throughout). In the steeper stretches, the fast water has already begun to dig its normal channels, deepest in the middle in the straight sections and in the outside curve on the turns. The result is the unusual situation that as the creek flattens out, it becomes bonier.

Most of the first 1.7 miles can be scouted from the road; there is also a public bridge with good access at 2.5 miles. There is one low-water bridge to be portaged (the Graves Mill Farm, at about 3 miles). A mile below that, a footbridge is followed by a pair of ledges with hydraulics at high levels – both can be run on the far left, and make good play spots at lower levels. After 5.6 miles, you reach SR 662, which is a much easier takeout than Va. 230. Garth Run enters after another 0.4 miles, and there is a play spot at the confluence. The river then divides twice, around two small islands, with most water going to the right. When you come to a dam, stop and scout. You could run the 3-foot drop (with speed, to escape the hydraulic) only at relatively low levels; otherwise, take a small channel that circumvents the dam on the left. Below, within sight of Va. 230, there are some excellent surfing waves with an eddy alongside.

The Va. 230 takeout is poor, because parking is very limited and you need to climb up some steep rocks and then carry a distance to your car.

The changes since the floods can be illustrated by comparison with Ed Grove's 1992 description: "If you like fences and downed trees, you'll love this 6 mile section of the Rapidan.... Trees (primarily sycamores) and ancient Pedlar granite boulders line the riverbank...." We encountered no fences and only two downed trees. But many of the sycamores and natural boulders are gone too.

GAUGE: Ruckersville should read over 700 cfs (projected 2 hours ahead) to start at the Park boundary, and 400 cfs to start at Graves Mill. Look for heavy rain within the past day at Big Meadows (Page County) on the Skyline Drive, Fork Mountain (Madison County) in the headwaters, and Graves Mill (Madison County) on the trip itself.

GARTH RUN: SR 718 (off Garth Run Road) to the Rapidan

Gradient	Difficulty	Distance	Area	Scenery	Strainers	Rating
45	II	1.0*	7	B	2-4/mi.	**

USGS Quad – Stanardsville/Rochelle; Source –Personal descent 9/04
N38 22.53, W78 22.77 to N38 21.23, W78 22.43

*(plus 1 mile on the Rapidan to Va. 230)

I had been searching for an additional Rapidan headwater to add to the standard list of five. Garth Run rises on the slopes of 3,500-foot Bluff Mountain, between the Rapidan and Conway valleys, and flows southeast for seven miles. Although it does not start on the Blue Ridge, it has a large enough drainage area to be occasionally runnable, and a decent gradient. Alas, for much of its length it is plagued by fences, visible from the road, so only the final mile, followed by a mile on the Rapidan, is worth doing.

This last mile is a pleasant trip, with nice scenery and almost continuous easy whitewater. But the creek is so narrow that visibility is limited and small branches hang down almost to the water in places, forcing you to duck and bash through. Around midway, you pass through a farm, guarded by fences at both ends; fortunately, they are in slow water and easily overcome.

The mile on the Rapidan, to Va. 230, has a few good play spots and a 3-foot dam to run over or around (see Rapidan section 2 above), but the takeout is poor.

GAUGE: If the stream is cleanly runnable at the put in, you will have enough water. Look for 1,000 cfs at Ruckersville (projected 3 hours ahead).

CONWAY RIVER

This creek, also known as the Middle River (between the Rapidan and South rivers), is a fabulous whitewater treat when not full of downed trees. Alas, it seems to attract wood like Bill Clinton attracted women – and they can cause just as many headaches. But then the strainers disappear again. After the flood of 1996, Virginia authorities bulldozed boulders and fallen trees out of its banks; this left the creek looking scoured, with intricate rock gardens replaced by gravel bars. The riverbed was also widened in the process, so it takes more rain to bring it up, but there is more room for maneuvering. Over time, both the good and bad features of the natural river will return. Strainers had returned by 1997, but after Hurricane Isabel in September 2003, we found the creek, especially section 1, almost completely clean, and it still looked pretty good from the road in 2012.

The Conway rises, like most upper Rappahannock tributaries, just off the Skyline Drive and the Appalachian Trail, on the opposite side from Naked Creek. A fire road parallels it for most of its early life, before SR 667 takes over. The river forms the boundary between Greene and Madison Counties, which helps prevent fences (we encountered none) because most properties end at the county line. There are wild brook trout in the upper reaches, wild brown trout down below.

There is a rough road access (SR 615) to the very upper Conway, just three miles from its source, but the river here is too steep (300 ft/mile) and boulder- and strainer-clogged. (Better to hike it, as well as its nearby Devils Ditch tributary, whose gradient is 600 ft/mile.) The next access, the northern end of SR 667, is a mile downstream, and is the start of section 1. I have divided the 7.5 miles of good paddling into two sections, based on their difficulty. Below section 2, the Conway continues for 2.3 miles of class II, at 35 ft/mile, to the Rapidan; however, you then face 5.2 miles of class I on the Rapidan, at only 12 ft/mile, to US 29. But you might try this some day when the Rapidan is high.

> The huge **"Northern Neck"** land grant, which was inherited by Lord Thomas Fairfax by 1719, was to include the land between the Potomac and Rappahannock rivers, and bounded in the west by a line "connecting the sources" of those two rivers. Many land disputes arose because of the vagueness of this description. Lord Fairfax's men succeeded in having (a) the North Branch defined as the Potomac, and (b) the Conway defined as the principal source of the Rappahannock. Together, this more than doubled the size of the land grant from 2.5 to 5.3 million acres, by, inter alia, including virtually the entire Rappahannock basin. The lawsuits continued.

Section 1: End of SR 667 to Kinderhook (SR 613)

Gradient	Difficulty	Distance	Area	Scenery	Strainers	Rating
110 (165)	IV-	4.0	10	B	0-2/mi.	!!!!

USGS Quad – Fletcher/Stanardsville; Source – Personal descent (last 3.3 miles) 9/03, and trip report (Jim Long - first 0.7 miles) 10/03
N38 25.01, W78 26.25 via N38 23.60, W78 25.96 (Fletcher) to N38 22.07, W78 25.74

When there is enough water, this is a wonderful run for those who can handle it. You can scout almost all from SR 667, and may want to put in lower down depending upon the conditions and your skill levels. I have seen the top part choked with strainers, but these were gone in 2003-4.

The first 0.7 miles averages 165 ft/mile and is continuous class IV-, but with no major drops. To get to this part, you have to cross a low-water bridge over the creek; you will need a high-clearance vehicle and a low water level. There are "no parking" signs around the put in, where the road ends, so you might want to unload there but leave your cars downstream. (As of 2012, this land all belongs to the Conway River Tree Farm, as part of a "stewardship forest" according to their sign.) Also, check carefully in advance both the low-water bridge you have driven over and one on a side road half a mile upstream, both of which are mandatory portages.

Below the bridge you have driven across (at 0.7 miles), the gradient is down to a mere 150 ft/mile, expended in a series of long, steep class III+ and IV- rapids. The hardest one, about the fourth in this part, is complicated by a series of only slightly covered boulders. The stream is enlarged (at 1.0 miles) by Pocosin Creek and its 4 sq. mi. drainage; there is a nice drop at the confluence. There are at least two more class III+ rapids, the second and more distinctive one marked by a huge mid-stream boulder with a ledge below, as well as lots of long, class III rock gardens, in the remaining mile (gradient of 120 ft/mile) down to the SR 675 bridge at Fletcher.

Below Fletcher (at 2.0 miles), the gradient drops to 85 ft/mile for the 2 miles to Kinderhook. A quarter mile below Fletcher, where the creek bends to the right, is a steep class III drop; most of the other rapids in this section are class III-. What is most memorable about the rapids, however, is their length – many continue unabated for over 100 yards, so swimming would not be fun. There are three bridges in this stretch, each of which has enough clearance at moderate levels. As of September 2003, this section was virtually strainer-free. Sycamores line the banks, but many of them are completely covered by kudzu.

GAUGE: Zero level is about 1,700 cfs on the Rapidan near Ruckersville (the most relevant gauge) and the North Fork of the Rivanna near Earlyville, both projected 3 hours ahead. We ran it 36 hours after 5 inches of rainfall at Lewis Mountain Camp (Page County) on the Skyline Drive and 3.5 inches at Fork Mountain (Madison County) on the top Rapidan, and had plenty of water – but 5 hours later it was becoming bony. Because the road follows the river, you can judge the level visually at many spots.

Section 2: Kinderhook (SR613) to Hood (Va. 230)

Gradient	Difficulty	Distance	Area	Scenery	Strainers	Rating
50	II+ (III+)	3.5	18	B	0-2/mi.	***

USGS Quad – Stanardsville; Source – Personal descent 9/03
N38 22.07, W78 25.74 to N38 19.94, W78 23.87

Below Kinderhook, the gradient eases up. And because the creek no longer follows the road, there was no need to bulldoze it to prevent road flooding. So the river is more natural than above, but has more problems with vegetation. The section starts off with a steep class II+ drop on a sharp left turn. Then the creek spreads out, with most of the water filtering through what had been fields, while the minority of it heads to the right, back to the original riverbed. Go with the GOP for the less-obstructed route. After the channels reunite, there are long twisty sections, with low gravel bars on one side and 4-foot high dirt walls on the other. The creek spreads out a few more times, and you have to paddle between bushes. Expect a few strainers and approach blind turns cautiously.

The rapids are no more than class II until about a mile before the end, when there is a lively class II+ stretch marked by a high cliff wall on river left. Shortly below, when the horizon line disappears, pull over above or onto the large flat rock on the left, to scout the class III+ ledge below. Most of the water goes to the far right into a big hole followed by a stopper wave. Prudent paddlers will stay center or left, perhaps scraping on the way down. The portage on the left is easy. Immediately below is a second ledge, with a class II+ sneak on the left (if you have enough water), or a class III+ plunge down the center/right. After that, the river returns to its milder, twisty way, down to the takeout.

GAUGE: You will need about 750 cfs on both the Rapidan near Ruckersville (the most relevant gauge) and the North Fork of the Rivanna at Earlyville, both projected 2 hours ahead.

> The **Conways,** originally from Ireland, were early settlers of the area. Eleanor Rose Nellie Conway was the mother of President James Madison.
>
> **Bent Canoe.** I first ran this with Ed Grove, when he wrote it up for his book. In one rapid, a branch snagged the string holding in one of my airbags, and I was spun sideways and dumped into the creek. The force of the water buckled my Blue Hole canoe, and although the ABS plastic tried later to regain its shape, the aluminum gunnel did not. That boat remains doglegged, and I explain that it makes left turns easier, while for right turns I rotate myself 180 degrees.

SOUTH RIVER

The South River, the southernmost Rapidan headwaters, flows 13.5 miles from the Blue Ridge to the Rapidan, starting steep and gradually flattening out. Early on, it plunges over the sheer 83-foot South River Falls, the third highest waterfall in the Park.

I had long ignored it because of Roger Corbett's description: "The South River is best described as a nine-mile long Class 2 gravel bar/rock garden.... It has a very steady gradient and there are no major rapids or big ledges ...." But he did add that after "the stream was channelized and cleared of briars, bushes, and downed trees ... the water velocity has already started reshaping the stream bed." Well, the creek must have changed considerably, for it now contains an interesting mix of rapids spread over nine miles of good to excellent paddling. Section 1 begins at the highest public access (a private road goes up a bit farther), where Entry Run adds about 60% to the flow, and the gradient drops to a mere 150 ft/mile. The division between sections 1 and 2 is somewhat arbitrary, except that the SR 637 low-water bridge is dangerous, so you would need to portage it in any case. Below section 2, it is 0.9 miles to the Rapidan, at just 18 ft/mile, and the 2.1 miles on the Rapidan are an even slower 10 ft/mile.

Section 1: SR 642/643 (Entry Run) to SR 637

Gradient	Difficulty	Distance	Area	Scenery	Strainers	Rating
105 (150)	III- (III)	2.8	8	C	0-2/mi.	****

USGS Quad – Stanardsville; Source – Personal descent 9/04
N38 22.01, W78 27.59 to N38 19.94, W78 26.83

This fast, steep run is mostly great fun. But even though we faced only a few strainers, be very careful approaching blind turns, because eddies are few and small. The class III rapid comes just 50 yards below the start, where a huge boulder divides the stream. Both channels are runnable, but scout first, and beware of currents that want to shove you into the boulder. After that, there are mainly long class III- rapids, some complicated by partial strainers. The gradient averages 150 ft/mile above the first bridge (SR 642, at 0.6 miles), 110 ft/mile until the third bridge (SR 634, South River Church, at 1.9 miles), and 70 ft/mile for the final 0.9 miles.

Soon after the second bridge (SR 647, at 1.4 miles), the creek flows left towards a large tree in the water along the left bank. Portage on the right. It may seem like you can avoid the tree, but the current is fierce. Three of us tried, but only one (not me) succeeded. At South River Church the flow is enhanced by Bull Yearling Run. This part is almost continuous class II+, with one 3-foot ledge at a private road crossing.

Be very careful at the SR 637 take out, so as not to get sucked into the culverts beneath this low-water bridge. Catch an eddy well above the bridge on river left, or have someone at the left end of the bridge to grab the boats.

GAUGE: A minimum 1,300 cfs on the Rapidan near Ruckersville and the North Fork of the Rivanna (projected 3 hours ahead) are normally needed. The rainfall gauge is Lewis Mountain Camp (Page County) on the Skyline Drive. The painted RC gauge on the downstream side of Va. 230 should read at least 6 inches.

Section 2: SR 637 to SR 619 (Dundee Rd.)

Gradient	Difficulty	Distance	Area	Scenery	Strainers	Rating
36	II+ (III-)	6.2	16	B	<1/mi.	***

USGS Quad – Stanardsville/Rochelle; Source –Personal descent 7/03
N38 19.94, W78 26.83 to N38 17.51, W78 22.35

Although the gradient averages 50 ft/mile for the two miles (to Va. 230) and just 30 ft/mile for the final 4.2 miles, the rapids do not change much – they just become more widely spaced. Indeed, the best rapid, a class III- rock garden, is about a mile below Va. 230. The ledges below Va. 230 are reminiscent of the Hughes, with good surfing. Partial strainers added spice to several of the rapids, but we had only one portage on my first trip and three on my second. (But, on the other hand, in May 2008 Ed Evangelidi reported a slew of new strainers, some of them quite dangerous because they were around bends with no eddies above them; so take this river very cautiously.)

A private road bridge a mile below the put in is dangerous in low to moderate water (at high levels, you could just paddle onto it), so scout it beforehand.

GAUGE: Look for 700 cfs on the Rapidan near Ruckersville and the North Fork of the Rivanna (projected 2 hours ahead). Lewis Mountain Camp (Page Co.) on the Skyline Drive is the rain gauge. There was a painted RC gauge on the downstream side of the Va. 230 bridge.

ROBINSON RIVER

The Potomac Appalachian Trail Club calls Whiteoak Canyon, with its six waterfalls, virgin hemlocks and prime brook trout fishing, "the scenic gem of the Shenandoah National Park." Just outside the Park, at the start of the Whiteoak Canyon Trail, Whiteoak Canyon Run joins with two smaller streams, Cedar Run and Berry Hollow Run, to create the Robinson River.

> On August 11, 2001, Bobby "ZoneDogg" Miller and Joe Stumpfel made the first known descent of part of **Whiteoak Canyon Run** – about a half mile, with a gradient of some 1,000 ft/mile. They started at the base of Two-Headed Wriekazoid (the third major waterfall from the top), and ended with Bobby getting knocked out of his boat at the base of the final waterfall, the 60-ft Flaming Moe. By that time, it was too dark for them to run the final 1.3 miles, at a mere 300 ft/mile. Together with Andy Maser and Ian Devine, they returned to run from the top, hiking down from the Skyline Drive, but strainers forced them to walk more than they paddled. Joe left the others and paddled the mile of class IV below Flaming Moe "before it peters out to cobble bars complicated by too many fallen trees to count," about a third of a mile above section 1 below.

From there, the Robinson flows 6 miles to its confluence with the Rose, and a further 24 miles to the Rapidan. The first 4.8 miles are seldom up, but when they are, it is an exciting trip (section 1). I have left out the final 1.2 miles above the Rose, because it had three fences (which you could carry around, with some effort). It is class II with a 42-ft/mile gradient. The 9-mile stretch below the confluence with the Rose, down to US 29, is a popular low-intermediate trip (section 2). Below US 29, the Robinson is a Piedmont stream at 10 ft/mile for the first 5.4 miles (to SR 632), and 6 ft/mile thereafter, with just one real rapid – a class II+ at the remains of an old dam, about 2 miles below US 29.

> Starting in 1724, **German settlers** moved into the Robinson valley, along the "German Mountain Road." Their chapel became Hebron Church, the first Lutheran church in the South, which operated what may have been the first public school in Virginia. Long before the Civil War, that community abolished slavery for itself. The Robinson was once called the Robertson River, consistent with Robertson Mountain, just west of Old Rag, at the northern end of the watershed. It is likely that the river is named after **John Robinson**, Speaker of the Virginia House of Burgesses when the area was first settled, but there have been so many Robinsons.

In the Schedule, I had written
"Robinson," for I am smitten
With a preference for running rivers new,
But I thought it disconnected,
For who'd ever have expected,
That the scheduled creek's the one we'd really do?

But the skies had been a-dumping,
And the creeks they were a-pumping,
It rained up to two inches the 5th of May,
So I figured that we oughta
Have more than sufficient water
To go run the Robinson with CCA.

So without the least hysteria,
We headed out toward Syria,
Past tiny, nameless drains that were a-flowing,
I felt a strong temptation
To engage in exploration,
But no, to the Robinson we were a-going.

We were seven open boats,
(Is there something else that floats?),
Phil DiModica, Doug White, Marion Dargon,
Dennis Seekins, Dickson Carroll,
All put on wet suit apparel,
While Brad White and I practiced our river jargon.

Now the most exciting part
Was the mile below the start,
(We put in 2.5 miles above the Rose),
It was non-stop fun and thrills,
And we even had two spills,
For at 60 feet per mile it really flows.

Soon the gradient declined,
But we didn't really mind,
With a foot of water this creek is a pleasure,
But it then began to pour
And frankly that was a bore,
As it left us little time for streamside leisure.

Now the middle Robinson
Is a pleasant, restful run,
With the hardest rapid not even a III,
But I must come back once more
The headwaters to explore,
Tiny Blue Ridge creeks like paradise can be.

Section 1: Source (SR 600) to 1.2 miles above Confluence with Rose River

Gradient	Difficulty	Distance	Area	Scenery	Strainers	Rating
90 (140)	III (III+)	4.8	10	C	1-2/mi.	****

USGS Quad – Old Rag Mountain/Madison; Source –Personal descent 1/03
N38 32.33, W78 20.81 to N38 29.36, W78 18.94

This must be a great run, because Jon Hauris and I did it in 40 degree, drizzly weather, had some mishaps and still enjoyed it. You can scout the bottom half from SR 600, and get a few views above that, including from driveways that lead to low-water bridges. I ran the last quarter of this trip when leading a CCA trip (see above doggerel) in 1989, but did not complete the run until 2003.

The put in is the most upstream bridge on SR 600, by the White Oak Canyon parking area, close to where the three headwaters meet. (We put in on Berry Hollow Run, but you can start on Whiteoak Canyon Run as well – they meet in 125 yards.) With no warm up, you are into class III rapids, which you can see stretching out ahead of you. There are no major drops, but hardly any pools either, lots of rocks to knock you off of your chosen line, and a 140 ft/mile gradient. Watch out for a pair of tricky spots just below the put in, and another where the creek drops steeply and blindly to the right, towards a pair of mid-stream trees. Also, check upstream from the next bridge to see if a dangerous strainer is still there.

After that bridge, at one mile, the gradient starts to decrease, to an average of 75 ft/mile for the rest of the trip. But the rapids aren't any easier, just more widely spaced. Watch out for a low bridge (as the back of my life jacket can testify), another with a single, narrow culvert that should be portaged, and a low-water bridge that you can scrape over but might better carry because of the drop below. Then, at 3 miles, is the hardest rapid – a steep, tight, twisting class III+ drop of about 5 feet, into a large eddy. The take out is another bridge over SR 600, before a series of fences.

For a creek this size, the density of strainers is comparatively low, but the steep gradient increases their danger. Be especially wary, of course, at high water levels.

GAUGE: At least 1,500 cfs on the Robinson at Locust Dale (projected 3 hours ahead) is normally required. The rainfall gauges are Skyland (Page County) and Syria (Madison County).

Section 2: Confluence with Rose River to SR 636 (just off US 29)

Gradient	Difficulty	Distance	Area	Scenery	Strainers	Rating
23 (45)	II+	8.8	33	C	<<1/mi.	***

USGS Quad – Madison/Brightwood; Source – Personal descent 1/98 (first 3.5 miles); 9/92 (remainder)

N38 28.17, W78 18.88 via N38 26.77, W78 16.16 (mile 3.5) to N38 24.08, W78 13.78

If you are not continuing from section 1 or the Rose River, start at the pullout 1/4 mile below the confluence, to avoid landowner problems. The first 3.5 miles, at 34 ft/mile, are alongside SR 670/231/609, and one can then take out where SR 609 turns sharply away from the river. There are many play spots and frequent class II and II+ rapids, including some lively waves early on and several nice ledges towards the end, especially just below the pillars of a destroyed bridge. This trip is harder at higher water. Keep your eyes open for zebras, run along with cattle by one farmer.

The remaining 5.3 miles averages just 16 ft/mile, and the rapids are far less common. But several of the class II drops may take you by surprise, if you have been lulled into thinking that the creek has become flat. The scenery is better, and the only intermediate access is SR 638, 1.2 miles from the take out.

GAUGE: Look for over 600 cfs on the Robinson gauge near Locust Dale (projected 1-2 hours ahead). The rain gauge is Syria (Madison County).

> In 1716, Virginia Governor Alexander Spotswood led an expedition of thirteen gentry (plus aides and servants) up the Rapidan and Robinson rivers to the Blue Ridge, and then down to the South Fork of the Shenandoah (which they called the "Euphrates"). Their success helped attract explorers, traders, hunters and settlers. The thirteen gentry became known as the **Knights of the Golden Horseshoe**, after the presents the Governor gave them upon return.

ROSE RIVER

The Rose (originally Rowe's) River and its tributary, Hogcamp Branch, rise in the Big Meadows area of Shenandoah National Park and flow over two lovely and popular waterfalls, Rose River Falls and Dark Hollow Falls, respectively. The valley is popular with hikers, trout fishermen and wine tasters (at the Rose River Vineyards). Four miles from its source, the Rose River leaves the Park, alongside SR 670. The next 0.7 miles, at 200 ft/mile, had many fallen trees and the access is across private property, so the recommended put in is where SR 670 crosses the creek.

Section 1: SR 670 to SR 648

Gradient	Difficulty	Distance	Area	Scenery	Strainers	Rating
120 (160)	?	1.2	10	C	1-2/mi.	?

USGS Quad – Madison; Source – Scouting from road
N38 30.61, W78 21.38 to N38 29.78, W78 21.04

The gradient of this *"explorers' special"* starts off at 160 ft/mile and drops only very gradually. Make sure you take the dirt road SR670 to the put in, not the paved SR 648.

GAUGE: About 1,350 cfs on the Robinson gauge at Locust Dale (projected 3-4 hours ahead) would be zero level. The rain gauges are Big Meadows (Page County) and Syria (Madison County).

Section 2: SR 648 to Robinson River

Gradient	Difficulty	Distance	Area	Scenery	Strainers	Rating
85	III (III+)	2.7	14	C	1-2/mi.	***

USGS Quad – Madison; Source – Personal descent 1/98
N38 29.78, W78 21.04 to N38 28.17, W78 18.88

Just above SR 648, Strother Run adds about 30% to the flow. Hurricane Fran (1996) and the subsequent clearing operations widened and scoured much of the streambed below here. Corbett was not enthusiastic: "This trip is NOT recommended for those who seek pleasure and freedom from fear and pain." Which means it is a lot like other steep Rappahannock headwaters. But it does have several quite dangerous spots, which you should scout beforehand, where possible

This section starts off with a class III- rock garden just upstream of the bridge, and never slows down much. The initial mile is fine – long class II+ and III- rock gardens, and nice scenery. Then comes the first dangerous spot, where a collapsed bridge left only a narrow, strainer-attracting channel on the right; eddy out on the left just above it. Half a mile below there is a low-water bridge to Graves Mountain Lodge; pull out well above and portage. Not long after comes a low weir followed by a short, steep class III rapid that contained a partially floating metal pipe (a strainer at low levels) and sometimes fallen trees as well. Make sure you scout this before running it, as the pipe (if it still there) can be quite dangerous. And then, after a class III rock garden and a short pool, the horizon line disappears. A pair of huge boulders split a class III+, 6-foot drop into 3 channels; the left one is tortuous, but the middle and right routes are more straightforward.

The final mile has been re-engineered to a uniform 50-foot width, with boulders on all sides, and horseshoe-shaped rock weirs (with openings in the middle) to control the destructive tendencies of high water with a 70-ft/mile gradient. Take out at the small dirt pullover a quarter mile below the confluence with the Robinson, at SR 649 in another quarter mile, or continue further down the Robinson.

GAUGE: About 1,350 cfs on the Robinson gauge at Locust Dale (projected 3 hours ahead) would be zero level. The rain gauges are Big Meadows (Page County) and Syria (Madison County).

On the **upper, upper Rose**, accessible only by carrying up the Rose River Trail from the end of SR 670, is a 4-500 ft/mile class 5.1(?) run, which has been done and written up, but it was more like boat-assisted hiking because of the numerous strainers and unrunnable waterfalls.

Jamie Deehan and I put on at SR 648 in the late afternoon, after 4-inch January rains. The Rose was running at over two feet, and was very pushy, with few eddies. I managed to catch a shallow eddy on river right just above the **collapsed Rose River Center bridge**, but Jamie, on river left, had too much water in his boat to hold his eddy, and had to run that narrow channel under only limited control. He managed to bounce over the low strainer there, but flipped and lost his swamped boat while getting into an eddy just below. Workers starting the repair of the Graves Mountain Lodge low water bridge rescued his canoe. And as I portaged the Rose River Center access, I found that the channel there was now completely blocked, as his passage had knocked the large branch there into an even worse position. Meanwhile, dusk was falling, so we took out at Graves Mountain Lodge, leaving the second half of the trip for a later date.

Three weeks later we were back, at close to zero level, along with Ed Evangelidi, Tom Gray and John Hauris, for the first Thursday Paddlers trip of 1998. The final mile was then a large **construction site**, where cranes and bulldozers were busy redesigning the river. We had to portage twice to get around the machine that was in the middle of the river, picking up boulders from one side and dropping them on the other, with obviously no intention of stopping for us.

Along the Rose and Robinson rivers is a unique semi-precious stone, **unakite**, composed of pink feldspar, green epidote and blue and green quartz. There are also copper-bearing ores, which were dug out of the Dark Hollow Mine in the headwaters, before the Civil War and again early in the 20th Century.

In those days, the Old Blue Ridge Turnpike went up the Rose River and through Fishers Gap. Robert Graves, whose descendents still own **Graves Mountain Lodge** (a good, moderately priced restaurant), lodged and fed many of those turnpike travelers. There was considerable local frustration that Fishers Gap was closed to vehicles when the Park was established.

Stonewall Jackson led his 20,000 "foot cavalry" over this pass in November 1862, after defeating several Union armies during his Shenandoah Valley Campaign, to join Lee in the east.

Thomas Shirley, one of the largest planters in the area, built a three and a half story house on the Rose River, from which he ran his 50,000-acre domain in the mid-19th Century.

Chapter 41:

RAPPAHANNOCK TAILWATERS

Unlike the headwaters in the previous three chapters, the lower Rappahannock Basin contains some of the most popular and easy-to-catch novice to low intermediate whitewater in the region, as well as little-known both flatter and steeper creeks.

The **Rappahannock** itself picks up a little steam between Remington and Kellys Ford (section 1), calms down for a pleasant 2-day novice canoe trip (section 2), and then has its hardest rapid as it descends the fall line at Fredericksburg (section 3). These sections, and the easy rapids of the lower **Rapidan**, are in previous guidebooks. Corbett also has a fine write up of the history and remains of the Rappahannock River Canal.

> This area, lying midway between Washington and Richmond, was the scene of frequent and major **Civil War** action. The Rappahannock and Rapidan were at several times the boundaries between Union and Confederate control, and the crossing of those rivers often marked the beginning or end of a campaign. Three major battles took place in this area: **Fredericksburg** (Dec. 1862), **Chancellorsville** (May 1863), and the **Wilderness** (May 1864). The first two were part of the string of Southern victories between Antietam and Gettysburg, whereas the latter marked the beginning of Grant's ultimately successful strategy of grinding down Lee's army and forcing it into defensive positions around Richmond and Petersburg. Following the Battle of the Wilderness, the armies moved farther south

The main tributaries of the lower Rappahannock and Rapidan are rather flat Piedmont streams. For the Rappahannock, the largest (the only one in Corbett) is **Mountain Run**, which despite its name, has only a 6-ft/mile gradient. **Marsh Run** is smaller, has a similar gradient (8 ft/mile), more truth in advertising and one long class II+ rock garden. Smaller still, but better in terms of both scenery and gradient (14 ft/mile), is **Deep Run**, which even has a brief class III stretch. The lower Rapidan's main tributaries are **Cedar Run** (15 ft/mile), site of the Civil War battle of Cedar Mountain, which has some nice class II rock gardens and some not so nice fences, another whimsically-named **Mountain Run** (9 ft/mile; its section 2 is the chapter's only "explorers' special"), and picturesque **Mine Run** (10 ft/mile), which was the center of an aborted Civil War campaign. The main complication with Deep Run, Mountain Run (Rapidan) and Mine Run is that there is no access near their mouths, so one has to paddle a considerable distance down the Rappahannock or Rapidan to a take out. (Access to those rivers is limited, as the land is being kept undeveloped to protect the source of Fredericksburg's drinking water.) The flip side of this is that these creeks can provide access to those rivers at useful places.

I have also included three very small (catchments 4-8 sq. mi.) downstream tributaries, which are steeper because they have farther to cut to get down to the Rappahannock. Below the confluence with the Rapidan, on the north side, is **Rocky Pen Run,** which has a short, steep and delightful gorge as it approaches the river; alas, it will soon be flooded out by a dam. On the opposite bank, **Hazel Run** flows more gently and less scenically through the Fredericksburg National Battlefield and the city, while **Massaponax Creek**, a little to the southeast, has a short whitewater section.

On the north side of the Rappahannock, across from Fredericksburg, are several tiny creeks with catchments of 3-4 sq. mi. and gradients of 30-50 ft/mile. **Falls Run**, in Falmouth, is the steepest of these (2 miles with a 50 ft/mile average gradient that starts out at 150 ft/mile); alas, quite a few strainers were visible. Downstream, **Claiborne Run** has a 40 ft/mile gradient for 2.5 miles, while **Little Falls Run** (1.8 miles, 33 ft/mile) has a nice ledge visible upstream from Md. 3. Only the last mile of **White Oak Run** (30 ft/mile) is safe because of a low-water bridge and fence on the upstream side of SR 603, while **Muddy Creek** offers a 2-mile trip at 32 ft/mile. Explore some of these if you live nearby.

A somewhat larger (7 sq. mi.) and further upstream creek is **Horsepen Run**. It could be run for a half mile with a gradient averaging 100 ft/mile (reaching 200 ft/mile), and looked class IV+, but was full of strainers, and would leave you a 4 mile flat paddle to Motts Run Landing. The **Horse Pen gold mine** operated from the 1830s until the early 20th Century. Nowadays, lower Horsepen Run is heavily (ab)used by **all terrain vehicles (ATVs) and dirt bikes**, which have cut trails up and down the steep banks of this and neighboring creeks.

GAUGES: For the two main rivers, the recorded gauges on the Rappahannock at Remington (619 sq. mi.) and Fredericksburg (1,595 sq. mi.) and the Rapidan near Culpeper (468 sq. mi.) are ideal, and they are somewhat useful for the larger tributaries as well, as are the gauges on Battle Run (26 sq. mi.) and the Robinson (179 sq. mi.). For the small, downstream creeks near Fredericksburg, the gauges on Aquia Creek (35 sq. mi.) and the South Fork, Quantico Creek (7.6 sq. mi.), 15-25 miles to the north, are usually the best (though very imperfect) choices. There are no on-line rainfall gauges in the area. In the table below, **gauge refers either to Remington (in regular type)** or to *Aquia Creek (in bold italics)*.

name	gradient	difficulty	length	area	gauge	rating
Rappahannock R. - Sec. 1	12 (35)	II+	4.5	625	250cfs	**
- Sec. 2	6 (25)	II	24.5	683	300cfs	*
- Sec. 3	13 (33)	II+ (III)	5.2	1530	200cfs	***
Marsh Run	8 (40)	A (II+)	3.7	38	*100cfs*	-
Mountain Run	6	I (II)	10.0	70	1000cfs	*
Deep Run - Section 1	25 (80)	II- (III)	2.0	8	*375cfs*	**
- Section 2	14	I	3.5	14	*140cfs*	*
- Section 3	9	I	1.7	26	*110cfs*	*
Rapidan River	6	II-	6.2	680	300cfs	*
Cedar Run	15	II	3.5	15	*215cfs*	*
Mountain Run-Sec.1	9	I	2.7	23	*110cfs*	*
- Sec.2	9	I (?)	4.0	30	*90cfs*	?
Mine Run	10	I	3.9	31	*90cfs*	**
Rocky Pen Run	55 (100)	III-	1.2	4	*600cfs*	***
Hazel Run	29	I	2.3	8	*250cfs*	-
Massaponax Creek	40 (75)	II- (II+)	0.9	8	*300cfs*	**

RAPPAHANNOCK RIVER (lower)

The Rappahannock ("current flowing in and out," a reference to the tides in the bottom part) flows for 80 miles, from springs on the Blue Ridge 5 miles southeast of Front Royal, down to tidewater at Fredericksburg, and then meanders east-southeast a further 100 miles to the Chesapeake Bay. The tidal part was explored in August, 1608, by Captain John Smith. The flowing section separates Fauquier and Stafford Counties on the northeast side, from Rappahannock, Culpeper and Spotsylvania Counties on the southwest. The first runnable sections are in Chapter 38. They are followed by 17.5 miles at just 3.5 ft/mile, until Remington; you can read about them in Corbett.

The 33.5 miles from Remington to Fredericksburg are normally divided into 3 trips. Sections 1 and 3, each 4.5 miles long, are rather flat until their final mile, when they produce delightful low-intermediate whitewater. The 24.5-mile section 2 (with its only midway road access being at a private campground) is an overnight novice trip; one can also do part of this by starting on one of several tributaries.

Section 1: Remington (Bus. US 29/15) to Kellys Ford (SR 620)

Gradient	Difficulty	Distance	Area	Scenery	Strainers	Rating
12 (35)	II+	4.5	625	B	0	**

USGS Quad – Remington/Germanna Br.; Source – Personal descent (often)
N38 31.81, W77 48.81 to N38 28.65, W77 46.84

This popular "Kellys Ford run" begins shortly after the Hazel River enters the Rappahannock, roughly doubling the flow. After a class II- rapid under the bridge just below the put in, the river is flat until the final mile. Then come several class I and II- rock gardens, followed by the class II+ Sandy Beach rapid, where most of the water is channeled to the right and then back toward the center between large boulders, into a hole. At levels above one foot, one can avoid the hole via the far right, while an easier route opens up on the left. After some more class II rock gardens, comes the other class II+, Piggly Wiggly, with the most interesting route on the far left. And then, too soon, you are at the take out.

There used to be access problems at the put in. Now, there is a narrow corridor between fences. There is no parking by the bridge, so leave vehicles in town, a quarter mile away, across from the nearest store.

GAUGE: You need 250 cfs on the Remington gauge to run this stretch; there are also RC gauges at both the put in and take out. In open boats, be careful above about 2,000 cfs, as the rapids become continuous with high waves.

> The **Armies of Northern Virginia and of the Potomac** faced each other across the Rappahannock around Kellys Ford for extended periods, and would both snipe and trade (Yankee coffee for rebel tobacco) across the water. Opposing generals were sometimes old West Point classmates or Mexican War colleagues, which did not make the combat any less deadly.

Section 2: Kellys Ford to Motts Run Landing

Gradient	Difficulty	Distance	Area	Scenery	Strainers	Rating
6 (25)	II	24.5	683	B	0	*

USGS Quad – GermannaBr./Richardsville/Storck/SalemCh.; Source – Personal descent 5/05 N38 28.65, W77 46.84 to N38 18.81, W77 32.45

This popular, novice overnight trip has three camping options: (a) Rappahannock River Campgrounds, after 10 miles, which has electricity, phone service, canoe rental, water and cold drinks; it is on the right bank at the bottom of a long rock garden, and the signs say "RRC." From April 1 to Labor Day, plus weekends through October, you can drive there by turning left at Richardsville on SR 638; (b) the G.H. Brumble campsite, between the two rivers at the confluence, after 16 miles; or (c) anywhere on Fredericksburg municipality land. The former public access at Scotts Dam, 4 miles below the confluence, is closed, unless you book a trip with Clore Brothers.

There are only riffles in the first 6 miles, about nine class II rapids over the next 12 miles (including the long Confluence Rapids at the Rapidan) and a final 6.5 miles with only riffles again. Unfortunately, there is no way to do just the middle 12 miles.

The scenery is mostly undisturbed woodlands, with a few fields and houses. It is a great trip for seeing bald eagles, ospreys, blue herons and other birds, as well as the remains of the locks of the Rappahannock Canal – a reminder of the commercial importance this river had during the great age of canal building before the railroads came.

The time needed depends largely on the river level. At 5 feet (1,250 cfs) on the Remington gauge, the trip took us 7 hours of moderate paddling (4 hours to the confluence, 3 hours below), including some time for playing and visiting tributaries.

GAUGE: At the zero level of 300 cfs at Remington, this would be a very slow trip; 1-2,000 cfs is preferable, even for novices. Some sources give 5 feet on Remington as a safe maximum, but at that level nothing is more than class II, and even at considerably higher levels, one could find class II routes by sticking to the shallower passages, except that Confluence Rapids would become class III.

Section 3: Motts Run Landing to Fredericksburg

Gradient	Difficulty	Distance	Area	Scenery	Strainers	Rating
13 (33)	II+ (III)	5.2	1530	C	0	***

USGS Quad – Salem Church/Fredericksburg; Source – Personal descent (often) N38 18.81, W77 32.45 to N38 19.13, W77 28.29

This popular trip has nice rapids and is usually runnable. After 3.2 miles of class I, you reach I-95. Until 2004, this was the start of the 0.8-mile backwater of VEPCO's Embry Dam. Now there are class II rapids here, highlighted by a 3-foot ledge with numerous routes (some class II+).

Just below the former dam, the creek divides for 0.7 miles around Laucks Island. Above one foot on the Fredericksburg RC gauge, you can take the left channel (turn just at the head of the island), which ends with a pair of nice drops (class II+).

The main, right channel is slow until a class II+ drop soon after you reach the road. The best drops (called the Falmouth rapids, after the town on the left bank) begin just before the two channels meet. There are a variety of routes (see Grove). The easier ones (class II) are to the left or middle, but you can stay far right for a class III slalom course. Several more class II rapids follow. The difficulty rises with the water level; even the easier routes become class III at 2 feet above minimum and class IV at 3 feet, with dangerous hydraulics on river right. There are excellent surfing spots. Blue herons love this area (I have seen ten at one time), as do bald eagles and ibises. Take out along Riverside Drive, beneath US 1 (or continue down to Old Mill Park). To run or play in the best rapids, you can put in on river right from Fall Hill Road, opposite Laucks Island.

GAUGE: Zero level is 600 cfs on the Fredericksburg gauge, but over 1,000 cfs is better. There is a color-coded RC gauge at the US 1 takeout; at 2,200 cfs (2 feet), this changes from green to yellow. To project the level a day ahead, combine the Remington and Culpeper gauges and add 25%.

> Having replaced McClellan as head of the 115,000-man Army of the Potomac, Gen. Burnside planned to seize Fredericksburg before the Confederates had time to defend it. Step one was to **cross the Rappahannock at Fredericksburg** on pontoon bridges. The first troops arrived November 17, 1862, but due to inefficiency and bad roads, the pontoons did not show up for over a week, which gave Lee time to gather his troops. Confederate sharpshooters disrupted the building of the bridges, until Union volunteers ferried across and seized control of the south shore. This further delay, to December 12, allowed Stonewall Jackson's corps to arrive, raising the Confederate strength to 78,000. The Battle of Fredericksburg consisted mainly of suicidal attacks by the North on strong positions. On the night of December 15-16, the beaten Federals retreated back across the Rappahannock, having suffered 12,600 casualties to the rebels' 5,300.

MARSH RUN: SR 668 to SR 661 (just before Rappahannock River)

Gradient	Difficulty	Distance	Area	Scenery	Strainers	Rating
8 (40)	A (II+)	3.7	38	C	3-5/mi.	-

USGS Quad – Remington/Germanna Bridge; Source – Personal descent 9/99
N38 30.49, W77 45.86 to N38 28.51, W77 46.36

This stream flows southward, a little east of Remington. The first mile is flat, but then comes a quarter mile long class II+ rock garden, divided into channels which are replete with strainers. This rapid would be easier when there is less vegetation blocking the view. And as suddenly as the rapid began, it ends. The creek leaves the woods and passes between cattle farms, where you can expect a few fences as well as more tree strainers.

Take out at SR 661, 300 yards before the confluence. If you continue to the Rappahannock, it is one-third mile upstream to Kellys Ford (difficult in high water).

GAUGE: Look for 800 cfs on the Hazel at Rixeyville and 75 cfs on Battle Run.

MOUNTAIN RUN [of Rappahannock]: SR 669 to SR 620

Gradient	Difficulty	Distance	Area	Scenery	Strainers	Rating
6	I (II-)	10.0	70	C	0-2/mi.	*

USGS Quad – Germanna Bridge; Source – Personal descent (1st half) 9/04; Corbett; trip report (Evangelidi) N38 28.06, W77 51.58 to N38 27.36, W77 46.25

This creek rises west of Culpeper and runs for 32 miles. As its gradient never varies much, stick to the lower part, where there are fewer strainers. It is a meandering trip – the direct distance is about half the river distance.

Corbett's coverage begins at SR 663, but as that is a difficult put in, I started 3 miles downstream, at SR 669, and paddled 5 miles to SR 672. From there it is another 5 miles to SR 620. We portaged 8 downed trees; in 1987, Corbett had only one portage in 13 miles. The scenery is a mixture of woods and farms. The creek has only occasional riffles, but just above SR 672, is a class II- rapid at the remains of a mill dam.

From SR 620 it is 0.6 miles to the Rappahannock, but if you do that final bit, you then have to paddle either 2.7 miles upstream to Kellys Ford or 7.3 miles downstream to the Rappahannock River Campgrounds. I have run that final 0.6 miles in order to cut 2 miles of flat water off the long paddle down section 2 of the Rappahannock.

GAUGE: You need at least 375 cfs on the Rixeyville gauge, 240 cfs on the Robinson at Locust Dale and 40 cfs on Aquia Creek.

DEEP RUN

For much of its length, Deep Run flows through a narrow, 50-100 foot deep valley – hence its name. It is rather flat, except for a one-third mile section on both sides of SR 617 (the start of section 1), in which it drops at 80 ft/mile. Section 3 is not too difficult to catch up, and is useful for access to the middle Rappahannock. For its final 4.7 miles, Deep Run forms the boundary between Fauquier and Stafford Counties.

> Deep Run was the center of a 19th Century **gold mining** district. A mile from the creek, in the town of Goldvein, Thomas Jefferson found gold-bearing rocks. The 30 mines were divided between Fauquier and Stafford Counties. The last one ceased operating in 1936.
>
> **Rock Run and Sumerduck Run,** just west of Deep Run, could be paddled in extremely high water (their watersheds above the put ins on SR 651 are each only about 6 sq. mi.) for 3-4 miles each, down to the Rappahannock, at 20 ft/mile. It is then one mile from Rock Run or two miles from Sumerduck Run down to the Rappahannock River Campground access, and a long shuttle via Kellys Ford or Fredericksburg. When the Campground is closed, you would have to go a further 14 miles down to Motts Run Landing, or pole up section 3 of Deep Run.

Section 1: SR 617 (Blackwells Mill Road) to SR 752 (Sillamon Road)

Gradient	Difficulty	Distance	Area	Scenery	Strainers	Rating
20 (80)	II- (III)	1.7	8.0	C	0-2/mi.	**

USGS Quad – Richardsville; Source – Personal descent 6/03
N38 29.20, W77 38.38 to N38 28.17, W77 38.05

Right below the put-in bridge is a 100-yard class III rapid, which begins with several narrow chutes that tend to catch strainers, and ends with a steep rock garden. (Members of the Southern Fauquier Hunt Club can legally scout that rapid beforehand from the rocky hill on river right.) Thereafter, the creek is mainly moving flat water, with a few riffles and small ledges. Towards the end, there is a two-foot ledge followed by an easy rock garden (class II-). Take out 100 yards below SR 752, where there is a good play spot at a ford and a rough dirt road to carry up along.

There is also a long rapid just above the put in, but access to it is an issue. You might start the trip a quarter mile upstream of the bridge, by parking alongside SR 617 and carrying down through the woods, but I could not find out whether this would be trespassing (there are no signs). The next bridge is two miles farther upstream, and the creek is really tiny and strainer-ridden there.

GAUGE: The South Fork of Quantico Creek should normally read at least 80 cfs and Aquia Creek (nearer but larger catchment) over 375 cfs.

Section 2: SR 752 (Sillamon Road) to US 17

Gradient	Difficulty	Distance	Area	Scenery	Strainers	Rating
14	I	3.5	14	B	0-2/mi.	*

USGS Quad – Richardsville; Source – Personal descent 2/00
N38 28.17, W77 38.05 to N38 25.83, W77 37.77

This is a pretty and pleasant novice run through the woods, past some beautiful cliffs, shaded by hemlocks and rhododendrons. Put in 100 yards below the bridge, where a primitive dirt road crosses the creek. This is a good surfing spot, with a hole on river right and a standing wave on river left. Just 100 yards later, the creek picks up a tributary, Green Branch (included in the catchment area). Riffles are frequent and well spread, with the longest one starting just below the only house visible, on a cliff on river left, about a mile into the trip. There is also a pair of 2-foot ledges in the first half of the trip. After 1.6 miles you cross SR 615 (Thompsons Mill Road), and the creek widens half a mile later, when Alcotti Run joins. The current slows down in the final mile. I had to exit my boat for only four strainers, which is better than average for such a small creek, despite considerable evidence of beavers. I also saw a flock of about a dozen turkeys taking off from a field alongside the stream. You can take out along the cement culvert on upstream river left, or continue down section 3 to the Rappahannock.

GAUGE: Zero level is when the middle concrete pier at the SR 615 (midway) bridge is just covered with water. The South Fork of Quantico Creek gauge should be at least 30 cfs and the Aquia gauge over 140 cfs.

Section 3: US 17 to Rappahannock River

Gradient	Difficulty	Distance	Area	Scenery	Strainers	Rating
9	I	1.7*	26	B	<1/mi.	*

USGS Quad – Richardsville; Source – Trip report (Ron Canter)
N38 25.83, W77 37.77 to N38 18.81, W77 32.45

*(plus 12 miles on the Rappahannock to Motts Run Landing)
Depending upon your time, poling skills and preferences, this section can be viewed either as a 3.4 mile paddling/poling round trip to the Rappahannock, or as a long downstream trip of 1.7 miles on Deep Run and 12 miles on the Rappahannock (to Motts Run Landing), with a few class II rapids in the first half of the latter. This access to section 2 of the Rappahannock can be useful during the fall

and winter, when the Rappahannock River Campground access is closed. The 13.7-mile paddle is a feasible day trip, whereas otherwise it is a 24-mile overnighter from Kellys Ford.

GAUGE: The South Fork of Quantico Creek should be at least 25 cfs and the Aquia gauge should be over 110 cfs. If you continue onto the Rappahannock, the Remington gauge should be 1-2,000 cfs, although strong paddlers could handle more.

RAPIDAN RIVER (lower): Elys Ford to Rappahannock River

Gradient	Difficulty	Distance	Area	Scenery	Strainers	Rating
6	II-	6.2*	680	B	0	*

USGS Quad – Chancellorsville/Richards./SalemCh; Source – Personal descent 4/01

N38 21.58, W77 41.15 to N38 18.81, W77 32.45

*(plus 8.5 miles on the Rappahannock to Motts Run Landing – see section 2 above)

This is a mild and relatively short trip to the confluence (where there is camping), but with the longer part (a few rapids and a lot of slow water) on the Rappahannock. It is a long day trip, best done tandem and/or when the water is high. (It used to be possible to take out at Scotts Dam, 3 miles down the Rappahannock, but the landowner closed that.)

There is a pair of class II- rapids on the Rapidan – the Haydens Ford ledge after three miles and Granite Shoals as you approach the confluence.

GAUGE: You need a minimum of 250 cfs at Culpeper for the Rapidan portion of this trip, and 500 cfs at Fredericksburg for the rest; however, more water on each makes for a much nicer trip, as the rapids are livelier and the flat sections faster.

CEDAR RUN: SR 652 (Mitchell Road) to Rapidan River (US 522)

Gradient	Difficulty	Distance	Area	Scenery	Strainers	Rating
15	II	3.5	15	C	1-2/mi.	*

USGS Quad – Culpeper W./Culp. E./Unionville; Source – Personal descent 3/99
N38 23.12, W78 00.39 to N38 21.54, W77 58.37

Cedar Run gathers the waters southwest of Culpeper for their brief trip to the Rapidan. That trip is rotten at first, but almost redeems itself in the second half. It is also a convenient trip, because you can take out just across the Rapidan, at US 522, and the shuttle is short. And, unlike nearby Piedmont streams in this chapter, it has real rapids.

Put in on the downstream, river-left side of SR 652; there is a sturdy board fence beneath the bridge. I encountered braiding and 4 other fences in the first half of the trip. The fences were in slow water, but all included barbed wire and required some effort. (One could avoid 3 of those fences and lots of flat water by putting in on Campbell Branch, the small river-right tributary that you cross on the shuttle and that enters Cedar Run after 1.3 miles, but I don't know if that quarter-mile cure is worse than the disease.)

But in the second half of the trip there are a half dozen class II rock gardens. None are steep, but they are long and intricate. There is usually a choice of routes, and although fallen trees blocked some passages, there was a clean route through each rapid.

The best take out, where you can drive almost down to the water, is an easy ferry directly across the Rapidan, right up by the last bridge piling. My wildlife highlight was a mink.

GAUGE: You will want at least 215 cfs on Aquia Creek, 1,100 cfs on the Robinson (1 hour later), and 1,750 cfs on the Hazel River (2 hours later). If the riffles just upstream of and beneath the US 522 bridge can be run cleanly, so can everything.

Battle of Cedar Mountain. Following his dazzling Shenandoah Valley Campaign of March-June, 1862, Stonewall Jackson was sent north again from Richmond two months later, to deal with General Pope's new Union Army of Virginia. On August 9, Jackson managed to concentrate his 22,000 troops against only 12,000 of the northern forces, who were spread across the farmland around Cedar Run, and to get artillery to a strong position up nearby Cedar Mountain. But his troops were being badly outfought until Jackson waded into the fight, waving his sword and battle flag, and rallying his soldiers. That, plus the arrival of Confederate reinforcements, turned the tide, and the Union forces fled back across Cedar Run toward Culpeper. Union losses were 2,500 vs. Confederate casualties of 1,400. This was Jackson's last independent command. Two weeks later, Robert E. Lee arrived with the rest of the Army of Northern Virginia, and they moved north to the Battle of Second Manassas.

MOUNTAIN RUN [of Rapidan]

This Mountain Run is almost as flat as the Rappahannock tributary of the same name. It also rises on a pretentious hill – Jerdone Mountain – a 269-foot behemoth, just east of Orange. After 2 miles, the stream makes a beeline northeast for 15 miles to the Rapidan. If you run section 2, you are committed to 5.8 miles on the Rapidan.

Section 1: SR 622 (Old Office Road) to True Blue (SR 611)

Gradient	Difficulty	Distance	Area	Scenery	Strainers	Rating
9	I	2.7	23	B	0-2/mi.	*

USGS Quad – Unionville; Source – Personal descent 3/99
N38 19.95, W77 55.55 to N38 21.21, W77 56.64

This section is pleasant, as it twists and turns with frequent riffles through the woods, with attractive cliffs generally on the right bank. We encountered few strainers, but the presence of beavers suggests that this could change.

The put in and take out have good parking, the mud is slippery at the former. You could begin two miles further upstream, at SR 621; from the topo map, it looks similar.

GAUGE: The USGS gauge at SR 611 should read at least 2.1, with Aquia Creek at 110 cfs and the Robinson at Locust Dale over 575 cfs.

Section 2: True Blue (SR 611) to Mine Run/Rapidan River

Gradient	Difficulty	Distance	Area	Scenery	Strainers	Rating
9	I (?)	4.0*	30	?	?	?

USGS Quad – Unionville/Mine Run/Germanna Bridge; Source – Scouting put in
N38 21.21, W77 56.64 to N38 22.75, W77 47.15

*(plus 5.8 miles on the Rapidan to Germanna Bridge/Va. 3)

Not every **"explorer's special"** is a tiny, raging brook. From the put in, it is 4 miles to the confluence with Mine Run and the Rapidan, plus 5.8 miles on the Rapidan to the take out at Germanna Bridge (Va. 3). The Mountain Run part is through a flood plain, with cliffs on river right. When Mountain Run is up, the Rapidan is likely to be high, and the 5.8 miles on it will pass quickly (see the Mine Run write up just below).

   GAUGE: The USGS gauge at SR 611 should read at least 2.0, with Aquia Creek at 90 cfs and the Robinson at Locust Dale over 475 cfs.

MINE RUN: Burr Hill (SR 611) to Rapidan River

Gradient	Difficulty	Distance	Area	Scenery	Strainers	Rating
10	I	3.9*	31	B+	<1/mi.	**

USGS Quad – Mine Run/Germanna Bridge; Source – Personal descent 5/98
N38 20.62, W77 51.56 to N38 22.75, W77 47.15

*(plus 5.8 miles on the Rapidan to Germanna Bridge/Va. 3)

It's too bad this creek has no rapids, for otherwise it's a delightful trip, and not too hard to catch. Almost the whole run is through the woods, with lovely rock outcroppings and steep slopes behind them. The high banks keep most of the fallen trees above head level, so we never had to portage, although there were a few tight squeezes. When the Rapidan is high, expect up to half a mile of backwater. Still, only 80 minutes of steady paddling took us to the joint confluence with Mountain Run and the Rapidan.

   From there, it is 5.8 miles down the Rapidan to Va. 3, with a 3-ft/mile gradient. Corbett lists the main hazard as "boredom," but when Mine Run is up, the Rapidan will usually be very fast – those 5.8 miles took us less than an hour (the Culpeper gauge was 3.5). The take out is at a small park on river right, 100 yards upstream of the Germanna Bridge. Make sure you know what to look for (chiefly a pair of islands in mid-stream), so that the swift current doesn't carry you past the small take-out eddy.

   One could put in 4.4 miles farther upstream, at SR 602, but the catchment there is only 15 sq. mi., the gradient is just the same 10 ft/mile, and it is less scenic.

   GAUGE: The USGS gauge visible on nearby Mountain Run should read at least 2.0 feet. Aquia Creek should be above 90 cfs, the Robinson 475 cfs.

> **Spotswood Furnace** along **Pipe Dam Run**, built around 1716 by Governor Alexander Spotswood, was the first fully equipped iron furnace in the colonies. It was half a mile from the Rappahannock, down which the iron was hauled to Fredericksburg.
>
> After Gettysburg, Lee retreated beyond the Rappahannock and Rapidan. In November 1863, he occupied strong defenses along upper Mine Run. Meade, with 70,000 troops, tried to dislodge Lee's 50,000 in the **Mine Run Campaign,** called "the great battle of the Civil War that never happened." After a week of skirmishing, the Union forces were poised to attack across Mine Run and up an open slope, when Meade realized that the Confederate position was too strong, and withdrew across the Rapidan; for his prudence, he received nothing but criticism. Lee discovered the Union withdrawal too late to intercept it, remarking: "I am too old to command this army. We should never have permitted those people to get away." Both armies then went into winter quarters. This was Meade's last independent command, before Grant joined him.

> Two small creeks flow out of the Battle of the Wilderness area and end in semi gorges. **Flat Run** is dammed to form Lake of the Woods, and might be paddled for 3 miles below this to the Rapidan, at 8 sq. mi. and 30 ft/mile. However, it will only come up when Lake of the Woods is full. **Wilderness Run** (17 ft/mile, 10 sq. mi) might be paddled 4 miles from Va. 3 to the Rapidan (plus 1 mile on the Rapidan, to Elys Ford). But it flows through an area of tangled scrub ("the Wilderness").

ROCKY PEN RUN: SR 654 to Rappahannock River

Gradient	Difficulty	Distance	Area	Scenery	Strainers	Rating
55 (100)	III-	1.2*	4	B+	1/mile	***

USGS Quad – Salem Church; Source – Personal descent 5/02
N38 20.63, W77 29.21 to N38 18.81, W77 32.45

*(plus 1.3 miles on Rappahannock to Motts Run Landing)

This creek is so tiny that you will be hard pressed to catch it, but if you do, don't miss the chance (or the put in). And do so soon; **the Rocky Pen Run Reservoir is in the construction stage, as a Stafford County water supply storage area for water pumped from the Rappahannock, and will eliminate the trip before completion in May 2013.** The first half has a 30-ft/mile gradient and is class II-, while the second half averages 80 ft/mile and is replete with rapids of up to class III-. The scenery is excellent, especially once you enter the gorge in the second half of the trip. All in all, it's a delightful paddle, but what a shame that it's so short and now short-lived.

From the confluence, it is 1.3 flat miles down to Motts Run Landing, on the other side of the river.

GAUGE: You need at least 125 cfs on the South Fork of Quantico Creek and 600 cfs on Aquia Creek. The rocks in the streambed just below the put in should be covered; if you do not scrape there, you will have enough water.

> For extreme paddlers, there is an even smaller (2.5 sq. mi.) tributary, **England Run**, where you can go just 0.4 miles with a 200 ft/mile average gradient that reaches 500 ft/mile. This cascade enters the Rappahannock on river left, a quarter mile above I-95.

🕪 HAZEL RUN: US 1 to US-BR 17 (Gunnery Road take out)

Gradient	Difficulty	Distance	Area	Scenery	Strainers	Rating
29	I	2.3	8	D	1-3/mi.	-

USGS Quad – Fredericksburg; Source – Personal descent 4/98
N38 17.27, W77 29.21 to N38 17.60, W77 27.55

This little creek runs an historic course along the edge of the Fredericksburg-Spotsylvania National Military Park, just south of the business district. It has no rapids, but good boat control is needed to avoid partial strainers and creek-wide strainers, some of which were tricky to portage because of high banks.

The scenery starts off very pretty, through Alum Springs Park, but deteriorates as first apartment buildings and then major highways appear alongside. There is good parking on the upstream side of the US 1 put in. Take out at the field off Gunnery Road, just before the creek flows under US-BR 17.

GAUGE: About 55 cfs on the South Fork of Quantico Creek and 250 cfs on Aquia Creek are minimal.

> In very high water, you can double the length of this trip by putting in on **Long Branch** at Harrison Road (2.4 sq. mi.), paddling one mile to the confluence (30 ft/mile) and then 1.3 miles on Hazel Run (60 ft/mile) to US 1. It looks like at least class III shortly above US 1, with hydraulics and pipes that could be dangerous.

> In the December 13, 1862, **Battle of Fredericksburg**, Hazel Run separated the Union left, commanded by General Franklin, from the right, under Generals Hooker and Sumner. Franklin made only a halfhearted effort with his 50,000 troops, while the 60,000-man Union right, channeled by Hazel Run and the Rappahannock Canal into a front only 1.5 miles wide, suffered 20% casualties in brave but futile attempts to reach the stone wall and sunken road at the foot of Marye's Heights. It was among the most one-sided Confederate victories. Six and a half months later, at Gettysburg, when General Pickett's troops staged an equally-doomed attack against a fortified position, the avenging Union forces chanted "Fredericksburg!"
>
> Hazel Run also figured in the May 1863 **Second Battle of Fredericksburg**, part of the Chancellorsville Campaign. After Gen. Sedgwick's 20,000 Union troops stormed Marye's Heights against only token resistance (600 Mississippians), Confederate forces under Jubal Early formed a defensive line along upper Hazel Run, while Sedgwick drove west to link up with the larger forces at Chancellorsville. The Southerners stopped that drive at Salem Church, and when Lee sent reinforcements, they sent the federals fleeing again across the Rappahannock.

🚣 MASSAPONAX CREEK: Va. 208 to SR 639 (Leavells Road)

Gradient	Difficulty	Distance	Area	Scenery	Strainers	Rating
40 (75)	II- (II+)	0.9	8	C	1-3/mi.	**

USGS Quad – Spotsylvania; Source – Personal descent 6/00
N38 14.52, W77 32.12 to N38 14.13, W77 31.59

Massaponax Creek flows eastward for 14 miles to Ruffins Pond. It is small and flat until Va. 208, southwest of Fredericksburg, five miles from its source. But then it makes a lively descent of the fall line, providing a short but enjoyable trip.

Put in on the northwest side of Va. 208, where the road (a divided highway there) is lower, and paddle through the culvert, after checking it for any trapped debris. (You can also slide down to the creek on the other side of Va. 208.) The trip starts off flat and then goes over three, widely spaced, 2-3 foot, man-made ledges; at high water, run them with speed to power through their hydraulics. Soon the action picks up in a little gorge, highlighted by a class II+ ledge and rock garden. That is followed by a quarter mile of continuous class I and II-, before the creek flattens out approaching SR 639.

For a longer trip, continue 1.5 miles through the woods, pass US 1 and take out immediately on river right, where there is parking at KFC. The gradient for this stretch is 15 ft/mile. Below US 1, the creek passes through commercial areas and is even flatter.

GAUGE: The South Fork of Quantico Cr. needs 65 cfs and Aquia Creek 300 cfs.

At the December 1862 **Battle of Fredericksburg**, the main Confederate forces, General Longstreet's Corps, was on the high ground southwest of town, with their right flank anchored at Hamilton's Crossing, near the marshy mouth of Massaponax Creek.

On May 21, 1864, after the Battle of Spotsylvania Courthouse, General Grant conferred with his leading commanders inside the **Massaponax Baptist Church** (in the creek's southern headwaters, south of Fredericksburg). Timothy O'Sullivan took a famous photograph of this war council, from a church balcony.

INDEX of STREAMS

Abrams Creek	279	*Big Run*	315
Accokeek Creek	423	Big Cove Creek	114
Accotink Creek	392	Big Pipe Creek	167
Alloway Creek	166	Big Rocky Run	412
[Anacostia River]	225	Blackrock Run	41
Northeast Branch	232	[Blue Run]	450
Northwest Branch	227	*Booze Creek*	201
Antietam Creek	120	*Borden Marsh Run*	331
East Branch	122	Braddock Run	101
West Branch	122	Brice Run	75
Aquia Creek	421	Brier Ditch	237
		Broad Branch	221
Babbs Run	273	[Broad Creek]	243
Back Creek	270	Broad Run (Above Great Falls)	358
Backlick Run	389	Broad Run (Catoctin Creek, Md.)	138
Baker Run	257	Broad Run (Occoquan)	402
[Ballenger Creek]	149	[Broad Run] (W. Montgomery Co.)	186
Batchellors Run	228	Brush Creek (Back Creek)	272
[Battery Kemble Branch]	226	Brush Creek (Wills Creek)	95
Battle Run	447	Buck Branch	199
Bear Branch	168	Bucklodge Branch	189
[Bear Creek]	109	[Buffalo Marsh Run]	298
[Beautiful Run]	450	Bull Run	408
Beaver Creek	127	Bullneck Run	372
Beaver Run	71	"West Branch"	373
[Beaverdam Creek] (Anacostia)	225	Bush Creek	172
Beaverdam Creek (Goose Creek)	352	Bynum Run	26
North Fork	352		
Beaverdam Run (Above Great Falls)	359	Cabin Branch	82
[Beaverdam Run] (Gunpowder Falls)	40	Cabin John Creek	196
[Beaverdam Run] (Occoquan)	415	Cacapon River	254
Beetree Run	38	[Cameron Run]	383
Bel Pre Creek	229	[Cannon Creek]	415
Bennett Creek	172	Captain Hickory Run	368
Bens Branch	171	*Carbaugh Run*	120
Bens Run	76	[Carroll Creek]	149
Big Creek	312	[Carsins Run]	24

Entry	Page
[Catharpin Creek]	409
Catoctin Creek, Maryland	134
Catoctin Creek, Virginia	339
North Fork	340
South Fork	341
Cattail Creek	83
Cedar Creek	297
Cedar Run (Occoquan)	404
Cedar Run (Rappa. Tailwaters)	472
"Cedar Lane Branch"	215
[Charles Branch]	88
Chestnut Lick	408
Chinquapin Run	47
Chopawamsic Creek	419
[Middle Branch]	421
[North Branch]	421
[South Branch]	421
[Claiborne Run]	466
Clark Run	248
Clarks Branch	360
"*Clarksville Branch*"	86
[Collington Branch]	88
Colvin Run	367
Cone Branch	138
Conococheague Creek	118
Conway River	453
Coquelin Run	218
Covington River	446
Cromwells Run	350
[Crooked Run] (Cacapon)	254
Crooked Run [north] (Goose Creek)	351
Crooked Run [south] (Goose Creek)	348
Crooked Run (Main Stem Shen.)	328
[Crooked Run] (Sideling Hill Creek)	109
Croyden Park Branch	213
Cub Run (Occoquan)	410
Cub Run (South Fork Shenandoah)	313
[Dargan Run]	131
Dead Run (Gwynns Falls)	61
Dead Run (Virginia Palisades)	375
Deep Run [north] (Patapsco)	71
Deep Run [south] (Patapsco)	76
Deep Run (Rappa. Tailwaters)	470
[Delaware Run]	40
Difficult Run	363
[Dillons Run]	253
[Dogue Creek]	383
Donaldson Run	380
Double Pipe Creek	167
Dry Run	317
Dry Seneca Creek	190
[Duck Run]	298
[Dueling Branch]	226
Dutchman Creek	339
East Branch, Antietam Creek	122
East Branch, Naked Creek	311
East Branch, Patapsco	71
East Branch, Sideling Hill Creek	110
East Branch, Winters Run	28
East Hawksbill Creek	316
[Elk Branch] (Back Creek)	269
Elk Branch/Elks Run (Opequon Cr.)	281
Elklick Run	411
[England Run]	476
Esther Run	114
Evitts Creek	104
Evitts Run	333
Fall Run	301
[Falls Run]	466
Fenwick Branch	219
Ficry Run	430
Fifteenmile Creek	107
[First Mine Branch]	39
Fishing Creek	161
[Flat Run] (Monocacy West)	149
[Flat Run] (Rappa. Tailwaters)	475
Flint Run	320
Flintstone Creek	106
"Forest Glen Branch"	217

INDEX OF STREAMS

[Foundry Branch]	226	West Branch	77
Fourmile Run	384	**Herring Run**	46
[Fourth Mine Branch]	39	West Branch	46
Friends Creek	153	*Hillegas Run*	96
Froman Run	302	**Hittles Mill Stream**	432
[Furnace Branch]	165	**Hogue Creek**	272
Furnace Run	301	**Holmes Run**	387
		[Hooes Run]	400
Gap Run	348	[Hopewell Run]	277
["Garlic Hollow Run"]	290	[Horsepen Run] (Above Great Falls)	357
Garth Run	453	[Horsepen Run] (Rappa. Tailwaters)	466
Georges Run	36	[Howellsville Branch]	332
Gilbert Swamp Run	249	**Hughes River**	438
Giles Run	397	[Hunters Mill Branch]	244
Gillis Falls	74	**Hunting Creek (Monocacy West)**	158
Gladdens Run	99	[Hunting Creek] (Va. Suburbs So.)	383
Gooney Run	321		
Goose Creek	346	[Indian Creek]	225
North Fork	351	**Indian Run**	390
Goshen Branch	188	**Isaacs Creek**	271
Grassy Lick Run	260	**Israel Creek (Catoctin Creek, Md.)**	132
Grave Run	36	*Israel Creek (Monocacy East)*	170
Great Falls (section of Potomac)	180		
Great Run	433	**James Run**	25
Great Seneca Creek	187	**Jeffries Branch**	350
Grindstone Run	137	**Jennings Run**	100
Gulf Branch	379	North Branch	101
Gunpowder Falls	32	[Jeremys Run]	319
Gwynns Falls	58	**Jones Falls**	52
Gwynns Run	63	North Branch	55
		Jordan River	431
Hammond Branch	86	**Josephs Run**	214
Happy Creek	326		
[Harlan Run]	277	[Kanes Creek]	400
Hawksbill Creek	315	**Kensington Hills Branch**	216
Hawlings River	83	"Kentdale Branch"	200
Hazel River	436	**Kettle Run**	403
Hazel Run	476	[Keyser Run]	446
Henson Creek	243	*Kimsey Run*	256
[Herbert Run]	77		
[East Branch]	77	*Laurel Run (No. Fork Shenandoah)*	392

481

[Laurel Run] (Wills Creek)	94	[Long Branch, Accotink Creek]	393
Licking Creek	113	*Long Branch, Fourmile Run*	386
Licking Run	407	[Long Branch, Hazel Run]	476
Linganore Creek	170	*Long Branch, Potomac Creek*	424
North Fork	171	Long Branch, Sligo Creek	231
Little River	353	Long Green Creek	41
Little Antietam Creek [north]	125	Lost River	256
Little Antietam Creek [south]	128	[Lubber Run]	386
[Little Beaver Creek]	128	Luzon Branch	220
Little Bennett Creek	173		
Little Brush Creek	273	*Maidens Choice Run*	62
Little Bull Run	409	Manassas Run	329
[Little Cacapon River]	253	Marsh Creek	143
North Fork	254	Marsh Run [north] (Antietam Cr.)	126
[South Fork]	253	*Marsh Run [south] (Antietam Cr.)*	120
Little Catoctin Creek [central]	138	*Marsh Run (Rappa. Tailwaters)*	469
Little Catoctin Creek [north]	135	[Marumsco Creek]	400
Little Catoctin Creek [south]	133	Massaponax Creek	477
Little Cove Creek	114	Mather Gorge (section of Potomac)	181
Little Difficult Run	366	[McIntosh Run]	242
Little Falls (Gunpowder Falls)	37	*Meadow Branch (Monocacy East)*	169
Little Falls (section of Potomac)	182	Meadow Branch (Sleepy Creek)	266
Little Falls Branch	203	[Meadow Brook]	298
[Little Falls Run]	466	"Michigan Park Hills Branch"	232
[Little Devil Stairs]	446	Middle Creek (Catoctin Cr., Md.)	136
Little Gunpowder Falls	42	Middle Creek (Monocacy West)	155
Little Hunting Creek	160	*Middle Creek (Opequon Creek)*	280
Little Isaacs Creek	271	*Middle Fork, Sleepy Creek*	265
Little Marsh Creek	145	Middle Patuxent River	85
Little Monocacy River	186	[Mill Branch]	253
[Little Owens Creek]	156	Mill Creek (Opequon Creek)	279
Little Paint Branch	235	Mill Creek (No. Fork Shenandoah)	289
Little Patuxent River	84	*Mill Run*	406
Little Pimmit Run	378	Milltown Creek	341
Little Pipe Creek	169	Mine Run	474
Little Seneca Creek	188	Mine Run Branch	361
Little Stony Creek	293	Miney Branch	153
Little Tonoloway Creek [north]	112	*Minnehaha Branch*	202
Little Tonoloway Creek [south]	112	[Monocacy River]	141
Little Wills Creek	97	Moores Run (Back River)	48
Littles Run	147	[Moores Run] (Cacapon)	253

INDEX OF STREAMS

"Morrisonville Creek"	341	Paddy Run	300
Morgan Run	72	Paint Branch	233
Mountain Run [of Rapidan]	473	[Painter Run]	290
Mountain Run [of Rappahannock]	469	Panther Skin Creek	349
Mountain Run (Sleepy Creek)	265	Pass Run	318
Muddy Branch	191	Passage Creek	303
[Muddy Creek]	466	Patapsco River	66
[Muddy Run]	435	East Branch	71
[Mulberry Run]	298	North Branch	69
		South Branch	73
Naked Creek	310	West Branch	70
East Branch	311	*Patterson Run*	113
South Branch	313	Patuxent River	80
West Branch	312	Pike Branch	391
Narrow Passage Creek	293	Pimmit Run	377
Neabsco Creek	416	Piney Branch (Rock Creek)	222
Needles (section of Potomac)	178	Piney Branch (So. Montgomery Co.)	194
Nichols Run	360	Piney Creek (Gunpowder Falls)	40
North Branch, Jennings Run	101	Piney Creek (Monocacy East)	167
North Branch, Jones Falls	55	Piney Creek (Sideling Hill Creek)	110
North Branch, Patapsco River	69	Piney River	444
North Branch, Rock Creek	212	Piney Run (NW Loudoun Co.)	338
North Fork, Beaverdam Creek	352	[Piney Run] (Gunpowder Falls)	40
North Fork, Catoctin Creek	340	Piney Run (Patapsco)	74
North Fork, Goose Creek	351	Pipe Dam Run	475
North Fork, Linganore Creek	171	Piscataway Creek	245
North Fork, Shenandoah River	288	Pohick Creek	395
North Fork, Thornton River	442	Popes Head Creek	413
North River	259	Port Tobacco Creek	247
"North Limestone Branch"	342	Portal Branch	219
Northeast Branch, Anacostia	232	Potomac Creek	423
Northwest Branch, Anacostia	227	Potomac River	177
		Potomac Run	425
Occoquan River	401	Powder Mill Run	61
Old Farm Creek	198	Powells Creek	417
Opequon Creek	278	[Prettyboy Branch]	34
[Overall Run]	320	Pughs Run	295
Owens Creek	156		
[Oxon Creek]	226	Quantico Creek	417
[Oxon Run]	242	South Fork	417

[Racer Run]	446	Sir Johns Run	264
Rapidan River (upper)	451	Sleepy Creek	264
Rapidan River (lower)	472	*Middle Fork*	265
Rappahannock River (upper)	430	*South Fork*	265
Rappahannock River (lower)	467	Sligo Creek	229
Red Run (Antietam Creek)	124	Snakeden Branch	199
Red Run (Gwynns Falls)	60	*Soapstone Valley Branch*	221
Redhouse Creek	48	South Branch, Naked Creek	313
Riles Run	292	South Branch, Patapsco	73
[Rivanna River tributaries]	450	South Fork, Catoctin Creek (Va.)	341
Robinson River	457	South Fork, Quantico Creek	417
Rock Creek (DC)	209	South Fork, Shenandoah	308
North Branch	212	*South Fork, Sleepy Creek*	265
Rock Creek (Monocacy North)	146	South River	456
[Rock Run] (Rappa. Tailwaters)	470	South Run	396
Rock Run (So. Montgomery Co.)	195	[Southlawn Branch]	208
[Rocky Branch] (So. Fork Shenandoah)	319	[Southwest Branch](Patuxent)	88
Rocky Run	368	[Sperry Run]	253
[Rocky Gap Run]	105	Spout Run (Main Stem Shenandoah)	332
Rocky Mountain Run	119	*Spout Run (Virginia Palisades)*	381
Rocky Pen Run	475	[Staunton River]	450
Rockymarsh Run	281	Stemmers Run	49
Roland Run	56	Still Run	236
Rose River	461	Stony Creek	290
Rush River	444	Stony Run (Jones Falls)	57
		Stony Run (So. Fork Shenandoah)	314
Sams Creek	169	Sugarland Run	359
[Sandy Run]	400	[Sumerduck Run]	470
Scott Run	373	Swan Creek	24
Scotts Level Branch	60	[Swover Creek]	290
[Second Mine Branch]	39	Sycolin Creek	353
Seneca Creek	186		
Seneca Rapids (section of Potomac)	179	Tearcoat Creek	260
Shaffers Run	97	Third Mine Branch	39
Shenandoah River	324	Thornton River	440
North Fork	288	North Fork	442
South Fork	308	Thumb Run	433
Sideling Hill Creek	108	[West Branch]	433
East Branch	110	[Tiber Creek]	226
West Branch	109	Tilhance Creek	274
Silver Run	168	Tinkers Creek	246

INDEX OF STREAMS

Toms Brook	295	[West Branch, Thumb Run]	433
Toms Creek	151	*West Branch, Winters Run*	28
Tonoloway Creek	112	Western Branch	87
Town Creek	105	Western Run (Gunpowder Falls)	40
[Town Run]	404	Western Run (Jones Falls)	56
[Trapp Branch]	403	White Run	147
Tripps Run	388	[White Oak Run]	466
Trout Run	257	[Whiteoak Canyon Run]	458
[Trout Pond Run]	253	Wildcat Branch	187
Tumbling Run	296	[Wilderness Run]	475
Turkey Branch	213	Wills Creek	94
[Turkey Run] (No. Fork Shenandoah)	298	*Wilson Run*	106
Turkey Run (Occoquan)	406	Windy Run	380
Turkey Run (Virginia Palisades)	376	Winters Run	27
Turkeycock Run	391	East Branch	28
Tuscarora Creek (Catoctin Cr., Md.)	139	West Branch	28
Tuscarora Creek (Goose Creek)	354	[Wolf Run]	400
Tuscarora Creek (Monocacy West)	163	Wolf Camp Run	98
Tuscarora Creek (Opequon Creek)	280	Wolftrap Creek	366
Venus Branch	331	Zekiah Swamp Run	248
Waites Run	256		
[Warm Springs Run]	263	**CODE:**	
Watts Branch (Anacostia)	237	*Italics* mean "Explorers' Special";	
Watts Branch (So. Montgomery Co.)	194	[Brackets] and not bold mean stream is mentioned but not written up fully;	
West Branch, Antietam Creek	122		
"West Branch, Bullneck Run"	373	"Quotation Marks" mean stream has no known official name;	
West Branch, Herbert Run	77		
West Branch, Herring Run	46	(Parentheses) indicate the chapter or the main stream of which this is a tributary.	
West Branch, Naked Creek	312		
West Branch, Patapsco River	70		
West Branch, Sideling Hill Creek	109		

485

Made in the USA
Middletown, DE
07 November 2015